HER WORKS PRAISE HER

D1444790

ALSO BY HASIA R. DINER

*Hungering for America: Italian, Irish, and Jewish Foodways
in the Age of Migration*

Lower East Side Memories: The Jewish Place in America

Jews in America

A Time for Gathering: The Second Migration, 1820–1880

*Erin's Daughters in America: Irish Immigrant Women
in the Nineteenth Century*

*In the Almost Promised Land:
American Jews and Blacks, 1915–1935*

————————

ALSO BY BERYL LIEFF BENDERLY

Jason's Miracle: A Hanukkah Story

In Her Own Right: The IOM Guide to Women's Health Issues

*The Growth of the Mind
(With Stanley I. Greenspan, M.D.)*

*Challenging the Breast Cancer Legacy
(with Renee Royak-Schaler, Ph.D.)*

*The Myth of Two Minds:
What Gender Means and Doesn't Mean*

Thinking About Abortion

Dancing Without Music: Deafness in America

HER WORKS PRAISE HER

A History of Jewish Women in America
from Colonial Times to the Present

HASIA R. DINER

~ *and* ~

BERYL LIEFF BENDERLY

BASIC
BOOKS

A Member of the Perseus Books Group
New York

Copyright © 2002 by Hasia R. Diner and Beryl Lieff Benderly

Hardback edition published in 2002 by Basic Books,
A Member of the Perseus Books Group
First paperback edition published in 2003 by Basic Books

All rights reserved. Printed in the United States of America. No part of this book may be reproduced in any manner whatsoever without written permission except in the case of brief quotations
embodied in critical articles and reviews. For information, address Basic Books, 387 Park Avenue
South, New York, NY 10016.

Books published by Basic Books are available at special discounts for bulk purchases in the United
States by corporations, institutions, and other organizations. For more information, please contact
the Special Markets Department at the Perseus Books Group, 11 Cambridge Center, Cambridge
MA 02142, or call (617) 252-5298, (800) 255-1514 or e-mail special.markets@perseusbooks.com.

Designed by Jeffrey P. Williams
Set in 10.5 Simonici Garamond by Perseus Publishing Services

A CIP catalog record for this book is available from the Library of Congress

ISBN-13 978–0–465–01711–9 (hc.); ISBN-10 0–465–01711–8 (hc.)

ISBN-13 978–0–465–01712–6 (pbk.); ISBN-10 0–465–01712–6 (pbk.)

*To Shira and Alicia
and their generation of American Jewish Women*

A woman of valor who can find? For her price is far
above rubies.

The heart of her husband doth safely trust in her, And
he hath no lack of gain.

She doeth him good and not evil all the days of
his life.

She seeketh wool and flax, And worketh willingly
with her hands.

She is like the merchant-ships. She bringeth her food
from afar.

She riseth also while it is yet night. And giveth food to
her household

And a portion to her maidens.

She considereth a field and buyeth it; With the fruit of
her hands she planteth a vineyard.

She girdeth her loins with strength and maketh strong
her arms.

She perceiveth that her merchandise is good; her lamp
goeth not out by night.

She layeth her hands to the distaff, and her hands hold
the spindle.

She stretcheth forth her hands to the poor, Yea, she
reacheth forth her hands to the needy.

She is not afraid of the snow for her household; For all
her household are clothed with scarlet.

She maketh for herself coverlets; Her clothing is fine linen and purple.

Her husband is known in the gates when he sitteth among the elders of the land.

She maketh linen garments and selleth them. And delivereth girdles unto the merchant.

Strength and dignity are her clothing; and she laugheth at the time to come.

She openeth her mouth with wisdom; and the law of kindness is on her tongue.

She looketh well to the ways of her household and eateth not the bread of idleness.

Her children rise up and call her blessed; her husband, also and he praiseth her:

'Many daughters have done valiantly, But thou exceedeth them all.'

Grace is deceitful and beauty is vain; but a women that feareth the Lord, she shall be praised.

Give her the fruits of her hands; and let her works praise her in the gates.

PROVERBS 31:10–31
From the Sabbath Evening Liturgy
(Jewish Publication Society 1917 Translation)

CONTENTS

PART   V

"BEYOND YOUR COMMAND"
Remaking Womanhood, 1964–Onward

INTRODUCTION

E very week for thousands of years, the Jewish people have welcomed the Sabbath into their homes. Personified in legend as a bride or queen bearing gifts of serenity and joy, the holy day of rest is said to provide the truest taste of heaven that humans can know on earth. As the sun sets on Friday, each woman welcomes the sacred guest by kindling Sabbath lights and reciting a special blessing. This act, one of the essential duties of womanhood, separates the bliss of holy time from the humdrum of the mundane. With the first flicker of the flame and the first word she utters, the Sabbath arrives.

As ordinary time recedes and sacred time begins, every Jewish husband traditionally recites verses from Proverbs 31 to his wife, the bride and queen whose cooking, cleaning, shopping, fretting, and candle lighting has brought the Sabbath's pleasures into their home. Whether in Spain or Lithuania, in Turkey or Poland or Morocco, in Iraq or America, whether in the tenth century or the twenty-first, he declares her an *asbet hayil,* a woman of valor, and enumerates the qualities that make a woman admirable.

She need not be beautiful, for "grace is deceitful and beauty is vain." Rather, she serves her family, and her husband "doth safely trust in her." Motherhood matters, and "her children rise up and call her blessed." She has charge of the domestic, and "she looketh well to the ways of her household." Virtue and industry rather than elegance or charm define her. "She worketh willingly." Indeed, "she is like the merchant ships [that] bringeth her food from afar." Above all, "she eateth not the bread of idleness."

Nor does the woman of valor fit any mold of delicate femininity. Rather, "strength and dignity are her clothing." She has a mind of her own, and the confidence to act in the world. "She openeth her mouth with wisdom." She also "considereth a field and buyeth it; with the fruit of her hands she planteth a vineyard." But always, "the law of kindness is on her tongue" and "she stretcheth out her hand to the poor." She is neither meek nor passive, but an activist, a doer, an accomplisher of deeds, and every Sabbath her grateful husband declares that "her works praise her in the gates."

Her Works Praise Her chronicles the millions of Jewish women who have lived in America from 1654 to the present day, and who have done much to make Jewish life in America possible. Whether they came from the Netherlands or Poland, from Bavaria or the Pale of Russia, whether they lived in colonial Savannah or suburban Los Angeles, on the Dakota prairie or the Lower East Side, their stories are cut from a single cloth. We explicitly tell that history as a women's story, a Jewish story, and an American story. Their works reflect both who they are, Jewish women, and where they are, the United States of America.

Whether immigrants or native born, the people in this tale have worked actively as Jews, as Americans, and as women to improve the world around them. When they have seen problems in society—be it a lack of Jewish education or the exploitation of factory workers—they have done what they could to solve them. When they have seen needs in their own homes, they have taken steps to fill them. Like their Biblical model, millions of Jewish women have "[laid] their hands" to all manner of work to get their loved ones proper shelter, clothing, food, education, and medical care.

American Jewish women's "works," in addition to their own homes and the welfare of their families, include Sunday schools, burial societies, orphanages, hospitals, old age homes, labor unions, summer camps, reform societies, settlement houses, vocational schools, and other institutions giving substance to the Talmudic injunction that "all of Israel are responsible for one another." Their "works" have also included stores they tended, corporations they founded, classes they taught, agencies they ran, shirtwaists they stitched, books they wrote, legal cases they argued, and patients they healed, as well as children they raised, meals they cooked, and homes they managed.

These works form a set of concentric circles. At the center stands each woman, entitled, as an individual, to the best that America can offer and cognizant that many countries offer very much less. Next is the wider circle of family, her parents, siblings, husband, and children, whose welfare is both her responsibility and the object of her ceaseless efforts, both paid and unpaid. Beyond this is the Jewish people, those nearby at her doorstep and those far away in the places of their distress. Whether in city tenements or gold rush mining camps, whether in elite suburbs or crossroads hamlets, American Jewish women have understood their historic obligation to Jews in other countries and continents. The pennies they collected, the clubs they formed, the picket lines they threw up in front of stores that gouged the public, all proclaim their answer to Rabbi Hillel's famous questions: "If I am not for myself, who is for me? If I am only for myself, what am I?"

But they have also seen themselves as Americans, connected to and concerned with their neighbors, and so the range of their "works" transcends religion and ethnicity. Jewish women formed labor unions, striving to help not only themselves and the other immigrant Jews who sewed for a living, but all the workers in the garment factories, regardless of their language, faith, place of origin, or skin color. Jewish women marched for suffrage and civil rights for oppressed minorities and organized to improve the public schools or establish city sewer systems, seeking better lives for Americans of every background. Looking back over the long history of Jewish women in America, one is struck by how little distinction they have seen between their private and public lives. Anyone who "look[s] well to the ways of her household" must nourish the community in which it lives. Family and community, home and public, Jewish and American have been inextricably bound together.

Her Works Praise Her views the women of a particular place, the United States, over the course of several centuries. By focusing on women rather than on Jews in general, we assert that women have had a distinctive history apart from that of Jewish men. The ways that they came to America, the ways they have encountered America and its opportunities, and the ways they have engaged with Judaism all bear the mark of gender. Whether in the context of education, family, work, or leisure, men and women have had fundamentally different options and expectations. In Judaism, for example, public religion has traditionally been a male domain. No one had to debate whether Jewish men could become rabbis or cantors, or if it is permitted for them to ascend the *bimah* (synagogue platform) and read from the Torah. Jewish men never needed to assert their right to be counted in the quorum needed for public prayer. Synagogue boards never had to vote on whether to consider men as members of congregations. Men were the norm, women a "problem."

In nearly all the many countries where Jews have lived and built the institutions that sustained their religious lives, women accepted the notion of separate Judaic spheres for men and women. In the United States, however, Jewish women responded differently. The first of their sisters to claim the synagogue as their space too, they pioneered institutions and practices that brought them down from the balcony, out from behind the curtain, and into the main arena of Jewish communal, political, and ritual life. More than in any other liberal, industrial, modern society—more than in England, France, Germany, Canada—*American* Jewish women have asserted their sense of entitlement to power, influence, and equality in the Jewish world. *Her Works Praise Her* therefore tells a story that differs from those of Jewish women in other lands, and it seeks to understand what in the American experience made it so.

America's Jewish women have, in addition, differed from other American women in ways that transcend religion. They come from a tradition that venerates the *ashet hayil* and a religion that invests enormous importance in the domestic, giving such matters as cooking and cleaning profound religious significance. America's Jewish women emigrated or descended from places where women routinely ran their own businesses and earned incomes distinct from men's. Both homemaking and earning formed part of the sacred work of Jewish womanhood, which is seeing to the physical, economic, and spiritual welfare of her family. They brought the strategy of separate earning, devised in places where Jewish life was precarious, across the sea to a land of plenty. Then they proceeded to bend, twist, and transform it to fit their increasingly middle-class lives. But the legacy of economic activism remains, and the quest for education, traditionally part of men's portion, became a female concern as well. American Jewish women's zeal for schooling and professional work—almost always in conjunction with marriage and motherhood—has distinguished them from many other immigrant nationalities. Their high levels of labor union activism, their enthusiastic embrace of birth control, their dynamic support for women's suffrage and for second-wave feminism all point to a singular story.

Some of the individuals we meet as we tell it—Rebecca Gratz, Henrietta Szold, Sally Priesand—are famous "founding mothers" and the subjects of many articles and books. Most, though, are less well-known, and their very obscurity gives their experiences and voices compelling resonance. They had little sense of themselves as pioneers or innovators, as heroes or notables, but their lives compose the course of Jewish women's accomplishments in America. How they set about making their homes, how they and their families planned and strategized to earn a living, how they banded together to build the institutions of Jewish life, and how they engaged with the society around them take us into the heart of Jewish experience in this country. For analytical clarity, we have divided their experience into five great epochs. Within each era we explore three major themes. For periods involving a migration, we first learn where the migrants came from and why they left. For all periods, we consider where Jewish women lived in America and how they made their American families, livings, and lives. And finally, we explore women's expression of their Jewishness and the ways in which their works molded a distinctively American Jewry and Judaism.

We chronicle a people who chose America, who cast their lot with the United States, who have worked in every generation to build the nation, because they have understood the limitations of so many other places. In this country, where people can tinker with tradition and experiment with institutions, over a third of Europe's Jews found a homeland and a home. By the end of World War II, for reasons inexpressibly horrible, but also because of energy, optimism, and hope, America had the largest, richest, freest Jewish community in the world, and one with an extraordinarily elaborate web of institutions and services devoted to transmitting tradition and alleviating distress.

This is largely the work of women fulfilling women's sacred role. Though the compilers of Proverbs could not have even remotely imagined the life that Jews would live in America, they nonetheless foretold the women who would carry an ancient heritage of action and responsibility into their lives and works in a new and unprecedented land. Each "woman of valor" in these pages has, as Scripture tells us, bravely faced her future, "laugh[ing] at the time to come." Each one has, in her own way, "done valiantly," indeed, "excell[ed] them all."

PART ONE

∞

"You Cannot Know What a Wonderful Country"

The Atlantic World, 1654–1820

1

"A GREAT MANY OF THAT LOT"

America's First Jewish Women Arrive

The dispute between Rycke Nounes and Asser Leveen began simply enough: she thought he had used her money to buy a boat ticket without her permission. He insisted that it was she who owed him money because of a debt incurred by her late husband. They ended up in court, with Master Leveen suing, the Widow Nounes countersuing, and the case a tangle of claims and counterclaims over "goods since sold at auction," a certain missing "Waistcoat and other things," and sums of money that the two claimants and their absent spouses may or may not have borrowed or lent.[1]

The judges found for her and ordered him to pay. Whether she actually saw any of her confiscated cash the record does not reveal. But it does clearly show that Rycke Nounes, newly arrived in New Amsterdam, entered history defending her rights.

Rycke and Asser had been in Peter Stuyvesant's colony less than two weeks when they found themselves embroiled in their lawsuit. From the moment that the two of them and twenty-one fellow refugees had disembarked on the town wharf at the foot of Manhattan island in the first week of September 1654, the group had struggled for recognition of their rights. The six men, seven women, and ten children had carried their meager belongings off the *Ste. Catherine,* doubtlessly viewing their arrival at a friendly port inhabited by fellow Dutch subjects as nothing short of deliverance. Their journey had begun in flight from a foreign invasion of their home in Brazil, when it had been a Dutch colony. They had spent anxious months partly on the ocean and partly in foreign ports waiting for passage on ships. Finally, it seemed, they had reached safety.

But on that late summer day, as word of unusual doings on the dock reached Governor Stuyvesant, the wayfarers could not have guessed the significance that others would see in their arrival. Stuyvesant saw the scene at the quayside not as a stroke of luck for some obscure individuals but as a threat to civil peace. And people centuries later would hail their arrival as a signal event in the four-thousand-year history of an ancient nation, indeed, as a pivotal moment in the modern history of the Western world. That is because the storm-tossed twenty-three were not only Hollanders but Jews. The village that would grow into the world's most populous Jewish metropolis, in the nation that would host history's largest, richest, and most successful Jewish community, had just received its first Jewish women.

A famously irascible man, the governor received the news with displeasure. The bedraggled newcomers, so destitute that they still owed the ship's captain money for their fares, belonged to "the deceitful race," Stuyvesant would write in a letter to the Dutch West India Company, which employed him and owned the colony of New Netherland. "Enemies and blasphemers of the name of Christ," they threatened to "infect and trouble this new colony."[2] For the sake of civil order he wanted them gone on the next outbound vessel.

But the little group, exhausted from their voyage but confident of their status as Dutch subjects, refused. They had the right to stay, they insisted, and Stuyvesant could not eject them except on the Company's authority. And even if the governor wrote for approval that very day, his request had to cross to Holland on a sailing ship and the Company's answer return on another. The Jews had found safe haven for several weeks or months at least.

And, as they wrote to the Company in a letter of their own, they were entitled to more. As "confirmed burghers" just like "all the other inhabitants of these lands," they asserted, they could live freely wherever the Dutch flag flew. Their people, they pointed out in a letter of January 1655, had done so in Holland and its possessions for generations. Jews, furthermore, had valiantly risked their "possessions and their blood" in the recent, unsuccessful defense of Brazil. And finally, the "principal stockholders of the West India Company" included "many of the Jewish nation" who had "lost immense and great capital" in the late Brazilian fiasco.[3]

Before long (at least as messages traveled in the days of sail) the Company vindicated the travelers' faith in Dutch tolerance and levelheadedness. In April 1655, a letter from Amsterdam instructed the chagrined Stuyvesant that, though the directors shared his concern about the "difficulties which you fear," barring these people from the colony was "unreasonable and unfair" because of Jewish Hollanders' "considerable loss" in Brazil, not to mention the "large amount of capital which they still have invested in the shares of this company."[4] The twenty-three refugees could stay, the letter ordered, so long as they looked after their own poor and expected no charity from Christians beyond what they had already received.[5] And so came to pass what Stuyvesant feared and generations of Jewish Americans would later celebrate: a continuous, unbroken, and often self-perpetuating Jewish presence in the territories that would become the United States.

We can't penetrate Stuyvesant's mind at three centuries' remove, but clearly something beyond routine anti-Semitism must have fueled his intransigence. He had, after all, admitted earlier Jewish arrivals to the colony. A few weeks before the *Ste. Catherine* nosed into New Amsterdam harbor, a ship called the *Peerboom* (Pear Tree) brought a Jewish merchant named Jacob Barsimon.[6] Other Jewish traders whose names we do not know also seem to have landed earlier that summer without objection from Stuyvesant.[7] What danger could be posed by this particular handful of storm-tossed mendicants?

His concern with "infection" offers the strongest hint. A sprinkling of proverbially shrewd male traders posed no danger to civil tranquillity, he seemed to believe, and might even benefit the colony's economy. But the presence of Jewish women and girls implied altogether different possibilities. They could transform a scattering of transients into the rudiments of a Jewish world in the midst of Stuyvesant's Protestant preserve. Jewish wives, mothers, and potential wives meant a living Jewish community, as opposed to the mere presence of Jewish individuals. Males might meet for Jewish worship—and scholars speculate that when the sundown of September 12, 1654, ushered in the holy day of Rosh Hashanah, the men and teenage boys from the *Ste. Catherine*, along with Barsimon and the various shadowy summer arrivals, may well have constituted this continent's first minyan, or quorum of ten adult Jewish males gathered for public prayer.

But reciting the liturgy in the company of coreligionists provides, for even marginally observant Jews, only the outer skin of Jewish life. The central, beating heart is the Jewish home, indeed an entire network of Jewish homes that creates the Sabbath atmosphere, the festive rituals, the necessary foods, and the spiritual sustenance that constitute the Jewish conception of holiness. Only a house cleaned and polished in honor of the holy day, only a table covered with a starched cloth and laden with traditional delicacies, only the presence or possibility of children to carry on the tradition, affords the necessary complement to the ritual of the synagogue. No man or woman is complete without a mate, the Talmud teaches. No man is exempt from the requirement to "be fruitful and multiply" and no community is possible without women. The little cluster of Jewish women sitting among their bundles on the dock thus introduced something totally new: the possibility of Jewish life in North America.

Later Jewish generations concurred, even reveled, in this insight. Exactly three centuries after the twenty-three made their inauspicious landfall, an American Jewish community 6 million strong uncorked a year of banquets, pageants, concerts, conferences, and books to mark the event. American Jewry reckoned its dawn from the *Ste. Catherine* landing and not from the day, almost seventy years earlier, when a very optimistic but seriously misinformed Bohemian mining engineer named Joachim Gaunse landed at Roanoke Island, Virginia, planning to help extract the mineral riches that everyone knew lay just beneath the new land's crust. Nor did the twentieth-century celebrants mark the moment in the 1640s when one Solomon Franco (of whom we know nothing but his name) stowed away to John Alden's Boston. Instead, American Jews feted the fact that Stuyvesant failed to "require" the twenty-three, "in a friendly way," to leave.[8]

The little band is American Jewry's legitimate forebears in the same sense that the arrival of the *Mayflower* at Plymouth Rock marks the spiritual, if not the strictly chronological, birth of the American nation. Itself sailing from a Dutch port, the *Mayflower* brought Pilgrim mothers who were likewise able and willing to stay. The various European powers had been dispatching numbers of soldiers, traders, explorers, and priests to outposts around the world. These solitary male sojourners might extract wealth and exert power, but they could never make a new continent their own. Only native-born generations can transmit, and transplant, an ancestral culture in a new land. And only female settlers can produce those generations. The profoundest and most beloved of American patriotic holidays asserts this same truth. The original Thanksgiving dinner with the Indians—if it really took place—celebrated the efforts of Englishwomen to make a home in a wilderness and thus to make the continent English and ultimately American. And even if the mythic meal never happened, the turkeys, pies, and casseroles eaten each November to this day mark the permanence that a female presence made possible.

Just as surely as American history begins at Plymouth Rock with Priscilla Mullins and John Alden, American Jewish history begins in lower Manhattan with Rycke (or Ricke, or maybe Rivke) Nounes (or Nunes), Judicq de Mereda (or possibly Judith de Mercado), and five other women whose names we do not know. Generations of arriving Jewish women and their native-born descendants would create in America a Judaism and a Jewry both faithful to ancient traditions and unprecedented in all of history. The strange new land, unimaginably vast to eyes used to measuring crowded European horizons and inconceivably open for souls nurtured on timeworn European restrictions, offered opportunities and posed dangers unknown, even unsuspected, in any Old Country beyond the sea. To this vast, uncharted terrain, newcomers brought long historical memories and the habits of heart and mind that their past had molded.

An ancient and treacherous path led these Jews to the North American shore. Along the way, Jewish women and men had forged a common life that differed in crucial respects from those of other peoples who came here. Their European experience afforded Jewish women American roles, responsibilities, and opportunities that differed in significant ways from those of other women, and made their encounter with America's freedoms and dangers unique in the history of both the Jewish people and the American nation. To understand where American Jewish women would ultimately arrive, we need to understand where they and their men had come from. Which takes us back to the little group on the wharf at the foot of Manhattan island.

The Path to New Amsterdam

No matter how momentous the arrival of the twenty-three might later seem, the refugees had not boarded the *Ste. Catherine* intending to launch a three-century-long golden age. Their minds were fixed not on future world history but on a far more pressing matter: They needed somewhere safe to stay. If the Brazilian towns in which they were living had not fallen to a hated enemy, we would probably know nothing about them at all.

Until very shortly before they set out on their journey into history, all seemed to have been quite unremarkable colonists in a smallish corner of the Dutch overseas empire, a colony that Holland had established in Brazil after conquering settlements formerly held by Portugal. But the Portuguese wanted their territories back, and this time the fortunes of war went their way. After a series of battles, Recife, the last Dutch redoubt in Brazil, fell to Portugal in the spring of 1654.

This military disaster meant that Brazil's Jewish population urgently needed to get out. The Portuguese were closely allied with Spain, so agents of the Inquisition, the dreaded purification arm of the Roman Catholic Church, were expected to arrive close on the victorious army's heels. Most Jews took ship for Holland, but others, for various reasons, sought refuge in other ports. Some, including the twenty-three, appear to have tried their luck first in nearby Caribbean islands, where they apparently met up, either as a group or as separate parties, with the *Ste. Catherine.* Among the available destinations, New Amsterdam was a rough and unprepossessing frontier outpost just forty years old. Along with Spartan living conditions, however, it offered the tolerance and protection that generations of Jews had enjoyed among the Dutch. The crude little town may well have struck the twenty-three as a very desirable haven.

The dangers taking shape in Brazil certainly helped the refugees over-look New Netherland's shortcomings. In addition to many decades of free-dom and prosperity under Holland's protection, by 1654 Jews had 162 years of bitter experience with the militant and oppressive brand of Catholicism that the Spanish crown favored. In the mid-seventeenth cen-tury many Jewish families considered themselves loyal residents of Holland but had originated in Spain, where a large, sophisticated Jewish community had prospered, mostly under Muslim rule, for a thousand years. The Iberian idyll ended suddenly in 1492, when King Ferdinand and Queen Isabella offered their non-Christian subjects the choice of bap-tism or expulsion. On a few months' notice, families that called Iberia home for forty generations had to decide whether to abandon their reli-gion or their country, whether they would become Christians or flee to Portugal, Turkey, Greece, Italy, or any other place that would have them. Those who remained in their beloved Iberian homeland mostly became unenthusiastic Catholic converts known as *conversos,* or New Christians. The Inquisition had been organized in part to root out from the unwill-ingly baptized any backsliders secretly practicing Jewish rituals.

When Ferdinand and Isabella expelled the Jews from their realms, their burgeoning empire also included the seven Dutch-speaking provinces of the Low Countries. In 1568, however, these newly Protestant lands rose against their hated Catholic overlords in a revolt that would last until they won independence some eighty years later. When Ferdinand and Isabella expelled the Jews, however, Spain's holdings did not include neighboring Portugal, where the authorities turned a largely blind eye to *converso* religious eccentricities. Displaced former Jews who settled there lived in relative comfort for another century. In 1580 this safe haven also vanished when dynastic maneuvering brought Spain and Portugal under a single unified crown and Portugal under the Inquisition's full sway. A new wave of formerly Jewish, now nominally Christian exiles spread out of Iberia to Italy, southern France, and North Africa. In their new countries, many of these families openly resumed their ancestral Jewish practices, identities, and names. These reborn Jews, however, were not deeply versed in Jewish law or lore. Three to four generations of life as unwilling Catholics had robbed them of earlier generations' intense familiarity with traditional Jewish texts and practices.

As these twice-uprooted people made major spiritual changes, moreover, many were also on the move physically, this time north to the Low Countries. By the turn of the seventeenth century, the Mediterranean and Iberian ports that had once grown rich from East Indian trade and West Indian treasure had begun to lose their commercial preeminence to the increasingly wealthy cities in northern Europe. New and growing centers of wealth attracted Jewish trading families of Iberian descent, now widely known as "Portuguese merchants," northward to mercantile, anti-Spanish, Protestant, relatively tolerant, and, most of all, booming Amsterdam. In addition, other Jews, with their own, quite different historical memories and language, were fleeing the Thirty Years War then ravaging Central Europe. These families, known in the Jewish world as Ashkenazim from the Hebrew word for Germany, also headed in large numbers to stable, peaceful, hospitable Holland.

Jews soon took a prominent part in the Dutch economy as artisans and small merchants; as craftsmen and businesspeople in the world's leading printing industry (then the cutting edge of communications technology); as physicians, scholars, and men of letters; even, in some cases, as substantial international traders and financiers. They thrived in forward-looking, industrious Amsterdam. Jews of Iberian descent (known as Sephardim, from the Hebrew word for Spain) generally dominated community life. By the time the *Ste. Catherine* landed at New Amsterdam, old Amsterdam's Jews had enjoyed three generations of security as residents of a city ranking among Europe's major Jewish centers. Though Dutch Jews rarely mixed socially with Gentiles, they suffered only minor religious and civil restrictions. This atmosphere of relative freedom and tolerance encouraged an elaborate network of synagogues, schools, charities, and even an institute of advanced Judaic studies.

But Dutch hostility to Spain never abated. The United Provinces mounted a worldwide effort to strip the combined Iberian crown of its overseas possessions and took Portugal's Brazilian colony at Pernambuco in 1630. Jews figured prominently among the Hollanders who sought business opportunities in Brazil, where people of Sephardic background found themselves at a unique advantage. Unlike either Dutch or Portuguese Christians, many Dutch Sephardim understood both Dutch and Portuguese, the colony's commercial languages, because Sephardic families generally used Ladino, a Hebraicized Spanish, as their home language. Since commerce played a central role in the Dutch idea of colonialism, successful businesspeople did very well in the Dutch colonies.

Dutch Jews had been preceded in Brazil by large numbers of New Christians hoping to put an ocean between themselves and the Inquisitors. When the Dutch Jewish newcomers arrived, speaking Ladino in addition to Dutch, they inspired many of these former Jews to return to their ancestral faith. By 1645, Dutch Brazil's Jewish community boasted more than fifteen hundred members as well as a school, various charities, and two synagogues. Recife's congregation claimed the New World's first fully qualified rabbi, the Amsterdamer Isaac Aboab de Fonseca. Leader of Congregation Zur Israel from 1642 to 1649, he helped numerous New Christians find their way back to Judaism, Jewish identity, and Hebrew names. His work was so admired on both sides of the Atlantic that when, four decades later, a volume of his Torah commentaries was published in Amsterdam, the title page honored him by referring to the biblical Isaac, who had, in the words of Genesis, "dug anew the wells that had been dug in the days of his father, Abraham." The Philistines later stopped up wells that Abraham had made, the Bible recounts, but Isaac restored them, once again calling them by "the same names his father had given them."[9]

In 1653 the Portuguese attacked Dutch Brazil, giving the colony's Jews, whether old or new in their faith, good reason to join the defense forces. When Brazil fell definitively to Portugal in 1654, some 650 Jewish colonists still remained and the former New Christians among them found themselves in great peril. Born Jews who had had never converted at least had lived unbaptized. But Jews who repudiated baptism were seen by the Inquisition as heretics to be burned at the stake. So every sort of Jew fled, most to the Netherlands. Some, including the twenty-three, tried their luck in other Dutch territories in the Caribbean and elsewhere. The exact routes that various members of the fateful band took from South America to the *Ste. Catherine,* as well as the route that the ship took to Manhattan, continue to inspire scholarly debate.[10]

A Grudging Welcome

New Amsterdam, Stuyvesant notwithstanding, provided the haven they needed, although they experienced considerable hardship during the first winter, before receiving final permission to stay. To get through the cold months, they begged "several hundred guilders" in emergency relief from Christians, as Reverend Johannes Megapolensis, a New Amsterdam pastor, reported to his superiors in the Dutch Reformed Church back home. He especially resented "the Jewish merchant" (whom historians generally take to be Barsimon, but who could, as we shall soon see, be another mysterious individual), who "would not lend them a single stiver." Several of the penniless refugees came repeatedly, "weeping and bewailing their misery," to the reverend's own house.[11]

These were not people used to penury. The Jews set out on the voyage to New Amsterdam with money and belongings, but pirates attacked the *Ste. Catherine* at sea and apparently stole most of what the passengers had salvaged from the Brazilian debacle. As soon as the ship anchored at New Amsterdam, the captain, Jacques de la Motthe, sued the twenty-three for unpaid fares. Those who still had any luggage, he demanded, should sell it to pay for the entire group's passage. At this point, a Jew already in New Amsterdam named Saloman Pietersz or Piers or Pietersen—presumably one of the traders who had arrived that summer—stepped forward to act as their attorney.

De la Motthe and the Dutch authorities held the Jews responsible for one another's debts, a view that the ship's passengers emphatically did not share. A New Amsterdam court quickly ruled that the group had to sell everything they owned to satisfy de la Motthe, but the resulting forced auction left them 107 guilders shy of the 2,500 he was owed. Any solidarity the little group might have felt dissolved as some people's possessions went to pay for other people's trips. Rycke Nounes, for example, had watched her luggage sold for an amount "over and above her own debt," with the remainder going, unjustly, she believed, to de la Motthe. Asser Leveen benefited from this series of transactions, and their legal squabble quickly followed.[12] Nonetheless, this nasty incident shows that Dutch law allowed a lone woman to hold her own in court against a man and that Rycke had the gumption to try.

When the Dutch West India Company decreed that the Jews accept no further charity from Christians, the twenty-three raised no objection. Like all seventeenth-century Europeans, they would have viewed the Jewish people as a nation distinct from other nations. Members of the House of Israel everywhere expected to provide for their own poor and accepted an inferior political status. Full, equal citizenship for Jews would not be achieved anywhere in the world for another century.

Stuyvesant finally executed the order to allow the twenty-three to remain, but with characteristic poor grace. "Giving [Jews] liberty," he gloomily—and accurately—observed, "we cannot refuse the Lutherans and Papists."[13] He did nothing to make the Jewish newcomers welcome and even tried to limit their business activities, forbidding them, for example, from trading along the upper Hudson River. He also refused to enroll Jewish men in the militia, an ordinary responsibility of male residents. The West India Company soon stymied the first restriction. The second evaporated as the colony needed every able-bodied defender against the Indians.

Events, however, soon confirmed the governor's worst fears: by the spring of 1655, more Jews were arriving in New Amsterdam, bringing word that "a great many of that lot would yet follow," Pastor Megapolensis wrote home with dismay.[14] Neither the reverend's nor Stuyvesant's religious misgivings carried any legal weight, however, and the new arrivals apparently faced no major obstacles to getting settled. They, in fact, seem to have enjoyed considerable social and business freedom in the colony, more perhaps because of the settlement's rough-and-tumble rawness than because of any policy assuring their rights. For whatever reason, however, in the mid 1650s, New Amsterdam's Jews were in fact among the freest on earth.

Though we can surmise something of their political situation, we know almost nothing about the daily life or personal lives of the six "Jewesses" on the *Ste. Catherine* or any of their coreligionists. Rycke and Judicq must have been widows because their names appear among the six heads of families listed in Captain de la Motthe's lawsuit. The litigious Leveen, Abram Israel, David Israel, and Moses Ambrosius were the males on that list. Wives presumably accompanied at least some of these men, and ten children or adolescents completed the group. No further details about these individuals, regarding their ages, their circumstances, or their relationships to one another, have come down to us.

It seems likely, however, that the twenty-three, like the great majority of their fellow colonists, were relatively young and had traveled either in family groups or with close friends. The twenty-three almost certainly included several households composed of a married couple, some children, and perhaps other relatives or dependents. At least four of the original group were single adults, and others could have been marriageable as well. Since we know neither the age nor the sex of the youngsters, we can't say whether any had already passed the Jewish age of majority, thirteen for boys and twelve for girls, which made them eligible to marry. Nor do we have any idea whether new Jewish families were started during the first New Amsterdam years. A religiously valid Jewish wedding requires the presence of Jewish witnesses but not a clerical functionary, so some of New Amsterdam's tiny handful of Jews could have wed at any time after they arrived.

Nor do we know exactly where or how the six "Jewesses," their traveling companions, and their coreligionists found lodgings in the colony. New Amsterdam's industrious inhabitants numbered about a thousand in 1650 and perhaps twenty-four hundred in 1660.[15] A drawing made a few years after the Jews arrived shows several hundred sturdy one-, two-, and three-story houses scattered in clusters along a gently sloping strand.[16] A windmill towers over an unmistakably Dutch skyline, close by the hulking outline of a military fort topped by a lofty flagpole. An oceangoing sailing ship rides at anchor in the picture's foreground, and a smaller, single-masted vessel makes its way along the coast. On the town's outskirts, not far from the water, a gallows proclaims the presence of European law.

Only four decades old when the twenty-three arrived, the colony had the rough look of the frontier settlement that it still was. As in any Dutch town, houses stood close to one another, their sides touching or nearly touching and their gable ends facing the street. How far each narrow structure stretched back depended on how many rooms the owner could afford. Most of those in the picture appear large enough to have a room or two per floor. Each facade, just wide enough for the front door and two or three close-set windows, rises to a steep peak with a single window at the attic level and a chimney at the rear. The streets that these houses face are nothing more than dirt lanes. Large stretches of open ground separate groups of buildings that seem to have been placed without concern for an overall town plan. Not a single tree shades a building as far as the eye can see; presumably all the nearby wood went to heat or build the houses. But it is clear that the colonists had advanced well beyond the bark huts that had sheltered Manhattan island's earliest Europeans, although few residents could yet afford brick or stone walls, tile roofs, or other signs of real prosperity.

Crossing a New Amsterdam threshold would have brought Rycke, Judicq, and the others into the familiarly dark, cramped, smoky world of seventeenth-century colonial domesticity. Like the narrow houses themselves, with their flat fronts and high stepped gables rising among the unfamiliar foliage of an alien continent, life in the colony would have struck the refugee women as at once comfortingly Dutch and exotically North American. The Ste. Catherinites would have recognized houses built for practicality, not for comfort, efficiency, or elegance. Dutch taste and values organized the daily round, but unaccustomed materials—animals, woods, fibers and the like—and unremitting labor in the face of real material scarcity added an edge of frontier crudity.

For all its failings, New Amsterdam must have seemed substantial indeed to new arrivals, especially after weeks or months on a cramped wooden ship. It was clearly a town and not merely a military camp or trading post. It had a life beyond the bare necessities of holding back the Indians, gathering furs to send to Europe, and loading and unloading ships. It was a place where people lived, not just a government base. We have little reason to doubt that before very long Rycke, Judith, and the rest of the Jews settled, whether as boarders, employees, or householders, in some of the tall, sturdy dwellings that looked so inviting from the pitching deck of the *Ste. Catherine.*

2

"OUR YOUNG AND RISING CONGREGATION"

Learning to be Jewish in America

What did going to North America mean in the seventeenth or eighteenth century? Rebecca Samuel knew as well as anyone.

"You cannot know what a wonderful country this is for the common man," she wrote to her parents in Hamburg, Germany, in 1790. In their new home in the little town of Petersburg, Virginia, Rebecca and her husband, Hyman, a watchmaker, had found possibilities and freedoms unimaginable for Jews back home. Hyman was enjoying financial success that far exceeded their hopes. "I believe ever since [he] has grown up he has not had it so good," Rebecca reported in Yiddish. He had even entered a second lucrative line of business. Although in Germany, "a watchmaker is not permitted to sell silverware . . . they expect a watchmaker to be a silversmith here."

Hyman worked unfettered by the discrimination and guild restrictions that limited Jews back home and was "well paid." He had more business than he could manage single-handedly and even enjoyed the amazing luxury of employing a journeyman silversmith, probably a Christian—something impossible for a Jewish artisan in Central Europe. The Samuels awaited the arrival of Rebecca's brother, Judah, who could join Hyman in the business and "become a watchmaker and a goldsmith, if he so desires."

So "now you know what sort of a country this is," continued Rebecca's rapturous description of Virginia, "the greatest province in the whole of America. And America is the greatest section of the world." In this "young country. . .it is amazing to see the business they do in this little Petersburg." Nor, she went on in astonishment, had she or Hyman experienced any problems with their Christian neighbors. "As for the Gentiles, we have nothing to complain about. . . . One can live here peacefully."

And yet, despite the Samuels' quite unaccustomed comfort and success, despite the goodwill of their fellow townspeople, despite the unparalleled frontiers of opportunity that lay open to them, Rebecca felt a great emptiness at the center of her American existence. "The way we live here is no life at all," she confided sadly. "Jewishness is pushed aside here." In free, friendly, booming Petersburg, "we do not know what the Sabbath and holidays are."[1]

Rebecca and Hyman, like all the young Jewish men and women who braved the ocean passage, had alighted not only at the edge of the known geographic world but in a different universe of time, space, and moral meaning. Gone was the European Jewish world they had known, where Jewish families lived in Jewish time and Jewish space, and often under Jewish law. Gone were the Jewish streets and quarters of London or Amsterdam, or the interlocking, intermarried families of small German or Polish towns, where life followed a rhythm set by custom and religion. In America a different tempo punctuated the passing days, one that Rebecca found strident and disturbing.

In the Europe of her girlhood, Rebecca, like virtually all European Jewish women, had learned to mark time by the law of Torah. A woman's week rose in a crescendo of work and anticipation toward the climax of the Sabbath. The cycle of feast and fast days, and the bustle of cooking and cleaning that preceded them, gave shape to the passing year. Every Friday, before the sun dipped, a housewife and her daughters had the house scrubbed and polished; the fish scaled, stuffed, and baked; the braided loaves shining and fragrant from the oven; the children dressed in clean clothes. Then the men and boys, all wearing their best, walked to the synagogue for evening prayers. The wife retired to change into her Sabbath finery. A lacy bonnet replaced the workaday kerchief or cap that covered her head throughout the week. She might slip on, over the ties or buttons holding her bodice closed, a special, embroidered band to assure the modesty of her apronless best dress. Then, with her daughters, their hair braided and beribboned, she spread the white cloth on the table and lit and blessed the lights. In the gathering dark, the men returned for the festive meal of wine and singing that began twenty-four hours of serene disregard for the shop or the peddler's round or the market stall.

Overlaid by the weekly round, the annual cycle of holidays, each with its own duties and delicacies, marked the housewife's year. Sweets, rich cakes, and special holiday loaves welcomed the new year each fall, as well as the family and friends who visited throughout a month of festivals. The year's shortest days were time for deep-fried foods, whether cakes or crisp pancakes, and the half-holiday of Hanukkah. In the late winter, as the days started to lengthen, the merry festival of Purim called for special three-cornered pastries and other goodies dispatched via laughing children to friends and neighbors. Immediately after Purim began the busiest season of the housewife's year, the month of preparation that culminated in the great Passover feasts.

A good manager would already be thinking about the special menus needed for the weeklong feast and preparing the special pickles and preserves it called for. But the real work began in an orgy of scrubbing and sweeping to clean house from top to bottom and find and discard every crumb or scrap of leavened food. All the everyday dishes, pots, and utensils had to be packed away or scalded in boiling water to make them fit for Passover use. And the family's entire stock of staple foods capable of rising or expanding in size—all the flour, barley, buckwheat, and the like, and for Ashkenazim, all beans and rice as well—had to be packed up, moved to storage, and "sold" to a cooperative Gentile, who would "sell" them back at the festival's end. Work began on special foods—cakes, puddings, and charlottes made of flours and meals used only at Passover—needed for the two huge Seder meals and the week that followed. On the great day, as budding branches and later sunsets proclaimed another spring, the family dressed in new outfits, supplied by housewives, often using their own needles. Crowds of relatives and friends assembled on two successive nights around tables set with the family's finest linens and tableware for the hours-long Seder service and the many courses of the year's choicest delicacies that followed it.

Arching over the external time of passing days and seasons was, for the married woman and her husband, the profoundest and most evocative time of all—the interior rhythm imposed by her body. The setting sun marked the onset of each Jewish day, and the full or new moon in the prescribed month announced each feast or fast. But the waxing and waning of the wife's monthly flow set the temporal boundaries of every couple's physical relationship. Judaism views faithful conjugal love as an unalloyed good that is as necessary to each spouse's health and happiness, and to the serenity of the home, as food, sunshine, and mutual respect. Physical satisfaction counts along with sustenance and shelter as every wife's right and every husband's duty. Apart from the modesty that dignified people observe in public, no sense of prudery or shame need spoil a married couple's mutual enjoyment. And for most couples, pleasure in each other, unhampered by the requirements of work, counted as the chief joy of the Sabbath night.

But every month, as regularly as the moon wanes, a pious wife must withdraw her physical presence from her husband, only returning to him, like the waxing crescent, nearly two weeks later. At the first sign of menstrual blood she becomes *niddah,* or prohibited to him, and any physical contact between them forbidden. They sleep in separate beds and, in the words of Ecclesiastes, "refrain from embracing" while waiting out the days of separation. Only after her period has ceased, and she is returned to ritual cleanliness by another flowing stream, is she allowed to return to her husband's embrace. Seven days after she noted the last sign of her bloody discharge, in the evening, she visits a ritual bath called a *mikvah.* Removing clothing, jewelry, ornaments—anything that can separate her body from the cleansing power of water derived either from rainfall or a naturally flowing stream—she immerses herself completely, recites a special prayer, and then immerses herself again. Finally, cleansed both physically and spiritually, she is again free to welcome her husband into her bed. Married life alternates between two states, the weeks of separation and the weeks of union, except when interrupted by the months of pregnancy. And because the days of *niddah* usually numbered approximately twelve, a wife returned to her husband each month at the time she was most likely to conceive. Another period of required separation followed each birth, and another visit to the *mikvah* marked her return to sexual life.

For every adult Jew, therefore, Jewish time ran in three separate but interlocking circles: the weekly round, the monthly cycle, and the turning year. Derived directly from biblical commandments, these regular alterations between the sacred and the mundane, the pure and the impure, tied the concrete acts of daily life into the moral structure of the universe, and moving in Jewish space, between the home, the synagogue, the *mikvah,* and the study hall, men and women did their part in the work of completing the Creation.

In seventeenth- and eighteenth-century North America, though, this ancient calendar and geography dissolved. In the strange new land, where small numbers of Jews found themselves scattered among Christians who accepted them as neighbors, life moved to a wholly different rhythm and the land spread out into a vast, and vastly different, realm of space. No Jewish quarters guarded the old ways. No streets of Jewish shops put up their shutters on Friday afternoon and then filled with men walking to synagogue. No market squares fell quiet for the fast of Yom Kippur or resounded with revelry at Purim. And, just as disorienting for many of the arrivals, no laws held Jewish men and women apart from the other inhabitants of their towns. No religious courts exercised jurisdiction over their daily lives. Here all white people answered to the same civil law, unlike many places in Europe where Jews and Christians answered to different court systems. Here Jewish men and women could enter whatever business they chose, unimpeded by guilds closed to non-Christians. Here they could own land, settle in a city or town without a dispensation from the local lord or bishop, and marry without bribing or pleading with an official for one of a limited number of marriage permits available to Jews.

In nearly all the colonies no official policies tried to keep Jews from prospering or multiplying or moving on the grounds that their very presence constituted a threat to the civic and moral order. Instead, as literate, able-bodied, energetic whites, usually having skills and often capital, they were welcome arrivals in colonies seeking settlers to turn the new continent's immense resources into wealth. And in a land where African slaves and Native Americans were permanently relegated to the society's bottom rungs, Jews were, for the first time in their experience with Christendom, no longer the denigrated Other, the sole, threatening outsider. In the rough, fluid, polyglot society of the port cities and frontier backcountry, the scattered Jewish residents were merely one of many emigrant groups trying to make a new life.

An Old Faith in a New Land

For the first time, Jews lived essentially as equals among Christians who were also new to the land. But, as rabbis in Europe repeatedly warned, no Jew could live piously in so strange and unsettled a country. To fulfill the minimum requirements of decency, an observant Jew needed a quorum of ten men to hold public prayer and establish a synagogue, religious judges and law courts to determine standards of behavior, ritual bathhouses where people can cleanse themselves in the required way, learned men to pursue scholarship and train teachers, traditional schools to pass on Jewish learning to the next generation, and assured sources of kosher meat, wine, and matzah. The boundaries of life called for someone competent to circumcise newborn boys and a cemetery located outside the town limits and enclosed by a fence. No town on the entire North American continent met all these requirements. Few offered enough of them to maintain even a shadow of Jewish observance. So the devout and learned stayed home in

Europe, and young men and women open to new ideas and new adventures were the ones who tested their luck and ingenuity in America.

And they needed plenty of both to transplant Jewish life onto such foreign soil. Many Christians arrived as congregations led by their own clergy and supported by church treasuries back home. Puritan, Anglican, and Roman Catholic clerics were among the first whites to set foot on the new continent. Christian houses of prayer and meeting were among the first, and certainly the grandest, colonial buildings to rise. But immigrants like Rebecca and Hyman arrived alone or in small groups, with no religious authorities to tell them how to go about being Jewish. No fully trained rabbi lived in America until the 1840s, almost two hundred years after the first Jews arrived.

For all the intervening generations, therefore, every Jewish prayer circle that met in a family's front room or at the back of some merchant's store, every group of children who gathered around an adult to learn their Hebrew letters and Bible stories, every band of worshipers who decided to rent or buy space to serve as a real synagogue, every committee that acquired a parcel of land for a Jewish burying ground, and everyone who asked neighbors to donate in aid of a widow and her children or a poor girl who wanted to marry—each Jewish person carrying out any pious act—did so not through some rabbi's direction but through the ad hoc efforts of individuals who had determined they would be Jews together. Many who cooperated in these projects had not known each other before they found, in America, that they shared a common religion. Many came from different countries and did not even share a common home language or liturgical tradition. When the time came to blow the ram's horn to welcome the new year, or to bathe and shroud the body of a dead neighbor, or to compose a marriage contract, or to interpret a line of scripture, or to circumcise a newborn, or to perform any of the countless other ritual acts that Jewish daily life required, the American settlers could depend only on their own resources of knowledge, imagination, and skill.

Jewish life can go on without rabbis, who, unlike some Christian clergy, do not occupy a sacramental position and have no power to stand between the individual worshiper and God or to transform the mundane into the sacred. A rabbi is simply a man who has devoted his life to religious learning and has reached a level of achievement recognized by ordination. His understanding of the Hebrew Bible and the commentaries in the Talmud equip him to guide his people toward a holy life. He functions not as prayer leader but as a teacher, in that word's broadest possible sense, working to educate his community in every possible way. He leads adult study groups, expounds Torah and Prophets to the whole community at religious services, counsels and advises about personal problems, oversees the schoolteachers who educate the children, provides a moral and spiritual model, and generally sets the tone of community life.

His wife—for in a traditional community a rabbi does not attain leadership without marrying—also fulfills a teaching function among the women and girls, organizing good works, serving as a moral and spiritual example, and even giving formal lessons in matters of religion. Routine religious tasks, such as leading set prayers, slaughtering animals, circumcising babies, teaching children Hebrew and Bible, and even officiating at weddings and funerals, do not require a rabbi's presence. Special functionaries—the *hazzan* (cantor), the *shochet* (slaughterer), the *mohel* (circumciser), the *melamud* (schoolteacher)—can do them just as well, and sometimes better. But the rabbi's guidance informs each of these jobs and assures the community that those who do them meet proper standards of knowledge, character, and piety.

In Europe, rabbis often also played the crucial role of legal authorities for their communities, a status backed by the power of the local ruler or state. In the old world, Jewishness was a legal status, not merely a spiritual choice; religious communities kept formal rolls of their members, which each individual entered at birth (or, very rarely, by official conversion) and could leave only by formally adopting another faith. Wherever a Jew's actions impinged on a Christian, Christian law obtained. But in areas that involved only Jews themselves—including such vast realms as family life, inheritance, many business dealings, and all the details of religious observance—Jewish law, codified as the *halachah* and interpreted by rabbis acting as judges, often held sway.

That detailed code governs not only large and obviously religious issues such as marriage and burial. It also controls countless smaller ones that secular people now consider matters of private choice: what you eat and wear; when you work and pray; how you deal with your parents, children, spouse, neighbors, employees, tenants, creditors; even when and how often you make love to your mate. "Can I serve a piece of meat that was placed mistakenly on the wrong dish?" a European housewife might ask her rabbi. "When, exactly, will the Sabbath begin two weeks from tomorrow?" a businessman planning a sales trip might inquire. "Is the schoolmaster teaching my child a correct interpretation of a Bible story?" a puzzled father might wonder. "Can we postpone our sickly son's circumcision from the required eighth day of life because he's ill?" anxious new parents might need to know.

But months on the high seas separated American Jewry from rabbis and rabbinic courts, and so only very large and not very immediate questions could ever be formally asked. For the countless small, daily conundrums of making a life in a new land, people had to depend on the opinion of the most learned Jew in the neighborhood or, very often, on themselves. By the time a query could cross the Atlantic and an answer return, the meat would have been eaten, the deceased buried, the baby circumcised, the Sabbath celebrated, the business dispute settled, the dress worn, and, even, perhaps, the sexual union consummated.

Beyond do-it-yourself *halachic* interpretation, Jews in America had to start every institution and practice from scratch and simply do the best they could with the knowledge and understanding they could muster. Even the largest communities, such as Charleston, Newport, New York, or Savannah, numbered at most a few hundred Jews who just happened to find themselves living in the same vicinity. Doing one's best often meant improvising to an extent that would have shocked friends and relatives back in Europe.

Fortunately, Jewish law grants wide latitude for acting within the law. If circumstances require, any individual with the requisite knowledge can lead a prayer service, conduct a burial, or even witness the legal agreements that create a marriage. But it's one thing occasionally to read the funeral liturgy or conduct Sabbath prayers with no nearby rabbi to consult. It's quite another to face the issues of daily life and establish a cemetery, a kosher abattoir, an elementary school, or even a synagogue with the nearest fully trained religious leader thousands of miles and many weeks away.

Even so, Jewish congregations sprang up even in towns like Petersburg with as few as a dozen Jewish families. The Jewish dead were often laid to rest in Jewish burying grounds, and at festival times people who traded along the frontier or worked in outlying hamlets converged on places where they could worship and celebrate among their fellow believers. For many, the desire to feel a sense of Jewish community and the shape of the Jewish year had crossed the Atlantic intact. But keeping the calendar and a sense of connectedness constituted a challenge even in the main cities; in many of the smaller places where people had followed business opportunity, Jewish time and Jewish space simply evaporated.

In Petersburg, for example, Hyman Samuel made precision timepieces that represented the pinnacle of high technology, but his wife, Rebecca, could not find a rhythm that resonated with her soul. "Hyman [has] made a clock that goes very accurately, just like the one in the Buchenstrasse in Hamburg," she proudly informed her parents. "Now you can imagine what honors Hyman has been getting here." But, to her deep shock, the only honors available in Petersburg were secular. "There are here ten or twelve Jews, and they are not worthy of being called Jews," she confided. "On the Sabbath all the Jewish shops are open; and they do business on that day as they do throughout the whole week." And even more appalling, "We have a *shochet* here who goes to market and buys *terefa* [unkosher] meat and then brings it home." What was more, "On Rosh Ha-Shana and on Yom Kippur the people worshiped here without one *sefer torah* [Torah scroll] and not more of them wore a *tallit* [prayer shawl] or the *arba kanfot* [ritual fringes] except Hyman" and his closest friend, a man they had met in Petersburg who had emigrated from Holland.

Rebecca and Hyman struggled to maintain the traditional ways. On the Sabbath, they did not "allow [their shop] to open. With us there is still some Sabbath. You must believe me that in our house we live as Jews as much as we can," but that, Rebecca obviously believed, was not nearly enough. No lone household, she found, can live a fully Jewish life nor any single family maintain the rhythm of the Jewish week or year when surrounded by neighbors who keep Christian time. A housewife cannot keep a Jewish kitchen or set a Jewish table if she cannot reliably get kosher food.

But even more worrisome than her own malaise was the future of Rebecca and Hyman's children, three-year-old Schoene and newborn Sammy, who had never known any old-world Jewish life at all. "Dear Parents," Rebecca went on in dismay, "I know very well you will not want me to bring up my children like Gentiles. Here they cannot become anything else." And so, she reported, she and Hyman had regretfully decided they must give up the thriving business they had built in Petersburg and move to Charleston, which had a "a blessed community of three hundred Jews. You can believe that I crave to see a synagogue to which I can go." Their Dutch friend, who had served as Sammy's godfather, "does not want to remain here any longer [either] and will go with us to Charleston." Their "whole reason" for leaving Petersburg, she emphasized, was "lack of *Yiddishkeit*" [Jewishness]. Indeed, Rebecca's Petersburg friends, mostly Christians, "say that it is sinful that such blessed children should be brought up here. . . . [where] they cannot learn anything . . . Jewish."[2]

Family Matters

We do not know whether Rebecca found the Jewish life she craved in the lush, deeply shaded gardens and sophisticated literary salon of that wealthy port city. No record of her experiences there survives. But keeping their children Jewish weighed heavily on the minds of many parents. As youngsters grew out of childhood, the issue often became painfully problematic. Abigail Franks, for example, an observant Jew brought to America as a child and married to one of New York's wealthiest and most prominent Jewish merchants, had to endure the shock of her daughter, Phila, secretly marrying a Christian in 1752. And not just any Christian, either; Oliver DeLancey was a scion of an old and distinguished New York family (which gave its name to a street later inhabited by countless Jews).

How did Phila and Oliver meet? Educated, wealthy, and at ease in the local culture, the Franks family moved freely in the city's uppermost business, literary, and social circles. New York Jewry seems to have been too small to inspire organized discrimination. In fact, Abigail preferred her Christian friends' company to that of certain Jewish women, who, she confided in a letter, were "a Stupid Set of people."[3] In the parlors of elegant Georgian townhouses, hers and theirs, she exchanged calls with such elite New Yorkers as the governor's family and the Van Courtlands, and often made extended summertime visits to country homes in the northern reaches of Manhattan island or even in bucolic Flatt bush, across the East River.

It was from that rural retreat that she wrote, heartbroken, to her son Naphtali Hertz (known within the family as Heartsey), a businessman and New York native who lived in London, to report his sister's duplicity. "I am now retired from town and would from my life, (if it were possible to have any peace of mind)," the grieving mother penned, "for the severe affliction I am under on the conduct of that unhappy girle [Phila]. Good God, wath a shock it was when they acquinted me she had left the hous and had been married six months. I can hardly hold my pen whilst I am writing it.... I gave noe heed [to rumors about the marriage] further than a generall caution of her conduct wich has always bin unblemish'd, and is soe still in the eye of the Christians whoe allow she had disobliged us but has in noe way been dishonorable, being married to a man of worth and character."

Phila, of course, had known in advance that marrying Oliver meant accepting Christianity, which in turn meant breaking her ties with the

Jewish people. But the young DeLanceys wanted to keep their bond with Phila's family. "Oliver has sent many times to beg leave to see me," Abigail's lament to Heartsey went on, "but I never would tho' now he sent word that he will come here. I dread seeing him and how to avoid him I know noe way, neither if he comes can I use [i.e., treat] him rudly [i.e., rudely]. I may make him some reproaches but I know my self soe well that I shal at last be civill, tho' I will never give him leave to come to my house in town, and as for his wife, I am determined I never will see nor lett none of the family goe near her." Nonetheless, Abigail added, "He intends to write to you and my brother Isaac to endeavor a reconciliation." And, she counseled Heartsey, "I would have you answer his letter, if you don't hers, for," she admitted sadly, ". . . nature is very strong and it would give me great concern if she should live un happy, tho' it's a concern she does not meritt."[4]

Much as Abigail bemoaned her daughter's union, however, this was not the first time a child of hers had taken a Christian spouse. Her son David, who became one of Philadelphia's pioneer Jewish residents, had married a Christian woman nine years before Phila's wedding. He never accepted Christianity, although he allowed his children to be raised as Christians. He took an active part in Mikve Israel, Philadelphia's first synagogue, throughout his life. Abigail's other daughter, Richa, seems to have had greater regard for her parents' feelings about intermarriage. She did not marry until she reached middle age and moved to England; her parents had already died. Apparently she found no suitable mate on a continent where, at any given moment, eligible Jews numbered at most in the hundreds.[5] We know that at least one Jewish suitor, David Gomez, of a large and prosperous New York Sephardic clan, doggedly sought her hand for several years. But that "Stupid wretch," Abigail predicted to Heartsey, would never win Richa's heart, and he eventually gave up and contented himself with a Sephardic wife.[6]

The very fact that a Gomez came courting a Franks shows once again how far American Jewry had traveled from the world Jews had known in Europe. David's ancestry was a tangle of Spanish surnames running directly back to the golden age of Sepharad, as Hebrew speakers call Spain. Richa's was purely Central European, or Ashkenazi. In the Old World such a match would have been unheard of. Jews arrived in Iberia with the Romans. For more than ten centuries, until King Ferdinand and Queen Isabella united their realms in marriage and the entire Iberian peninsula under Christian rule, Jews lived and prospered in the territories that ultimately became Catholic Spain. For seven of those centuries a succession of Muslim rulers held most of the peninsula, and according to their religion's teachings, granted Jews and Christians toleration and protection, though not full legal equality. While Rome's Christian heirs fell into barbarous decline throughout northern Europe, all around the Mediterranean littoral Muhammad's followers erected brilliant, cosmopolitan civilizations.

In cities and princely courts aglow with poetry, philosophy, science, mathematics, music, and all the other arts of high culture, Iberian Jews flourished as scholars, writers, traders, artisans, doctors, politicians, even advisers to the rulers. Their community and religious life blossomed and their devotion to Iberia's land and culture grew deep and sincere. They even developed their own form of medieval Spanish, known as Ladino, which became the Jewish home language. Educated Jews commonly wrote and read Arabic and Hebrew in addition. They built elegant synagogues in the Moorish style, where, amid Arabesque colonnades and geometrically tiled walls, they chanted their prayers to sinuous Arab tunes. Jews who refused to relinquish their tradition and had to leave when Ferdinand and Isabella expelled them went mourning as if the temple of Jerusalem had been laid waste a third time.

Wherever these exiles found refuge—in France, Italy, Turkey, North Africa, and later in Holland, England, and the Caribbean—the sons and daughters of Sepharad (the Sephardim) kept alive the memory of their lost home. They preserved their Hebreo-Spanish tongue, their liturgy, their family names, and their sense of themselves as a select clan within the House of Israel. Jews of Iberian blood called themselves the Nation and worked to keep their bloodlines unsullied by Jews of less genealogical distinction. They never denied their kinship to their less privileged and unsophisticated brethren from backward Ashkenaz—the northern Christian lands generally coterminous with the German language—but the Sephardim emphatically denied those less worldly and less wealthy Jews access to their synagogues, their neighborhoods, their social lives, and especially to their families through marriage. Preserving the Nation's purity had such importance that in 1615 the Amsterdam Sephardic community organized a fund to ensure that even Sephardic maidens in financial need had the means to marry a proper son of Iberia. The Holy Company for Providing Dowries of Orphans and Young Girls (or Dotar) staged an annual lottery to award money needed to make respectable matches. Deserving girls from around the world submitted applications, a judging committee made its selections, and each year a small number of brides married at the Dotar's expense.

As a full-blooded son of the Nation, why was David Gomez trying to woo a girl whose antecedents ran back to some petty realm of Central Europe and not to the Golden Age of the Abassids and Almohads? As befitted his New World birth, if not his Iberian heritage, David was simply acting like a North American and was doing what Jews of every background had done from the earliest days in Peter Stuyvesant's New Amsterdam. He was treating all his fellow American Jews as if they considered themselves one community. They felt this way both because they were so few in number and because the larger Christian society viewed them as one people in any case. In Europe the Sephardim had remained stubbornly distinct; in 1697 the Amsterdam community decreed ostracism to any man who wed an outsider. As late as the early nineteenth century it refused to bury a Portuguese Jew who had taken an Ashkenazic wife.

But in America, Sephardic Jews increasingly married other American Jews regardless of ancestry. Of the generation coming after David Gomez, at least two members of the family chose Ashkenazic spouses. Indeed, the 942 Jewish marriages that occurred in America between 1686 and 1840 show a similar pattern: the longer a Sephardic family lived on this continent, the more of its young people found husbands and wives outside of the Nation.[7]

Even before David Gomez began calling on Phila, Abigail Franks had seen such a match in her own family, the Levys. The dashing Isaac Mendes Seixas, newly arrived from London, had caught the eye of her sister Rachel Levy, Abigail wrote to Heartsey in 1738. But Isaac's people back in England, as well as "the Portuguese [Sephardim] here are in great fermenth about it And think Very Ill of him," she went on. When the couple defied this opposition and married two years later, "the Portugueze here" went into "a Violent Uproar abouth it," made all the worse, Abigail gleefully added, by the fact that the groom "did not invite any of then to ye Wedding."[8]

But these hard feelings did not last. Within a decade Isaac was a leader in the New York Jewish community, serving on the executive committee (or *manahad*) of the city's only (and now its oldest) Jewish congregation, Shearith Israel, still called the Spanish and Portuguese synagogue. The congregation has always followed the Sephardic liturgy, though it served a mixed membership from the beginning. No one more clearly symbolized the new and distinctively American Jewry formed out of melded European strains than the son of Rachel and Isaac's scandalous union, Gershom Mendes Seixas, who in 1768 became Shearith Israel's first American-born *hazzan*, or cantor. With no rabbi on hand, the *hazzan* functioned as the congregation's religious head. Until his death nearly forty-eight years later, this offspring of a controversial "mixed" marriage not only headed New York's leading Jewish religious group but served as the community's quasi-official representative to its Gentile neighbors.[9]

In the place of hereditary distinctions that carried great weight in Europe and of religious authorities who told European Jews not only whom they could marry but what they should wear, read, and see at the theater and opera, American Jews acted on their own sense of what was proper and reasonable. Their self-confidence and inventiveness arose in part from necessity; if American Jews were to have any religious life at all, they had to will it into existence themselves. It also rose from an atmosphere of personal freedom that people in Europe could not even imagine. In Jewish law, for example, communities have the power to ostracize members who flout their practices or beliefs. In 1656, for example, Amsterdam Jewry imposed *herem* (excommunication) on Baruch (later Benedict) Spinoza, a Sephardic lens grinder who made blasphemous statements about his ancestral faith and is also known to world history as a great modern philosopher. For a man of Spinoza's intellectual gifts, the community's power to deny such rights as Jewish marriage, burial, and education for his children might have carried little terror. But for more ordinary men and women, who had nowhere to turn except the Christian world, *herem* served as an effective control on all kinds of behavior.

But in America, whose booming coastal cities and open frontier beckoned the ambitious and determined, *herem* meant very little. Whether people even identified as Jews, whether they stayed put where they first landed, or whether they struck out for new horizons, was essentially a matter of personal choice. Many men and women of every religious persuasion moved time and again after they arrived in the country, seeking newer and better opportunities. Many of the customary distinctions that had separated Jews from one another and from the non-Jews around them simply didn't survive the Atlantic crossing. In Europe, for example, Jewish women generally dressed according to a code of modesty that the rabbis enforced. Bodices came to the neck and sleeves at least to the elbow. Kerchiefs or caps hid a wife's hair from all eyes but her husband's. But in this astonishing new world, Jewish women "go about with curled hair and

French finery such as is worn by ladies of other religions," marveled a German mercenary soldier stationed in New York during the Revolutionary War. Equally amazing, he found that, unlike their bearded coreligionists back home, New York's Jewish men also "dressed like other citizens [and] shaved regularly." No Jew of either gender had to bow to a rabbi's opinion requiring modesty or to a civil law requiring distinctive badges or hats, as some European governments still demanded. Here people's wardrobes were dictated by their own taste and pocketbook.

Thus a confident Phila Franks, dressed in a fashionably low-cut gown, gazes at us from a portrait made before her marriage. Her wide, scooped neckline reveals a long throat and a delicate cleavage. In another portrait, her maternal grandfather, Moses Levy, an Ashkenazi who reached New York in the early 1700s, has the wig, waistcoat, and clean-shaven face of a colonial gentleman, while the ship in the picture's background indicates the source of the family's wealth. Paintings of Grace Mears Levy, Moses's second wife, and of Sarah Lopez, who married Newport's most prominent Jew, reveal every bit as much chic as Phila's and, in Grace's case, a good deal more décolletage. Grace wears a dress with a plunging, off-the-shoulder neckline perfectly appropriate for a ball attended by aristocratic Gentiles, but utterly shocking to traditional Jewish sensibilities. What's more, both of these married ladies show their dark, lustrous hair. Sarah wears hers piled on her head and adorned with a swatch of lace, but Grace's elaborately coifed tresses are bare.

As Abigail Franks's comment on David Gomez make clear, parents recognized that their daughters had a right to marry, as well as dress, as they chose. In Europe that choice lay largely with the older generation. A young man might suggest that his father inquire about a girl who caught his eye, and a girl could reject a match proposed by her parents, but young people did not simply wed whom they wished. For young Americans, elders' opinions carried much less weight, in part because the fluid new society gave individuals far more personal freedom and economic opportunity and in part because a marriageable white woman was a far scarcer and more valuable commodity than in the Old Country. A good many more young men than women streamed off the incoming ships, swelling the already lopsided supply of suitors vying for local girls. We don't know the exact sex ratios of Jewish arrivals or, indeed, of the Jewish community at large. (Censuses and city directories enumerated people as members of households. Because eighteenth-century law did not grant females anything close to legal equality with males, only heads of household were

listed by name. Except for a scattering of widows, those names are exclusively male.) Still, we have no reason to suspect that Jewish proportions
differed greatly from those of the population at large.

We do know that Jewish women married men considerably older than
themselves. New York records, for example, indicate brides as young as
fifteen, and a first wedding for a woman over thirty was rare. A Jewish
woman typically came to the *chuppah* (marriage canopy) at twenty-three or
twenty-four; the man awaiting her under the silk or linen covering had usually reached his early thirties. Although the method of choosing a mate had
undergone a sea change, families tried to retain the old rituals when they
solemnized a match. Thus, when Rachel Phillips of New York wed
Michael Levy of Virginia in 1787, "four young men . . . who had put on
white gloves for the purpose" held poles at the corners of "a beautiful
canopy composed of white and red silk," according one of their wedding
guests, the eminent Philadelphia physician, Dr. Benjamin Rush, who
described the scene in a letter to his wife. "At one o'clock . . . sixty or forty
men assembled in Mr. Phillips' common parlor" to recite prayers and witness the groom and the bride's father sign a marriage contract written in
Hebrew. The bride then entered, "accompanied by her mother, sister and
a long train of female relations." Her "veil . . . reached halfways down her
body. . . . Innocence, modesty, fear, respect and devotion" mingled in her
face. "She was handsome at all times, but the occasion and her dress rendered her in a peculiar manner . . . most lovely and affecting. . . . I gazed
with delight upon her" as two bridesmaids led her to her fiance's side
under the *chuppah*. The couple faced an officiant whom Rush calls "a
rabbi" and "a priest" but was doubtlessly a *hazzan*, perhaps Gershom
Mendes Seixas himself. The Christian Rush understood none of the
Hebrew ceremony, but he watched the couple sip wine from a single gob-
let, the bride receive a ring, the groom smash a glass, and the guests give
"a general shout of joy," whereupon everyone adjourned for wine and
cake. The happy couple meanwhile went upstairs, where, in greater privacy, they "supp[ed] a bowl of broth together" to break the fast, "agree-
abl[e] to the custom of their religion," that they had begun the night
before. Rush's medical duties prevented him from staying for the dinner
that followed, but as he made his farewells the bride's mother, Mrs. Jonas
Phillips, "put a large piece of cake into my pocket" for the doctor's wife
and sent warm regards to her from "an old New York acquaintance."[10]

But many American Jews did not have a traditional wedding—or any
wedding at all. As many as a quarter of them, like Richa Franks, remained

single. In addition to the small numbers of potential mates, the social differences between long-time residents and newcomers made matchmaking difficult. Recent Ashkenazic arrivals, often poor in both education and finances, held little charm for native-born girls of established families.[11] Phila's grandfather Levy may have started the family fortune as an itinerant peddler fresh from Germany, but it's hard to imagine her, two generations later, choosing a small-time trader just off the boat.

Some Jewish bachelors wanted to deal with the shortage of suitable partners by marrying a Christian woman willing to adopt his faith. But a daunting obstacle barred the way to the *chuppah*: no one on the entire continent had the qualifications to perform the conversion that must precede such a wedding. Even in Europe a Christian who became Jewish was a real rarity, and nearly all such cases involved not true proselytism but a Gentile woman who wanted to marry a Jew. But the 1655 law permitting Jews to live in Britain expressly prohibited seeking converts among Christians (although no such restraint applied in the other direction), and colonial congregations wanted to avoid even the appearance of violating it. Still, law has little sway in affairs of the heart, especially among people torn out of their accustomed ways and thrown together with strangers, as were many new Americans. Despite both Jewish and civil law, some Jews and Gentiles wanted to marry and form Jewish families. American communities had to figure out how to deal with them.

Some conversions seem to have taken place. Reverend Ezra Stiles, a leading Protestant clergyman, may have witnessed or heard an account of the process, for he accurately noted in his diary that for men it entailed immersion and circumcision.[12] For women, immersion alone sufficed. In 1793, Moses Nathans, a Jewish Philadelphian, brought a poignant request to the board of the city's Mikve Israel congregation. Having lived with a Gentile woman for almost a decade, he wanted to marry her and legitimate their daughter and two circumcised sons. Couldn't the congregation accept her as a convert so that they could have a wedding recognized by Jewish law (as well as civil law—a fact that accorded Jewish clergy legal equality with their Christian counterparts)? Benjamin Nones, the synagogue's president, sympathetically passed the question on to the *bet din* (religious court) in London. It was an issue, his letter emphasized, of the greatest importance "to Jewdaisme at large and to our young and rising congregation in particular."[13] The couple married under Jewish law the following year.

Not long afterward, a Gentile woman named Anna Barnett petitioned Mikve Israel for permission to convert. She had missed "the happiness to be born a Jewess and favoured imediatly from the God of Israll as you are," she wrote, and longed to "liv[e] up to the divine precepts of the Bible." An unmentioned desire to marry a Jewish man may well have figured into her wish.[14] In the custom of the time, a wife accepted her husband's religion, so conversions probably involved a Christian woman marrying a Jewish man. Such matches, of course, did nothing to improve the chances for unmarried girls like Richa who wanted to stay within the faith; their odds of finding a Christian man willing to accept Judaism were essentially nil.

Though many young couples may have suffered for lack of rabbis to perform conversions, the situation greatly enhanced the standing of the men holding the post of *hazzan* in the new congregations. Functionaries traditionally charged with leading prayers and perhaps teaching children found their roles expanded far beyond anything known in Europe—into the official heads and spokesmen of American Jewish communities. Catholic Christians regard marriage as a sacrament, and only an ordained member of the clergy can solemnize a union. British law therefore recognized only weddings performed by ministers of religion or justices of the peace. (The sole exception was Quaker Pennsylvania, where members of the Society of Friends could wed in their accepted fashion, without officiants.) Jewish law, on the other hand, regards wedlock as a civil contract. Just as Michael Levy did in the Phillips family's parlor, the groom and a male representative of the bride sign before witnesses a contract called a *ketubah*, which lays out the couple's agreed-upon rights and obligations. By accepting a token (traditionally a ring), as Rachel Phillips did, the bride assents to his promise to live with her and support her in the manner appropriate to a Jewish husband. This mutual consent, not any special power vested in a religious officiant, makes them spouses. The wine and prayers serve to sanctify the occasion, not to create the marriage. Any individual, ordained on not, who knows the procedure (or can read it out of a book) can preside over this bare-bones exchange and perform a perfectly valid wedding.

But if the British authorities wanted a "minister" designated by each Jewish congregation, then a "minister" they would have, the Jews decided, even if that person was just a previously humble *hazzan* now endowed with unaccustomed prestige and power over who could marry "according to the law of Moses and Israel." Naming such an official assured that Jewish marriages would have civil status equal to Christian ones, a privilege denied in much of Europe, since unions performed under Jewish law often lacked legal standing.

Reinventing Ritual

Though they had to invent much of it themselves, many American Jews lived active religious lives in the seventeenth, eighteenth, and early nineteenth centuries. A considerable number of "the seed of Abraham," for example, assembled at Shearith Israel for Yom Kippur prayers, as a visitor from Annapolis, Maryland, Dr. Alexander Hamilton (not the first secretary of the Treasury), wrote in a 1744 letter home. The "doleful hymns" haunted him for weeks afterward and the "veil[s] of some white stuff" that the men "threw over their heads in their devotions" gave the entire affair a note of decidedly exotic piety. And numerous female worshipers, he noted, occupied a special gallery above.

The letters of Abigail Franks testify to her devotion to traditional ways. She cautioned Heartsey, for example, to eat only bread and butter at the London home of one of her brothers, who, she suspected, did not keep a strictly kosher house.[15] As much as she loved keeping in touch with her far-flung kinfolk, she refers in letters to putting down her pen because the Sabbath approached, when writing would become a forbidden form of work. Even though she might miss a chance to send a letter with someone traveling to a far-off place, she chooses not to break the Sabbath rest. Two other Jews loath to abandon their religion, L. E. Miller and his wife, Polly, sent Shearith Israel a plaintive note begging "any Yehuda" to buy the indenture that bound them to a Christian master. They longed to complete the term of service that had paid for their passage to America under a Jewish master who kept the Sabbath and a kosher home. Otherwise, they, pleaded, they faced years in their present, "very deplorable situation amongst Goyim."[16]

But for many other Jews, like the Samuels' Petersburg acquaintances, Judaism had by the eighteenth century become a "once-a-week" ritual rather than the all-embracing and distinctive way of life it had been—and would long remain—in much of the Old World.[17] To varying degrees they had abandoned strict observance. Among the women "who stood up in a gallery like a hen coop" at Shearith Israel, Dr. Hamilton spotted some "very pritty" ones.[18] Unlike many traditional European synagogues that sequestered the women's section behind curtains, grates, or lattices, this

American house of worship gave any casual visitor to the main-floor men's section a clear and revealing view of the ladies above. When the congregation built a new house of worship in 1817, a traditionalist faction tried—but failed—to include a concealing screen across the women's balcony. They also attempted, unsuccessfully, to bar unmarried women from the front, and most visible, row.

America's Jews also seem to have become lax in a matter unknown to Dr. Hamilton that was utterly crucial to traditional married life. We have no idea how—or whether—seventeenth- and early eighteenth-century Jews met the requirements of marital purity. A *mikvah* stood on Shearith Israel's grounds from at least 1731 on.[19] Newport's Touro synagogue also possessed a "Bagnio (bath) where there are Stairs and one stands to his neck in Water," Reverend Stiles noted in his diary. "Most strict Jews baptize religiously by trine Immersion three Times a year" in preparation for major holidays such as Yom Kippur, he added, although "such strictness is not exacted."[20] As to the women's habits he says nothing. Not until 1784 do we have evidence that the members of so prominent a congregation as Mikve Israel, Philadelphia's oldest, felt the need for a proper *mikvah*. (The synagogue's name, incidentally, derives from a different word and means "hope of Israel.")

In that year Manuel Josephson, a German immigrant noted for both religious and secular learning, organized a petition to the congregational board expressing "great sorrow and regret" at a failing that "cannot affect but with astonishment and horror every judicious and truly religious mind." The "want of a proper mikve [sic] or bathing place," such as commanded in Leviticus 20:18, degrades much more than the congregation's women and their sexual partners, the document argued. "The very children born from so unlawful habitation," must be "deemed bene niddot [children born during menstruation, i.e., in a state of ritual uncleanness]," the petitioners warned. Should Jews in other lands learn of this grave blemish on "not only the parents, but their posterity for generations to come," they "would not only pronounce heavy anathemas against us, but interdict and avoid intermarriages with us, equal as with [a] different nation or sect, to our great shame and mortification."

And even more dangerously, the petitioners went on, the congregation was neglecting the duty to "manifest our gratitude" to God for the blessings of life in America that "we enjoy far beyond many of our brethren dispersed in different countries and governments." Only by punctiliously following divine law could the community hope to avoid the "severe tremendous sentences" brought against it. The synagogue needed to build a *mikvah* for its "sole use" without delay.[21] Offering to pay for the project out of their own pockets, the signers "flatter[ed them]selves that every married man will use the most persuasive and every other means to induce his wife to a strict compliance with that duty so incumbent on them, so that the Almighty might look down in mercy upon us and send the Redeemer of Zion in our days."[22] Within two years, the congregation had a bathhouse in operation, with Josephson supervising.

Did Philadelphia's Jewish wives actually frequent it? And what had they done for the sixty years that elapsed before Josephson's innovation? The mention of Mikve Israel's "sole use" might imply that the congregation had shared a facility with others. Had they, for example, met their ritual obligations in a river or creek that their Christian neighbors used for more mundane washing? Any freely flowing natural stream meets the religious requirements as to water source, but probably not the congregants' desires as to privacy or comfort.

A natural spring near Shearith Israel, for example, may have served in the early years, some historians suggest. But can we imagine someone similar to Abigail—or even to one of her "Stupid" fellow members—doffing their wigs and petticoats and ducking under the surface completely nude? Even if the ladies agreed to such a crude arrangement, they surely would have demanded some sort of wall or fence for privacy. But no mention of such an arrangement in the early decades of the eighteenth century survives (if such a thing ever stood on synagogue grounds), perhaps because the community ignored the question or perhaps because they considered it too delicate to discuss.

But we do know for sure that colonial Jews kept another central element of traditional piety, the dietary laws. For a woman trying to provide her family kosher food, everything to do with their sustenance rises to the realm of the holy. Going to the market, raising chickens in the yard, churning butter and making cheese, seasoning a cut of meat, turning it on the spit, planning a day's meals, setting the table, clearing the dirty dishes, washing, drying and putting them away—each of these deceptively ordinary acts brings her in touch with the ultimate law of the Universe, as commanded by God and written in the Torah. Biblical injunctions forbid eating *treif,* or nonkosher, foods and mixing milk and meat. Some animal foods, such as pork, shellfish, and the hind quarters of any mammal, are *treif* by definition; others become so unless slaughtered according to *halachah* and handled in a way that keeps them safe from contact with *treif.*

So, bending over her kneading board or gingerly sampling a soup, skimming the cream from the morning's milking or picking the plumpest chicken to send to the *shochet* to be killed for the Sabbath dinner, she guards her household's sanctity—and the spiritual state of their table—by punctiliously following the rules. Did she prepare meals that a pious person could eat without compunction? Could guests partake at her table in confidence? The ritual state of a family's kitchen could make the smallest details of cooking, serving, and storing into matters of public import.

In 1744, for example, Shearith Israel accused the widow Hetty Hays of keeping "a Treffo [ritually unclean] house," and her alleged infraction became a community issue.[23] A member of a large, contentious clan often at odds with synagogue leaders, Hetty not only fed her own household but ran a boarding house catering to Jewish travelers. Her alleged use of (probably cheaper) unkosher meat thus threatened not only the rectitude of the Hayses but the reputation of the congregation. Either she must immediately restore the *kashrut* of her kitchen or risk losing a lot of business. As it happened, a London rabbi and a Dutch *shochet* were visiting New York at the time, so Hetty had expert supervision while she cleansed all her pots, dishes, tables, and cooking and dining utensils to the congregation's satisfaction. We don't know whether she chose to boil, scald, or sear her things or bury them in the ground—both approved methods of "kashering" equipment—but we do know that she complied.

Hetty seems to have failed in a crucial aspect of maintaining *kashrut*—allowing only kosher food to enter her kitchen. But she also would have had to segregate meat and dairy foods, as well as the dishes and utensils used to store, prepare, and serve them, from foods or implements of the other category. Families needed special meat and dairy sets of kitchenware and tableware, as well as habits of cooking, washing, serving, and storing that keep them scrupulously apart. Beyond the demands that the dietary laws place on the homemaker, they also require every community of any size to provide a source of kosher meat.

Only a pious man trained in the law can serve as a ritual slaughterer. In small communities, he might do this job part-time, when, for example, children or servants would arrive each Friday with a clucking, struggling chicken in their hands and leave with a headless bird ready to be plucked and cooked for the Sabbath dinner. Larger settlements might provide steadier work preparing cows, sheep, and poultry for the market. However they managed it, providing for kosher meat and also for a supply of Passover matzah ranked among every synagogue's most important responsibilities. Even in places too small for a full-fledged congregation, committed individuals sometimes looked after these needs on their own, often becoming in the process the hubs of informal communities.

Every Sabbath for decades during the eighteenth century, for example, the dinner table of the Simon family in little Lancaster, Pennsylvania, became the center of Jewish life between Philadelphia and the frontier. At sunset every Friday, and at the set times in every season, men who peddled and traded throughout the surrounding backwoods gathered with the Simons for the prayers and festive meals that ushered in the Sabbath and the festivals. At the High Holidays in fall and at Passover in the spring, this ad hoc congregation convened for prayers and fellowship. As long as Joseph Simon ran his trading company in the thriving commercial town, men passing through to sell their goods or replenish their supplies joined the prayer group that met regularly in the shop. When Joseph died, Lancaster's Jewish life died too. But the tradition of religious initiative lived on. As we will see, his daughter, Miriam, who married into the Gratz family of Philadelphia, herself raised a daughter who pioneered distinctively American institutions during the mid nineteenth century that became central to the nation's Jewish life.

Formal congregations have left extensive records regarding the men they hired as *shochets*, as well as the salaries they paid, the terms of service they arranged, and the other duties the *shochets* performed. But no good evidence tells us how individual families managed *kashrut* in their own homes. People rarely record the ordinary details of everyday life—how they clean their cookware, for example, or where they store their leftovers. We can only infer that a fair proportion of Jewish homes were observant, given that communities went to the trouble and expense of employing kosher slaughterers. Rebecca Samuel, after all, bemoaned the laxity she saw in Petersburg, and Abigail Franks cautioned Heartsey to take care at the home of his lax London uncle.[24] But Abigail also socialized with a wide circle of Christian friends. What she ate when calling on them in town or staying with them in the country we do not know. Perhaps they planned their menus to accommodate her. Perhaps she brought food with her, or perhaps she tried to follow the advice she gave Heartsey. Perhaps she improvised, avoiding pork or shellfish but eating what she could of her friends' unkosher food off their unkosher plates. Or perhaps, as many colonial visitors did in a time when housewares were scarce and expensive, she brought her own dish and knife. She may even have followed the practice, common in modern times, of keeping kosher at home but not away.

Although we can only guess at the mechanics of colonial *kashrut*, we can surmise that they must have affected spouses' roles as well as their daily fare. Responsibility for the kosher kitchen fell to women. But kosher slaughter and the bureaucratic arrangements surrounding it were the affair of men, since females could neither vote as synagogue members nor, usually, carry out the traditional role of *shochet*. Jewish gender roles thus differed from Gentile roles in this domestic matter, just as they did in earning a living, as we shall see in later chapters.

Transforming Tzedakah

Keeping kosher at the edge of the known world took ingenuity, but preserving another of Judaism's central tenets led individuals and communities deep into unknown territory. The community's obligation to provide for the poor, and the individual's duty to contribute to the effort, goes back in Jewish law at least to the reign of King David. This responsibility binds every Jew, rich or poor, young or old, male or female, who is not currently suffering utter destitution. Even those living on community relief gave their mite for people still less fortunate. A sick neighbor, a penniless decedent, a needy widow or orphan, any oppressed or distressed individual, has the right to the protection and care of every member of the House of Israel, an obligation that extends to Gentile needy as well. From their earliest days in the New World, a land where colonial authorities from Stuyvesant on expected the Jewish community to take care of its own, Jewish men and women banded together to keep a roof over the fatherless, to arrange proper burial for the indigent departed, to buy medicine for the needy sick, to feed and house the old or frail or friendless.

The Hebrew word for these monetary donations is *tzedakah*, from a root meaning righteousness; it translates into English as something close to "social justice." Unlike such Christian terms as "alms," which comes from the Greek word for mercy, or "charity," from the Latin for love, *tzedakah* implies no special religious or spiritual merit, but only the decency to do one's fair share, rather like paying taxes. Indeed, in many parts of Europe the organized Jewish community had the backing of the state to collect from each family the funds it needed to pay for orphanages, hospitals, schools, old people's homes, widows' and orphans' mites, poor girls' dowries, and all the other needs of a community that included many poor members. But the ethic of *tzedakah* went much deeper than a formal responsibility and wove itself into the ordinary rhythm of the week, the year, and the lifetime. Before lighting the candles that begin every Sabbath and festival, a woman slips money into the family's *tzedakah* box. Children devote some of their Hanukkah money—given by parents in memory of the currency coined by a long-ago independent Jewish state—to the poor. Every Sabbath and Passover table should, if possible, include the needy among its guests. And the more bountiful one's blessings, the greater is the obligation to give as lavishly as possible. Generous giving has always played a large role in the determination of social standing among Jews.[25]

But arriving from Europe, where the work of collecting and distributing *tzedakah* was a function of an official community, Jews landed in a country that considered charity a private matter largely centered in churches. In the absence of authority or custom, Jewish newcomers fell back on instinct and ingenuity. Their old assumptions about the need to care for the unfortunate remained, but they had to invent new ways of putting them into effect. So, when a Jew died where there was no Jewish cemetery, or an invalid couldn't pay his doctor bills, or a family lost their possessions in a house fire, or any of the countless other catastrophes of life struck one of their number, Jewish individuals and small groups passed the hat or sometimes simply paid out of their own pockets. Thus they bought many of the early burying grounds, as well as necessities of life for the unfortunate. In 1740, for example, three years after arriving in Philadelphia, Nathan Levy—one of the city's first Jews and a business partner of Abigail Franks's son David—bought a piece of land for family burials. Before long he opened it to the whole community.

In *tzedakah,* as well as in many other aspects of life, Jews also noted the example of their Christian neighbors. As soon as a makeshift prayer or study group meeting in a home or behind a shop began to organize itself into a formal congregation, it took on the task of coordinating *tzedakah* in its locality. And since only men served on synagogue governing boards, a community's formal good works were initially in male hands.

But only women can perform some of the tasks that need to be done. Besides such ordinary necessities as bringing food to a house of mourning or seeing a neighbor through childbirth, a Jewish woman might have to prepare a relative, a friend, or even a stranger for the grave. In traditional Judaism, the formal and sacred task of cleansing, bathing, and shrouding the dead falls to an honored voluntary association known as a *chevra kadisha* (holy society). In Europe such associations of men functioned almost as fraternal societies, with annual dinners, badges of office, and special washing bowls and beakers decorated with the group's name or pictures of the funeral rites.

Respect for the dead requires that a person of the same gender perform the intimate rituals of purification and dressing. So, alongside men's associations, but without all the banquets and insignia, women organized themselves to assure each other the dignified treatment due every human being in death as well as life. *Tzedakah* in the new land probably functioned in this traditional way at the beginning. But by the latter decades of the eighteenth century, American Jewish women were doing something unprecedented in European experience: taking a prominent and public role in charity projects of their own. This activity stems partly from the New World penchant for taking personal initiative. But it also owes much to social changes affecting Gentiles as well as Jews.

For many families of every background, the hardscrabble days of scratching a living out of a newly settled land were decades or generations in the past. The Atlantic port cities enjoyed vigorous trade, and many of their enterprising citizens enjoyed a level of wealth and comfort unknown in the early years. A number of wealthy, established families, Jews as well as Gentiles, had elegant homes staffed by servants and furnished in the beautiful Georgian or Federal styles. Household labor and the struggle to make a living no longer dominated their days. The women of these families now had time for more prestigious concerns, such as the stylish new pastime sweeping the colonies, the ladies' afternoon tea party. Behind red brick facades facing Philadelphia's most select squares, under New York's best high tiled roofs, on Charleston's finest deeply shaded verandahs, or in Newport's choicest Chippendale parlors, privileged Jewish wives, mothers, and daughters—like their Christian friends—devoted more and more of their energy to making calls, planning entertainment, keeping up with fashion, and refining their manners.

For prosperous Christian women, this shift was especially pronounced; indeed, it signaled a newly emerging ideal of womanhood. The lady, with her delicate sensibility and elevated tastes, replaced the thrifty, competent housekeeper busy at her spinning wheel or butter churn. Fine needlework occupied the hands of visitors in fashionable parlors, where once women had bent over workaday sewing or mending. A wife and mother sheltered from life's ruder realities began replacing the stern father as the family's moral guide. But many of these well-off and often well-read women of good families, recently liberated—or cut off—from hard, practical concerns, sought to do serious work in the world and found an outlet for their considerable energies in Christian concern for the poor. Charity provided the one form of socially accepted work a lady could do outside her home.

Because this modish new model of womanhood won over the socially prominent, it beguiled the aspiring middle classes as well. The prestigious new occupation of philanthropist thus held great attractions for prosperous Jewish women. Charitable concerns—not identical to but certainly compatible with Christian ideas on the subject—also lay at the heart of Judaism. But because men dominated the public aspects of *tzedakah*, Jewish women first entered American-style charity work through nonsectarian causes organized by their Christian friends. At tea tables up and down the seaboard during the last decades of the eighteenth century and the first decades of the nineteenth, the Jewish "Lady Bountiful" began to emerge alongside her Gentile sister.

As Jews had already done in so many other spheres, these women remained Jewish by becoming wholeheartedly American. Like Rebecca Samuel, Abigail Franks, and others of the preceding generations, native-born daughters of affluence in the early years of the nineteenth century cherished their Jewish heritage and strove to preserve it in characteristically New World fashion. Indeed, the first American Jewish woman known for her own accomplishments rather than her wide correspondence or prominent husband created her lifework by creating new and authentically American forms of *tzedakah*. Born in 1781 of the union of two prominent Pennsylvania merchant families, the Lancaster Simons and the Philadelphia Gratzes, Rebecca Gratz founded—indeed, invented—institutions that have played a crucial role in American life for almost two centuries.

She carried on the spirit of religious devotion and public service that had animated her maternal grandparents, the Joseph Simons, but Rebecca had other arresting qualities as well. Her intelligence, character, and bewitching charm convinced some Jews that she had inspired the beautiful Rebecca in Sir Walter Scott's *Ivanhoe*, though independent evidence does not confirm this belief. Unlike the literary heroine, the real Rebecca never married, instead spending her entire long life in the service of her community. She began at an early age; by twenty she belonged, along with her mother, Miriam Simon Gratz, and two sisters, to the founding board of the Female Association for the Relief of Women and Children in Reduced Circumstances, a nonsectarian society of prosperous Philadelphians. Rebecca's deep piety and strong ties to Mikve Israel soon expanded her interests to meeting specifically Jewish needs, and in 1819 she and several friends founded the Female Hebrew Benevolent Society.

Organized to aid small numbers of "their indigent sisters from the House of Israel," it was the first American Jewish charitable association not formally connected with a synagogue.[26] As its work expanded into the broader concerns of poor Jewish families and involved women from various sectors of an increasingly diverse Jewish community, it provided a model, both in form and content, for countless organizations since. But Rebecca did not remain content simply carrying out the Jewish tradition of *tzedakah*. Through pioneering achievements in religious education, she also worked for the survival of the American Jewish community.

That she and others could build the distinctive culture and institutions of American Jewry was possible because the seventeenth- and eighteenth-century Jews who came before them had explored a new world of piety and community as adventurously as their era's sailors and frontiersmen explored the unknown continent. Landing on a mysterious shore whose spiritual outlines they could only barely discern, they led the way to forms of Jewish life and expression unprecedented in history but well suited to this unprecedented new land.

3

"I MAKE EXCEEDINGLY WELL"

Making a Living and a Life

S ecure in her family's comfortable home in her native city of Charleston, Penina Moise experienced neither oppression nor intolerance. Her merchant father, Abraham, originally from Alsace, had found business success first on the Caribbean island of St. Eusticius, where he had married the daughter of a rich local family in 1779. He also prospered in Carolina, where he, his wife, Sarah, and their four young sons fled twelve years later to escape a slave uprising.

Their sensitive younger daughter Penina, born in 1797 as the second of five children born to the Moises in the United States, nonetheless felt the anguish of her coreligionists across the sea. In 1820, she penned one of the first poems by a Jewish woman ever published in the United States, an invitation "To Persecuted Foreigners" to seek the freedom and safety her parents had found in America.

"If thou art one of that oppressed race," begins the nearly forgotten poem's best-known stanza,

> *Whose pilgrimage from Palestine we trace,*
> *Brave the Atlantic—Hope's broad anchor weigh*
> *A Western Sun will gild thy future day.*[1]

For immigrants of every background, prospects in the new land did seem golden. Gentiles saw a boundless vista of opportunity, with vast expanses of virgin acreage and untouched fields and forests stretching as far as the eye could see or the mind could imagine. Gone were the fences, hedgerows, and walls that delimited an old-world farmer's holdings and economic opportunities. Gone were the rules of inheritance, rent, tradition, and class that kept so many ordinary Europeans from even hoping ever to till soil of their own. In their place the new continent offered limitless horizons of fertile cropland, full barns, dignity, and prosperity.

For Jewish newcomers, the geography of hope had a special shape. Though their Christian shipmates were overwhelmingly country folk looking for a chance to farm, nearly all the Jews from Europe descended from generations of town dwellers who had provided goods or services to farmers. Whether from a metropolis like London or Amsterdam or a tiny hamlet deep in the German mountains, Christendom's Jews had for centuries functioned mainly as middlemen between city producers and the peasantry, between foreign markets and local populations, and even, in large stretches of Eastern Europe, between landlords and their own tenants. Forbidden to own farmland in nearly every European country, generally banned from joining Christian craft guilds, Jews traditionally had sought their livelihoods as traders or small artisans.

Family-owned businesses provided most Jewish households with often meager livings, with men and women alike trading from little shops, market stalls, or pushcarts. Jewish peddlers with their stocks of notions, tinware, and household sundries trudged the back roads of a dozen nations. Jewish rag and bone dealers, the recyclers of the preindustrial age, rode their wagons through the towns, buying and selling the raw materials for paper, buttons, and other products. Jewish tailors, metalworkers, and other small tradesmen met the needs of both Christian and Jewish customers.

Would-be colonists brought to America skills, tools, and sometimes capital acquired back home, and this usually intangible cargo molded their chances in the new land. Because European Jews had lived differently from the Christians surrounding them, their American lives also tended to take a distinctively Jewish course. The great majority of men and women landing at colonial ports hoped to find homes and work in the countryside, but the sprinkling of Jews among them gravitated toward town occupations and town life. And as was true in European market squares and shopping streets, a striking number of Jewish women entered business in the New World as well. From their earliest days as Dutch colonists, Jews worked as traders, whether in little shops or substantial stores in the towns, from peddler's carts or trading posts in the countryside, or by ship in the ever growing Caribbean and transatlantic trade.

The daring and ambitious of every religious persuasion found tremendous opportunities. Dominating fine natural harbors, New Amsterdam,

Savannah, Charleston, Baltimore, Philadelphia, and Newport gave access to the continent's unfathomable riches. Stuyvesant's little settlement, for example, served as the main port for a colony that stretched from the Hudson River at today's Albany to the shores of the Delaware River near Philadelphia. It enjoyed vigorous trade with both the mother country and the flourishing Dutch colonies of Surinam, on the South American coast, and Curaçao, astride the shipping lanes of the Caribbean. Sugar, hides, fur, timber, rum and other New World produce flowed toward the Old World. Manufactured goods and slaves flowed back.

So rich was the transatlantic trade that the British decided to take it from the Dutch, capturing New Amsterdam in 1664 and the rest of New Netherland soon after. Dutch colonists, Jews and Gentiles alike, abruptly and unexpectedly found themselves residing in an English town renamed New York and in a British colonial empire newly extended from Massachusetts to Virginia. The takeover's timing proved very propitious for Jewish New Yorkers. Late in the thirteenth century England expelled all Jews from its home islands. In 1655 it readmitted some, over the objections of potential business rivals in the City of London. Within two years of their arrival, London's new Jewish residents had gained permission to hold public worship, a right that had taken five decades to attain in Holland. Within five years of readmission, Jewish Londoners totaled thirty-five Sephardic households; within thirty years Sephardic families numbered almost a hundred. Indeed, so many Jews from all parts of Europe came to live in England that within a half century the Jewish community—by then three-quarters Ashkenazic—topped seven thousand souls.[2]

When Holland ceded New Netherland, toleration of Jews was still a relatively new idea in England; nonetheless, the Articles of Capitulation between the two powers granted freedom of conscience to all the colony's residents. The British Crown had taken a similar attitude when, in the same momentous year, 1655, it captured Jamaica from Spain. In 1661 it extended to all of that island's white inhabitants and their children, including the Jews who had begun arriving shortly after the Spanish departed, the status of "free denizens" with rights equal to "natural born subjects of England."[3] The British Crown had in fact gone so far as to proclaim in the 1663 charter of Rhode Island colony that "noe person within the sayd colonye at any tyme hereafter shall bee in any way molested, punished or called into question" because of religious views or practices unless they "actually disturb the civill peace of our sayd collony."[4]

A desire to attract to vast and underpopulated colonies every able-bodied person willing to make the dangerous ocean voyage and take up the often arduous life of a new settler probably motivated His Britannic Majesty far more strongly than any abstract interest in the religious rights of non-Anglicans. Among Britain's North American colonies, only Massachusetts and Connecticut imposed any doctrinal requirements for residence. Developing the colonies' wealth demanded so much labor and talent that the colonial powers could not entice sufficient numbers of workers across the ocean, and they began to import slaves from Africa.

In their general enthusiasm to recruit settlers, the British admitted religious dissenters of all kinds, including some who were persecuted back home. Quakers, Catholics, Lutherans, Presbyterians, German Pietists, deists, and nonbelievers all flocked to the New World in hopes of living and worshiping (or not) as they chose. Criminals, debtors, and other social undesirables also found a new chance on the Atlantic's far side. As more, and more varied, emigrants continually landed, all the port cities except religiously restrictive Boston became increasingly cosmopolitan, polyglot clusters of mostly young, often adventurous, individuals from innumerable and frequently unknown backgrounds. Once arrived in the colonies, settlers—who had, after all, wrenched themselves out of their accustomed lives in the home country—continued their footloose ways, many moving repeatedly in search of ever more enticing opportunities. In this volatile atmosphere of hope and ambition Jews found that their long honed commercial skills could take them down promising new paths.

Getting Started

For the entrepreneurs who organized and financed the vast oceangoing exchange among the colonies and the mother countries, profits could flow very abundantly, and from early on Jews sought a share. Throughout the seventeenth century, Jewish families had pursued trade in London, Amsterdam, and such Caribbean islands as Jamaica, Barbados, St. Barthélemey, St. Eustatius, and Curaçao.[5] In the same entrepreneurial spirit, Jews began reconnoitering North American possibilities beyond New Amsterdam soon after the twenty-three arrived from Brazil. By the early 1660s, a quarter century ahead of William Penn's Quaker settlers, Jewish traders were traveling down the South River, which we know as the Delaware, to call at newly declared Dutch territories that had recently been New Sweden and would soon be Pennsylvania. Jewish merchants also appeared in the leading British ports of Newport in 1685, Charleston in 1697, and Savannah in 1733.

The burgeoning seaports where these women and men first tried their luck grew within a generation or two from hardscrabble frontier outposts into thriving cities complete with substantial businesses, wealthy mercantile and financial firms, lively cultural scenes, and small but active Jewish communities. Jews took part in all spheres of commerce, from itinerant peddling to large-scale overseas shipping and in artisan trades ranging from simple tailoring to elite silversmithing. As far as we can tell, married couples, sibling groups, and lone individuals all started concerns and many Jewish wives, mothers, sisters, and daughters had full, adult shares in their family businesses.

For generations in Europe, wherever a Jewish man tried to turn a shilling or pfennig or kopeck, chances were good that a Jewish women worked beside him. More often than their Christian counterparts, Jewish women, whether married or single, were active in business, either in cooperation with male relations or on their own. Husbands and wives worked together in the shop or stall. Male peddlers traveled their country routes, but their wives stayed in town, often dealing on their own in dry goods or notions or groceries or baked goods from the family's front room or a booth in the marketplace or door-to-door among their Jewish and Gentile neighbors. A German-Jewish contemporary of the twenty-three, a matron called Glueckl of Hameln (1645–1724), is the entrepreneurial woman we know best because she left a memoir detailing both her commercial exploits and the doings of her large brood of children and grandchildren.

In the seventeenth century, of course—and well into the nineteenth—European and American women of all religions and social strata, except the very richest, did work crucial to the household's economic and physical survival. They spun, wove, and sewed the clothes their families wore, and then repeatedly scrubbed the garments clean. They knitted the socks that made the period's often ill-fitting shoes wearable, along with the mittens, scarves, and caps that made work possible in cold weather. They rendered and molded tallow for both soap and candles. They grew gardens and preserved the produce, raised chickens and collected the eggs. They raised cows and made butter and cheese. (Gentile women also kept pigs, which in early colonial days ran free in the towns, living on foliage, garbage, and scraps.) Women of all faiths cooked the meals and baked the bread. They nursed the sick and saw one another through childbirth. They labored from morning to night running complicated households almost devoid of mechanical aids. A colonial woman's marriageability depended on her skill at these essential tasks. The needlework samplers so familiar to us, with their verses and pictures created out of fancy stitching, were intended not to decorate but to display a girl's ability to do, or at least to supervise, the sewing that would clothe her future family.

A nimble needle could even feed a household. Frances Sheftall, for example, the wife of a prominent Jewish merchant, slaveholder, and patriot in Georgia, found herself the sole support of several children and responsible for several slaves when, from 1778 to 1780, the British authorities imprisoned her husband, Mordechai Sheftall, and their eldest son, Sheftall Sheftall, for their Revolutionary War activities. Most American Jews patriotically favored independence. Many fought in the army, including members of the self-styled "Jew Company" of South Carolina. Jewish merchants helped provision the Continentals, including Mordechai Sheftell, who was captured while attempting to run goods through the British blockade. The Jewish banker Haym Solomon helped finance the struggling new government. A Jewish physician tended the sick at Valley Forge.

Frances, meanwhile, stripped of the family's assets, sought safety in Charleston, where she, her children, and her slaves endured the three-week British siege of the city. All her charges caught smallpox, Frances reported in a letter to her prisoner husband, and one of the slaves died. Meanwhile "[cannon] balls flew like haile," and "whear [hard currency to pay the rent] is to come from God only knows. . . . I am obliged to take in needle worke to make a living for my family, so I will leave you to judge what a livinge that must be."[6]

Breadwinning ladies were, of course, nothing unusual in the colonial period, especially during crises like the Revolutionary War. Abigail Adams, who urged her husband, John, to "remember the ladies" and their right to fair treatment "in the new code of law which I suppose it will be necessary for you to make" for the new country, ran their family farm for years on end while he was off helping to found the nation.[7] In normal and extraordinary times alike, however, Jewish wives and daughters appear to have played a larger and more direct role in commerce than women of other backgrounds. Typical is the resourceful Frances, who, in another of her letters to the British prison, told Mordechai that she had received "the 2 thousand pounds" owed the family by a Mr. Cape, "with which I make exceedingly well out by doing a little business," presumably trading. She also reported commissioning a Mr. Levy, who planned to travel shortly to

North Carolina, to buy her some gold coins "as thay are much cheaper thare than [they] are here."[8] These she soon used to buy relief supplies that she sent to her imprisoned husband and son.

As in the Old Country, both Jewish and non-Jewish artisans and traders generally started out doing business from home, working at their crafts, storing their stocks of materials and merchandise, and even waiting on customers either in the same cramped houses that their large families inhabited or in outbuildings right nearby. As Gentile families prospered, the practice of living "above the store" (or behind it or next to it) tended to wane. Jewish families, however, retained the custom a good deal longer, often even after they had achieved considerable financial success, which allowed women to remain active in family businesses.

We can name a considerable number of Jewish businesswomen among the tiny colonial Jewish population. In addition to her questionably kosher boardinghouse, Hetty Hays, the fractious eighteenth-century New Yorker, also ran a dry goods shop, as did her fellow Manhattanite Hannah Moses. Charity Cohen kept another New York boardinghouse. In 1791 Ann Sarah Alexander of Charleston received from her husband, Abraham, the right to act as a trader on her own account.[9] Esther Pinheiro, who inherited her husband's shipping business and ran it from her home base on the Caribbean island of Nevis, operated on a grander scale, calling regularly during the eighteenth century in the ports of Boston and New York on her sloop, *Neptune,* and becoming a well-known figure in both towns. Abigail Minis of Savannah ran both an unspecified commercial concern and a plantation worked by more than a dozen slaves. Frances Polock of Newport oversaw a "substantial establishment" active in the import-export field.[10] "Rachel the Widow and Relict [survivor] of Symon Mendez," along with an otherwise all-male group of "other Jews fforeigne born," successfully defended themselves in court against charges by Newport's British authorities that they had violated the Navigation Acts, infamous laws that limited trade in the colonies stringently enough to encourage the colonists to revolt against the Crown.[11]

Jewish Geography

The *Ste. Catherine* twenty-three may even have chosen New Amsterdam because it offered, in addition to Dutch tolerance, business opportunities as yet untapped by Jewish entrepreneurship. Jewish merchants, mostly Sephardic, were numerous and prominent in the Caribbean by the 1650s.

By the end of the seventeenth century, Jews constituted at least 80 percent of the traders, merchants, and brokers in wealthy Curaçao and owned over two hundred trading vessels home-ported there.[12]

By striking out for a place without Jewish merchants, the twenty-three and those who followed them were pursuing a venerable tradition. Starting commercial outposts in new territories was a road to wealth that enterprising Jews had followed for centuries, at least since the days when they were traders sending camel caravans along the Silk Route to China. Their strategy, in the days before overnight express mail, international wire transfers, and computerized credit reports, was to deal in faraway places as much as possible through trustworthy trading partners. But how could a trader in London or New Amsterdam tell whom to trust in Curaçao or Newport? The best ways were knowing the person's reputation, family, and background; checking bona fides with trusted and knowledgeable associates; and bringing any missteps to the attention of people able to exert effective sanctions. But whose family and background does one know better than one's own? And who can enforce sanctions against dishonesty or sharp practices better than someone related to both the principals to a deal?

Not long after Abraham set out from Ur with his flocks, Jewish traders deduced that the most trustworthy and easily accessible commercial correspondents were relatives, friends, and friends of friends. In a world where Jews generally lived in tight, inbred local communities but stood at a social remove from the surrounding non-Jews, their long-distance dealings often involved relatives, or at least putative relatives, at both ends of the transaction. In the days of the Silk Route across Central Asia, Jewish traders tried not to leave home without letters of credit written in Hebrew script. To this day, whether on New York's 48th Street, in Antwerp, or in Hong Kong, Jewish diamond merchants seal agreements with a handshake and a Yiddish phrase (practices now widespread among Hindu traders as well). In the same spirit, Jewish colonial traders preferred, if at all possible, to entrust their transatlantic or trans-Caribbean shipments to other Jews, and most preferably of all, of course, to kin.

Just as the founder of the House of Rothschild dispatched four of his five sons each to a different European capital in the late eighteen century, other seventeenth- and eighteenth-century Jewish families with designs on intercontinental commerce sent out sons, grandsons, nephews, and cousins to settle in places where the family wanted a commercial presence. If an appropriate relative could not be tapped to make the move, or if the

family hoped to strengthen ties with a commercial house already established in a faraway town, what could better ensure harmonious dealings
than becoming relatives? Marrying the daughter or granddaughter or
niece or sister of one family to a promising young man of the other house
could serve both groups' business interests while also solving Jewish parents' eternal and pressing problem of finding suitable Jewish mates for
their children when many local communities were too small or too inbred
to offer many eligible candidates.

In the late seventeenth century, for example, Louis Moses Gomez, born
in Madrid about 1655, emigrated by way of France to New York. There he
married Esther Marques, a New Yorker with family ties to Barbados,
including a stepfather and brothers living there. The sons of Louis Moses
and Esther eventually married Rebecca Torres, daughter and sister of
Jamaican merchants; the Curaçaoan Esther Levy; and Esther Nunes of
Barbados. Louis and Esther's son Daniel did business with his Curaçaoan
brothers-in-law Aaron Da Chaves and Jacob Da Joshua Naar during the
1740s, and with Jamaicans Isaac and Benjamin Gomez. Benjamin, possibly
a brother of Daniel's, also married a girl named Esther Nunes, of Jamaica.
Daniel's business associates also included one Miguel Gomez, of the
Spanish island of Madeira, perhaps also a relative.[13]

Daniel's brother Mordechai, meanwhile, sired seven children in New
York, of whom only a daughter, Eve Esther, married a fellow New Yorker,
the Ashkenazi Uriah Hendricks. Mordechai's sons Isaac and Moses found
wives in Curaçao and Jamaica, respectively. Moredechai's son Moses M.
married Esther Lopez, daughter of the leading Newport merchant Isaac
Lopez. Esther Lopez Gomez's sister Abigail then wed Moses M.'s nephew,
Isaac Gomez Jr. Mordechai's other daughter, meanwhile, settled down
with a husband in London.[14] Other families had equally far-flung in-laws.
Sons of Rachel and Isaac Mendes Seixas, Abigail Franks's sister and
brother-in-law, married into Newport and Charleston families; their
daughter wed a Londoner and a niece a Jamaican man.[15] Down the coast,
in 1761, the future patriot Mordechai Sheftall of Savannah wed his
Frances, a Charlestonian. Six years later Mordechai Sheftall's brother Levi
married a girl from St. Croix, and in 1774 their fellow Georgian, Philip
Minis, wed a daughter of Newport.[16]

These long-ago social notes reflect the importance of colonial "Jewish
geography." It constituted vital intelligence for families hoping to prosper,
expand their business options, and above all help their sons fulfill the mitzvah (commandment) of being fruitful and multiplying while also remain-

ing Jewish. Judaism places the duty to reproduce on males rather than females. "A man may not refrain from fulfilling [it] unless he already has children," the Talmud states.[17] His obligation to find a wife is so strong that a bachelor traditionally could not become a teacher, judge, rabbi, or community leader. The word *hazzan*, usually translated "cantor" or "prayer leader," is an acronym of three Hebrew words that define job requirements far more important than a good singing voice: *hacham*, wise or learned; *zakayn*, old or mature; and *nasui*, married.

To fulfill the obligation properly, the wife a man found must be Jewish; regardless of the father's piety or pedigree, only the child of a Jewish mother traditionally counts as a Jew. Parents of daughters naturally hoped that they would marry, and women saw marriage as a very desirable state. But staying single carried no religious opprobrium for women. Though Jewish tradition regards marriage as the ideal situation for all adults, a woman's inability to wed reflected her parents' inability to provide her a match or the community's failure to ensure her a dowry, rather than any fault of her own.

The mercantile and matrimonial mechanics of long-distance match-making worked best when sentiment backed up financial connections, so women often played central roles in engineering matches. Arranged marriages were the norm throughout Jewish Europe, but parents could only organize them if they heard about one another's children. The *shadchen*, or marriage broker, a perfectly respectable member of nearly every Jewish community, could belong to either gender. Although the young couple's male relatives may have carried out the public part of the negotiation, female relations or friends often had a hand in seeing that the right people happened to meet or learn of one another. Female members of many colonial trading families, in a tradition at least as old as that biblical business-women, the "woman of valor" described in Proverbs 31, took an active part in wide-ranging exchanges of news and goods, and they doubtlessly used far-flung intelligence networks of sisters, cousins, aunts, sisters-in-law, daughters, and childhood playmates in the cause of matrimony.

Women also bore much of the emotional cost of the long-distance marriages they worked to devise. "I wish but for the happyness of Seeing you," Abigail Franks wrote to Heartsey in 1741. "I fear I never Shall [see you] for I dont wish you here And I am sure there is Little probability of my Goeing to England," she lamented.

"If parents would Give themselves Leave to Consider the many Difficulties that attends the bringing up of Children there would not be such Imoderate Joy at there birtth I dont mean the Care of there infancy thats the Least but its affter they are grown Up and behave in Such a manner As to Give Satsfaction then to be bereaved of them in the Decline of Life when the injoying of them would be Our greatest happyness for the Cares of giting a Liveing Disperses Them Up and down the world and the Only pleassure wee injoy (and tats intermixt with Anxiety) is to hear they doe well Wich," she added, in the spirit of countless Jewish mother before and since, "is a pleassure I hope to have."[18]

Extant Franks family letters, as well as other collections of letters, diaries, and records, confirm two important facts about colonial Jews. First, in those days before the telephone, scattered kinfolk took their correspondence seriously. Second, Jewish women, especially the native-born, navigated easily in American society. Like Abigail, they generally were literate, and sometimes highly literate for their time and place. Despite her irregular spelling and punctuation, Abigail wrote like many cultured people of her era. The inconsistencies reflect not lack of schooling but rather the casual attitude toward linguistic niceties customary in a society where printed matter was scarce and costly. Abigail must have read widely, though, because she peppered her correspondence with quotations— sometimes a bit inaccurate but still to the point—from such popular contemporary authors as Addison, Dryden, and Pope.[19]

Keeping up with the latest literature implies more about Abigail than an inquiring mind. She obviously had the leisure to read extensively and either the means to buy books or access to affluent friends who could lend them. Since books were very upscale luxury goods well into the nineteenth century, at least some members of North American Jewry—along with North America's economy and cities—had come a long way from the mud and deprivation of New Amsterdam in the 1650s.

Real Cities

By the turn of the eighteenth century, in fact, the main ports, where most Jews lived, were much more than hardscrabble hamlets. Month after month, boatloads of strong young newcomers came ashore, adding to the booming populations of the port towns and their hinterlands. The large families typical of Americans of all religions also helped the colonies grow. New Yorkers, who had numbered an estimated thirty-nine hundred in 1690, were seven thousand strong by 1720, and eleven thousand—which would have rated as a significant urban population even in England—only twenty years later. Philadelphians increased even faster, from four thousand in 1690 to thirteen thousand in 1742. With that city's protected harbor and easier access to its fertile backcountry, it would soon overtake Boston as the continent's metropolis. Even little Newport almost tripled, from twenty-six hundred in 1690 to sixty-two hundred in 1740. Charleston, doyen of the lush, semitropical low country, had expanded explosively, from eleven hundred to sixty-two hundred in that same period, despite repeated calamities of fire and hurricane.[20] As the towns became cities and businesspeople found even more scope to make money, some individuals and families, both Jewish and Gentile, become well-to-do and even rich. Certain Jewish women were by now owners of prosperous businesses and matriarchs of propertied clans.

Shina Etting, for example, the widow of a successful Indian trader in the frontier settlement of York, Pennsylvania, recognized that a sizable town held more opportunity for an enterprising businesswomen. In 1758 she and her five daughters moved to Baltimore. Overshadowed by neighboring Philadelphia and not yet a major center of Jewish settlement, Baltimore nevertheless had a busy port. Etting opened a boardinghouse on Calvert Street that became one of the city's most popular. Her success eventually drew her three brothers from Germany to Maryland, where she ran her business and presided as head of a sizable extended family.

But it was in Charleston, the elegant city behind the fortified seawall, that the nation's largest Jewish community grew to "about six or seven hundred individuals," according to *The History of the Jews* published in 1812, a two-volume work written by Hannah Adams, a Christian and the new nation's first female professional writer. Endless flat, fertile, semitropical acres and an equally endless flow of slaves from Africa laid the foundation for the fortunes of plantation-owning low country families—and of the merchants, financiers, and artisans, many of them Jewish, with whom they traded. "Chiefly Carolinians," Adams noted, "descendants of German, English and Portuguese emigrants," and loyal fighters for independence, "the Hebrews of this city pay hearty homage to the laws, which guarantee their rights and, consolidate them into the mass of a free people."[21]

Nothing better shows Charleston Jewry's degree of "consolidation" (and wealth; "most [of them were] rich," according to Adams) than the synagogue they constructed in 1795 to house Congregation Beth Elohim. Except for the absence of a cross, the building's exterior, complete with tall windows and steeple, was indistinguishable from a stylish Anglican church. Inside, though, a traditional layout—the carved wooden ark for the Torah scrolls in its customary place on the eastern wall, the reader's platform at the center of the main floor, nearby men's seating, and women's seating in galleries above—provided an unmistakably Jewish setting for worship.

Newporters prayed amid even greater architectural distinction. The town's few public buildings included two exceptionally fine religious structures, a 1726 church adapted by a local architect from a plan by the great Englishman Christopher Wren and a synagogue that is still in use to this day, the oldest continuously used Jewish house of worship in the United States. Built in 1763 by the twenty families of Congregation Yeshuat Israel, the structure is now known as the Touro synagogue, after a family of philanthropists who supported it.

The community commissioned one of the era's leading architects, Peter Harrison, who introduced the classically inspired Palladian style to North America. He created a stone and wood structure of chaste and exquisite symmetry. Newporters of all persuasions hailed the facade, which featured tall, arched windows and a porch composed of a classic pediment and Corinthian columns, as a distinguished addition to their city. Though the exterior carried no indication of the building's religious function, the interior skillfully adapted Palladian principles to traditional Jewish practices, expressing both the congregation's comfort in its American home and its strong ties to religious tradition. Though unmistakably American, the space recalls the proportions and materials of the great Sephardic synagogue in London.

After commissioning this architectural gem, however, the congregation opted for traditional Jewish values over modern purity of design. Harrison's much admired building lacked space for a school. To his intense chagrin, his clients insisted that he add a classroom wing to one side. The architect's sole consolation at having to wreck the gorgeous symmetry was that, because his masterpiece sits at an angle to the street, the addition is not visible to passersby. The school building "completely spoilt" the otherwise admirable design, opined Reverend Andrew Burnaby after a visit to the new building, but "the Jews, insisted on having [it] annexed," Burnaby went on, "for the education of their children."[22]

Educated Women

Newporters were not the only colonial Jews who made strenuous efforts in the cause of schooling, both religious and secular. Some, like Abigail and

Jacob Franks, provided their daughters educational opportunities on a par
with their sons'. Jewish boys generally received instruction at least as good
or better than that provided by Gentile families of comparable standing.
In most places poor boys got only rudimentary schooling, but better-off
families, especially town dwellers, generally used private tutors or private
schools, often run by religious congregations but sometimes by enterprising schoolmasters.

"Those Jewish children intended for the professions, receive a handsome classical education," Hannah Adams noted in Charleston. In addition to "the French, Italian, Latin and Greek languages . . . together with
other branches of learning" taught to both Christian and Jewish boys in
that city's academy, Jewish Charlestonians also used the services of "The
Rev. Cavalho, [who] also teachest the Hebrew and Spanish languages."[23]
No girls and very few boys went on to higher education in those days, but
at least one eighteenth-century Jew graduated from Kings College (later
Columbia University) in New York, and another from Franklin's
Academy in Philadelphia, the future University of Pennsylvania. In a day
when signing one's name marked a person as literate, perhaps one Gentile
male in eight was illiterate, but only about one Jewish man in eighteen.
Girls of all communities tended to get somewhat less education than boys,
but virtually all Jews of both sexes born in the colonies learned to read,
and nearly all had more education than their parents.[24] Living in towns
and mostly preparing their children for lives in trade, Jewish parents had
both the incentive and the opportunity to provide at least minimal schooling, and synagogues generally provided some religious training to their
members' children.

During the 1730s, for example, Phila Franks studied with George
Brownell, who gave private lessons in reading, writing, arithmetic,
accounting, Greek, Latin, embroidery, and dancing.[25] She also received
instruction in French and Spanish.[26] Her brother Moses studied with
Alexander Malcolm, a mathematics teacher who gave classes both pri-
vately at his home and at a school chartered by the colonial assembly. Phila
and Moses's sister Richa may even have attended the school run by
Shearith Israel, which offered both secular and religious studies under the
congregational *hazzan*, whose duties included serving as schoolmaster. He
received an income from the tuition paid by parents who could afford to
and from congregational subsidies paid on behalf of children whose parents could not. By 1793 the school was routinely accepting girls, and seven
studied Hebrew there that year.[27] During the 1808 school year, the twenty-

two students in schoolmaster E. N. Carvalho's Hebrew and English classes included six girls. All but one of them won academic honors, but only three of the sixteen boys did that well.[28]

Still, the Frankses were probably unusual in giving their daughters as well as their sons a chance at serious academic studies. Well-to-do families of all religions tended to send their daughters for advanced work in such ladylike "accomplishments" as music and embroidery. Those of more modest means probably provided girls basic studies. American-born Jewish women, however, generally read both English and Hebrew, the former at a level of useful literacy and the latter at least well enough to follow, if not necessarily to understand, home and synagogue prayers. Many Jewish New Yorkers, for example, named women to execute their wills, thereby giving the strongest possible testimony to their confidence in female literacy and acumen.[29]

Like Penina Moise, some Jewish women reached quite elevated intellectual levels. Though her formal education ended at age twelve, when her father died, her broad reading and creative writing continued while she nursed her sickly mother and asthmatic brother. In the late eighteenth and early nineteenth centuries, Charleston nurtured one of the continent's largest Jewish communities as well as its liveliest literary scene. It was, as Penina rhapsodized in "To Persecuted Foreigners," a city "where every Muse has reared a shrine, / The aspect of wild Freedom to refine."[30] A poet and essayist whose work appeared in both Jewish and general publications across the nation, Penina was prominent among the cultivated Jews of both sexes who moved easily in those circles. From the cosmopolitan and cultured salons of the city's elite also emerged Grace Seixas Nathan, another of the earliest Jewish women to gain notice as a published poet.

Cultivated Jewish women also pursued literary interests in smaller towns and more isolated locales. In Wilmington, North Carolina, for example, Rachel Mordecai Lazarus, a teacher and a member of a distinguished family of educators, for two and a half decades maintained a transatlantic correspondence with the popular Anglo-Irish novelist Maria Edgeworth. In 1812 Rachel wrote to her favorite author to express her hurt and dismay that Edgeworth's latest book, *The Absentee*, involved a character who not only embodied the timeworn stereotypes of Jewish crassness and stinginess but bore the name of Mr. Mordecai. Stung and chastened by this devoted fan's courteous, sincere, and literate critique, Edgeworth extended a double apology. She promptly wrote back expressing her regret and then proceeded to devote her next book,

Harrington, to exposing the fallacy of anti-Semitism. Over the ensuing years, from opposite sides of the ocean, the two women weighed the great political issues and literary events of the day. A native southerner, Rachel nonetheless shared Maria's strongly expressed distaste for slavery but argued against immediate freedom for the South's human chattel, suggesting that a "gradual and judicious emancipation" would prove ultimately more humane than abrupt liberation. Any move toward immediate freedom, she believed, would so lift the slaves' hopes that they might rise up against their masters in their impatience, only to be "exterminated in self defense."[31]

Few eighteen- or nineteenth-century Americans, men or women, matched the accomplishments of Rachel and her intellectually adventurous family. A daughter of the educational pioneer Jacob Mordecai, she played a pivotal role in the first school in the South (one of the first anywhere on the continent) to offer young women of all religions not mere "accomplishments" but solid academic studies resembling those available in the best schools for young men. Though we know more about Jacob than the women of his family, their crucial contributions to his revolutionary academy are beyond doubt.

Born in 1762 to a merchant family newly arrived from Germany, Jacob got his own early education at private schools in his native Philadelphia and at home with his father, who was devoted to Classical scholarship. He served as a soldier in the Revolutionary War and as an apprentice in trade under David Franks (Abigail's son) before entering business in New York. In 1792 he and his wife, Judith Myers, originally a New Yorker, decided to strike out on their own and establish a store in Warrenton, North Carolina, about one hundred miles from Richmond.

The little county seat, with its unpaved streets, scattered houses, and lone courthouse, seems an unlikely spot for groundbreaking education. Several years before the Mordecais arrived, however, the town had chartered the Warrenton Male Academy, which quickly gained an excellent reputation. A Mr. Falkner ran a short-lived young ladies' boarding school nearby. The town lay next to the main federal road between Richmond and Columbia, South Carolina, and stagecoach service connected it through those centers to Philadelphia and Charleston. Businesspeople thus could easily send their merchandise, and well-to-do parents their sons, to Warrenton.

For a number of years the Mordecais ran their business, prospering along with their new hometown. The hub of a thriving tobacco- and horse-raising region, Warrenton began attracting wealthy out-of-towners to its racetrack and cock ring. Before long, fine two-story houses, an up-to-date public market, and new public wells bespoke the town's growing stature, and Judith and Jacob established themselves among the substantial local citizens.

In 1806, however, the Mordecais' fortunes suddenly collapsed, along with some disastrous tobacco speculations of Jacob's. The family now numbered fifteen children, including the eight born to Judith before her death from complications of childbirth. Her half-sister Rebecca had come to help out in the crisis and stayed on after Judith died. She married Jacob and bore him seven more children. Unlike most parents of their time and place, the Mordecais made sure that each child, regardless of sex, received an education worthy of the best schools. Their progeny eventually included a clutch of teachers, a prominent Raleigh lawyer, a successful Richmond merchant, a physician in Mobile, and, as we shall see, perhaps America's first two female professional educators.

An observant Jew and head of the only local Jewish family, Jacob enjoyed a reputation as an erudite and upright man, and Rebecca was also literate. With their family business gone and their comfortable home sold for their debts, Jacob took a post that called on their learning and fine character, though it paid only a meager salary. In the spring of 1807, he, Rebecca, and the children still at home moved into cramped accommodations at the Warrenton Academy, where he became supervisor of the school's newly built residence hall and Rebecca served as housemother. The family reportedly bore this severe drop in social standing with notable dignity.

Despite its new dormitory, the Male Academy soon closed for lack of sufficient enrollment. But during the summer of 1808, a group of prominent local men came to the jobless Jacob with a surprising proposition: if he, the town's leading intellectual, would reopen the failed academy as a nonsectarian girls' school, they would back him financially. Jacob accepted their challenge, and the following January the Female Academy welcomed its first class, with Jacob, Rebecca, and twenty-year-old Rachel splitting the teaching duties among them. A flyer they circulated that first year announced a program designed not only to cultivate ladylike accomplishments but "chiefly to form the mind to the labor of thinking upon and understanding what is being taught."[32]

Though already well educated under her father's supervision, Rachel spent the summer and fall before the school opened preparing for her new job by studying the books her older brother Solomon had used at the Male

Academy. Whenever she had time off from her chores in a family with ten members still at home, she readied herself to teach the radical curriculum that Jacob was determined to introduce gradually and by subterfuge. Along with needlework, music, and other usual ladylike attainments, he intended to present real intellectual work; the *Iliad* in Greek, for example, would climax the ancient history program. Jacob planned to attract bright students and then, quietly and over time, simply allow them to demonstrate that they could handle advanced studies as ably as boys. As his concern for his daughters' education had shown, his confidence in female intellects went back many years. Some historians have even suggested that he located his school in North Carolina rather than in neighboring Virginia because it afforded women more legal rights.

Rachel and her younger sister Ellen, another faculty member, were intellectual pathfinders in their own right because they broke professional ground as full-fledged teachers in a true winter school, and one whose excellent reputation spread throughout the region, even attracting the admiration of Charleston literati like Penina Moise. Well into the nineteenth century, Americans generally considered teaching at every level a male profession. Schoolmasters dispensed serious learning; schoolmarms held class in the distinctly second-rate summer schools run for girls while boys took time off to work in the fields.

The Mordecais' school attracted the daughters of prominent families, the great majority of them Christian, from across the South.[33] Its alumnae soon vindicated Jacob's faith in their potential, becoming authors, teachers, and community leaders. At fifty-six, though, after ten years of hard work and increasing success, Jacob felt ready to retire. In 1818 he sold the Warrenton Female Academy, by then one of the best-known schools in the South, to Joseph Andrews and his son-in-law, Thomas Jones, two well-regarded Philadelphia schoolmasters. The Mordecai family moved to Richmond, where, for the first time in a quarter century, they could fully participate in a vigorous Jewish community.

The pioneering work done by Rebecca, Rachel, and Ellen reflected the traditional Jewish concern for education. But it also foreshadowed the new institutions that Jewish women would create across the continent during the next phase of American history, as Jewish life, like the nation itself, spread west from its original Atlantic seaboard base.

PART TWO

"The Length and Breadth of the Union"

The Central European Migration, 1820–1880

4

"LITTLE SHORT OF IMPOSSIBLE"

Leaving Central Europe

Jeanette Hirsch did not join the American people until 1864, when they were well into their century-long project of turning a small seacoast republic into a vast continental nation. By the time she arrived from Bavaria, two generations of pioneers had labored over the Appalachians and across the plains, prairies, and mountains. Many thousands more had risked the ocean passage around Cape Horn. Farms and ranches and mines and towns already dotted the immense territory that Americans considered theirs by right. But in the way that Jeanette came and in the life that she found, she stands as a model for many hopeful Jewish arrivals between 1820 and 1880. Just as the American people were inventing themselves and their culture in countless settlements from the Ohio Valley to the Pacific Northwest, Jeanette and scores of thousands like her helped devise a whole new way of being an American Jew.

Later generations would call Jeanette a member of the "German" migration. These people would be seen as prosperous Jewish emigrants who rejected their ancient religious heritage, first in favor of Teutonic, and then of American, culture. In these German Jews' rush to assimilate and grow rich, future generations would believe, men and women eagerly discarded much that had made Judaism distinctive and substituted for that vibrant, authentic tradition an ersatz, Protestant-flavored, Victorian middle-class respectability.

Jeanette and her relatives and friends probably would have found this description puzzling. They did not see themselves as coming from Germany or being Germans, for two very good reasons. No country of that name yet existed, and the people who had long claimed Germanic language and culture as their own had long refused to include Jews among their number. Nor were most of the Jews who came in Jeanette's time very prosperous. Calling them enthusiastic assimilationists belies the effort they put into living as Jews under conditions totally unsuited to any Jewish life they had ever known.

They carried Judaism and Jewish values to the far reaches of the United States. "The descendants of the patriarchs can be found through the length and breadth of the Union," wrote a mid–nineteenth century historian. Had they been asked, Jeanette's generation might have even pointed out that, far from abandoning their birthright, they made themselves Americans and made Judaism American in deeper ways than any previous generation had accomplished. They built on the experience of established families like the Gratzes and devised ways to stay Jewish that fitted this totally unprecedented land of religious tolerance and social mobility. Organizations and ideas that Jeanette's generation invented still structure the largest, freest, most religiously creative Jewry in the ancient people's history. And many who led that transformation were women.

Jeanette's own journey to her American self probably began in her parents' front room in the small Bavarian town of Ellerstadt, one day in 1863. Few details of her first twenty years survive. We can't say, for example, whether she, like so many young people of her time, place, and background, dreamed of trying her luck in the new land. Nor are we sure what she thought of the thirtyish man in foreign-cut clothes who came to call on her father. We do know that her father was acquainted with a local family named Meier whose son, Aaron, was in Ellerstadt visiting his widowed mother after eight years away. When Aaron returned to his home in the astoundingly distant settlement of Portland, in the amazingly exotic territory of Oregon, on the westernmost reaches of the American continent, Jeanette went with him as his bride.

Aaron's life, as was so often the case for nineteenth-century men, is far better documented than Jeanette's, as men's lives often were in the nineteenth century. He had first left Ellerstadt for America in 1855 at the age of twenty-four, following two older brothers, Julius and Emanuel, who left home to try their luck in the California gold fields. The brothers do not seem to have sought their fortune directly at the diggings, however, but rather behind the counter of a dry goods store, providing the prospectors flooding into California the gear and supplies they would need to strike it rich. Aaron joined Julius and Emanuel in Downietown, where they had established their own business. He worked there for a while, but before long he was on the road as a peddler, driving a mule-drawn wagon loaded with notions, sundries, housewares, and dry goods among the scattered settlements and homesteads of Oregon Territory.

Aaron apparently prospered on his rounds, in part, according to local legend, because of his kindness and generosity. A story told by a Gentile pioneer's granddaughter, for example, has him arriving in the isolated hamlet of Pass Creek Canyon late one November, where he quickly learned the sad fate of the single darning needle that the settler families had been sharing. First the precious needle had been temporarily lost. Then it had been permanently broken, making mending impossible until somebody came up with a replacement. The astute Aaron reached into his pocket for a pack of needles and, the story goes, bestowed on each Canyon lady a holiday gift of her own personal darning needle—despite the fact that, as he reportedly explained, "My people do not celebrate Christmas."[1] Whatever the truth of this tale, within two years Aaron accumulated enough capital to trade the hard life on the road for the comfort of a store of his own.

In 1857 he took a steamboat up the Willamette River to Portland, then a boomtown of thirteen hundred inhabitants, most of them busily prospering by provisioning prospectors. Twelve years old and growing fast, Portland had forty-two retail establishments when Aaron and two partners opened the doors of a dry goods and clothing emporium that scarcely measured thirty-five by fifty feet. For the next six years the business grew with the town until, thirty-two years old and ready for life's next big step, Aaron went back to visit Ellerstadt.

From the distance of a century and a half, Aaron's early rise to prosperity seems almost automatic, but in fact the Meiers' American success story included painful and unexpected setbacks. Passing through New York on the way back from Europe, Aaron sank his remaining funds into a large supply of merchandise that he and Jeanette took with them on the long trip to Oregon. When they finally reached Portland in 1864, Aaron found, instead of the prosperous store he had left, a defunct business bankrupted by one of his erstwhile partners. To make matters worse, local merchants he had counted on to buy some of the New York merchandise failed to make good on their promises.

Before long, though, the Meiers were back in business, in larger premises across the dusty street from the original location. They set up housekeeping in an apartment close by, where each day Jeanette cooked a hot meal to eat in the store. The following year she had their first child, Fannie, and soon the family moved to their own two-story house. There Jeanette gave birth in turn to Abe and Julius, who, like their older sister, lived to adulthood, and to Hattie, who died in infancy. Jeanette and Aaron faced the challenge of creating a family life as two of a mere hundred or so Jewish settlers in a raw frontier town of two thousand.[2]

The business kept growing, and Aaron and Jeanette decided they needed more help. Once again they looked to Ellerstadt and soon several Hirsch relations—cousins, nephews, Jeanette's half-brothers—were working behind the counter on Front Street. Then, in 1870 Aaron made a business trip to San Francisco and met a young man named Emil Frank. Impressed, he offered Emil a clerk's job and three years later, in 1773, made him a partner. In that same year, however, Front Street, along with most of the rest of the downtown business district, went up in flames. The Meiers once again had to start over almost from scratch.

The new, brick Meier & Frank store, which opened its doors later that year, filled a whole city block. Then the partners unwittingly laid the groundwork for another future long-term merger by bringing Emil's twenty-three-year-old brother Sigmund from San Francisco. Fifteen years later his marriage to Fannie strengthened the link between the families. Not long afterward, Sigmund replaced Emil as a partner in the business.

As the years passed, the Meiers became substantial citizens and Meier & Frank became—and remains—Portland's premier department store. Aaron, however, witnessed only part of the rise to preeminence. Widowed at forty-six, Jeanette spent her remaining thirty-six years active in the business as both a day-to-day manager and final arbiter of every decision. "Tante Jeanette," recalled her great-nephew Harold Hirsch, held court each Sunday evening at her impressive home, where the crowd of close and distant relations working in the firm gathered for a command performance social-cum-business dinner. From his seat at the children's table, Harold watched as she "got up at the head table and told each of the men exactly what they were going to do and how they were going to do it. When there were arguments, [she] would 'bang their heads together'" until an agreement emerged.[3] As head of a prominent family, Jeanette also ranked among Portland's leading philanthropists.

The Hirsch relations also thrived. Jeanette's nephew eventually left the family firm to join Harry Weis in the canvas business. At first their company, Hirsch-Weis, outfitted ships, and then Alaskan gold prospectors, with water bags, tents, and other gear. A later generation added a line of men's sportswear as well as a new, nationally advertised trademark that punned on the founding partners' names: White Stag. To cap the family's

American success story, Julius Meier, Jeanette and Aaron's younger son, was elected governor of Oregon.

A Crossroads of Opportunity

Relatively few immigrant families ended up with major department stores, national clothing brands, or members who lived in the state house. Yet the great majority of Jews who trace their American ancestry to the middle decades of the nineteenth century can look back to stories much like Jeanette and Aaron's. The Meier-Hirsch saga differs from other family stories only in scale, not structure. Aaron and Jeanette's ascent from the peddler's pack to prosperous entrepreneurship in fact includes essentially every important element of the period's typical Jewish immigrant experience: the small-town origin; chains of brothers and sisters bringing one another to America and into small, family-run businesses; the early years hawking goods in the hinterland; the series of dry goods, clothing, or general merchandise stores; the marriage between an up-and-coming shopkeeper and a much younger hometown girl; subsequent unions further cementing family partnerships; and the couple's growing success, both financial and social, in their new town and nation.

The details vary from family to family and from place to place. The old hometown may have been in Bavaria or Bohemia or Byelorussia. The peddler may have trudged the back roads of Michigan or Missouri or Montana. The stores may have stood in Boston or Buffalo or Boise or Biloxi. The spouses may have met in New York or New Mexico or New Orleans.

But the remarkable uniformity of Jewish immigrant experience in this period is no coincidence. The archetypal story reflects not the random luck of individuals but the common reactions of people from extremely similar backgrounds to a particular set of circumstances that arose at the intersection of two immense, simultaneously occurring historical processes. On the one hand, the social, economic, and political worlds in which Central European Jewry had long lived were rapidly collapsing. On the other, the United States was rising to the status of a transcontinental industrial power. On the eastern side of the Atlantic, forces unleashed by industrialization and political modernization were shaking the foundations of traditional European culture. On the western shore, a huge, immensely rich, and drastically underpopulated continent was becoming, in a matter of decades, a leading industrial power and the world's first great popular democracy. Open to essentially unlimited European immigration, the new land offered unimaginable opportunity to almost any white person who had decent health, the price of a ship ticket, and the gumption to try his or her luck.

In Europe, great reservoirs of dissatisfied young people who had been dammed up in outmoded economic and social structures began to flood across the Atlantic in a torrent of ambition, enterprise, and daring. From villages, farms, and cities across the rapidly changing countries of northern and central Europe came men and women of a dozen nationalities, languages, and denominations, each bringing the particular skills and attitudes that the group's history and circumstances had formed. From the vast array of possibilities that the new continent presented, Jewish newcomers generally pursued a limited number of commercial patterns. And to succeed in America, they had to transform themselves and their religion into something they had never been before, a people and a faith adapted to middle-class life in a dynamic, diverse, secular democracy. To understand how they did this and who they became, we must first know who they had been and why they had come.

A World Dissolves

In 1820 the Jewish population of the United States stood at two to three thousand. Sixty years later, it numbered more than 250,000. During those six decades, at least 150,000 Jewish men, women, and children left their homes, journeyed to a European port, booked passage to an American destination, and endured a dangerous and uncomfortable voyage that could, on the sailing vessels still in use in the first decades of this period, last six weeks or longer. They arrived, usually almost penniless, in a land where they spoke little of the language, understood almost nothing of the culture, and knew at most a handful of people. But they made that challenging journey in numbers that dwarfed all the Jewish arrivals during the previous two centuries put together.

This migration drew Jews from different sources. No longer did the typical arrival hail from a western European city like London or Amsterdam or from a Caribbean island such as Curaçao. No longer was he or she as likely to carry a Sephardic name as an Ashkenazic one. No longer did the fortunes of transatlantic trading families play a role in most decisions to come. People of such backgrounds did, of course, continue to arrive throughout this period, but the great bulk of those now making the crossing had more in common with Aaron and Jeanette Meier than with Isaac

Mendes Seixas or Rycke Nounes. Like the Meiers, they typically were young, with modest education and finances, and hailed from rural towns or villages in the lands that would become part of Germany or the German cultural sphere.

No polity unified the territory now known as Germany until 1871. Before German-speaking lands were united under the kaiser, a variety of local rulers, nobles, and town councils ruled a patchwork of duchies, counties, principalities, free cities, and other small entities. Residents of these states and statelets lived under the laws established and enforced by their particular lords or legislators. Masses of Jews also left Central European areas we do not now consider German, such as Poznan—the historically Polish enclave absorbed for a time by Prussia—as well as Galicia, Moravia, and Bohemia. Some came from territories that owed allegiance to the imperial house of Hapsburg, which, from its capital in German-speaking Vienna, ruled a vast, polyglot empire that included speakers of Hungarian, Czech, and a dozen other languages.

Although Jews' political circumstances varied from place to place, in the first decades of the nineteenth century their cultural and religious loyalties did not. Until midcentury the great majority shared a language and a national identity, neither of them German. Among themselves Jews spoke Yiddish, which, though based on medieval Low German, was written in Hebrew characters and contained many Hebrew words. In their own, and their Gentile neighbors' eyes, further, Jewish people were nothing more or less than Jewish—in Jewish eyes, the Ashkenazic branch of the House of Israel; in Christians', the benighted descendants of those who had denied Jesus.

Jews occupied a distinct and inferior status in all the Christian polities they inhabited. In 1820 no Central European Jews, even those descended from numerous generations native to their home place, held citizenship in any political entity. But from Alsace in the west to Russia in the east, early nineteenth-century Yiddish-speaking Jews shared a uniform culture, with similar customs, values, and expectations shaping the lives of individuals and communities. Except for a tiny, wealthy elite who had gained the special favor of Christian rulers or aristocrats, the Jewish people of Central Europe remained what their ancestors had been for centuries past: traditional, pious, generally poor *Dorfjuden*—village Jews.

They lived in small clusters of usually related families among the Christian populations of countless hamlets and little towns. In the shadow of Christian churches and homes, Jewish families observed the compli-

cated rules of traditional Judaism and the customs of a distinctive folk culture. In matters that did not involve Christians, they lived under Jewish
law and the authority of the rabbis who interpreted and administered it.
When issues arose that involved Christians, such as taxation or legal dis-
putes, Jews were represented before the larger society by an officially recognized Jewish community that enrolled individuals at birth.

Baptism offered the only way out of this cramped Jewish sphere and
into the wider world beyond. Entrance into nearly every prosperous and
prestigious career lay on the other side of conversion. With agriculture,
most guild-based crafts, and other more secure and lucrative occupations
traditionally forbidden to them, Central European Jews overwhelmingly
earned their often meager livelihoods as minor traders, small-scale money-
lenders, or petty artisans in such crafts as tailoring. For centuries, however,
this narrow and denigrated economic niche had at least provided the possibility of earning a living.

In the static world of the premodern agricultural economy, Jews occupied
the crucial, if widely criticized, position of middlemen among various elements of Christian society. In Central Europe they gathered the produce of
the countryside—grain, vegetables, livestock, timber, eggs—and sold it to
residents of towns and cities. They also brought the products of the cities—
notions, dry goods, liquor, tools—to the countryside. They shuttled between
the peasantry and townsmen, and between the citizenry and the government, assuming the risks of these transactions and living off the price differ-
entials and fluctuations among these various markets. Though the social and
economic theories of the time defined such activity as parasitic because it
produced no tangible goods, Jews acting as intermediaries and market makers provided essential services that permitted the economy to function.
Some even managed to make a good living. Jewish communities also supported small numbers of functionaries—rabbis, Hebrew teachers, kosher
slaughterers and bakers, circumcisers, prayer leaders, *mikvah* attendants,
synagogue caretakers, and the like—who met specifically Jewish needs. Few
of these posts paid a living wage, however, and many required that their
incumbents do some kind of business on the side.

But by 1880, throughout the lands that became Germany, as well as in
other areas of Central Europe, the lives of Jews had undergone an epochal
transformation. No longer a collection of changeless agricultural locali-
ties, the kaiser's realm was a mighty, dynamic industrial and scientific
power. Instead of forming a distinct class of small traders in scores of little country towns, many Jews had become middle-class business (and in

some cases professional) people living urban lives in major cities and towns. Similar trends were also unfolding, if more unevenly, in areas beyond Germany.

Instead of using Yiddish among themselves, these newly modern, newly bourgeois Jews now spoke, depending on their location, German or Polish or Czech or Hungarian both at home and in the street. Instead of sending their sons to learn the Hebrew texts at traditional, Yiddish-speaking heders and yeshivas, they now sent both sons and daughters to learn science, mathematics, history, and literature in the national language at public schools and, for a handful of the exceedingly able and fortunate, at universities. Instead of all observing the same set of time-honored religious practices, Jews now belonged to any of several different versions of Judaism, each with its own ideas about which of the old rules to obey and how to obey them. Sabbath, *kashrut, niddah,* Hebrew language, the nationhood of the People Israel, no longer bound Central Europe's Jews into a single, unified nation but rather sundered them into an array of feuding denominations.

An equally drastic change overtook their political status. Instead of belonging to the local *kahal,* the corporate community that represented Jewish people and Jewish interests to the civil authorities and society at large, Jews were now citizens or subjects of any of several states or empires. Each person now owned allegiance to the country of citizenship as an individual rather than as a member of a community or class. In nation-states like the new Germany, where a uniform national culture and language formed crucial elements of national unity and identity, people could only participate fully if they made that language and culture their own. For the great majority of Jews, this entailed a revolutionary change in self-concept and lifestyle. No longer a separate nation set apart from the alien and unwelcoming society around them, they were now legitimate, if rather anomalous, members of that society—legitimate because they held citizenship, but anomalous because they lacked one of the basic elements of full participation, Christianity. And the pressure to leave behind the "primitive" and "uncivilized" usages and values of Judaism and to adopt the "modern," "civilized" manners of respectable Gentiles grew more intense the higher one climbed in the newly modern social structure.

Such sweeping social change in a few decades meant turmoil and upheaval within Jewish communities, Jewish homes, and Jewish hearts and minds across Central Europe. But not all Jews could find a place in the new European social and economic scheme when their old economic niche vanished. With the traditional rural economy collapsing under the weight of technological and political change, the Christian peasants who had been the main customers of the *Dorfjuden* found themselves increasingly shaken from their accustomed homes and occupations. Many of these displaced country folk were either pulled toward the growing cities as industrial workers or pushed toward them as the dispossessed poor. Others left for America in hopes of rebuilding rural lives in a new land. As the old peasant way of life disappeared from the countryside, so did the need for rural middlemen that had sustained generations of Jews. The possibility of eking out even a minimal living disappeared for countless *Dorfjuden*. Poor young men like the Meier brothers found themselves tossed aside by economic revolution, their opportunities increasingly constrained and their futures increasingly bleak.

The answer, obviously enough, was to leave the countryside. The best and most prestigious and promising opportunities lay close by in rapidly growing cities like Berlin, Hamburg, and Vienna. But grasping those possibilities meant becoming "modern" and culturally German, which in turn required the kind of education that taught modern academic skills and good German manners. And that sort of schooling cost more, in both money and time, than poor rural families could provide. The costs of setting up a household and getting into business in a city were vastly higher in capital and contacts than filling a pack or wagon with notions and yard goods. As increasing numbers of Jews abandoned their old village homes, the better-off, better-educated, and more Germanized headed for the Central European metropolises. The poorer and less educated—like Aaron, Emanuel, and Julius—set out for America.

Just such a hopeful *Dorfjud*, twenty-one-year-old Seligmann Heilner, made his way to America in 1845. By the early 1850s, after an unsuccessful attempt at gold prospecting and various other misadventures, he was running a dry goods store in Crescent City on the northern California coast. In 1854 her wrote to his father Aron, back in little Uspringen, Bavaria, inviting his younger brother, Sigmund, to join him in the business at a salary of $60 a month. Aron, who worked three jobs—schoolteaching, moneylending, and part-time farming—and barely supported his wife and the four children still at home, answered in amazement. "Anyone that can pay that much money in one month must be wealthy. In two months, that is more than I make in one year." And if Seligmann had become rich, his father went on, the family needed his help with an urgent problem. The "situation" of Seligmann's sister Regina "rests very heavily on my heart," Aron gloomily confided.[4]

Regina still lived with her parents and suffered from the frustration and distress common to Jewish young people across Central Europe. Even if a village man or woman could find a way to earn a living, marriage was almost impossible. The governments of Bavaria, Württemberg, Hesse-Kassel, and other states wanted to limit the number of Jews within their borders. An efficient method of doing that was to limit the right of Jews to move about and, by extension, to establish new households.

Bavarian Jewish communities, for example, had to maintain an official register, known as the *Matrikel*, that listed all the families legally entitled to reside in any given place. A new family could join the list only when an old one vacated its space, either by death or departure. Jewish couples therefore could marry only when and if they secured official permission and a coveted, exceedingly rare vacancy on the *Matrikel*. "The register makes it little short of impossible for young Israelites to set up house-keeping in Bavaria," a Jewish newspaper reported. "Often their head is adorned with gray hair before they receive the permission to set up house and can, therefore, think of marriage."[5]

"Regina must get married soon, but for that much money is needed," Aron Heilner reminded Seligmann, though whether to pay a dowry or to convince an official to grant a position on the *Matrikel* he did not specify. But Aron's religious duty to provide his marriageable daughter a match had become extremely pressing, probably because of her advancing age. So dire was the situation, Aron continued, that brother Sigmund had written from New York offering to send all the money he had "for Regina," even though "his entire savings consist of only 199 f. I hope that you will also help me if you are in a position that you can."[6] Seligmann apparently failed to respond with the needed funds, and several more years passed before Regina managed to wed Feiffer Guttman. By telling contrast, however, no such difficulties hampered the wedding plans of Aaron Meier, new American, and his bride, Jeannette.

Setting Out for a New Life

From the 1820s on, Central Europe was awash in news of America. Heinrich Heine and other leading German writers echoed the themes of freedom, vigor, and adventure that they had read in tales of Washington

Irving and James Fenimore Cooper. Heine, a born Jew and an ambivalent convert to Christianity, considered both America and most European Jews crude and vulgar. But he nonetheless admitted that the new land afforded a great advantage: "everyone over there can find salvation in his own way." He foresaw that "even if all Europe should become a single prison, there is still another loophole of escape, namely America, and, thank God! the loophole is after all larger than the prison itself."[7] Before long, writers aiming at Jewish readers were also spreading these ideas in Yiddish and Hebrew books and newspapers. One particularly enthusiastic 1822 pamphlet, for example, carried a Hebrew title that translates as "Chronicles of the Days of the Messiah."

But by far the most influential reading matter, of course, was the glowing report that arrived by mail from the venturesome souls who actually made the trip. One "Bavarian Israelite" had received just such a letter from a brother in New York, the *Allgemeine Zeitung des Judentums*, a leading Jewish periodical, reported in 1840. This unnamed new New Yorker "highly extols his present situation and his trade (he is a shoemaker) guarantees him an ample livelihood." Even more importantly, he "rejoices particularly" that "his children have an opportunity to learn a lot" and that, "along with full civil liberty, an Israelite has the opportunity to comply—unhindered—with all religious prescriptions," with handy access to "three synagogues and all other Jewish institutions." The happy emigrant "invites his brother also to come over, since he will surely find a situation [job] there."[8]

Similar invitations began arriving all over Central Europe, not from an anonymous newspaper story but in the handwriting of trusted relatives and friends. More and more of the recipients read their mail, packed their bags, and took their destinies in their own hands by accepting the offer. Leaving singly or in small groups of siblings, cousins, or friends, these travelers were initially mostly young, single, impecunious, modestly educated, and male, although a number of single women also went. Letters also came asking wives to bring the children and join husbands who had gone ahead. Others inquired whether any of the marriageable girls still at home (or perhaps some particular hometown girl) would be willing to become an American wife. Perhaps such a query preceded Aaron Meier to Ellerstadt.

Before long, going to America had changed from an intriguing possibility or a daring adventure to a large, spontaneous, self-sustaining mass movement. As emigrants multiplied, so did the enticing envelopes bearing American return addresses. In Galicia, Alsace, Baden, Württemburg,

Hesse, Posen, Moravia, and in every locality where young Jews faced legal restrictions or economic stagnation, "emigration fever" seized entire communities. The accounts of previous departures became a contagion infecting the entire young generation. Among the two hundred Jewish families in the Swabian town of Ichenhausen, the newspaper *Israelitische Annalen* reported in 1840, sixty individuals were actively contemplating the trip, as were twenty more among the twenty-five Jewish families of nearby Osterburg.

Emigration became so widespread and so common that it distorted the demography of the communities left behind. "If the present tendency is to continue," mused the *Allgemeine Zeitung* of Würzberg in 1839, "numerous small communities will be compelled to close their synagogues and schools. . . . In many a place, out of a Jewish population of 30–40 families, 15–20 people have emigrated, mainly the young and employable."[9] By the 1820s and 1830s, in small towns across rural Central Europe, marriageable Jewish women markedly outnumbered potential suitors. The crisis became severe enough to bring the traditional matchmaker, or *shadchen,* back into vogue.

But rather than sit at home and hope someday to wed, many young women followed the flow. Bella Bloch, for example, took her parents' advice and left her home village for Hamburg to learn millinery, a trade they heard would be in demand when she reached America. For the first decade or so the Central European migration appears to have been heavily male, but by the 1820s, single women already formed a substantial proportion of the migrants—45 percent of those who left the town of Kissingen in that decade, and just about half of those who left all of Bavaria, a total of 12,806 males versus 11,701 females.[10]

Not only did poor girls face bleak marriage prospects in man-starved, *Matrikel*-bound Central Europe, but industrialization and rural economic change were drying up the traditional sources of employment for unmarried women: sewing, small family businesses, and domestic service. Since the poorest Jews in the most depressed trades and businesses were the most likely to leave, the size of the Jewish lower classes began to shrink. In many places the *kahal* raised the local average income by paying the fares of poor people who could not afford to emigrate. "Pattern it gilt wet!" (It's worth the money to be rid of them," the Yiddish saying went.)

In the end, the emptying of the Jewish countryside proved unstoppable. Even as Jews gained more legal rights and the hated marriage restrictions were rescinded in the 1850s and 1860s, the outflow to America continued to swell. The faster, safer, more comfortable steamships in service by the 1860s only made the trip more desirable. "The second-class cabins of the steamer which is to leave Bremen . . . are completely booked by Jews from Prague," an observer noted in 1871. "The captain was willing to accommodate them with a kosher table."[11]

America ranked first among desired destinations, but some emigrants, especially those hailing from Posen and points east, did not manage to get all the way across the Atlantic on the first leg of their trip. Many stopped for months or years at intermediate staging points such as German cities or London. The latter, of course, had the added advantage of permitting the sojourners to arrive in America already speaking English. Many Jews from Poland, Galicia, and elsewhere in Eastern Europe who had earlier sought opportunities in German-speaking cities also thought better of their plans and joined the mass exodus across the Atlantic. No one knows for sure how many East Europeans came in the "German" migration, but their numbers were substantial, probably over fifty thousand. "There is virtually no family in Poland that has no relatives in America," according to an 1869 article in *Ha-Melitz*, a Hebrew-language magazine published in Odessa.[12]

Woman's Lot

Whether, like Jeannette Meier, a small-town Jewish woman emigrated with her husband, she went to meet or marry him in America, or whether, like Bella Bloch, she expected to live unmarried after she landed, she brought a very particular set of expectations molded by the life she had known in Europe. First, she had worked hard helping her mother with the time-honored tasks of Jewish womanhood. Beyond household duties, a good daughter did what she could to contribute to the family's income. She might work in the family's shop—often its front room—or mind younger children while her mother did the accounts. She might also bake or sew items to sell and might also start a small business of her own. And if worse came to worst, she would hire herself out to clean another family's house, cook or serve another family's meals, or tend another mother's children.

A small-town girl learned many tasks from her mother, who, if formal girls' classes were not available locally, might also teach her to read Yiddish, do sums, and understand something of the lore of the Bible and traditions. Women also spoke, and sometimes could even read, the local language used in trading with Christians. Only rarely, however, did a girl

attain any real proficiency in Hebrew, the *lishon ha-kodesh* (holy language). The *mama-loshen* (mother tongue) sufficed for women to conduct their daily lives, read popular religious and secular books, and
repeat their daily devotions out of special little volumes that combined
well-known Hebrew prayers with Yiddish translations. Nor did females
often enter the masculine intellectual world of sacred texts in the sacred
tongue. Cheder taught all boys to read Bible stories in Hebrew, but only
the gifted and prosperous few continued past late childhood to higher
studies at a yeshiva.

A girl also learned, from observing her parents, what she could expect
from the marriage that they endeavored to arrange for her. In seeking a
son-in-law, fathers and mothers strove for the best available combination
of financial security, sacred learning, piety, and distinguished ancestry,
although obtaining a gifted scholar or a scion of wealth generally involved
a handsome dowry and, to snag a young man destined to attain a promising yeshiva career, an agreement to support him, his wife, and children.[13]
Most families contented themselves with more modest matches. Although
Jewish law gives a woman the right to refuse a man her parents propose,
few daughters exercised it. Romantic love played no role in marriage plans.
Marital affection, prospective brides knew, would arise over time as the
spouses built their life together, each fulfilling a preordained role within
the home, the extended family, and the community.

The intense connections among their large networks of kinfolk and in-
laws provided a social life. The husband, in his role as the family's leader
in religious matters, attended synagogue and carried out home devotions
that included daily prayer and the special observances for Sabbath and the
festivals. His wife, meanwhile, kept a scrupulously kosher home, meticulously guarded the couple's sexual purity, prepared the biblically commanded challah loaves each Friday, kindled the lights that usher in each
Sabbath and festival, and made the many special foods for feast days.

Along with piety, thrift and good management marked the worthy wife.
"We live, as you know, very simply," Aron Heilner reminded his son
Seligmann in a letter. "We save what we can and especially our dear
Mother is so efficient in this."[14] A Jewish wife usually had to be. If she married an impecunious middling scholar, she might have to bear the entire
burden of supporting the family. If she married a man who worked hard
but earned little, she might join him in a combined business venture or go
into business on her own. Unlike nineteenth-century American or English
wives, who lost control of their assets at marriage, a wife under Jewish law

could own property and make contracts in her own right. And even a village girl fortunate enough to marry a man with a comfortable income expected to help in the business as needed, perhaps keeping the account books or serving as cashier, and certainly running a home that reflected the family's status and economized its resources.

As women across Central Europe packed their clothes, their prayer books, and perhaps a brass candlestick or embroidered challah cover for the long trip to their new lives, they brought along a set of assumptions and experiences that differed in important ways from those of non-Jewish Americans. How the values they had learned in places like Ellerstadt served them in Portland, Providence, or Peoria would have unexpected and far-reaching consequences for themselves, their new hometowns, and the future of American Jewry.

5

"TO THE END OF THE WORLD"

Jewish Women All Across the Nation

When the long-awaited letter came, beckoning Amelia Ullmann to join her husband, Joseph, in the "new and thriving town" of St. Paul, it was so little known that, Amelia would recall decades later, in order to write him from St. Louis saying she was coming, she had to "go into several shops before I found a person who could inform me in what state or territory it was situated."[1] Not that the St. Louis waterfront was itself a very prepossessing place that May day in 1852. It consisted of a "graveled river bank piled high with a mass of merchandise: bales of cotton, hogsheads of sugar and molasses, stacks of wood, and great stores to be transported to the military posts and new settlements up the Mississippi and Missouri Rivers."[2] From the nearby "low wooden buildings, mostly with flaring signs of groceries or cheap restaurants" Amelia saw "drunken men stagger[ing] out upon the sidewalk."[3] But the levee was where the steamboats departed, so that's where Amelia went to buy her ticket.

She went on her own, just as she would travel up the Mississippi to her new home. Getting to the rough riverfront district, finding the booking office, and arranging her passage would have been "neither an easy nor a pleasant experience for a young woman familiar with American life, and it was especially trying to me, new to the land and customs," she remembered. Her family had arrived fairly recently from their native Rhineland, and her father still did not speak English and so could not help her with the arrangements. But Amelia had already met daunting challenges. In addition to the "difficulties and inconveniences" that all travelers faced on the "long journey" to America, from "Coblenz on the Rhine to Rotterdam, and thence by way of Liverpool and New Orleans to St. Louis," she had traveled alone except for a younger brother in her care. But that hard trip nonetheless had its advantages. Amelia had reached St. Louis with "more confidence than as a girl in a quiet Rhine town, I had thought myself capable of possessing."[4]

The same optimism and self-reliance had shone when she agreed to marry Joseph, an Alsatian immigrant. He had lived in New Orleans but fled a yellow fever outbreak, then in Louisville and New Albany, Indiana, and finally in St. Louis, where he had worked in the liquor business and met and married Amelia. He made yet another move after their marriage to escape the oppressive Missouri summers, finally coming to rest in St. Paul. Son of a well-to-do family and better educated than most young Jewish immigrants, he may have expected a handsome dowry. But Amelia recounted long afterward, that, though she did not know how much money her father had, "I do know that I shall take nothing from him as he has a large family to care for. In America, though, anyone who will work and be economical can earn money for themselves. We are young and . . . I will follow you to the end of the world." So Joseph went ahead to the frontier town in the "young Northwest," where he made a start as a fur trader.[5] Four days after Amelia got his letter, she walked to the dock, once again in charge of young travelers. She, her three-month-old son, and her younger sister boarded a steamer for St. Paul. "When we started up the river on that bright May day, I did not think that the time to go to 'the end of the world' had come so soon."[6]

For more than fifteen days they steamed through wilderness only occasionally interspersed with tiny settlements, stopping "wherever there appeared to be the least excuse and even, at times where there was none. Wherever there were a few houses was a 'city.'"[7] At last they reached their destination, Amelia's son decked out in a stylish short dress for his father. When Amelia's new hometown came into view, she noticed with dismay that "there were no houses nor cultivated fields to be seen, only the prairie with the early spring verdu[r]e and wild flowers" and "a low marshy tract" filled with "tall swamp grass" and "ponds coated with green scum." In the distance stood a pair of bluffs. "A few wooden shanties" could be seen in that vicinity. Beyond them lay the cluster of somewhat more substantial buildings that made up the town.

Through the crowd that had gathered for the steamer's arrival—a great event in a pioneering river settlement—came her smiling husband. Riding a bit later in Joseph's wagon up the muddy track to town, Amelia spied, among the "rough, unpainted" buildings that he described as the main business district, several "tall, erect, wild-looking" individuals "wrapped up in colored blankets and adorned with feathers braided in their long, black hair." Seeing her first Indians on St. Paul's main street, this daughter of the Rhineland thought her new home "not at all favorable for a place of either business or residence."[8] Her family's hard years in the rough settlement proved her right in the short run. But in the long run, St. Paul and hundreds of other cities and towns across the nation would provide mid–nineteenth century Jewish women and their families secure homes and ample livings and the opportunity to make themselves and Jewish life American.

American Journeys

In 1820, with America's westward expansion beginning in earnest, all but a handful of the nation's three thousand Jews lived in six old seaboard cities: Newport, New York, Philadelphia, Richmond, Charleston, and Savannah. Just thirty-one years later, when Reverend Samuel Myers Isaac traveled from New York to help dedicate the first synagogue in the up-and-coming outpost of Chicago, "not a village on my route was without an Israelite," he reported in an English newspaper, the *London Jewish Chronicle,* "much less towns, such as Detroit and Ipsilanti [sic], each containing 20 families, Kalamazoo and Marshall 10 and others in proportion."[9] Eight years after Reverend Isaac's trip another Jewish traveler, Israel Joseph Benjamin II, began a journey that resulted in his book *Three Years in America*, which detailed encounters with Jews in both great cities and such unexpected spots as mining camps and hamlets along the Great Lakes. An entry in the 1872 book *A History of All Religions* claimed that "whether we travel in the New England States, or in the distant regions of the West," one meets "the outcasts of Judea."[10]

Like the Ullmans of St. Paul, the Meiers of Portland, and their scattered coreligionists throughout the hinterland, many Jews who came to America between 1820 and 1880 behaved rather differently from most earlier arrivals. Almost 200,000 Jews landed during those sixty years, but only half of them settled in such large East Coast communities as New York, Philadelphia, Boston, Baltimore, and New Jersey. The rest fanned out to cities, towns, villages, and crossroads trading posts the length and breadth of the country, from New Hampshire to New Mexico, from Washington, D.C., to Washington State.

Already used to living in small groups among Gentiles, Central European Jews like the Meiers and Ullmans generally had few compunctions about arriving among the early settlers in hundreds of American places. Their long experience as low-status outsiders may even have given them an advantage in finding their way in a rough new country. Lowly *Dorfjuden* had no expectations of social standing and eagerly took whatever opportunities came their way. In their early years in America many Jews tried one business after another and one town after another until they found something that worked. The 1819 Baltimore city directory, for example, listed Joseph M. Levy as a painter and glazier with premises at the corner of Barre and Hanover Streets. The 1822 edition found him in the grocery business at 145 Sharp Street. From 1824 on, he was back among the painters.[11]

The nation's established Jewish communities were still small at the outset of the 1820–1880 period. The largest, Charleston, numbered only six hundred in 1825.[12] But as newcomers poured off incoming ships year by year, Jewish communities in a number of places grew into a substantial urban presence. By 1860 New York, which had long since eclipsed Philadelphia as the nation's premier metropolis and Charleston as its leading Jewish center, had a Jewish population topping forty thousand. Baltimore and Philadelphia followed with eight thousand each, and Boston with twenty-three hundred.[13] Elaborate networks of commercial ties and communal institutions bound these Jewries into organized communities. And in embryonic cities already poised for rapid growth, like Chicago, Cincinnati, San Francisco, Cleveland, and Washington, the founders of future major Jewish centers were already on hand.

The immigrants of these generations differed from their precursors in some respects, but there was one crucial resemblance. As striking as American Jewry's rapid growth and geographic dispersion was its strong preference for urban, usually commercial occupations. As in earlier American centuries, Jews, both newly arrived and native born, overwhelmingly shunned agriculture, the occupation favored by the vast majority of Gentile Americans, in favor of business, usually retail trade. Even the few Jews who tried their hand at farming generally did some trading on the side.

As cities mushroomed with immigration and the frontier rolled over the Appalachians and across the prairies and plains, and as gold fever lured thousands to California, the same small-scale Jewish commercial skills that Europe found redundant turned out to be just what the new country needed. In crowded city neighborhoods and tiny settlements springing up in the wilderness, on main streets and backcountry trails, America's town dwellers, scattered settlers, slave plantations, and even Indian tribes needed the yard goods, tools, notions, knives, cookware, and other manufactured articles that a peddler could carry or a small store could stock. In a country alive with moving and building and exploring, the skills and attitudes that had made the *Dorfjuden* obsolete in Europe proved crucial to their economic progress in America. On the growing edges of American society, thousands of small traders found their own chance to strike it rich or at least earn a decent living in a new home.

And even beyond the frontier's enticing commercial possibilities, many Jews saw that it offered other opportunities unavailable in either Europe or the older, more established American places. In 1862, for example, Bertha Roman eagerly agreed to marry Mark Levison of Placerville, California, so that she could live far from the anti-Semitism she had known in East Prussia. Hannah Greenebaum left Philadelphia in 1858 for the California home of her new husband, Lewis Gerstle, in part because she wanted to be near her sister and three brothers, who already lived in the West. Merchant Henry Lesensky would confide to his son many years later that "I had not a very severe task to induce you mother to accompany me" in 1867 to the small New Mexico town where he was living.[14] Until their wedding Henry's twenty-year-old bride Martha, her sister, and their widowed mother had lived in poverty in New York. Marlchen Deutsch arrived in America in 1869 from Karlsruhe, Bavaria, and went straight to Davenport, Iowa. As she recalled decades afterward, "I had relatives there, so that offered me an *Anfangspunkt* [starting point] to America. I was married there to Mr. Deutsch, and we came to Minneapolis in 1873 ... because we heard that it was a thriving community."[15]

Despite the West's attractions, however, many found the decision to brave its dangers and discomforts hard to make. In 1869, new American Ichel Watters visited his hometown of Rogassen, Prussia, hoping to find a wife. Augusta Graupe caught his eye, and he tried, with tales of his success in fast-growing Utah, to convince her parents that he could offer Augusta a happy life in Salt Lake City. The thought of their daughter in the wilds of Indian country horrified the elder Graupes, and Ichel returned to America still a bachelor. The letters he exchanged with Augusta over the succeeding months did nothing to change his personal situation.

Meanwhile, the political situation in Salt Lake City was deteriorating rapidly. Growing animosity between Mormons and non-Mormon "Gentiles" boiled over into fights and disturbances. Idealistic Ichel spoke up publicly for reason and tolerance but got for his trouble a pair of beatings that almost cost him an arm. The news of his injuries reached Augusta and, aghast, she persuaded her parents that she had to go and nurse her courageous suitor. Of course, by the time Ichel traveled to Wyoming to meet Augusta and bring her back to Salt Lake, he had completely recovered. The couple married in 1871.

Both Bertha Roman's hopes of acceptance and the senior Graupes' fears of danger proved justified, as many westering pioneers discovered. Alighting from the boat at St. Paul, Amelia Ullman saw that "many of the men" (overwhelmingly Gentiles) "greeted my husband and showed a kindly interest in my arrival. New residents were much sought for the struggling new towns, and anyone who came with the intention of becoming a settler was sure of a hearty welcome."[16] The prejudice, discrimination, and social isolation that plagued Jews in Europe found no place in the rough, fluid, democratic life on the frontier. People—at least white people—judged one another by individual character and behavior, not by religion or background. Regardless of religion, "we dwellers in St. Paul, from being thrown so much together, became as one big family living under many different roofs," Amelia found. "Among us there was a geniality and a cordiality that was most agreeable."[17]

The same midwestern neighborliness prevailed in Urbana, Illinois, according to Jerome Sholem, whose great-aunt settled there in the mid-nineteenth century. When the Christian women who lived next door came to visit for the first time, they politely posed a question. "Are you a Jewess? . . . We have never seen anyone before who was Jewish. We just never have." The aunt invited them in to "look me over. See if I have horns or a tail or whatever you wish. Come on in." The callers, who soon became friendly with the Jewish newcomers, accepted the invitation to satisfy their curiosity.[18]

Living conditions, however, were often as harsh as the Graupes feared. "Only a conscientious housewife, only a devoted mother who had lived in St. Paul in those days know[s] all the inconveniences and miseries I was forced to endure in my efforts to do what I felt to be my duty," Amelia wrote. "No servants, no house help of any kind was to be obtained" to aid with the baby or the housework—a considerable hardship in a time when every household task required arduous labor and in a place where very little was available for purchase. "Every drop of water had to be carried across the prairie from a well in a livery stable," Amelia recalled. "My child was ill much of the time for lack of proper nourishment, for good, wholesome food was difficult to obtain. Fresh vegitable[s] [sic] and fruit were unknown. These things being brought up from St. Louis by the boats, they were often in such a condition upon their arrival at St. Paul [as to have] been deleterious to health."[19]

The town boasted a single cow, but the owner chose not to sell its milk. The Ullmann family moved from one dismal shack to another until Joseph secured a pair of ramshackle rooms behind a storeroom, where they set up house. St. Paul lacked any amusements other than what the residents could make for themselves. The winter brought cold so severe that even when wrapped in buffalo hides—which, being "plentiful and not costly" were the preferred dress in that season—anyone venturing outdoors risked injury or death. Amelia eventually learned, "as had many another woman who had left the comforts of civilization to go into the new lands of the Great West, that many vexations and privations must be nobly born."[20]

Amelia's surroundings, however, were less crude than those of Hannah Austrian. With her husband, Julius, and their children, Hannah lived for twelve years on Madeleine Island, near Bayfield, Wisconsin, with Christian missionaries and members of the Ojibway tribe as their only neighbors. Amelia's despair was no deeper than that of Anna Freudenthal Solomon, who emigrated from Inowrolclaw in Prussia in 1872, the day after her wedding to Isadore Elkan Solomon, known in his new country as I.E. Four years in the livery business in Towanda, Pennsylvania, brought the Solomons a growing family and a failing business, so they decided to join Freudenthal relatives in faraway New Mexico Territory. Selling "everything we possessed except our three children" to finance the trip, they journeyed by train to La Junta, Colorado, and then, for six days and nights, on a cramped, jolting stagecoach to the settlement of Las Cruces. Anna and the children stayed there with cousins while I.E. reconnoitered business possibilities in the region.[21]

Within months, he was in the business of making charcoal to sell to a copper mine in the Gila Valley of Arizona, in the middle of Apache country patrolled by soldiers from nearby Fort Thomas. Another arduous round-the-clock trip, this one in a wagon crammed with the children and all their bedding, clothing, food, and other belongings, brought a frightened Anna through Indian Territory to the house that I.E. had rented. She had no inkling, despondently viewing the ramshackle, isolated old adobe building in the desert, that she stood at the center of the future Solomonville, destined to become the seat of Graham County and the site of the Anna's celebrated hotel and I.E.'s prosperous charcoal factory. On that first night, Anna cried herself to sleep on the dirt floor of the new home she had struggled so long to reach.

Nor did Anna's fear on her desert journey rival that of Hannah Phillips on her isolated homestead outside of Fargo, North Dakota, on the day her daughter Sarah was born. Her husband was off on his peddling rounds and "the rain had cut a hole in the roof of the sod farmhouse," according to their grandson, Henry Fine. "My grandmother was about to give birth to her fifth child. She was in pain and obviously suffering. My mother [one of Hannah's older children] remembered the scene well. All of a sudden two Indians appeared in the house. They looked at my grandmother, saw the condition she was in, and without saying a word turned and walked out. Within ten minutes two squaws were in the house and they delivered my aunt Sarah. They never knew where those Indians came from, but after that my grandmother insisted on moving off the farm."[22]

And not even Hannah's travail matched that of the legendary Rebecca, a Jewish woman said to have journeyed west with a sickly brother to marry trader Isaac Goldstein. The siblings reportedly fell into the hands of Colorado Indians who used Rebecca for a human sacrifice. The distraught Isaac, the tale continues, then became a kind of Jewish Flying Dutchman, peddling throughout Colorado Territory as he searched vainly and ceaselessly for his lost fiancée at every Indian camp he found. The tragic drama reportedly concluded with his death on September 29, 1879, at the Indian battle known as the Mill River Massacre. Whatever the truth of this gruesome saga, the fact that it was widely known and believed reveals the depths of trepidation and dread felt by many of the women making their way to a new life in the West.

The Way West

Because of the distance, difficulty, and danger, women were a minority among the first waves of whites on the frontier. "There were not many young children nor aged persons," among Amelia Ullmann's fellow St. Paul residents, "and the women were a small percentage of the entire population," she wrote. "The majority were young and middle-aged men who were able to build well and firmly the foundation of a new city."[23] This description holds true not only for the settlers of western and southern towns but also for the Central European Jewish immigrants they attracted in the early years. The first arrivals were overwhelmingly young men starting out in business, usually out of a backpack or wagon. In 1840 peddlers constituted 40 percent of all Jews in the United States. They accounted for 70 percent ten years later, reflecting the large number of impecunious new immigrants who arrived in the intervening decade. Of the 125 Jews in Iowa in the 1850s, fully one hundred followed the peddling trade.

Wherever they worked, the peddlers' business development followed a course we have already observed. Phillip Goldsmith, to take one well-documented example, arrived at the age of eighteen in Milwaukee, where he stayed with an uncle and aunt. We know the details of his career because, during that very first summer, thirteen-year-old Sophia Heller, a local Jewish girl who had come as an infant with her parents from Bohemia, spied a handsome newcomer one day at a swimming school in the town. She and a girlfriend giggled over his good looks and the black mole on his back but then, as young girls will, promptly forgot him. Some weeks later, friends of Sophia's parents, Mr. and Mrs. Pereles, came to call at the Heller home, bringing their sons Franklin, Madison, and Jefferson and a newly arrived nephew. "Behold, who was it but the handsome young fellow with the mole on his back," Sophia wrote in her old age. "My heart gave a bound. . . . He had come from the old country. That I could see from his clothes."[24]

The two met occasionally while swimming or at dances, but Sophia knew little of Phillip's personal life. One day that winter, they unexpectedly met on a downtown street. She was going to the post office, and he had "a large tin notion box in one hand and a large heavy bundle of dry goods tied in a striped ticking on one shoulder, peddling. We were both embarrassed" by his lowly trade. Within a year, however, Phillip had advanced to a more prestigious job, clerking in a downtown store while living alone in a hotel, apparently forgotten by "the rich uncle and aunt Pereles."[25] Before long he moved to Waukesha, a small town west of Milwaukee, to clerk at a store owned by a Mr. Klein. Though friends had once assumed that Sophia and Mr. Goldsmith "would be couple," he showed little interest and she thought of him no more. But three years later Sophia moved to Chicago to work in her brother Albert's brand-new dry goods emporium. She expected to "assist my sister-in-law to sew little clothes, as well as assist in the store, as they could not afford help." She did not expect to find that the store next to Albert's belonged to Phillip Goldsmith and his brother Alex.

A courtship began in earnest, culminating on a crowded Chicago street among the huge throng that had come to pay respects to the recently assassinated President Lincoln, who lay in state at the courthouse. "Mr. G. insisted I take his arm as the crowd was so large," but the modest Sophia hesitated because "in those days if a girl was seen on the arm of a gentleman, she was considered to be . . . engaged." Finally, "in order not to be separated" in the press of people, Sophia had no choice. Phillip immediately made her move official by proposing. Sophia's parents consented and her father came to Chicago to bestow his blessing, as "Mr. G. could not leave his business at that time." Chaperoned by her mother, Sophia returned to Milwaukee where, three months later, at the age of sixteen years and nine months, she became twenty-one-year-old Phillip's bride.

Phillip's family connections in America and his early rise in business, from hawking goods on a street corner, to a clerking job in a second town, to keeping his own store in yet a third, mirrors the course followed by countless young men. So does his decision to marry once he had established his store as a going concern, as well as his and Sophia's involvement in family businesses. That the Goldsmiths ultimately moved to Covington, Kentucky, and started a factory manufacturing doll heads and baseballs is rather less typical, as is the fact that later generations built the company into MacGregor, a major manufacturer of sports equipment.

But the course of Phillip's romance with Sophia still ran more smoothly than many other men's. He had the good luck to find an eligible Jewish girl—the American-raised daughter of successful businesspeople—in his very first American town. Heller's ability to make a wedding gift of $300 a decade and a half after his own arrival in America attests to his prosperity. It also gave the newlyweds, by the standards of their time, a comfortable start in married life; their first meal in their first Chicago apartment was ice cream and cake! What's more, fortunate Phillip married in his early twenties, avoiding the more typical wait of years or even decades. And his wife was within several years of his own age, whereas most Jewish men took wives considerably younger than themselves.

The marked shortage of eligible Jewish women in the United States, and especially on the frontier, forced many a lonely merchant to far greater lengths than Phillip went to find a Jewish bride, either to an East Coast city or, like Aaron Meier and Ichel Watters, all the way back to Europe. Men willingly undertook such efforts because most placed a very high premium on marrying within the faith. Fewer than a quarter of the Jewish marriages recorded in Los Angeles County in the turbulent years between 1850 and 1876 involved a non-Jewish partner, for example, and almost no mixed marriages occurred in Portland.[26]

Eager bachelors who chanced to find a suitable girl nearby sometimes used extraordinary tactics to win her. Isadore Strassburger, for example, met Rachel Cohen in 1867 in a rather unlikely place—the Virginia City,

Montana, mining camp. Seventeen years old, she lived with her parents, who had decided to move to another town. As the day of the Cohens' departure neared, Isadore thoughtfully offered to help with the move, even more thoughtfully arranging for Rachel to ride with him in his own carriage. Falling a discreet distance behind the others, he asked her to marry him. When she accepted, he instantly turned his horse and raced the carriage back to town, where a judge promptly performed the ceremony.

Sheer luck, often combined with family ties, produced many other matches. Peddlers moving from town to town and merchants making partnerships met other Jews, some of whom had marriageable relatives. A young Bavarian named Roth, who boarded with a Milwaukee family between peddling forays into the countryside, for example, ended up as his landlords' in-law when he married their daughter soon after opening his own store in Monroe, Wisconsin. Samuel Rosenwald, who peddled along the Winchester Trail in Virginia, got his goods from Jewish wholesalers named Hammerslough. Initially his creditors, the Hammersloughs became his brothers-in-law when he married their sister. A store to run in Peoria was the young couple's wedding present from the bride's family.

One lucky day an immigrant merchant, William Frank, was riding a train from Philadelphia to his store in Kilgore, Ohio. "A young man, no doubt observing that I was a follower of Abraham, moved next to me," he remembered. "During the conversation [he] said he could scarcely await the train's arriving in Lancaster, as he had been married six weeks before and had been away for several weeks. I told him that if I could meet a desirable girl, I would like to marry also." At the Lancaster station both men's wishes came true. William's new acquaintance introduced Paulina Wormser, his wife's cousin. William immediately "knew that she would make a good wife" and two weeks later married her.[27] And in a family connection that had historic consequences, Chicago shopkeeper Jacob Rosenberg married Hannah Reese in the new town's first Jewish wedding. His business partner, Levi Rosenthal, soon became his brother-in-law by marrying Hannah's sister. Some years later all of Chicago rejoiced in these Reese family ties. The women's brother, Michael, a childless bachelor, left to the city of Chicago, where he had never lived, a fortune he had amassed in California, including a hospital that was dedicated in 1881 and named for him, its first benefactor.

Occasionally Jewish men tried underhanded methods when legitimate ones failed to secure a bride. On an 1858 trip east after a lonely decade in Oregon, Portland merchant Nathan Cohen met an Ohio girl, Fanny

Hyman, who was planning a move to Portland to live with relatives. Cohen volunteered to serve as her guardian on the trip to the West Coast. But once they arrived in New York to catch a ship to Oregon, Cohen abused his position of trust by giving Fanny the choice of marrying him or being abandoned alone and penniless in the unfamiliar metropolis. She refused him. In cahoots with a relative of hers, Cohen decided to hold Fanny prisoner until she agreed. After four months the desperate girl relented and underwent a hasty wedding shortly before the ill-matched couple sailed. Reaching Oregon, however, she instantly escaped to her uncles, who quickly arranged a divorce. Cohen's fellow Portlanders nonetheless appeared to forgive their nefarious townsman. He eventually became a respected local citizen and, in the 1870s, another woman's husband. Poor Fanny's fate is lost to history.[28]

Fanny's travail indicates how far many Jewish women had traveled from European marriage traditions. Many quickly adopted the American custom of choosing their own mates. Hannah Marks, whose Polish-born parents left her an orphan in New Bedford, Massachusetts, was sent to live with an uncle and aunt, David and Judith Solis-Cohen in Philadelphia. Hannah found their Orthodox home confining and longed for the freedom her brother Bernhard described in letters from California. (Her Aunt Judith, however, was herself an independent-minded woman. When she married the Ashkenazic Myers David Cohen in 1837, she insisted that he add her Sephardic surname to his own, establishing what would become a distinguished Philadelphia family name.) Unhappy and rebellious, Hannah found a job in a store, which allowed her to move out of her uncle's house. Even so, he insisted that she live in a kosher boardinghouse that was far from her work and too costly for her means. In 1853 she leaped at the marriage proposal of a lonely California bachelor who offered to pay her passage west if she agreed to wed him.

Once she met her fiancé in the flesh, however, Hannah ended the engagement. Her horrified eastern relatives insisted she go through with the wedding. But Hannah stood firm and Bernhard backed her up. "That cattle matching project," he declared, was "not exactly consistent with the spirit of an American education in the 1850s."[29] Hannah took a job in San Francisco teaching school and in 1862 married the man of her choice, Gershom Mendes Seixas Solomons, grandson of the famous New York *hazzan*. In retrospect, however, she might have done better with her original suitor. Though a respected San Francisco religious leader, the younger

Gershom was also an alcoholic, and Hannah ended up the sole support of their family of seven children.

Despite some Jewish bachelors' best efforts, whether honest or otherwise, demography conspired with geography to keep everyone from finding a Jewish spouse. Faced with intermarriage or bachelorhood, quite a number of men appeared to choose the latter. Others, however, married non-Jewish women, including Isadore Friedman of Washington Territory and Prussian-born Solomon Bibo of Santa Fe, who took Indian wives. Married at Acoma Pueblo by a Catholic priest and accepted into his wife's tribe, Solomon, the son of a *hazzan,* nonetheless insisted that his children have a Jewish education and moved his family to San Francisco to obtain it.

Intermarriage was common in America from the earliest colonial days, but by the 1820s it was becoming increasingly controversial. With growing immigration and ever larger numbers of native-born offspring, Jewish communities, at least the major ones, were now large enough to offer a reasonable choice of potential marriage partners. Some parents began to insist that their children take spouses within the faith. Hillel Moses Anker, for example, who died in Philadelphia in 1837, left a will that divided his substantial property among his wife and children. But it also stipulated that if any "child or children should marry out of the Jewish faith; or die leaving no issue born in the Jewish faith then I give my whole estate to my wife absolutely."[30] A Denver Jewish father, Solomon Nathan, pleaded temporary insanity to a charge of assaulting a minister who had conducted the wedding ceremony in which his daughter married a Christian. Attacked inside a local bank, the minister insisted that the couple was determined to run off with or without benefit of clergy. Unimpressed by Nathan's defense, the judge fined him $40.

And as in earlier days, some Gentile wives embraced Judaism. European-born Marcus Spiegel, for example, met a Quaker girl named Caroline on his peddling rounds in Ohio. They married and he brought her to Chicago, where in 1853 she became one of the city's first Jewish converts. Eleven years later Marcus died in the Civil War battle of Vicksburg, but Caroline remained loyal to her new faith for the rest of her days. (At the time of his death, Marcus was intending to go into business with his brother Joseph. Joseph went ahead and opened the planned store, which eventually grew into the Spiegel catalog company.)

Given the odds they faced against making a suitable marriage, some Jewish men pursued nonmarital liaisons with non-Jewish women. Tucson businessman Barron Jacobs fathered a baby out of wedlock by a local Mexican woman but then arranged for a sixteen-year-old Jewish girl to come from New York to become his wife. Yetta, still in pigtails but wise beyond her years, learned of the situation and made sure that the child had a proper upbringing. In early Los Angeles, merchant Bernard Cohen, though maintaining an Orthodox home with his wife, Esther, and their three Jewish children, assimilated to local culture in adopting the practice of *la casa chica*. For many years he maintained a second household for his mistress Delfina Verelas and their four Catholic children.

Women in the West

Regardless of how they traveled, of course, or why they came, the advent of a settlement's first Jewish women marked a milestone in its life. Portland's initial Jewish arrivals, Lewis May and Jacob Goldstein, for example, came in 1849, followed by brothers Jacob and Simon Blumauer in 1851 and by brothers Charles, Kalman, and Samuel Haas and their cousins Jacob and Abe in 1852. But it wasn't until the next year that the first Jewish woman in the territory, a Mrs. Weinshank, brought a touch of Jewish home life to these Central European Jewish men by opening a boardinghouse catering to bachelors. Not long afterward Simon Blumauer brought another important change to Oregon's infant Jewish community. Traveling to New York in 1854, he married Mollie Radelsheimer, like him a native of Bavaria, who bore Louis, Oregon's first Jewish child. Other women arrived gradually, and in 1858 Marjana Bettman and Simon Baum stood under Portland's first *chuppah* and were married by Samuel Laski, apparently a local layman who knew enough Hebrew to lead prayers. The bridal couple issued invitations in their own names printed on a elaborately cut-out paper adorned with an appropriately western pair of cows and a rather incongruous palm tree. To attend the *simcha* (joyous occasion), the guests—perhaps including Aaron Meier—climbed a flight of stairs to a loft over a blacksmith shop and livery stable that a group of Jewish men rented to use as a prayer hall.

But Jewish women brought more than domesticity and formal social events. As they had in earlier years in the East, they also made a major (in many cases crucial) contribution to businesses, both those ostensibly belonging to their husbands and those they ran on their own. Following a pattern going back at least a century to New York's slipshod landlady, Hettie Hays, Mrs. Weinshank and her counterparts in towns and cities across the country built a livelihood out of the need of rootless young peddlers and other Jewish travelers for a stable, familiar refuge from the rigors of life on the road.

Such a business required relatively little capital and no special skills beyond those a competent homemaker already possessed. Demand was brisk, given the constant influx of young male transients who had grown up in kosher homes. Philadelphia widow Esther Hart, for example, supported a family of ten through the boardinghouse she ran in the 1820s.[31] Because the often cash-strapped immigrant traders generally dealt in ordinary household goods, landladies often took a peddler's wares in lieu of rent, allowing both parties to get what they needed even if neither happened to have much ready cash. Jewish women, such as Annie Stargarth Mitchell, also provided accommodations for non-Jewish travelers. Her outstanding cooking attracted guests to the White River Hotel, which she ran for four decades with her husband, Levi, in Tailholt, California, in the Tulare County mining country. After Levi's death in 1885, Annie supported their four children as sole manager of the hotel.

Many a landlady's skill in the kitchen contributed to her business success, and in one case a Jewish woman's frontier recipe became the basis for a national company. Baltimore native Rosana Dyer Osterman moved to Galveston with her husband, Joseph, in 1838. There the couple combined a general store with some import business. Galveston, like all nineteenth-century port cities, saw many immigrants heading inland. Through their dealings with members of the Comanche tribe, Rosana got the idea of combining dried, powdered buffalo meat with cornmeal and beans to make dry but very nourishing biscuits that stayed edible and nutritious even after long periods in a saddle bag or on the back of a wagon. With financial backing from the Ostermans, their friend Gail Borden worked at perfecting the traveler's biscuit as a commercial product and in the process came upon an even more lucrative food idea, condensed milk.

Women across the country opened their own retail businesses, often selling items they made themselves. In the 1830s, the widow Sarah Hart ran a stationery shop on Philadelphia's Walnut Street that supported her household of eight. Two decades later, Bella Bloch found that the millinery skills her parents urged her to acquire paid off when she put them to use in the shop she opened in Newark, New Jersey, in the 1850s. Gustav Kussy, a young butcher who peddled fresh kosher meat around the town and its suburbs, began stopping by, though it's doubtful that he needed a fancy lady's hat. In 1858 the couple married. Their wedding presents, which included a washtub and a stove that lacked legs, gave some indication of their own and their friends' tight finances. The newlyweds set up house-keeping on the $200 remaining to them after they paid for the wedding.

Bella then closed her store, pooled her capital with Gustav's, and joined him in the meat business. While he continued to peddle through the streets, Bella, according to their son, Nathan, "waited on customers in the butcher shop, cooked, washed and sewed for the family."[32] Though Bella's contri-bution to the family business was vital to its success, only Gustav's name appeared in the city directory and, by the convention of the time, only he was considered a business owner. A married woman, as a legal extension of her husband, ordinarily did not have independent economic standing.

Sarah Nathan Goldwater, an ancestor of the prominent Arizona retail-ing and political clan and grandmother of U.S. senator and Republican presidential candidate Barry Goldwater, was one wife who did establish financial independence from her husband. Born in London in 1850, she married Michael Goldwater, originally from Konin, Poland. Standing six foot three, "Big Mike" had dreams as large as his stature. In 1851 he set off with his younger brother Joseph ("Little Joe") to strike it rich in California. Left behind to care for their two children, Sarah spent three years in London before rejoining her husband in 1854. Far from striking gold, however, Mike was running a fruit store in Sonora, Tuolumne County. He soon lost the business but optimistically started up another one, this time using Sarah's name, but was again quickly bankrupted. By 1858 the brothers, now in Los Angeles, had run several more enterprises into the ground.

Sarah decided she had to take her children's economic destiny, as well as her own credit rating, in her own hands. She declared in a statement filed in the Tuolumne County courthouse that "from and after this date I intend to transact in my own name and on my on account, [and, by exten-sion, not in Michael's] the business of tailoring and merchandising. . . . I will be personally responsible for all debts contracted by me in said busi-ness" but, by extension, not for those contracted by Michael in any of his.[33] While the brothers continued their string of financial disasters, both in Los Angeles and later in the mining camp of La Paz, Sarah, first in Los Angeles and after 1868 in San Francisco, ran her own successful dressmaking con-cern, supporting a brood that eventually numbered eight. Eventually, how-ever, Michael and his sons achieved success in Arizona Territory, founding the firm that grew into the Goldwater's Department Store chain. Michael visited San Francisco often to be with Sarah. But she, according to legend, declined ever to visit the region where her name and descendants would become so influential.

But perhaps the most striking example of a wife's success in her husband's shadow involves a woman born to a rabbi and his wife as Mary Ann Cohen in 1848 in Scheveningchen, Holland. Mary Ann grew up in London, where at sixteen she married twenty-three-year-old Isaac Moeijan, son of a Russian father and Dutch mother who had taken him to America as a child. Isaac had peddled in New Mexico and Texas, fought in the Civil War, and ultimately emigrated to London, where he became a dealer in art supplies. Twelve years after their wedding, the family, now numbering nine, took the long voyage from London around the horn to San Francisco.

In his first California job, Isaac carved and gilded picture frames in the Oakland workshop of Solomon Gump. In their home, meanwhile, Mary Ann put her exquisite needlework skills to work crafting luxurious baby clothes to sell. Decidedly more ambitious than the dreamy, philosophical Isaac, she convinced him to leave a position that she considered menial in favor of the presumably more promising career of selling clothing, at first from a pack on his back. By an odd chance, for the brief period that Isaac worked for Gump in Oakland, the bearers of what would become the two most famous names in San Francisco retailing labored under the same roof. Isaac and Mary Anne had by that time Anglicized their surname. Not long afterward, they crossed the bay, settled in San Francisco, and opened a small shop to sell the elegant children's wear and women's undergarments that Mary Ann made. They followed the convention of their time and gave it the husband's name: I. Magnin.

Whatever they called it, the business was from the very beginning unmistakably Mary Ann's. A shrewd businesswoman with subtle taste and a keen eye for style and fabric, she stocked the store with luxurious silk lingerie and blouses sewn under her supervision to her specifications. In a city newly rich on gold rush money, both the shop's reputation for the highest quality and the demand for its exclusive goods quickly grew. Though the 1880 census lists Isaac as the owner of a fancy goods store and Mary Ann as a housewife, he cared more about philosophizing than fabrics, and the firm's swift rise to preeminence reflected Mary Ann's determination and drive and the business and dressmaking training she insisted that the young generation of retailing Magnins receive.

Moving Up

Though many enterprising Jewish women and their menfolk succeeded in traditional commercial businesses, others soon took advantage of America's opportunities to move into fields unattainable, or even unimaginable, to their Old World foremothers. In most Jewish families, newfound prosperity quickly translated into better educational opportunities for the children. The combination of ready cash, traditional Jewish respect for learning, and the growth of both girls' schools and coeducation opened the world of higher education to at least some Jewish women. As far back as the late eighteenth century, Rebecca Gratz's sister Richea had enrolled, along with their brother Hyman, in the first class to enter Lancaster's Franklin College, later known as Franklin and Marshall. Rebecca appears to have attended Philadelphia's Young Ladies Academy, the first girls school chartered in the United States. Other girls across the country followed Richea, America's first female Jewish college student, to campus. Native New Yorker Esther Jane Baum Ruskay took her degree with the first class to graduate from New York's Normal (now Hunter) College in 1875. Across the continent, Polish-born Mary Goldsmith Prag finished San Jose Normal School.

Like Hannah Marks Solomons, who for a time was the youngest person and the only woman serving as a San Francisco school principal, Esther and Mary, along with counterparts across the nation, chose teaching as their career. As early as the 1840s, twenty-year-old Judith Peixotto set out to support her widowed mother and seven siblings by apparently becoming the first Jew to teach in the New York City public schools. In this she followed the example of her physician father, Daniel L.M. Peixotto, son of a Shearith Israel *hazzan* and a holder of Columbia University bachelor's, master's, and medical degrees. Leaving New York, he became Ohio's first Jewish professor and first Jewish physician, then served as the first president of the institution that became the Ohio State University medical school. Judith's sisters Sarah and Zipporah also joined the city system, and the three bearers of an old Sephardic name appear for a time to have been its only Jewish faculty members.

When Judith began her career, "schoolmarms" were replacing the school masters in classrooms across the country, especially in the generally coed public systems. Willing to take lower pay than men, women held half the teaching jobs in the Northeast by midcentury. Unlike Roman Catholic immigrants, who distrusted the largely Protestant-run public systems and created an independent educational system mirroring the one supported by the taxpayers, Jews generally used the public schools that were rapidly multiplying across the country. Wealthy families, of course, used either private tutors or the private academies also favored by elite Christians.

Positions as teachers or even principals represented significant professional attainments for nineteenth-century women. But a handful of Jews managed to join an even more prestigious profession. Elizabeth Cohen, a mother of five and the wife of New York physician Aaron Cohen, lost a young son to measles. Tormented by the thought that she could have done more to save him, she decided to "become a doctor myself and help mothers keep their little ones well."[34] Her husband moved his medical practice to New Orleans in 1853, but thirty-three-year-old Elizabeth went to Philadelphia to enroll in the Philadelphia College of Medicine, the nation's first medical school for women. Graduating sixth in a class of thirty-seven in 1857, she joined her husband in New Orleans as a doctor in her own right—the fourteenth physician, and the first female, in the state. The city directory did not list her as a physician until twenty years later, calling her first a midwife and then a "doctoress." Nonetheless, at the end of her career she recalled little actual discrimination, perhaps because she specialized in caring for women and children and pitched in when the 1857 and 1878 yellow fever epidemics ravaged the city.

Dr. Fanny Berlin had an even more illustrious medical career. Born Stefanija Berlinerblau in Cherson, Ukraine, in 1852, she entered the Faculty of Medicine in Zurich in 1870, taking her medical degree five years later from the University of Bern. Two years after that she came to America to serve a residency at the New England Hospital for Women and Children in Boston, the only hospital in the city that employed women as doctors. She was named one of its four female staff surgeons two years later. When the Massachusetts Medical Society excluded her because of her sex, she founded the New England Women's Medical Society in 1878; the all-male group accepted her for membership eight years later. Known for her writings on prolapsed uterus and fluent in several languages, Fanny focused her hospital work and her later private practice on serving the city's immigrant women.

For most educated Jewish women, however, professional careers in the public arena lay many decades in the future. But one prestigious field did lend itself to nineteenth-century notions of homebound female propriety. Several Jewish women, primarily native-born daughters of prosperity, became writers and attained widespread recognition and substantial readerships during this period. Most important was Emma Lazarus, immortal

for the lines engraved at the base of the Statue of Liberty. Her 1883 son-
net "The New Colossus" envisions the "Mother of Exiles" lifting her
"lamp beside the Golden Door" to light the way of the "huddled masses"
into America. Born in 1842 to wealthy Sephardic parents who traced their
descent to the *Ste. Catherine* landing 182 years before, Emma lived in a
New York and Newport world of governesses, private tutors, and French,
German, and Italian lessons. From adolescence on, she published scores of
poems, essays, and translations in a stream of books and periodicals, both
Jewish and general, including such influential journals as *Century* and
Scribner's. The family attended Shearith Israel, but in early decades of her
life Emma's "religious convictions . . . and the circumstances of [her] life
. . . led [her] somewhat apart from [her] people," she later admitted.[35] By
1871, when she published a book of poems that included "In the Jewish
Cemetery at Newport," Jewish identity took a larger role in her creative
life. Though both she and her readers considered her first and foremost an
American writer, she used her powerful literary voice and national stature
to express both her growing devotion to her Jewish heritage and her passion for the promise of America.

Poet and historical writer Leah Cohen Harby came from a long-estab-
lished southern family that had fought in the Revolutionary War and
included several other literary women. Rebekah Gumpert Hyneman, on
the other hand, did not descend from prominent Jewish dynasties but had
a non-Jewish mother and a Jewish father. We don't know for certain what
sort of religious life she experienced in her parents' home in her native
Philadelphia, but her marriage to Benjamin Hyneman, a practicing Jew,
brought her into the Jewish orbit and Judaism into the center of her life.
Though widowed only five years into her marriage, she hewed firmly to the
"faith of [her] adoption" for the rest of her life.[36] Her stories and poems
looked deeply into the lives of Jewish women, especially those tempted to
leave the faith for Christianity. Steadfast loyalty to their religion ultimately
yields her courageous Jewish heroines and heroes the rewards of riches
and love.

A few Jewish women gained national attention in fields considered controversial, even notorious, in the Victorian era. Polish-born Ernestine Rose
spent her early adulthood in Europe and England and arrived in New York
in 1836, just in time to take an active role in the movement for women's
rights. A rabbi's daughter, she had the chance—denied the great majority of
women both here and in Europe—to study religious texts in the Hebrew
language. Great intellectual ability and a striking independence of mind

revealed themselves early. In childhood she questioned the justice of a God who exacted frequent religious fasts. At fourteen, based on what she had already learned, she denounced both women's inferior status and the texts supporting it. At sixteen, she rejected the fiancé her parents had chosen and successfully sued in civil court for the return of the dowry given him. Using part of that money, she left Poland for Prussia. Her extravagant exploits in the next few years included successfully petitioning the Prussian ruler for an exemption from the law that required Jewish arrivals to have a Christian sponsor, inventing a room deodorant that generated proceeds sufficient for her to live and travel independently, and becoming a disciple of the prominent English socialist Robert Dale Owen.

Once in the United States with her English husband, fellow Owenite William Ella Rose, she continued the public speaking career she had begun in England by lecturing about a number of progressive causes. She also took part in every important women's rights conference during the seminal midcentury period and knew all the leading figures of the suffrage and abolition movements. Touring the speakers circuit with Susan B. Anthony, she even devised Anthony's signature slogan, "Agitate, agitate, agitate."[37] Among the signal successes Rose achieved before returning to live in England was a successful fifteen-year drive that culminated in 1869 with the passage of property and guardianship rights for New York State wives.

The theatrical stage rather than the speaker's platform was where two other Jewish women made famous careers and large fortunes. Both born in 1835, Adah Isaacs Menken and Rose Etyinge were national stars. Menken caused a sensation by appearing onstage "nude," though actually clad in flesh-colored tights. Eytinge was the highest-paid actress of her time, earning a then astronomical salary in three figures. A third, and possibly even more flamboyant individual, Josephine Sarah Marcus, also used the stage as her route out of the ordinary. Born in New York in 1861 and raised in San Francisco, at eighteen she ran away with the Pauline Markam Theater Company. In Arizona she met and became involved with the already married (at least in the common law) Wyatt Earp, beginning a relationship as fiery as the famous gunfight at the O.K. Corral. Both the celebrated cowboy lawman and his Josie lie buried with the Marcus family in a San Francisco Jewish cemetery.

But most mid–nineteenth century Jewish women, like most women of their time, shunned the limelight as scandalous and lived far more conventional lives. By the 1870s, the lives of the Central European immigrants and their native-born daughters showed patterns that would typify later generations of American Jewish women. Central European Jews and their offspring quickly achieved economic success, aided by the choices they made in their personal lives. Like Fanny Meier and Sigmund Frank in Portland, many couples chose spouses with an eye to strengthening business ties. A small percentage of Jews, such as the group of friendly and ultimately intermarried San Francisco clans who called themselves the "Golden Circle," had by then achieved great wealth. Most of their coreligionists had climbed into the lower or even the upper reaches of middle-class respectability.

At the same time, Jewish families were becoming smaller. In the early 1800s, Americans typically had seven children; by 1860, Boston Jewish couples averaged 3.8 children each.[38] A decade later, typical Jewish mothers were bearing as few as two or three babies. We're not sure what methods they used to control their fertility, but the practice of withdrawal seems to have played a part, along with animal-skin condoms and a variety of "female preventatives," including douching, vaginal sponges, and suppositories.[39] Though Jewish law expects couples to have children, it permits even the highly observant to limit family size. It places the obligation to reproduce on men and raises no objection to contraceptive techniques that protect women from conceiving. Preserving the mother's health is an overriding concern. Smaller families allowed parents to concentrate more resources on preparing each boy and girl for life as an upwardly mobile American rather than as a member of a struggling immigrant group. It also freed time for their increasingly educated mothers to devote themselves not only to the family business but also to the community, and to projects that would transform American Jewry and Judaism.

Perils and Patriots

Wherever they settled during the nineteenth century, Jews generally became active, loyal members of their local communities. Flora Spiegelberg, a member of a prosperous New Mexico Jewish clan, was, for example, a close friend of the archbishop of Santa Fe, Jean Baptiste Lamy, often conversing with him in his native French. When the Civil War split America, Jews, as Americans, supported both sides, either as passionate proponents of the Union or devoted sons and daughters of the Confederacy. Many of Rachel Mordecai Lazarus's fellow southern Jews, for example, rejected the abolitionist opinions that she had expressed to

Maria Edgeworth, staunchly favoring the southern way of life. Eugenia Levy Phillips, wife of U.S. Congressman Philip Phillips of Mobile, Alabama, spoke out for it so vehemently that Union officials imprisoned her, first in Washington in 1861 and later in New Orleans after she was exiled from the nation's capital. In occupied Natchez, Ophelia Meyer, daughter of a prominent business family, wrote a letter calling General Brayman, the Union commander, a "miserable tyrant." Denounced to the authorities, she soon found herself under arrest in the city hall. Despite their rebel sympathies, however, Ophelia's relatives were willing to use the good offices of Yankees (specifically, Jewish ones) to win her release. Isaac Lowenberg and Henry Frank, two northern Jews associated with the occupation and acquainted with the Meyers, convinced army officials to free Ophelia.

Henry Frank's influence also proved helpful when the Meyers needed to get warm clothing and new boots to two soldier sons who had written begging for help after the battle of Vicksburg. It is not clear, however, that Frank fully understood his role in smuggling the contraband supplies through Union lines and into Confederate hands. At the Meyers' request, Frank arranged for documents allowing Ophelia's mother and two of her sisters to pass through army checkpoints and visit friends living on the out-skirts of town. As Union troops inspected their papers, the ladies sat demurely in their carriage, the clothing and boots hidden under their enor-mous hoop skirts. They paid their call with apparent nonchalance and the friends forwarded the clothes to the needy Meyer boys.

Eugenia Phillips's sister, Phoebe Yates Levy Pember, was meanwhile arranging far more significant aid for thousands of wounded Confederates as the matron of Richmond's Chimborazo military hospital. The daughter of well-to-do parents and the widow of a non-Jew, Thomas Noyes Pember, she called herself Phoebe Yates Pember (dropping the telltale Levy) and moved in elite Christian social circles. Her friendship with the wife of the Confederacy's secretary of war, George R. Randolph, led to her appointment.

In Texas, meanwhile, the ever enterprising Rosana Dyer Osterman, another loyal southerner, not only comforted wounded soldiers but also, according to popular legend, confounded Union plans to hold occupied Galveston. Over seventy years old, the widowed Rosana stayed in her home after the city fell to Union forces. She made her house and grounds a hospital, just as she had done during a yellow fever epidemic in 1853. As she worked on the wards, a northern patient told the grandmotherly

Rosana how a runaway slave had given the Union army a Confederate plan to win back strategically important Galveston island in an attack scheduled for January 12, 1863. Rosana tipped off the southern forces, who attacked on January 1 and took the occupiers completely by surprise.

Rosana, the Levy sisters, and the Natchez Meyer daughters were not, of course, recent immigrants but rather the American-born descendants of earlier migrant generations. But they, like Jews throughout the country, both newly arrived and long established, saw themselves as wholehearted Americans and fashioned their lives and identities in response to an American reality quite unlike anything Jews had ever experienced elsewhere. The commercial and family patterns that had isolated and impoverished *Dorfjuden* in the declining economy of the Central Europe countryside fitted Jewish immigrants and their descendants to grasp the astonishing opportunities offered by the rising American economic colossus. The skills and attitudes that Jewish women had used for generations to help their families survive in Europe helped their families thrive and prosper in the new land. As they found their place as Americans, the women of both newcomer and native generations would use those skills to shape not only successful American families but Jewish communities and institutions uniquely suited to the new American world.

6

"THE BUDDING BRANCH"

Inventing an American Judaism

Like many young Jews setting out for America, Abraham Kohn left his Bavarian hometown on June 15, 1842, with a mixture of hope and trepidation, faith and regret. "I wept bitterly as I kissed my dear mother, perhaps for the last time," he confided to his diary. He knew his future lay beyond the sea, but his heart remained in Wittelshofen as he pressed "her hand and commend[ed] her to the protection of the Eternal, Father of all widows and orphans."[1] Abraham did not know that the lifelong separation he feared would never come to pass, nor realize that his devotion to his mother would play a significant role in the life of an entire American community.

His brother Moses and a boyhood friend accompanied Abraham across the Atlantic. He next spent some time peddling in the rural hinterland of Boston. Within a couple of years, however, he and Moses, along with a third brother, Julius, had found their way to the booming new settlement of Chicago, where they started a clothing store on busy Lake Street. The proceeds soon let them bring over a sister, three additional brothers, and their much loved mother, Dilah.

Dilah had given her children a strong sense of Jewishness in her religiously observant home. On Abraham's second day in America, for example, he had found his way to New York's newest synagogue, Shaar Hashomayim on Attorney Street, to attend Rosh Hashanah services. The congregation he chose followed the liturgy he knew from home, the Central European Ashkenazic style rather than the Sephardic favored by Shearith Israel.

In addition to reciting set devotions from the prayer book, Abraham contemplated the fateful juncture of beginning the "new career before me" in a new country at the start of a new year. He "prayed to the Almighty, thanking him for the voyage happily finished and asking for good and abiding health for my dear mother and brothers and sisters" as well as "for my own good health." Finally, he "asked for all of us good fortune."[2] In time, Abraham's prayers would be amply answered in all but one important respect. His mother's poor health would have long-lasting consequences for all of Chicago Jewry.

Whether in Bavaria or Illinois, Dilah's piety proved unshakable. Though she had come to a frontier town almost devoid of Jewish institutions, she strictly kept the dietary laws. With no one in the territory competent to slaughter meat or poultry to kosher standards, she staunchly refused to eat flesh of any kind. Her children worried about her declining health and thought a more balanced diet might build up her strength. The only way to get Dilah to eat meat was to get a *shochet* for Chicago, which would take a sizable group of people willing to pitch in to pay his salary. The time had come, the Kohns decided, to start a synagogue.

On November 3, 1847, about twenty men, a fifth of the local Jewish population (out of a total population of 17,000), met to discuss the possibility. Jacob Rosenberg and Levi Rosenthal, not yet married to the Reese sisters, hosted the gathering in their store. By evening's end this group of Central European immigrants living in the westernmost good-sized town then under the American flag had transformed themselves into Kehilath Anshe Maariv, or Congregation of Men of the West. The following day, fourteen of these self-proclaimed westerners, including Abraham, Julius, Jacob, and Levi, signed the synagogue's constitution. But even though this was the first time Chicagoans had formed a Jewish congregation, it was not the first time they had gathered for Jewish worship. The Kohn brothers counted among the scant minyan that had met in a room over a store on Yom Kippur of 1845. A slightly larger group reconvened the following year at Rosenberg and Rosenthal's. A Jewish Burial Ground Society that had come into being in 1845 paid $46 the following year for an acre of lakeside land.

But by starting KAM the founders declared themselves not only residents of the frontier but members of a group distinct from their non-Jewish neighbors and determined to practice Judaism on a regular, formal basis. The group secured a meeting hall, a rented room on the third floor of a building otherwise occupied by an auction business, at the corner of Lake and Wells Streets, and fitted it out as a synagogue. Under the congregation's auspices, Abraham traveled to New York and recruited thirty-seven-year-old Reverend Ignatz Kunreuther, a learned, European-born son of an old-country Orthodox rabbi, to serve as KAM's spiritual and prayer leader and Chicago's *shochet.* Soundly trained in Talmud and strictly observant, Kunreuther served as a role model of traditional religious life. Many KAM members tried to follow his example. On Sabbath and the festivals, they closed their businesses, threaded their way through a passage cluttered with the auctioneer's merchandise, and climbed the stairs to services. Congregational activities further expanded three years later when Leopold Mayer, a graduate of a German teacher's institute, arrived to teach Hebrew and religion.

KAM soon outgrew the auction house loft and leased a lot at the corner of Quincy and Clark streets. To raise funds for their planned building, Abraham, Levi, and fellow member Leon Greenebaum sent a letter "to the Israelites and friends of the House of Jacob throughout the United States" asking "in the name of the God of our fathers" for donations toward the proposed "house of worship, so that this and generations to come, may pray to the Lord of Israel in the same, and that he may pour out his blessings on you and all the descendants of Jacob forever."[3] The $12,000 structure, with a traditional east-facing ark and seats for 450 worshipers, was dedicated on June 13, 1851, with dignitaries in attendance, including Reverend Samuel Myer Isaacs, traveling all the way from New York.

Dilah, of course, had catalyzed the congregation's founding and even before that had sent her sons the Torah scroll used in the original Yom Kippur services. She had also inspired the arrival of the *shochet* who served all Chicago Jews, whether synagogue-goers or not. But as a female, she would never count as a synagogue member. Nor did she ever number in the quorum needed for public prayer. Devout woman that she was, she contented herself with sitting in a section set aside for women in the Lake Street loft. Her 1848 death in a cholera epidemic kept her from ever enjoying the ample women's balcony that would run around three sides of the Quincy Street shul.

As both a pivotal figure in building the Chicago Jewish community and a marginal participant in traditional public worship, however, Dilah typified countless other pious women of her time, who energized Jewish communities across the country but took no role in public religious practice. Rosana Dyer Osterman, for example, played an equally dynamic role in Galveston, arranging the island's first-ever visit by a rabbi to consecrate its first Jewish cemetery. But five years later, when a minyan of Texans met for the state's first known Jewish religious service, a man, Rosana's brother

Isadore Dyer, led the proceedings. This pattern repeated itself across the nation, with men founding synagogues and women sparking inclusive, community-wide institutions that, though unprecedented in Jewish history, allowed an ancient people to put down robust roots in a new land.

Synagogues Across America

Making his way to KAM's Quincy Street dedication, Reverend Isaacs met, in town after town and hamlet after hamlet, scattered small clusters of Jews. "All of these" Jewries, he believed (the score of families in Ypsilanti and Detroit, the dozen each in Kalamazoo and Marshall), "are destined to be congregations."[4] Indeed, in cities, towns, and villages across the nation, Jewish men were joining together to form synagogues, just as they had in the seaboard Jewish centers in an earlier era. Many places that had only a dozen or so Jewish settlers had a congregation before many years had passed, and not too long after that, a synagogue building where they could meet for worship and study. Whether newly arrived or native born, and wherever Jews ended up as they spread across the continent, they continued the long-standing American practice of figuring out how to create some form of Jewish life. In many cases, sadly, a graveyard was the first milestone of a nascent community. In 1859, for example, three years before St. Paul's Mount Zion Hebrew Congregation was formally chartered, Amelia and Joseph Ullmann laid a child to rest in the Mount Zion Hebrew Association cemetery, the first Jewish burying ground in Minnesota Territory.

But no matter how earnestly laypeople came together to found a fledgling congregation or bury a friend in newly purchased ground or pass the hat for a comrade in need, knowledgeable, traditional religious leaders, especially those born and trained in Europe, found their efforts inadequate. When he met the twenty-eight male members of KAM, for example, Hebrew teacher Leopold Mayer (known in his new community as "Lehrer," or teacher, Mayer) thought their "instruction in both the tenets and morals of Judaism . . . lacking." Equally distressing, "already at this period the Sabbath was more or less violated. . . . Most of the women and many of the men" regularly attended Saturday morning services, "but the latter as a usual thing, left hurriedly for the their places of business. Many stores were already open, and the younger men, engaged as clerks, were invisible in the synagogue."[5]

However justified on *halachic* grounds, this criticism nonetheless missed an important, specifically American point. Though unlearned and haphazard in synagogue attendance, this small band of people living thousands of miles from home, thrown together essentially by chance, and struggling to establish themselves in a foreign country, had, at their own initiative and expense, sought each other out and organized a Jewish communal life. They may not have reproduced European patterns exactly, but they wanted a Jewish community badly enough to build one as best they could. Across the country, people who could easily have jettisoned their Jewish identities and assimilated unnoticed into the American mass clung to practices and obligations that bound them to certain of their new neighbors and distinguished them from the rest. Young men and women who had moved great distances to new places in order to adopt a new way of life, and, generally, a new language and culture as well, still took the effort to preserve what they could of an ancient tradition. In cities that had sizable Jewish populations, immigrants even chose to live near other Jews rather than among Christian immigrants who hailed from their own native regions. In the 1850s and 1860s, for example, Jewish and Christian immigrants from Holland lived in different parts of Chicago.[6]

"To the praise of the Jews here," Lehrer Meyer acknowledged, "I must say, that they clung together in sorrow and in joy. The good fortune of one was the happiness of the other, while the gloom of one cast a shadow over all. Thus, on my first Friday in Chicago, I watched, with one of my brothers, [presumably, one of his brother Jews, rather than one of his own relatives] at the bedside of the sick child of a friend." In other words, he joined with Chicagoans fulfilling the important mitzvah of *bikkur cholim*, visiting the ill.[7] Despite their deficits in formal learning, Chicago Jews not only understood but practiced one of their faith's fundamental teachings.

Even in places with far fewer Jews than greeted Mayer, elements of tradition survived. On her remote Wisconsin island, Hannah Austrian sang her children Hebrew songs, accompanying herself on the banjo. In distant Santa Fe, the six mercantile Spiegelberg brothers—Elias, Emanuel, Lehman, Levi, Solomon Jacob, and Willi—along with their wives, formed the nucleus of New Mexico Territory's far-flung but nonetheless functional Jewish community. In 1878 a rabbi hoping to provide religious leadership to Santa Fe arrived unannounced with his wife, all the way from Dallas. Realizing that the town could not sustain a real synagogue, the Spiegelbergs helped the couple move on to try their luck in Kansas City. Not for another eight years would New Mexico have a formal synagogue, Congregation Montefiore, founded in Las Vegas by merchant Charles Ifeld. But even without a trained leader, Santa Fe marked the Jewish year.

At each major holiday, one or another of the Spiegelberg households hosted prayers and feasting, with invited coreligionists gathering from far and wide. Despite (or perhaps because of) Flora Spiegelberg's polyglot friendship with the archbishop, her family's religious identity was clear to their Catholic neighbors. Local Spanish speakers considered them (reportedly favorably) "la misma gente que nuestro redentor Jesus Cristos [sic] (The same people as our Redeemer Jesus Christ)."[8]

In occupied Natchez during the Civil War, the patriotic Mayer family supported Jewish life along with the Confederate cause. When Yankees Henry Frank and Isaac Lowenberg arrived in town as members of the U.S. commissary department, they promptly called on John Mayer "at his store," recalled John's daughter, Melanie Mayer Frank, "making themselves known as Jews, and father, the president of the Hebrew [Hebra] Kadusha [Holy Fellowship] Congregation, invited them to attend the services during the Holy Days." John (originally Jacob) Mayer had, as a twenty-seven-year-old French shoemaker, met fifteen-year-old Jeanette Reis and her parents, also French Jews, aboard a sailing ship making the grueling three-month passage from Havre de Grace to New Orleans in 1833. They married two years later, and in 1841 they moved with their first three children to Natchez, where they established a successful business and had eight more offspring. Natchez had "no temple [building] nor weekly services," Melanie recalled, but "during Roshashona and Yom Kippur some of the members officiated at services held upstairs in the old engine house on North Union Street."[9] Jeanette's role in Natchez Jewish life was as active as John's, with "her home . . . the center of all Jewish festivities, and at the long dining table," Melanie remembered, "there were often seated as many as thirty-five guests on Passover Eve, the feast of Seder, which was always celebrated with much pomp and ceremony."[10]

The nation's widely scattered Jews also took pains to enter their newborn sons into the Covenant of Abraham by arranging for ritual circumcision. Larger communities generally had a specially trained functionary, or *mohel*, to perform the mitzvah of *brit milah* on the eighth day after the birth. (In many places he was the same individual who did the honors as prayer leader, meat slaughterer, and Hebrew teacher.) But in remote areas, a *mohel* might not arrive until long after the mandated time for the ritual had passed. Several unfortunate Santa Fe boys, for example, underwent the ceremony at "an advanced age" in 1872 at the hands of Reverend M. A. H. Fleischer, who had specially come from Denver.[11] "Under the impact of English-American prudery," a visitor from Germany observed in the

1850s, American circumcisions often took place in the privacy of the home rather than publicly in the synagogue, as was customary in Europe. But far more important than the ceremony's setting is the fact that this uniquely Jewish rite, which lacks any parallel in either American or Christian practice, in fact took place and that American Jews often went to considerable trouble and expense to ensure that it did. Families also arranged ceremonies to mark their son's reaching the age of bar mitzvah. New Mexico's Jewish community first extended this honor to a Spiegelberg nephew, Alfred Grunsfeld, in 1876.

Marking the great events of the life cycle and the religious year helped scattered Jews retain their religious identity. But a number of other practices important to traditional piety occur not once in a lifetime or once in a year but several times each day. Reciting prayers the required three times daily presented no tremendous difficulties, as individuals can quite correctly say them alone, in an undertone, wherever they happen to be. Anyone who wishes can also repeat the traditional blessings for eating, drinking, and other activities.

But the content of those meals raised important issues. America had far too few people trained in *shechita* (ritual slaughter) to meet the needs of Jews who wanted a source of reliably kosher meat, and not everyone had Dilah Kohn's luck in getting one to come to town. In the single issue of the *American Israelite,* published on September 15, 1865, for example, congregations in Alabama, Kentucky, California, Illinois, Ohio, and Louisiana ran ads offering jobs for *shochets.* Congregation B'nai B'rith (Sons of the Covenant) in Los Angeles employed its own slaughterer as early as 1861. Even smaller places such as Elmira, New York; Portland, Maine; Fort Wayne, Indiana; and Akron, Ohio, succeeded, at least intermittently, in doing the same. In communities without their own *shochet,* people sometimes tried to order kosher meat from elsewhere. Mary and Samuel Kobey, who came to little Crystal City, Colorado, in the 1860s, had it sent from Denver. But the meat arrived spoiled so often that they gave up the attempt and adopted vegetarianism, which they gave up when they moved to Denver, where Samuel became rabbi of the Orthodox Congregation Agudas Achim.

In great stretches of the country, even meat of dubious *kashrut* could not be had. Like Dilah Kohn and the Kobeys, some people chose to live as vegetarians. Peddlers in the Carolinas were called "egg eaters" by their Cherokee customers. But other Jews made other choices, often out of desperation. "My parents got tired of eating potatoes," recalled Isadore Pitts, son of northern plains homesteaders, "and prairie dogs weren't kosher."[12] As in previous immigrant generations, many families made elastic interpretations of *kashrut* rules. Some people who ate nonkosher meat, for example, drew the line at pork. Marcus Spiegel's Civil War letters indicate that he ate just about everything else. Aaron Haas recalled that in Atlanta in the 1850s "it was impossible to keep a kosher table, [but] there was never a piece of hog in my father's house, nor was milk or butter on the table with meat."[13] But when ice blocked the Mississippi at St. Paul and cut off shipments from St. Louis, Amelia Ullmann, anxious over her frail son's health, fed her family bacon.

Nor do we know very much about how the practice of *niddah* fared. Even at New York's Shaaray Tefila, a bastion of Orthodoxy in the 1840s, *hazzan* Samuel Isaacs berated the women of his congregation for ignoring the synagogue's *mikvah,* which had been built with care from specifications of Baltimore's Rabbi Abraham Rice. Several recent deaths of young children, Isaacs proclaimed, represented God's anger at young wives' disregard for the requirements of ritual purity.

Organizing Women

Along with improvising their Judaism, this generation of American Jews continued another long-standing pattern traditional in both American and Jewish life: scanting the contributions of women. Though Aaron Haas credited his father for his family's avoidance of pork, it was more likely his mother who figured out how to manage without her region's most easily available meat. Although synagogue charters and cemetery association bylaws bear male signatures, it was women who pioneered many of the innovations that most profoundly shaped the future of American Jewish life.

First and most famous among these innovators was Rebecca Gratz of Philadelphia, whose Female Hebrew Benevolent Society blended the emerging American model of the ladies' charitable association with the ancient Jewish responsibility to perform *tzedakah.* She created something new in Jewish history as well as a prototype duplicated across the nation. Apart from groups dedicated to preparing deceased women and girls for burial, female-run organizations devoted to fulfilling major religious obligations were as unknown in Central Europe as they had been among the seventeenth- and eighteenth-century Sephardim of London,

Amsterdam, or the Caribbean. In Bavaria and Bohemia, as in Britain or Barbados, official Jewish institutions were the exclusive province of men.

In early and middle nineteenth-century America, men continued to take the lead in organizing traditional religious groups. The larger Jewish communities boasted a variety of philanthropic and social groups, burial societies and cemetery associations. Literary circles met to discuss books and ideas. *Landsmanshaftn,* clubs whose members hailed from particular old-country towns or regions, attracted immigrants to socialize, catch up on hometown news, and generally afford mutual support. Among a growing number of Jewish men, American-style fraternal orders held lodge meetings replete with arcane rituals and secret handshakes. Since 1843 B'nai B'rith, Sons of the Covenant, the first and longest-lived of these social-cum-charitable brotherhoods, has combined fellowship and philanthropy in a Jewish atmosphere. The Order of B'rith Abraham (Free Sons of Israel), founded in 1843, and Kesher Shel Barzel (Bond of Iron), founded a year later, had similar aims.

Just as Abraham Kohn had sought out a High Holiday service that resembled the ones he had known at home, each of these orders, like many of America's synagogues, appealed to men of a particular cultural or regional background. The first B'nai B'rith lodge began when a dozen relatively new New Yorkers from Germanic lands decided to formalize their Sunday evening get-togethers at Sinsheimer's Saloon on Essex Street. Poles and other Eastern Europeans, on the other hand, gravitated to Kesher Shel Barzel, and Hungarians and Austrians to B'rith Abraham.

But when a town's Jewish women gathered to discuss what help they could give a new widow, or when to bring meals to a sick mother's family, or how they could aid new arrivals to set themselves up as seamstresses, they generally paid less attention to where people hailed from or the liturgy they followed. Men planning services or hiring a *hazzan* had to choose a particular prayer book or musical style, thus sharpening the distinctions among people from different regions or countries. But women— who were not considered synagogue members in any case—met to deal with problems that affected people regardless of background—childbirth, poverty, matchmaking, arranging people to sit with the sick or keep watch over the dead. Just as Gratz's society aimed to serve all needy Jewish women in Philadelphia, in towns and cities across the country, groups of Jewish women, at first informally and later as officially constituted organizations, did the same.

Many of these incipient organizations' members probably had not heard of Gratz and had no conscious intention of imitating her. But the model she developed fit American conditions so perfectly that various people across the country may well have discovered it on their own. It used the time-honored and characteristically American pattern of the voluntary association to meet the specifically Jewish challenge of carrying out humanitarian functions that the traditional corporate Jewish community had fulfilled in Europe.

But by joining their own charitable groups, women gained much more than the opportunity to do good works. Consider, for example, the night in 1852 when a group of Newark husbands attended a meeting of Frauenverein Naechstenliebe, their wives' local Jewish women's association. The male guests spoke up on some issues and "for some unknown reason the participation of the men . . . arouses the ire of their hostesses," reported Nathan Kussy, son of Bella, the ex-milliner, and Gustav, her butcher spouse, both presumably present at the session. "Perhaps the women feel that the presence of the men robs the meeting of that mystery and secrecy so characteristic of women's organizations," Nathan speculated. "Perhaps the men, instead of being silent spectators, open their lips, like Balaam's ass, and speak. Or perhaps—who know?—the startled husbands, beholding the unwonted spectacle of dutiful wives and mothers cultivating the art of public speaking, are suddenly confronted with a vague but gruesome specter of female emancipation, glimpsed through the mist of years, and having come to scoff, begin to bray. Whatever the cause, the dutiful wives become of a sudden undutiful, fiery, incensed, as though determined to repel the plebian mob of husbands that has ventured to invade, as it were, the sacred Temple of Diana. Breathing defiance to the trembling males, the outraged women decide that never, never, never thereafter shall men be invited to meetings of the organization."[14]

Meetings seldom ended in shouting matches, but the "unwonted spectacle" of the Newarkers and their counterparts learning to be public people through their organizations repeated itself in scores of places across the country. Running their own organizations—whether a local chapter of the United Order of True Sisters, first begun in New York in 1846; a local association like Hartford's Deborah Society, started eight years later; the First Hebrew Ladies Benevolent Society, founded in 1864 in Portland, Oregon; or the Baszion Benevolent Society, begun in Minneapolis in 1876—gave women a vehicle for independent action not otherwise available in Jewish tradition or American life. This model did not fit anything in the Jewish past, but it matched a notion gaining wide currency in Victorian America. Though countless pioneer women, farm wives, immigrants, and members of the urban and rural poor did all kinds of work to support themselves and their families, the respectable middle-class ideal limited the proper sphere of a "true woman" to her home. There, in a realm of supposed moral and spiritual uplift, she was to pursue femininity's higher and more refined purposes safe from the contaminating masculine hurly-burly of money, business, and public life.

Though foreign to traditional Judaism, the notion of women as men's moral superiors had penetrated American Jewry by midcentury. "You are a wife and mother," rhapsodized the *Israelite* of April 5, 1861, to its female readers, "and therewith your position is nobler and grander than that of the master mechanic, the merchant prince, the man of letters, the soldier and the statesman of the land; your position gives you the power to sway over all; but do you use the power which civilization and nature have bestowed on you, rightly?" That power was wholly moral because Jewish women who fully adopted the housewifely ideal relinquished their power as earners. The magazine writer admits as much by advising that "if you are true to your husband, if you take a lively interest in his occupations, if you are economical and do your best to live below his income; if you strive to be worthy of his entire confidence; if you advise him to what is good and noble; if you speak kindly to your children, reason with them and impress upon their minds that 'Honesty is the best policy,' if you bring them up domestically; if you set them a good example of sweet temper and good manners . . . then you are worthy of your exalted position; then peace and harmony prevail in your house; your husband gathers strength in your loveliness, in your noble counsel and your manners. . . . he earns abundantly because he is a happy man, and a happy man is a host within himself."[15]

A huge gap in expectation and perception separated this paragon of domestic sweetness, this cheerful counselor and soothing homemaker, from the savvy, competent, independent trader praised as the Bible's "woman of valor," whom observant husbands lauded every Sabbath eve, as well as from the hardy, practical Jewish merchant women streaming off the immigrant ships. But as Jewish families moved up the American economic ladder, they aspired to a corresponding place on the social one as well. To gain that, they often moved toward this bourgeois ideal (which was also gaining ground among their upwardly mobile coreligionists back in Central Europe).

In one crucial respect, the biblical heroine and the Victorian lady overlap. In her role as a responsible adult, the woman of valor generously provisions the needy (as would a prosperous man). In her role as the angel of the hearth, the "true woman" compassionately cared for the sick, weak, and helpless while her coarser menfolk, lacking her sensitive nature, brave the rough-and-tumble of the business world. For groups of midcentury ladies to join together to pursue such purposes appeared to be an extension of an unassailably feminine concern, and thus well within the proper purview of respectability. Indeed, a concern for the less fortunate was both a requirement and a proof of Victorian respectability and thus became the duty of every successful man's wife.

By creating formal societies to do good, even the "truest," most ladylike of ladies could turn a mainstay of domesticity—compassionate regard for others—into a platform for influence in the wider community. Baszion Rees, for example, started the benevolent association that bore her name—appropriately enough, "Daughter of Zion" in Hebrew—in 1876 to provide Minneapolis's fledgling Jewry with a needed cemetery. The town's first congregation, Shaari Tof (later called Temple Israel), was still two years in the future. Once the graveyard was established, a new philanthropic challenge arose. "In order to build a fence around this plot of ground, so that the cows would not eat the geraniums," recalled Marlchen Deutsch, an association cofounder, "the Ladies Benevolent Society gave a charity ball, at which sixty dollars was raised, with which was erected a wooden fence. The ball was attended by Jew and Gentile alike."[16]

Though regarded by some as a worthwhile pastime for good-hearted, though basically ineffectual, housewives, female benevolent associations became an influential force in Jewish communities across the country, as well as in American society at large. Detroit's Ahabas Achjaus (Love of Sisters) society donated $250 to Temple Beth El in 1859 "with the proviso that steps be taken speedily toward the earnest realization of the long-discussed building of the synagogue," reported the congregation's Rabbi Liebman Adler in the magazine *Die Deborah*.[17] The Ladies Hebrew Association of Baton Rouge, meeting on June 28, 1874, donated money to "the Gentlemen's congregation" on the condition that they "not use the money collected for rent of lot [at the]Cor[ner of] North and Church [but only] for purposes of the Building Fund."[18] On May 25 of the following year, a group of Richmond women wrote to their synagogue board requesting certain changes in the service. They closed their letter with what a local community history calls "the very politic statement that they understood that the Board contemplated the building of a new synagogue in a more appropriate location, and promised their co-operation."[19] Later the same year, the men organizing Hebrew Union College to train rabbis called on the Ladies Educational Aid Society to help finance the venture. In 1859, when fifteen Chicago charitable groups and synagogues joined together to form the citywide United Hebrew Relief Association, four of the constituent entities were female: the Ladies Sewing Circle, the Frauen Wohlthaetigskeit Verein, the Young Ladies Hebrew Benevolent Association, and the Sisters of Peace.

Two years later, when the Civil War began, American women of all faiths faced an unprecedented philanthropic challenge. Ten thousand Jewish men served in the conflict, seven thousand Northerners and three thousand Southerners. Along with Union Colonel Marcus Spiegel, some five hundred died. Jews enlisted in numbers that exceeded their proportion in the total population, placing a special strain on Jewish communal resources. Conditions were often harsh, both for the soldiers in the field and the families they left behind. Marcus, like thousands of others fighting far from home, wrote to his Caroline pleading for some new boots and adding that "something nice to eat in the Box [and a] bottle of something to drink wouldn't hurt anybody." And as he lay near death, his surgeon recalled, a weeping Marcus cried, "This is the last of the husband and father, what will become of my children and family?"[20]

All across the country, home front communities organized to answer that question. An appeal from the Jewish community in Washington, D.C., published in the *Jewish Messenger* told their more numerous New York coreligionists that "unlike you, we have no fund to support the families of poor soldiers, and the unhappy consequence is, the wives and children of these poor men are in *abject want*" (emphasis in original).[21] In Baltimore, Cincinnati, New Orleans, and countless towns on both sides of the Mason-Dixon line, the families of fighting men and war dead became the main focus of the existing Jewish women's benevolent societies.

Marcus's plaintive letters from the front and those of the Natchez Mayer brothers reveal that the members of both armies, even high officers like Colonel Spiegel, were pitifully short of such everyday essentials as warm socks, dry boots, gloves, scarves, and bandages. Dry socks could save an infantryman's feet, clean bandages could save a casualty's life, a scarf or sweater or gloves could save a soldier from freezing. Since nine-teenth-century women generally knew how to make the simple items that could ease combatants' suffering and even aid their survival, knitting, sewing, lint picking, and bandage rolling for the troops became constant occupations in kitchens, parlors, and shops across the nation. Moving the huge masses of donated materials handmade on the home front required large-scale organizing.

The combination of their men's desperate need and women's industri-ous handiwork and experience at philanthropy led to America's first major female-run national organization, the Women's Branch of the United States Sanitary Commission, which provided warm clothing, bandages, and other items of care and comfort to Union soldiers. Sewing circles and benevolent societies in hundreds of towns kept up a constant stream of goods, and women themselves arranged for shipping and delivery to the troops. In 1863, for example, Women's Branch Visiting Committee head Mary Rose Smith wrote to Mikve Israel's *hazzan,* Sabato Morais, asking the Philadelphia congregation to name a representative to the commission. Mikve Israel's women chose Matilda Cohen for this post, proceeded to organize themselves for war work as the Ladies Hebrew Relief Association for the Sick and Wounded Soldiers, and recruited 250 members in the first month. By war's end two years later, it had dispatched ten crates of sup-plies. Jewish women also pitched in on nondenominational work for the war effort. A Philadelphia-wide fund-raising fair, for example, sold needle-work done by a Jewish needlework circle called Alert, formed specifically for this purpose by nine young women.

But raising money and supplies was the easy part. Wherever fighting happened or large numbers of men congregated in camps or bivouacs, the wounded and sick needed medical care, often provided in hastily requisi-tioned, primitive hospitals located in public buildings or even private homes, with local women doing much of the nursing. Mikve Israel was only one of countless institutions, North and South, that turned their buildings into hospitals. In the besieged Confederate capital of Richmond, local Jewish women "fed the hungry, clothed the poor, nursed the sick and wounded, and buried the dead. The wives and mothers and sisters did valiant work in the hospitals," according to an address to Richmond's Rimon lodge of B'nai B'rith.[22] The fact that Herbert Ezekiel offered this tribute fifty years after the war's end conveys the deep impression that the women's service made on their community.

From Generation to Generation

Organizing benevolent societies, as Rebecca Gratz and many others discerned, gave Victorian women a perfect protective cover for exerting influence in the larger community while appearing to remain within the ladylike confines of their domestic concerns. An even bolder move by Gratz brought female leadership into the very heart of traditionally male Jewish life. As Rebecca was growing to womanhood in a proudly Jewish— though not very Jewishly learned—home during the century's first decades, her Christian neighbors were undergoing the beginnings of a major religious change. Eighteenth-century Americans were generally God-fearing but not very formally devout. No more than 10 percent of the Revolutionary generation, for example, officially belonged to a Christian church.[23] By the time Rebecca reached her early twenties, a new evangelical fervor was taking hold, particularly among Protestants. Many more became active in church life, and the desire to bring the unchurched to Jesus excited religious people. Religion, along with morality, charity, and spirituality, was becoming increasingly prominent among the concerns of the respectable "true woman."

Gentile sinners, scoffers, and backsliders, of course, abounded, providing evangelists copious opportunities for their efforts. Proselytizers, many of them women, used a variety of means to spread Christian teachings. Relief organizations, for example, began to provide the needy "improving" sermons and lectures along with—or even as a condition of—their soup kitchen meals and secondhand clothes. But Jews, as principled and traditional holdouts against the gospel message, were particularly attractive targets for missionary zeal.

Whether Christian evangelism actually constituted a serious threat to the Jewish community is debatable. Christian missionaries had spent "$50,000 over five years for the conversion, real or supposed of *five* Jews," reported *Niles' Weekly Register* in 1816. Still, the proliferation of associations dedicated to distributing Christian Bibles and publications and of meetings intended to bring people to Christ convinced many Jews that the danger was real. It was, in fact, Protestant ministers and missionaries' attempts to convert the poor—including needy Jews—to Christian practice that inspired Gratz and her friends to form their Female Hebrew Benevolent Society in 1819. Unaffiliated with any congregation, it became both a model for independent organizations and a strong unifying force in a Jewish community that was becoming more culturally and socially diverse as it grew ever larger.

As Christians' interest in spreading their religion grew, many American Jews began to realize that they knew far too little about their own religion. Here again Rebecca Gratz took the lead, deciding, in 1818, to hire a tutor to teach her Hebrew. The man she engaged, Solomon I. Cohen, came to Gratz's home, where she arranged for a number of female relatives, both adults and children, to attend the lessons. "Elkalah Cohen, Maria and Ellen Hays and [eleven] little ones . . . have been for the past month outlining pronouns etc. with as much zeal as success," she wrote to a family member a few weeks after Cohen began the informal afternoon classes. "I expect we shall make out very well if [he] continues here long enough to take us through the grammar."[24] Rebecca also read a book on Judaism that Cohen had written and gave copies to friends.

Just two years before Rebecca began her little home Hebrew school, Joanna Graham Bethune, a Protestant, did something similar, but much grander, in New York. Bethune started a female-run independent Sunday school—the nation's first—that in a single year grew from one location to twenty-one, with a total of 250 teachers instructing over 3,000 students of both sexes. Judaism, on the other hand, had traditionally considered the religious education of boys a male concern. In Europe, the heder schools where curly-haired three- and four-year-olds learned their first Hebrew letters and older children studied the Bible, as well as the yeshivas, where academically gifted adolescents pursued Talmud, had exclusively male faculties and student bodies. Though girls might learn to read (but not generally to understand) the Hebrew prayers (and learn, meanwhile, the letters used to write Yiddish) under a rabbi's wife or other relatively learned woman, females rarely delved into the holy books that are at the core of Jewish learning, and they never taught boys. In America some early synagogues established schools that enrolled both sexes. Much American religious education, however, focused on preparing boys for bar mitzvah, teaching them to read the Hebrew prayers and chant from the Torah scrolls, but not necessarily to understand much about what they read.

Nineteenth-century America, however, cut up the world quite differently from the way European Judaism had. Jewish tradition had recognized no distinction between private, domestic religious life and public economic and political life, both coming under the sway of *halachah*. American life, however, increasingly made each of those worlds the realm of one sex or the other. As the masculine world of business and the feminine one of domesticity pulled apart, the moral and educational lives of children were drawn into the female orbit. Earlier generations of Americans had considered the family's religious standing and the moral development of the children to be mainly the father's responsibility. But Victorian men busy with the serious, manly business of working—and occupied all day at an office, shop, or factory separate from the home and even in another part of town—increasingly left to their wives the care and training of the young.

It took a number of years, during which Gratz was busy with the FHBS and other philanthropic ideas, for her to expand her experiment in Hebrew instruction into a plan for a new kind of Jewish religious school. Like Bethune, whose work Gratz knew, she decided that this school should be run by women who had the time and inclination to mold the young, rather than by men whose business concerns kept them too busy. Unlike existing Jewish schools, hers would not concentrate on teaching children to carry out ritual practice but on arming them to defend Judaism, and their own loyalty to it, against the evangelists. Her new school, like Bethune's, would be independent of any particular congregation. Like the FHBS, it would serve the entire community, offering people from different parts of Europe and diverse economic standing a similar, American-style educational experience.

On February 4, 1838, Gratz called a meeting to establish her Hebrew Sunday school. Classes started exactly four weeks later, on March 4, with six women teachers and fifty students. By the fall of that year, an additional twenty youngsters had enrolled. Families that could paid tuition. Donations made up the rest of the budget. She had obviously identified a genuine need because Philadelphia families flocked to enroll their children. By 1841, the Hebrew Sunday school had twenty-five women teaching 250 children. Gratz soon adopted the practice of hiring the school's own graduates as its teachers.

Faculty members took their responsibilities seriously, assigning weekly homework and requiring annual exams. "The instruction must have been primarily oral," recalled Rosa Mordechai, who as a girl in the 1850s came every Sunday to classes held on the upper floor of the firehouse on Zane Street (later Filbert Street). Later she taught in the same school. Before climbing the stairs to their classroom, she and her schoolmates would "linger . . . to admire the beautifully kept" fire engines until they would "catch a glimpse of Miss Gratz approaching . . . [who] says, 'Time for school, children!'"[25]

With about ten youngsters seated on each bright, yellow-painted bench, "Miss Gratz always began school with the prayer, opening with, 'Come ye children, hearken unto me, and I will teach you the fear of The Lord.' This was followed by a prayer of her own composition, which she read verse by verse and the whole school repeated after her. Then she read a verse of the Bible, in a clear and distinct voice." After dividing into separate classes, the school came together again for "closing exercises [which] were equally simple; a Hebrew hymn sung by the children, then ... simple verses, whose rhythm the smallest child could easily catch as all repeated."

Each year around Purim, close to the anniversary of the school's founding and Gratz's own birthday (both March 4), the annual exams were held. They took place in Mikve Israel's sanctuary on Cherry Street, with its "circular benches and deep gallery facing the large open space between the *tebah* and the *hechal* [the reading desk and the ark]," arranged Sephardic fashion. "It was with something like awe that we women [teachers] took possession of the ground floor," where women were not ordinarily permitted. "A small table was placed in front of the reading-desk for Miss Gratz. The classes were all arranged in the men's seats and were called to 'Stand and recite!' ... The classes were arranged in a semi-circle. . . . One teacher stood at the center, giving the questions. . . . Thus every child was really examined, and each book recited in whole or in part." Prize winners received Bibles and other books "most carefully chosen by Miss Gratz herself, and handed to each child herself with a kind, encouraging word, often with a written line on the fly-leaf. As the happy children went out orderly by class, through the back door, each was given an orange and a pretzel."[26]

In addition to encouraging the pupils, Gratz also encouraged "courting" of the young women on her faculty. "'Having never tasted the delights of matrimony,' Miss Gratz . . . naturally wished all [her] young charges to enjoy connubial bliss," Mordechai recalls. "Tradition says that it was in Sunday school" that Hazzan Morais, then "young, active . . . full of enthusiasm [and] always ready to lead the Hebrew hymns or take the class of an absent teacher," first became "attracted to his beautiful young wife, who was one of the most beloved teachers." Other matches made at Sunday school included an unnamed teacher of Mordechai's, whose "husband was first drawn toward her, by her gentle manners to her young pupils. Other successful and unsuccessful lovers will always retain pleasant memories of the old Sunday school, and of their walks to and from it."[27]

This was an educational institution quite unlike any the Jewish world had known before. In place of men deeply versed in the Hebrew Bible, the

Talmud, and other commentaries, the teachers were American-born women highly literate in English but with little or no mastery of the holy tongue. "Of all the inflexible demands which his religion and his duty make on each Israelite, the first and foremost is to give his child a good education," the traveler Israel Joseph Benjamin II informed his readers in his book *Three Years in America* (1863), published in German in Hanover.

> The American schools . . . certainly guarantee this in part; but it is much to be regretted that, because they exclude all religion and confessions of faith—not with an unwise purpose—I must say with the deepest regret that the study of the Holy Scriptures . . . is much neglected among the daughters of Israel. Jewish boys after a fashion—for that is the established way—are instructed in their religion, as is also the case with the sons and daughters of Christians. The Jewish boys attend some Hebrew school or other, or are instructed privately; but in this respect. what does the situation look like for the daughters of Israel? How sad is the provision for the religious instruction of these Jewish housewives and mothers of the future! How little do they learn of their duties toward God and man! . . . It is with regret and astonishment that one learns that half of the American Jewesses are at present unable to undertake and fulfill worthily the place in life for which they are intended.

Indeed, he noted with horror, when many an American girl reaches the end of her education, she can only "continue to recite in English the few prayers which she has learnt from her mother. Should she, quite by accident, attend synagogue, she takes a book in the same language."[28]

Some schools tried to teach girls the sacred language, often with limited success. Since girls would not celebrate a bar mitzvah, they were often not seen as "needing" to read Torah in the same way that boys did. At the religious school of Cincinnati's B'nai Yeshurun in the 1850s and 1860s, recalled Emily Fachhimer Seasongood many years later, "We were taught Hebrew and English. The *Chumash* [Pentateuch] I could not understand, and told my beloved father I could not see why it was taught to us [in Hebrew] and please have the teachers do away with it. As he was president of the congregation then, he brought it before the board, who quite agreed with me, and I was very happy after it was removed from our studies."[29]

Benjamin probably accurately described the religious education that most American-born women and girls received, but he greatly underestimated the devotion that many felt to Judaism. In their determination to provide Jewish education to American children, Gratz and her colleagues did not see their own ignorance of the traditional texts as an obstacle. Instead of using books written by rabbis and religious scholars, they taught from materials of their own devising, which drew not on deep Judaic scholarship but on their own ideas of what Judaism taught and meant. Sisters Simha Peixotto and Rachel Peixotto Pyke, who ran a Philadelphia girls academy and in whose family home Gratz's Sunday school originally met, were among those who wrote texts for the school. A catechism—a set of religious questions and answers—compiled by Pyke proved especially influential. "Many old scholars can still recall the question: 'Who formed you, child, and made you live?'" Mordechai remembered, "and the answer: 'God did my life and spirit give'—the first line of the admirable 'Pykes Catechism,' which long held its place in the Sunday school, and was, I believe, the first book printed for it. The 'Scripture Lessons' were taught from a little illustrated work published by the Christian Sunday School Union. Many a long summer's day have I spent, pasting pieces of paper over answers unsuitable for Jewish children, and many were the fruitless efforts of those children to read through, over, or under the hidden lines."[30] Books by the British Jewish author Grace Aguilar, especially *The Spirit of Judaism* and *The Jewish Faith,* were also prominent in Sunday school lessons.

An immediate success, the Sunday school also grew into an enduring and significant Philadelphia institution. By 1900, it had instructed four thousand students, and it lasted as an independent entity until 1993, when it merged with another school. As it grew, the Sunday school continued to hire its own female graduates as teachers. The corps of women that Gratz trained became the first women in Jewish history to set curriculum and teach both sexes in religious schools. Other educated American women soon followed the Philadelphians' example. In Charleston, poet Penina Moise applied her skills to Jewish themes. In 1845 she became the second person to serve venerable Beth Elohim as superintendent of its Sunday school. Over a long career she composed 190 hymns that her own and other Reform congregations used in services. They proved so enduringly popular that thirteen appeared in the *Union Hymnal,* which the Reform movement published in 1932, fifty years after her death at age eighty-three.

Many Jewish children attended religious school on Sunday, the Christian Sabbath, rather than on the more traditional Jewish one, because they generally attended American schools, which held a half day of classes on Saturday. New York, for example, provided free public education from 1842 on. A heavy Protestant emphasis pervaded public education in many places, however, and some parents, especially new immigrants, wanted their children to learn in a Jewish atmosphere. This led to the founding of a number of day schools, mostly run by synagogues, in New York. But when reforms enacted in the 1850s did away with much of the overt Protestant content, Jewish parents, unlike the Roman Catholic immigrants also arriving during these years, generally cast their lot with the public schools.

Guardians of Tradition

"I went to the synagogue Sabbath morning, and found besides the Vice-President . . . who took the place of the absent Hazzan, nine more men, five boys (three of them mourners) and one lady," wrote Rabbi Isaac Mayer Wise of a disheartening stop in Sacramento during a visit to the West Coast in 1877. This Orthodox service, conducted according to *Minhag Polen,* the Polish rite, had, in other words, very close to the absolute minimum congregation needed to hold public prayer. The ten adult males formed a bare minyan. The three bereaved boys probably attended to fulfill the requirement that they recite the Kaddish prayer in public daily during their mourning period. Neither they, their two other companions, nor the lone woman counted toward the required quorum. And even worse, "I was told that all over California this is the case."[31]

As Lehrer Mayer had noticed decades earlier and thousands of miles to the east, American men were eager to remain Jewish, but not to practice strict Judaism. "As a general thing the ladies [in California] must maintain Judaism," Wise observed. "They are three-fourths of the congregation in the temple every Sabbath and send their children to the Sabbath schools. With very few exceptions, the men keep no Sabbath."[32] Boston men attended lodge meetings but left synagogue-going to their wives, sneered Solomon Schindler. In Newark in the 1860s, Gustav Kussy "was not as deeply pious as [his wife Bella]," recalled their daughter, Sarah, "but was nonetheless ardently Jewish. During his early married life he had kept his shop closed on Sabbath. As the growing neighborhood brought with it increasing business competition, he yielded to the pressure of circumstances and kept it open."[33] Here again, American Jews were mirroring Protestant patterns, and from the 1830s on, church and synagogue attendance became an increasingly female affair.

Wise believed he had a solution to the apparent decline of Jewish practice in the face of American life. Rather than cling to Orthodox rites developed centuries before in entirely different circumstances, he was pushing
a movement to reform Judaism, to make it, as a later generation would say,
relevant to the realities of nineteenth-century American life. While women
were remaking Jewish community and education to fit America, men—
both lay synagogue members and European-trained immigrant rabbis like
Wise—joined them in the project of remaking Jewish worship and ideology. American Judaism, of course, had always been an eclectic project,
with scattered bands of laypeople creating institutions on their own and
only calling in religious specialists when the task was already well under
way. In America, synagogues were independent entities and rabbis their
employees, so congregants' desires held far greater sway than in Europe,
where authority lay with the traditional corporate community and with the
rabbis. What many congregants desired was a Judaism that fit into their
lives as Americans.

The first organized attempt to fulfill this wish happened at Charleston's
Beth Elohim Congregation, one of the nation's oldest and most prestigious. A faction of the membership, organized as the "Reformed Society
of Israelites for promoting true principles of Judaism according to its
purity and spirit," requested a shorter service, English translations to certain prayers, and other minor changes. Lay members of some of the city's
leading Jewish families, they believed that "from time to time" they should
have the right to modify "such parts of our prevailing system of Worship,
as are inconsistent with the present enlightened state of our society, and
not in accordance with the Five Books of Moses and the Prophets."[34]
When the congregation's board turned them down, the dissidents withdrew for a time but later returned.

But the Beth Elohim revolt was followed by many others. Across the
country, congregations grappled with the problem of managing Jewish ritual in American settings. Often, for example, congregations found that the
most practical way of acquiring a building was buying an outgrown
Protestant church. These structures' lack of the large balconies or specially
demarcated women's sections found in traditional synagogues, of course,
presented the immediate problem of where people should sit. The presence of organs provided the possibility for instrumental music during services, which violated Jewish tradition but figured importantly in the
worship of the congregation's Christian neighbors.

Laypeople facing these quandaries generally had no particular program or vision in mind. They just knew what they did and did not like and what they did and did not want: perhaps more English for those who did not understand Hebrew; maybe an inspiring sermon, like the ones Christian clergymen preached, and not merely a commentary on the weekly Scripture portion; possibly a choir to beautify the service with hymns. Decorum and congregational prayer, rather than the tradition of worshipers praying at their own pace, seemed more dignified. Congregational boards often hashed out agreements on these issues on their own, according to the membership's traditional and pragmatic impulses, and presented the rabbis they hired with faits accomplis.

These changes matched another important aspect of American life, the shift in gender roles that was moving religion generally away from the male-centered tradition toward the Victorian model of morality and spirituality as female concerns. One of the first reforming steps in many congregations ended the physical separation of the sexes by allowing men and women to sit together in "family pews" as the Christians did. "Is it not a rudeness of the meanest kind that a female is considered a nobody in respect to persons in religious affairs not only in the Synagogue, but even at the table in the family circle?" Rabbi Wise exclaimed. "If it was a custom among us that a man with his wife and children should go to the Synagogue and occupy their seats together, the whole would be improved, decorum and devotion would be gained, and a ready attendance would be secured."[35]

Mixed seating not only expressed a more "modern" concept of family relations, it also helped fill the main-floor seats with worshipers, even if they were women and children rather than the traditional men. As such home-centered, private (and traditionally female) observances as *kashrut* and *niddah* lost importance in many households, the public, synagogue-centered (and formerly mostly male) practice of attending services became an increasingly important area of women's piety. On Sabbath mornings in Sandusky, Ohio, in the 1860s, recalled David Philipson, "the boy [himself] attended divine service with his mother, as he had done for years."[36] Significantly, because the often heated debates on seating took place among synagogue members, women had no part in them. But women's increasing visibility in the sanctuaries, along with the financial influence their organizations wielded, brought them more and more into the center of synagogue life.

This change became explicit in many congregations as they adopted the practice of confirmation—a ceremony and concept new in Judaism—in place of or in addition to bar mitzvah. Unlike the traditional adolescent ceremony, which involved chanting from the Torah scroll at the reader's desk and was exclusively male, confirmation from the outset involved both boys and girls. Based on the Christian practice of "confirming" one's faith in Jesus, the Jewish version involved a period of study that culminated in a synagogue ceremony performed by the young people, often at the festival of Shavuot in the late spring. Rabbi Max Lillienthal officiated at the nation's first confirmation in 1846, for which a group of twelve-year-old boys and girls had prepared by attending special classes twice a week for five months. New York's influential Emanu-El adopted the practice in 1852. Ten years later, Beth Israel of Hartford became the first congregation to substitute the mixed confirmation ceremony, accompanied, significantly, by a mixed choir, for the male bar mitzvah. In many confirmations, such as Rabbi Mayer May's 1878 class in Portland, Oregon, the girls outnumbered the boys.

Indeed, "the modern confirmation is entirely the opposite of . . . bar mitzvah," Wise wrote in 1854. "The first day of Shebuoth, the day of the revelation of Mount Sinai, is appointed for this purpose in almost all modern synagogues. . . . On the anniversary of that epoch when our fathers received the law we give it to our sons and daughters; when the Covenant between God and Israel was renewed, we receive our sons and daughters into the same covenant."[37] Strikingly, of course, only males traditionally entered the covenant, and they did so through circumcision.

By the middle of the nineteenth century, Judaism's "most devout friends, the most sensible of its devotees," its women, had moved from the periphery of ritual life toward its center.[38] That a rabbi, even one as innovative as Wise, could use these terms to describe women shows how radical a sea change had occurred in their role. Instead of the domestic helpmeet of the main religious actors, American Jewish women were now widely regarded as the true guardians of Jewishness in both home and community. "The women of Israel have at all times been the conservators of our hallowed creed," announced the usually traditionalist *Jewish Messenger* in 1876.[39] Poet Rebekah Gumpert Hyneman caught the mood exactly in "Miriam's Song," a poem published in the magazine *Occident* in the late 1840s: "Oh woman! weak and powerles, yet unto thee is given / The task to prune the budding branch, and bid it bloom for heaven."[40]

As European-trained rabbis began trickling into the United States, especially in the 1850s and later, the desire for a more modern Judaism took on an ideological cast. Similar desires had surfaced in Central Europe, as the stay-at-home kinsmen of America's Central European immigrants busily transformed themselves from *Dorfjuden* into middle-class, bourgeois business and professional people, and a new generation of young, university-trained rabbis had developed a conceptual framework for reforming Judaism in light of modern knowledge. Central European states had begun requiring that all clergy be university graduates, exposing would-be rabbis to Western philosophy, literature, and comparative religious studies.

Invitations to lead American congregations brought Wise and a number of other new-style rabbis to this country. Wise ultimately led the moderate wing of American Reform. David Einhorn took a more radical approach. Max Lilienthal, Samuel Adler, and Kaufmann Kohler also played prominent roles in fashioning change. Meeting at conferences in Cleveland in 1855 and Philadelphia in 1869, these rabbis gave form to their movement. Einhorn, for example, edited a reformed prayer book entitled *Olath Tamid,* and Wise edited one called *Minhag America* (American customary practice), explicitly placing American preferences on a par with the venerable European styles of worship. In 1873 these rabbis formed the Union of American Hebrew Congregations, and in 1875 they founded the Hebrew Union College to train rabbis and cantors, asserting the view, radical in the context of Jewish tradition but arguable in the context of nineteenth-century modernism, that they had the right to amend and even nullify part of the ancient body of Jewish law.

The changes they made corresponded, they believed, to the reality of their progressive, rationalist, modern, scientific age. For example, although Jews outside of Palestine had observed a second day of all major festivals ever since the Babylonian Exile in 586 B.C.E., the Reform rabbis declared that one day sufficed in their technological age. The tradition arose to permit Diaspora communities to be sure they observed the holidays on the correct days. But modern clocks and calendars obviated this need, the rabbis argued. Why should American Jews continue to mourn the Jewish people's long-ago exile from Zion and the destruction of the Temple in Jerusalem by observing the fast day of Tisha B'Av, the ninth day of the Hebrew month of Av? Americans no longer lived in exile in foreign countries, the rabbis argued, but in the freedom and prosperity of a chosen land.

Also unnecessary, the rabbis believed, were many of the rules regulating personal behavior, such as *kashrut* and sexual purity. These ancient practices, though possibly useful in former times, no longer suited modern, rational people. The Bible itself, rather than the enormous accretion of commentaries and legal decisions known as the Talmud, was the valid source of Jewish thought, the reformers argued, and ethical values rather than inherited rules formed the essence of Judaism and a proper Jewish life. Members of many reforming congregations, and the congregations themselves, gave up the attempt—or the pretense—of following these traditions. Mt. Zion synagogue in St. Paul, for example, hired a *shochet* shortly after its founding in 1856. By the mid-1870s it no longer employed one.

Later generations of Jews have seen the early period of Reform as an era that rejected Jewish tradition and abandoned many of the central elements of Jewish life and of Judaism itself in favor of Gentile-style American practices. The Jewish community, once unified by ritual and belief, had become a collection of individuals and congregations thinking and doing things in many different ways. But to the people making the decisions that added up to both capital R Reform ideology and small r reforms of congregation and family practice, the changes probably more accurately, represented a way of staying Jewish while becoming American. They found that the American reality of living as equal and upwardly mobile—but minority—citizens in an officially secular republic nonetheless permeated by Christian custom and belief made the complicated code of traditional Judaism at best onerous and at worst unworkable. Faced with what many saw as the choice between altering and abandoning Jewish identity, they chose to remain loyal through adaptation.

Traditionalists

Despite the manifold benefits of confirmation and other innovations, "still, strange enough, this improvement has found numerous adversaries," Wise marveled; "our modern men with olden views object to it because they do not know what it is; they never saw it ... and know that their fathers did not know anything of it."[41] Although many Americans eagerly embraced some or all of the reforms, others, both men and women, did not. Traditionalist members sued New York's Congregation B'nai Jeshurun over the decision to adopt mixed seating, and dissension over the issue rocked other congregations as well. Many Orthodox-leaning factions withdrew from reforming synagogues to start new, more traditional groups. "Our rabbis . . . should call attention to the wives and mothers of Israel to that portion of the holy law . . . specifically addressed to them . . . and it should be the duty of our women to attend to it, instead of forcing themselves into positions which our religion wisely does not open to them," opined *Occident* editor and prominent educator Isaac Leeser.[42]

Women also kept to the old ways. The first Jewish cookbook published in the United States, Esther Levi's 1871 *Jewish Cookery*, sought to dispel the notion that "a repast, to be sumptuous, must unavoidably admit forbidden food."[43] Along with etiquette tips, sample table settings, advice on supervising servants, such unmistakably American dishes as okra gumbo, and other invaluable information for the upwardly mobile housewife, Levi included only kosher recipes. In the Cincinnati home of Sarah and Wolf Cohen in the 1870s, the strict Orthodoxy of Sarah's widowed mother, Lena Auer, prevailed. No family member did any work from sundown Friday to sundown Saturday, though the two Gentile maids, Minnie Miller and Tillie Taylor, "were not prevented from carrying the heavy scuttles of coal up three flights of stairs to keep the open grate fires, with which the house was heated in winter, blazing, the lamps and candles lighted, the kitchen stove hot and the Saturday meals well-cooked," according to Sarah and Wolf's granddaughter, Sarah M. Wartcki.

In fact, "Grandma Auer had consented to the marriage of her daughter, Sarah, to . . . a non-observing Jew, only when he gave a solemn promise he would not work on the Sabbath." Wolf was as good as his word but had the last laugh on his pious mother-in-law. He closed his tailor shop faithfully at five o'clock each Friday. Saturday mornings, however, found him not at synagogue but in the courtroom of a Gentile judge who was a friend of his. These visits "gained a more lenient sentence for many a 'good Jewish boy' who was in trouble with the police," Warcki claims.[44] Undeterred by her son-in-law's impiety, Lena made elaborate Sabbath preparations, exchanging her everyday *scheitel* ("the wig that all Orthodox Jewish married women wore constantly to cover their natural hair") for an elegant black Sabbath model. This she would "comb every Friday on its wig stand and adorn with a delicate black lace cap with modish ribbon rosettes over the ears. Grandma Auer was too 'frum' (religious) to comb her wig on Sabbath."[45]

Similar piety prevailed in the Nathan home in 1860s New York. Maud Nathan recalls that her aristocratic Sephardic family strictly observed the Sabbath, the festivals, and "other hardships which seemed to differentiate us from our playmates."[46] The Nathan children "were brought up to keep the Sabbath day holy, according to the literal rendering of the commandments. Therefore, we walked to and fro, in order that no horse should be compelled to work for us." They attended Shearith Israel where, "in our Orthodox synagogue, the women, according to oriental custom, are relegated to the gallery, while the men sit below. My mother and I toiled up the high flights of stairs, and I was told to sit on the stairs, next to my mother's seat."[47]

Whether in elite, traditional Shearith Israel, with its pre-Revolutionary Sephardic families, in large midwestern Reform congregations of Central European immigrants, or in little synagogues on the northern plains or the California coast, by 1880 America's Jews had devised distinctively American ways of being Jewish. A Jewish presence—be it a handful of families that gathered at a private home for seder and Kol Nidre or a community scores of thousands strong and honeycombed with congregations, clubs, and charities—now existed in hundreds of cities, towns, and hamlets across the continent. Jewish women had combined the values of their heritage with the opportunities of their new country to attain a level of influence and prominence in community life previously unknown.

The Central European immigrants found characteristically Jewish ways of being American. Transplanting commercial skills developed in Europe, a few families grew rich as merchants or traders, or in such related areas as banking, cotton factoring, cattle dealing, clothing manufacture, and even ranching and mining. Many more attained modest but comfortable livelihoods as storekeepers, wholesalers, and various kinds of businesspeople. Some still peddled from a pack or wagon along back roads and city streets. And immigrants' native-born descendants were moving beyond commerce into teaching, law, medicine, and other professions. Wherever they went, Jewish women and men had entered the commercial, political, and social life of their new hometowns, becoming recognized as local citizens while retaining a special loyalty to their fellow Jews. By the late 1870s, wealthy Jews trying to enter elite American circles had begun to feel some social discrimination, as old-line Christian families moved to protect their privileged position by raising caste barriers against the more recently rich. But blackballs by the most exclusive clubs and rejections at the priciest hotels hardly affected the much larger body of Jews who couldn't afford such luxuries in any case.

Though the Central European Jews had not penetrated the highest reaches of society or the industries at the core of the American economy, such as the railroads, they had in general reached a level of prosperity and acceptance unparalleled in the Old Country. They fashioned American families and raised American children. They used their opportunities to craft institutions that gave their Jewishness a usable American shape. They improvised both Jewish communities and a version of Judaism to meet their own needs. The opportunities and demands of becoming Americans had brought women to the center of religious and philanthropic life. But they had created their American lives for their own purposes, never suspecting that the sturdy structures that they built could (and very soon would) face and ultimately withstand and channel to creative ends one of the greatest upheavals in all of Jewish history.

PART THREE

"The Golden Door"

The Eastern European Migration,
1881–1924

7

"AMERICA IN EVERYBODY'S MOUTH"

Fleeing the Pale

Malka Chernikovsky came to America forty-five years after Jeanette Hirsch, and she walked down the gangplank into an entirely different country. No longer were pioneers venturing into uncharted western lands. The railroad and telegraph now sped goods and messages to all but the remotest locations. Where once hopeful newcomers had sought their fortunes in the wilderness or the gold fields, now millions followed their dreams of prosperity and success to rapidly growing cities.

After crossing the Atlantic on her own with a label marked "New York" pinned to her coat, thirteen-year-old Malka carried her bundles—feather comforters tied around a few of her clothes and her mother's candlesticks, samovars, and a silver thimble—onto a wharf where the immigrant traffic almost never ceased. When the Ellis Island officials who daily quizzed hundreds of dazed and anxious new arrivals questioned her, she answered in Yiddish, the only language she spoke except for a smattering of Russian words. She stepped from the Manhattan ferry into the teeming bustle of New York's Lower East Side, and into a city and an economy larger and more fast-paced than anything known back in Russia.

Much probably confused and puzzled the girl as she joined her older brother Morris, her older sisters Ida and Sophie, and brother-in-law Sam, who had preceded her to America. But two things must have been immediately clear: "Malka," the Hebrew word for "queen," did not suit the American girl she intended to become. And nothing about the life of the newly renamed Molly—neither the people she would meet nor the tenements she would live in nor the jobs she would take—would be at all regal. Yet Molly, like millions of other Jews, knew that her future, and her people's future, lay not back across the sea where their families had lived for centuries but here, in this strange, noisy, urgent, hectic, legendary, and, most of all, promising new country.

Molly was a tiny drop in the greatest wave of foreign arrivals ever to break on America's shores. The flow of people like Molly lasted from 1881 until 1924, but its first ripples gave no hint of what was to come. In the second week of February 1882, for example, a message from England reached the Philadelphia branch of the international charitable group L'Alliance Israelite Universelle. On the eleventh of that month, the organization learned, the steamship *Illinois* had cleared Liverpool harbor, bound for Philadelphia with 225 Russian Jewish refugees aboard. The city's Jewish community, which in a century and half had gradually grown to fifteen thousand members, had less than two weeks to prepare to receive a group of unexpected, undoubtedly traumatized, and probably destitute new arrivals who would increase Philadelphia Jewry by 1.5 percent.

By the time *Illinois* steamed up the Delaware River after twelve days at sea, not only Philadelphia's Jews but the city at large had rallied to its passengers' aid. Local and state officials hastened to the wharf to welcome them ashore. Citizens of all faiths, appalled by the anti-Semitic atrocities that had driven the newcomers from their Russian homes, donated $20,000. The Academy of Music, the city's most prestigious public hall, rang with speeches denouncing the pogroms sweeping the czar's empire. Jewish philanthropies geared up for the emergency, several organizing women's auxiliaries and committees of lady visitors to handle the practicalities of settling needy families into new lives in the City of Brotherly Love.

But what Philadelphia Jewry did not—indeed could not—do that busy winter was realize that the *Illinois* represented not an isolated influx of unfortunates but the leading edge of a gathering torrent. A vast, unstoppable tsunami of Jews fleeing Russia, Poland, Lithuania, Galicia, Romania, and other East European realms would soon inundate, then overwhelm, and finally utterly transform Jewish life in America. On the day the *Illinois* arrived, 250,000 Jews lived in all of the United States. By the time Congress would cut off mass East European immigration forty-two years later, that many would live in Philadelphia alone.

Two and a half million Jews would pass through American ports during the intervening years. A total of four and a half million—a number probably inconceivable to the Philadelphians preparing for the *Illinois*—would one day inhabit the nation as a whole. Just about every Jewish community on the continent would experience an influx. New York would become the largest Jewish settlement on earth. From an exotic outpost of the Diaspora, with perhaps 5 percent of the world's Jews, America would rapidly emerge as a major center of Jewish life, home to nearly one of every four Jews worldwide. American Jewry would change from a small, prosperous, Americanized community of mostly Reform mercantile families into a large, religiously diverse, heavily working-class, strongly Yiddish-speaking ethnic group.

Over a period barely longer than the biblical Children of Israel would wander in the desert, one in every three Jews living in Eastern Europe—home to half the world's Jewish population at the migration's outset—would make a journey in some ways as profound as that of the ancients. They would leave a deeply traditional region where their ancestors had lived for centuries to seek better lives in foreign parts, 80 percent of those emigrants arriving, either directly or after intermediate stops in England, Germany, or elsewhere, in the United States. The movement out of Eastern Europe to America ranks among the epic migrations of Jewish history, comparable in scope and import to the Babylonian exile or the Spanish expulsion. Massive as it was, however, it counted for only a small part of a far more gigantic transfer of talent, hope, and humanity from the Old World to the New. For the two generations bracketing the turn of the twentieth century, the economically distressed regions of Europe would hemorrhage poor people from their rural villages and urban slums into the cities, farms, factories, and mines of the rapidly industrializing United States. By the time the Congress dammed off this essentially unlimited flow, some 50 million souls, belonging to scores of nationalities and denominations, had made the crossing.

The deluge of newcomers forever changed the character of this nation, its cities and countryside, its culture and politics, its vision of itself and its place in the world. For the first time, the people streaming off the immigrant ships hailed mostly from Eastern and Southern Europe—from Poland, Italy, Russia, the Hapsburg empire, and Greece—rather than from the British Isles and Northern or Central Europe. For the first time, large numbers brought religious convictions and customs formed in Mediterranean, Slavic, and Orthodox Christian lands. For the first time, a major group bore the memory of staying Jewish under the czars, a heritage that would divide them from, rather than unite them with the coreligionists they found here.

The new land indelibly changed those who arrived. No matter where their ships tied up or which hamlet or metropolis became their home, the newcomers encountered Americans who had come, or whose ancestors had come, on earlier voyages. The institutions that these established Americans built over generations channeled the immigrants' energies, defined their opportunities, taught them new lives, and ultimately allowed them to become Americans in their turn. Generations earlier the Gratzes, Seixases, and other early families had helped show Central American *Dorfjuden* how to be Americans and American Jews. Now the descendants of Central European peddlers marshaled the skills, education, and resources gained on this side of the Atlantic to help the newest comers find their way. In their turn, this newest generation of immigrants, like all who had come before them, adapted what they learned here in ways that established Americans could not have foreseen. Though often inharmonious and difficult for participants on both sides, this encounter created a people utterly distinctive in world history: the largest, strongest, richest, freest, and arguably the most powerful and creative Jewry ever known.

Fleeing the Czar's Domain

As the emigrating Jewish millions lugged their bundles onto departing steamers, or strained at ship railings to glimpse the approaching skyline, or stammered their answers to immigration officials, they could not foresee what they and their descendants would become. But they knew what they were leaving behind—poverty, privation, oppression, hopelessness bordering on despair. Malka, for example, had been born near Odessa, Ukraine, in 1886, the youngest of eight children. The exalted name her parents gave her suited life in their small town even less than it would her future in America. By the time she boarded the ship for the New World, three of her siblings had died of disease. She spent her childhood helping put food on the family's table, gardening in their vegetable plot and working in her mother's struggling retail business. On market days the girl joined in spreading a cloth on the bare ground of the marketplace, arranging as attractively as possible the meager wares her mother assembled, and waiting on any potential customers who happened by. For twenty-three years, the family's neighbors, friends, and finally its own members had been leaving for America. It must have seemed inevitable from the outset that Malka—soon to be Molly—would join the flow.

As thousands upon thousands of Jewish men, women, and children crowded onto trains or bounced in wagons or tramped back roads to the German or Belgian or Dutch ports where the ships for America tied up, they knew that something important—something larger than any individual or family hopes or ambitions—was happening to their people. The Jewish tide out of Russia and surrounding lands was so vast and forceful that "every emigrating Jew realized that [he or she] was involved in something more than a personal expedition," recalled Abraham Cahan. As a youth in Vilna, Cahan had hoped to be a rabbi, but as an adult in New York he became a universally recognized voice of East European immigrant Jewry. The wayfarers knew, Cahan observed, that they formed "part of an historical event in the life of the Jewish people" as they "joined . . . the move westward to start a new Jewish life. They did so with religious fervor and often with inspiring self-sacrifice."[1]

Emigrating Jews traveled in hope. "I will not bury my best years here [in Poland]," a girl named Anna Kahan told herself when not much older than the emigrating Malka. "I must go to the big, wide world where I can learn, experience life. . . . I see myself in the United States, dressed neatly, walking to school with books in my arms," no longer mired in the deprivation and misery she had known at home. "I am sure that in the new country I'll have a chance to study, to make something of myself. . . . Now [because of her family's desperate poverty] all I can think of is work. . . . work hard enough and long enough to earn enough money to pull my dear ones out of the pit. . . . I must provide for . . . myself and our parents and the younger children. When I think of the coming winter with its lack of bread and fuel, I see a bottomless abyss, and I shudder. And we [her sister and herself working] over there [in America are] their only hope."[2]

Jews also traveled in fear. "We left Russia because every month or week some other bandits came and . . . began to kill the people from [our] town," fourteen-year-old Edith Modelevsky recounted in one of the first compositions she wrote as a Minneapolis schoolgirl. Violent men "came to Zhitomir and . . . began to kill the [Jews]. . . . Five soldiers came to our house and said to my mother that she should give them all the money that we have. . . . They took the hundred dollars [that her father had sent from America to pay for his wife and children's passage] and threw them in my mother's face and said it wasn't enough for them. My grandmother . . . told them that we haven't got any more money so they can do what they please. . . . They told us to stand near the door and they are going to kill us. . . . I was trying to run out and call someone for help. While I was [running] to the door one bandit pushed me so hard that I fell. . . . They took the guns to shoot us [but] one soldier said something to the rest of them and they did not shoot us. They took away the hundred dollars and took away all our clothes and they broke our furniture and they went away."[3]

Countless migrants agreed with eighteen-year-old Rachel Bella Kahn, a penniless domestic servant in the Ukraine, who in 1894 decided that the "future seemed hopeless."[4] The travail of East European Jewry in the age of the great migration stands in American Jewish folk memory as the culmination of unbroken centuries of Old World suffering. And, in fact, anti-Jewish sentiment and action—as well as the number of Jews living in hopeless poverty—reached new heights in those years. But the source of East European Jewry's immediate troubles, and of the migration itself, lay not in traditional racial or theological hatreds but in economics and technology, in the same massive technological, economic, and social changes that had earlier demolished traditional rural and village life in Western and Central Europe. The forces that a generation or two earlier had transformed the German-speaking lands and sent scores of thousands of Jews to America were now rolling remorselessly eastward, triggering a similar collapse of a long-stable rural society.

Across great reaches of countryside, which had been Polish and later Russian, generations of Jews had earned their living serving the Gentile peasantry and rural gentry. Like the *Dorfjuden* of Central Europe, East European Jews of both sexes were middlemen, selling town goods to the peasants and country produce to the towns. They served the gentry and nobility as tax collectors and estate managers, ran inns and taverns along country roads, and worked as artisans in such trades as shoemaking, tailoring, and liquor distilling. As elsewhere in Europe, they formed a separate society within the larger Christian one, with Yiddish as their language and traditional Judaism as the central reality of their way of life. Compared with their Central European brethren, though, they lived even more intensely Jewish lives in local Jewish communities that were considerably larger than the ones in the countries to the west.

Rather than scattered families in overwhelmingly Christian villages, Jewish communities often formed substantial portions or sometimes even the entire population of small market towns—known in Yiddish as a shtetlach (plural of shtetl, a Yiddish diminutive of the German *Stadt*). Jewish traders maintained shops or stalls where the peasants came to buy cloth, tobacco, boots, or tools on the market days when they rode their produce-laden wagons to town. Less prosperous Jews eked out a living selling goods door to door in town or peddling house to house in the countryside.

With hundreds or even thousands of Jewish residents, each shtetl maintained an array of Jewish institutions supported by mandatory contributions. The wide range of schools, shuls, law courts, *mikvahs,* relief services, and the rest was the outward expression of a rich, inner communal life. Traditional East European Jewry existed as a people apart not only because their neighbors shunned them but also because living a holy life—following the laws of Torah and Talmud, and striving to attain the sacred in the everyday—was the goal and meaning of a believing Jew's time on earth. People punctuated their activities with blessings, pronouncing prayers of thanksgiving each time they ate, drank, saw a rainbow, put on a new garment, or performed countless other everyday actions. They marked time by the Hebrew calendar, their days adding up to weeks crowned by the Sabbath, their weeks to the months adorned by the festivals, their months to years numbered from the Creation rather than from the birth of Jesus. As naturally as flowers bend toward the light, the values of traditional East European Jewish culture inclined toward piety and the pursuit believed to lead there most directly—the study of the holy books. No activity had more social prestige than religious learning. No individuals attained higher social status than outstanding religious scholars. No families claimed more distinguished pedigrees than those with generations of learned men among their forebears.

Intense pressure encouraged any male equipped for study, whether by aptitude or financial resources, to try to do so. People lacking the time or talent for books could gain honor by supporting a worthy scholar at his holy task. Men with intellectual promise but without economic means could often find others—the community at large, a wealthy father-in-law, a hardworking wife—eager to underwrite days spent in learning. Though wealth certainly counted socially, a man's ability to support his family contributed far less to his position in the community than his achievements in the house of study. This emphasis on religious learning allowed a downtrodden, religiously stigmatized minority to evolve a system of social values and prestige entirely independent of—indeed, at odds with—the values of the surrounding Christian society.

Religious learning was, of course, a wholly masculine pursuit. Women expressed their piety not by participating in scholarly discourse or synagogue worship, but through the sacred work of making the home that made a man's scholarly life possible. If they had time, they could recite prayers from Yiddish translations of the Hebrew prayer book either at home or in the women's section of the synagogue. "The household tasks which for the Jewish housewife are sanctified, because they have a religious significance," would have been "mere drudgery without it," observed Sarah Cohen Berman, who left Russia early in the twentieth century. "The preparations for the Sabbath and the festivals, even the house-cleaning for Passover, were performed in a spirit of religious exaltation. The hard-working housewife was the priestess performing the commands of God. She was not a mere drudge."[5] Indeed, through her labor the family transcended the everyday and moved into the sacred.

"Thursday, I used to help [my mother] baking bread and fixing the house," recalled Sophie Katz of their home in the Ukrainian town of Berdichev in the 1890s. "And I used to tell myself, tomorrow is Friday. Tomorrow is Friday night. My father comes home, he goes to the [public] bath, puts on a clean shirt and fixes himself up, puts on holiday clothes. Mother is bathed and washed. . . . she wore a little scarf to protect her hair, because she's supposed to wear a wig. . . . And I used to come home Friday a little earlier from work [which she began at age nine]. And it was so peaceful. The challah, the beautiful bread that she finished baking, and it was so clean and every child was washed and dressed, and it was so beautiful it gave me the greatest thrill in the world. . . . [Mother] had a little money, but she used it for the Sabbath. . . . Monday there is no bread. . . . And I used to many times feel so low down, but I went to work, and it went on, the week. And usually the week was for worries."[6] But through the sacred work of a Jewish homemaker, the Sabbath was for beauty and holiness.

For the great majority of shtetl women, that sacred work of making a Jewish home included making some or all of the money that supported it. Of course, all poor women in Russia, regardless of their religion, worked hard to care for their families. But only Jewish women—and men—considered it appropriate for a wife to act in addition as breadwinner for a scholarly husband. Isaac Bashevis Singer's "saintly" mother, for example, "never assumed that it was her husband's duty to support her," recalled her son, the Nobel Prize winner. "She left him to his beloved Torah and . . . herself traveled to Warsaw to buy goods and earn a living for her family, since her husband's wages [as a rabbi] could not keep a bird alive. . . . It never occurred to her that one day her precious son would be expected to earn a living. She always considered that a wife's responsibility."[7]

Fulfilling that responsibility, Jewish wives across Eastern Europe found many ways of earning money, most often by selling things they produced themselves or bought to resell. Some kept cows, chicken, or geese and provided customers with milk, eggs, butter, or cream. Some sold the surplus vegetables from their gardens. Some baked bread or bagels or rolls. Some baked matzah at Passover time. Some sewed or wove or knit. Some altered clothes or decorated hats. Some dealt in notions or cloth or pots and pans or whatever else they could wangle, doing business from a room in their house or a stall or space in the market, or even door to door. But whether they provided all or only some of their family's livelihood, they had a grasp of economic realities and a sense of importance and self-confidence women often lacked in traditions that considered only men acceptable breadwinners. Like Singer's mother, Jewish women traveled about the countryside and carried out business deals on their own. Dickering with suppliers, haggling over credit, attracting customers to their market stalls, closing deals, and making collections required an assertiveness and bluntness that some other social traditions considered pushy, crass, and unladylike. But in the world of Eastern European Jewry they seemed sensible and normal.

Jewish religious literature and tradition and Jewish family life were theoretically patriarchal, however, and women often deferred symbolically to their male relatives. Men, after all, sat at the head of the Sabbath table, recited the blessings over the braided loaves and the wine in the silver cup, and debated the fine points of doctrine at the Passover seder. The women scurried about bringing their menfolk the delicacies they had cooked. But in practical reality, the breadwinning mother, responsible not only for the household's daily functioning but often also for its finances, frequently dominated family decisionmaking.

"We were very poor," remembered Solomon Bailin, who left the Ukrainian village of Sosnitz in 1911. "My mother had two cows, and from two cows she managed to feed seven of us. The butter, cheese and milk she sold . . . paid for our schooling in the little village. My father sold cattle and had no money." Once, though, "he finally struck a piece of luck." He and two partners happened to get a very good price on some lots of cattle and quickly arranged for the special permission needed to take them to market in St. Petersburg. Bailin's father came home with more money than he ever possessed. "Naturally, [he] was overjoyed. . . . My mother was overjoyed. The first thing she did was pay her debts . . . [and she] bought some clothes for the family and we were all happy. My father stayed at home for about a week or ten days. Then he thought he was very smart and decided to go back and try his luck again with his partners." He took part of the remaining cash out of the suitcase where it was stored. "About three weeks later he came home without a penny in his pocket. . . . My mother was a very clever woman and knew what she was doing. She told him, 'Nothing doing.'" No more of the precious cash would go toward trying to recreate a once-in-a-lifetime stroke of luck. "'You are not getting [the rest of the] money.' [she told him.] 'We have been poor long enough. With this money we are going to America.'"[8]

Despite women's indispensable canniness, though, the patriarchal ideal meant that boys—whose arrival occasioned a festive circumcision ceremony—were more valued than girls—whose birth was officially noted only by a single prayer during services at the synagogue. Boys could bring their family *yiches* through learning and righteousness, whereas girls would cost their parents money for their dowries. Girls were expected to help with the household work, whereas boys were expected to study. Most of the husbands that parents found for their daughters, of course, were not scholars. Only a minority had the talent; only a handful had the financial backing. Most boys, like their brethren in Central Europe, ended their education about the time of their bar mitzvah, began an apprenticeship, and from then on worked hard at trades or businesses that did not provide a very ample living. Thus their wives and often their children also had to work. In the world of the shtetl, working to support the family was not a male or a female role, not an adult's or a child's role. It was simply a human being's role.

A Jewish World

Nine centuries of Jewish life in the lands that came under Russian rule or domination produced not only separate Jewish communities but an entire, separate Jewish world with great centers of Jewish learning, a venerable folk tradition, and a religious culture of unparalleled richness that anchored daily life. By the middle of the nineteenth century, however, the world of the shtetl, and of the rural Christian society on which it depended, had begun to come apart. In 1861 Czar Alexander II emancipated the serfs, in part hoping that that they would leave the land, move to the cities, and become the industrial workers of the modernizing economy he hoped would develop.

Some of the newly freed peasants did abandon their native countryside, exchanging rural for urban poverty and decreasing the customer base of their hometown Jewish traders. Other ex-serfs traded their former legal servitude for a more up-to-date financial bondage of large land mortgages, which kept them at home but also reduced the money they had to spend on goods from nearby Jews. Meanwhile the railroads had begun to penetrate the countryside, carrying goods between factories and farms and bypassing small-town markets. Wheat from the immensely productive American Midwest also began appearing in East European cities at prices cheaper than locally grown grain, a further blow to rural middlemen. Many of the market towns dotting the countryside, and the traders, brokers, and agents who did business there, were rapidly becoming obsolete.

In the early and middle nineteenth century, the Jews of Central Europe had faced a similar crisis and the social disintegration it entailed. Many had used their capital and literacy to transform themselves or their children into bourgeois Berliners or Viennese. But Eastern European Jews had much less hope of building acceptable alternate lives in the prosperous, growing cities nearby. The Central Europeans had faced anti-Jewish prejudice, but nothing that compared to the remorseless and vicious anti-Semitism of Eastern Europe. To protect the regime's stability in a time of social unrest, the Russian government systematically cultivated anti-Jewish hatred, using people who were legally and socially separate from Russian Christian society as convenient scapegoats for all the empire's troubles.

Jewish economic prospects, furthermore, were often even more dismal than those of many ordinary Christian Russians. Industrialization came late and fitfully to the czar's backward domains. Since 1791, imperial decrees had confined all but a handful of the Jews under czarist rule to a territory known as the Pale of Jewish Settlement. From the Latin *palus,* meaning "stake" or "pole," the word originally denoted both a fence and the area it encloses. Modern English speakers mostly know that "beyond the pale" means "outside the ordinary boundaries of reason, safety, or law." What lay beyond the Russian Pale were the great cities, with their business, educational, and cultural opportunities. What lay inside, crowded into twenty-five provinces that the czars had acquired from Poland and the adjacent Ukraine, was a rapidly growing Jewish population competing for severely limited opportunities. Few people could arrange the special permission needed to live outside the Pale and practice certain trades or attend particular schools. One Jewish woman who wanted to stay in Moscow to attend university reportedly registered as a prostitute—a line of work that qualified her for a residency permit.[9]

The ultimate goal of the containment policy was not geographic restriction but social and cultural annihilation, the forced blending of a traditional, devoutly Orthodox, Yiddish-speaking populace into Russian-speaking, Christian society. The regime devised various means, some odious, some merely irritating, to persuade individual Jews to abandon their traditions and adopt Gentile ways. Between 1827 and 1850, for example,

Jewish communities had to meet annual draft quotas of men and boys—
who could be as young as seven or eight—to serve twenty-five years in the
army under a harsh discipline intended to convert them to Christianity.
Perhaps the most hated of all czarist laws, it fostered the nightmarish practice—still vivid in Jewish folk memory—of recruitment by kidnapping.
Paid agents known as *khapers* snatched poor children off the streets or
from their houses. Wealthy families, meanwhile, used their money and
influence to shield their sons and send others instead.

In 1874 the government adopted a new policy to lure Jewish boys into
secular Russian-language schools. In addition to exemption from military
service, enrollment often earned the entire family the right to live outside
the Pale. It enticed many families away from traditional Yiddish- and
Hebrew-based religious schools and, in some cases, away from their religious heritage as well. "As soon as we settled in Petersburg, I had to discard the peruke [wig] which pious Jewish women wore," recalled Pauline
Wengeroff, the pious mother of one such student, "[and after a struggle
with my husband] I ceased to keep a kosher kitchen. . . . [Then] what a
time of heartbreak when my son attended the gymnasium [secular academic high school] . . . But ought I to expect that my children, growing up
under such alien influences, would follow the ways of their mother? . . . I
felt alone and abandoned."[10]

By the late nineteenth century, oppression began drawing many newly
secular young Jews into underground opposition movements struggling
against the regime. Having jettisoned the hope of messianic deliverance
along with the rest of traditional religion, many secularists retained, disguised by fashionably scientific new terminologies, Judaism's perennial
yearning for social and political justice. Redemption would come, these
dissidents believed, not through their ancestors' faith but through his or
her particular brand of revolutionary theory. And "her" fit a significant
portion of the dissenters. At a time when Jews composed about 4 percent
of the entire imperial population, they made up 13 percent of the individuals and 64 percent of the women arrested or tried for subversion.[11]

Finally, one band of young radicals, the Narodnaia Valia (People's Will),
hatched a fateful scheme to overthrow the government. This mostly
Gentile group decided to ignite a general popular uprising. According to
the plan, pogroms—government-sanctioned attacks on Jewish communities—would provide the needed spark. Once anti-Semitic violence had
broken the bounds of civil order, the aroused peasantry and proletariat
could easily be convinced to expand their attacks beyond Jews to govern-

ment targets. The desperately desired revolution would finally begin. To get things rolling, in 1881 Narodniks engineered the assassination of Czar Alexander II. The actual killer had lived for a time in the home of a Jewish woman named Hessia Helfman, and the group had some other Jewish members as well.

The regime seized this pretext to blame the plot on the Jewish community at large. To distract the Christian poor from thoughts of further antigovernment action, officials unleashed assaults on Jewish settlements that were savage even by Russian standards. The non-Jewish Narodniks, still eager to jump-start their revolution, joined in. The planned larger uprising, of course, never came, though the government's effort to contain the danger by diverting attention to supposed Jewish perfidy worked perfectly. Officially sponsored broadsides alerted mobs to "the harm caused the Christian population by the activity of the Jews with their tribal exclusiveness, religious fanaticism, and exploitation." Circulars asked, "Who takes the land, the woods, the taverns from out of your hands?" Then they supplied the obvious answer: "The Jew curses you, cheats you, drinks your blood."[12]

That year and the next, more than 225 cities and towns, including major centers like Kiev, erupted in anti-Jewish violence. Rioters sacked more than a thousand Warsaw homes, businesses, and synagogues. Mayhem and murder stalked communities across the Pale. But simply inciting mobs to loot and burn did not satisfy the regime. Supposed Jewish culpability for Alexander's death served to justify new restrictions more draconian than any yet seen. "With regard to all Russian subjects, with the exception of the Jews, the fundamental principle is that everything not prohibited by law is allowed," observed an astute aristocrat in 1884, as the first wave of pogroms finally died down. "Whereas for the Jews, the maxim is that everything which is not positively allowed is considered prohibit[ed]."[13] Official boards of inquiry quickly concluded that the wave of anti-Semitic pillaging had itself arisen from "Jewish exploitation." The list of things not positively permitted expanded drastically. Beginning with the May Laws of 1882, a series of harsh decrees deprived hundreds of thousands of Jews of their homes, trades, businesses, chances at higher education, and any hope of tolerable lives.

These new laws came on top of the thousand or so special restrictions and requirements already in force. This mass of regulation not only limited people's actions but entangled them in the constant need to seek licenses and permits and exceptions for even the most mundane purposes.

Changes in the czar's mood and the political climate compounded the confusion as periodic bursts of liberality alternated unpredictably with stretches of repression. "Pray for the present czar," Jews used to say; the next could be even worse. "Lord keep the czar" they would recite, and then, in a whisper, "far away from us!" In their shtetlach and villages, Jews (indeed, all Russians) lived at the mercy of corrupt and capricious bureaucrats, with bribery and favoritism weighing more heavily than the letter of any law in determining an individual's or family's fate.

In May 1882, a set of particularly onerous decrees called the Temporary Rules ejected half a million Jews (including a fictitious dairyman named Tevye and his wife Golde, Sholom Aleichem's immortal creations) from rural villages and towns across the Pale. Masses of country artisans, traders, and innkeepers lost their livelihood. Soon even elite Jews with special privileges lost their right to live in cities outside the Pale. By 1891 the new residents forced into the already crowded Pale topped 700,000, including 20,000 who formerly lived in Moscow. Then liquor distilling, long a Jewish specialty, became a government monopoly, throwing further thousands out of work. Jews competed with one another and with uprooted Gentiles for what work could be found in an economy hardly noted for its prosperity or stability. Employers, however, often preferred Christians, who had no reputation for sharp dealing and no inconvenient desire to rest on Saturdays.

By 1898 the Pale's 5 million Jews, traditionally small-town dwellers, were a predominantly urban people, 51 percent of them living in cities. In the Polish city of Lodz they numbered eleven in 1797; 100,000, or 32 percent of the total population, in 1897; and 166,000 in 1910. About thirty-five hundred Jews lived in Warsaw as the eighteenth century ended. A hundred years later, the city's 220,000 Jewish residents constituted a third of its total. Another nearly 200,000 lived in Odessa, along with large numbers in such centers as Grodno, Berdichev, Lublin, Kovno, Kiev, Minsk, and Vilna.[14] In Bialystok, just under two-thirds of the population were Jews.

Jews constituted three-quarters of the Pale's merchants, including almost 90 percent of those in Grodno and Minsk provinces.[15] But their small, independent businesses could not succeed in cities clogged with sellers who had no hope of finding buyers. At Passover of 1898, almost a fifth of Pale families needed charity simply to buy their holiday food.[16] In the previous four years the number of Jewish paupers had risen by 30 percent, and fully 40 percent of Jews in the Pale were *luftmenshen* who, in the ironic Yiddish phrase, lived on air (*luft*, as in German) because they had no dependable means of support.

"The observer is struck by the number of Jewish signs in Bessarabian towns," observed the governor of that Russian-held region, his tone implying that the government bore no responsibility for conditions. "The houses along second-rate and even back streets are occupied in unbroken succession by stores, big and small shops of watchmakers, locksmiths, tinsmiths, tailors, carpenters, and so on . . . amidst shocking poverty. They toil hard for a living so scanty that a rusty herring and a piece of onion is considered the tip-top of luxury and prosperity. There are scores of watchmakers in small towns where the townsfolk, as a rule, have no watches. . . . Competition cuts down their earnings to the limit of bare subsistence on a scale so minute as to call into question the theory of wages."[17]

Women's Work

Unnoticed by this official, along with the legions of men hopelessly plying their trades in hovels and shacks, Russia's skilled Jewish artisans included many women, especially dressmakers, milliners, and seamstresses who, as teenage girls, had apprenticed with experts. "My mother had a philosophy," remembered an immigrant named Yetta Brier after she had come to America. "Everyone should have a trade. If you're rich you won't practice the trade—if you're poor you'll make living by it."[18]

But for countless Jews, survival now depended not on finding customers for their craft skills but on jobs in the factories that were multiplying in the urban centers. Once overwhelmingly independent artisans or merchants, Jews by 1898 constituted between a fifth and a third of the Pale's industrial workers.[19] The 1897 Russian census found factory work the predominant Jewish occupation. The 37.9 percent of Jews employed in manufacturing edged out the next highest category, trade and transport, by almost three percentage points. Another 20 percent of Jews worked in generally low-paying domestic and personal service. The relatively lucrative and prestigious professional occupations trailed with a meager 5 percent.[20] "About 90 percent of the whole Jewish population . . . come near being a proletariat," found an 1888 Russian government report.[21]

Men and unmarried women toiled long factory shifts for meager pay—often at piecework rates rather than hourly wages—with women accounting for just under a quarter of Russia's factory operatives and in some places nearly half of textile plant employees.[22] Females often made cigars or artificial flowers, but the commonest jobs for employed Jews of all ages and both sexes were in the needle trades, sewing and assembling clothing or, for those with very good skills and even better luck, as pattern makers or cutters. Married women also sought industrial work but usually did the actual labor at home. As contractors rather than employees, they collected bundles of precut pieces, carried them home, and spent the hours not consumed in household tasks sewing for pay. The treadle sewing machine, invented in the mid-nineteenth century, expanded women's income opportunities because owning or renting one of these high-tech marvels made possible factory work at home. Many other women and men continued as traditional artisans, cutting, constructing, fitting, and often even designing entire dresses, cloaks, jackets, and suits from start to finish or making complicated alternations on existing garments. Expert dressmakers, seamstresses, and tailors, however, had increasing difficulty finding private clients willing to pay prices corresponding to their skills.

Still, even in backward Eastern Europe, industrialization created wealth for factory owners, and some of the new rich were Jews. But the mass of workers without capital, no matter how hard they labored and how many members of their families went into the factories, grew steadily poorer. As conditions worsened, Jewish workers throughout the Pale and beyond became active in labor unions, organizing scores in various cities and industries. The labor movement's class consciousness and socialist ideology gave countless Jews some hope of a new day; for many, they replaced traditional religion as a guiding philosophy.

Still, these struggling new urbanites and their children continued to see themselves as Jews. Vilna brush makers, for example, began a strike by taking their oath of solidarity on a Torah scroll. Bialystok unionists publicized plans to boycott Janovsky's tobacco factory with announcements in the local synagogues. Tanners in Krynki ended a two-hour outdoor strategy meeting—held in a downpour—by swearing solidarity with comrades fired in a recent strike on the sacred Torah passages contained in a pair of phylacteries. Union activists extended the traditional concept of *herem*, religious excommunication from the community of the righteous, to apply to strike breakers, unfair employers, and other workplace renegades. Though Orthodox practice became less uniform, Jewishness, expressed by some in terms of secular, cultural *Yiddishkeit* and by others in terms of newly developing political and cultural Zionism, remained the bedrock of individual and group identity.

The surrounding Christian society never ceased viewing Jews as Jews, and in 1903 the pogroms began anew. Thousands of government-supported publications printed anti-Semitic materials, including the infamous fabrication, *Protocols of the Elders of Zion*. The attacks not only destroyed Jewish property but took large numbers of Jewish lives. "At our door they hanged four Jews, and I saw that with my own eyes," Marsha Farbman remembered from the pogrom that drove her from Russia in 1903. "The Gentiles were running and yelling, 'Kill the Jews! Beat them!'"[23] The notorious Kishinev pogrom of April 1903 cost forty-seven Jews their lives and hundreds of others severe beatings. One young girl hiding from the mobs that year was five-year-old Golda Mabovich, a future Milwaukee schoolgirl. Under her Hebraicized married name of Golda Meir, she became prime minister of Israel. Another twenty-nine Jews died in Zhitomir two years later, also in April—a particularly cruel month for Jews in those times. The liturgy of Easter, combined with the libel that Jews used the blood of Christian children to make matzah, provided common pretexts for mass fury. But anti-Semitism observed no particular season. A July pogrom in Kiev killed one hundred, an August pogrom in Bialystok took sixty, and an October outbreak in Odessa, eight hundred.

This campaign of savagery and oppression was the latest version of the long-standing czarist effort to do away with Jewry as a separate group and ultimately absorb it into the Russian people. "One-third of the Jews will convert," opined Konstantin Pobedonostev in 1891. This high official of the Russian Orthodox Church also predicted that an additional "one-third will die, and one-third will flee the country."[24] He proved at least partially prescient. The vast majority of Jews continued to shun the baptismal font and managed somehow to stay alive. But between 1881 and 1924, just about the number that he foretold did take flight. In the first year after the 1880s pogroms began, thirteen thousand Polish and Russian Jews, including the *Illinois* refugees, fled across the Atlantic—half the number that had gone to America during the entire preceding decade. Three times as many left during the following year. Across the Pale, amid penury and violence, countless Jewish women and men were concluding that Jewish life had become impossible in Eastern Europe; nearly a thousand years of Jewish history there had reached a dead end. As the citizens of Philadelphia and other cities throughout the United States would learn, the tidal wave of East Europe's huddled masses did not abate for four decades.

Bound for the Golden Land

Once under way, the East European migration, like that out of Central Europe over the preceding two or three generations, became a self-sustaining mass movement, but this time on a scale the world had never before seen. The basic motives for flight had existed before the 1880s—although the pogroms sharpened the element of fear that figured in many people's decision to emigrate. But a major difference was that the great masses of the European poor, both Jewish and non-Jewish, now had the means and opportunity to make the move. No longer did travelers have to spend months on a rolling sailing ship. No longer did they have to pay hefty fares for cabins on the newer, faster steamships. Instead, late–nineteenth-century emigrants could make a one-way Atlantic crossing in less than two weeks aboard fast steam vessels specially—if crudely—outfitted to carry lots of people paying very little money.

Albert Ballin, a German Jewish shipping executive, invented the vehicle of their salvation while trying to solve a business problem facing his company: the need to find a cargo to fill empty holds on the outbound run to America. Homeward-bound vessels of Ballin's Hamburg-America Line came laden with timber and other New World raw materials, but Europe had nothing bulky yet profitable to ship to American ports except, Ballin realized, the emigrating poor. Furnishing the great spaces below decks with multideck bunks and installing a few primitive latrines, he created accommodations (if that is the word) that large numbers of would-be emigrants could afford. The name of these cramped, airless compartments comes down to us heavily freighted with suffering and dread. Originally, though, it was a simple descriptive term for the area near a ship's rudder: the steerage.

Passengers traveling steerage class began their sea voyage to freedom and prosperity by crowding into fetid, often filthy spaces along with hundreds of strangers of both sexes and many religions and nationalities. They slept on straw, lived in public, and ate cheap, unappetizing food unless, like many Jews, they carried their own kosher provisions for the trip. Everyone used water closets that early in the voyage usually overflowed with stinking waste. As the ships heaved across the rough North Atlantic, seasickness made the areas open to steerage passengers ever filthier and more wretched. The crossing would live in millions of memories as an episode of horror and distress. "We were huddled together in the steerage literally like cattle—my mother, my sister, and I sleeping in the middle tier, people being above and below us," recalled Morris Raphael Cohen, later a famous philosopher and a leading professor at New York's City College, of his youthful passage on the steamship *Darmstadt*. "We could not eat the food of the ship, since it was not kosher. We only asked for hot water into which my mother used to put a little brandy and sugar to give it a taste. Towards the end of the [fourteen-day] trip when our bread was beginning to give out we applied to the ship's steward for bread, but the kind he gave us was unbearably soggy."[25]

The hardships went beyond the physical. "On board the ship we became utterly dejected. We were all herded together in a dark, filthy compartment in the steerage," remembers an immigrant named Kasovich. "Seasickness broke out among us. Hundreds of people had vomiting fits, throwing up even their mother's milk. . . . As all were crossing the ocean for the first time, they thought their end had come. The confusion of cries became unbearable. . . . I wanted to escape from that inferno but no sooner had I thrust my head forward from the lower bunk than someone above me vomited straight upon my head. I wiped the vomit away, dragged myself onto the deck, leaned against the railing and vomited my share into the sea, and lay down half-dead upon the deck."[26]

The steamship companies did little to lessen the misery of their steerage passengers. "On many ships, even drinking water is grudgingly given," reported Edwin Steiner, a minister from Iowa who investigated the outbound passage for his 1906 book *On the Trail of the Immigrant*. "On the steamship *Staatendam,* we literally had to steal water for the steerage from the second class cabin, and that of course, at night. On many journeys . . . the bread was absolutely miserable, and was thrown in the water by the irate immigrants." When the ships did provide the steerage passengers something they were willing to eat, "the food, which is miserable, is dealt out of huge kettles into the dinner pails provided by the steamship company. When it is distributed, the stronger push and crowd." The area where the people had to stay "lies over the stirring screws, sleeps to the staccato of trembling steel railings and hawsers. Narrow, steep and slippery stairways lead to it." And in that noisy, vibrating space were "crowds everywhere, ill-smelling bunks, uninviting washrooms. . . . The odors of scattered orange peelings, tobacco, garlic, and disinfectant meeting but not blending. No lounge chairs for comfort, and a continual babble of tongues—this is steerage."[27]

Eventually the outrage of critics like Steiner resulted in some improvement, but Ballin's shrewd guess proved to be sound business for several decades. Purveyors of these dismal accommodations had few worries that poor service or bad word-of-mouth would scare away repeat business; few customers on the routes from the German ports would ever make the voyage more than once. The supply of new passengers wanting desperately to come to America and able to afford no other way proved inexhaustible. Appalling though life aboard ship might be, life in the Old Country was more appalling still—and at the end of the relatively brief ordeal lay America. The tickets kept selling. The ships kept sailing with full loads of hopeful humanity. The mass migration was on.

As in the 1820s, 1830s, and 1840s, the migration quickly became self-sustaining. The emigrants flowed west, filled with dreams and trepidation, and the letters flowed east, filled with reports of plentiful jobs, free public schools, running water, the right to worship, the right to speak—and, occasionally, the money for a ticket. For a young girl in Poland named Kaila Simon, later to be the writer Kate Simon in New York, "my life was filled with images of raisins and chocolate, cookies and dolls, white slippers and pink hair bows, all waiting me in a big box called America."[28] Indeed, "America had been in everybody's mouth," remembered novelist Mary Antin, who reached Manhattan in 1891. "Businessmen talked of it over their accounts; the market women made up their quarrels that they might discuss it stall to stall; people who had relatives in the famous land went around reading their letters for the enlightenment of less fortunate folk . . . children played at emigrating; old folks shook sage heads over the evening fire, and prophesied no good for those who braved the terrors of the sea and the foreign goal beyond it; all talked of it, but scarcely anyone knew one true fact about this magic land."[29]

Well, maybe just one, as the writer Anzia Yezierska noted. The American cities might not actually afford the easy life or instant riches that some of the more enthusiastic correspondence reported, but it was just about certain that "there is no czar in America."[30] And that was enough for almost 3 million Jews to uproot themselves and leave. As in previous migrations, those who left were neither the poorest, who could not afford the trip, nor the richest, who had relatively tolerable lives at home. Nor were they generally the best educated or the most pious, who feared they could not retain their faith in a *treife medina* (unkosher land). They were young—mostly between sixteen and forty-five. A relative handful of these emigrants reached final destinations other than the United States— Canada, Cuba, Palestine, Western Europe. But when mothers across the Pale sang to their babies about the fathers who had gone far away to prepare a new life for the family, the lullaby often went:

Sleep, my baby, sleep. Your father is in America.
In that wonderful country he eats white bread every day.
When there is a sound at the door, he does not flinch.
It is not the officers of the Czar but only the wind.
Sleep, baby, soon you will join him.[31]

Sending a member or members ahead to scout the territory and make preparations for the rest was how most families managed to finance the trip. Someone—often the father, but also frequently daughters or sons—would get work in America and send money or tickets home for others to follow. Malka Chernikovsky's brother Morris, for example, earned what the family back home considered amazing riches as an auctioneer on the Coney Island boardwalk. This wealth permitted him finally to send for his baby sister, the last of his siblings to come. Chains of migrating family members bound America to the Pale. Similar chains also tied it to Ireland, Italy, Greece, and many other places in Europe. But the Jewish migration out of the Pale differed from that of nearly every other nationality. Italy, Greece, Christian Poland, Hungary, and most other nations sent many more men than women. A large number of their immigrants came with the intention of working for a while, saving a nest egg, and returning home to invest it in a farm, a home, or a business—and a much improved life in their native place. Theirs was mostly an economic migration, a movement of a certain underemployed sector of the local workforce.

But East European Jews came with the steadfast, even desperate, intention to stay and make new lives as Americans. For the great majority of them, there was no going back and nowhere to go back to. Thus they sent not only young men but women and children and even some old people. It was the movement of a whole people to a new home, not of workers to a new labor market. Fifty-six percent of Italian immigrants, 59 percent of Slovaks, and 64 percent of Christian Hungarians returned to their native lands, but only 2–3 percent of East European Jews.[32] Because whole Jewish families came, the proportion of females in their migration was 43 percent, twice as high as in other Eastern or Southern European groups.[33] Only the Irish, who were also fleeing a hopelessly poor and politically hostile land of no return, sent more women—52.9 percent of their total migrants.

Historians and American Jewish folk memory traditionally date the East European migration's beginning to the first summer of pogroms after the assassination of Czar Nicholas, and certainly fear for physical safety played a part in many decisions to leave. But in fact the migration was not strictly a flight from the marauding Cossack bands of so many family legends. In its first decade, an average of twenty thousand Jews arrived in America each year. In the following decade, when the first wave of pogroms had died down and the second one had not yet begun, the average annual rate rose to thirty-seven thousand, and in the decade after that, to more than twice that figure. Seventy-six thousand East European Jews entered the United States in each year of the decade in which Malka arrived.[34] The numbers fell off during World War I but rose again in the peacetime years until the open door to America closed in 1924. Jews came in large numbers not only in years but also from regions not subject to widespread pogroms. The 5 percent of the Russian empire's population who were Jewish constituted 50 percent of emigrants from Russia. But Jews also accounted for 60 percent of those leaving Galicia, where pogroms were virtually nonexistent, and 90 percent of those leaving Romania. Terrible economic conditions and the prospect of avoiding the military draft probably drove away more Jews than did Cossack horsemen.

But even if most people were not strictly fleeing for their lives, leaving was not an easy step to take. "My little flock of birds," cried Charles Losk's mother on the "beautiful, balmy sunshine morning" of April 2, 1905, when her sons and daughter, with their spouses and children, got on the train that would take them from Odessa. "I have sheltered you all these years under my wings and now in a few minutes you will all fly away from me and perhaps I will never see you again." All the friends and relatives gathered to see the voyagers off "broke down and cried," Losk remembered many decades later.[35] Benjamin Berger's weeping mother stood in the railway station beside her husband, who cried the first tears his departing son had ever seen him shed. "Just before I got on board, Mama took my arm and stopped me. . . . She raised her hands above her, over my head, and 'benched' [blessed] me. She asked in this blessing that the good angel watch over me and take care of me for all time, wherever I went."[36]

Once the emigrants had wrenched themselves from the hugs and kisses of the loved ones left behind and said good-bye (in many cases, as Mrs. Losk foretold, forever), they faced an often arduous journey to their ship. Crossing the border out of Russia, Romania, or Galicia generally had to be done in secret. Few people could pay the high price for a passport and men of draft age probably couldn't have gotten one even if they had spent the money. Instead, emigrants paid smugglers to sneak them across the borders or bribed officials not to notice when they tried. From 1888 on, the Russian authorities, always intent on making Jewish lives miserable, increased the bureaucratic obstacles to getting a passport but nonetheless turned a blind eye to the millions leaving the country in defiance of the law.

Jews traveled by whatever means of transport could get them to the ports. Many went by railroad, but others rode in horse carts or walked all or part of the way. In 1899 idealistic young Romanian Jews organized themselves into bands of *fusgeyer* [hikers]. They marched hundreds of miles to Hamburg, singing as they went and turning down offers of donations from people they met along the way. Instead, they put on musical shows and orations to raise funds for the trip. For many people, the journey to the ship was itself a major ordeal, exhausting the meager resources that many emigrants had painfully scraped together, often by selling all they had. "Sell my red quilted petticoat," one woman declared after hearing a letter describing conditions in America. Sell the samovars and feather bed too, her children proposed. "Sure, we can sell everything," their mother decided. And they did.[37]

The forced illegality of many departures put the travelers at the mercy of unscrupulous bureaucrats and shady operators of all kinds, in addition to the usual perils—bandits, thieves, swindlers, confidence artists, white slavers, and other scoundrels who preyed on inexperienced and unsophisticated travelers, most of whom were known to be carrying either valuable tickets or the cash to pay for them, along with their most valuable possessions. The vast number of people on the move made transportation and lodging hard to find. The Austrian city of Brody, one of the main crossing points out of southern Russia, was repeatedly overwhelmed by the masses of fleeing Jews, who sometimes outnumbered the local residents. Thousands were temporarily quartered in stables and factories, while Brody's Jewish population struggled to shelter some of the wayfarers in their homes.

Some financial help to Brody and other places where emigrants congregated came from such Jewish charities as the Alliance Israelite Internationelle and the Baron de Hirsch Fund. An immensely wealthy financier and railway tycoon descended from bankers who had served the royal court of Bavaria, Baron Maurice de Hirsch made the East European migration the object of vast philanthropies. His Jewish Colonization Association, founded in 1891, did much to encourage Jews to emigrate. German Jews also organized the Hilfsverein der Deutschen Juden (Aid Association of German Jews) to help speed the hordes of their impoverished coreligionists moving through their country. They provided information and referrals to individual travelers, and also persuaded railroads and steamship companies to offer lower prices and governments to help expedite the journey to the ships. The Hilfsverein helped almost a third of the 700,000 Jewish emigrants who passed through Germany between 1905 and 1914.[38]

Next came the voyage, for most people in steerage, and then the huge lines, unfathomable questions, confusion, and anxiety at the American ports of entry. From 1855 through 1891, foreigners arriving in New York, the destination of the overwhelming majority of East European Jews, were first received at Castle Garden at the bottom of Manhattan island. This large building soon proved inadequate to the flood that passed through it—5 million people between 1881 and 1891.[39] In 1892 operations were moved to far larger facilities out in New York Harbor, on a bit of land known as Ellis Island, not far from the islet where Emma Lazarus's Mother of Exiles held aloft her lamp.

But even the new buildings and expanded staff could not keep pace with the crush of humanity waiting with their bundles and their dreams in long, snaking queues and vast, congested halls. Five thousand people passed through on a typical day, but on April 17, 1907, the busiest day in the island's history, officials struggled to process 11,745 individuals.[40] Here on the "Isle of Tears" the newcomers submitted to the inquiries and examinations that would determine their fitness to enter America, and here the unlucky ones judged feebleminded, tubercular, afflicted with trachoma, or otherwise ineligible were sent, shocked and disconsolate, to ships that would take them back across the ocean.

But the great majority passed their ordeal before the inspectors and were admitted. Even up to the very last moments of the journey, the road to the Golden Door was for most people paved with worry, discomfort, and travail. And the fabled, proverbial door, when they finally reached it, was not exactly decked with shiny yellow metal. But at least it stood open, and at least the great majority of them could walk through it. And beyond it lay something far more glittering: the deceptive, exhilarating, terrifying, heartbreaking, glorious, beloved, cruel, and altogether unimaginable landscape that would be their America.

8

"EVERYTHING POSSIBLE"

Immigrant Women at Work

Molly Chernikovsky left Russia knowing that her big brother Morris had made a success in America. But as she peered over the ship's railing toward the indistinct hump gradually growing on the horizon, her own prospects for doing likewise must have seemed less bright. Apart from her mother's few household treasures, she brought nothing to New York that the bustling, burgeoning center of commerce, finance, and manufacturing valued: not English, capital, or industrial skills—nothing, in fact, but the memory of working hard in the old country and the willingness to work just as hard in the new.

But she brought the assurance, based on Morris's example, that in the new country a Jew could rise from poverty. Like her brother and millions of other newcomers, Molly would see her chances and take them. And like so many of the great immigration, she found them in the teeming world of East European immigrants like herself. At the beginning, though, she had to take a job she considered far beneath her true standing as a merchant's daughter. But in the land of opportunity, she soon discovered, even a humble job as a servant could offer a clever girl a way to move up. Her employers, an East European immigrant family who had already made good, owned a sewing machine. While in their employ, she learned to use it.

Before long she had landed better paying and less restrictive work as a seamstress in the Philadelphia garment plant that employed her older sister Sophie. No longer confined for long hours to a Yiddish-speaking household, Molly quickly picked up English, made friends with fellow factory girls, and found a social life. She spent her Sundays with other young people, picnicking in Fairmount Park or going to dances. "Believe me," she reminisced long afterward, "it was better than it was in the Old

Country."[1] For one thing, in the American fashion, her circle included young single men.

One of them caught her eye, a Russian Jew who had, since arriving, transformed himself into an "American type." A tailor at her factory, he did union organizing and "wasn't scared of nobody." Marrying when she was twenty, they had merry times with their friends, young working couples and singles who took in the latest Yiddish plays, chatted late over coffee at the Automat, thrilled to amusement park rides, and took promenades along the Schuylkill River or past the strange creatures at the zoo. A son, born within the year, ended Molly's factory career. A daughter came two years later. The young family "didn't have much money, but it was enough to get along and we enjoyed. Sometimes in the summer we went to Atlantic City for a week. Always on Saturday night there were people in our house." The regulars included Sophie and her husband, Meyer, she keeping everyone up-to-date on her union activities, he dancing up a storm. "Everybody brought their *kinder* [children] and we put them to sleep on the floor or on chairs we pushed together," Molly remembered. "Everybody had a good time" laughing and telling stories, noshing on herring and potatoes and drinking a little shnapps.[2]

But suddenly Molly found her herself widowed, without insurance or any other means of supporting her young children. Being her mother's daughter, she started a tiny retail business with what she had at hand. A milkman, an egg man, a bread man, and a bagel baker agreed to deliver their wares to her house. Her neighbors began coming to buy at an impromptu store in her cellar. While she waited on her customers, "the children stayed with me in the store or played in front. I managed."[3] Before long she expanded into fresh produce and her luck also seemed to take a fresh turn. The man delivering her twice-weekly supply of vegetables and fruits "fell in love with me, so I married him. I thought enough struggling, now I would have somebody to take care of me and the family. But what he brought in, you could do without. So I kept the store open and I still ran it alone. And I had right away two more children—two girls."[4]

Molly's outlook and finances took another disastrous turn one Friday evening some years later. That sundown, as always, she lit the Sabbath candles. Somehow the flames spread, destroying the family's house, belongings, and livelihood—as well as Molly's religious belief. "What kind of God would take away the home and business of a person who observed?" she asked herself. "I'm not one who thanks God for bringing *tsores* [sorrow]."⁵ Thenceforth, she resolved to rely on human help. She began the very next day, taking a bus to New York. Morris and their other sister, Ida, advanced Molly the down payment on a building she'd noticed in her neighborhood, one that had a real store on the ground level and living quarters above.

Molly soon resumed her grocery business at the new location and gradually expanded into other fields. With her shrinking religious scruples and growing bankroll, she took some shadier profit opportunities, posting bail bonds for neighborhood no-goodniks, collecting bets for numbers racketeers, trading on the black market during World War II. Doing "all right" in these ventures, she put the proceeds into additional real estate.⁶ And her husband? "Don't ask. . . . He was nothing when I met him and so he remained."⁷ Molly was the breadwinner. But growing prosperity never surprised the girl who had helped keep store in the mud of the shtetl market square. "*I knew I could always make something out of nothing*," she said.⁸

Big City Chances

For all of Molly's enterprise, resilience, and self-reliance, though, she didn't exactly make her success out of nothing. Like countless fellow "greenhorns" who managed to better their lot in their new land, she used the opportunities that early–twentieth-century America's economy afforded, as tempered by the skills and values that East European immigrants brought with them from the Old Country. A specific web of contacts and resources, for example, permitted Ida to help rescue Molly from the disastrous fire. She had used the available opportunities, though in a different combination, to become, in her own estimation at least, quite astonishingly well-to-do. She arrived in 1903 with her husband, Sam, as penniless as Molly would be three years later. The couple spent their first American weeks lodging on New York's Lower East Side with a cousin of Sam's who also provided something even more crucial than a bed: contacts among the many tiny, marginal manufacturing businesses operating out of cramped tenement rooms throughout the teeming, largely Yiddish-speaking neighborhood. Soon Sam was stripping tobacco for a cigar maker in a dingy, airless workshop, one of the thousands whose bosses "sweated" long days of piecework out of their immigrant help. With Sam's earnings, Ida went looking for an apartment.

The three-room, sixth-floor walkup flat that she found at the back of a nearby tenement house was by far the finest home she ever had, even if the vista of the airshaft from its three sunless windows seemed terrifyingly high. She made the first rent payment with money borrowed from a *landsmanshaft* and spent the little left over on furniture. Morris also bestowed some cast-off pieces. A table and straight-backed chairs went into the kitchen, a painted iron bedstead and bureau into her and Sam's bedroom. That left a cot, a night table, and a straight chair to start their inaugural American business venture. Sam asked around at the plant and a coworker even "greener"—newer to America—than Ida and himself agreed to pay $3 a week to sleep in the third room and eat the meals that Ida cooked. Before long a second male boarder was spending his nights on a cot in the kitchen, also eating with Ida and Sam, but paying only $2.25 a week for his rather less private accommodations. Then a woman who slept elsewhere began coming to dinner for a daily $.25.

If all went well, these paying guests brought in over $5 a week (some of it, however, needed to cover expenses), at a time when about $15 a week would decently support a workingman's family.[9] Shrewd shopping at the pushcarts lining the curb outside their door let Ida control her costs. Perhaps the women hawking edibles along her street reminded Ida of her own mother calling out to potential customers in that faraway marketplace. She befriended many of these sidewalk saleswomen, who taught her the ropes. "They saved food for me; they told me who had what and how much I should offer."[10]

Sam and Ida made their home on Hester Street, a main commercial thoroughfare of the densely Jewish immigrant quarter, but before long they could have been forgiven for imagining they had found their way instead to Easy Street. Ida had a second salable skill. As an experienced midwife, she commanded $5 each time she attended a tenement delivery, and calls came as often as twice a month. The demand for her dinners grew as well. She cooked in an authentic old-country style but created dishes tastier than those possible in Russia. "You could find everything on Hester Street—herring, beets, apples, dried fruit, fresh fish packed in ice like I never saw." More and more people showed up to dine at Ida's, often introduced by the pushcart women. "Suddenly," Ida remembered, "I'm having a restaurant—six or seven people at my table." Though she only accommodated people she knew, "sometimes I had to serve in shifts."[11]

Life was good in every respect but one. After helping scores of women become mothers, Ida learned that she could not be one herself. This grieved her deeply, although Sam seemed content to remain childless. But then, in 1911, he made a proposition so astonishing that Ida thought it would have been impossible—even inconceivable—in Russia. "'Ida,' he said, 'let's buy a building.'" She was amazed. "Me, with a building? I couldn't believe it. In the old country Jews didn't own. So I said, 'Sam, buy it. We're in America, everything is different here, everything possible.'"[12] So he did and they moved in, keeping space for their own home, their boarders, and Ida's restaurant, and renting out the rest to tenants.

Now a landlord, Sam quit making cigars. He managed the rentals, maintained their tenement, and helped in Ida's businesses. A year later, with savings and a loan, they bought the building next door. Soon their holdings expanded to include a country place that they ran as a summer boardinghouse. One day Sam declared, "We can afford to live like people now."[13] A woman of property need not rush out at all hours at the behest of laboring mothers or stand over a stove making meals for customers, he believed. Ida agreed to give up midwifery, but she loved the cooking and the company and kept running the restaurant. Their savings paid for more buildings, including some in more prestigious neighborhoods uptown. By the time Molly rode the bus from Philadelphia, something over three decades after Sam and Ida had landed in New York, they were rich beyond the imagination of the two young "greeners" they had been.

For millions of Jews living in the United States today—perhaps as many as eight or nine in every ten—the tale of Ida's and Molly's American rise sounds as resonant as a myth, as intimate as a bedtime story, as familiar as a family dinner. Some version of it has echoed, first in Yiddish-accented voices and then in American-sounding ones, through three or four or five generations of American lives. The ancestral protagonists might not have grown as wealthy as the childless Ida or as crooked as the cynical Molly. They might have come from Poland or Lithuania or Galicia rather than from the outskirts of Odessa. They might have landed at Boston or Baltimore rather than New York, stitched men's suit jackets or peddled kosher meat rather than strip tobacco leaves and sell butter and eggs. But the essential trajectory and backdrop of their stories are almost always the same. Years of unremitting labor and relentless saving, of little businesses and arduous jobs, of *landsmanshaftn* and labor unions, of evenings at Yiddish plays and mornings in little shuls, passed in the hectic, crowded immigrant quarters of industrial cities and towns.

Rather than fan out to every remote settlement that might possibly support a general store, as the Central Europeans had done, rather than devise an impromptu Jewish life in mining camps and prairie hamlets, East European newcomers crowded into city enclaves that mimicked the densely Jewish communities they had left behind. New York's Lower East Side, by far the largest of these districts, was for all practical purposes a transplanted shtetl, though one rather larger than the market towns of the Pale and surrounding regions. Yiddish theaters and newspapers, public baths and kosher butchers, synagogues and matzah bakeries abounded along its crowded streets. In the congested blocks east of the Bowery, north of Monroe Street, and south of Houston Street, a Yiddish speaker could find all the cultural, social, and religious resources needed to live as an Eastern European Jew.

From the 1870s on, the great majority of Jews who landed in New York went first to this most Jewish of American neighborhoods, and many of them went no further. As poor immigrant Jews began flooding into the district, the established German, Irish, and Central European Jewish families already in residence, many of them middle class, retreated to more spacious quarters uptown. But so rapidly was New York's Jewish population growing that, despite losing its better-off Jewish residents, the Lower East Side by the early 1890s was nonetheless home to three-quarters of New York City's Jews. As the new arrivals made good, they in turn flowed out of the neighborhood, leaving its crowded tenements and noisy street markets to the most recently arrived. By 1903 the Lower East Side housed only half of the city's Jews and by 1916, only a quarter.

For countless immigrants or their descendants, the East Side was a way station on the route to more spacious and sedate neighborhoods in Harlem or Brooklyn. As early as 1916, two-thirds of the Jews in the city who had first lived on the Lower East Side were making their homes elsewhere. But so vast was the immigrant tide that the old neighborhood's Jewish population continued rising even as its percentage of the city's total Jewish population fell steadily. The high-water mark came in 1910, with 542,000 Jewish Lower East Siders.[14] Had the neighborhood been a city in itself, it would have ranked as the nation's fourth largest.[15] Within this gigantic, transplanted, Jewry, people who originated in different countries gravitated toward particular areas, the Romanians clustering between Allen and Chrystie Streets, the Hungarians along Houston, the Russians south of Grand.

And the district was not only densely Jewish, it was just simply astoundingly dense, packing in more human beings per acre than any city in the world at that time except Calcutta and Bombay. Tens of thousands of enterprising housewives like Ida crammed into their apartments as many boarders as the stuffy rooms could hold and still leave space for their large broods of children and sundry relatives. Nor did all these landladies offer accommodations as luxurious as Ida and Sam's. Some gave bargain rates for the right to sleep on boards placed nightly over a couple of chairs. One former boarder who occupied a two-room apartment along with five other paying guests and the eight members of a cantor's family remembered not only the crush of humanity but the shoemaking and dressmaking businesses his flat mates pursued. On a typical day, he recalled, the "cantor rehearses, a train passes, the shoemaker bangs, ten brats run around like goats, the wife putters in her 'kosher restaurant.' At night, we all try to get some sleep in the stifling, roach-infested two rooms."[16]

In the last decade of the nineteenth century and the first decade of the twentieth, as many as 730 or even 1,000 persons lived on each acre in some sectors of the Lower East Side. In 1906, thirty-seven of the area's blocks housed over three thousand souls each.[17] The tenement houses "seemed to sweat humanity at every window and door," a contemporary observer noted.[18] Along Orchard Street, "the crush and stench were enough to suffocate one," observed another.[19] Conditions were no better on Suffolk Street, where a pedestrian "had to pick and nudge his way through dense swarms of bedraggled, half-washed humanity, past garbage barrels rearing their overflowing contents," and beneath "tiers and tiers of fire escapes barricaded and festooned with mattresses, pillows, and feather beds not yet gathered in for the night."[20]

Not surprisingly, this teeming and alien district held few attractions for non-Jews or Jewish Americans prosperous enough to live elsewhere. Apart from schoolteachers, police, merchants, social welfare workers, socially conscious reporters, and factory bosses, many Lower East Siders who stayed close to home rarely encountered anyone unlike themselves. "The East Side . . . was a completely Jewish world," recalled Zalman Yoffeh, one of its sons. "The newspapers that came into our house were Yiddish. The store signs were all in Yiddish. The few Gentiles we dealt with [the janitor in the tenement, the barber around the corner, the policeman on the beat] spoke to us out of their smattering of Yiddish. Small wonder that after twenty years in America my mother could not speak a complete English sentence. Or that I, born in America, did not know a single English word until I was five years old!"[21]

Other cities had their own Yiddish worlds crowded with newcomers and their children. Some fifteen thousand Jews lived in Denver's West Colfax district in 1921, and forty-five thousand in Newark's Prince Street area in 1924.[22] Chicago's Maxwell Street, Boston's North End, and South

Philadelphia's Jewish immigrant communities were larger still. None of
these districts, however, or the similar ones in other cities, matched the
Lower East Side in numbers of Jews or depth of *Yiddishkeit*. Except for
the absence of hopeless poverty, heartless oppression, and established religious authority, each was in most respects a remarkably complete replica
of an old-country shtetl of similar size.

The Jewish residential concentration continued as immigrants and their
descendants made good. Families might move on to neighborhoods more
prosperous and prestigious than those that sheltered them just off the
boat, but they still clustered in identifiably Jewish districts of the major
cities, especially those near the coasts, the Great Lakes, and the great
inland river thoroughfares—in other words, the urban regions where
industrialization was taking place most rapidly. In the mid-1920s, with the
great immigration over, New York City had 1,765,000 Jewish residents, 44
percent of the nation's total. Chicago was next with 325,000, or 8.0 percent. Philadelphia followed with 270,000, or 6.7 percent, and Boston with
90,000, or 2 percent. Jewish populations ranging from 85,000 to 35,000
lived in Cleveland, Detroit, Los Angeles, Pittsburgh, Baltimore, and San
Francisco. Milwaukee, Cincinnati, New Haven, Rochester, and Providence
had Jewish communities numbering in the twenty thousands.[23]

The impulse to concentrate in cities rather than disperse across the
country carried fateful consequences. It arose from the politics of the
East European past and reflected the economics of the American present; and it powerfully influenced the American future of the immigrants
and their descendants. The larger a city's concentration of East
European Jews, the more intensely Jewish—and less typically
American—was its residents' daily experience and the fewer their opportunities to know Gentiles. The Central Europeans had grasped opportunities that meant venturing into places with few other Jews, living among
American Gentiles, and inventing consciously American ways of being
Jewish. Their growing ease in American culture let them follow fortune
where it led, often to town after town.

But the East Europeans, mostly from cities and towns, found opportunities multiplying in America's industrial urban centers. Less accustomed
than their immigrant predecessors to living among Gentiles and often
scarred by memories of brutal anti-Semitism, they tended to seek refuge
among their own kind, unwittingly trading geographic, economic, and
social mobility for cultural and religious comfort and security. The East
European Jews who settled in smaller communities often rose faster and

earned more than their *landsleyt* in the great centers. New York, Chicago, and the other main centers bubbled with commercial possibilities, but had far too many East Europeans for all or even most to succeed as traders in business for themselves. This meant that the great majority had to look for jobs. But huge numbers, limited knowledge of American possibilities, and the constant arrival of ever "greener" competitors drove down wages for the work that best suited the immigrants' skills and cultural background.

Going to Work

As it happened, though, one burgeoning big-city industry was ideally suited both to profit from the East Europeans' abilities and to take advantage of their weaknesses. It needed large number of workers able to do exacting work, accustomed to sitting for long periods, and willing to take low pay. Who could suit better than town-bred artisans and merchants used to endless hours in cheder and shul and loath to venture very far from their new homes? Even better from the immigrants' standpoint, the bosses were often Jews, though longer-established, richer, and more Americanized than those streaming off the boats. Taste and technology, ethnicity and economics thus combined to create a labor force perfect for mass-producing ready-made clothes.

Along with electricity, gas stoves, canned food, running water, telephones, indoor plumbing, and internal combustion, mass-market ready-to-wear clothing was one of the industrial innovations remaking everyday American life. The Civil War forced millions of men, the great majority of whom had worn garments made at home or by individual tailors, into identical outfits. It also galvanized the government to pay for them. Menswear, especially in the North, changed almost overnight from an artisan craft to an industrial business. By the time the great wave of East European Jews began, sixteen years after the last battle, the ready-to-wear suit, consisting of a jacket, trousers, and vest, was standard town attire for American men, as were junior versions with short pants for their sons. By 1909 more than 190,000 people earned their living making men's clothes.[24]

American women continued to wear homemade or sewn-to-order dresses and gowns for some years after their menfolk became accustomed to buying off the rack. At the start of the Civil War, about six thousand people earned their livings making women's clothes; only hoop skirts and cloaks were usually bought ready to wear.[25] But as the great wave of East European Jews came streaming through Castle Garden, rising incomes, falling prices, and changing tastes were encouraging women to buy more and more of the underwear, dresses, skirts, jackets, and coats that manufacturers had begun to offer. Tastes changed because lives had. Many more women and girls now went out in public than in the past, to school, to stores, and to jobs as teachers, office workers, sales clerks, and factory operatives. They needed outfits more presentable than home-sewn dresses and more practical than the fussy, constricting clothes Victorian ladies preferred.

By 1890 the cotton or linen shirtwaist—better known to us as the blouse—provided the answer. This light, comfortable, washable, inexpensive button-front top allowed a fresh, neat appearance each day without the cost of owning and maintaining many different full-length frocks. Boldly man-tailored and daringly devoid of the frills and furbelows of former eras, it fit the mood of women who considered themselves modern. The era's fashion icon, the dashingly up-to-date, unmistakably well-bred, impeccably respectable "Gibson Girl," cemented the look's popularity. Illustrator Charles Dana Gibson pictured his wildly admired and widely imitated creation bicycling, motoring, sipping ice cream sodas, and enjoying other modish pleasures in a crisp shirtwaist and skirt, often with a matching jacket. For forward-looking American women, a shirtwaist and suit became standard wear for daytime in town.

With increasingly prosperous Americans of both sexes, all ages, and a wide range of incomes now wanting ready-to-wear, the burden of clothing the family was passing from the housewife with her needle to the retail store and mail-order catalog. With garments costing less than many home sewers could achieve and styles changing from season to season, household needlework alone could no longer keep a woman and her daughters even modestly abreast of fashion. Owning at least some store-bought clothes was now a requirement for anyone who aspired to urban respectability. By 1909 the ready-made women's and children's wear industry employed more than 150,000.[26]

Many industry owners were Jews, mostly of Central European descent. When mid–nineteenth-century American men began buying their new, more extensive wardrobes in their hometown dry goods and general stores, progressive local merchants—often Jewish—often expanded from selling cloth to making clothes. Tailors and dressmakers started to fashion manufacturing firms and small workshops grew into large concerns. In Chicago, for example, Sinai Congregation, a prosperous and prestigious Reform temple, counted among its members the partners Harry Hart,

Joseph Schaffner, and Marcus Marx, as well as their fellow menswear tycoon B. Kuppenheimer, Sears Roebuck head Julius Rosenwald, and shoe magnate Siegmund Florsheim. (The congregation was founded in 1861 when twenty-six men withdrew from KAM in order to worship with organ music, uncovered heads, more decorum, and less Hebrew.)

Hart, Schaffner, and Marx employed six thousand in their huge Chicago plant, but many of their competitors got by with many fewer workers and far less capital. Unlike owners in such rapidly growing industries as railroads, steel, and automobiles, garment manufacturers could get the cost and time savings that modern equipment made possible without huge investments in factories and machines. Entrepreneurs could set up as independent suppliers, whether to retailers or larger clothing firms, with nothing more than the rent for a few sewing machines and a workroom, the loan of some cloth and thread, enough cash on hand for a few weeks' wages, and a contract to deliver goods. If the staff were the owner's family and the workplace their kitchen, the initial investment could be smaller still. Countless would-be industrialists set up in lofts, tenements, and private houses in the larger cities and towns. So many succeeded in creating going concerns that, according to the 1914 census, 60 percent of the nation's garment firms were small operations employing fewer than thirty workers. "Hundreds of small 'insects' of employers" entered and left the business each year, noted one of its labor leaders.[27]

Large numbers of small firms produced intense competition, but also a dynamic industry with many opportunities for the daring, lucky, and alert. This was especially true in New York, by 1860 well established as the nation's leading garment-making center. By 1909, its residents stitched 40 percent of the clothing worn by American men and its companies ranged from elite fashion houses to producers of the cheapest of mass-market ready-to-wear. Most significantly for the Eastern Europeans, by 1890 some 90 percent of the city's garment industry belonged to Jews of Central European origin, with 80 percent of its production located in the old neighborhoods south of 14th Street, close by the area most attractive to new Jewish immigrants.[28] By the turn of the twentieth century, nearly half the garment workers in New York were immigrant Jews.[29] By 1925, they constituted 65 percent of that workforce.[30] As early as 1890, almost 60 percent of immigrant Jews with jobs worked in the needle trades.[31]

Those who didn't make clothes often worked, as Sam had, in similarly dismal factories making other products. In 1890 manual work and artisanship in the printing, tobacco, shoemaking, carpentry, and blacksmithing

industries employed 15 percent of New York's Jews. A scant handful pursued intellectual occupations like teaching, music, the rabbinate, and the
cantorate (though often at very low incomes). The rest of the immigrant
workforce consisted of petty merchants and traders. Over time, more and
more Jews went into business for themselves, so that eventually up to half
of Jewish husbands were their own bosses. Many of those counted as
entrepreneurs continued making a living in the garment trades, perhaps
even doing identical work for the same companies. Now, however, they
stitched and cut as contractors rather than direct employees. Very few of
them attained real financial success.[32]

Taking an American manufacturing job, often at piece rates, could drastically affect women and men who in Europe had considered themselves
self-employed. It hurled them into the unaccustomed status of proletarians, members of the working class. Some Jews had worked for wages in
Europe, but many had considered that a short-term expedient. Most Jews
arrived in America still picturing themselves as independent traders or
artisans, perhaps forced by temporary adversity into becoming employees.
But the American factory quickly destroyed many such illusions. Geared
to mass production, most shops laid little stress on the expert old-world
artisanship of highly skilled dressmakers and tailors who knew all the steps
needed to create a coat, dress, or pair of pants.

Manufacturers found economies of scale by breaking processes down
into simple steps carried out by people with lesser—and cheaper—skills.
A worker might spend all day, every day, attaching sleeves, stitching hems,
or sewing on buttons. Jobs that required expertise, such as cutting the fabric that became large numbers of identical garments, went to a relatively
small number of better-paid specialists, overwhelmingly men. In 1913 an
agreement arbitrated in New York known as the Protocol in the Dress and
Waist Industry defined cutting as a male trade paid at $27.50 a week for a
fully fledged worker and $21.00 for a top-grade trainee. Pressing, also lim-
ited to men, paid $23.00 a week. Both sexes could be ironers, but men
made $17.00 while women got only $13.00. Draping and sample making
were female specialties, paying $15.00 and $13.00 respectively. Cleaners
were young girls, earning as little as $6.00 a week to start.[33] That same year,
the U.S. Bureau of Labor Statistics found that 100 percent of New York's
dress and waist cutters were male, and 100 percent of the garment cleaners and finishers were female. Buttonholing, sleeve setting, skirtmaking,
hemming, tucking, marking, and many other jobs occupied people of both

sexes, however, putting men and women in direct competition for many jobs, and making them shop floor colleagues through long working days.

For some of the people who landed these American garment jobs, life as an interchangeable cog instead of an individual recognized for skill entailed a severe loss of status and self-respect. Zalman Yoffeh's father, a Torah scholar unable to find intellectual work, "drifted into the clothing shops [where] he was very unhappy," the son recalled. Eventually Yoffeh Sr. realized that he had no future in the needle trades. Next he tried his hand at peddling fruit, but with limited success. This left Zalman's mother, Chaye Itte, daughter of a prosperous merchant who had made her a "glorious match" back home in Yablonyi, unexpectedly struggling to feed and clothe a large brood in New York. "When [Chaye Itte's] grandfather [had gone] to Bialystok and got [her the] scion of a long line of rabbis and 'learners' [as her husband] the entire district celebrated," Zalman explained. "Such learning and piety mated to such beauty and wealth. A perfect combination."[34]

But the riches proved fleeting and the "golden land" harsh, and Chaye Itte "suffered severely. How could she be expected to realize that it was just because he did not work and could do no work, that my father had been considered such a good match originally? She simply knew that children were coming one after the other, and that it was hard to raise them." Divorce, which her brothers urged, lay equally beyond her ken.

Her husband, no matter what happened, was her husband, and to him and her children she must devote her life. So with our one dollar a day she fed and clothed an ever-growing family. She took in boarders. Sometimes this helped; at other times it added to the burden of living. Boarders were often out of work and penniless; how could you turn a hungry man out? She made all our clothes. She walked blocks to reach a place were meat was a penny cheaper, where bread was a half-cent less. She collected boxes and old wood to burn in the stove instead of costly coal. Her hands became hardened and the lines so begrimed that for years she never had perfectly clean hands. One by one she lost her teeth—there was no money for dentists—and her cheeks caved in. Yet we children always had clean and whole clothing. There was always bread and butter in the house, and wonder of wonders, there was usually a penny apiece for us to buy candy with. On a dollar and quarter we could have lived in luxury.[35]

Try though Chaye Itte might, she could only stretch her husband's mea-ger earnings so far. Like the great majority of new arrivals, she found her-self suddenly in a new and unfamiliar economy based almost exclusively on cash. Unlike most places in the Pale, lower Manhattan provided no space for a kitchen garden or milk cow or chicken coop. Nor were there neighbors or peasants willing to barter skills and services for daily necessi-ties, nor yards where families could build on an extra room or two to accommodate additional members. Here there were only the landlord, the electric company, the butcher, the grocer, all demanding cash, as one "green" housewife learned from her more established neighbors, for "the rent . . . for the light, for every potato, every grain of barley."[36]

But even if Chaye Itte had married a more practical man, one, perhaps, of her own commercial background, he probably would have found him-self hard-pressed to support his family all by himself. The major industry employing immigrant Jews was a highly erratic source of income. The gar-ment business ran in "seasons," which differed somewhat among different types of clothing. For most workers, slow periods and layoffs alternated with rush seasons. Only one in five immigrant husbands—as opposed to almost two in three of the native born—managed to earn enough to main-tain what contemporary economists considered a "normal standard of liv-ing" for a working-class family, according to 1907 figures. In that year, the housing, food, clothing, fuel, transportation, and other purchases suitable to a respectable working man's household cost $800, but the Russian Jewish men living in eight American cities earned on average only $463, according to the U.S. Immigration Commission. New Yorkers were slightly more affluent, making an average of $520, but Bostonians averaged only $378.[37]

The difference between a father's wages or profits and a family's expen-ditures came, as it had in Europe, from the labor of other relatives. In the early decades of the great migration, all immigrant sons and daughters old enough to work—which in those days meant from early adolescence on—were expected to contribute to the household exchequer. A family's need for a second, third, and even fourth income drastically curtailed the older children's chances to go to school, even though in America schools charged nothing and accepted everyone. In large, poor, newly arrived fam-ilies, youngsters who could land jobs generally took them, often within days or weeks of disembarking. Only their younger brothers and sisters would get the chance to sit in a classroom learning the accentless English and academic skills that could equip them for more prestigious white-collar jobs or sometimes even for college. Not until 1920 were children required to stay in school until age sixteen.

School Days

For children who could go to school, however, it changed their lives. Thirteen-year-old Mary (née Maryashe) Antin, a native of the Pale town of Polotsk, for example, entered the Boston public schools in 1904 speaking no English at all. Starting at the kindergarten level, she graduated grammar school four years later, "an illustration of what the American system of free education and the European immigrant could make of each other," according to an admirer.[38] That same year, an account of her family's passage to America that she had written appeared as a book, *From Plottzk to Boston.* With the earnings from her memoir, she enrolled in elite Girl's Latin School. Meanwhile, she came to the attention of such prominent Bostonians as Edward Everett Hale, a noted man of letters, and several wealthy Jewish philanthropists.

At twenty, and as a noted, educated American, she married Amadeus William Grabau, a Lutheran and a Harvard Ph.D. They moved to New York, where he taught geology at Columbia and she studied at two of the university's branches, Barnard and Teachers Colleges, and gave birth to a daughter. She never completed a degree, but her successful writing career continued in such prestigious outlets as the *Atlantic Monthly.* Her memoir of Americanization, *The Promised Land,* became a national best-seller and she a nationally known figure shortly after it appeared in 1912. This paean to the opportunities she found in her new country, this account of a shtetl girl's transformation into "an American among Americans . . . a daughter of Israel and a child of the universe," sold almost eighty-five thousand copies.[39]

Missing from the epic of her ascent, however, was the figure of her sister, Fetchke. Mary saw herself as one of the "certain class of aliens" who could build new lives in the "open workshop" that was America. "I only had to be worthy and it came to me . . . my friendships, my advantages and disadvantages, my gifts, my habits, my ambitions . . . were the materials of which I built my after life." Her success, she suggested, arose inevitably from the encounter between her talent and American opportunity. "Steadily as I worked to win America, America advanced to lie at my feet. . . . I was a princess waiting to be led to the throne."[40]

But no such royal summons came for Fetchke, who was called Frieda in the Boston sweatshop where she labored during Mary's school years.

While Mary raced through the elementary grades and their father, Israel, failed at business after business, Frieda uncomplainingly brought home her pay envelope so that the family could eat and the younger children study. The marriage her parents eventually arranged for her also failed, and she later spent some years running the Grabaus' home in New York. None of the brilliant chances that shone on Mary ever dawned for Frieda, or for the countless immigrant girls who went to work instead of to class.

The gulf separating the Antin sisters probably yawned more starkly than in most families. But for children of the immigrant generation, birth position in the family made the difference between a lifetime as a Yiddish-sounding, working-class wage earner or an accentless American with a chance at something better. Dignified careers as bookkeepers and secretaries were imaginable for girls able to finish high school. The professions of nursing and even schoolteaching beckoned those who managed to proceed to higher studies. The near certainty of manual labor loomed for those who could not. Economic conditions being what they were, by age sixteen, Jewish immigrant girls typically worked, most often in factories. In 1911 the Immigration Commission found that 89 percent of Boston's unmarried Jewish females over sixteen held jobs, as did 74 percent of New York's. Another fifth of the New York young women it described as being "at home," perhaps helping with family businesses or younger children. Six percent were students.[41]

American society, however, did not generally appreciate the crucial role of young women's wages in families' economic survival. The conventional wisdom saw them as earning "pin money" until marriage. "Many people . . . secretly believe that women come into industry in a casual way; that they are not earnest about it; that their chief desire is to obtain through it extra spending money; and that men are their natural protectors," stated Elizabeth Dutcher of the Women's Trade Union League, an association of middle- and upper-class women supporting the labor movement. But an examination of the finances of young Jewish and Italian working women produced "a shock and . . . a revelation," Dutcher went on. Far from buying trifles, their wages "were supporting old fathers and mothers, both in this country and abroad; mothering and supporting younger brothers and sisters, sending brothers to high school, to art school, to dental college, to engineering courses."[42]

"All week long I wouldn't see the daylight," recalled Clara Lemlich Shavelson of her eleven-hour workdays as a teenage factory girl. "Once, when things were slow, they let us out in the middle of the day." That pedestrians filled the streets during working hours surprised a youngster who spent her daylight hours peering at pieces of cloth in a sunless workshop, not out the window at passersby. "'What,' I said, 'are all the people on strike?' I had never realized that there were so many out during the daytime."[43]

Working Women

Long, arduous sweatshop days went hand in hand with thoughts of strikes, not only for young Clara but for hundreds of thousands of other Jewish working women. Though forced to take hard jobs that often paid little in either wages or respect, few Jewish working girls believed they deserved such treatment. Rather, most saw themselves as worthy, active individuals whose earning power gave them adult roles in their families and control over their own lives.[44] Nearly all who lived at home turned their pay envelopes over to their mothers, often keeping back just enough to pay for transportation and sundries. Others waited to be given an allowance for their daily expenses. Prominent labor movement figure Rose Schneiderman first felt adult freedom when she began pocketing one of the six dollars she earned each week as a cap maker before handing the rest over to her mother.

Jewish working girls knew that their contributions to their households were real and recognized, but their strong sense of self did not arise solely from helping bear the burden of financial support. Many families helped foster it by treating young workers as young adults. A girl named Anna Kahan, for example, had to choose between a hat making job she loved and an offer from a relative's "dirty little shop" that would pay $10 more each week. With her father too sick to work, the family's need for the higher wage was dire. The old job was "a pleasure," Anna remembered. At the new one, "I knew I'd have a harder time." Financially she had no real choice, but her parents still strove to assure her that emotionally she did. "You have to decide," her mother insisted, declining to force the decision.[45] So when Anna changed jobs, she acted as an adult assuming her family responsibilities, not as a child obeying her elders. Young Jewish working girls showed "an unusual development of independence," noted an American writer at the turn of the century.[46]

The immigrants, however, had not sold their belongings, left their relations, and come halfway round the world merely to continue their traditions. Crossing the ocean meant casting one's lot with the New World, and most wanted, often intensely, to become up-to-date. Being a modern American meant, above all, looking and sounding American. For many a female newcomer, the first act in the new land was replacing the home-made frocks and kerchiefs worn across the Atlantic with store-bought shirtwaists, suits, and wide-brimmed hats selected with the advice of the relatives who provided the first American bed. A studio photograph in the new attire marked many a passage from emigrant to immigrant. The trans-formation of a typical daughter of the Pale into a Semitic-featured Gibson Girl was a striking change. But for a bearded, side-locked, soft-hatted Jew to become a clean-shaven, stiff-collared, Derby-topped man-about-Manhattan could be shocking. "I didn't recognize him," one former green-horn recalls of the apparently unknown American gent who came in place of the uncle she expected to claim her at the immigration station. "And he comes to the gate, and they open the gate and call his name and mine, and I wouldn't go" until convinced that this dapper stranger was indeed her own uncle in New World dress.[47]

Acquiring English, another crucial mark of Americanness, took more effort, but many people quickly gained some minimal mastery, even though that often entailed learning an entirely new alphabet, different from both the Hebrew letters used for Yiddish and the Cyrillic ones used for Russian. Knowledge of the language serves as a particularly sensitive gauge of commitment to a country, and one showing that Jews were vastly more committed to America than they had ever been to Russia. Under the czars many never learned usable Russian. By 1914, however, a random sample of New Yorkers who read Yiddish newspapers found that almost two-thirds regularly read English ones as well.[48] Young people, of course, enjoyed a real advantage over their elders in picking up American speech, which gave them confidence, enhanced their standing in their families, and encouraged them to look to their peers rather than their parents for guid-ance on living in this new land. One girl who preceded her parents to America "became a regular Yankee and forgot how to talk Yiddish" in the few years until the rest of the family arrived, her mother later complained. "She says it is not nice to talk Yiddish and that I am a greenhorn."[49]

Fortunately for many would-be new Americans, factories could serve as training schools. Young workers could meet Jewish, Italian, Polish, German, and other immigrants, some of whom spoke English, some of whom had even spent time in American public schools or evening classes, and most of whom knew lots about American life. Occasionally a worker could even meet native-born Americans. Stitching shirtwaists in Boston in

1912, the girls at adjoining machines liked "to sing to each other," a former garment maker recalled. "We used to sing Russian songs and Yiddish songs and the American songs. I liked very much the American songs, the 1912 songs. I loved it there and I learned there." And especially important, "They used to teach me English."[50]

After work, informal education continued along Houston, Grand, Stanton, or Delancey Streets or comparable thoroughfares in other cities, where young working women and men enjoyed "the glare of lights and the blare of music."[51] With a little money in their pockets and the American notion of easy sociability between the sexes in mind, Jewish young people heard the latest songs, did the newest dance steps, saw the most popular movies, and generally immersed themselves as deeply in American popular culture as their time and their English would allow. (Had she known these independent-minded young women of her former religion, Phila Franks DeLancey probably would have approved of their spirit and of the fact that they found fun and adventure along the street bearing her husband's family name.) In 1911 a live theater, eight movie houses, two recreation centers, nine dance halls and dancing academies, ten pool halls, seventy-three soda shops and stands, and one hundred restaurants filled the one-third of a square mile of New York bounded by Suffolk, East Houston, Chrystie, and Grand Streets.[52]

More conventional educational opportunities enticed women with the energy and curiosity to study after work. Settlement houses, labor unions, public school systems, and other groups offered night school classes at the elementary, high school, and even more advanced levels. Public lectures provided intellectual stimulation without the commitment of a formal course. Well before radio brought information and enlightenment into people's homes, thousands of people went out to public lectures in the evening. In New York in 1904, reported the *Forward*, the city's leading Yiddish daily, "during the winter there are several hundred lectures. Big societies have series of lectures; the tiny ones have single, irregular ones. . . . There are thousands and thousands of Jews coming to be educated. . . . They come to hear about socialism on East Broadway, about literature on Forsythe Street, about a play in Harlem, and even a lecture in Russian on Grand Street. Although they hardly know the language, it doesn't matter. They sit and sweat and listen."[53] A million spectators sat through the five thousand adult free lectures sponsored by the People's University of New York State during the 1903–1904 season alone. The People's Institute of Cooper Union presented its own wide array of well-attended talks, as did Workman's Circle, Socialist and Zionist associations, and many other groups.

Among those eagerly absorbing insights into German literature, Hindu society, the dialectic of Hegel, correct breathing, electricity, ancient Greece, and always, and above all, "How to Be an American," a striking number were Jewish women. They accounted for fully 70 percent of Philadelphia's night school students in the 1920s.[54] At least two different studies by Gentile sociologists remarked on this disproportionate representation, as compared with women of other nationalities. Jewish women felt they had every right to enjoy the freedom of their neighborhood streets, a portion of their own earnings, and their people's traditional thirst for knowledge. "I go to lectures, and I like to listen to the speaker," said a New York shirtwaist worker who had no formal schooling when she came alone from her native Galician town at nineteen. In her new home, through her own informal efforts, she became, in her friends' eyes at least, "an educated woman." Her method was simple: "I listen, and I learn."[55]

The Union Makes Us Strong

Beyond individual workers' efforts to improve their lot by learning, many Jews of both sexes felt a need to raise the condition of workers in general through structural changes in the terms of their labor. Jewish women and men already had a good deal of labor union experience in the East European union movement. Young, single women made up a third of the membership of the Bund, the major Jewish workers organization in the Pale.[56] But the overwhelmingly male American labor movement, with its emphasis on protecting skilled workers from competition rather than all workers from exploitation, did not initially welcome women.

Jewish factory girls, many in their early teens, soon played a major role in changing those attitudes. Whether because of Judaism's traditional emphasis on social justice and community or East Europe's Socialist labor movement, Jewish workers tended to understand the hardships they faced as examples of class conflict rather than as personal problems, as injustices afflicting the great mass of working people rather than as misfortunes affecting particular individuals. Low pay, long hours, unsafe and uncomfortable workplaces, discrimination, harassment, arbitrary treatment, and general loss of control over their lives, they believed, reflected immigrant workers' lack of bargaining power, not a lack of personal worth. Workers could most effectively better their lives, this analysis went, by organizing

for concerted action, not by individually winning the boss's favor or finding a better job.

Jewish women's exceptionally high degree of class consciousness struck
the Gentile author Mary Van Kleeck during the research for her 1910
study, *Artificial Flower Makers.* For Jewish women workers, raising the
condition of the working class fit easily into their roles as females and family members. The whole purpose for spending their days in crowded, dirty
sweatshops, after all; the whole reason for straining their eyes and bending
their backs over buttonholes or flower petals or tobacco leaves; indeed, the
whole need for bringing home a wage packet in the first place, was to fulfill a Jewish woman's inherent and lifelong obligation to ensure her family's
well-being. That Jewish women should have to face exploitation and
degradation while carrying out this duty—and especially at the hands of
fellow Jews—violated their sense of social justice and communal responsibility to the needy. The cause of the immigrant worker was thus the cause
of the immigrant family, and that was every woman's most sacred concern.

What's more, the hardships that Jewish immigrants endured in the
sweatshops violated another of their basic beliefs: the promise of liberty
that had drawn them to America. Arriving Eastern Europeans "were
struck by the atmosphere of freedom here. But then they went into the
sweatshop," observed labor leader Fannia Cohn, herself a former sleeve-
maker. "The sweatshop was not only a physical condition, but moral and
anti-spiritual. They found there was no Bill of Rights off the street, in the
shop. They were thrown out if they mentioned the Bill of Rights in the
shop."[57] For some newcomers to the Land of the Free, labor activism and
democratic freedom seemed one and the same thing. In his book *Children
of the Poor,* Jacob Riis, the pioneering journalist who helped awaken
America to the shocking truth of "how the other half lives," described "a
little working-girl from an Essex Street sweater's shop attending an
American history class." The teacher asked, "'When the Americans could
no longer put up with the abuse of the English who governed the colonies,
what occurred then?' 'A Strike!' responded the girl promptly. She had
found it here on coming and evidently thought it a national institution
upon which the whole scheme of government was founded."[58]

Jewish working men, of course, shared the class consciousness of their
laboring daughters and sisters, as well as their desire for social justice (and
perhaps also their confusion about American history). Early on men began
to organize, creating such labor groups as the United Hebrew Trades (a
socially conscious umbrella organization) and the International Ladies

Garment Workers Union (a union of people who made women's clothing). Initially, perhaps following the American approach, Jewish unionists seldom encouraged female membership. During a 1905 walkout, for example, women did not qualify for the strike benefits that the men received, possibly on the American assumption that they were not "really" supporting families as male breadwinners did.

But young factory girls put the lie to such notions. Fifteen-year-old Dorothy Jacobs, a native of Latvia who had already spent two years as a $3-a-week Baltimore buttonhole maker, organized the women of her men's coat shop into Local 170 of the United Garment Workers of America. In Chicago, another fifteen-year-old, newly arrived from Lithuania and named Bessie (née Bas Sheva) Abramowitz, tried to organize the shop where she earned the same scanty wage sewing buttons sixty hours a week. Fired as an agitator and blacklisted, she needed an alias to get work at Hart, Shaffner, and Marx. But when the giant firm cut a quarter of a cent from the four-penny piece rate it paid its button sewers, Bessie, now twenty, led fifteen of her coworkers in a walkout. At first the company's eight-thousand-strong workforce, including a twenty-four-year-old Lithuanian cutter named Sidney Hillman, mostly laughed at the band of upstarts and its leader.

But Bessie persisted. Within a month most of Hart, Shaffner, including Sidney, was on strike in sympathy, as were thousands working for other manufacturers around town. Sidney became deeply involved in the strike's leadership and in a romance with Bessie. A landmark agreement ended the walkout, but the courtship continued, although the need to send money to relatives in Europe prevented them from considering marriage. For several years they held jobs with separate unions, but another major strike made them collaborators once more. The year afterward, as the garment workers' brigade marched in Chicago's 1916 May Day parade, Bessie and Sidney led the way arm in arm—in those days tantamount to announcing their engagement. They married two days later.

Once a wife, Bessie withdrew from full-time employment. She remained active through volunteer labor work, serving the Amalgamated Clothing Workers of America, a union formed by dissidents from the more conservative United Garment Workers, both as a member of committees and boards and as an unpaid organizer in the Midwest and Upstate New York. She also bore two daughters. Sidney, meanwhile, rose to national prominence in the labor movement. Bessie returned to paid employment thirty years after her marriage, as a widow with a scanty inheritance from a husband who never lived any more lavishly than the union cutters he represented. A well-known activist in her own right, she accepted the full-time post of Amalgamated's vice president for education and continued her union work for her twenty-six remaining years. But she never forgot who was the real labor pioneer in the family. "I was Bessie Abramowitz," she pointed out, "before he was Sidney Hillman."[59]

Young women in Chicago, Baltimore, and other cities led many dramatic labor actions, but it was in New York, center of the nation's garment trade and Jewish immigrant life, that Jewish factory girls made their greatest impact. When twenty-one-year old, Polish-born Rose Schneiderman brought her shop into the United Cloth Hat and Cap Makers Union, for example, she was already a veteran of eight years as a worker. Standing well under five feet tall and crowned with flame-red hair, she did not initially impress her union's male leadership as a potentially gifted organizer. But her success in signing up members and delivering fiery speeches—in an era when political oratory ranked as a popular form of free entertainment—soon won her the first national office ever held by a woman in any U.S. labor union.

She next won office in the New York Woman's Trade Union League, whose prosperous, reform-minded members supported the labor movement. Irene Lewisohn, a liberal uptown lady from a wealthy Jewish banking and industrial family, so admired Rose that she offered to support her while she completed her long-interrupted education. Rose declined, mindful of the countless workers without rich benefactors. Irene next proposed paying Rose to serve as chief labor organizer for NYWTUL, an offer she swiftly accepted. By 1908 she was working to unionize the chaotic Lower Manhattan garment industry.

She had many allies. Nineteen-year-old Clara Lemlich, for example, had no sooner arrived from her native Ukraine and found a job making "white goods" (shirtwaists, underwear, nightgowns, and the like) than she began organizing the shop. The men who held the great majority of better-paid skilled garment jobs (mostly in shops making tailored clothing rather than white goods) were still trying to stem the growing influx of young, less-skilled women into the established unions. But Clara saw the potential for female power. The shirtwaist workforce was 80 percent female, 70 percent aged sixteen to twenty-five, and 65 percent Jewish.[60] The immigrant girls, she believed, had the numbers and the spirit to make effective action possible. In 1906, a scant year in America, Clara first led her coworkers out on strike. Next, she and eleven other upstarts—five women and six men—

founded a small white goods workers' group called Local 25 and managed to talk their way into the ILGWU.

Factory owners, meanwhile, tried to resist the scattered strikes hitting the industry. The Jewish-owned Triangle Waist Company, for example, one of the nation's largest shirtwaist producers, decided to undercut the unions' appeal by starting its own Triangle Benevolent Association, a workers group beholden to management and closed to union supporters. As Jews prepared for the High Holidays of 1909, the Association voted grants of $10 each to the needy breadwinners among its members. But Triangle's bosses balked, insisting the Association make loans, not gifts. Angry Association members consulted with United Hebrew Trades. The company retaliated by laying off suspected dissidents, claiming to lack work for them even while advertising job openings. Local 25, with six Jewish women on its fifteen-member executive board, accused Triangle of perpetrating a lockout. On September 27 it called a strike and threw up picket lines. Workers at the Leiserson factory, where Clara Lemlich worked, joined the walkout.

As fruitless picketing stretched into mid-October, the strikers' spirits, energy, and finances began to flag. Beaten by thugs working for Leiserson, taunted by prostitutes hired by Triangle, harassed by police, and increasingly desperate for their pay envelopes, the girls on the lines found it harder and harder to keep going. Biased judges slapped them with fines and even terms in the workhouse. "You are striking against God and Nature," one jurist proclaimed.[61] Scrutiny by uptown supporters might help curb abuses, Local 25's strategists reasoned, and welcomed ladies from NYWTUL to join them on the picket line. The police arrested NYWTUL president Mary Dreier after an argument with a would-be strike breaker, and the city's attention finally focused on the sidewalk drama playing out on Greene Street.

The Yiddish press and many organizations supported the strike, but by early November it was near collapse. Poverty and the fear of violence or arrest drove many workers back to their machines. The companies had meanwhile suffered very little, maintaining their cash flows by contracting with small shops to do their work. With $4 left in the Local 25 strike fund and imminent defeat looming, the hundred-member union and its allies in Hebrew Trades decided on a drastic step: they would ask all of New York's thirty thousand shirtwaist makers to declare a general strike in solidarity. They announced a mass meeting where the workers could decide.[62]

ILGWU officialdom demurred, but Local 25 forced the issue by making flyers inviting workers to the Cooper Union meeting hall on November 22.

That evening many more waist makers than the large space could hold converged to hear Mary Dreier, United Hebrew Trades head Bernard Weinstein, and various other dignitaries declaim at length on the need for caution despite the rightness of the strikers' cause. Two hours into these orations, a frustrated Clara Lemlich mounted the stage and asked to speak. Some objected to hearing the slip of a twenty-three-year-old, who appeared much younger and had a reputation as a hothead. The chair nonetheless recognized her.

"I am a poor working girl," she began in a Yiddish statement that became an instant legend, "one of those on strike against intolerable conditions. I am tired of listening to speakers who talk in general terms. What we are here for is to decide whether we shall or shall not strike. I offer a resolution that a general strike be declared—now."[63]

In seconds the great crowd, overwhelmingly young and Jewish and heavily female, "was on its feet," recounted the *New York World*, "everyone shouting an emphatic affirmative, waving hats, canes, handkerchiefs, anything that came handy. For five minutes perhaps the tumult continued; then the chairman asked for a seconder of the resolution. Again the big audience leaped to its feet, everyone seconding."[64] Then the chairman cried, "Do you mean faith? Will you take the Jewish oath?" Thousands of hands went up, thousands of voices declared traditional words: "If I turn traitor to the cause I now pledge, may this hand wither from the arm I now raise."[65]

The phenomenon known as the Uprising of the 20,000 began the next morning. By nightfall of November 23, fully that many garment workers— 90 percent of them Jewish, 70 percent of them women—were picketing factories throughout the Lower East Side. The district "was a seething mass of excited women, girls and men," reported the New York *Call.* Total participation soon rose even higher, perhaps to thirty thousand. The first days were a thrilling chaos, filled with meetings, rallies, crowds, confusion. "All over the East Side a sea of excited faces, a mass of gesticulating women and men, blocked the streets," the excited article went on. Not only low-paid girls but skilled men walked the lines, effectively shutting down the industry. Some smaller employers quickly settled with their workers in hopes of getting a jump on bigger competitors still on strike. "The vast crowds" broke "into storms of applause as the word that another boss had settled with the strikers was passed along."[66]

At shops that wouldn't settle, the customary hired thugs had plenty of work. The police did too, arresting as many as 723 strikers in a single month. Clara Lemlich alone underwent seventeen arrests and suffered six broken ribs. The courts, as usual, hit the strikers, but not the owners, with fines eventually totaling more than $5,000, as well as heavy bail requirements averaging $2,500 a month. One court sentenced a ten-year-old girl to the workhouse after a trial devoid of testimony. In all, the strike cost the colossal sum (colossal to the strikers, at least) of $100,000. Cash to support it came in tiny sums from East Siders and bigger wads from socialites, including $1,000 collected by Wellesley College students.[67] Uptown sympathizers, led by the WTUL, held fund-raisers, marched on the picket lines, and rallied at Carnegie Hall, City Hall, and the Hippodrome to highlight the struggle and its ties to the larger national drive for women's rights. "It is no mere accident that in this fight the striking Jewish and Italian girls, the poorest of the poor, have the sympathy and active support of the suffrage workers of all classes," observed labor lawyer Morris Hillquit. "There is a certain common bond between women fighting for industrial rights and women fighting for social justice."[68]

Through the bitter winter of 1910, thousands of hungry, ill-clad factory girls stood in the cold handing out leaflets, trudged the icy sidewalks with their signs, and exhorted passersby. Young strikers who had barely enough money to feed themselves spent their days collecting funds, getting strike benefits to those in greatest need, and organizing rallies and meetings. Clara Lemlich, Rose Schneiderman, and other immigrants scarcely out of their teens emerged as strategists, orators, parliamentarians, and public relations operatives. Some called on experience as political radicals in Europe, but many more got their first feeling for politics in the uprising.

The Association of Waist and Dress Manufacturers, however, proved as resolute as the unions. For eleven weeks they adamantly refused to consider the closed shop (the requirement that all those working at a company belong to the union), a demand the workers believed nonnegotiable. Unless owners were required to allow unions, the workers feared, no agreement could be enforced. But even without winning on this point, the negotiations produced notable advances—which highlight the workers' dire situation before the strike. Three hundred thirty-nine of the 353 AWDM member companies eventually settled with the union, agreeing to cut the work week to fifty-two hours, pay overtime for hours worked above that total, provide four annual paid holidays, end punishment for supporting unions, furnish materials and tools to workers at no cost, divide available work equitably during slow periods, and determine pay scales through negotiations rather than by fiat. The union also made signal gains. By mid-February, ten thousand shirtwaist makers, 85 percent of the industry's entire New York labor force, belonged to Local 25.[69] But finally, as the winter wore on, the thousand or so pickets still on the street could endure no longer. On February 15, the epic uprising came to an end. As if from exhaustion, the strike simply petered out. Triangle's workers went back with no agreement.

The revolt, however, overturned a great deal more than some employers' most exploitative practices. Countless young women workers discovered that they could, to an extent that astonished many, fashion their own fate. Though "economic conditions force us to fight our battle side by side with men," shirtwaist maker and Local 25 member Mollie Schepps would later proclaim, women workers "cannot play the simple idiot and worship men as heroes. . . . We refuse to play the silent partner any more."[70] Until 1909 women had negligible influence in the American labor movement. A little over a decade later, some 169,000 women, or 46 percent of the industry's females, belonged to unions, compared with only 10.2 percent of the women doing other kinds of manufacturing. The garment trades alone accounted for 42 percent of the nation's female union members.[71]

The immigrant community at large also realized the strength and bravery of "unzere vunderbare farbrente maeydlekh" (our wonderful fervent girls).[72] Male unionists acknowledged that women possessed both the courage "to stand together in the struggle to protect their common interests as wage-earners" and the capacity "as strikers to suffer, to do, and to dare in support of their rights," as Samuel Gompers told the convention of the American Federation of Labor.[73] "It was mainly women who did the picketing, who were arrested and fined, who ran the risk of assault, who suffered ill-treatment from the police and the courts," wrote the ILGWU official historian, Louis Levine. "In fact, though the principal union officials were men and the direction of the strike was in the hands of men, the women played a preponderant part in carrying it through." And they did more than march and picket. Hundreds upon hundreds of women whose names we do not know stepped forward to carry the message of the strike to anyone who would listen. "Into the foreground of this great moving picture comes the figure of one girl after another, as their services are needed," Levine recorded. "With extraordinary simplicity and eloquence, she will tell any kind of audience, without any false shame, and without self-glorification, the conditions of her work, her wages, and the pinching poverty of her home and the homes of her comrades. Then she withdraws into the background to undertake quietly the danger and humiliation of picket duty or to become a nameless sandwich [sign]-girl selling papers in the street, no longer the center of interested attention, but the butt of the most unspeakable abuse."[74]

Americans far beyond the Lower East Side cheered the strike and the strikers, and they began to understand something of what poor working women had to endure. New York *Sun* reporter McAlister Coleman, for example, witnessed a "dozen tough-looking customers, for whom the union label of 'gorillas' seemed well chosen," attack a double line of marching girls who sang "Italian and Russian working-class songs as they paced . . . before [a] factory door." The "thugs rushed the line," knocking down pickets to let a "group of frightened scabs" into the plant. A bevy of "fancy ladies from the Allen Street red light district" stood by, cheering on the attackers. The resulting "confused melee of scratching, screaming girls and fist-swinging men" ended only when "a patrol wagon arrived." As they "thugs ran off," the police arrested several "badly beaten girls." The remainder retreated to "the union hall, a few blocks away," where those whose families included small children each received "one bottle of milk and a loaf of bread." Shamefacedly, and "for the first time in my comfortably sheltered, upper West Side life," Coleman recognized "real hunger on the faces of my fellow Americans in the richest city in the world."[75]

Calamity

Even as newly invigorated unions called strikes in garment plants across the country, some companies, notably Triangle, were recalcitrant. Firing most of its union employees, it resumed business as usual in its cramped, littered lofts on the eighth, ninth, and tenth floors of the Asch Building, a reputedly fireproof structure at the corner of Washington Place and Greene Street, near Washington Square. Neither official citations for fire code violations nor warnings from insurance company inspector P. J. McKeon, a Columbia University instructor in fire prevention, convinced Triangle's Jewish owners, Isaac Harris and Max Blanck, that overcrowding, illegally locked fire doors, and a complete lack of fire drills posed any serious risks. McKeon suggested an expert to advise on correcting the deficiencies and even contacted the specialist, who sent Triangle a letter offering his consulting services. No answer came from Harris or Blanck.

Close to a thousand workers, six out of seven of them young Jewish and Italian women, jammed Triangle's shop floors during its busy seasons. About half that number were bent over their work at 4:40 on Saturday, March 25, 1911, several hours after the other manufacturers in the building had closed for the day. City authorities would later surmise that someone must have accidentally dropped a lighted match into a bin full of cloth. As flames suddenly shot up and smoke filled the congested rooms, Harris and Blanck left their offices and made for safety across the building's roof. Some of those working on the tenth floor fled by the same route and were rescued by New York University students atop an adjacent building. Some employees on the eighth floor managed to race down a flight of stairs or ride a freight elevator to street level before smoke made those routes impassable.

But for the workers on the ninth and for many on the other floors, there was no escape. To prevent unauthorized breaks by employees and visits by union organizers, Harris and Blanck kept stairway doors illegally locked, and the door to the single fire escape had rusted shut. Desperate hands finally forced it open, but so many of the trapped clambered through that the fire escape collapsed. Others tried jumping for their lives. The firemen gathering below stood by helplessly, equipped with ladders too short to reach the windowsills where doomed women and men anxiously stood.

One chance passerby "looked up at the burning building, [and] saw girl after girl appear at the reddened windows, pause for a terrified moment, and then leap to the pavement below, to land as a mangled, bloody pulp."[76] Many more never left the blazing lofts, perishing there of smoke or burns. It was "all over in half an hour," the *New York Times* reported, despite the efforts of the four fire companies that raced to the scene. One hundred forty-six workers died, "mostly girls from 16 to 23 years of age . . . Most . . . could barely speak English. . . . Almost all were the main support of their families," the *Times* went on.[77] No one ever reliably totaled the injured. As the bodies hurtled toward the pavement, frantic crowds struggled against police lines in the streets below. "It's the worst thing I ever saw," one veteran policeman, a "seasoned witness of death," mournfully told a *Times* reporter.[78]

It was, in fact, among the worst industrial disasters that New York or the nation had ever witnessed. Many agreed with witnesses on the sidewalk who called the dead "not so much victims of a holocaust of flame as . . . victims of stupid greed and criminal exploitation." Adding to public outrage, the building did, as advertised, prove to be fireproof. Afterward it showed "hardly any signs of the disaster," the *Times* noted. "The walls are as good as ever; so are the floors."[79] The only damage was to furnishings and occupants.

When people recalled that Triangle had held out against the uprising, many wondered with Morris Hillquit "if the magistrates who sent to jail the girls who did picket duty in front of the Triangle shop realized . . . that some of the responsibility may be theirs. Had the strike been successful, these girls might have been alive today and the citizenry of New York would have less of a burden upon its conscience."[80] William Shepherd, covering the disaster for United Press, "looked upon the heaps of dead bodies and . . . remembered these girls were the shirtwaist makers. I remembered their great strike of last year in which the same girls had demanded more sanitary conditions and more safety precautions in the shops. These dead bodies were the answers."[81]

The immigrant community reeled in grief and shock, many Jews comparing the toll to the largest and deadliest of pogroms. The news raced to *shtetlach* across Eastern Europe and to villages throughout southern Italy. In a paroxysm of guilt and horror, better-off, progressive New Yorkers held meetings and organized committees to collect funds for the victims' families and to demand reform and retribution. On May 12, Anne Morgan, of the family that ruled New York's social and financial worlds, rented the Metropolitan Opera House for a standing-room-only protest called by WTUL. But working-class fury was not to be so easily assuaged. After an array of luminaries had detailed their distress and sorrow as well as their proposals for safer factories, Rose Schneiderman took the stage, her voice choked with tears.

"I would be a traitor to those poor burned bodies, if I came here to talk of good fellowship," she cried out to the packed audience of well-meaning labor supporters and sympathizers. The working poor had "tried you good people of the public and . . . found you wanting. The old Inquisition had its rack and its thumbscrews and its instruments of torture with iron teeth." But in the present day, "the iron teeth are our necessities, the thumbscrews the high-powered and swift machinery close to which we must work, and the rack here is the fireproof structures that will destroy us the minute they catch fire."[82]

The publicized blaze was "not the first time girls have been burned alive in this city," she went on. Each week brought "the untimely death of one of my sister workers. Every year thousands are maimed. The life of men and women is so cheap and property is so sacred. There are so many of us for one job it matters little a hundred-forty three [sic] of us are burned to death." The good citizens may donate "a couple of dollars for the sorrowing mothers and daughters and sisters as a charity gift," but whenever the working poor strike against "unbearable" conditions, "the hand of the law is allowed to press heavily upon us. . . . Too much blood has been spilled" to talk of fellowship, the "Red Rose of Anarchy" railed at the assembled prosperous progressives. "I know from my experience it us up to the working people to save themselves. The only way . . . is by a strong working-class movement." [83]

Many immigrant Jews agreed. On April 5, as the last seven unidentified victims were buried, half a million people joined in a march of mourning and protest organized by Local 25. The trauma inspired some marchers to devote all their energies to the union movement. One garment worker living near the Asch Building, Fannia Cohn, witnessed the carnage and later became the first female member of the ILGWU executive board and a lifelong labor activist. "It was the Triangle fire that decided my life's course," she remembered. [84]

Most immigrants, of course, did not choose to devote their lives solely to the labor movement, but support for working people's rights to organize and strike was broad and deep in the Jewish community, as it was for concrete efforts to aid those who exercised their rights. When unions called walkouts, individuals donated to strike funds. Storekeepers extended strikers credit. Family members joined in strike actions. During one 1911 Cleveland walkout, "the wives of [cloakmakers] marched in a body in the parade with their children," a pleased union official noted. "Two wagon loads of children" also participated, "carrying banners which read, 'Our Fathers and Mothers Are Striking to Give Us a Better Education.'"[85] In Chicago, worker's wives "struggled in [behalf of] the union" even if they did not belong to it themselves.[86] The broader society also took to heart at least one lesson of the fire. Safety regulations in factories were tightened and governmental bodies established to suggest and enforce improvements.

Workplace Perils

In a fundamental sense, though, Rose Schneiderman was right. All the uptown goodwill and solidarity did not change the basic conditions of immigrant workers' lives. Harris and Blanck stood trial but were acquitted, and they blamed anti-Semitism for the ignominy they suffered. Their fire insurance made good their losses. Garment factories may have been equipped with more accessible fire escapes and less cluttered passageways, but garment workers still lived with danger and exploitation. And women were subject to indignities over and above the woes endured by all who earned their bread at a sewing machine or in a cutting room. The unions did not recognize gender issues as distinct from class issues, so discrimination against women in job opportunities and pay, as well as sexual harassment by male coworkers and supervisors, was rampant.

Male coworkers' dirty jokes and vulgar language so rattled Anna Kahn, for example, that "I got headaches. I rushed myself and I stuck my fingers. Three of my fingers got infected." An owner's wife, jealous of her husband's attraction to employee Elizabeth Herskowitz, insisted she be fired. Gussie Agines's boss "tried to hug me, and I was so ashamed I didn't know what to say or do. No man had ever kissed me except my father." Rose Cohen endured pinches and poking at various jobs, despite having mastered, as her very first phrase in her new tongue, "Keep your hands off please." Even so, she lost one job when she declined to cuddle with the boss and quit another when the men's talk became intolerably crude.[87]

At times the abuse turned violent. When Pearl Adler's prosperous parents sent the eldest of their nine children from their small Pale town of Yanow to attend school in Massachusetts, they had no idea that an aggressive foreman would determine her life's course. When World War I prevented her parent's checks from reaching her, Pearl had to leave school and move in with cousins in Brooklyn, Lena and Yossell Rosen, who helped her find a garment job. Three years later, she lost her heart to a good-looking, flirtatious foreman. Against friends' advice, she accepted his invitation to Coney Island. Instead of squiring her to the Boardwalk, he lured her to a deserted cottage, knocked her out, and raped her.

Back at Lena's the next morning, Pearl invented a tale about taking a fall that left her too bruised to go to work. Eventually, though, she had no choice, though the man now ignored her. When she discovered she was pregnant a month later, she insisted that this "dangerous reptile," marry her, but he refused. A friend located an abortionist willing to take the little money that Pearl had, $35 saved for a fur cape. After hearing her story, Dr. Glick insisted she keep $10 of her nest egg. Lena, however, proved less sympathetic. No girl lodging in her respectable home would stay out all night, she announced. Pearl "wrapped my clothing in a newspaper and went." On the way to the subway, the bundle came apart, showering her shirtwaists and stockings all over the platform. Back in Yanow "I'd had a good stout potato sack . . . to carry my possessions," Pearl thought with a bitter laugh. "So far, I had certainly racked up a row of goose eggs in the Golden Land. I had failed in my quest for . . . education . . . I had lost my virginity, my reputation and my job. All I had gotten was older."[88]

Now a fallen woman, she left Brooklyn for Manhattan, where she returned to garment work but never to respectability. She shared lodgings with another young woman and soon began the career that would bring her national notoriety as Polly Adler, a leading madam in New York's expensive demimonde.

In her new trade, as in the factory, Polly again found herself among Jewish working girls. Women of the night were a conspicuous presence on the Jewish Lower East Side, as in poor districts everywhere. "Stay away from Allen, Chrystie, and Forsyth Streets when walking your wife, daughter, or fiancee," the *Forward* advised its respectable readership, lest they see the "official flesh trade in the Jewish quarter. In the windows you can see flesh instead of shoes."[89] Indeed, prostitutes brazenly displayed their wares on the streets they shared with upright passersby. "On sunshiny days the whores sat on chairs along the sidewalks," remembered one son of the Lower East Side. "They sprawled indolently, their legs taking up half the pavement. People stumbled over a gauntlet of whores' meaty legs."[90]

Demand for Jewish tarts extended far beyond the boundaries of the immigrant quarters. To San Francisco's Gentile johns, "a redheaded Jew girl was supposed to be pure fire and smoke," recounted former Bay Area procuress Nell Kimbrell. That city's "big Jewish madam," Idoform Kate, had in each of her twenty or so houses "a genuine Jewish redhead [who] swore [that] the hair was natural and [that] each girl [was] a pious Jewess saving to bring a husband, mother and father to the U.S.A."[91] Prostitution did in fact provide the funds that twenty-eight-year-old Lena Meyers dutifully sent to her parents back in Cracow. Sending thanks for the money, her mother asked, "Lena. Why don't you get married? Do you want to be an old maid?"[92] Not long after, Lena prevented that eventuality by drinking carbolic acid. The Mazet Committee, an investigative group appointed by the New York legislature in 1899, found a number of other young Jewish prostitutes (among other nationalities) who also died by their own hand.

Like Lena and Polly, the immigrants who found their way into this life usually lacked close family in America. Sometimes these unprotected girls fell prey to organized Jewish racketeers who befriended women traveling alone from Europe or struggling on their own in America. Pimps and white slavers abducted some victims and "attracted [others] by promises of honest jobs and so . . . lured [them] into the trade," Kimbrell reported.[93] But other young women willingly took up a line of work that they viewed as less onerous than ceaseless stitching in a sweat shop. Their heartbroken parents often performed the rites of shivah, the traditional mourning for a death in the family. Having tasted "the easy life that immoral living brings," for example, Maimie Pinzer found herself not "moral enough to see where drudgery is better than a life of easy vice."[94] Polly Adler gradually realized that providing a love nest for a gangster she met through her roommate and procuring women for his friends afforded a much better income than any garment job. She resolved to go straight after her first arrest in 1922 but failed in a legitimate lingerie business and returned to a surer and more lucrative form of selling.

"Most of the Jew girls were snappy but willing," Kimbrell found. "They learn quickly, and they gave a john the act [as if] he was impressing them." Indeed, they were so enterprising—or perhaps so imbued with the commercial values that inspired so many Jewish immigrants to start their own businesses—that "a great many of them soon became madams."[95] Vice could even be a family business. "Mother Rosie" Hertz, whose chain of Lower East Side brothels thrived for more than three decades, ran the business along with her husband, Jacob, and several brothers and cousins. Jewish women were also prominent in other branches of crime. New York's "Mother" Marm Mandelbaum, for example, won local fame as a leading fence. Like any group of prudent merchants, Lower Manhattan's bordello owners and procurers banded together into the Independent Benevolent Association, which supplied its members the medical coverage, funeral insurance, and "assistance in case of necessity" offered by any other immigrant mutual-aid society.[96]

Polly, however, had uptown—even upstate—ambitions. Priding herself on the elegance of her establishments and a clientele that included major crime figures along with leaders in more respectable fields, she followed New York's social elite to the fashionable summer resort of Saratoga Springs, where she opened a luxurious retreat. She always strove to be the "best goddam madam in all America," she confided in *A House Is Not a Home,* her best-selling memoir later made into a movie. After she retired to Burbank, California, and before she died at sixty-two, she even fulfilled the immigrant dream that had brought her to America, finishing her high school education and taking college courses.

9

"OF THEIR OWN MAKING"

Building American Families

Most young Jewish women bent over sweatshop sewing machines escaped industrial drudgery in a less lurid way than Polly Adler. "In the beginning," recalled Clara Lemlich, long after she had become a Brooklyn housewife married to printer Joe Shavelson, immigrant girls started their careers in the needle trades "full of hope and courage. Almost all of them think they will be able to get out of the factory and work up. Continuing to work under long hours and miserable conditions, they lose their hopes. Their only way to leave the factory is marriage."[1]

Clara, however, was an exception to her own rule. After the uprising no manufacturer would hire so notorious a troublemaker, so, instead of sewing, she worked as an organizer for the suffrage movement. But her undiluted working-class radicalism alienated the middle-class reformers leading the drive for votes, and the job ended. Her organizing continued, however, after she and Joe set up housekeeping in 1913 in the Brownsville section of Brooklyn, and while she raised their son, Irving, and daughters, Martha and Rita. Her attention turned from workplace issues to pressing domestic concerns, such as the prices that ordinary families had to pay for food and rent. By the late 1920s, she had helped organize the United Council of Working-Class Housewives (and joined the American Communist Party).

She remained an energetic leftist to the end of her ninety-six years. At eighty-one she moved to the Jewish Home for the Aged in Los Angeles, where she convinced the management to observe the United Farm Workers boycott of lettuce and table grapes and helped the orderlies who staffed the home start their own union.

But in her personal life, this consistent, fearless, and legendary leftist followed a far more decorous course. She hewed to the conventions of her era that Jewish wives did not work in factories and that respectable women married the men they lived with. She did not resume garment work and union activities until her late fifties, after Joe had fallen seriously ill. As a seventy-four-year-old widow, she married Abe Goldman, a long-time labor movement comrade, and lived with him until his death seven years later.

Making Modern Marriages

Clara's ideological commitments took her much farther left than most women of her generation, but her personal life followed the course trod by countless girls of the great migration who arrived in America unmarried. Like so many others, she spent a period as a factory worker and took part in union activities. She married a fellow Jewish worker. She became a housewife and mother in a heavily Jewish neighborhood. She took an active role in ensuring the family's economic well-being.

The families those immigrants built, like Clara's, were self-consciously American. Founded on the ideal of marriage for love and fed, clothed, and furnished according to American fashion and dedicated to upward mobility, they departed in many ways from old-world conventions. But in their ferocious determination to give their American children the new country's fullest blessings, these immigrant housewives—*balebustes* in Yiddish— embodied a value central to Judaism: the work of making a proper home has transcendent worth.

For immigrant girls, their parents, and the whole community, the *chuppah* offered a factory girl's most promising gateway to a better life. A lasting escape from drudgery depended not only on marrying but on landing "a good provider"—a husband earning enough to free his wife from the need to supply or even supplement the family income. Because Jewish men were mostly literate skilled workers, many eventually accumulated job experience or established businesses that enabled them to provide the main support for a decently working-class or lower-middle-class home— especially if they chose a wife who could shrewdly squeeze maximum value out of every hard-earned dollar and even bring in a few themselves. The steady flow of Jewish families from the noisy, crowded blocks where immigrants first settled to more commodious and respectable neighborhoods testified eloquently to Jewish couples' abilities to earn and economize.

Although the *New York Tribune* noted in 1901, "the son-in-law for whom the soul of every East Sider pines is a professional man—a doctor preferably," most families settled for men of more modest prospects.[2] The possibility of above-average earning power naturally increased a bachelor's allure. A woman named Frieda saw her chance, appropriately enough, while attending a wedding. The man in charge of the refreshments "asked me to dance with him," she recalled. Later, "he asked me to stay until he closed up the place. And when I heard that it was his place—I was ready" to wed. She had long sought a husband, but at twenty-seven ("in those days, that was very old but . . . ") she knew that "I couldn't marry just anyone." She and her single sisters wanted to marry well-off men who could help them care for their parents. By marrying this apparently prosperous caterer, Frieda thought, "I'd make my father and mother rich."[3] Her mother was gravely ill, in danger of dying without having fulfilled the Jewish parent's traditional duty to raise each child for "Torah, *chuppah*, and good deeds"—an obligation that endured, at least as far as the *chuppah* was concerned, even in families that had discarded Torah-based observance. But Frieda and her caterer gave the sick women the satisfaction of seeing at least one daughter suitably settled.

This traditional consummation was achieved, however, through decidedly modern means. Frieda had made the caterer's acquaintance by chance and on her own. Neither a marriage broker nor a family connection had brought them together, but rather an invitation to dance. Their turn around the ballroom carried deep cultural implications. Both parties to the impromptu introduction had an understanding of dignified flirtation and a passable command of current dance steps.

Such a meeting would have been highly unlikely in the traditional world of Jewish Eastern Europe. At the simplest level, wedding guests did not twirl in the arms of a stranger of the opposite sex, but danced in larger groups with members of their own. From single-sex schooling to synagogue seating, every aspect of custom and culture strove to keep unmarried males and females from meeting. The job of introducing them belonged to family members or the marriage brokers they hired. The prerogative of selecting spouses belonged to parents, who exercised it long before a daughter reached Frieda's advanced age. But American society strained in exactly the opposite direction. Mixed schools and workplaces, easy sociability, and the rituals of chaste flirtation encouraged the unmarried to meet and choose their own mate.

The change set in soon after the immigration began. "This has been a hard year for the Cupids of the Ghetto, as the matrimonial agents of the Jewish quarter might be called," the *New-York Tribune* reported in 1900. "Unless the marriage business picks up the broker is going to drop out of sight. Already he is branching out into other ways of making a living, . . . [writing] letters for the illiterate, [interpreting] in business transactions, or [doing] odd jobs at the synagogue."[4]

The earliest wave of immigrants included some who had plied the ancient trade in Europe and intended to continue it in America. Within the first decade or two in the New World, however, young people rebelled. The old emphasis on tradition and family respect had given parents the authority to organize their children's adult lives, but the American devotion to individualism—and the younger generation's greater ease in American culture, as well as their independent earning power—transferred that authority to the young, at least in the children's opinion.

"I would starve to death in a month if I depended on matchmaking for a living," complained a Hester Street practitioner to a *Tribune* reporter. "Once I lived on the fat of the land," with customers clamoring for him to "make them happy for life." His erstwhile clients now believed "in love and all that rot" and "learned to start their own love affairs from the Americans." But he wondered, "How can a Jewish couple expect to be happy in a marriage of their own making when it has been the custom of their fathers and mothers for ages not to see each other until after marriage?"[5]

But happiness in love, as depicted in the movies, romantic novels, and popular songs, was exactly what forward-looking young immigrants counted on. The careful old-country weighing of *yiches*, scholarship, dowry, and piety was replaced by the American fashion of sizing up potential partners by going out on dates. In the traditional, family-based system, newlyweds assumed that affection, even devotion, would grow in time as the couple built a home and family. But if love never come, a man and woman could still live a perfectly satisfactory married life, just as their forebears had, if both observed the rules of traditional respect and *sholom bais* (peace of the house, or civil, courteous behavior).

But now the deal was sealed by the wholly subjective reactions of youngsters, not objective considerations weighed by adults with long experience at life and marriage. "I think all my generation married for love," surmised Ruth Katz, who came to Chicago at sixteen in 1913.[6] The first girl in her family to choose a husband in the American fashion, she met him the second year after she arrived and married after five years of courting in public places. The dance halls, cafes, theaters, and movie houses that checkered the immigrant neighborhoods offered limitless opportunities to mix with members of the opposite sex, as did workplaces of all kinds. Country boardinghouses, such as the one that Ida and Sam ran, also provided their guests, along with summertime scenery and kosher meals, an assortment of potential mates they might otherwise not get to know. Many a young worker skipped lunches or walked instead of taking the trolley in order to save for a week among new marriage possibilities in the mountains or at the shore.

Before long many marriage brokers stopped trying to manage negotiations among parents and retooled as dating bureaus that charged for introductions instead of earning a percentage of the dowry. Once introduced, the clients went on dates and determined any future steps for themselves. "We bought a nickel ice cream cone; for twenty-five cents we went to Jackson Park and you took a boat for an hour," Ruth Katz recalled. "Sometimes . . . a movie. . . . Who was chaperoned? Not in this country."[7]

As Polly Adler learned to her sorrow, though, the new American freedom did not liberate a girl from the burden of maintaining her reputation and virginity, still crucial to her chances for a good match. The definition of what a virtuous girl could do changed, and parents no longer chaperoned their daughters in the traditional way. However, they insisted on certain proprieties. A young man escorting a respectable girl was expected to call for her at home and meet the adults in charge, who used the opportunity to assess his social standing, acceptability, and prospects. He, meanwhile, tried to impress them with his desirability as a companion and possible future husband for their daughter.

Young women bore the burden of safeguarding their own purity. Immigrant girls often had to manage this without accurate knowledge of sex, which many mothers withheld until the wedding day. Until a coworker assured her otherwise, for example, Fannie Edelman believed that sitting beside a man could make her pregnant. Armed with the assurance that this threat was imaginary, Fannie began accepting dates, which raised the thorny question of, as one woman put it, "How far is it permissible to give into your feelings?"[8]

Young women who dated and hoped to marry faced "a great deal of fear," another immigrant recalled. "We did not know how to take care of ourselves. Fear lived in my heart always that I might get pregnant."[9] This worry may have increased as Jewish courting couples came ever closer to American patterns. By the 1920s, "necking" had won wide acceptance. In a day when many poor married women could not easily learn about birth control, a girl who cared for a man had to learn to say, as one woman remembers, "You want to have me and I want to have you, but it can't be outside of marriage."[10]

As early as 1903, young Jews believed that, in the words of a letter published in a popular advice column in New York's *Yidisches Tagblat* (Jewish Daily News), "It is every woman's right to decide who shall be her life's partner. Who would tear that right from her and force her to a loveless marriage is—inexpressible."[11] The columnist who published those heartfelt words strongly agreed and two years later herself became a nationally celebrated icon of marriage for love. Perhaps not coincidentally, Rose Harriet Wieslander had been born in Augustova, Poland, of a loveless union. Her mother, Hindl, had loved a Pole but married the Jew her parents chose. When daughter Rose was only three, Hindl left her husband and took her child to England. In the immigrant slums of London's Jewish East End, she met and married one Israel Pastor. By the time he moved the family to Cleveland, Ohio, in 1890, Rose, then eleven, had younger half-siblings and three years' experience in factory work. She soon found unskilled work in a sweatshop tobacco factory. Eventually Hindl's marriage to Pastor also failed, and Rose supported her mother and four siblings.

After twelve years making cheap cigars, Rose's fate took a turn as fantastic as any plot twist in romantic fiction. She, in fact, probably thrilled to such tales of delirious transformation because, despite only meager formal schooling, she loved to read. One day she noticed an invitation in the *Yidisches Tagblat* for readers to write in about their lives. She responded and in 1901 the paper published the first of her essays. Before long, under the pen name Zelda, she was regularly contributing "talks for girls." Her counsel on job problems, family relations, social life, and other issues facing immigrant working girls won her so loyal a following that *Tagblat* took her on as a regular staff member at the handsome sum of $15 a week. In 1903 she moved to New York, her mother and siblings following soon after.

From her new base on the Lower East Side, Rose expanded her topics to broader political and social concerns. She praised Theodor Herzl and his Zionist followers as courageous pioneers and denounced "Jew-baiting and Negro lynching [as] two blunders well worth being freed of. Kishineffing [a reference to the horrific Kishinev pogrom of 1903] outside the land of Kishineff is a greater blot upon civilization than in that hell's kitchen, Russia."[12]

Then she began a series on the reformers who worked in the settlement houses serving the immigrant poor, and her life underwent a second fairy-tale change. At the Henry Street Settlement she interviewed Lillian Wald, a plump, middle-aged Jewish lady who had brought health care to the Lower East Side poor. At the University Settlement she spoke with James Graham Phelps Stokes, a charming, handsome, tall, college-educated thirty-two-year-old Episcopalian, a supporter of the reform movement and a multimillionaire scion of an old-line upper-class Manhattan family. Rose's story on their conversation cemented a friendship that was at first intellectual and philosophical.

By the late summer of 1904 their friendship became romantic, and on April 6, 1905, the *New York Times* front page carried an unaccustomed—and astonishing—social note: "J.G. Phelps Stokes to Wed Young Jewess," the headline ran, "Engagement of Member of Old New York Family Announced—Both Worked on East Side."[13] The formerly working-class reporter was suddenly "the Cinderella of the sweatshops," the heroine of a fairy tale that captivated the city.[14] The *Times* story went on to detail two separate worlds: his upbringing in cultured leisure among the nation's most privileged elite and her early hardship and toil among the struggling poor.

The question of their disparate religions, however, attracted even greater attention. "The Israelitish maiden" did not strike most of Graham's relatives as a suitable addition to their family circle and some tried to scotch the match. Rabbis meanwhile fretted that this famous romance would glamorize intermarriage. The *Times,* however, hailed the couple as "demonstrating the ideal of universal brotherhood." And the smitten Graham declared that few people possessed "the qualification which Jesus asked in larger measure than Rose." For Rose, their union of "riches and poverty, Jew and Christian" was "an indication of the new era."[15]

At last they married, Rose wearing a cross, reportedly as a goodwill gesture to her new in-laws. Though the newlyweds had originally planned to continue their ties to settlement work and the Lower East Side, disillusionment soon set in and they transferred their reforming zeal to the Socialist Party. Rose's connection to the downtown immigrant world gradually dissolved as she moved into broader realms of labor activism and social reform, for example, providing crucial support to the new and controversial birth control movement. She was a newsworthy and virtually arrest-proof advocate for many causes, but a 1918 speech denouncing the U.S. entry into World War I brought her arrest in Kansas City, Missouri, followed by a sensational trial, a conviction, and successful appeals. By 1919 she was a leader in the American Communist Party. Long before this, however, the profound differences between Graham and Rose had begun to assert themselves. Divorce ended the storybook marriage in 1926.

Coming Apart

Divorce ended many less prominent Jewish women's marriages as well. Thousands of couples who immigrated after marrying found that the unions they had contracted in the Old World could not survive in the New. A husband who preceded his family to America might find that the wife who followed months or years later, with her shawl and wig and accent, her old-country ways and total ignorance of English, did not fit into his newly American life. A wife might come off the boat to discover that a derbied, mustachioed English speaker had replaced the bearded Yiddish speaker she had kissed good-bye—and that a more desirably American woman had replaced her in this stranger's affections.

Other families disintegrated under the burden of earning a living and making a life in an unforgiving foreign city. The crossing stripped many people of the status and identity they had known at home. Countless small businesses failed, destroying not only an immigrant family's hopes and painfully accumulated savings but a man's self-respect and sense of independence. Many husbands who wanted to support their families found themselves depending on sons, daughters, and wives. Low wages, lack of traditional authority over children, reverses of all kinds undermined masculine self-respect. "I left Europe and I was a man, and here I am a what?" one despondent father asked his daughter.[16] "He couldn't seem to really find himself" in the new land, another daughter recalled of a father who had to do work he disliked. "It rankled him. . . . I think he was ashamed of himself."[17]

Some troubled would-be breadwinners allayed their misery with infidelity or drink. Some released their anger by beating their wives and children. Some abandoned the effort of being a husband. No ethnic group had a higher divorce rate than Jews in New York City in the early 1900s.[18] Immigrants of every nationality faced similar disappointments and defeats, but despondent Catholic spouses lacked the option of ending their miserable marriages. Some Jewish family breakups, usually among the well-to-do, involved official civil and religious divorces. Thousands of other husbands, who could not afford lawyers and documents and hearings, opted instead for a "poor man's divorce" and simply disappeared.

So many wives found themselves abandoned that the *Forward* regularly printed a photo gallery of fugitive husbands. Twenty-five hundred cases a year came before the National Desertion Bureau, a Jewish charity that tracked missing spouses. New York's United Hebrew Charities each year spent about ten percent of its relief funds on deserted families. Destitute, abandoned wives sent pitiful pleas to the *Forward*'s "Bintel Brief" letters column. "Max! The children and I say farewell to you," one pathetic reader wrote in. "You left us in such a terrible state. For six years I loved you faithfully, took care of you like a loyal servant, never had a happy day with you. . . . Max, where is your conscience? . . . I was a young, educated, decent girl when you took me. You lived with me for six years, during which time I bore you four children. Then you left me." Sadly, only two of those children had survived, "living orphans," with no father to support or care for them. "Have you no pity on your own flesh and blood?" On the assumption that the despicable Max did not, she warned that "in several days I am leaving with my two living orphans for Russia. We say farewell for you and beg you to send us enough to live on."[19]

The majority of such "orphans" remained in the United States, however, some living in orphanages run by the Jewish philanthropies along with the youngsters of parents too sick, too poor, or too addled to care for them. Pleas from desperate parents for people willing to foster their children were another recurring feature in the *Forward* and similar newspapers, along with inquiries from children seeking the parents who had left them and from parents seeking children they had left.

Keeping the Family Jewish

The vast majority of immigrant girls emulated the sweatshop Cinderella by marrying for love but stopped short of intermarrying, however. Flirtations occurred between Jewish men and women and their Italian or Polish coworkers or neighbors but rarely led to serious commitments. Immigrant parents of all origins insisted that their children marry within their faith, and often within their nationality as well. An eighteen-year-old who signed herself "Broken hearted," for example, poured out the misery of a mixed romance in a 1903 letter to *Yidische Tagblat*. Though she was "in love with a young Christian man [who] loves me, too, and . . . wants to marry me," her father insisted that "a Jewess should marry a Jew." This "old-fashioned man" ignored all of the young man's "good qualities," including striking good looks and a promise to make his sweetheart a happy wife. "What would you advise me to do?" the rebellious daughter begged. "Marry my Christian lover or listen to my father?"[20]

"I do not intend to advise you because I do not think you need my advice," the writer of the "Just Between Us Girls" column astutely answered. "If you had decided to marry a Christian, if you had thought it right and 'nice' (as you express it) to marry a Christian, if you had thought your father was wrong to object, you would not have asked my advice. It is because you know it would be wrong to marry him" that the pitiful query had been penned.

"You will break your father's heart . . . you will break your mother's heart," the columnist, Zelda, went on, warming steadily to her subject. Indeed, the Jewish parents of lower Manhattan objected as bitterly to a child's marriage out of the faith as Abigail Franks had a century and a half earlier. Parents who had fled across an ocean to escape anti-Semitism, who had remained Jewish despite relentless official pressure to convert, who had seen homes burned or friends killed by anti-Semites, regarded a child's choice to abandon Judaism in the land of liberty as treachery and disgrace. Immigrant families touched by intermarriage often observed the formal rites of mourning, which marked the transgressor's death to the family circle. "Can you bear to do this to the two beings whom God has commanded you to honor?" Zelda asked.

Nor did passion offer any excuse for such behavior, the *Tagblat*'s popular young staffer, Rose Pastor, insisted from behind her pseudonym. "You are not happy though you try to make yourself believe you are," she warned. "You will respect your father's wishes and do the thing most worthy of a loyal daughter; you will give up your Christian lover and save yourself and your parents the life-long misery that is in store for you if you do the contrary."[21]

Immigrants and their children overwhelmingly followed Pastor's advice and not her example. Most couples, despite their devotion to romance, probably did not match the intense initial passion between Rose and Graham. Many an immigrant girl with few alternatives to the sweatshop fell as deeply in love with the prospect of fleeing the factory as with the charms of the young worker courting her. "When [such young women] met a young man who fell in love with them, they were very glad to get out of having to work as they did," an immigrant woman recalled. "They made a home, had children immediately, and were content with that."[22]

Home Comforts

Many women who had experienced poverty and oppression in Europe or the burden of supporting parents or siblings in America found themselves quite content with such modest attainments. Legend and literature remember the immigrants' surroundings as grim, dirty, oppressive, and unsafe; their days as hard and monotonous; their prospects as limited. Viewed from our time and standard of living, three or four tenement rooms several winding flights above a street jammed with pushcarts, chattering neighbors, and shouting children have little appeal.

But viewed through the memory of the Pale, with its drafty huts on unpaved shtetl lanes and its unheated rooms overlooking fetid city courtyards, a tidy tenement flat, complete with a private kitchen and bathroom, ever flowing water taps, steam heat, electricity, a gas stove, and an icebox, afforded a housewife astonishing, even miraculous, comfort. With a gas range standing in her kitchen—an appliance that the *Yidische Tagblat* termed "a true delight and God's blessing for ever"—she need not lug wood or coal to make the fire or haul the ashes away. With faucets gleaming in both kitchen and bathroom, she no longer dragged buckets of water from wells or pumps. With electric lights shining and radiators steaming, families need not cluster around lanterns to see at night or stoke fires to keep warm. Nor did anyone ever again have to empty nightsoil or visit an outhouse. Even in the poor sections of American cities, these crushing, age-old chores simply vanished.

This luxury flowed from an industrializing economy that grew rapidly for most of the period in which the immigrants came. Recessions and even depressions occasionally intervened, but the upward economic trend that had begun decades earlier had already made the American standard of living the envy of the world. The average U.S. worker's discretionary income far exceeded what his or her counterpart earned in the most advanced European countries, let alone the pittance in Russia or Poland.

In 1900, food took less than half of the American's pay, but 60 percent of a comparable worker's in France, one of Europe's richest countries. Ten years later, American workers ate for as little as 37–47 percent of their total wages, though similar workers in wealthy England had to spend 61–67 percent of theirs. Young, single American workers, beneficiaries of the world's most dynamic industrial system, often kept three-quarters of their incomes after feeding themselves.[23] Americans' relatively smaller expenditures bought them a far better diet than people in rich countries abroad could afford. They got twice as much meat and fish, twice as many eggs, and four times as many fruits and vegetables as even their English counterparts, among Europe's most favored, in 1910, and vastly more than their brethren in Eastern Europe.[24] Luxuries like roasts and delicatessen meats—beyond the means of comparable Europeans—appeared routinely on the tables of American wage earners.

As early as 1870, a thrifty American housewife could enjoy objects that a generation or two earlier had demarcated the modestly well-to-do. Such erstwhile luxuries as bed linens, rugs, dishes, flatware, mirrors, china cupboards, dining tables, and clocks furnished even relatively humble homes.[25] By 1888, such "comforts of life" as pictures, lace curtains, and upholstered chairs and sofas were "found in the vilest tenements," according to the U.S. Bureau of Labor.[26] By 1910, shop girls and factory workers were adorning themselves with silk underwear and their parents gracing their apartments with pianos.

This "new style of poverty" startled the novelist Henry James; though such people had less than other Americans, they did not suffer dire want. The immigrant neighborhoods supported platoons of merchants offering stylish, up-to-date consumer goods and national brands of soaps and foodstuffs. Others provided their working-class clientele with cheaply made knockoffs of higher-priced fashions and housewares; deeply discounted seconds, irregulars, or other "schlock" (from the Yiddish for "broken"); or appliances and furniture available on "easy" credit terms. In 1904, after twenty-two years abroad, James returned to his native New York to witness the Lower East Side's "blaze of the shops addressed to the New Jerusalem wants."[27]

More striking than this commercial bounty, James perceived, was "the splendor with which these [goods] were taken for granted" by the immigrants thronging the shabby, congested streets.[28] Young Jewish women in particular attained a reputation for superstylish, even flashy, dress. Grand Street, a major Lower East Side shopping strip, "out-Broadways Broadway [a fashionable uptown shopping thoroughfare]," commented the *New-York Tribune Illustrated Supplement* in 1900. "Does Broadway wear a feather? Grand-st. dons two, without loss of time. Are trailing skirts seen in Fifth-ave.? Grand-st. trails its yards with a dignity all its own. . . . Grand-st. is

Broadway plus Fifth-ave., only very much 'more so.' Its wide sidewalks show more fashion to the square foot on a Sunday than any of part of the city."[29]

The tenement housing available to Jewish workers, though often crowded and poorly maintained, improved steadily throughout the immigrant period. In the 1890s, East Siders had to pay $8–$10 a month for a sunless "room and bedroom" apartment, plus sanitary facilities down the hall that they shared with neighbors. But soon buildings were going up in the neighborhood with four- and five-room apartments, often including electricity and private bathrooms. By 1902, a year after the New York Tenement House Act mandated a bathroom for every apartment as well as layouts providing better light and ventilation, five- and six-room apartments were the norm in new Lower East Side construction. A decade or so later, twenty-two thousand "new law" buildings housed a million and a half New Yorkers of modest means.[30]

Along with their impressive plumbing fixtures and miraculous kitchen appliances, many immigrant apartments contained an even more remarkable American invention, a parlor or "living room." A room devoted not to working or sleeping but to "living"—entertaining visitors, leisurely chatting, reading the newspaper, listening to music—had existed only in well-to-do Eastern European homes. From the early years of the great migration, however, countless Jewish households strove to have one of their own. Often they did so by maintaining "the interesting fiction" that their apartment had "specialized divisions," observed Marcus Ravage, who saw his first New York tenement in 1900.

The relatives who took him in when he arrived from Europe had five rooms, all of which were crammed each night with sleeping family members and boarders. But every morning the bedding was whisked from sight and an American-style layout emerged. "Here was the parlor with its sofa and mirror and American rocking chairs; then came the dining room with another sofa called a lounge, a round table and innumerable chairs, then the kitchen with its luxurious fittings in porcelain and metal; then the young ladies' room, in which there was a bureau covered with quantities of odoriferous bottles and powder-boxes and other mysteries; and, last of all, Mrs. Segal's and the children's room."[31] The grandeur and Americanness of his landlady's apartment also impressed the newly arrived Abe Cahan in 1882. A widow who supported her children by peddling, she presided over a parlor with furniture and rugs rivaling those owned by the affluent back in Cahan's native Vilna.

By the turn of the century, a great many Jewish parlors sported the pinnacle of immigrant householders' acquisitive ambition. A piano, usually bought on credit and paid off in small amounts over a period of years, stood as a gleaming testament to prosperity and cultural aspiration. "What is a Home without a Piano?" a Yiddish advertisement asked.[32] And what is a piano without someone to play it, wondered the countless Jewish parents who scrimped to pay not only the piano dealer but the piano teacher who gave the children lessons.

Despite this dedication to upgrading the household, however, most Jews longed to abandon it for a week or two when the weather grew hot. At the beginning of the great immigration, summer vacations were a long established custom among prosperous Americans. Jewish newcomers quickly made it their own. About seventy thousand people, mostly well-off and native born, vacationed in the Catskill Mountains north of New York City in 1883. By 1906, some 400,000 summer visitors, a great many of them foreign-born Jews, enjoyed the region's rustic delights. Far more than any other immigrant group, Jews of modest means flocked to mountainsides, lake shores, and ocean beaches. "One would never think of an Italian laborer, or an Irishman working on a street railroad, sending his wife and children [on vacation] for the summer," mused a 1903 *American Israelite* article. But "year after year," Jewish garment workers did exactly this.[33]

To provide summer playgrounds for all these would-be vacationers, Jews began buying rural acreage, including, between 1900 and 1910, some thousand farms in the vicinity of the Catskill town of Ellenville.[34] "Nearly every one of the purchased homes is used as a summer boarding house," the *Ellenville Journal* reported.[35] Malka and Asher Selig Grossinger, for example, bought a rundown country property in 1914. Reaching New York from Galicia in 1887, Selig spent three years working to bring over Malka and their daughters, Jennie and Lottie. Jennie arrived at age eight and took a job five years later making buttonholes in the factory where Selig worked. But Selig, the son of an old-country estate agent, longed for a rural life. After several failed attempts to start businesses in New York, he moved the family to the Catskills, planning to support them as a farmer. But his luck proved no better in the country than it had in the city.

To help out, Malka started a business of her own. She was an excellent kosher cook and the daughter of innkeepers, one of East European Jewry's traditional trades. With the help of Jennie, by now married to a cousin, Harry Grossinger, she began taking in paying guests. The old farmhouse lacked heat, electricity, and indoor plumbing, but people came for Malka's meals and Jennie's vivacious hospitality. Harry helped recruit customers while he worked in New York, visiting his wife on his days off. Within five years Malka and Jennie were doing well enough for the family to sell the farm and buy a nearby hotel. Over the next fifty years, Jennie and Harry would expand from that single building into the vast, world-renowned resort that made their name a synonym for lavish, "Borscht Belt"–style vacationing.

Few families advertising spare rooms with meals or "kochalein" (cook alone) cottages attained the Grossingers' legendary success. Many Jewish summer hotels and boardinghouses were slapdash affairs, run by people with little or no previous experience as hoteliers. But like Grossinger's, establishments large and small emphasized good eating and a "haimish" atmosphere where immigrant Jews could feel at ease. As early as 1903, "there [were] towns in this state, in the Catskill region, and along the seashore whose summer population is made up almost entirely of East Siders," according to the *American Israelite*. "A Sunday afternoon spent on the boardwalk at Averne, or on Ocean Avenue, Long Branch or Bath Beach, will attest . . . that the entire East Side has closed up home and has gone to the seashore."[36] Even Jewish workers who couldn't afford or arrange a summer respite on their own could call on charities specially organized to help. From 1892 on, for example, the Jewish Working Girls' Vacation Society each summer sent a thousand young women for a restorative week on Long Island or in the Catskills, at accommodations that met even the most stringent parent's standards of propriety and *kashrut*.

For the immigrants, such formerly unattainable luxuries as parlor spinets and seaside holidays meant a good deal more than merely enjoying greater physical comfort. Newfound trappings of prosperity symbolized rising social position and increased ease in America, especially when American financial success overturned old-country status rankings. A family dinner, for example, celebrated the engagement of Leah Chotzinoff, the granddaughter of an East European rabbi and daughter of a New York Hebrew teacher, to a young housepainter who had followed his father into that far less prestigious but more lucrative trade. The Chotzinoffs' superior scholarly *yiches* earned Leah's father the seat of honor at the head of the table. But as her brother Charles remembered, their mother's ersatz mother-of-pearl jewelry "appeared insignificant alongside Mrs. Kalb's gold watch and chain" and fashionable outfit.[37]

In another sartorial ambush described in the *Forward* in 1906, a woman who had been poor in Berdichev now spent her husband's princely insurance company salary of $40 a week on expensive, ostentatious ensembles that she wore to call on her Ukrainian *landsleyt*. One disgusted woman she visited, the wife of a mere wage earner, plotted revenge. Inviting the show-off to come again in two weeks, the hostess managed, through saving and savvy shopping, to greet her guest in even more lavish and showy finery, vanquishing her, at least temporarily, in the status competition.

Owning American possessions meant more than just outdoing fellow immigrants. To a people excluded for millennia from the full life of the countries in which they resided, America offered the hope of joining the nation by acquiring its consumer goods. In this country, generations of newcomers had become citizens. Centuries of immigrants had raised American children. This entirely new kind of country did not reckon nationhood by blood, but rather received as its adopted sons and daughters all who gave it their loyalty and adapted to its ways. Or so the East European Jews thought; few newcomers had ever wanted as fervently to join the American people.

Bargain-Hunting Balebustes

Among the very first established Americans to welcome Jewish immigrants into their new national identity were industrialists with goods to sell. Recognizing that Jews outpaced other groups in their desire to be American, firms soon tapped into their longing by advertising extensively in the Yiddish press. Borden's Milk, a company perhaps sensitized to the Jewish market by Joseph and Rosana Dyer Osterman's early involvement, was among the first. Within three years of inventing Crisco in 1910, Proctor & Gamble informed Yiddish readers of a product "for which the Hebrew Race has been waiting for 4000 years."[38] Maxwell House coffee's giveaway Passover haggadahs, with Yiddish and Hebrew or English and Hebrew on facing pages, lent the traditional seder an up-to-date American touch. Yiddish cookbooks from Pillsbury and Crisco divulged the secrets of preparing American meals.

Clothing played an especially crucial "part of the process of becoming Americanized," the *New-York Tribune Illustrated Supplement* recognized in 1901. "The girl whose Russian mother knew but the wig of the religious Jewess and a soft shawl . . . [feels] vastly fine in a 'three story hat' which might well vie with the historic coat of Joseph. In the land of equality shall not one wear what another wears? Shall not Fifth Avenue and Grand Street walk hand in hand . . . ? It would be rank heresy to insinuate that there is anything faulty in the process of 'Americanizing' as it goes on on the East Side."[39]

Jewish housewives saw nothing amiss in getting their families what other people had, indeed, the very best goods possible. In America, acquiring prestigious possessions depended not on birth or background but on ability to pay. As the sensibility formed in East European marketplaces reinforced the all-American love of a bargain, deep discounting became the hallmark of retailing in the Jewish immigrant shopping districts, and careful comparison shopping the pride of every self-respecting Jewish customer. "The psychology of the Jewish customer" required "more 'money's worth' with less ta-ra-ras," commented the *Yidische Tagblat.*[40]

"The women of the Jewish race are rarely deceived when trading with the vendor," a U.S. government document observed.[41] A canny eye for quality and a network of contacts could, for example, get a woman an attractive costume for very little cash, the *New-York Tribune Illustrated Supplement* observed. "The skirt her brother-in-law, who 'works in skirts' had made for her at odd times, and it cost, getting the material wholesale, $2.50. Her hat her 'chum' made at an expense of 60 cents. To the uninitiated, the costume represented an outlay of $20, at least, although she achieved it at an expense of $3.30, and was able to go abroad without proclaiming to the world the dire poverty at home. . . .There are many such on the East Side."[42]

Vigilance in bargain hunting and wheedling the best price—skills honed in shtetl market squares—were hallmarks of the able and effective *balebuste.* Far from a simple housewife who cooks and cleans, or a mere housekeeper who organizes domestic tasks, she acted as her family's chief executive officer, financial overseer, and social arbiter; the active, dynamic, assertive, and, above all, central figure responsible for creating and maintaining the physical, spiritual, and emotional well-being of everyone under her care. With buying American so closely tied to becoming American, the wives and mothers of the immigrant generation faced the honorable and essential challenge of cooking, scrubbing, cleaning, haggling, sewing, earning, and saving in ways that made the most of their families' chances in the New World. It was a responsibility they discharged with pride, determination, energy, and grit.

In 1892, for example, the kosher butchers of Boston's heavily Jewish North End formed a trust and hiked their prices. Neighborhood women reacted furiously to this calculated attack on their purchasing power. In a pattern also followed in other cities over the years, outraged shoppers organized to protest. A mass meeting in a local synagogue, mostly of *balebustes*, demanded a return to former pricing and accused the butchers of selling *treif*.

Ten years later, when a similar New York meat cartel announced a 50 percent price rise, from twelve cents to what their customers considered an extortionate eighteen cents a pound, the Lower East Side's reaction went far beyond speeches and rallies. The Ladies Anti-Beef Trust Association formed to meet the emergency. "These women are in earnest," the *New York Herald* declared. "For days they had been considering the situation, and when they decided on action, they perfected an organization, elected officers . . . and even went so far as to take coins from their slender purses until there was an expense fund of eighty dollars with which to carry on the fight."[43] For the next three weeks, across the Lower East Side and in neighborhoods throughout upper Manhattan, Brooklyn, and the Bronx, angry *balebustes* boycotted kosher meat markets. Tussles broke out, display windows mysteriously shattered, kerosene splashed over butchers' wares, and policemen made arrests. The uproar is remembered as the kosher meat riots, but the protesters disavowed accusations of hooliganism. "We don't riot," declared one of those arrested. Looting was rare and demonstrators insisted on their dignity. "If all we did was weep at home," the boycotter continued, "nobody would notice it. We have to do something to help ourselves."[44] That same year women in Newark, Boston, and elsewhere took to their own streets in the same cause.

Rising rents met with similar resistance. Six hundred Lower East Side women marched in 1907 and 1908 to demand rollbacks. Clara Lemlich Shavelson, active in the 1907 kosher meat boycott, led New York women in organizing against gouging landlords two years later. In many cities, Jewish women repeatedly used the vocabulary of democracy and the strategy of the labor movement to protect what they saw as their right to fair commercial treatment.

Inspired by, and often veterans of, labor strikes, the *balebuste* "strikers" knew that individually they had little power against those selling the things their families needed. But they saw themselves as active agents of their own financial fate and individuals entitled to equitable treatment and a decent standard of living. In Europe, eating meat had been an occasional luxury. For *balebustes* in America, buying it regularly at prices that working families could afford had become something akin to a right.

Balebuste *Businesswomen*

Even in the hands of the most tireless, resourceful, and energetic shopper, a dollar could stretch only so far. Immigrant wives and mothers not only saved money but usually had to earn it too. When she married, Ruth Katz remembered, her husband "couldn't give me anything. The boys weren't prepared to support us; they also came [from Europe] unprepared."[45] But an American wife had to earn without shaming her husband. In the Pale, a man's scholarly career justified his depending on a female breadwinner. In America, almost devoid of old-fashioned religious scholarship, it seemed that virtually nothing did. "At the time I came [to the United States], the woman was home cooking and cleaning and raising the children," according to Ruth. "Women weren't supposed to go out to work" at jobs for wages. Once, with her husband unemployed, she got a job as a saleswoman. "'Not as long as I live.' He wouldn't let me go. That was a disgrace."[46]

Like countless other immigrant wives, Ruth found an invisible job, a source of income that didn't involve taking pay from a boss and that grew from her role as a *balebuste*. Quite apart from masculine pride, immigrant wives had their own good reasons for not spending their days in factories or shops some distance from home. First babies often arrived in the first year of marriage, and the grandmothers who could help with child care in many cases remained across the sea. Young girls, who in the Pale might have pitched in as baby-sitters, spent their days at school or jobs. No matter how much of the family's income a wife earned, her husband generally did no more housework in the New World than in the Old. A *balebuste* needed employment that kept her close to home and that gave her some control over her schedule. If she earned at home, she needed something safe to do with youngsters around. If she went out, she needed somewhere she could take her children.

Ruth found the work she needed in the series of small businesses she ran either on her own or with her husband. Official statistics disguised wives' roles as earners by assuming that the "true" owners of family businesses were male, with females merely "helping out." But both Katzes knew that he could not support them alone. When they decided to marry, "we had nothing to start with. My husband didn't have at that time a trade. . . . He used to pick up odd jobs, so I said to [him], 'I'll work and you work, and whatever we can, we'll arrange a life.'" She had been run-

ning a tiny candy story and living in the backroom. "That little candy store
. . . paid my rent. The only thing that I didn't like working is, when I lived
in the back of the store, my company were rats."[47]

But they married, rats and all. Within three months of the wedding, "I
became already pregnant and the room was cold. I stayed there for seven
months [then] . . . sold the store for $500. Then I thought that with $500
I was a rich woman. $500! I took a little apartment, and I had my daugh-
ter and raised her in the back of the business—selling bakery goods—and
when my daughter was ten weeks old, my husband bought a little delicatessen, and I lived at the back." Now the couple became business partners as well as marriage partners, working together in what amounted to
their front room. "My husband used to go to the market, and buy a barrel
of apples and I used to keep my daughter on one hand and dip the apples
in taffy with the other—sold them a penny an apple. Ten cents a corned
beef sandwich, and they used to say, 'Put a little more corned beef on.'"
Soon, though, the delicatessen folded, and "when my daughter was about
three years old . . . I had a little cigar store and I lived in the back and my
husband used to go out and do *any* kind of a job."[48]

Four years later, with the help of friends and relatives, a big opportunity
came their way: the chance to buy a small department store in an area of
German and Lithuanian Gentiles. The store's owner, a friend of Ruth's,
was selling out because she thought living among Christians was "not good
for her children; especially no young [Jewish] man wanted to come out to
that neighborhood to take the younger daughter out and bring her back in
the evening."[49] Ruth weighed the difficulty of raising a Jewish child among
non-Jews against the promise of modest prosperity at last. Finally she
decided, "'If I'll succeed as a mother, I'll succeed there. If I fail, I'll fail
anywheres.' We wanted that store and soon made the move." A year later
the Katzes "had a merchandise of $18,000. We really did tremendous."
Dealing with their non-Jewish clientele, "there was always respect. I was
never insulted as a Jew and neither was my husband, because [we] would
never cheat, never take advantage."[50]

But the store did not survive the Depression. By the mid-1930s, the
Katzes were running a much smaller women's and children's clothing
shop. It eventually prospered, but then Ruth took seriously ill. One
evening at the hospital, her husband announced that "he's liquidating
the business. I said, 'Who kills the goose that lays the golden egg?'" But
he preferred being "poor . . . here [to being] rich . . . in the cemetery."
With the proceeds, "we bought a little real estate so I wouldn't have to

work." Rentals provided their income and "my husband took care of [our] apartment."[51]

But many immigrant businesswomen could not start out in a shop, even a tiny rented one. By peddling from a pushcart, though, they could clear $15 to $18 a week in the early years of the century and enjoy the status of independent entrepreneurs.[52] Thousands of women, some in partnership with their men, some on their own, sold clothing, notions, sundries, pots and pans, and every kind of foodstuff from carts lining the gutters and curbs of the Lower East Side and the other Jewish immigrant quarters. "Women are among the most successful merchants on Maxwell Street," concluded the pioneer Chicago sociologist, Louis Wirth, from his study of that bustling outdoor market. "They almost monopolize the fish, poultry and herring stalls."[53]

The elite class of market women held proper licenses, owned their own carts, and sold a particular line of merchandise at an established spot on the pavement. Below them, in both standing and income, came the traders who rented their carts but still usually did business in a set location. Further down the pecking order were the "trundlers," many of them trading illegally without licenses, who moved about hawking whatever merchandise they could get. A winsome small child, either the peddler's own or the "borrowed" offspring of a friend and neighbor, often helped in attracting customers and heading off police who inquired too closely about legalities. At the very bottom of the sidewalk business hierarchy were outright professional beggars who worked to appear as pitiful as possible, the better to fleece softhearted passersby. "Some of them would hire a neighbor's child and take it with them to increase their appeal, particularly in the shopping and market districts," noted *New York Times* writer Meyer Berger. The usual rental for a baby was twenty-five cents a day.[54]

Even more numerous than the street sellers were the legions of wives who literally worked at home. In 1909, well over half of New York's *balebustes* took in boarders, and the practice was widespread wherever Jewish immigrants lived.[55] Many wives, especially in the earlier years of the migration, also did garment work in their bedrooms or kitchens or parlors, sometimes enlisting the aid of children and other relatives. With nothing more than a sewing machine, either rented or purchased on time, plus the knowledge of how to run it, a woman could set herself up as a contractor, a subcontractor, or a sub-subcontractor to a manufacturing firm. She collected bundles of cut garment pieces from the factory or sent a child to get them for her. Then she stitched sleeves or made buttonholes or attached buttons for endless hours in her apartment, returned the finished goods, and received payment by the completed piece. "The kitchen gave a special character to our lives: my mother's character," wrote literary critic Alfred Kazin of his New York tenement boyhood. "All my memories of that kitchen are dominated by the nearness of my mother sitting all day long at her sewing machine. . . . Year by year, as I began to take in her fantastic capacity for labor and her anxious zeal, I realized it was ourselves she kept stitched together."[56]

A few of the little businesses that grew out of women's experience as women, as *balebustes*, and as Jews made their owners rich. Lena Himmelstein, for example, built a company out of a nearly universal feminine embarrassment. Born in 1879, she came to the United States in 1895 and took her first job as a sixteen-year-old seamstress at a dollar a week. Eventually her skill earned her a wage fifteen times that figure. Despite this success, she left the garment trade to marry a Russian jeweler, David Bryant. Soon, though, she had to return to it as a young widow with a baby to support. In 1904 she again quit factory work to open her own small dress shop, complete with an apartment at the back where she lived with her son, Raphael. A misspelling on a bank account produced an enduring trademark: Lane Bryant.

Lane's commercial success began in a customer's confidential question about a sensitive personal problem. With visible pregnancy considered unfit for public view, respectable women had to either hide their condition under confining clothes or spend months stuck at home. Could Lane perhaps concoct an outfit to meet both an expectant mother's need for easy wearability and society's insistence on ignoring or disguising her physical state?[57] Lane experimented with various styles, finally hitting on a garment with an elastic waist and accordion pleats that expanded along with the wearer while attractively camouflaging her form. No newspaper would carry an ad for so indiscreet an innovation, but each delighted client told all her friends. This first-ever commercially available maternity outfit quickly became the shop's biggest seller.

In 1909 Lane married Albert Maslin, gaining a partner to handle the business side of a shop grossing $50,000 a year while Lane concentrated on design. Two years later the *New York Herald* finally agreed to advertise her special dresses; their stock sold out completely the first day the ad ran. That same year the Maslins issued a thirty-two-page mail-order maternity catalog; within five years they were doing over a million dollars of business annually. Lane next added styles sized for stout figures, a line that eventually eclipsed maternity wear as the company's largest seller. She made her designs based on studies of thousands of women to determine correct sizing. By 1923, the large-size line accounted for half of the company's $5 million annual sales.

On the way to establishing a major company, Ida Cohen Rosenthal helped resolve another intimate female issue. Born in 1886, she watched her mother run a small shop in her native Rakov, Russia. At sixteen, she apprenticed to a Warsaw dressmaker. Her hometown sweetheart, William, a devoted Socialist, took off for America in 1905, just ahead of his draft notice. Ida followed shortly afterward and opened a small dressmaking shop in Hoboken, New Jersey. She and William married the next year, forming a business and personal partnership that would endure for over half a century. Together they ran Ida's dress shop while raising their two children. In 1918 they opened a more fashionable location in Manhattan.

A partnership with a fashion designer named Enid Bissett, begun in 1921, soon led to a revolution not only in the trio's finances but in women's wear around the world. The flapper look then coming into vogue demanded a boyish figure, which women tried to create with brassieres— at that time, tight bands of cloth—that flattened the breasts. Fuller-figured women found this approach uncomfortable and unflattering. To provide those customers something more suitable, Enid took one of the so-called bandeaus and sewed on cups to support rather than constrict the breasts. William developed a range of sizes, and the partners' shop, Enid Frocks, began giving away a new-style brassiere with each dress. Soon customers were clamoring for their support garments, not their dresses. The Rosenthals and Bissett formed the Enid Manufacturing Company—later renamed Maidenform—to meet the demand.

The need that Regina Horowitz Margareten's successful business met was religious rather than sartorial, but was as central to a Jewish woman's American life as properly fitting clothes. Coming to New York from her native Hungary in 1883 as a twenty-year-old bride, Regina opened a grocery on Willet Street on the Lower East Side with her husband, Ignatz. For their first American Passover, the Orthodox Margaretens, along with Regina's Horowitz relatives, baked their own matzah. Their customers noticed, and before long matzah making had eclipsed their other business, with Regina mixing, baking, and selling the unleavened cakes. Working by hand in a rented bakery, they started out using fifty barrels of flour a year. By the 1930s, Horowitz Brothers and Margareten, the company Regina and Ignatz ran with Regina's brothers Joseph, Leopold, Moses, and

Samuel, and her mother, Mirel Chayah, was taking in a million dollars and using forty-five thousand barrels of flour each year. It also added noodles and other kosher foods to its product line.

For over seventy years, Regina went to the factory at 8:30 each morning except on the Sabbath, Jewish holidays, and her summer vacation. Each morning she sampled the day's production before turning to her other work as a company executive. She also attended the duties of a devout Jewish woman. Her six children and their own families vacationed for many years at Margareten Park, a Catskill compound Regina bought near Hunter Mountain. She supported scores of charities and did practical *tzedakah* at the plant; no one asking for food at the factory, she told the staff, should ever be turned away. Many of those working in the business were family members she had helped bring from Hungary.

Families They Could Afford

Every *balebuste* knew that one thing was even more crucial to her family's welfare than her earning and scrimping: the number of children that an income had to feed. With the average Jewish couple producing five children in the twentieth century's first decade, the "women of the poor" waged "a fierce struggle against frequent pregnancies," wrote the famous radical, Emma Goldman, who had worked as a midwife.[58] Various types of reasonably effective contraception existed; however, both the devices and compounds, as well as the act of informing people of their existence, had been outlawed by the late 1870s as politicians became alarmed at the gap between the dropping birthrate of native, old-stock Americans and poor immigrants' often enormous families. Educated and well-to-do wives found ways to learn about and obtain contraceptives, but poor immigrants generally could not.

Sadie Sachs, at twenty-eight expecting her fourth child, was one of those struggling immigrant wives. One day in July 1912, her truck-driver husband, Jake, came home to a scene of horror in his Grand Street tenement flat. His three children were weeping and their mother was unconscious. Jake sent for a doctor, who brought along a nurse. The patient, wracked with septicemia, had tried on her own to abort her pregnancy. Instead of sending Sadie away to a charity hospital, where she would be one desperate, dying patient among many, Jake committed the family's meager savings to the slim chance that nursing her at home could pull her through. Within two weeks she began to recover, but her spirits were low. A week later, as the nurse and doctor prepared to depart for the last time, she finally voiced the question tormenting her: Could she survive another pregnancy?

The doctor assured her she could not. But how, Sadie shyly begged, could she avoid it? Heading for the door, the doctor answered, "Tell Jake to sleep on the roof."[59]

Sadie desperately turned to the nurse, beseeching her to share "the secret" that she had heard some women knew. But the nurse said she knew no such secret and went her way.

Three months later, another anguished call came from Jake. With heavy foreboding, the nurse returned to the tenement. Up the same three flights, she found the scene she had feared: the weeping children, the frantic husband, and Sadie on her bed, comatose. Minutes later she died.

Leaving Jake wailing in his apartment, the nurse spent the night wandering the darkened city. As the sun rose, she resolved that Sadie was the last immigrant mother whose tenement death she would attend. She would find the answer to Sadie's question and tell every wife who wanted to know it. Margaret Sanger, née Higgins, was neither Jewish nor an immigrant, but once she started the first clinic offering "birth control"—a term she coined—women like Sadie were her most avid clients, and Jews of all persuasions the most enthusiastic proponents of making it available to all wives, regardless of education, background, or economic standing.

Poor women, terrified of another mouth to feed and another one after that, could only resort to what Sadie tried. They shared ideas on how to bring on abortions, including "herb teas, turpentine, steaming, rolling downstairs, inserting slippery elm, knitting needles, shoe-hooks," Sanger reported.[60] Druggists and midwives were afraid to reveal anything they knew and many, like Sanger, did not know much. Immigrants lined up by the hundreds to patronize abortionists charging a few dollars. Others died as Sadie had.

In 1916, in a storefront in the heavily Jewish Brooklyn neighborhood of Brownsville, Sanger started up the nation's first open source of contraceptive devices. Flyers in Yiddish, Italian, and English attracted a steady stream of clients, most of them Jewish. But before two weeks were out, the police closed down the storefront operation, despite fervent support from the neighborhood's *balebustes*. Sanger and her sister Edith Byrne, a Mount Sinai Hospital nurse, were sentenced to a month each in prison for fitting devices, and Fania Mindell, a Jewish social worker on the clinic staff, received a $50 fine for distributing forbidden information. On appeal, however, Sanger established a crucial legal principle and a desperately needed loophole. Doctors could now legally prescribe birth control when they determined that a woman's health was affected. Though the medical profession generally stood aloof, the number of specially established, free-standing clinics dispensing diaphragms and other devices began to grow.

If medical men remained skeptical, immigrant Jewish women were convinced, eagerly reading Sanger's pamphlet *What Every Woman Should Know* in its Yiddish edition. Before they learned to "use Margaret Sanger," many had struggled fiercely to limit their families, repeatedly running the risks of illegal abortions.[61] At one clinic serving poor Jewish women in the 1920s, fully half the clients had histories of abortions. The author Kate Simon, whose *Bronx Primitive* and other works chronicle the privation and travail of growing up in her immigrant family, reported that her own mother had undergone thirteen. Nor was this an unusual number in the neighborhood, her mother assured her.[62]

Prosperous Jewish men and women with progressive leanings supported Sanger's efforts. A responsum (Jewish religious judgment) by Dr. Jacob Z. Lauterbach, a leading Talmudic scholar at the Reform movement's Hebrew Union College, provided *halachic* support for the notion that contraception was permissible in certain forms and under certain conditions. Because Judaism considered sex a good and natural part of married life, and because men, but not women, were commanded to be fruitful and enjoined against spilling their seed, barrier contraceptives used by the female, such as a diaphragm, could be construed as conforming with Jewish law. Acceptance was far from universal in the Jewish community, however, especially among Orthodox-minded men. Still, a decade after Sadie Sachs died, the birthrate among Jewish immigrant women had begun to fall, as it had already among the better-off descendants of Central Europeans. Within a generation of Sadie's death, Jewish women, who once bore more children than the American average, were giving birth to fewer.

Educated Girls and Women

On June 27, 1906, at the close of a month in which rampaging hoodlums murdered seventy Jews in Bialystok, the Lower East Side saw an astonishing spectacle: "great mobs" of Jewish mothers, some clutching babies and all "intent on rescuing their children," were swarming "down on [public schools] all over the lower East Side," reported an astonished writer in the *New-York Tribune*. Throughout a "riot belt . . . from

Rivington Street to Grand, and from the Bowery to the East River," hordes of enraged *balebustes,* fierce Cossacks pillaging a defenseless shtetl, "stoned the school houses, smashing windows and door panels, and except for the timely intervention of police reserves from several precincts, would without doubt has done serious injury to the frightened women teachers."[63] The battle only subsided when the school officials "dismissed their pupils, and the sight of the multitude of uninjured children stifled their mothers' wrath."[64]

What roused thousands of mothers to fearless violence was the dread of what the reporter termed "Russian massacres here." An "absurd story" had swept through the neighborhood "that children's throats were being cut by physicians in various East Side schools."[65] To women who knew of murderous attacks by government-sanctioned thugs, the possibility that officials could harm Jewish innocents sounded anything but absurd. In a reference that revealed more about the *Tribune* writer's ignorance of Jewish culture than about the mothers' state of mind, he admitted that rumors of an impending "slaughter of the innocents surpassing Herod's [Mt. 2:16]" had been circulating for days. Though few Lower East Side women had probably ever heard of that New Testament tale, many seemed to have gotten wind of an unusual summons issued to certain parents by Miss A. E. Simpson, the principal of Public School 100, at the corner of Cannon and Broome Streets.

Their children, Miss Simpson must have explained to the mystified Yiddish-speaking parents in her precise, schoolteacher's English, suffered from a condition that the *Tribune* story termed "adenoids, a fungus growth at the back of the mouth and nasal passages." The youngsters, the school system had decided, needed "a simple operation" to remove it.[66] If the families did not wish to use their private physicians, Miss Simpson could arrange for board of health doctors to do the procedures at school. "Most of the parents probably misunderstood," the *Tribune* speculated in the article's only understatement. Children's reports of the operation turned into the suspicion that "throats were being cut."[67]

But the frantic mothers, along with a few fathers who had also rushed to the scene, harbored no animus against the public schools. When the youngsters came through the doors, healthy and safe and probably thrilled at the unexpected early dismissal, the uproar subsided "as suddenly as it had risen," according to the *Tribune.*[68] In the history of Jewish immigrant parents' relationship with American public schools, this frantic episode is a revealing aberration. On the one hand it tells how little the native administration understood of their East European Jewish students' ancestral culture. But on the other, it shows that thousands upon thousands of Jewish parents had entrusted their children's future to the classrooms and teachers that this amazing new country quite remarkably provided to everyone free of charge. Many of the Catholics pouring through the immigration stations, in even larger numbers than the Jews, felt that Catholic schooling represented the only safe course for believing parents. But from the mid-nineteenth century onward, Jewish immigrants had overwhelmingly opted for public education in the belief that it would make their children American while permitting them to remain Jewish.

The public schools fulfilled the first goal with remarkable efficiency. Both teachers and parents saw English as the key to children's Americanization, and pressure to learn it was relentless and extremely effective. Julia Richman, named school superintendent for the Lower East Side in 1903, developed immersion classes that immigrant children attended for the six to eight months they needed to attain fluency. The first Jew and the first Normal School graduate to serve as principal of a New York grammar school, this uptown daughter of Central European immigrants banned Yiddish in all classrooms, corridors, lunchrooms, restrooms, and playgrounds under her purview and decreed demerits for children backsliding into their mother tongue. Recalcitrant offenders had their mouths washed out with soap—kosher if necessary. Under her stern rules, children not only became fluent in their new language but brought it home as well. Far beyond learning to speak like Americans, public education was for many immigrant parents the meaning of America, the promise that had brought them across the ocean, the hope for their American future. More than any other immigrant group, Jews pinned their dreams on study. The intense passion for learning, which in the shtetl focused on the Torah and Talmud, now shifted to the secular curriculum of the public schools. The reverence that had long invested the yeshiva boy now shone brightly on the college student. Perhaps the proudest boast a poor immigrant could make was not that a son had grown rich or a daughter was beautiful, but that a child was excelling in the courses that would lead to becoming a teacher or a lawyer or, most exalted of all, a doctor. Italian and Polish immigrants saved their arduously earned pennies so that they could buy a house or a piece of land. But East European immigrants lived in rented quarters and scrimped and borrowed and tolerated boarders and kept the store open long hours and worked extra factory shifts and did without for years on end so that a child could spend as many years as possible in school.

Apart from its abstract value, education was viewed by many Jewish parents, especially for their sons, as a means to higher social status for the entire family. Education was thus an investment that would pay off in a better life for everyone. Jewish boys on average stayed in school longer than their Irish and Italian counterparts, and many parents struggled financially to keep them, especially if they were younger sons, out of the factories and at their books. Jewish girls stayed in school too, as long as holding them back from the workforce did not impose a severe hardship on the family. But the realities of thousands of budgets sent daughters into the factories so that a brother could study.

"The odds in life are from birth strongly against the young Jewish-American girl," a Christian journalist opined in 1909. "The chief ambition of the new Jewish family in America is to educate its sons. To do this the girls must go to work at the earliest possible date, and from the population of 350,000 Jews east of the Bowery, tens of thousands of young girls go out into the shops. There is no more striking sight in the city than the mass of women that flood east through the narrow streets in a winter's twilight, returning to their homes in the East Side tenements." No admirer of the Jewish people, this man added that "the exploitation of young women as money-making machines has reached a development on the East Side of New York probably not equaled anywhere else in the world."[69]

But that flood did not carry all East Side daughters. Contrary to the writer's opinion, Jewish immigrants were more willing than any other immigrant group to educate girls. Foreign-born Jewish boys graduated high school at double the rate, and foreign-born Jewish girls at triple the rate, of any other immigrant group. Among the American-born children of Jewish immigrant parents, boys and girls graduated from high school in equal numbers.[70] Far more than gender, a child's relative age in the family and the size of the household income determined his or her chances of going to school. How long he or she stayed also depended on family finances too, because many poor parents willingly sacrificed to educate daughters.

A fourteen-year-old-girl, for example, the eldest of seven children, put an anguished question to Bintel Brief. Two years in this country, the entire family depended for support on their father, "a frail man. I go to school, where I do very well. But since times are hard and my father earned only five dollars this week, I began to talk about giving up my studies and going to work in order to help my father as much as possible. But my mother didn't even want to hear it. She wants me to continue my education. She even went out and spent ten dollars on winter clothes for me. But I don't enjoy the clothes, because I think I am doing the wrong thing. Instead of bringing something into the house, my parents have to spend money on me. I feel a lot of compassion for my parents," this loving daughter went on. "My mother is now pregnant, but she still has to take care of the three boarders we have in the house. Mother and Father work very hard and they want to keep me in school."[71]

To this would-be "money-making machine" desperate to be "exploited," the *Forward* gave an unequivocal answer: the best way to respect her parents' willing sacrifice was to follow their wishes and continue to study. At fourteen, this girl was among the older children still attending class. Of the children who started public school in New York in 1913, only a third reached the eighth grade.[72]

Immigrant schoolgirls, no matter how many years they spent in school, had before them the example of the American schoolteacher, in the lower grades almost always a woman and in every grade a model of independence, authority, propriety, and professional success. Traditional Jewish schools were taught by males, but America entrusted the training of its young largely to women. Girls who did well in school had a clear path to higher status: high school, a teacher's college, and a career with a school system. Many thousands of Jewish daughters pursued that course into the educated American middle class. By 1920, youngsters could not drop out of New York public schools until they turned sixteen—placing a good student within sight of the precious high school diploma and the vast horizon of respectable, sometimes prestigious, white-collar jobs that it opened, and even the vastly more precious possibility of going on to higher education.

In New York City, public, tuition-free, all-female Hunter College could make that a reality. Founded in 1870 and first known as the Normal School of the City of New York, the "Jewish Radcliffe" already had a substantial Jewish presence by 1889, as well a fine academic reputation.[73] When President Benjamin Harrison visited New York to celebrate the centennial of the U.S. Constitution that year, the Hunter student chosen unanimously by her classmates to make the welcoming address was Jewish. So were that year's class valedictorian, four of the six students who read prize-winning essays on commencement day, and fifty of the three hundred women receiving degrees.

Gradually increasing opportunities for women in higher education had already allowed a small number of Jewish women to enter professions. As early as 1902, the journalist Hapgood Hutchins found "successful female dentists, physicians, writers, and even lawyers by the score." By 1905, 25 percent of unmarried female Jewish immigrants in New York held white-collar jobs, whether in teaching, which required higher education; book-keeping, in those days considered a professional occupation; and as office clerks, salespersons, and shopkeepers. Within the next decade, Jewish women appear to have overtaken the Irish as the largest group of teachers in the city's public schools.[74]

Of the ten thousand Jews in college in 1915, a thousand were female; by 1917, imitating the social sisterhoods fashionable among Gentile colle-gians, five national Jewish social sororities existed on the nation's cam-puses. Jewish women were making beachheads in the professions all across the nation. Teachers numbered "far beyond the thousand mark," accord-ing to 1923 survey of eighty-seven cities outside the Jewish metropolises of New York and Chicago. Next came social services, "with a host of able executives and professional workers," noted the study's author, Estelle Miller Sternberger. "Twenty-three cities together reported 69 lawyers" and "two boasted 15 and 14 respectively." In addition, "nineteen cities enu-merated 40 physicians," with Boston and Baltimore accounting for five each and Philadelphia for four, plus a medical professor. Sternberger also found businesswomen galore, "a very great proportion of them" owners. Twenty-four professors taught at seventeen different colleges, and twenty-nine authors labored in fourteen different cities. Significant numbers worked as nurses, dietitians, and hospital superintendents.[75] Smaller groups practiced journalism, dentistry, advertising, librarianship, design, architecture, psychology, and interior decorating, all fields, Sternberger presciently opined, that "suggest avenues and opportunities that have not yet been fully appreciated by our women."[76]

Although educated Jewish daughters may not have ventured into every professional field, immigrant mothers fully appreciated where their fami-lies' opportunities lay: in getting as many of their children as possible through school and into the white-collar middle class. If the Yiddish gen-eration that crossed the sea could not enjoy those advantages, *balebustes* would dedicate themselves to seeing that their American children did.

10

"FULL OF THE TROUBLES
OF OUR NEIGHBORS"

Responding to the Great Migration

A cold autumn rain was falling, but Frances Wisebart Jacobs knew that a sick baby needing medicine couldn't wait for better weather. So she left her large, comfortable house that day in November 1892, and set out in the downpour on another of the countless errands she made for Denver's suffering poor. Perhaps she picked up an infection at the child's bedside. Perhaps she returned home drenched and chilled. At any rate, she came down with pneumonia, and on November 3, two days after falling ill, she died. She had spent decades bringing medical care to others, but the doctors could not save her.

The funeral held for the city's "mother of charities" attracted two thousand of her fellow citizens to Temple Emanuel. Denverites gathered again the next week at the First Congregational Church for another service honoring this Jewish woman. Some years later sixteen stained glass windows were installed in the dome of the Colorado state capitol, each one bearing the portrait of a pioneer who rendered a signal service to this frontier community. The only female face is Frances Jacobs's.

Frances was a pioneer three times over. One of Denver's early settlers, she arrived when the town numbered perhaps five thousand. As it exploded to more than eighty thousand over the next twenty years, she pioneered its social services, helping to establish institutions crucial to both her own Jewish community and the population at large. Along the way, she helped pioneer a new style of female philanthropy capable of coping with the East European immigration. Frances died in the early years of that epic passage—just over a decade after the czar succumbed to his wounds—and also early in her own lifespan, at the age of forty-nine. But she had nonetheless begun to transform the small-scale *tzedakah* practiced by earlier generations of American women of her Central European background. Had she lived, she might well have helped lead the dramatic shift in role and consciousness that would soon sweep over American-born Jewish women struggling to cope with the apparently unstoppable influx of needy coreligionists. From this effort would emerge definitions of womanhood, Judaism, and Jewishness that continue shaping American and world Jewry to this day.

Born in tiny Harrodsburg, Kentucky, in 1843, Frances was the second of seven children and the eldest daughter of Bavarian immigrants Leon and Rosetta Wisebart. While she was small, the family moved to Cincinnati, where Leon did tailoring and the children went to public school. There Frances's brother Ben befriended classmate Abraham Jacobs. In 1859, the two young men set out for the booming Colorado mining country to try their hands as traders. Once Abe had established himself as an owner of a general store and an operator of a stagecoach to Santa Fe, he returned to Cincinnati to marry his eighteen-year-old sweetheart, and his partner's sister, Frances. The newlyweds lived first in the bustling mining town of Central City, some thirty miles from Denver, where Abe and Ben took active parts in local civic life. The Jacobses had a daughter and two sons, one dying in childhood. We know little else about Frances's life in these years except that she made a Jewish home in that mountainside frontier settlement.

She, Abe, and the children moved to Denver in 1870, and she quickly emerged as a civic leader in her own right. By 1872, among a Jewish community of fewer than two hundred, she founded and assumed the presidency of the Hebrew Ladies' Relief Society. Her interests soon expanded beyond her own people's needs, and two years later she achieved prominence in the wider community as well, as vice president and main public speaker of the newly organized, nonsectarian Denver Ladies' Relief Society. Her dynamic presentations and work on numerous projects earned her a wide reputation. In 1880, for example, she helped establish the city's first kindergarten. In 1887 she joined with Monsignor William O'Ryan and Reverend Myron Reed to establish the citywide Charity Organization Society, whose twenty-four federated groups later evolved into the Denver Community Chest.

The federation was needed because, though thousands of miles separated Denver from the torrent of impoverished humanity inundating the East Coast ports, a turbulent tributary of that flood had reached the growing city. Large numbers of "lungers," mostly penniless and many Jewish, constantly arrived in the mile-high metropolis of the Rockies seeking to breathe the clear mountain air then considered the best hope of curing tuberculosis. Besides striking many gentile Americans, the "white plague" afflicted many Jews, including twelve out of every thousand Lower East Side Jews in 1906. "The Jewish disease," "the tailor's disease," it seemed to spread with particular ease among pale, ill-nourished folk crowded into dank, sunless workshops. Before antibiotics able to kill the bacterium responsible, a long rest cure at a high altitude, accompanied by an excellent diet and careful nursing, was the best treatment that medical science could offer. Prosperous sufferers spent months at specialized sanitoriums but often died anyway.

The destitute ill formed a plague all their own, overwhelming Denver's hospitals and charity clinics. Too weak to work, often with ragged, hungry children in tow, haggard men and women filled cheap lodgings until their rent money ran out. Then they camped or squatted in the open. They collapsed in the streets, they lay hemorrhaging on the sidewalks, they perished in the alleys. Frances Jacobs was prominent among the compassionate Denverites who stopped to aid the fallen. She comforted anyone she saw and paid for strangers' doctor visits and hospital stays. She brought food, blankets, medicine, and coal to the slums where wretched newcomers lay coughing themselves into the grave. But individual charity could not stem the tide of misery, she soon saw, nor could the combined efforts of Denver's existing organized philanthropies.

The only possible solution was a proper TB hospital that would treat indigent patients. Frances led a fund-raising drive that lasted years and did the plain work of caring for the suffering as well. A familiar figure in the city's slums, this prosperous lady cooked sufferers' meals, changed their bedsheets, dressed them in new clothing, and spread relentless merriment. On October 9, 1892, the Jewish Hospital Association of Colorado laid a cornerstone in a plot it had purchased east of town. Three weeks later Frances set off to see the baby that infected her. The sanitorium opened in 1899 as the Frances Jacobs Hospital. In 1900, with support from B'nai B'rith, it became the National Jewish Hospital.

But not even the new sanitorium could meet all the needs for health care that their tubercular brethren imposed on Denver Jewry. Seven years after Frances's dream became reality, Denver's Jewish population was nearing five thousand, the great majority poor East Europeans concentrated in the West Colfax neighborhood, and many affected by TB.[1] When one of these unfortunates took his own life, leaving two young children, a local twenty-five-year-old matron named Fannie Eller Lorber decided that she, like Frances, had to do something for all the "poor kids from New York" suffering in her city.[2] To care for children whose sick parents could not, she spearheaded a drive to build the Denver Sheltering Home.

Russian-born Fannie had been in Denver about a decade. There she met her husband, Hungarian-born Joseph. She worked with him in their shoe business, bore two sons, and came under the powerful influence of Frances's example. The home opened in 1906 with eight young residents. By 1912, with Denver Jewry topping twelve thousand, it sheltered twenty-eight children in newer, larger quarters. Like the hospital, it provided services regardless of religion, although most of the children living there were Jewish.

Fannie also took a cue from Frances Jacobs's aggressive fund-raising. In 1920 she cast her net beyond Denver, establishing an office on the Lower East Side. Soon a network of women's auxiliaries in Jewish communities across the country began providing a steady stream of support. Hundreds of children lived in the home free of charge over the years, many receiving treatment for lung diseases. In the half century that Fannie devoted to her charges (while Joseph ran the business), TB was driven from the nation's slums, and the renamed National Jewish Medical Center, with which the Sheltering Home eventually merged, achieved international recognition as a leader in treating asthma and other lung and immune diseases as well as TB.

A Humanitarian Emergency

Emaciated paupers expiring on the sidewalks was a problem that most Jewish communities did not face. But in the early years of the great migration, in cities across the country, Jewish women came to the same conclusion as Frances Jacobs and Fannie Lorber. The independent, local Hebrew ladies' benevolent or relief societies that for two generations had provided *tzedakah* to America's Jewish poor simply could not cope with the new crisis. The old methods of collecting money through subscription and extending informal loans or relief through voluntary committees did not begin to provide for all the impoverished, unassimilated Jews turning up everywhere. They fit neither the new realities of the immigrant slums and sweatshops nor the problems and perils facing unprotected female immigrants, abandoned and orphaned children, non-English speakers, the destitute ill, and many other vulnerable or helpless Jews. The networks of

prosperous, Americanized commercial families who had until then composed America's Jewish communities had long absorbed the earlier, more
manageable, stream of newcomers from Central Europe. Now they found
themselves unprepared for both the sheer numbers of the new needy and
the depth of their deprivation.

These uninvited brethren also challenged the established Americans'
view of themselves and their responsibilities. The penniless, Orthodox,
Yiddish-speaking refugees from East European shtetlach obviously
belonged to the same religious tradition as the well-off, Reform, English-
speaking, business-owning voters and householders from the better
neighborhoods of many American cities. But these noisy, pious, uncouth
exotics threatened the image of progressive Americanness that the
Central Europeans had worked hard to establish. "The relationship
between the Russian and Polish Jews and the German [sic] Jews was anything but amicable," remembered Bernard Horwich, a Chicagoan who
arrived from the Pale in the 1880s. "The latter group . . . engaged in more
sophisticated business enterprises, and practicing Reform Judaism, were
looked upon as Germans rather than Jews [by the new arrivals]. The
Russians and Polish Jews maintained that the reformed religious ideas . . .
made them really 'substitute' or 'second-hand' Jews, and that their Rabbis
were almost like Christian ministers. Some even asserted that they
regarded the Christian ministers more highly than the Reformed rabbis,
since the former were believers and preached their religion truthfully and
faithfully, while the latter tried to deny their Judaism, so as to ingratiate
themselves with non-Jews."[3]

Most attending decorous Reform services, however, were sincerely
practicing what they saw as a legitimate, even enlightened, form of their
faith that also happened to fit the life their families had made in America.
To the East Europeans, though, the continuity between services featuring
English sermons, mixed seating, uncovered heads and organ music and
their brand of traditional, all-Hebrew devotion was far from obvious.
Rather than adopt what they saw as Reform's *goyische* affectations, the East
Europeans clung, to the extent they could, to the forms they knew from
home. Many immigrant *balebustes* preserved as much of the old piety as
the bustle of the New World would allow. They often gave up the married
woman's wig, or *sheite,* and, although more than two dozen Lower East
Side *mikvot* gave New Yorkers ample opportunity to observe the mitzvah,
the practice appears to have declined markedly.[4]

But more visible public observances endured. The great majority of immigrant *balebustes* carefully maintained *kashrut* and made elaborate preparations for the holidays. In many homes the New Year each fall began with family feasts and exchanges of greeting cards. Two weeks later, tenement roofs and yards sprouted flimsy little booths decked with fruits and greenery during the festival of Sukkot. Hanukkah was the highlight of winter, and the custom of gift giving was quickly grafted from the Christian December holiday onto the Jewish one. Purim brought children onto the streets in costumes. Passover brought families dressed in new outfits to lengthy seder services followed by enormous meals. In the great majority of East European immigrant households, the Friday night candles continued to greet the Sabbath, that evening's festive dinner often being the only meal in the whole busy week that had all or most of the family around the table together. A *balebuste*, who often had a great deal of control over her own time, could if she wished pause from her work to observe the day of rest or to recite the prayers and psalms that gave her comfort throughout that day and the rest of the week. Other family members, however, usually found traditional piety and Sabbath observance much harder to maintain. Saturday became another workday for many, even most, East Europeans. In the Pale, "Father had been the most pious Jew in our neighborhood," immigrant Rose Cohen remembered. But in New York, she saw to her shock, he "touched coin on the sabbath."[5]

Many other old customs also faded. Fewer and fewer men strapped on phylacteries (called *tfilin*) and donned a prayer shawl (or *talis*) for daily prayers. Even fewer probably said the prayers at all, and fewer still came to synagogue to recite them in the company of a minyan. As Sabbath observance fell, so did synagogue attendance, membership, and Torah study. The many amusements available in the immigrant districts on Friday night and Saturday lured people to the theater or the dance hall rather than to shul. By 1906, fewer than 10 percent of East Europeans remained strictly Orthodox, in the sense of observing the many rules, requirements, and restrictions of the faith.[6] By 1912, only about a quarter of Lower East Siders kept a work-free Sabbath.[7] A 1913 survey of two thousand Lower East Side stores found 60 percent of them open on Saturday.

Along with the traditional Sabbath, the traditional concern for Jewish learning faded under the intense glare of Americanization. Not that Jewish parents lost their zeal to educate their children. But the East European method of transmitting the religious tradition—heder and yeshiva for boys, minimal Yiddish classes or none at all for girls—did not fit the reality of America, where women rather than men often bore the real burden of handing on Judaism. American children, unlike those in Eastern Europe, did not absorb Jewish ritual, custom, history, and belief from the air. Almost every Jewish child whose immigrant family could manage it went to public school, but no more than a quarter got any systematic Jewish education. Orthodox groups tried to establish religious day schools, but Jews largely shunned them. In 1917 the New York public schools enrolled some 277,000 Jewish students, but the city's three Orthodox day schools enrolled only 1,000.

Very few of the immigrants busy making their way in the new country gave any thought to the future danger that this trend implied. "We immigrants have made a mistake," observed an article in *Di froyen-welt* (Woman's World), a Yiddish magazine that claimed to be the "Jewish Ladies Home Journal." "We thought that free public education would solve all the problems of our children. . . . They had no Jewish education but a factory education instead. Because of this mistake we have lost an entire generation or even more." This complicated the Jewish woman's crucial role of educating her own children, the article noted. "She must see to it that her children, whose education lies in her hands, not be torn loose from our people. Into her hands is entrusted the fate of the future of our own history." The only solution lay in a "healthy Jewish education" for all girls.[8] By the 1890s, Orthodox religious leaders had come to the same conclusion. In a break with old-world custom, they began to establish after-school classes for girls attending public school, along with the ones they ran for boys. But the observant Orthodox were rapidly becoming a minority persuasion.

As strict religious observance waned, however, emotional loyalty to Orthodoxy and respect for its customs endured. Immigrants refused to follow their uptown brethren into Reform Judaism. Rather, they saw themselves as Orthodox Jews unable to maintain observance. "The orthodox Jews who go to the theater on Friday night . . . are commonly somewhat ashamed of themselves," journalist Hapgood Hutchins observed. They "try to quiet their consciences by a vociferous condemnation of the actions on the stage." Actors lighting up cigarettes on stage, for example, were "frequently greeted with hisses and strenuous cries of 'Shame, shame, smoke on the Sabbath!' from the proletarian hypocrites in the gallery."[9]

But religion was not the only source of friction between Central and East Europeans, and scorn flowed in both directions. "The Russian and

Polish Jews, having come from countries where oppression took the place of education, were considered 'half-civilized,'" Bernard Horwich observed. "The attitude of the German Jews towards their Russian and Polish brothers was one of superiority and unpleasant pity. They tolerated them only because they were Jews, and one could hear the German Jews bewailing their fate—that they, Americanized businessmen, had to be classed in the same category with the poor, ignorant, ragged Jewish peddlers on the other side of the river, on Canal Street."[10]

Before long, the established Americans realized that not only the teachings of their faith but the opinion of their Gentile countrymen required them to aid these less fortunate coreligionists. A large, needy population of unassimilated Yiddish speakers reflected badly on those in a position to help. The Central Europeans wanted *unsere Leute* ("our people," but in German, not Yiddish) to become, as one Chicago newspaper put it, "sufficiently Americanized to be tolerable," even though accomplishing this would prove "a very difficult task in cultural labor."[11]

Women Take Charge

That labor ultimately, if sometimes grudgingly, began in cities and towns across the country. Though the great bulk of East Europeans clustered in certain large urban centers, few Jewish communities of any size were immune from the crisis posed by penniless Yiddish speakers appearing in their midst. Even Philadelphia Jewry, with one of the nation's oldest and most extensive networks of Jewish philanthropies, found itself under stress almost from the time the *Illinois* arrived. The institutions that Rebecca Gratz had devised to meet her tiny community's social and educational needs proved as unequal to the current predicament in her hometown as anywhere else. The women who began casting around for solutions soon found, as had Frances Jacobs and Fannie Lorber, that they had to step outside the traditional mold.

A Philadelphia group called Ezrath Nashim (Help of Women), for example, "aid[ed] and assist[ed] poor Jewish women during confinement." That work began in 1873 when some charitably minded ladies learned from a local *mohel* (ritual circumciser) that in the modest homes he visited he sometimes found a sick or impoverished new mother in urgent need of competent, friendly, compassionate care. A group of women met at Anshe Emeth Synagogue to discuss the situation and established the society with a board of seven women to run it. The founding president, Esther Amram, held that post through twenty-two years of growth and change. Her husband, David, expressed his support for the project by becoming the society's first male subscriber. Members each paid a monthly subscription of twenty-five cents, and for the first fifteen years they took turns accompanying doctors and nurses into tiny back alley houses and up winding tenement stairs to the bedsides of birthing Jewish women. Like the great majority of similar benevolent societies, Ezrath Nashim did its work informally, without any permanent offices, staff, or storerooms.

By the mid-1880s, the migration had completely swamped this style of individual, ad hoc charity. There were simply too many pitiful cases to visit. In 1891 the society officially transformed itself into the Jewish Maternity Home, ten of whose sixteen directors had to be female. In a building it purchased at 354 Spruce Street, it created a central facility where mothers could come for help and care. In the following four years, the organization that had begun as a band of women making personal calls on impoverished families evolved into a constellation of specialized institutions including a nurses' training school, the Seaside Home for Invalid Women and Children, and a nursery where children could stay temporarily under the care of a professional staff. A sewing circle also met regularly to make supplies for the various facilities. Though men now ran the association's business and financial affairs, women continued to make the philanthropic decisions.

Philadelphia's United Hebrew Charities also struggled to cope with the immigrant influx through old-fashioned "friendly visiting." An individual woman or a small group would try to "take care of a family who are in destitute circumstances . . . see that they are properly employed and . . . look to their general interest."[12] But because the numbers of people now begging for aid were so high, simply offering food, funds, and advice no longer sufficed.

Fanny Binswanger, the widely traveled, well-educated, Philadelphia-born, twenty-three-year-old daughter of a prominent local Jewish family, had an idea for providing the more focused and effective help the new age demanded. She invited thirty other single Jewish women to join her at the Young Men's Hebrew Association on February 5, 1885, to discuss it. From that gathering came the Young Women's Union and, less than a month later, the first phase of Fanny's plan, an English-speaking kindergarten for immigrant children. The youngsters, initially numbering fifteen, were taught by YWU members and received meals, clothing, and medical care as part of the program. YWU teachers also visited the students' homes, to meet and win over their parents.

Before the year was out, the kindergarten had outgrown its original Pine Street quarters. The students and their families had also outgrown the impromptu ministering of YWU members. Several moves to larger buildings followed as the group sought an adequate facility. Finally, in 1900, at 422–28 Bainbridge Street in the South Philadelphia immigrant district it found a permanent home. By then the YWU had started a household school for girls, where ten- to thirteen-year-olds learned sewing, cutting, millinery, household skills, and typing during the day, and working girls studied English, arithmetic, and reading by night. Services now included two-week summer vacations for children and day care, including a complete series of vaccinations, for the offspring of ill or working mothers. Other projects included a Penny Savings Bank, art classes, evening literature lectures, and a Working Girls Club to broaden the horizons of young women who spent their days in factories or shops.

Across the country, the female members of congregations also began organizing to help immigrants, In Charleston, forty-five single sisters and cousins who belonged to venerable KK Beth Elohim, by now Reform, joined together in 1889 as the Happy Workers, pledged "to care for as many poor [Jewish children] as funds will allow."[13] Within the next several years, they were visiting and aiding several hundred Jewish families who lived among the poor black residents of the waterfront area at North King Street.

That daughters of privilege wanted to be known as workers rather than as ladies expressed something powerful about a new generation and its approach to *tzedakah* and social action. Young women wanted to give not only money but personal labor, not only of their wealth but of themselves. At New York's tony Reform Temple Emanu-El, the group that undertook to serve the Lower East Side called themselves the Sisterhood of Personal Service, a name that spread to similar groups in many other congregations as well. Members of an old-fashioned benevolent society had promised to donate a set amount of money each month or year, wrote Hannah Bachman Einstein, the Emanu-El sisterhood's president for twenty-five years. But sisterhood members committed themselves to "devote a certain fixed portion of their time to a definite task and attend to it herself; the chief object being the bringing together of the well-to-do and the poor— the 'haves and the have-nots.'"[14]

The "definite tasks" included running nurseries and religious schools, youth clubs, vocational training programs, and health clinics; evening classes in English, citizenship, sewing, and cooking; summer camps and resorts, libraries, job referral agencies, sports programs, and the like. Some even established their own full-scale settlement houses. In San Francisco, the women of elite Temple Emanu-el, including Bella Seligman Lilienthal, of the prominent banking family, and Bertha Haas, of the family that controlled Levi's, organized their own sisterhood in 1893. Within a few years, they had established a settlement on Folsom Street. At 86 Orchard Street in New York, a center sponsored by Shearith Israel, the original Spanish and Portuguese congregation of colonial days, offered, along with the usual range of clubs, classes, and clinics, a little house of worship called B'rith Shalom. It was, in the synagogue sisterhood's words, "the only settlement house in the country in which a fully organized synagogue, holding the old traditional services on Sabbath, the festivals and holy days, is an integral part of the work."

Settling the Slums

Settlements were founded all over the country in the late 1880s and 1890s. Middle- or upper-class reformers "settled"—literally went to live—in poor districts in hopes of knowing the people they served, and their problems, as neighbors rather than as visitors from "better" parts of town. Like-minded residents of more elite neighborhoods also often pitched in, either as nonresident staff members or volunteers. But the core of these efforts were the "settlers," women and men, often college educated, who believed that baffled or hostile newcomers would come to trust people they saw day after day on the staircase or stoop, shopping at the same pushcarts and shops, sharing the life of the tenements and streets. The reformers would come to understand the conditions of immigrant lives not as abstract social issues but as daily hazards, frustrations, and perils faced by real, rounded, individuals and families. Unlike the immigrants scrabbling to survive, however, the educated idealists who "settled" the slums generally paid their bills with the help of philanthropic backers, many of them wealthy, established Jews such as financier Jacob Schiff.

The settlement workers hoped to teach the immigrants, and especially their children, what it was to be a competent American. In young lives darkened by poverty and toil, the settlements could be a "bright vision of freedom," remembered Lucy Fox Robins Lang, who studied English and citizenship at Hull-House after long days laboring in a cigar factory or caring for four younger siblings. Her tradition-oriented parents, Moshe and

Surtze, had brought her to New York at nine, and then on to Chicago, where Moshe found work as a gilder and Lucy found new horizons that the Hull-House Settlement opened to her. One was ballroom dancing, a practice considered immodest by traditionalists back in the Pale. In Chicago, it entailed the further violation of contact with Gentile boys. Jane Addams, the settlement's Gentile founder, asked Lucy to help in a dance class. Lucy answered that only a personal visit from the celebrated head of Hull-House could wrest permission from her scandalized parents.

Such disregard for Jewish custom and even, in the eyes of many immigrants, for Judaism itself, convinced some parents to keep their children at a distance from the settlements, at least initially. Many settlement workers were not Jewish, some observed the Reform version, and many observed no version at all. Some had even gone over to the nonreligious Ethical Culture movement. For such Americans, an apparently inoffensive custom like a Christmas party at a nondenominational settlement house seemed merely a pleasant feature of American life, though to observant Jews it suggested Christian missionizing. At New York's Henry Street Settlement, a Christmas party complete with a tree incensed the devout Jacob Schiff, a major benefactor. At Hull-House too, Yuletide struck terror into the hearts of youngsters like Hilda Satt Polacheck, who feared that she would die if she attended the settlement's 1896 holiday festivities.

Finally she joined the guests, welcomed by Addams and cheery strangers. "Bigotry faded," she later recalled. "I became an American at that party."[15] For the next ten years Hull-House became a second home where she studied and played. In 1904, through Addams's influence, she entered the University of Chicago. That same year, she became a teacher of English where she had once been a student. Perhaps half of those attending Hull-House lectures, taking its classes, and joining its clubs were Jews. Others preferred the activities and services of the Maxwell Street Settlement, founded by a Jewish group led by social worker Minnie Low, or the Chicago Hebrew Institute, which in 1903 opened its own community center for the Maxwell Street area on Blue Island Avenue. Five years later the generosity of Julius Rosenwald, the Sears Roebuck magnate and donor to countless Jewish institutions, provided a new six-acre site with buildings set among attractive gardens.

The American settlement movement had begun in 1886, when Stanton Coit founded the Neighborhood Guild to serve Lower Manhattan's Italian and Jewish boys. On nearby Rivington Street, the College Settlement offered similar services to girls; the two organizations eventually merged to form the University Settlement. In 1889, Jane Addams "settled" at 800 South Halstead Street in Chicago's Maxwell Street area; her Hull-House eventually grew to encompass thirteen buildings. Other groups offered similar services outside the strict settlement model, and the term "settlement house" eventually applied to community service centers, whether or not they had begun, strictly speaking, as "settlements." In 1883, New York's ten-year-old Young Men's Hebrew Association, originally a literary and cultural society, started a downtown branch to serve immigrants, said to be the first institution of its type for Jews in the country. Five years later, led by Julia Richman, a short-lived auxiliary called the Young Women's Hebrew Association came into being. After merging with two other groups, the YMHA ultimately became the Educational Alliance, a major force for instruction and Americanization on the Lower East Side. By the start of World War I, more than four hundred settlements and neighborhood centers (service organizations whose staffs resided elsewhere) were bringing education, recreation, and social work to the nation's immigrant districts. An estimated seventy-five of these had Jewish staffs and supporters; an equal number, staffed and supported by Gentiles, catered to Jewish populations.[16]

For all the useful education they provided, for all the crucial assistance they rendered, for all the compassion they felt, many of the well-to-do helpers could not mask their condescension toward their less-favored brethren. Nor could many recipients hide their resentment toward these self-appointed benefactors. Some of the reformers, such as Minnie Low, head of Chicago's Personal Service Bureau, subscribed to philosophies like scientific philanthropy, which viewed alms as corrupting. The goal of charity must be to foster self-sufficiency, Low believed (as had the great Jewish thinker Maimonides, who placed helping a person to gain a livelihood at the top of his ladder of charitable actions). Among the agencies Low built to further this aim was the Women's Association, which at its height lent more than $30,000 annually to help immigrant women run their own businesses.[17] To ascertain that their aid built self-sufficiency, scientific philanthropists and other givers felt justified in closely investigating their beneficiaries. The Philadelphia Maternity Home, for example, maintained a Ladies Visiting Committee charged with assuring that "only the deserving and needy receive assistance." They felt justified in examining immigrants' personal affairs because they saw themselves as bringing each needy woman "into an atmosphere of cleanliness, refinement, calm and peace such as her life [had] never known before." They further hoped that a new mother would leave with the "lessons of cheerfulness and cleanliness and of order impressed on her mind."[18]

Many poor immigrants, however, did not particularly appreciate having their minds impressed by middle-class notions of cheerfulness. They viewed themselves as impecunious, not morally, socially, or culturally inferior. Often the rich do-gooders were offensively patronizing. "It is far too common in our settlement houses and elsewhere, even in tenement houses themselves, to find wealthy women very expensively dressed attempting to encourage the so-called unfortunates by visiting them and telling them what they should do," Rose Pastor Stokes reported in 1906.[19] The *Forward* also berated the volunteer work of women who come to the slums and settlements "with their bediamonded hands more to show their delicate alabaster fingers with well-manicured nails than really to save the unfortunates."[20]

But from these alabaster hands flowed the funds that supported many charitable institutions, and from the settlements and centers grew not only dense webs of social services but a new profession. Lillian Wald coined the name and created the reality of public health nursing because of a "baptism of fire" she experienced one day in 1893. A trained nurse in her mid-twenties and a first-year student at New York's Women's Medical College, she began giving part-time home nursing classes to Lower East Siders. As she ended one bed-making lesson, a little girl told Lillian about her sick mother. A new baby had arrived, Lillian gathered, but the mother seemed not to have recovered. Taking some clean linen, she asked the child to show her the way.

Through a cold rain, they threaded their way along crowded streets, "past odorous fish-stands, . . . past evil-smelling, uncovered garbage cans." Finally "the child led me though a tenement hallway, . . . where open and unscreened [water] closets were promiscuously used by men and women, up into a rear tenement by slimy steps." The family clustered in the sick-room "was neither criminal nor vicious." The crippled father did his best to earn what he could as a peddler—or, more accurately, a beggar. Still, they were people "sensitive to their condition," struggling to do their best by their children, and so grateful for Lillian's efforts that "at the end of my ministrations they kissed my hands." She emerged shaken, stricken, that she belonged to a "society that permitted such conditions to exist."[21]

"Within half an hour," her life had changed course forever.[22] "Deserted were the laboratory and the academic work of the college, I never returned to them." By the end of a sleepless night in her comfortable dorm, she had come to the "naive conviction . . . that, if people knew things—and 'things' meant everything implied in the condition of this family—such horrors would cease to exist" and that her "training in the care of the sick . . . would give [her] an organic relationship" to the poor who needed her care.[23] Acting quickly on her new resolve, she and a friend and fellow nurse, Mary Brewster, moved into the College Settlement on Rivington Street. Soon they had moved again, to a tiny fifth-floor apartment in the tenement at 27 Jefferson, an unlikely address for a graduate of Miss Cruttenden's French-English Boarding and Day School for Young Ladies who was the daughter of a wealthy Reform optical dealer from Ohio.

A gifted student, Lillian had received a broad general education but no formal Jewish training. At sixteen she applied to Vassar College, only to be turned down as too young. Several more years of studying and socializing followed. In her early twenties, seeking more significant work, she came to Manhattan to enter the nurses training program at New York Hospital. She spent her first professional year nursing at the New York Juvenile Asylum, a dismal, abusive orphanage. Frustrated with work as an institutional nurse, she turned her sights to medicine and entered the Women's Medical College. Not long afterward, home nursing classes started. Not long after that, the little girl led her on the walk that would change her life, and the nursing profession, forever.

The new tenants at Jefferson Street began by calling on their neighbors and setting them "to sweeping, cleaning and burning the refuse. In some rooms swill was thrown on the floor, vessels standing unemptied after the night's use."[24] Though some distrusted the two young Americans, suspecting them of being missionaries in disguise, "nursing was [an] open sesame" that unlocked confidence and affection, noticed their friend and soon-to-be colleague, Lavinia Duck.[25] Soon people were coming to the nurses' apartment for help or calling them out to the bedridden. Before long the visits and requests came in an endless flood. From those who could pay something, the nurses accepted a modest fee. From those who could not, they asked nothing at all. In 1895 the Nurses Settlement moved to larger quarters, an entire house at 265 Henry Street. By this time, Mary had resigned in exhaustion, but other colleagues came to continue her work, some declining the weekly $15 salary. Programs besides nursing also began to fill the house, which abandoned its original name at the behest of its boys' baseball team, mortified to be known in the neighborhood as the Nurses.

"We are full of the troubles of our neighbors," Lillian wrote in one of her monthly reports to Jacob Schiff, who quietly supported the project.[26]

To the Henry Street Settlement, as 265 Henry was now known, came the unending pleas for help, and from it, tirelessly, went the nurses. By 1898, nine were climbing the endless tenement stairs to sickbeds and childbeds, or cutting across countless tenement roofs to avoid the long trudge down to the street and then up into a neighboring building. Two years later, there were fifteen nurses, six years after that, twenty-six. By 1926, more than one hundred professional women were doing the work that Lillian and Mary had started alone, carrying medical bags and expertise into poverty-stricken sickrooms nearly a quarter of a million times each year. The Visiting Nurses Service, as the effort came to be known, was spending $150,000 annually.[27]

For Lillian Wald, healing her neighbors' troubles extended beyond treating sickness to preventing it in the first place through education in health, sanitation, and nutrition. In 1902 she pioneered the practice of placing nurses in schools. By 1910 a department at Columbia University Teachers College based on her precepts was teaching nursing and health. In 1912 she assumed the presidency of the new National Association of Public Health Nursing, a name, an association, and a profession that she had invented.

But her work went beyond all this. The "organic relationship with the neighborhood" that nurses enjoyed "should constitute the starting point for a universal service to the region," she believed.[28] The settlement grew into a village of buildings, bursting with activities of all kinds. "The poor trust her absolutely," wrote Jacob Riis, the pioneering chronicler of New York's slums. They "trust her head, her judgment, and her friendship. She arbitrates a strike, and the men listen. . . . When pushcart peddlers are blackmailed by the police, she will tell the mayor the truth, for she knows."[29] She served on boards and commissions, gave talks and lectures, struggled for decades for better working conditions, better housing, better sanitation, and the right of the poor to more decent lives. She chastised her wealthy, uptown contributors about their condescension and contempt toward the immigrants, whom she considered "new life and new blood for America."[30] More than a century after Lillian Wald moved to Jefferson Street, taking the principle of *tzedakah* with her, the settlement she founded continues to serve new generations of the poor and the tempest-tossed, no longer from the Pale of Russia, but from Asia, Latin America, and the lower reaches of American society.

The shocking scenes of want and deprivation that visitors witnessed in the immigrant slums inspired many well-off ladies besides Lillian Wald to do good works, if generally less brilliantly and selflessly than she did. Countless middle- and upper-class matrons and young, single women living with their families also volunteered in the settlements, sometimes spending a few token hours a month, sometimes making virtual careers of funding and running complex agencies. Milwaukee native and lifelong resident Lizzie Black Kander, for example, combined ingenuity, entrepreneurship, and traditional household skills to produce a permanent stream of support for the Settlement, the first such agency to serve her city's poor immigrants.

Her career in philanthropy began when she volunteered with the Ladies Relief Sewing Society the year she graduated from Milwaukee High School. By 1896 Lizzie was a forty-two-year-old wife and the Sewing Circle had grown into the Milwaukee Relief Mission, which founded the Settlement. She assumed the Settlement's presidency in 1900, teaching cooking to immigrant women and girls, among other activities. The following year, she and a friend put together a little recipe booklet for their cooking students, but the board of directors refused to pay for printing. "The way to a man's heart is through his stomach," Lizzie had whimsically written on the cover. She also found the way to the hearts of the city's businessmen, who pledged enough money to underwrite a thousand copies. Those her students did not need were sold at a department store for fifty cents apiece. By 1903 the original collection of Jewish and American recipes, household hints, and etiquette advice had grown to 180 pages and its sponsor list to sixty-five. The book's appeal and customer base continued to grow as Lizzie brought out edition after edition of *The Settlement Cook Book: The Way to a Man's Heart*—twenty-three in all—while she served as head of the Settlement Cook Book Company. The profits supported the Settlement and built both an expanded facility, the Abraham Lincoln House, in 1911, and the Milwaukee Jewish Community Center in 1931. Generations of Jewish cooks fed their families American meals from its pages. Almost 2 million copies of the white-covered volume with its double line of little stylized chefs stood in American kitchens by 1984. In a new edition, it remains in print today.[31]

The New American Jewish Woman

The immigrants' plight motivated Lizzie Kander, Lillian Wald, and many other Americans who found their way into both the new, organizational style of philanthropy and endeavors and neighborhoods new to respectable womanhood. But there were many who responded to more than the demands of the great migration. These women generally came from family traditions of *tzedakah*, expressed a generation or two earlier by the benevolent societies their mothers and grandmothers had founded and served. Their families had achieved financial security and often donated substantial funds to the general good. These new-style philanthropists were women completely at home in their native land. Many, indeed, had far better grounding in general American culture than in traditional Judaism. Like their middle- and upper-class Christian friends, they had an expanding sense of female possibility, a confidence that women could and should count for far more in the wide world of the coming century than they had in the past.

Education, at least through high school, was now a commonplace of middle-class and wealthy girlhood. Growing numbers of coed and women's colleges had brought higher learning into the realm of possibility, though respectable daughters were still overwhelmingly expected to find promising husbands, not independent professions. Still, the very early marriages that their mothers had contracted had passed from fashion and pressure to accept a proposal did not usually become severe until a girl reached her early to mid-twenties. That hiatus provided space to pursue a paid premarital career, however brief, as a teacher, nurse, or typist, or else an engrossing job as a volunteer.

After they wed, middle-class matrons enjoyed far more free time than their mothers and grandmothers had. By the turn of the twentieth century, American-born Jewish women under the age of forty—who by then composed only a small percentage of the nation's Jewry—mirrored very closely the domestic patterns of the Protestant middle class among whom many of them lived. In their early to mid-twenties they married men with good financial prospects who were four to seven years their senior. These couples had only two or three children, lived in their own houses, and employed at least a servant or two to take care of them. Despite the long-standing Jewish tradition of nearly universal wedlock, about a fifth of native-born Jewish women over thirty now remained single—a departure that reflected the growing number of female high school, nursing school, business school, college, and university graduates opting to be professionals rather than wives.

The New Woman, with her independent career and decision not to marry, was the most talked-about American female of the age. Clad in her tailored clothing, pedaling her bicycle, tapping on her typewriter, poring over her books, working at her job, demonstrating for the vote, she rejected many of the constraints that had limited her mother's movements, activities, and influence. Well-born Protestant reformers such as Jane Addams led the way, soon followed by Jewish comrades. Residing as independent single women rather than members of conventional male-headed households—sometimes even with female partners in so-called Boston marriages—female settlement workers embodied a new vision of honorable womanhood based outside of matrimony and masculine protection. Knowingly violating the rule that respectable women lived with their families, they counted on their high social origins and exalted purpose to preserve their standing as "good" women. During the years when suffragists sought the vote for those excluded by outdated laws, when unionists demanded economic justice for those oppressed by exploitative employers, and when reformers brought social services to the slums, the New Woman stood for equality and accomplishment in a dramatically middle-class form.

Society at large did not immediately accept the notion of prosperous men's wives and daughters being active outside the traditional boundaries of feminine concern. Though Fannie Binswanger's father was a leading figure in Philadelphia Jewish education, he did not permit her to go to college—an attitude he shared with many respectable parents across the country. Learning the refined accomplishments of a young lady would fit a girl to marry and make a home for an educated man—as Fannie would become the wife of attorney Charles I. Hoffman. Earning a degree struck conservative opinion as an unfeminine excursion into activities appropriate to the stronger sex. Many doubted that females had the capacity to grasp complex material or learn unladylike subjects. Ill-advised mental exertion even threatened childbearing, or so late-nineteenth-century medical authorities taught. Respected doctors commonly believed that exercising the brain stole energy needed by the female reproductive organs, rendering a scholarly woman less fertile than one who confined herself to less taxing pursuits.

Teaching Themselves to Be Jewish

Across the country, intelligent, curious, literate, and cultured women with free time wanted to learn. If they couldn't pursue education formally, some began to discover, they could work together to educate themselves—and do so under the nose of often skeptical men. Beginning in the latter decades of the nineteenth century, groups of middle- and upper-class ladies, both single and married, met in "study circles," often in one another's homes and often adapting the form of the social visit or ladies tea to the subversive new purpose of expanding their intellectual horizons. They explored various subjects, often religious, historical, or literary, through self-organized programs of readings and discussions, or with members researching and writing papers to present at meetings. Many circles had the support of clergymen eager for mothers capable of imbuing the next generation with proper religious values. The great majority of circles were Christian, but Jewish women of intellectual bent also gathered to learn. Among New York's active groups was the Hadassah Study Circle, which used the Hebrew form of the name of Queen Esther, the biblical heroine. Its members included a scholarly night school teacher, an editor and writer named Henrietta Szold, who joined at the suggestion of Judah Magnes, a Reform rabbi.

Study circle membership often overlapped with the rosters of local philanthropies. Sometimes members of charitable societies formed study groups to investigate particular conditions they wished to improve. Sometimes friends who met to learn about the Bible, history, literature, or social issues joined forces to attack a social problem that disturbed them. By the late 1880s the twin streams of female self-education and new-style philanthropy began to flow together into an organizational movement powerful enough to carry thousands of women to unprecedented levels of accomplishment.

"The whole country is budding into women's clubs," the prominent feminist writer Charlotte Perkins Gilman proclaimed.[32] Large numbers of middle- and upper-class women were eagerly joining, convinced that becoming a club woman meant something entirely different—much bolder and more modern—than belonging to an old-fashioned ladies society. "To join an organization of 'women'—not ladies—and one which bore the title 'club' rather than 'society' was in itself a radical step," announced Hannah Solomon, who went on to play a crucial role in the lives of Jewish club women.[33] A member of an old-fashioned ladies society was a "passive agent, like the child that follows the path laid out for it," stated Sadie American, another Jewish club leader. Club women, on the other hand, "refused to be used merely to act as figureheads in the management of sewing societies and ladies' auxiliaries."[34] By the 1890s, more than 100,000 women had come together into dozens of clubs.[35]

Club women insisted on running their own organizations under their own names and on setting their own goals, devising their own agendas,

planning and carrying out their own programs. They held meetings by parliamentary procedure, established official structures of officers, boards,
and committees, formed wide networks of affiliated chapters, and spoke
out and acted on a broad range of issues facing the nation at large. Ladies
benevolent societies had done valuable community work, many club
women acknowledged, but members of the new movement insisted that
female groups could no longer stay in the background and confine themselves to an exclusively female realm. "Women's sphere is in the home,
they told us," Hannah Solomon declared. But, she insisted, "women's
sphere is the whole wide world, without limit."[36]

Well, not exactly without limit. The great majority of club women, as
the wives of businessmen or professionals, did not hold paid jobs. Those
who did, usually unmarried women, worked mostly in caring professions
such as teaching, health care, or social service. Unlike certain radicals of
the period, club women believed that the boundaries of that role must
markedly expand. For us, after a turbulent century of social change, it may
be difficult to perceive anything revolutionary about a group of corseted
ladies in feathered hats holding earnest discussions or rolling up their
sleeves to make beds or serve food. But from the perspective of their own
time, club women forcefully asserted that they had abilities and responsibilities worthy of serious notice.

As the club movement tried to engineer a major expansion of women's
public role, "there was much unreasoning objection to women's public
activities," recalled Rebekah Kohut, another Jewish leader of the club
movement, of the early days.[37] Rebecca Gratz and her generation had rev-
olutionized Jewish education, philanthropy, and synagogue life by redefin-
ing them as "traditional" female domestic concerns. Under the guise of
nurturing children and spirituality—legitimate female concerns according
to nineteenth-century American culture—they had moved into areas of
religious and community life never before open to the women. But in the
last decades of the nineteenth century and the first decades of the twentieth, American women were making an even bolder claim and many opponents challenged it, some subtly, some openly. The threat that these new
activities would distract wives and mothers from their duty to make proper
homes seemed particularly acute to Jewish leaders who recognized the
home as basic to community and continuity.

"We need Jewesses to give us . . . Jewish homes, Jewish men, a Judaism
spiritualized," said prominent Reform rabbi Kaufman Kohler.[38] Rabbi
Israel Levinthal denounced the "Jewish woman [who] is forsaking the

Temple—of which she is the Priestess—her home."[39] Beyond harming the families and communities that needed their quiet self-sacrifice, wives and daughters with outside interests were injuring their own chances for genuine satisfaction, warned Rabbi David Marx, urging women to realize that their "happiness lies at the family fireside" and that "Judaism emphasizes the hearth and that the woman's place is in the home."[40] None of these rabbis, of course, perceived any threat to Jewish continuity or domestic sanctity in the auxiliaries and benevolent societies that worked quietly within their synagogues and communities. The danger lay in the new public style.

A few men, however, encouraged women seeking a larger role. At a meeting where philanthropist Julius Rosenwald supported Goldie Tuvin Stone for financial secretary of Chicago's new Federated Orthodox Jewish Charities, one Orthodox rabbi quashed criticism by proclaiming, "Was not Miriam a Prophetess and Deborah a Judge in Israel?"[41] How much the millionaire philanthropist's presence influenced the rabbi's snappy comeback we will never know. But his quick defense of Mr. Rosenwald's protégé indicated that the new female activism was forcing American Jewry's male leadership to confront a paradox. On the one hand, throughout the Jewish world, from the haughtiest, most refined Reform pulpit to the grittiest little storefront prayer hall, the positions of public power remained exclusively male. Women did not lead congregations, whether as rabbis, cantors, presidents, officers or, except in rare cases, even board members. At Orthodox services they sat in balconies or behind curtains. Even in Reform temples, girls did not come to the Torah to celebrate their entrance into adulthood. The world's first bat mitzvah did not occur until 1920, when Rabbi Mordechai Kaplan, the founder of Reconstructionism, decided that his daughter, Judith, deserved the same synagogue honors as a boy of her learning and age. But the practice did not become widespread for more than half a century. The brilliant Henrietta Szold, eldest daughter of a Baltimore rabbi and editor of major works of Jewish scholarship, could only get permission to study at New York's Jewish Theological Seminary by agreeing to renounce in writing any ambition to seek ordination, despite an intellect that clearly qualified her for it.

Nonetheless, American Jewish men had, in the American way, abdicated much of the nuts-and-bolts work of religion to their wives and daughters, who staffed many of the religious schools, raised much of the money that supported congregations, and organized the celebrations and social events that bound them together. The community also needed Jewishly knowledgeable women to nourish and hand on the tradition outside the synagogue—even as they filled the pews within it. But the existing system of Sunday schools and bar mitzvah–oriented Hebrew instruction was not doing a very good job of educating them, and many girls were not getting even the inadequate Jewish schooling generally available.

Americanized Jewish women also faced pressure from missionaries, and even their own friends, to become Christian. Many realized that, to resist, they needed more than the simple catechisms, scattering of prayers and glosses of Bible stories they had learned as children. They needed a mature understanding of their faith and its precepts, one developed from grappling with religious issues with an adult's mind and experience rather than a child's. Rabbis therefore often encouraged their female congregants—usually the synagogues' most enthusiastic members—to study their religion and learn to interpret it to their children and integrate it into their homes.

For American women newly delving into Judaism, especially in the Reform version that ignored *kashrut*, strict Sabbath observance, marital purity, or other marks of traditional piety, the principles and practice of *tzedakah* emerged as a strong basis for religious identity and practice. Hebrew was a mysterious, inscrutable code. Much traditional practice seemed arcane and foreign. But the traditional Jewish idea that the community owes its needy members care and sustenance as a matter of right rather than as an expression of individual virtue meshed perfectly with the interest in social reform that was growing throughout the country. Study and good works, it appeared, were the twin hallmarks not only of a Jewishly committed woman, but of a modern American one; in fact, of a club woman. Together they allowed her to be at once American and Jewish, at once modern and traditional, at once practical and spiritual. As prosperous Jewish women watched their towns and cities fill with impoverished coreligionists, and as club membership gained increasing prestige in the nation at large, Jewish women across the country began to combine these elements into a club that changed not only their own lives but the life of American Jewry.

Frances Sheftall took over her family's business while her husband languished in a British prison during the American Revolution. She did not just keep herself and her children alive, but served them all well with her resourcefulness and business acumen. (Jacob Rader Marcus Center of the American Jewish Archives)

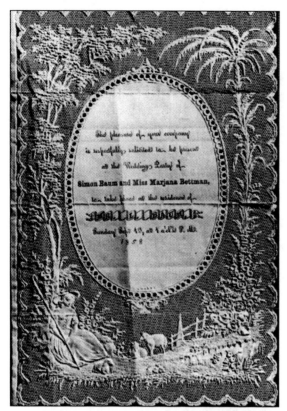

Jewish communities in America, from the eighteenth century on, were held together by the bonds of marriage and the ties of family. The first Jewish wedding in Portland, Oregon, was that of Simon Baum and Marjana Bettman in 1858. (Beth Israel, Portland, Oregon, Courtesy, Syndey Baer)

Reform Judaism sought to broaden public roles for Jewish women. The confirmation ceremony adopted in the mid-nineteenth century, like this one in Portland, Oregon, in 1878 at Congregation Beth Israel, gave young Jewish women a chance to learn and to participate in leading services. (Beth Israel, Portland, Oregon, Courtesy, Sydney Baer)

Like many immigrant women Lena Leiderscheider came to America without her parents. Just before her 1918 wedding in North Dakota, she hung their pictures on the wall of her new home. (Jewish Historical Society of the Upper Midwest)

The Feinstein family of Zeeland, North Dakota, in the 1890s.
(Jewish Historical Society of the Upper Midwest)

Jewish small business, a fixture of small towns and large cities, involved the labor of all. Women played a crucial role in managing these businesses and in supporting their families through their work in the stores. (Jewish Historical Society of the Upper Midwest)

Women of the Amalgamated Strike (Jacob Rader Marcus Center of the American Jewish Archives)

Jewish residents of Boston's immigrant West End participate in an early twentieth century food protest. Jewish women understood the home and their responsibilities as mothers to be political. (Boston Public Library)

Elizabeth Blume Silverstein, born in 1892 in Newark, graduated from the New Jersey Law School in 1911. A criminal lawyer, she was elected to the American Jewish Congress in 1916. In addition to her law practice and her family, she belonged to the Zionist Organization of America, the Malbish Arumim Society, Hadassah, and the boards of the Jewish Orphan Asylum, the Talmud Torah, and the Hebrew Free School. (Courtesy, Nathan Royce Silverstein)

By 1925 the confirmation class in Sioux Falls graduated five young women but only one young man. Women also made up the majority of synagogue adult education classes and in fact outnumbered men as teachers in Jewish schools. (Jewish Historical Society of the Upper Midwest)

A group of immigrant Jewish women in Cleveland. (Courtesy, Jane Rothstein)

After the strike. The penciled Yiddish inscription on the back of this photo—probably taken in Chicago in the 1920s—says, "In remembrance of our strike. Hannah Lenski." (Courtesy, Hasia Diner)

On the eve of migration, young Jewish women in Rypin, Poland, in the 1920s, belonged to an array of voluntary associations, attended schools, formed themselves into Zionist clubs, and participated in much of modern, western culture. Helen Fenster (seated alone) born in 1904, left Rypin just as immigration restriction cut off the Jewish migration to America. Standing to the far right in the photo below, she had participated in the "People's University In Rypin," in 1921, a place where young women and men mingled and learned about the world around them. (Courtesy, Martin and Steven Diner)

A garment worker in New York City's blouse factories, Fenster did not marry until her late thirties. In the interim she hitchhiked across America, returning to New York via the Panama Canal, enjoyed days at the beach with her friends, and spent some time in 1935, despite the rigors of the great depression, to pose for the camera at the left-wing Camp Nitgedaiget—or "do not worry." For this young woman from a small town in Poland, the migration to America from Poland was an unmixed success. (Courtesy, Martin and Steven Diner)

On Chicago's West Side an elderly immigrant woman from the Ukraine, Chasya Kite, stares straight at the camera. She, unlike any of her daughters, kept her hair covered in accordance with Jewish laws of modesty for married women. (Courtesy, Hasia Diner)

Her daughter Esther, born in 1902, took her first steps on the road to modernization when she enrolled in the gymnasium—or high school—in Mirgorod. She studied mathematics, science, history, and literature; a far cry from the limited and domestic oriented education Jewish women of her mother's generation had received. (Courtesy, Collection of Museum of the Jewish Heritage—A Living Memorial to the Holocaust)

Once in America this immigrant woman partook of much of American and American Jewish life. She left her parents' home in Chicago to work as a milliner in Los Angeles where she was an active member of her union and participated in Labor Zionist activities. Unlike her mother, she covered her head to give herself a bit of shade at a day at the beach in Venice. (Courtesy, Hasia Diner)

Jewish women in Sioux Falls, South Dakota prepared a festive Passover meal, a seder, for the Jewish soldiers stationed at the nearby army air base in April 1943. (Jewish Historical Society of the Upper Midwest)

Women at the Workmen's Circle —the Arbeiter Ring— knit for soldiers at the front during World War II. The wall poster on the far left proclaims American patriotism, while the picture on the far right is that of Yiddish writer Sholom Aleichem. In the middle, above the knitters, is Karl Marx. (Courtesy, Jane Rothstein)

Jewish women created their own autonomous communal institutions. In their free loan associations, like this one from St. Paul, Minnesota, Jewish women helped each other get through crises or take on the challenges of new opportunities. (Jewish Historical Society of the Upper Midwest)

The women of Temple Emanu El in Bellefaire, in Cleveland, staged a play in 1947. A few men joined in as well. (Courtesy, Jane Rothstein)

The Women's League of St. Paul's Temple of Aaron combined the fervor of World War II patriotism with the images of Jewish women's traditional roles in this pageant. Women's auxiliaries or sisterhoods helped make the American synagogue possible as a place of Jewish leisure and social life as well as a place of worship. (Jewish Historical Society of the Upper Midwest)

Bess Narod surveys her new Seattle neighborhood from her front porch in 1946. Her husband Milton moved the family into their new home during the same week that their first child was born. (Courtesy, Beryl Lieff Benderly)

The last class to be confirmed at this downtown Newark Congregation Oheb Shalom poses with Rabbi Louis Levitsky in 1957. The next year the Conservative synagogue, like much of American Jewry, moved to the suburbs. (Courtesy, Beryl Lieff Benderly)

Pearl Jacobs Lieff, Ph.D., teaches sociology at the City University of New York's Borough of Manhattan Community College in 1968. She interrupted her graduate work, begun in 1936, to raise three children. She resumed it in the late 1950s and retired from BMCC with emerita status in the mid–1980s. (Courtesy, Beryl Lieff Benderly)

"Yoo-hoo, Mrs. Bloom!" From 1929 to 1948 Molly Goldberg's signature call rang out on radio, and then again from 1949 to 1956 on television. Acted, written, produced, and directed by Gertrude Berg, the saga of the Goldberg family was daytime radio's most durable serial. (Photofest)

Ethel Greenglass Rosenberg and her husband Julius were convicted of atomic espionage and executed in a case that became a Cold War cause celebre. Julius, a devoted Communist who spied for the Soviets refused to bargain for his wife's freedom by implicating others, even though she played a most a trivial role in the conspiracy. Their deaths orphaned their two young sons. (Photofest)

Twenty-one year-old Bess Myerson became the first, and only, Jewish Miss America in 1945, just weeks after the end of World War II. Though she experienced anti-semitism during her reign, her victory thrilled and inspired Jews around the world. (Photofest)

Belle Miriam Silverman, born in Brooklyn in 1929, won international fame as opera singer Beverly Sills. Retiring from the stage at fifty, she served for ten years as the New York City Opera's first female director and then as chair of New York's prestigious Lincoln Center. (Photofest)

Esther Pauline Friedman Lederer, born in 1918, assumed the pen name Ann Landers when she began writing a Chicago Sun Times advice column. Three months later her identical twin, Pauline Esther Friedman Phillips became her chief competitor in the guise of Abigail Van Buren. Both sisters are now syndicated across the country. (Photofest)

The first Jewish woman named to the Supreme Court, Ruth Bader Ginsburg, born in 1933, spent the sixties and seventies demolishing the legal foundations of gender discrimination. (Photofest)

Jan Kaufman stands outside of New York's Temple Emanu-El with her grandmother in the spring of 1979. Kaufman had just received her rabbinical ordination from Hebrew Union College–Jewish Institute of Religion, a seminary of the Reform movement. When in the 1980s the Conservative movement agreed to ordain women, she became the first woman admitted to the Rabbinical Assembly. (Courtesy, Rabbi Jan Kaufman)

Thirty-nine-year-old Rosalie Mandelbaum, a member of the egalitarian havurah Kehila Chadasha, reads from the Torah at her adult bat mitzvah ceremony which she shared with two other women in College Park, Maryland, in 1985. (Courtesy, Beryl Lieff Benderly)

Simply stated, Sally Priesand reversed several thousand years of tradition when she became the first woman to be ordained a rabbi. (Courtesy, Jacob Rader Marcus Center of the American Jewish Archives)

11

"TO DO AND TO DARE"

Club Women Make a Revolution

B etty Meirovitz had watched enough young women pass through Ellis Island to know potential trouble when she saw it. This one, she thought, had given her heart to the man who came to meet her altogether too quickly for her own good. The girl had arrived from Europe alone, had not yet been admitted to the country, and was asking to be released to someone she knew only from letters but with whom, she insisted, she had fallen in love at first sight.

In 1911, Betty knew, resourceful white slavers prowled for naive young immigrants. Before this one went anywhere with her newfound swain, Betty decreed, she would have the full protection of American law. To ensure that the ardent pen pal did not seduce her, thereby ruining her marriage prospects, and then lure her into prostitution, the girl would enter on the condition that the sweethearts immediately wed. After pronouncing this decision, the sharp-eyed "Mrs. Meirovitz got worried," an associate of hers with the unlikely name of Sadie American reported to a group of interested women later that year.[1] The fact that the would-be husband "came from a little place in Pennsylvania" aroused her suspicions. In the end, Betty and Sadie's extensive network of contacts saved the day. A friend of a friend knew someone in the Pennsylvania town, and a quick query brought back "word that the man was all right."[2]

Twenty years before that day, when a Chicago club woman named Hannah Greenebaum Solomon had acceded to a friend's request that she chair yet another committee, she could not have foreseen Betty Meirovitz's encounter with the Ellis Island lovers. Nor could Hannah have known that this new committee assignment would change life not only for her but for tens of thousands of others. Her decision resulted in Betty's action and afforded thousands of other vulnerable female travelers the protection of savvy and experienced Americans. It provided countless needy people of all ages and many nationalities and religions an unprecedented range of aid. And it gave an entire generation of American Jewish women a new vision of themselves as women, as Americans, and as Jews.

What Hannah did know that day in 1891 was that Ellen Rotin had just offered her a plum job. Twenty years after the great fire that destroyed much of their downtown, Chicagoans were preparing to welcome the whole world to their rebuilt and vastly expanded hometown. Ostensibly celebrating the four hundredth anniversary of America's discovery, the World's Columbian Exposition of 1893 would salute American industrial might and innovation, American culture and democracy, and the dynamic, exciting metropolis that seemed to embody all that was new. Plans for the fair, to be held near Lake Michigan on the city's South Side, had already engrossed city leaders for years. Prominent citizens served on a myriad of committees, which, in the custom of the time, were divided into men's and women's groups. An elaborate schedule of congresses, each prepared and presented by authorities, would highlight many facets of American life. The World's Parliament of Religions, for example, would bring representatives of faiths from around the world. The city's major rabbis were already busy planning four days of scholarly papers, panel discussions, and lectures for the Jewish denominational congress.

Ellen Henrotin, a leading Christian club woman and cofounder of the Chicago Women's Club, the city's premier female organization, held one of the fair's top posts as head of the women's section of the General Committee on the Religious Parliament. Right now she needed a subcommittee chair for each major denomination. Initially she sought female clergy or leading suffragists but found none to fill the Jewish slot. Then she thought of her old friend, Hannah Solomon.

A native of the brash, bustling home of the nation's second largest Jewish community—seventy thousand of the city's 1.5 million residents—Hannah belonged to two of Chicago Jewry's oldest families. Her mother, Sarah, was a sister of the late Civil War soldier, Colonel Marcus Spiegel. A Greenebaum had been among the fourteen original signers of the constitution establishing the KAM synagogue. Others had built a major bank. Almost as long as there had been a Chicago, Greenebaums and Spiegels had played prominent roles in its civic, commercial, and Jewish life. A thirty-three-year-old wife and mother of three, Hannah was a former high school and religious school student, a trained pianist, a committed suffragist and social reformer, a regular at prestigious Reform Temple Sinai, and an activist in Jewish organizations. Fifteen years earlier, she and her sister Henrietta became the first Jewish members of the Chicago Women's Club. Along with a solid and respected record of service and a wide network of family and social connections—including relatives among the founders of Chicago's five original Reform congregations—she also had a taste for bold, principled action inherited from her father, Michael, who had violated the Fugitive Slave Law and helped an escapee get to freedom. The assignment Ellen offered—organizing Jewish women's participation in the exposition—would require all Hannah's stamina, connections, and skill. What she made of it would change the Jewish world forever.

Making the Woman's Congress

Thrilled at the chance to advance understanding and to present Judaism, for the first time in history, "on an equal footing with Christianity," Hannah quickly agreed to Ellen's offer.[3] She seems to have envisioned the fair as a gigantic study circle, with learned and accomplished women presenting papers, panels, and lectures on major contemporary and historic issues. A convinced member of Reform, she wanted Jewish women portrayed as members of a religious denomination rather than a distinct people. Although she shared the suffragist orientation of the feminists organizing events at the Women's Building, she was troubled by some of their views. In her book *Woman's Bible,* for example, the suffragist Elizabeth Cady Stanton blamed Judaism for oppressing Western women by "teaching that woman was an afterthought in creation, her sex a misfortune."[4] The place to present a positive and forward-looking image of Judaism and Jewish women, Hannah decided, was not the Women's Building but the Parliament of Religions.

The male Jewish organizing committee did not agree. Unlike various Christian denominations whose exhibits included contributions by both sexes, the rabbis refused to schedule presentations by or about women. "Yes, Mrs. Solomon, you can be a hostess," one man is said to have told her.[5] When the men's committee invited Hannah to one of its meetings, the chairman told her that the program already "seems complete" without any female contributions.[6] But welcoming guests and pouring tea at a male event did not fit this staunch club woman's vision, so she determined to organize a separate Jewish Women's Congress, independent of the men's, as part of the religious parliament. For the very first time in world history, she decided, women would gather, as Jews, in a formal organizational setting to discuss and learn about their religion through lectures and programs presented by women.

Hannah recruited a committee of friends, relatives, and women she knew from charitable and synagogue work. They began publicizing their congress in Jewish magazines and newspapers and seeking appropriate speakers not only in Chicago but among authors, lecturers, and club women in other cities and towns. The search involved hundreds upon hundred of handwritten letters; Hannah herself penned more than ninety. This intense effort produced discouragingly few names, however. Indeed, the committee learned to its distress that "hundreds of Jewesses disclaim affiliation" with the Jewish people, and "hundreds proclaim indifference and confess absolute ignorance of Jewish history and literature."[7] The failure of education and identity seemed so profound, and the loss of ritual practice so pervasive, that the very survival of Judaism in America appeared threatened.

To the staunch club women of the committee, education was the obvious key to Jewish survival, and a single congress lasting a few days could not provide what was needed. "The difficulty we experienced in reaching Jewish women for organized effort made it apparent that a national organization was necessary to obviate such difficulties in the future," Solomon later wrote.[8] What better vehicle for launching such an organization than a national congress at a world's fair? Establishing the organization became "an integral part of the plan of the Congress . . . at one of the [committee's] earliest meetings."[9]

The committee now focused on galvanizing women to attend. More than two thousand letters, each one mentioning that "an attempt would be made to effect permanent organization," asked women in cities across the country and as far away as England to gather in their own communities and choose delegates to the congress. Despite the initially disappointing search, women in twenty-nine cities and towns wrote back saying they would send a total of ninety-three delegates. The search for speakers also continued, eventually producing enough women—a number of whom would make their public speaking debuts in Chicago—to fill a four-day program. The Jewish Women's Congress, as increasingly excited organizers gradually came to realize, might become, like the discovery the exposition commemorated, the beginning of a whole new world.

A Revolution Begins

On September 4, 1893, the great event opened to unanticipated crowds. "Women elbowed, trod on each other's toes, and did everything else they could without violating the proprieties to gain the privilege of standing in a hall heavy with the fragrance of roses," reported the *American Israelite*. "They filled all the seats some time before the opening of the Jewish Women's Congress. By ten o'clock all the aisles were filled; ten minutes later there was an impassable jam at the doors that reached down the corridor."[10] From its first moment, the congress astounded everyone present. It began with twenty-seven-year-old journalist and lecturer Ray (Rachel) Frank intoning the first female-uttered benediction that all but a handful of her listeners had ever heard. Three years earlier, this San Francisco–born great-great-granddaughter of the scholar known as Gaon of Vilna had caused a sensation by presenting not only prayers but a sermon to a thousand Jews and Christians at a Yom Kippur service in the Opera House of Spokane Falls (later Spokane), Washington, a town whose small Jewish community lacked a synagogue. The proceedings so moved one Christian in the audience that he stood up and offered to finance the construction of a synagogue. Ray's fame grew as she lectured and preached in many places throughout the West, inspiring Jews to organize congregations. She also studied at the new Hebrew Union College.

In the electric atmosphere of the congress, the so-called Lady Rabbi asked the God "through Whose justice and mercy this first convention of Jewish women has been permitted to assemble" that "this glorious [event] shall broadcast a knowledge of Thee and Thy deeds" and foster "that which is in accordance with thy will."[11] Ellen Henrotin and Hannah Solomon then rose to welcome an audience far larger, Hannah said, than even her "fondest expectations" to a meeting "as enthusiastic as the [sparsely attended men's congress] was cheerless," according to the *Jewish South*.[12] "Enthusiastic" only mildly describes the women's mood. The congress tapped into a longing far deeper and more widespread than its organizers realized. Standing-room-only crowds followed each event. Talk about the possibilities of the proposed new organization intensified. Rapt attention and rapturous ovations greeted every paper on biblical history, women's role in religion and American society, religious ritual and practice, the challenges of charity work, and other topics.

Then, on the fourth day, Sadie American, a thirty-one-year-old, unmarried settlement worker, rose to give the culminating talk. The Chicago-born daughter of a Central European immigrant who took his distinctive surname to express his gratitude to his adopted country, she had graduated from high school but had been forbidden to attend college. Her long and busy career in social reform and civic work included stints at the Maxwell Street Settlement and on many boards and commissions. Her paper, intended to kick off the projected national organization, began as if addressed to opponents of the idea rather than an energized throng frantic for the project to begin. She carefully described the good that women's groups had already done in America and the advantages of nationwide collaboration over isolated local action—a scheme of local chapters consisting exclusively of Jewish women and allowing not only individuality along with unity, but also Jewish solidarity without insularity and female initiative and authority that did not threaten men.

Finally, giving way to her intense excitement, she proclaimed, "Friends, a great opportunity is ours." To cheers she continued, "Let us understand it. Let us live up to it. Others have died for Judaism; let us live for it—a harder task. . . . On the wings of a mighty purpose let us soar above and beyond . . . every obstacle. The Congress has clarified for us the things that were dull or blurred. Let it not be like a meteor in the sky, leaving no trace behind." With her listeners shouting their approbation, she cried, "Let us be the first to do and to dare."[13]

With Sadie's thundering ovation still ringing out, Hannah was on her feet, calling a business meeting to order in the best parliamentary style. She recognized Julia Richman, who made a formal motion: "Whereas, It is desirable that the zeal, energy and loyalty to the cause of Judaism which has been evinced by the Jewish women of America in the preparations for and the discharge of the duties connected with this Congress be turned to permanent good. . . . Resolved, That this Congress resolve itself into a permanent organization to be known as the Jewish Women's Union, for the purpose of teaching all Jewish women their obligations to the Jewish religion."[14]

Everyone present knew that the long-awaited new organization was on the verge of creation, but the parliamentary discussion of Julia's resolution threatened to dissolve into a debate about its name and the exact phrasing of the founding statement. To save the day's matchless emotional momentum, Sadie American now rose and placed before the assembly her own version: "Resolved, that we, Jewish women, sincerely believing that a closer fellowship will be encouraged, closer unity of thought and sympathy and purpose, and a nobler accomplishment will result from a widespread organization, do therefore band together in a union of workers to further the best and highest interests of Judaism and humanity, and do call ourselves the 'National Council of Jewish Women.'"[15]

The idea and the name won quick acceptance, although many listeners wanted a clearer and more specific founding statement. Still acting as the meeting's chair, Hannah Solomon quickly named a small group to immediately draft a new formula. While they worked, she read aloud congratulatory messages from around the nation, from Toledo, Ohio, civic activist Pauline Perlmutter Steinem; from Sabato Morais, rabbi of Philadelphia's Mikveh Israel and a founder of New York's Jewish Theological Seminary; from his daughter, Minneapolis community leader Nina Morais Cohen; and many others. Then the committee returned with a resolution that the assembly adopted by acclamation:

> Resolved, That the National Council of Jewish Women shall (1) seek to unite in closer relation women interested in the work of Religion, Philanthropy, and Education and shall consider practical means for solving problems in these fields; shall (2) organize and encourage the study of the underlying principles of Judaism; the history, literature and customs of the Jews, and their bearing on their own and world's history; shall (3) apply knowledge gained in this study to the improvement of the Sabbath Schools, and in the work of social reform; shall (4) secure the interest and aid of influential persons in arousing general sentiment against religious persecutions, wherever, whenever and against whomever shown, and in finding means to prevent such persecutions.[16]

A purer statement of the club woman's creed could not have been written. Education and social action together would give America's Jewish women the tools to understand and advance their religion, solve society's problems, and turn the nation away from prejudice and toward understanding. Women would seize the initiative, turning their talents and energies to the great issues facing their people and nation. Everyone jamming the hall understood the unprecedented import of the moment. "A heady sense of independence, a thrill, a feeling that one was taking part in the best kind of revolution" suffused the great gathering, one of those in attendance later recalled.[17] Next the entire assembly rose unanimously, as one woman, to acclaim Hannah Solomon the Council's first president. They elected every other officer unanimously as well, with nominees declining consideration rather than contesting a choice. The post of first national secretary went to Sadie American.

A benediction by Ray Frank ended what Sadie American called "an epoch making day . . . to [woman] it accorded for the first time the recognition of her individuality, her independence of thought, and of her right to represent these herself and not by proxy."[18] Those present at Council's creation sensed a break with the immemorial, submerged past of Jewish womanhood far more profound than people of our time may be able to imagine. "To have opinions and speak them out in a public meeting!" remembered Rebekah Kohut many years later, long after she had achieved national recognition as a Council leader, noted lecturer, and founder and headmistress of a respected private school. "One would have to belong to my generation to understand."[19] The delegates and onlookers at that unforgettably decisive congress, now Council members, streamed back to their home cities and towns filled with exalted fervor, boundless optimism and hope, and the certainty that they were part of something that would permanently alter American Jewish life.

Council in Action

It very soon did. American Jewish women had been waiting, it seemed, for a women's club of their own. Across the nation, not only community leaders and women already active in charity and reform work, but hundreds of the "Jewesses" who had only recently "disclaimed affiliation" with the Jewish people or "proclaimed indifference and confessed absolute ignorance" hastened to join. Each city with a Council presence organized as a single local section. From this main group radiated various committees and work groups that undertook projects according to the members' interests. The national board, based in Chicago, provided overarching structure and unity to the scattered units. In some places, existing literary societies, study circles, charitable organizations, or sewing circles simply became Council sections. In others, returning delegates recruited friends to entirely new entities affiliated with Council.

Hannah Solomon led the way. Her own Sinai Congregation offered its assembly hall at no charge for the Chicago section's organizational meeting. Three hundred women turned out for a program that included remarks by five of the rabbis who could not find room for Hannah on their congress program. Backed by the city's most prestigious Reform temple, as well as prominent religious leaders, Council had obvious appeal to Americanized women comfortable in a Reform setting. Hannah's cousin Lizzie Barbe, daughter of Marcus and Caroline Spiegel, became one of the section's long-standing leaders. Twelve other cities organized sections, and a total of 1,324 women joined Council that first year, many encouraged or galvanized by visits from national board members. In city after city, women already active in social service and Jewish learning eagerly joined. Fanny Binswanger Hoffman hosted Philadelphia's first Council study circle in her home on fashionable Centennial Avenue. Lizzie Kander signed on in Milwaukee, Pauline Steinem in Toledo. Most Council women were well-off and well-established. Sections often held afternoon meetings, obliviously cutting out those who had to work. Sometimes speakers discussed such issues as "The Attitude of Women of Leisure to Their Wage Earning Sisters."[20]

Growth was very rapid. When 250 women from across the nation gathered at New York's Tuxedo Hall for Council's first national convention in November 1896, the organization already had fifty sections and more than four thousand members. Membership continued to rise steeply for decades to come, reaching ten thousand by 1905, twenty thousand a decade later, and fifty thousand a decade after that. After a dip during the Great Depression, the sharp ascent resumed. Council membership reached a historic high of 110,000 in 1970. Hundreds of sections functioned across the country, in hamlets and metropolises, on the coasts and in the heartland. Big-city sections could number hundreds of members, small-town ones fewer than ten. Sections whose leaders had club experience conducted meetings strictly according to parliamentary procedure. Those growing out of sewing circles often retained more casual ways. Various committees and groups under the sections also developed their own styles of operating. In communities from coast to coast, however, Jewish women learned the skills of leadership, the attitudes of social activism, and the confidence to innovate by choosing, organizing, and carrying out countless educational and service projects.

Over the next decades, the work that Council sections undertook varied as much as their organizational styles. Many groups built their own educational programs for members, often based on the study circle model. Most identified gaps in the social services, religious institutions, or educational offerings in their home communities and devised methods to fill them. In San Francisco, Jessie Peixotto, who held a University of California Ph.D. in sociology, led a study of local poverty. In Santa Fe, Flora Spiegelberg designed a solid waste disposal plan and spent two decades working with town officials to get it under way. In Marion,

Indiana, Council members founded the town's original synagogue. In Newark, a Council offshoot called the Reciprocity Club ran Americanization classes. The Portland, Oregon, section, numbering 298 in 1907, helped build the Neighborhood House Settlement in South Portland. Hartford's section ran a clinic and a milk fund; its Americanization classes provided the first child care ever offered in the local Jewish community. In Philadelphia, a section that chose Rebecca Gratz's niece Laura Mordecai as its first president organized a sewing school for immigrants and worked to combat missionaries.

Before long, Council service projects were concentrating more and more on immigrants. Section after section undertook work in settlements and clinics, as friendly advisors to newly arrived families or as advocates for the oppressed poor. By the first decade of the twentieth century, this general interest had begun to focus ever more sharply on a grave but largely ignored issue crucial to the welfare of countless immigrant women: the perils facing those arriving alone or living without the protection of families. "In those days, white slavery was very imminent in this community," recalled Nettie Goldman, cochair of the Hartford section's immigrant aid committee. "We wanted to be sure that none of [the immigrant girls] got into trouble."[21] And if danger stalked naive arrivals in a small East Coast city like Hartford, confused and penniless travelers faced much greater risks of falling into the hands of determined and unscrupulous men on the docks and in the byways of the great ocean ports or on long, lonely train rides to distant relatives in the hinterland.

Nettie Goldman did not exaggerate. With masses of the European poor making their way by foot, rail, and horse cart to the emigrant ports, often with barely enough money to pay for their food, let alone their passage, a criminal trade in women flourished on both sides of the Atlantic. In 1886, for example, "an attractive young girl, seventeen years of age" landed at Philadelphia, whereupon she was "urged by a suspicious-looking man to go under his care to New York," reported Moses Klein of the Association for Jewish Immigrants of Philadelphia at that year's annual meeting. A sharp-eyed association agent—perhaps Klein himself—"interposed" himself in the conversation. Questioning revealed that the girl "had an uncle in Chicago." The agent "took charge of her, procured her food and a railroad ticket, and telegraphed to her uncle to meet her, despite the vexation and chagrin of her would-be betrayer."[22]

An even closer call befell a "very prepossessing young woman destined for San Francisco [who] was induced to go to a beer saloon to await intelligence of her husband," Klein continued. Luckily, "she fell under the notice of our agent while accompanied by the saloon keeper and another man. Her genteel dress and handsome appearance attracted general attention and there was evidently a concerted effort made to detain her. Our agent inquired why she remained in the saloon and where she was to go. She replied that she wished to go to her husband in California, but that all her money was spent and she had acted on the advice of these gentlemen to notify her husband and remain at the saloon until she received money to proceed. He then asked if she wished to go at once, to which she quickly assented."[23]

Not all vulnerable travelers were so lucky. Gullible young immigrants were kidnapped outright, hoodwinked into fake marriages that wrecked their virtue and placed them in men's power, or snared by fraudulent employment agencies that sent them to brothels rather than the well-paying legitimate jobs promised in flashy leaflets. Some of the men running this commerce, and many of the women traded within it, were Jews. In 1909, for example, half the prostitutes in Buenos Aires were East European Jewish women.[24] Because of the relatively independent role that women played in Eastern European life, Jewish parents were more prone than others to send daughters on the long voyage alone. Klein's group and others such as the Hebrew Immigrant Aid Society did what they could, but they were unable to concentrate their attention on solitary women and girls.

For Council women like Nettie Goldman, the protection of defenseless young women seemed an obvious task to undertake. No other Jewish group had made a major commitment to combating white slaving. In the eyes of Council women, those lured or forced into prostitution were not evil or fallen but the victims of well-organized and well-funded conspirators. Only equally well-organized, well-funded, concerted, practical action, Council women decided, could foil them, taking Jewish girls out of their clutches and seeing them safely on their way to final destinations. In the early 1900s, members of the New York section began appearing at Ellis Island to help shepherd Jewish women through the trials of arrival. New York's United Hebrew Charities already supported representatives at the immigration station to help arriving Yiddish speakers, but they did not pay special attention to the particular problems of women.

In 1904 they were joined by a paid, full-time female agent of Council's New York section. In that official, professional role Betty Meirovitz intercepted the love-struck young greenhorn in 1911. The money for the agent's salary came mainly from the Baron de Hirsch Fund and the impetus for her presence mainly from Sadie American, who had moved east in 1901. In 1905 she became Council's paid national executive secretary and later president of the New York section. From these twin positions in the nation's greatest port, she masterminded Council's growing service to immigrants.

"Many girls are misled into immoral lives, and others are subjected to great dangers because of the lack of some directing and protecting agency in Ellis Island," Sadie had written to the Baron de Hirsch Fund in the letter that proposed support for Council's initiative. "It is in order that there shall be a complete chain of protection that the Council now asks to maintain a woman at Ellis Island . . . and the Council would be very glad to supervise the work of such a woman if you desire . . . and also to engage other women's organizations in assisting to fully protect and safeguard our immigrant sisters."[25]

The "complete chain of protection" started before a girl ever set foot on American soil. Council's agent arranged to receive from the shipping companies and the federal immigration service the names of women and girls between fourteen and thirty-five years arriving alone or with children. She met them after they landed and did what was necessary to see them safely on their way. Those planning to stay in New York who had no respectable relatives or friends waiting were taken to the Clara de Hirsch Home or some other protected residence, where they could stay until they got their bearings. Those making their way to other cities were escorted to the appropriate train. With its nationwide reach, Council had agents in 250 communities across the country. A telegram giving all the details of the woman's journey preceded her to her destination. When her train pulled in hours or days later, whether to a great metropolitan terminal or a prairie whistlestop, a Council volunteer would be waiting at the track, ready to help the newcomer make her next connection or find her destination. In one year, 1909–1910, Council representatives met almost five thousand new arrivals at Ellis Island.[26] Between 1909 and 1911, Council's paid workers and volunteers helped a total of 19,377 girls, 4,020 women, and 6,427 children.

Council agents also helped unsnarl snafus at Ellis Island, explaining the immigrants to the immigration officers and the immigration officers to the immigrants. Chaya Blocker, for example, arrived with a false passport in the fake name she assumed to mask her illegal exit from her native country. The immigration inspector refused to release her to the purported fiancé who came to meet her. The Council agent learned from the man that he was Chaya's husband, and that a marriage certificate in her correct name was in her luggage. Learning the true situation from the agent, the inspector quickly admitted Chaya. Eventually, any girl met by a fiancé was released to Council agents, who would arrange a civil wedding at city hall "for [the girl's] protection."[27]

Council helped immigrant women with countless other vexing details, answering questions, tracking down relatives, and assisting in the search for housing. Its Department of Immigrant Aid published a booklet, *What Every Emigrant Should Know,* and issued monthly bulletins on current conditions. In 1910 Sadie American attended the International Conference on Suppression of Traffic in Girls and Women, held in London by the British Jewish Association for the Protection of Girls and Women, and the International White Slave Trade Conference in Madrid. Of all American Jewish organizations, only Council sent a delegate to both meetings. Sadie was instrumental in preventing these conferences from becoming forums for general attacks on Jews by anti-Semites who blamed the entire problem on Jewish racketeers. In a speech at Madrid, she insisted that prostitution had an ancient pedigree and that its onus should not fall so heavily on women. She boldly called for "a single standard of morals, which shall raise men up to the standard of women." Otherwise, she predicted, "we shall continue to have white slaves."[28] She later traveled to Rome to advise the Italian government on improving protections for their own women immigrating to the United States.

Council's "chain of protection" stretched well beyond the boat dock, immigrant station, and train platform. After young women had safely arrived in Hartford, for example, "we used to follow them up and ask them to report to us," Nettie Goldman explained. "The young girls had to report to us every week as to what they were doing and who their friends were."[29] In New York, Council made provisions for immigrant girls who slipped from the straight and narrow, despite the efforts of their would-be protectors. Therese Loeb Schiff, wife of Jacob and herself a prominent philanthropist and community activist, provided $10,000 in 1906 to permit Council to acquire a home for wayward girls at Lakeview on Staten Island. Sadie American considered it "unwise" to "call the work of Lakeview work for immigrants," she wrote to the Baron de Hirsch Fund, because she did not want to advertise the prevalence of unwed pregnancy and prostitution among Jewish newcomers. Still, she admitted, only a fifth of the "inmates" were American-born and another tenth immigrants who had spent more than five years in America.[30]

Beyond immigrant protection, Council sections across the country accumulated other concerns. Margaret Sanger credited it with being the first organization to join her in pressing for legal birth control, out of concern for the health and welfare of mothers and families. The 1911 convention heard Dr. Rosalie Morton call it a "crime to allow any girl to reach the menstrual period without having her understand before the time is at hand what it means."[31] Other programs pioneered services to the blind and to Jews living in rural areas.

Council had been founded not only to serve society but to preserve and enrich Judaism and to build Jewish identity and understanding. Many women eagerly joined specifically because it was Jewish. Like Hannah Solomon in the Chicago Women's Club, they could find ample opportunities to do good works among Christians. But few had any other opportunities to study Jewish subjects in a systematic way. In the early years, study circles were the core of many members' Council activities, and many who attended craved a deeper connection with Jewish tradition, ritual, and spirituality. Esther Jane Baum Ruskay, a writer, teacher, and journalist who graduated with Julia Richman in the first Normal College class, told the meeting that founded Council's New York section, "We have in Judaism and the Jewish life all of divine comfort and consolation."[32]

It amazed and dismayed her that many of her Jewish contemporaries would reject the practice of their own traditions and "seek in Ethical Culture and its kindred cults the answer to our prayers." This universalistic movement, led by Felix Adler, son of the rabbi at New York's Emanu-El, was then attracting large numbers of educated, Americanized Jews away from Reform. A charismatic speaker who had once studied for the rabbinate, he explained to huge audiences each Sunday morning at his Society for Ethical Culture that ethics, not separate peoplehood, should be the goal of proper living. But Ruskay believed in Jewish ritual and tradition. American Jews should teach their children Hebrew, the ancient language of prayer and scripture, "in the same spirit of educational fervor that we give the Latin and Greek for their classical training."[33] To her, "Ethical Culture is neither more nor less than the expression of the wide humanitarianism of the Mosaic creed, as the ethics of all religions are the outcome of their faiths. Ethics is the tail of the kite. Religion is the kite itself."

Many Council women, adherents of Reform in its more radical version, did not share her view of the centrality of Jewish ritual. After the first, fervid years of Council's existence, its religious emphasis gradually declined and was replaced by a focus on service as an expression of Jewishness. As early as the first convention in 1896, dissension over religious practice began to appear. Traditionalists like Esther Ruskay and Rebekah Kohut, wife of a non-Reform rabbi, argued that Council should support family Sabbath observance as a keystone of Jewish life and an expression of the centrality of the Jewish home. "Sabbath! That is a work which we, as Mothers in Israel, must brave again," Kohut told the gathering. "When down Sinai's mighty heights the Lord's voice rang out in thunder tones, 'Remember the Sabbath day to keep it holy,' even the women joined in the answer, 'We will do and we will harken.' This be the spirit of the convention," she urged. "Let us not only harken, but let us do."[34]

For Hannah Solomon, Sadie American, and others of the radical Reform persuasion, however, the traditional Saturday rest did not fit American reality. Better, they argued, that Jews should cease work on the day the entire country did than struggle to maintain a outmoded custom simply for the sake of tradition. Since in America most who worked had to do so on Saturday, keeping it as the Sabbath deprived most families of the opportunity to devote the Sabbath day to worship, study, and family. Celebrating Sabbath on Sunday, when Americans did not work, would allow families "to consecrate that day of rest in accordance with the spirit of Judaism and its message," Henrietta Greenebaum Frank argued. "Not the choice of the calendar day, but the manner of its observance makes it a Sabbath. . . . We keep our religious ideals more alive by devoting a part of the day of rest to the study of Judaism, its history and evolution, its message to us and the world, than by wasting it and celebrating the traditional Sabbath-day more in the breach than the observance."[35]

Challenged for Council presidency by members who thought that a woman who did not observe the Saturday Sabbath should not represent Jewish womanhood, Hannah Solomon retorted, "I forbid the council or any member of it to be a censor over me as to what day I shall keep. I do consecrate the Sabbath. I consecrate every day."[36] Only the withdrawal of the Saturday faction candidate, Minnie Louis, prevented a vote to oust Solomon that might have shattered Council. With religion so acrimonious an issue among the leadership, Council began to concentrate more and more on service—the area on which members could agree. The conflict came to a climax when the 1913 convention put support for traditional Judaism to a vote, and the traditionalists lost. Rather than continue in an organization that they believed had abandoned the religion that was its reason for being, many traditionalists began to abandon Council.

The Daughter of My People

In the two decades since the glorious dawn at the congress in Chicago, Council had taught thousands of women across the country to organize, to study, and to lead. By the time major defections began to occur, Council had, largely through its own success, already ceased to be the only organization offering women opportunities to learn and serve in a Jewish setting. Many had taken its lessons and applied them to founding and building other organizations. Many synagogues now had sisterhoods with active programs of education and service. Just a year before the decisive vote, a little group that met regularly in New York to explore religious issues affecting women formed a new organization that would make the name of their Hadassah Study Circle known throughout the world.

For Henrietta Szold, Jewish scholarship was as central as community leadership was for Hannah Solomon. Born in Baltimore the year after her parents had emigrated from Hungary, she was the oldest of the five daughters of Rabbi Benjamin Szold and his wife, Sophie Schaar. Her father was a liberal-minded scholar who led the prominent Oheb Shalom synagogue, and Henrietta grew up in a household devoted to Judaism, learning, and independent thinking. Reaching their new home just before the Civil War, the Szolds disregarded Baltimore's Confederate leanings and supported Lincoln and emancipation. Benjamin encouraged his daughters to develop their own ideas. As adults, Rachel worked for woman suffrage, Bertha supported socialism, and Adele favored communism.

Henrietta shared her father's passion for Jewish scholarship. A brilliant performance at Western Female High School indicated her intellectual gifts, but her early immersion in her father's work deepened and broadened her education. Arthritis deprived Rabbi Szold of the normal use of his right hand, and he came to depend on his talented eldest child as a research assistant, translator, editor, and secretary as he prepared his sermons and other writings. Before she even finished high school, this work taught her German and Hebrew and produced a wide knowledge of Jewish texts and thinking. While Benjamin Szold upheld the traditions of Jewish scholarship, Sophie exemplified its dedication to service through community activities that included work at a home for the aged. Together, the Szolds raised their daughters in a home dedicated to traditional Jewish practice.

Right out of high school, Henrietta accepted two jobs, teaching math, German, and French at the Misses Adams English and French School for

Girls and Jewish subjects in Oheb Shalom's religious school. A trip to
Europe with her father when she was twenty-one strengthened her sense
of kinship with the Jews of Europe and her desire to serve Jewish women.
As the great migration started and East Europeans began to appear in
Baltimore, Henrietta taught Americanization and English at a night school
she helped to establish. She also expanded her editing activities from her
father's writing to works being prepared for press by the new Jewish
Publication Society. In 1888, JPS, which soon became a major intellectual
force in American Jewish life, named Henrietta as the only woman on its
nine-member publications committee. After working on several major
projects, she was named the committee's full-time, paid secretary (actually
executive director) in 1893. During these years she began publishing articles under her own byline and the pseudonym "Shulamith" in the New
York *Jewish Messenger* and other publications.

Her father's death in 1902 inspired her to prepare his writings for publication, but she felt her Jewish knowledge inadequate. She applied to New
York's Jewish Theological Seminary, which admitted her subject to her
promise not to try to become a rabbi. Here she met Louis Ginzberg, a
thirty-year-old bachelor and brilliant scholar, who became the love of her
life. She threw herself into editing and translating his masterpiece, *The
Legends of the Jews*. After years of accepting Henrietta's work and adula-
tion, Ginzberg abruptly married a woman a generation her junior.

"Wretched and despondent" over her Louis's defection and her own
"failure to live a full women's life," Henrietta did not know that her true
life's work still awaited her and would shortly begin.[37] In 1909, not long
after the wedding that broke Henrietta's heart, she joined a study circle
composed of women, some of them the daughters or wives of seminary figures, and devoted to learning about Zionism. That same year, she and her
mother took a trip to Palestine, her first visit to the ancient home of the
Jewish people. They saw both the old religious cities and the Zionists' pioneering settlements. The primitive living conditions and inadequate education and medical care under the backward Turkish regime distressed her
as much as the ancient holiness of Zion inspired her. Back in America, she
became active in Zionist activities. On February 14, 1912, she and six
friends from the Hadassah Study Circle constituted themselves as the
Daughters of Zion—Hadassah Chapter. Though some in the male-dominated Federation of American Zionists thought that Henrietta had
founded a potential ladies' auxiliary for the existing group, she had no
such intention. "The time is ripe for a large organization of American

Zionists," the founders declared.[38] Ten days later, thirty-eight women gathered in a room at New York's Emanu-El; more than twenty of them left that meeting as officers or board members of the new organization. Henrietta now headed a group of Jewishly committed and knowledgeable women, many of whom had prominent husbands and extensive experience in Council, sisterhoods, and other organizations.

In building what would become the largest women's organization in American history—with a membership almost twice as large as Council would ever achieve—she and her collaborators combined two of the great female achievements of their era: Council's organizational structure and Lillian Wald's public health nursing. Unlike either of those endeavors, however, they infused their work with a deep love of Jewish peoplehood and a fervent devotion to rebuilding the ancient homeland. The group adopted as its motto the Hebrew phrase *aruchat bat-ami* (the healing of the daughter of my people). By the following January, 122 women had joined. With the $542 in dues that they had accumulated, plus $5,000 donated by wealthy Chicagoans, it dispatched two young Jewish nurses, Ray (Rachel) Landy and Rose Kaplan, to establish a Daughters of Zion–funded Nurses Settlement. But instead of renting an apartment on the Lower East Side, they rented a house in Jerusalem and posted a placard reading "Hadassah Chapter, Daughters of Zion" over the door. Like Lillian Wald and Mary Brewster's neighbors in the early days on Jefferson Street, Jerusalemites at first distrusted the newcomers, certain that they intended to missionize. Before long, however, a steady stream of poor people were coming for help. Though Szold wanted this initial settlement to lead eventually to a community nursing system on Lillian Wald's model, she envisioned facilities to train local women in nursing, not merely a continuing American presence.

Eight Daughters of Zion chapters existed within the next year, including chapters in Baltimore, Boston, Chicago, Cleveland, Newark, Philadelphia, and St. Paul, each affiliated with male-run Zionist organizations as well as with each other. Like Council, Daughters of Zion permitted only one main group in each city, though smaller committees devoted to special interests could radiate from it. Unlike Council, it was "composed not of swell, nor of the very poorest class of people" but of those "who have regard for the meaning of a dollar," said Sarah Kussy, leader of the Newark group and daughter of early Newarkers Bella and Gustav Kussy.[39] Quite a number of those sensible, hardworking women were Yiddish speakers, and the single-chapter structure brought native-born and immigrant women together as equals in a common organization.

For Szold, this strengthening of ties among Jewish women at home fit with the healing she had in mind. "We are an organization of Jewish women who believe in the 'healing of the daughter of the people' in the healing of the soul of the Jewish people as well as its body."[40] American Jewry was wracked by dissension over religious practice, with many Jews assimilating and others locked in rigid Orthodoxy. "We need Zionism as much as those Jews do who need a physical home," she believed. And Judaism needed it too; Zionism would build a Jewish homeland in which Judaism could "be changed back from creed to a way of life." Through study and service, Hadassah members could build not only a geographic Zion but a "restored Zion in [their] hearts."[41]

By 1914, the nurses' reputation for physical healing was already wide-spread in Palestine, and the organization changed its name to Hadassah, by then almost a synonym for "nurse" in Jerusalem. Hadassah had twenty-one hundred members in thirty-four chapters when the United States entered World War I, but it had to close the original Nurses Settlement because of political pressures arising out of the conflict. With the war over, however, it helped organize and fund the American Zionist Medical Unit, which sent a score of nurses and eventually organized medical and dental clinics, a nursing school, X-ray services, child health stations, and other facilities based on American models and aiming at American standards. In 1920 Szold arrived to supervise the effort, which became the Hadassah Medical Unit. She continued in that role for three years, despite initial resistance. After a visit home, she returned in 1925 and spent the remaining twenty years of her life building the homeland whose independence she did not live to see. A major international figure in her mid-sixties, Szold remained Hadassah's spiritual leader. But running the organization—which counted more than thirty-eight thousand members by the late 1920s—was now in the hands of a younger generation of leaders. As the organization's activities spread beyond health care to social work, education, and rescue in Palestine and later in Israel, it retained its twin emphases on building the homeland and building Jewish consciousness and education among its membership.

By the mid-1920s, female-founded social services had become a major and permanent feature of American Jewry. Care for the poor and dispossessed, both in Palestine and at home, had begun as the voluntary effort of community women. Over the decades in which the great migration coincided with American's reform-minded Progressive era, it gradually became more organized and bureaucratic. By the second and third decades of the twentieth century, it had grown into the profession of social work. Fewer leaders of service agencies were now earnest club women and many more were university-trained specialists. Fewer of the agencies they worked for were now financed by female fundraising and more by city-wide federations. As these trends advanced, social service was seen less as an extension of "natural" female nurture and compassion and more as an instrument of community or government policy. With social service agency budgets now large, control of both philanthropic money and the work it supported increasingly passed from women, still generally defined as well-meaning amateurs regardless of the decades they spent as effective organizers and administrators, to men, who defined themselves as the real custodians of society's serious business. No longer a matron's avocation, social work was now an official profession. In the agencies—as in the nation's hospitals and schools—women did the great bulk of the frontline work, but males controlled policymaking, budgeting, and leadership.

By 1915, three decades after the Chicago congress, Minnie Low was complaining to David Bressler, president of the National Association of Jewish Social Workers, about that organization's failure to choose even one female speaker among the thirty-one persons scheduled to address the group's conference. "Women not only like to vote, but they also like to talk once in a while," she wrote to him, "and particularly in the presence of a crowd of brilliant coworkers of the other sex. In fact, if you want to retain the interest of the rank and file, you must give women a chance to be heard. It is not a question of favoring my sex, but it is merely a question of justice, because surely you could have found one fair dame in the width and breadth of this land who could bring something valuable to the Conference."[42]

For the veterans and heirs of the great Chicago revolution; for the stalwarts of Council, Hadassah, the settlement houses, the sisterhoods, and the many other women's organizations that had pioneered large-scale social service; and also for the rising generation of American-born and educated daughters of immigrants, something had permanently changed. Men might not acknowledge women's decisive move into the public sphere, but club women and career women, working girls and college girls had felt the shift. "We have earned the title to larger responsibilities," Rebekah Kohut told Council's 1917 convention. "It is now that woman can show for all time that she is able to meet the greater demands, not only in the social spheres, but in the productive fields of work as well."[43] Through a generation of work and learning, "the scope of [Jewish women's] activities had broadened to include every phase of that world-wide movement of revolt against artificial barriers which we call feminism," declared Mrs. Carl Wolf of Terre Haute, Indiana's convention delegate.[44] In women's own estimation, the old value of *tzedakah* had successfully expanded into the new world of effective public action. "The spirit of the work has remained unchanged," Hannah Solomon said, "even though the work itself has changed."[45]

Something else had changed too. The Immigration Act of 1924 ended the era of essentially unlimited European immigration to the United States. The Golden Door swung shut on Eastern and Southern Europe, barring millions of Jews, Slavs, Italians, and others who yearned, as desperately as those who came before, to breathe the air of freedom. The Jews who had made it through the fabled portal, who were busily making themselves Americans, and whose children were born Americans, could only thank the merciful God of Israel, if they believed in Him, or the inevitable forces of history, if they did not, for bringing them safely to a new land that would, at last, allow Jewish people fully to belong.

It fell to a son of a Russian shtetl called Temun, who landed in New York as a child in the 1890s, to put into words what millions of his ancient tribe and his new countrymen felt. "God bless America" was the very least that Israel Beline could pray for the "land that I love." By the time he penned that lyric to a ditty that instantly became a beloved patriotic anthem, the Golden Door had been closed for fifteen years. By then, with the flood of newcomers cut off, U.S. Jewry included as many native-born Americans as it did one-time greenhorns. Fully half of its people, and an entire young generation, claimed the United States not as a gift but as a birthright, not as a mysterious land of promise but as the homeland that held their inalienable futures. Millions of its freeborn sons and daughters now sang along with the renamed Irving Berlin, truthfully and in unaccented English, of what the Goldene Medina had become: "God bless America, my home sweet home."

PART FOUR

"My Home Sweet Home"

American-Born East Europeans Remake Jewish Life,
1925–1963

12

"ALWAYS A STEP IN THE RIGHT DIRECTION"

The Great Migration's Children Join the Middle Class

One day in the late spring of 1944, Frances Slanger helped open the way for thousands of other young American Jews to return to the continent that their parents or grandparents had so hopefully and gratefully abandoned. Frances, a daughter of Boston's Roxbury district, reached the European coast after a short trip from Britain on a crowded ship. She disembarked into the English Channel's choppy waters and then waded through the waves onto the sandy shore of northern France. The date was June 6, the stretch of sand was the Normandy beachhead, and Lieutenant Frances Y. Slanger was one of four U.S. Army nurses to land with the greatest and most decisive amphibious invasion in the history of the world.

As the Allied armies pushed toward Germany from the logements they won during that longest day, Frances and her colleagues of the Forty-Fifth Field Hospital followed them into Belgium, caring for an endless stream of wounded soldiers in makeshift canvas wards. Their patients were, she wrote in a letter to the GI newspaper *Stars and Stripes* four months after D-Day, "brought in bloody, dirty with the earth and mud and grime, and most of them so tired." But all, she knew, were "somebody's brothers, somebody's fathers, somebody's sons." She delighted in "seeing them gradually brought back to life, to consciousness." Sweetest of all was the moment when "their lips separate into a grin [and they] say, Hiya, Babe, Holy Mackerel, an American woman—or more indiscreetly, how about a kiss?"[1] Bending over her letter paper at two o'clock that cold October morning, she noted that "the wind is howling, the tent waving precariously, the rain beating down, the guns firing." The three other nurses who shared her canvas quarters slept peacefully in their coal stove's fading warmth.

Each of the lives entrusted to their care, Frances went on, resembled the flame still glowing among those slowly dying embers. "If it is not allowed to run down too low, and there is a spark of life left in it, it can be nursed back. . . . It is done all the time in these field hospitals and the other hospitals of the [European theater of operations]." Recuperating GIs, she continued, constantly praised the nurses—all volunteers—for the work they did and the conditions they endured. But, Frances told her future readers, she did not believe that the nurses deserved the soldiers' praise. "We wade ankle deep in mud—you have to lie in it. We have a stove and coal. We even have a laundry line in the tent. . . . but in comparison to the way you men are taking it, we can't complain nor do we feel that bouquets are due us. But you—the men behind the guns, the men driving our tanks, flying our planes, building bridges—it is to you we doff our helmets." Patients generally spent about two weeks with the Forty-Fifth. During those stays the nurses "have learned a great deal about our American boys and the stuff he is made of. The wounded do not cry. Their buddies come first."[2]

Stars and Stripes published the letter for soldiers across Europe to read. Some months later its last two sentences appeared again, this time engraved on a tombstone over the English and Hebrew names of Fraidel Yachet Bat David Wolf, thirty years old, a noncombatant shot by a German sniper an hour after she finished writing the lines. Frances's own life flickered out before her buddies in the Forty-Fifth could save it. The U.S. hospital ship *Frances Y. Slanger* would carry on the lifesaving work of caring for casualties more fortunate than she.

The GIs who blinked awake and smiled up at Frances had come to the Belgian battlefields from cities, farms, and villages across the nation. But their varied origins never stopped them from recognizing a Jewish woman of East European ancestry as a genuine American "babe." If they noticed any accent at all, they could kid her about Boston's flat vowels and vanishing Rs, not about the other speech commonly heard in her part of town, the guttural consonants of the Russian Pale. And beyond Frances's unmistakable Americanness, the soldiers also recognized her—as they did all women in the military—as a volunteer for hard, hazardous duty. For its part, the army gave her the recognition due an officer and a professional, a lieutenant and a registered nurse.

Frances was a proud and courageous patriot, an enlistee in the fight against Hitler, an educated product of a middle-class neighborhood, an American. From our more distant vantage point, we can also see that she

was something more: a woman who belonged to a pivotal Jewish generation. Americans born to East European immigrants carried East European
Jewish life into the American middle class and deep into the American
dream. First they filled all-American (though nearly all-Jewish) neighborhoods in the great cities, and then they moved on to the exploding postwar suburbs. The Jewish ways of making a family life and the Jewish
religion went with them. Both were transformed by American-born
women, who in turn were also transformed.

Frances had grown up in the midst of a vibrant Jewish community during the years when the first American-born East European generation
moved en masse out of their parent's immigrant world and into their own
birthright as Americans. The period presented these young people
remarkable challenges and opportunities. Children during a time of
extraordinary prosperity, they came of age during depression and war.
After these cataclysms, they moved on to a new, postwar land of prosperity and mobility unimaginable during the preceding decades of deprivation
and struggle. Imbued with the values of their East European forebears and
inspired by the promise of their American future, these largely native-born
sons and daughters managed a massive cultural and social transformation.
Their efforts, and that of their parents, transformed a community of struggling wage laborers and marginal traders into an educated, upwardly
mobile, and extraordinarily creative branch of the American middle class,
in little more than a generation. In the process they remade more than their
social situation; like the Jewish generations who had preceded them into
American respectability, they also reinvented the Judaism that they had
inherited. Combining what their families had brought from Europe with
what they found here, they transformed customs, ideas, and organizations
suited to the Pale or the immigrant enclaves into institutions and programs
that were compatible with middle-class American homes and communities
and remain viable today.

Moving in so little time from proletarian hardship to petit bourgeois
comfort demanded drive, determination, ingenuity, and sacrifice,
although, of course, Jews enjoyed the benefits of white skin and the openness of American opportunity. Much of the energy and inventiveness that
went into this new version of Jewish life owed, as in the past, to countless
unsung women. Perhaps because these transformations happened against
the backdrop of tumultuous and trying times, or perhaps because the
women who did so much to achieve them stayed largely within the ladylike conventions of their era, this entire period of American Jewish history

somehow lacks the nostalgic glamour that folk memory has bestowed on earlier immigrant days. Historians have not paid to Jewish life in this era anything like the attention lavished on the great migration. Still, as Frances's generation came of age, the Great Depression and World War II put the American people to severe and unprecedented tests. Plunged into the despair of economic collapse, they had to rouse the confidence to save themselves from poverty and financial chaos. Then they had to rally the courage, ingenuity, selflessness, and determination—along with the vast productivity of a revitalized economy—to save the nation and the world from barbarous tyranny.

For many observers, the agonies and glories of those titanic struggles dwarf the drama of aspiration and achievement that played out in countless Jewish families during those years. Compared with the vivid travails of the immigrant era, the trek to the middle class may appear banal. Becoming a bookkeeper or a pharmacist or a schoolteacher has little of the heroic grandeur of an illegal border crossing or a harrowing ocean voyage to escape the czar. Furnishing an elevator-building apartment lacks the moral weight of going out on strike against exploitation in the dead of winter.

Yet Frances's Jewish generation does not lack its own moral and heroic dimensions. They served in large numbers in the armed forces during World War II, found the means and motivation to pursue higher education in very hard times, raised themselves to the ranks of white-collar and pro-fessional workers, retained and reinterpreted their sense of Jewishness, and vindicated their immigrant forebears by making for themselves and their children the decent, hopeful, dignified lives that European Jews had come to America to find.

During Frances's childhood and youth, the enormous generation raised in immigrant homes grew up to be Americans. Mostly native born (some born in Europe but arriving young enough to learn English without an accent), they were educated in American schools and formed their con-sciousness on American sidewalks and playgrounds. Most lived in big cities of the nation's northeastern quadrant, and especially in neighborhoods like Frances's Roxbury, filled with East European families who had made their way, if only barely and recently, into the middle class. As they attained adulthood, this generation quickly came to dominate American Jewry, set-ting its economic and social course and its cultural tone. Their path into American life became American Jewry's permanent trajectory.

The immigrants remained numerous for decades, as most of them had arrived in their teens or twenties. Their Yiddish speech and old-world consciousness endured for years in Jewish communities across the nation. But early on it became clear that the American Jewish future lay not in elaborating that old culture but in embracing the new. The Yiddish universe that the immigrants had built, with its newspapers, theater, literature, and film; its labor rallies and *landsmanshaftn,* its needle trades and free loan societies, began to fade even as it flourished. The children born into it knew Yiddish from infancy but by childhood largely chose not to speak it, at least among themselves. The *mama-loshen* (mother tongue) might bear the adults' memories and legends, but for young Americans the new, English world that poured out of the radio and off the movie screen all but drowned it out.

By the mid-1920s, furthermore, the former flood of young, vigorous Yiddish speakers no longer replenished the immigrant population. World War I effectively shut off unlimited immigration. Even the reduced flow that resumed with the Armistice stopped altogether in 1924, leaving American Jewry marooned, cut off from its demographic, cultural, and religious sources in the Yiddish-speaking lands of Eastern Europe. New European infusions occurred from the late 1930s to the early 1950s, but the refugees from Hitler's persecution and the survivors of the Nazi annihilation who came to America totaled only 415,744 souls.³ A sprinkling of Hungarian, North African, and other Jews admitted in the mid-1950s numbered fewer still. From 1924 on, therefore, American Jewry grew steadily more native born and ever more strongly, self-consciously, and self-sufficiently American.

Seeking an American Life

Even as children, Frances's generation understood that they were heading somewhere their parents could not go, that the world was wide but their lives in their parents' homes were somehow narrow. Philadelphia's Marshall Street, for example, was a scruffy retail strip where working-class East Europeans, Gentiles of half a dozen nationalities as well as Jews, did their shopping. After school or on Saturday mornings Jewish youngsters sat behind the counters of their immigrant parents' little stores, ears to the radio or eyes on comic books. These reluctant young salesclerks would "shout to friends across the street, and discuss the programs," one of them recalled long afterward. "Parents would scream bloody murder: 'Get in the store! Tend to the customers!' We wanted to dream. A different life. Not Marshall Street and the store. There had to be something different."⁴

A Marshall Street girl named Rebecca got a glimpse of what that some-thing could be early in her first year at Philadelphia's academically selec-tive Girls' High School, a public school that drew students from across the city. Rebecca's family lived above their small store. The little business consumed nearly all of her immigrant parents' waking hours and kept Rebecca herself sitting at the cash register whenever she had free time. But even its long hours and the small income it produced represented a step up from the sweatshop where Rebecca's mother had begun her work-ing life. As a child, Rebecca had loved the warmth of her noisy block and its friendships.

But "once I reached . . . Girls' High," she recalled, "I hated Marshall Street. My contemporaries were not from the neighborhood. I went to houses and saw how people sat down at the table together for dinner. They lived in [more prestigious and prosperous] Olney. They had family din-ners," something she "never saw" at home because someone always had to be available to serve any customer who might show up. "I never invited a friend to my place. How could I? I felt sensitive about my surroundings. That was a decision I made—not to invite friends. They would have walked through the store. The living room was on the second floor."[5]

Compared with the Marshall Street crowd, "some of them poorer than we were, we were not deprived," Rebecca knew. "There was always food, family" at her house.[6] But there was also, she now could see, something lacking, something wrong, something not up to the Olney standard. Looking back to the sweatshops or the Old Country, her parents could see how far they had come. But members of Rebecca's generation looked for-ward to measure the distance between themselves and the dinner tables of places like Olney. Once the realization of that distance dawned, people who felt at home in America no longer believed that economic survival was enough. The goal of crossing the Atlantic was not only to live in America but to live in some sense like Americans, to have the life of dignity, pros-perity, and freedom that was theirs. By the 1920s, more and more Jews were determined that they—or failing that, then certainly their children—would attain that life by joining the American middle class.

Such essentially materialistic ambition, of course, contradicted the rhet-oric of working-class radicalism prominent in the labor movement. Garment workers negotiating with their bosses might loudly proclaim the dignity of honest toil. Union members on their picket lines might fervently cheer the solidarity of the working class. Few of them, however, actually wanted either for their offspring. The chance for social mobility, as much as for freedom, had been for many immigrants basic to the meaning of America. Working-class consciousness had served not as an ultimate goal but as a strategy for acquiring the means of moving their children into the white-collar world. Unlike immigrants of many other nationalities, skilled Jewish workers strove not to train their sons or daughters in the family trade but to prepare them to rise above it.

Still, native-born daughters—except for the few whose families struck it rich in the Golden Land—knew that they, like their mothers, would work before they married and "help out" as needed afterward. But they expected to do so in much better jobs—as clerks or bookkeepers or even nurses or teachers. The Jewish ascent into the middle class was happening very fast. By the mid-1920s, a New York Jew was five and a half times more likely to do white-collar work than an Italian and only one-seventh as likely to be unskilled.[7]

The economic boom of the 1920s provided many reluctant former pro-letarians the perfect opportunity to resign from the class struggle and take their place among the "alrightniks," those who were doing all right, thank you very much, here in America. By 1924 New York's Jewish social welfare agencies were serving 50–75 percent fewer clients than they had ten years before.[8] As the 1920s ended, most Jews had reached the promised land of a white-collar occupation.[9] About 40 percent of them, as opposed to only 14 percent of the general population, worked in trade, though often as employees rather than owners.[10] By the mid-1930s, 47 percent of New York's Jewish youngsters came from white-collar families and a third from households headed by a proprietor, manager, or official, a rate twice that of any comparable group. By then only four in ten members of the ILGWU were Jewish and only three in ten Jews did manual work.[11] As the 1940s began, Jews constituted about a third of New York's population but they owned two-thirds of the city's thirty-four thousand factories and 104,000 retail stores and wholesale houses.[12]

In smaller places that lacked large numbers of garment jobs, this com-mercial concentration was even more pronounced. The predominantly East European Jews of Johnstown, Pennsylvania, for example, represented 1.5 percent of the local population, but 10 percent of those self-employed in services and trade. Most sold clothing or shoes—some as prominent haberdashers, others as tailors and shoemakers. The rest dealt mainly in furniture, food, jewelry, or notions.[13] Not all Jewish Johnstowners were prosperous (though some were quite well-off indeed), but almost none of them were proletarians.

Countless immigrant Jews, of course, had, like Rebecca's parents, long been capitalists of a sort. But American-born sons and daughters who aspired to high school or even college did not foresee taking over the family pushcart or peddling route or spending their working lives behind the counter of some mom-and-pop store. Young people aiming at retail careers looked to run enterprises that were substantial and modern, that dealt in finer merchandise and served more prosperous customers in more prestigious parts of town. Better-quality ready-to-wear and luxury goods such as furs and jewelry were popular fields for Jewish entrepreneurs. As the economic boom boosted the demand for more and better housing and the furnishings to fill it, others found opportunities in construction and real estate and in all manner of light manufacturing. Many other young Jews looked forward to careers in sales or in such prestigious fields as social work, teaching, accounting, bookkeeping, stenography (then considered professions), nursing, pharmacy, and even, for the most ambitious, law or medicine. In 1935, a third of New Yorkers between sixteen and twenty-five were Jewish, but that third included 56 percent of the age bracket's proprietors, managers, and professionals, 43 percent of its clerical and sales workers, and 37 percent of its professionals.[14]

The Doorway to the Middle Class

The most direct route to realizing any of those ambitions lay through the classroom. The academic or business-track high school diploma had become the door to the white-collar world, and the college degree the gateway to the professions. The effort, begun in the earliest immigrant days, to keep as many children in school as long as possible intensified as rising incomes allowed more families to provide education and rising aspirations made it ever more necessary. Immigrant parents could teach their children many things: to persevere, to turn adversity into advantage, to run a business on a shoestring, to wrest the maximum value from every penny earned, to sell and to sew. These skills could take an ambitious, disciplined child a good way toward middle-class status. But foreign-born mothers and fathers could not teach the rest of what a youngster needed: how to speak English fluently and correctly; how to spell and punctuate it accurately; how to write it grammatically in a clear, legible hand; how to converse in it knowledgeably on the books, sports, politics, and other mysteries that interested Americans; how to dress and act and look and just generally be a convincing white-collar American.

Those were the basic requirements for entering the world of work beyond the immigrant quarters. The better jobs demanded even more: specialized skills like typing, shorthand, double-entry bookkeeping. Its best jobs—careers, actually—also called for expertise in abstruse fields like pedagogy, the rules of evidence, the tax code, the pharmacopoeia, or the techniques of surgery, as well as diplomas and test scores to prove that one possessed it. All that an immigrant mother or father could contribute was the faith that staying in school was honorable and necessary and justified the long hours behind the counter or the sewing machine that could free a student to stay at the books.

By the 1930s, a high school diploma was the minimum expected of youngsters from respectable Jewish families. Even if older brothers and sisters had to quit day classes to help support the family, most tried to complete high school in the evening. Many graduates continued on, as Frances Slanger had, to further study in a technical school, business course, or college. During the 1930s, nearly three-quarters of the Jewish girls in New York City studied bookkeeping and stenography (the art of taking shorthand dictation), many in high school business programs and others in special secretarial schools.[15] Even a half-year postgraduate business program qualified a girl for what many families considered a fine job as a shorthand typist, private secretary, or bookkeeper, elite office workers in the days before word processing and spreadsheet programs, an occupation that would enable young women to meet promising young white-collar men.

Others aimed even higher. "I had dreams of going to college," recalled a Philadelphian named Susan. "Temple University was close by, but it seemed out of the question. My father was adamant. 'A girl should get married. What does she need college for? I'll send you to secretarial school. Learn to be a secretary, a bookkeeper. Work in an office.'" A sixteen-year-old high school graduate, Susan had no choice but to comply, although her mother "knew my dreams, but only bit her lip to avoid an argument." Several years as a shorthand typist, however, yielded enough savings to pay for a freshman year. When Temple accepted Susan, her father "didn't say a word. I told him I would work during school and in the summers at secretarial and bookkeeping jobs, and that's what I did."[16] Aiming to become a doctor, Susan took a demanding premedical curriculum, each course filled with fiercely competitive classmates who knew that Jews faced discriminatory admissions quotas at the medical schools. Doing less than very well was not an option.

Susan loved her course in anatomy, which included extensive practical work. "We each received our own cat to take home in a shopping bag," she remembered. "It was dead, of course. Preserved in formaldehyde. We had to skin it by boiling" in order to study the musculature and skeleton. Her parents, not surprisingly, "were appalled at the idea of cooking a cat in the house. It wasn't kosher. It was impossible." But the demands of Susan's education overcame her mother's religious qualms. A compromise was devised. Her mother "would buy a separate pot, allow me to cook the cat, but I must hang the shopping bag with the cat inside on the clothes-line" that ran over a pair of pulleys between Susan's bedroom window and a pole across the yard. "That would be perfect" because it allowed the *treif* carcass to be outside the house but within easy reach. For days a strange odor hung over the house and "customers asked what in the world we were cooking."[17] Each night Susan reeled in the shopping bag for study and then reeled it back out for storage. Finally, to her parents' tremendous relief, the semester ended and the cat made its final exit via the garbage can.

Few parents had to endure foul odors in the cause of their children's advancement, but many made other compromises. Declaring a false address, for example, was a common strategy for giving a child from an undesirable neighborhood a chance to attend a superior public school. "To me, the most important thing was that [my children] should go to college," recalled an immigrant Philadelphian named Sora, voicing an opinion shared by many. Sora had entered this country as a young wife. As a mother she spent most days behind a store counter and many evenings learning to read and write English in adult classes at her children's elementary school. But Sora's youngsters could expect little help with college costs from their hard-pressed parents. Like many young Jews of their time, they "worked and saved money. They worked and went to college. All of them. I couldn't ask for more."[18]

Countless Jewish parents agreed, especially in the large cities. Constituting less than 4 percent of the nation's population, Jews in the 1920s were 9 percent of the nation's college students and nearly 50 percent of New York City's.[19] In New York, Jewish students finished high school and college twice as often other groups. In the 1930s, more than half of the city's female college students were Jews. Twenty-one percent of its college-age Jewish women were students, as opposed to 12 percent of Americans of college age and 9 percent of comparable non-Jewish New Yorkers.[20] As early as 1920, Jewish students constituted 80–90 percent of the enrollment at public, tuition-free Hunter and City Colleges and 93 percent of the Washington Square campus of private New York University in lower Manhattan. When Hunter established a coed branch in Brooklyn in 1926, it too had an overwhelmingly Jewish enrollment. Adele Bildersee, a Jewish woman with degrees from Hunter and Columbia, was dean of women. In 1930 the branch became Brooklyn College, the third of the city's tuition-free campuses (a fourth, Queens College, opened in 1937). Bildersee served as Brooklyn's dean of students and later its director of admissions.

In addition to New York's free public colleges, Jewish applicants armed with excellent records besieged the undergraduate and graduate admissions offices of elite eastern colleges and universities, especially those in or near cities with large Jewish populations. By 1920, 14 percent of the students in 106 law schools were Jews.[21] Few of the people reading their applications, however, were Jewish. To schools that had long catered to the upper-middle- and upper-class offspring of old-stock American families, the eager progeny of East European immigrants often seemed too intensely intellectual, too academically precocious, too impecunious, insufficiently mannerly, athletic, and "clubbable," and, above all, too numerous and competitive, to fit into the social character and academic climate of schools traditionally geared to preparing the nation's gentlemanly and ladylike Protestant elite. Harvard President James Lowell told a Jewish alumnus that Jewish and Christian students "just don't mix." To become real Americans, he opined, Jews would have to become Christians because "to be an American is to be nothing else."[22] And perhaps even more to the point, Jewish applicants' superior records threatened to win them places that would otherwise go to the children of well-to-do Gentiles.

Restrictions against Jews had for some decades been spreading at prestigious resorts, social clubs, and neighborhoods, though only the minority of Jews with the means to afford them were affected. Jews of all classes knew that they were unwelcome where well-to-do Christians gathered socially. To safeguard their aura of social exclusivity from the taint of allegedly uncouth and inarguably non-Christian candidates, as well as to ensure places for academically less qualified but socially more desirable students, Harvard, Yale, Princeton, and many other elite private men's and women's colleges established quotas, often 10–15 percent of the student body, on Jewish enrollment. The number of Jews admitted fell far below the number who qualified on academic grounds. Half the applicants to the nation's medical schools were Jewish in the mid-1930s, for example, but fewer than a fifth of them got in.[23]

Many schools excluded Jews not through explicitly religious tests but through newly established subjective criteria of character, refinement, and social suitability that effectively disqualified youngsters raised in immigrant homes. Even Columbia, hard by the nation's largest Jewish population, cut its Jewish enrollment sharply. Jewish applications to Radcliffe, the women's division of Harvard, rose between 1936 and 1938, but Jewish admissions fell from 24.8 percent to 16.5 percent. At the New Jersey College for Women (NJCW), later known as Douglass College, Jewish enrollment dropped from 17 percent in 1928 to 11 percent in 1932, even as the state's Jewish population rose, along with the Jewish enrollment at nearby Rutgers College for men. In 1930, NJCW accepted 61 percent of 635 applicants but only 31 percent of the Jewish ones, although "their scholastic standing is usually better than that of the other students," according to the school's Committee on Admission and Freshman Work. Harsh admissions quotas only held sway in elite northeastern schools, however. But with almost 40 percent of the nation's Jews in New York City and most of the rest in the Northeast, relatively few Jews sought admission to the midwestern and western universities that generally welcomed them.[24]

The first American generation's intense hunger for education, folk memory relates, simply bubbled up from deep within Judaism. Reverence for learning, the recollection states, had always permeated a religion based on sacred texts. The values of that ancient faith—whose rituals and requirements so many immigrants had discarded and whose sacred books so few had actually read—were, this argument held, what drove the immigrants' children to cram geometry and chemistry, U.S. history and Gregg shorthand, and the parents to insist that they do so. The evidence, however, suggests something less romantic. The ferocious drive for high grades and diplomas expressed not venerable piety but modern ambition, not a devout tradition of scholarship but a devout desire to turn large investments of time and small ones of money into white-collar status. Nineteenth-century Central Europeans, for example, though heirs to the same sacred tradition, put little energy into spurring their American offspring to comparable academic heights. By late adolescence, most of their children were accumulating not college credits but practical experience in the family business. In that earlier era, most occupations, including some that now require university training, could be learned through apprenticeships or on the job. Colleges and even high schools generally enrolled only students who had ample spare cash, exceptional academic talent, or plans to enter one of the learned professions. Well into the first decades of the twentieth century, joining the white-collar middle class could be managed through practical skills rather than schooling.

By the 1920s, however, the American economy had changed. Technical, professional, and bureaucratic jobs multiplied as cities grew and businesses and government became more bureaucratized. Middle-class opportunities began to contract for those without formal education. More and more occupations began to require diplomas, certificates, and degrees, boosting the value of schooling as a means to land a good white-collar job. Young people aiming at middle-class occupations began staying in school longer and longer, through high school and even college.

If the fervor for education that burned among New Yorkers and other big-city Jews had in fact arisen mainly from religious tradition, it would, of course, have glowed as brightly among Jews elsewhere, and especially in those closest to the old-fashioned faith. Jewish families of little Johnstown, Pennsylvania, for example, were on average much more religiously observant than New Yorkers. Nearly all those with East European backgrounds originated in traditional shtetls rather than the secularized cities that many New Yorkers hailed from. Though closer to old-world Judaism than most New Yorkers, Johnstowners sent fewer of their children to college—only about 12 percent during the 1920s and 17 percent during the 1930s—rates higher than the nearby Slavic and Hungarian blue-collar families, but lower than the Anglo-Saxon and northern European Protestants who constituted the local middle and upper classes.

In fact, Jews flocked to campus in large numbers only in big cities where white-collar jobs were plentiful, education gave an advantage in getting them, and nearby colleges were inexpensive or free. Economics, not religion, played the most crucial role in educational plans. Johnstown's Jewish families generally earned middle-class incomes, but few were wealthy, and nearby University of Pittsburgh cost $400 to $500 a year in the 1920s, far more than New Yorkers had to pay. What's more, Johnstown collegians had to live away from home, too far to help out in the family store between classes. A woman named Vivian, for example, would have liked to study nursing after she finished Johnstown High, but what her father earned in a wholesale business "was not enough for college."[25]

Some local parents managed to save or borrow enough for their children to matriculate; Johnstown's Jewish collegians came overwhelmingly from families that placed an unusually high priority on advanced education. Back in Europe, all of these parents had some secular education, an experience unusual for shtetl youngsters. Still, only about half of Johnstowners who began college graduated, many dropping out because they could not pay the bills or because their labor was needed at home.[26] Even after the university opened a junior college branch in town, Jews did not attend at a rate any higher than other local people. Completing a degree still required years at the main campus.

"When I finished high school I went to work for my father, this was the thing to do then, to go to work in some kind of business," one Johnstowner recalled.[27] The local steel-town economy afforded Jewish graduates nowhere near the range of white-collar opportunities that comparable New Yorkers enjoyed. Unlike New York's huge, job-rich school system and civil service and its vast array of Jewish-owned manufacturing, commercial, publishing, entertainment, shipping, and other businesses, the steel company that dominated Johnstown, along with many of the town's smaller Gentile firms, generally hired only Christians in white-collar posts. Four out of five American-born Jews—including two out of three who had been to college—therefore ended up working in hometown Jewish businesses, often for their own families.[28] Except for youngsters aiming at professions such as law, medicine, and dentistry, or considering the unusual step of moving away from their homes and families, a relatively costly campus sojourn did not appreciably increase their chances of getting the kind of white-collar job that already awaited them in a family business near home.

Instead of going to college, therefore, most of Johnstown's American-born Jews received a solid business training at the institution they jokingly called "Gee Bee Tech." Glosser Brothers Department Store, the area's second largest, employed over five hundred people, a third of them Jewish. Founded early in the twentieth century by five sons of Antopolie, a shtetl near Grodno in Byelorussia, it hired just about any Jewish high school student who applied for part-time or summer work. Many stayed on full-time after graduation, often for several years before joining their own families' businesses, but sometimes for an entire career. Unlike their college-bound big-city brethren, Jewish Johnstowners eschewed the campus but nonetheless found their own cost-effective route into the white-collar middle class.

Big-city immigrant families, of course, could not afford private college tuition or the expenses of living on campus any more than their Johnstown *landsleyt* could, especially during the Depression. Instead, New Yorkers thronged the commuter campuses that their city provided free of charge, and residents of other cities did likewise at whatever local schools were cheap and accepted Jews. "We were the children of peddlers, tailors, first-chance Americans," recalled a 1934 Brooklyn College alumna. "Everybody pointed to the city colleges and said, 'This is your opportunity. Take it.'"[29]

Close to 50 percent of the New Yorkers who eagerly did so were female, a percentage that was a good deal higher than in places where students had to pay tuition. As many Johnstown girls as boys graduated from high school, generally with good grades, but only about half as many went to college.[30] Jewish families that could only afford to send some of their children generally favored boys. By working and living with their parents, though, New Yorkers from even quite modest homes could often eke out what they needed to stay enrolled. Nearly all college girls of the first generation, whatever city they lived in, traveled to campus each day from their immigrant parents' homes.

The very first subject that these urban scholars had to master was what Hunter graduate Rae Lieberman called "the art of studying while strap-hanging."[31] For the typical Hunter student, traveling to and from school took half as many hours as did all her classes and labs combined. Rae spent more time on the subway than she did on campus. And once she got home, she "had to help with the cooking and cleaning to help my mother who worked in our store."[32] So many Hunter girls had part-time jobs at Macy's Department Store, especially on Thursday evenings and Saturdays, that their yearbook dubbed it the college's "Saturday branch." And to get the Depression-era Macy's sales job that let her go to college, future schoolteacher and best-selling author Bel Kaufman had to pass a written exam that she remembered being "almost as difficult as my Masters."[33]

For most commuting students, the demands of travel, work, and home left little time for campus activities, especially during the desperate 1930s. Radical politics and an idealistic peace movement roiled the nation's campuses throughout that Depression decade as young people struggled to understand and cope with the poverty wracking the nation. Many, for example, supported the Oxford Pledge not to serve in any war. In the mid-1930s, 39 percent of American college students told a survey that they would refuse to fight for their country under any circumstances, and another 33 percent said they would do so only if America were attacked.[34] Protest rallies and student demonstrations, sometimes attracting tens of thousands of people, were commonplace, handbills and petitions ubiquitous. First-generation Jewish students, often from strongly unionist and socialist families, naturally sympathized with the left-wing and peace groups active at the colleges. The public campuses in New York were the nation's most intensely political, their students keeping up on political issues "with an eagerness generally associated with a World Series," in the words of a Hunter official.[35] But few could spare much time to join or work for radical organizations during long days crammed with subway rides, classwork, waiting on customers, rushing to the library, cleaning house, and late-night cram sessions over the kitchen table.

In the end, all the sacrifice and dedication paid off in much more than white-collar credentials. A child's academic attainments vindicated the years of parental self-denial and toil, bringing them honor, joy, and *nachas*, that special pleasure that mothers and fathers feel at a child's success. When Mildred Herman's four-year grind of endless subway trips, odd jobs, and long shifts in her family's little luncheonette finally ended in June 1935 with her Hunter graduation, her parents arrived with a bouquet of roses for the family's first college graduate. Half a century after the splendid Carnegie Hall ceremony, Mildred remembered weeping at so glorious an extravagance in that bitter Depression year. She carried the precious blooms as the family returned home to the Bronx in triumph, where they received the stream of friends and relations who came throughout the day to pay congratulatory calls on the new holder of a coveted teaching degree and her *kvelling* parents.

Another immigrant Bronx couple, housepainter Louis Myerson and his wife, Bella, were also parents whose income couldn't stretch to cover their children's college costs. Their talented middle daughter, called Bassia in the Yiddish the family spoke at home, had studied piano and flute at the prestigious, selective High School of Music and Art. At Hunter, her music studies demanded a high-quality piano, a luxury far beyond the means of a working-class family of five. Then Sylvia, the eldest of Louis and Bella's three daughters, had a bright idea. Without asking permission, she mailed her sister's picture to the Miss New York competition, suspecting that the stunning, five-foot-ten-inch brunette might win the money prize.

The outcome proved far better than she hoped. In the late summer of 1945 Sylvia's kid sister, who had grown up among the 250 socialist Jewish union families in the Scholem Aleichem Cooperative Houses and had attended afterschool classes at the socialist-leaning Scholem Aleichem Yiddish Folkschule, arrived in Atlantic City as New York State's candidate for a $5,000 scholarship and the title of Miss America. All of Jewish America, including her parents' left-wing neighbors, was wild with excitement, oblivious to the decadent and counterrevolutionary materialism inherent in this most sexist and capitalist of spectacles. Total strangers cheered her on the street. A New York fashion house donated her wardrobe of evening gowns, stitched, perhaps, by Jewish workers *kvelling* over their sewing machines.

As the elimination rounds proceeded, the Bronx's favorite daughter remained in the running. Then, just hours before the climactic final judging, pageant officials suggested that Beth Meredith might be a more suitable name for the nation's ideal of pulchritude—and might, incidentally, improve the New Yorker's chances of winning the coveted check and tiara. But in "the most important decision [she] ever made," twenty-one-year-old Bess Myerson declined to alter her surname and deny her heritage. That evening, just six days after the Allies defeated Japan and exactly three months after they defeated Hitler, Bess Myerson defied the officials' predictions and became the first (and to date the only) Jewish Miss America.

With her sparkling crown, her ermine-trimmed robe, her refusal to conceal her Jewishness, her dazzling looks, and the imprimatur of the American establishment, Bess was a breathtaking combination of a movie star and the biblical Queen Esther—instantly the best-known Jewish woman in the world. As far away as the DP camps in war-ravaged Europe, Jews rejoiced. If a first-generation East European daughter could be declared the epitome of American womanhood, then every Jewish parent's child could succeed in America. For young women and girls, the effect was simply electrifying. Bess, who had dark hair and dark eyes, had done nothing to tamper with her Jewish looks—and still had won. "Bess Myerson was the most important female image in your life," remembered a woman in her teens on the great day. "We didn't just know about her. We *felt* her."[36]

In her year-long public reign Bess lived up to her people's exalted expectations. A dignified and well-spoken Hunter graduate, she embarked on a schedule of official appearances in aid of various good causes. But in private, her reign had some "painful" moments. In Wilmington, Delaware, to promote the sale of war bonds, she overheard the woman in whose home she was staying, a prominent local matron, fret that "we cannot have Miss Myerson at the country club reception in her honor. . . . We never had a Jew in the country club."[37] Miss America instantly packed her tiara and left. Certain veteran's hospitals also found that their young patients would do better without morale-boosting visits from the young woman officially certified as the nation's most beautiful because, she remembered, "some of the parents didn't want me—[even though] their sons had lost arms and legs fighting a war to save the Jews."[38] Three out of five of the pageant's national sponsors mysteriously declined to use the current Miss America in their ads, despite initial plans to do so. Her official travels also introduced her to the reality of legal racial segregation in the South. For Bess, who initially "couldn't imagine why" her name might be a detriment to success, the course was clear.[39] She became a frequent headline speaker against racism and anti-Semitism for the Anti-Defamation League. Despite these disappointments, Bess's star did not dim. Decades after her year as Miss America ended, she became a familiar presence on TV, modeling a mink coat on *The Big Payoff,* bantering with fellow panelists on *I've Got a Secret,* and cohosting the Miss America Pageant.

Moving Up and Moving Out

The apotheosis of the immigrant dream, Bess Myerson was, like Frances Slanger, an unmistakably American "babe." She had become so in an unmistakably American world. By the 1920s, East European families were not only moving up—out of poverty. They were also moving out—away from the immigrant quarters. Members of the middle class, as they could plainly see, did not live on noisy streets jammed with pushcarts, in cramped tenements or decaying alley houses. They did not lug their groceries up multiple flights of splintery stairs. They did not use multifamily toilets or outdoor privies. Rather, they made their homes in the bright, airy apartments of buildings with elevators and stylish lobbies or in the solid, roomy houses that lined quiet, tree-shaded streets. Their windows looked out on private yards or public parks, not on air shafts and alleys clogged with trash cans. Sleek porcelain fixtures gleamed in their tiled bathrooms. The newest refrigerators and ranges stood at the ready in their up-to-date kitchens. Polished hardwood covered their floors, brass sconces and stained glass panels adorned their walls, decorative beams crisscrossed the ceilings of their eighteen- by twenty-two-foot living rooms. In America, even successful members of the working class made their homes not in dismal slums but in bright and modern—if smaller and more modestly appointed—flats and houses.

Nor did dwellings fit for respectable middle-class Americans crowd against one another along the narrow, littered thoroughfares of old city centers. By the 1920s, American families who had attained a measure of financial success preferred homes along the broad boulevards, imposing avenues, and landscaped side streets of new sections specifically planned for people of standing, and the building industry was working overtime to accommodate them. In New York alone, between 1920 and 1930, some 152,772 new apartments went up in the Bronx and 144,905 in Brooklyn—twice as many as during the preceding decade.[40] New houses and apartments also multiplied on the outskirts of many other cities and towns. The outer boroughs of New York City and the outlying sections of other cities, only recently considered semirural hinterlands, now became desirable home sites. By the 1920s Americans could conveniently live farther from their work than ever before. More and more people owned motor cars. More and more cities built or extended transit lines out into districts that had been countryside a few years before. Residents of the new sections could now travel swiftly to business in the morning and back to their green, airy suburban retreats at night.

Prestigious new neighborhoods beckoned Manhattan Jews, who responded in the hundreds of thousands to the lure of living in "the country," or at least among the open fields and empty lots of what journalist Konrad Bercovici in 1923 called "the wilds of the Bronx" and Brooklyn.[41] Cheye Itta Yoffeh, for example, the stalwart Lower East Side *balebuste* we met earlier, "heard of a wonderful bargain in then sparsely settled Brownsville—four rooms with a private bath," and the Yoffehs became early emigrants, her son Zalman recalled. But life on the frontier proved harder than his parents had imagined. "What a horrible experience," Zalman reported. "Our nearest neighbor was over fifty yards away. At night the street was deserted and quiet. Gentiles lived across the way; one had to walk two and three blocks to reach a store. What self-respecting Jew could live in such a neighborhood?"[42]

Chaye Itta became so homesick that the Yoffehs returned to their old neighborhood, arriving, as it happened, in mid-August. "The street we moved to was filled with pushcarts," Zalman remembered. "A continual roar arose from the occupants and it was with difficulty that one made his way through the crowds. Here and there were heaps of rotting fruit. The stench and heat were, as I look back on it, unendurable. Yet we were all happy to be back. Back on the East Side, back in a Jew's world."[43]

For old-world woman like Chaye Itta, who had grown to adulthood in Poland, the barren wastes of middle-class American comfort were simply too foreign. More important than the amenities Brownsville offered—private bathrooms, good ventilation, modern steam heat, extra space for her family of eight—was the familiar immigrant ambience. But for young couples more comfortable in America, a neighborhood full of *landsmanshaftn,*

Yiddish signs, and tiny *shtiebl* shuls held little attraction. More alluring by far were brand-new apartments on brand-new streets—some so new that the builders had to shoo goats from the construction sites. At $100 a month on an impressive boulevard or as little as $70 a month on a rather less grand but still pleasant side street, a four-room apartment with all modern conveniences was within the reach of many Jewish New Yorkers and seemed a fine place to raise an American family. Coops financed by labor unions or other nonprofit groups charged even less. And so, by the mid-1920s, when Bess was a baby, settlement workers were noting that, as one put it, "the young married people are going to outlying districts of the Bronx and Brooklyn."[44]

Vast numbers of them went. Between 1920 and 1930, the Jewish population more than doubled in Brooklyn's Flatbush and more than quadrupled along the Bronx's fashionable Grand Concourse, where middle-class Irish and old-stock Protestants also lived.[45] Jewish residents increased sevenfold in the Bronx's Pelham Parkway, and large numbers also moved to Coney Island, Midwood, Sheepshead Bay, and other outer borough areas. By the mid-1920s, as many Jews lived in Brooklyn as in Manhattan and the Bronx combined.[46] Across the Hudson River in New Jersey, Newark's Jewish community, the nation's seventh largest, was also on the move, out of the immigrant quarter around Prince Street in the Central Ward and into more prestigious Clinton Hill. From there, families of East European background moved on to the large two-and-a-half flat houses, park view apartments, and single-family Sears Colonials of leafy Weequahic, there to be immortalized by novelist Philip Roth, the neighborhood's most celebrated son. Newarkers with Central European roots moved even farther out, to suburban areas beyond the city limits.

Jewish Bostonians had already abandoned their first immigrant settlements in the North End. By the mid-1920s well-to-do Jewish families, many of them Central European, were enjoying large private homes in the elegant suburbs of Brookline and Newton, and seventy-seven thousand people of moderate means—half the city's Jewish population—lived in more modest comfort in the row houses, apartment houses, and three-flats of Roxbury and Dorchester.[47] Jewish Chicagoans were also moving en masse to West Side areas like Lawndale-Garfield, home of 110,000 Jews in 1931, or to Westown-Humboldt on the Northwest Side, or to Kenwood, Woodlawn, and Hyde Park near the University of Chicago on the South Shore. Philadelphians were flowing north and east, to Olney and Logan and across the Schuylkill River to West Philadelphia. Even in Johnstown,

Jewish families were moving from their first homes near the train station up the hill to the larger houses of better-off Westmount. In Portland, Oregon, young marrieds like Diane Nemer were leaving the South Portland streets of their childhood for tree-filled Irvington or Ladd's Addition on the city's east side. They had "the feeling of moving up from one area to the next," she remembered. "Always a step in the right direction. . . . Each one of us married and moved away from South Portland to where we felt the homes were better, to a better district. It was sort of something you were striving for."[48]

But upwardly mobile couples didn't want just new neighborhoods, they wanted Jewish neighborhoods. "Ninety out of every hundred Jews . . . seek a Jewish [apartment] house situated on a Jewish block in a Jewish neighborhood," the *Forward* reported in 1926.[49] Overwhelmingly, they got their wish. As Jews arrived in their new neighborhoods, the Gentiles who had preceded them soon made way and most Gentile would-be residents looked elsewhere. By 1930 three out of four Jewish New Yorkers lived in newly built, predominantly Jewish areas—a higher level of ethnic concentration than had existed in the immigrant quarters. The richest and the poorest families remained in Manhattan, in the tenements of the Lower East Side, where annual income averaged $1,000, or in the brownstones and luxury apartments of the Upper West Side, where it averaged $8,000. The great mass in the middle chose the newer areas of Brooklyn, the Bronx, and Manhattan's Washington Heights, where average incomes ranged from $2,000 in Williamsburg to about $4,200 in Flatbush.[50]

As they filled with families, many of the new Jewish neighborhoods became intensely Jewish indeed. By the 1930s, Jews constituted well over half of North Lawndale's residents.[51] Roxbury, Weequahic, and many similar sections in other cities had similar majorities. With time, Jewish concentration continued to grow. In 1920, neighborhoods at least 40 percent Jewish were home to 54 percent of New York's Jews. Nine years later, 72 percent of the city's Jews lived in such places.[52] Even families who had to move repeatedly during the Depression, just ahead of rent collectors or eviction notices, tended to find each new apartment in the same Jewish parts of town.

Middle-class Jews flocked to neighborhoods like Flatbush or Pelham Parkway in part because Jewish builders worked to lure them there. The booming construction industry attracted more and more Jewish entrepreneurs and workers until in the 1920s it ranked second only to the garment trade as an employer of Jews. Many New Yorkers—even those who could afford to buy a single-family house—preferred to rent, in part because they were accustomed to apartment living and didn't care to maintain a house, and in part because renting rather than buying left capital free for business. Jewish builders knew Jewish tastes and could select exactly the luxury appointments and Art Deco or Moderne decorative touches that appealed to their market of first-generation and immigrant strivers. Then, with the building finished, the general contractor became the rental agent eagerly filling his building with Jewish tenants, and finally the landlord collecting their reliable rent checks.

But having a coreligionist for a landlord was not all that persuaded Jews to congregate in these areas. In large parts of America, especially in the major population centers, many neighborhoods were closed to Jews. Along with colleges, clubs, and summer resorts, renters and sellers of apartments and houses had the legal right to exclude people on the basis of race and religion, and many did. Beyond the prejudices of individual property owners, title deeds often contained special clauses called protective covenants that bound owners to sell the property only to white Christians. Other owners in the neighborhood or subdivision had the right to enforce the bans in court. Newspaper ads thus commonly indicated the religion, race, or ethnicity of the desired tenant or buyer.

When Molly Rosenberg moved from Newark to the heavily Gentile town of Montclair in the late 1930s, for example, "I encountered anti-Semitism when using a party phone line" that was shared by a number of nearby households. One woman "said something like 'You Jews. You are always taking over.'" Then the Rosenbergs "tried to buy a house in [even more exclusive] Upper Montclair." They looked at one that interested them. "When we left, the owner of the house called and asked us if we were Jewish. We said we were and asked what difference it made. She said it did not make any difference to her but that she could not possibly sell her house to Jews. Her neighbors would not like it."[53]

But in Lawndale or Midwood or Weequahic or Roxbury, one need never worry about exclusion or feeling out of place. Everyone was Jewish and everything Jewish was normal. Stores and eateries stocked foods unknown in other parts of town—kosher pickled cucumbers and green tomatoes out of aromatic barrels, thick slices of greasy kishka, copper-skinned smoked whitefish, chicken schmaltz, kasha varnishkes, chopped herring, farmer cheese, pastries filled with prunes or poppy seeds, fresh-baked bagels, dill and chicken feet for making soup, challahs each Friday and matzahs at Passover. In its heyday, the Ashkenaz Restaurant in

Chicago's Rodgers Park sold more than half a ton of corned beef each month.[54] Synagogues and other institutions were also close at hand. Lawndale readers could borrow from the excellent Yiddish and Hebrew collection at the Chicago Public Library's Douglas Branch, where a young Milwaukee woman named Golda Mabovitch Meyerson (later Hebraicized to Meir) worked for a time as a librarian. The neighborhood's high school grads could take college courses inexpensively at Theodore Herzl Junior College.

Nor did anyone find it odd that local public schools, with enrollments 80–90 percent Jewish and heavily Jewish faculties, were nearly empty on Sukkot or Shavuot, or had few volunteers for the role of Santa Claus in the mandatory Christmas play. Along with Bess, youngsters grew up unaware of the need to dissemble about who they were to advance their prospects. Though, like Bess's parents, most people were not highly observant, the Jewish clock and calendar still held sway. If, early some evening, a synagogue found itself a man or two short for the quorum needed to recite the daily *minchah* prayers, "the *shammas* [sexton] came outside to find a few teenage boys to complete the minyan," a Philadelphian named Bella recalls. "The boys . . . lounging or playing ball in the street, couldn't scatter fast enough when the search began. The *shammas* would grab a few by their sleeves and reprimand them for not coming to *shul* on their own accord. They would disappear with him for an hour to *daven* the service. When they came out grinning, we would hear them brag about drinking wine and eating cookies after the service. Girls were exempt from the *minyan*. As they were being pulled by their sleeves, the boys often yelled, 'You're lucky you're a girl.'"[55]

But Bella and her friends didn't need daily prayer to remind them who they were. "We girls knew we were Jewish and that was that. We lived and breathed it every day."[56] A neighbor named Lillian recalls that she and her parents "were not religious or synagogue-going Jews," but the neighborhood "gave me my identity as a Jew, culturally." Its life and "environment gave me my sense of family and resourcefulness for getting along in the world."[57] In the East Bronx neighborhood where journalist Vivian Gornick grew up as the daughter of a bookkeeper and a presser, "on *Pesach* and Yom Kippur we did not have to be 'observing' Jews to know we were Jews. The whole world shut down, everyone dressed immaculately, and a sense of awe thickened the very air we breathed."[58]

Parents sent their children to class confident that the daily Bible reading required by state law would not be from the New Testament and that the music teacher would not object if glee club members declined to pro-nounce certain climactic words in the required Christmas carols. No child risked exclusion from Scout troops, sports teams, or neighborhood clubs with heavily or wholly Jewish memberships. Few youngsters faced the temptation to date non-Jews, as they rarely met any. In New York and a number of other cities, the great majority of Jews almost never socialized with anyone but fellow Jews. When summer came, families simply adjourned to their community's vacation quarters—New Yorkers to the Catskills, Philadelphians and Newarkers to heavily Jewish towns on the New Jersey shore, Chicagoans to the Indiana dunes or towns on the east-ern shore of Lake Michigan reached by daily boats from the city. Chicago's Central Europeans favored Lakeside and Coloma, where many had sum-mer homes, while its East Europeans preferred Union Pier or South Haven, with its thirty-one hotels and resorts, ranging in pretension from the Biltmore and Plaza hotels to the Workman's Circle cottage colony.[59]

All-American Icons

Along with Pesach and Purim, Hanukkah and the High Holidays, another sacred schedule also ordered neighborhood life. Opening day and the World Series, Thanksgiving and the Fourth of July also divided up the year. The adventures of Jack Benny and Will Rodgers marked the passing weeks. Within the world of these middle-class Jewish districts, East Europeans and their children lived lives at once Jewish and American, simultaneously full participants in the United States of America and full members of the People Israel. The very "atmosphere" breathed on these streets and in their shops, schools, homes, and synagogues "told us who we were, gave us boundary and reference, shaped the face of the culture" through which individuals defined themselves, Vivian Gornick recalled.[60] Public life was largely conducted in English. Dress was American. Children played baseball and hopscotch and read comic books. Families listened to the radio and went together to the local movie house. Soap opera heroines and baseball teams inspired intense conversations on neighborhood streets.

For many first-generation youngsters, the rough democracy of the base-ball diamond perfectly expressed the American promise of opportunity open to all. During the 1930s the rise of Detroit Tigers second baseman Hank Greenberg to the pantheon of the national pastime gave American Jews their first national icon of ethnic pride. In their eyes, however,

Greenberg's true glory lay not in his commanding statistics or his two seasons as the American League's most valuable player, but in his quiet decision to sit out a single game in the 1934 season. During a close pennant race, he spent that crucial day at Shaarey Zedek synagogue observing Yom Kippur rather than at Tiger Stadium helping clinch first place. His choice inspired Jews across America to ecstatic pride and Edgar A. Guest, the nation's most popular poet, to congratulatory doggerel in the *Detroit Free Press*. Though the Yankees took the game 5–2, Guest led the city—which was also the center of Henry Ford's notorious anti-Semitic propaganda— in saluting the hometown hero. The essentially unobservant Greenberg had hit two homers on Rosh Hashanah. But then, Guest rhapsodized,

> *Came Yom Kippur—holy feast day world wide over to the Jew—*
> *And Hank Greenberg to his teaching and the old tradition true*
> *Spent the day among his people and he didn't come to play.*
> *Said Murphy to Mulrooney, "We shall lose the game today!*
> *We shall miss him in the infield and shall miss him at the bat,*
> *But he's true to his religion—and I honor him for that!"*[61]

More honor was heaped on Greenberg when he returned to the game in the spring of 1945 after spending forty-nine months in World War II military service. Though skeptics doubted his prospects after so long a hiatus, he hit .311 that season. And then, a week after Bess Myerson won her crown, neighborhoods like Greenberg's own Crotona Park in his native Bronx again went wild as he batted the grand slam home run that won the American League pennant, then went on to hit over .300 as he led the Tigers to a World Series win.

For many American Jews in that fateful summer and fall, Greenberg's and Myerson's symbolic victories seemed to echo the Allied victory over the Axis powers, which both ended Hitler's war against Europe's Jews and began to reveal the unspeakable toll it had taken in Jewish lives. Throughout the war years, and even before, a deep and frantic desire to stop Nazi persecution had combined with American patriotism to make Jews fervent supporters of the fight against Hitler, both overseas and on the home front. When the czar had called them up to fight in his army, countless Jewish men had hit the roads for the emigrant ports. When Uncle Sam called on their children and grandchildren to resist Hitler and Japan, hundreds of thousands came forward to battle for America and the Jewish people. Serving in every branch of the armed forces, Jews represented 8 percent of America's World War II military, a figure more than twice their representation in the general population. Some thirty-five Jewish families had six or more members serving.[62] Three Liberman sisters, Eva, Charlotte, and Miryon, joined the navy. Staff Sergeant Matilde Blaustine served in the army along with her daughter, Bernice. Thirty-six thousand Jewish men and women won decorations for distinguished service, and forty thousand gave their lives in the conflict.[63] Hank Greenberg led the way into uniform, trading his Tigers knickers for khaki even before Pearl Harbor.

The wartime draft affected all military-age men, but every one of the 340,000 American women who served in the armed forces was a volunteer. Thousands of Jewish women responded to a recruitment slogan and came forward to "Free a Man to Fight."[64] In 1942, twelve of them—four Philadelphians, three New Yorkers, three Chicagoans, two girls from Buffalo, and one from Seattle—graduated in the very first officers training class of the Women's Auxiliary Army Corps, precursor of the Women's Army Corps (WAC). From the very start, Jews of both genders were in the thick of the struggle for victory, both in the military and on the home front. Like their fellow Americans of every background, Jews in uniform and in the war industries went places, did things, and met people they would never had encountered in peacetime.

Countless young Jewish men and women who had grown up almost exclusively among their own people spent years sharing living quarters with and depending on buddies and coworkers from the many nationalities that made up America. Youngsters who had never ventured far from their home neighborhoods suddenly found themselves in New Guinea and Alaska, in North Africa and the Canal Zone, in Italy and Japan, and in every part of the forty-eight-state Union. Members of an overwhelmingly urban, white-collar, and commercial population learned to shoot guns, drive tanks, drop bombs, build runways, storm beaches, sail ships, and repair airplanes, among many other unlikely tasks. They brought back from the war a broader and deeper sense of themselves as Americans.

The GI generation came home to an array of government benefits that altered their lives and the life of the entire nation. Generous education payments that covered both tuition and living expenses permitted the veterans to flood the campuses, filling the nation's colleges and technical schools far beyond their prewar capacity, and in the process drastically democratizing higher education in America. Hundreds of thousands who never thought of studying now pursued that dream. Equally generous mortgage assistance put a private home within the reach of millions who never imagined buying a house of their own. Back home after two or three or four years of wartime hardship and danger that had followed a full Depression decade of frustration and want, the veterans demanded nothing less than the full American lives they had thus far been denied in the homeland whose safety and freedom they had fought for and won. Young couples separated "for the duration" rushed to marry or to start families, producing, within months of V-J day, the first members of the enormous generation that became known as the baby boomers.

Depression-era deprivations and wartime shortages, long acknowledged as inevitable and accepted with forbearance, no longer seemed tolerable. The apartments and houses that young couples had reluctantly shared with parents or other relatives during Depression-era penury or wartime housing shortfalls would no longer do. The war was won and the nation's industrial bounty was no longer earmarked for the battlefield. Bank accounts bulged with savings. For years industry had run at full tilt, workers had put in long wartime hours, and very little had been available for them to buy. In more than ten Depression years only small numbers of new homes had been built because few could afford to buy or rent them. During four wartime years all new construction had gone for the war effort. Suddenly Americans had the means to build and to buy all the homes they had longed for and to fill them with all the consumer goods they could imagine.

The veterans had hardly returned before factories that had turned out tanks and jeeps were retooling to make refrigerators and cars. Woods and farm fields surrounding major cities quickly filled with bulldozers and construction crews. A New York builder, Abraham Levitt, along with his sons William and Alfred, had been putting up houses since 1929. Wartime projects on military bases had taught Levitt and Sons how to put up large numbers of inexpensive housing units using mass-production methods rather than old-style techniques. In 1946 the company undertook, in a potato field near Hempstead, Long Island, the largest private housing project the nation had ever seen. Levittown was not the country's first tract suburb or even the first built after the war. But it was the one that became the model and the mantra for the demographic earthquake that began in the late 1940s and rumbled on for decades to come.

With their GI mortgages in hand and their babies in tow, the veterans and their wives rushed to buy what the Levitts were offering. Acre after acre, block after block, mile after mile of nearly identical little one-story houses stood on treeless muddy plots almost, it seemed, as far as the eye could see. But these houses were new and modern and clean. They had up-to-date fixtures and appliances. They had big windows and room to expand. Each had its own front and back yard. They were within commuting distance of jobs. And, most importantly of all, they were priced so that a young family with one breadwinner could afford them. Mr. and Mrs. Veteran looked at them, saw their family's future, and signed on the dotted line. The houses sold like hotcakes. The race to the suburbs was on.

In the decade following World War II, 10 million new houses became home to 40 million Americans.[65] The Levitts built other Levittowns, and other builders built them too, under other names, until brand-new towns ringed every major city. Young families poured out of the old urban neighborhoods, in which they had grown up, into the new single-family frontier, to gardens of their own, and someplace to park, and no nosy upstairs neighbors, and picture windows, and swing sets in the yard, and space and privacy and light. They abandoned settled communities thick with extended families and ethnic institutions for raw settlements where the houses were almost all the same, the trees were almost all saplings, and everyone was a middle-class newcomer.

The new suburbanites included Americans of many backgrounds. Near the great polyglot cities that had received large numbers of immigrants, thousands of young native-born couples shook themselves loose from ethnic enclaves and moved in next door to people of unknown, and very likely of different, backgrounds. In the new subdivisions they now called home, these residents were all Americans among Americans, not Italian Americans among fellow Italians or Irish Americans among fellow Irish or Polish Americans among fellow Poles, or Jewish Americans among fellow Jews. In 1948, the U.S. Supreme Court declared protective covenants invalid. The new suburbs lay open to Jews along with everyone else (or at least to everyone else who was white).

Jewish New Yorkers, Philadelphians, Chicagoans, Bostonians, Clevelanders, and residents of many other cities joined the move. From the late 1940s on, the center of Jewish life began to shift away from the solidly Jewish city neighborhoods of the 1920s and 1930s and toward the newer suburbs. As Jews moved out, in many cities African Americans, who were undergoing a massive demographic transformation of their own, moved in behind them, taking over the lower-middle-class neighborhoods that young, aspiring Jews now felt that they had outgrown. By the late 1960s, this pattern of succession would take on a strong and often hostile racial charge as Jews who had lived in neighborhoods for decades watched them become, in their eyes, denuded, unfriendly, and unsafe. In the 1950s, unscrupulous real estate operators called "blockbusters" used the threat of oncoming blacks to frighten Jews into selling. In the late 1960s, riots in dozens of American cities finished the job of scaring out those who remained. At the beginning, though, the Jews who moved from the old neighborhoods to the suburbs did so because they wanted to, because they sought and could afford better housing in what they perceived as better areas beyond the city limits.

By the mid-1950s, Dorchester, Roxbury, and nearby Mattapan in Boston were losing not only families but institutions. By the mid-1950s, Jews had largely abandoned Newark's Clinton Hill. Many had already gone on to the suburbs, but others favored remaining in Weequahic. The city's YM-WHA closed the Beaux Arts building in the old Third Ward and moved to Weequahic, not foreseeing that the neighborhood would endure as a Jewish community only another ten years. Lawndale in Chicago was seeing similar changes. With few single-family houses, it could not hold families who had done well during the war and now wanted more commodious and prestigious homes in the suburbs to the north. The change happened quickly, starting in the late 1940s; within ten years, the Jewish community was gone from Lawndale. Eighty-five percent of Cleveland Jews lived beyond the city limits by 1958.[66] Not everyone could or would leave their homes of many decades, however, any more than Cheye Itta Yoffeh had been able leave the Lower East Side. But the young and the prosperous went, leaving the older and poorer behind.

As the Jewish population in the old neighborhoods thinned, the institutions that had made neighborhoods into communities also moved on or closed, and not just synagogues or schools or religious institutes. As the Jewish community that supported the merchants along once-prosperous Blue Hill Avenue departed, "the action was not longer in Dorchester," one of its sons, Mark Mirsky, recalled in the *Boston Globe*. Instead, it was "out in Newton, Brookline, Sharon, where the girls were wealthy, their ranch houses dazzling brick after the brown wooden bunkers on the avenue. Jack and Marion's [deli restaurant] in Brookline was the place to take a girl, not the [old] G&G [in Dorchester], their sandwiches were bigger, the decor 'fabulous.' The G&G by comparison looked sad, old-fashioned." Dorchester still remained "comfortable, a bit run down but not seedy. It was friendly, a community," but by the 1950s it was doomed. "Fashion, and its silent patron, marriage, dictated that it must crumble. No girl was going to be left behind on Blue Hill Avenue. No matter how high the rent or mortgage, Brookline, Ho! A flight of families with eligible girls began." Soon it was a "rout, a panic-stricken rush. In a few years my friends who had sisters were all gone. Fled. The ranks in the G&G were not yet thinned noticeably but the seed crop was gone. The loins of Israel sat in Jack & Marion's."[67]

It was indeed the "seed crop" who led the way into the suburbs—the families with rising incomes and young children to raise. In 1949 Evelyn Rossman moved to the Boston suburb of Sharon, where "streets reaching like tentacles from the main thoroughfares meet each other in the woods and fields." But the fields were filling with tract houses, and the tract houses with "middle-income people for the most part, salesmen, professionals and small businessmen."[68] Fewer than a hundred of those families were Jewish when Evelyn and her husband bought a house and moved in.[69] For people like them, the move to the suburbs represented not the loss of a communal past but the gain of an even more promising American future. This time, moving up meant moving out in every direction.

Jews were not just moving to new suburbs but to whole new cities and parts of the country. Now the struggle for schooling during the 1920s and 1930s paid off. Jews had more education than most Americans, and anti-Semitism was declining in the face of revelations of the Nazi atrocities. With solid credentials and American manners, Jews could now avail themselves of career opportunities closed to them in decades past. By 1949, New York, New Jersey, Connecticut, and Rhode Island had outlawed job discrimination, and other states were considering similar laws. In 1964 the U.S. Congress banned it nationwide. By the 1960s, a third of all Jews had moved to the metropolitan areas from somewhere else.[70]

A number of those migrants had grown up in small towns or small Jewish communities, where their families had run small stores along the main streets. These places had meant opportunities when the Jews had first arrived in the nineteenth or early twentieth centuries, and the businesses they built supported their families for a generation or two. But the younger generation was looking beyond their parents' life to the new opportunities that now lay open to them. More and more young Jews went to college from the 1940s on, many away from home. By the 1960s, the rate had reached 80 percent.[71] Able young people were leaving small towns and not coming back. The smaller hinterland Jewish communities had been losing their young people for decades. Between the 1920s and the 1940s, for example, the community in Portland, Oregon, dropped from ten thousand to seven thousand members.[72]

Cities in the West and South attracted many of the newly mobile, with Los Angeles Jewry more than tripling between 1945 and 1968, from a mid-size community of 150,000 to a mammoth one of 510,000.[73] San Diego also grew quickly, and by the late 1940s Sacramento and Stockton had large enough Jewish populations to establish federations of local agencies, as did Orange County in the 1960s. Florida also experienced massive growth, especially in the Miami area; Orlando and St. Petersburg also had Jewish federations by 1950, and Clearwater and Broward County in the 1960s.[74]

By the 1950s and 1960s, the immigrants' children had traveled far from where they had started out, from the densely Jewish eastern city wards of their childhood to the sunbelt and the suburbs, through Depression and war to prosperity unprecedented in history, from being the daughters and sons of foreign Jews to the mothers and fathers of second-generation native-born Americans. And along the way they were to remake Jewishness and America in their own image.

"SO GOOD YOU WOULD NOT KNOW"

Finding a Career by "Helping Out"

A mong the millions of Jews who deliriously *kvelled* as Bess Myerson
won her tiara or Hank Greenberg prayed for atonement might have
been a family living at 1038 East Tremont Avenue in the Bronx. Like all
the other tenants in their apartment building, like all the friends and relatives in the neighborhood, Molly, Jake, and their children would have
rejoiced to see people so unmistakably Jewish playing roles so central to
American life.

Molly and Jake appeared to be ordinary lower-middle-class Jews. He
went out to work in his little garment business, earning just enough for her
to stay home, keep house, and care for the kids. Though Molly's days
weren't glamorous, they were full, and she had plenty to discuss over the
urban equivalent of the all-American back fence with a good friend who
lived in a nearby apartment.

Almost every day Molly, a plump, aproned *balebuste,* would lean from
her kitchen window and issue a singsong greeting, "Yoo-hoo, Mrs.
Bloom!" From a nearby windowsill would come an answering call. But
when Molly sang out, not only Mrs. Bloom but the entire nation listened.
For almost thirty years, Molly Goldberg, the very model of the modern
Jewish mother, was perhaps the most familiar Jewish woman in America, a
daily presence not only in the Bloom apartment but in homes across the
country, in cities thick with Jews and in rural areas where no Jew lived for
a hundred miles.

Millions felt they knew Molly and her family and friends as intimately
as they knew their own people. But this warm-hearted, not terribly educated, somewhat provincial housewife did not, in fact, live at that fictitious
number on that real Bronx thoroughfare. Rather, she existed in the imagi-

nation of a shrewd and canny media professional who had learned her craft in the Catskills and at Columbia University. The central character of *The Rise of the Goldbergs* radio program and later of *The Goldbergs* on TV, Molly was the creation of Gertrude Berg, who for three decades wrote, produced, and starred in the shows. She played Molly with such realism and warmth that for the nation at large, Molly's identity subsumed her own. Speaking in a quizzical Yiddish inflection rather than a full-fledged Yiddish accent, Molly and Jake Goldberg were not broad ethnic stereotypes from the vaudeville stage but sympathetic and sensitively drawn participants in a believable panorama of ordinary middle-class life. Through their apartment came an array of relatives, neighbors, and friends facing problems recognizable to people everywhere—shy single people unable to find the right mate, quarreling relations too proud to apologize, parents who felt slighted by their uppity children, children who felt pressured by their ambitious parents, individuals whose past mistakes had caught up with them, and many others—all of whom ultimately benefited from Molly's good-hearted, even inspired, meddling.

That these people happened to be middle-class, urban Jews who went to Kol Nidre services on Yom Kippur and ate such exotic delicacies as gefilte fish enhanced rather than diminished their humanity for their overwhelmingly Gentile audience. Stripped of all bitterness, travail, and frustration, urban Jewish life as lived by the Goldbergs served as a touching reminder of both the commonality of all human beings and the openness and tolerance of Americans. In her scripts, Berg consciously eschewed "anything that will bother people . . . unions, politics, fundraising, Zionism, socialism, intergroup relations . . . I don't stress them. After all, aren't such things secondary to daily living? The Goldbergs are not defensive about their Jewishness, or especially aware of it. I keep things average. I don't want to lose friends."[1] As the Goldbergs worked to attain the American dream—ultimately moving to a single-family house in the mythic suburb of Haverville and sending the kids to college—they maintained sound moral values, thanks to Molly's warm heart and good sense. "Jake wants the children to have everything money can buy, and I want them to have everything money can't buy," Gertrude, in the guise of Molly, told a reporter.[2]

For all of Molly's lovable, comforting warmth, however, the person behind her was not an earth mother dispensing chicken soup and kitchen wisdom but a businesswoman smart enough to develop an enduringly marketable product and tough enough to keep creative and financial control throughout its three-decade run. Starting at $75 an episode, she eventually earned $7,500 a week from the program alone. Of the major female stars in radio's golden age and television's early years, only Lucille Ball, who devised and embodied the madcap and even more enduring and lucrative Lucy Ricardo, managed a similar creative and financial doubleplay.

Gertrude Edelstein Berg was barely thirty years old when she persuaded the NBC Blue network that the matronly Molly belonged on their airwaves. Married at twenty and the mother of two children, Berg had already experienced both family life and show business. Born in Harlem, she grew up there and in the Catskill town of Fleischmanns, helping her parents run their summer hotel and putting on skits and programs to entertain the guests. Writing courses at Columbia honed her skills after she finished Wadleigh High School. A gasoline ad in Yiddish was one of her few radio credits at the time she read one of her original scripts to the executives who agreed to give the Goldbergs a trial run. *The Rise of the Goldbergs* debuted on NBC Blue in 1929 and switched to CBS in 1938. By 1941, with 10 million daily listeners, it was the most widely distributed show on radio. In the late 1940s, Gertrude took Molly on stage, first in a touring performance and then to Broadway in the show *Me and Molly*. In 1949, Molly, in her dark dress, pearls, and apron, her black hair pinned up on her head, made the jump to television. For the next five years, she seemed to lean into viewers' living rooms as she called to Mrs. Bloom. Other projects included a movie and the *Molly Goldberg Cookbook*.

Molly Goldberg's life provided the enduring popular image of American Jewish womanhood between the 1920s and the 1950s, but Gertrude Berg's life was in many ways a more realistic example of how Jewish women actually managed their lives. Berg created an icon of domesticity, a womanly woman who devoted all her energies to her family and friends. Molly the nurturant homebody perfectly matched her era's socially accepted vision of a middle-class wife. But within her creation, Berg also created something not overtly included in that conventional social role: a serious business and creative career marked by high achievements in three very competitive fields—acting, producing, and script writing. Rather like a set of Russian nesting dolls, her career also contained yet another aspect of her identity, her own private family life as a wife and mother. Berg rarely presented herself publicly as the complex figure she actually was, however, usually slipping into the persona of the motherly, matronly, slightly dizzy Molly.

For countless less famous Jewish women from the mid-1920s through the early 1960s, the outward forms of middle-class housewifery also disguised the multiple demands of family and paid work. Whether in the densely Jewish middle-class city neighborhoods built in the 1920s and 1930s or in the suburban developments put up after World War II, many Jewish families counted on not only a breadwinning husband but also a wife who "helped out"—whether she brought home token sums or a handsome salary. The Jewish community also needed women who "helped" build the institutions of middle-class Jewry. Throughout this period, educated, middle-class women did serious work in an ever broadening array of fields, but the conventions of the time required them to be wives first and professionals second, and not to exercise authority over men. Thus they were nurses but rarely doctors, teachers but rarely superintendents, religious teachers but not rabbis, sisterhood presidents but not synagogue presidents, and partners—often silent ones—with their husbands in businesses large and small.

When the boom times of the 1920s abruptly collapsed into the Depression of the 1930s, husbands' unemployment or business failures made multiple workers once again a necessity of survival in many homes. Then Pearl Harbor abruptly turned the tables and suddenly would-be breadwinners no longer scoured their hometowns for jobs and employers no longer turned away hordes of overqualified applicants. Millions of men went away to military service for years on end. With the nation's vastly enlarged industrial sector running at full capacity to meet wartime demand, and with the military and other government agencies clamoring for staff to run complicated systems of rationing, procurement, and other aspects of the all-out global conflict, employers, both public and private, found themselves desperate for workers. Intense propaganda trumpeted war work as a patriotic imperative for any civilian capable of holding down a job.

The Commission on Fair Labor Employment Practices, established by a presidential executive order in 1941, was encouraging employers to hire ability and skill rather than religion or race. Workers previously excluded from many well-paying fields—especially women and racial and religious minorities—suddenly enjoyed unprecedented opportunities to put in long hours for high wages at tasks that, mere weeks or months earlier, were considered fit only for white males. Rosie the Riveter became a national icon as women donned hardhats and work boots to take the places men had vacated at aircraft factories, shipyards, and other industrial plants. Decked out in police uniforms, farmers' overalls, welders' masks, carpentry belts, and more customary suits and dresses, they also did many other jobs ordinarily considered the province of men. Massive numbers of southern blacks abandoned rural Dixie's backward economy and legalized segregation and streamed north to Detroit, Pittsburgh, Chicago, and other industrial cities that fairly glowed with the promise of high pay and better lives. Jews, with their higher than average education and white skin, suddenly found themselves able to land some jobs that discrimination had previously made off-limits.

Then, as abruptly as the war had begun, it was over. Millions of veterans came home, expecting to return to their old jobs or better ones. Suddenly Rosie's patriotic duty was to put down her rivet gun, tie on her apron, and return to her home (or move to a new one in the suburbs) and have all the babies delayed by the Depression and war. As the postwar boom stretched on and little Jewish baby boomers began to go to school, their mothers became increasingly active outside the home. Often the wives of prosperous business or professional men, thanks to the many years Jewish families had invested in education, many American-born Jewish women took advantage of the opportunities afforded by the expanding economy to use the business and professional skills that they too had developed in school.

First-generation American Jewish women had, of course, grown up watching their immigrant mothers earn and manage money while running homes and raising children. But the middle-class American culture that these native-born daughters joined divided earning and household responsibilities between the two spouses, one the breadwinner and the other the homemaker. Middle-class American married women certainly did not rent out rooms to boarders or stitch in their kitchens on subcontract or mind the cash register in a corner store. They most emphatically did not hold garment factory jobs. Nor did the economy provide the opportunities for the kind of home work that so many immigrant wives had done. Nonetheless, for many American-born Jewish couples, the daily reality in these decades clashed with the requirements of respectability. To fulfill their traditional role of caring for their family's welfare, the women of this new Jewish generation continued to balance the requirements of work and family, although now they earned their money in ways considered more suited to their identities as full-fledged middle-class Americans.

Getting Through the Depression

The great economic crisis of the 1930s began, according to American folk memory, with the stock market crash of October 1929. At that time, however, the great majority of Americans, including American Jews, did not own stocks. For them, the reality began to dawn somewhat later, and sometimes gradually, as the economy inexorably slowed and increasing numbers of husbands found it difficult to support anything approaching a middle-class lifestyle on their own. For the huge New York East European Jewish community, true economic calamity struck in December of the following year, when an even more important financial institution—for them at least—went under. On that "terrible day," young Irving Howe, the future writer and literary scholar, "sat in our apartment listening to my aunt and grandmother wailing over the loss of the few hundred dollars they had scraped together" over years of labor and frugality.[3] They had entrusted their savings to the Bank of the United States, whose impressive name seemed to share the strength and grandeur of the nation itself. Behind that name, however, stood not a venerable national institution but a bank founded seventeen years earlier by a pair of East European immigrants. Cries like those in Howe's apartment rang out across the city as 400,000 other depositors—thrifty households, industrious laborers, store owners, wholesale distributors, garment firms, and other businesses—saw their accounts evaporate. Frantic crowds besieged the bank's sixty branches, battling for a chance to demand their funds. The bank that had symbolized its depositors' faith and hope in the new country finally settled with them for a fraction of their money.

The bank took many Jewish businesses, and the jobs they produced, down with it, and across the country, other banks were doing the same. The *Forward* promised traumatized readers that "America, to be sure, is not going under," but many of those relatively new Americans and even newer members of the middle class were not so sure about their own social standing.[4] As the national economic crisis deepened, more and more enterprises of every sort began to fail. Dealers in luxuries like furs, tobacco, jewelry, furniture, and entertainment—all heavily Jewish industries—were among the hardest hit. In the two years after Black Friday of 1929, half of New York's jewelers closed their doors.[5] Eight thousand of the city's furniture stores, mostly Jewish owned, went under between 1929 and 1933.[6] Mom-and-pop groceries, another Jewish staple, meanwhile, faced growing competition from spreading chain stores, whose lower prices lured hard-pressed consumers. Mostly small independent merchants, white-collar Jews struggled to maintain their hard-won foothold in the middle class.

Many other Jews who had arduously acquired white-collar credentials discovered that degrees and diplomas did not guarantee white-collar incomes. Because established Gentile law firms generally refused to hire Jews, thousands of lawyers struggled to earn anything at all as obscure sole practitioners. Because Gentile hospitals often did not extend practice privileges to Jews, some doctors had trouble attracting patients. Lillian Cantor, a young social worker for the Workman's Circle New York service center, spent long days working to help the Jewish jobless. She found a promising possibility at the Works Progress Administration, a federal New Deal agency designed to provide employment. In one of its programs, "a taxi company could hire men three afternoons a week at fifteen dollars if those men were certified by a social service agency," she wrote. "I placed 300 doctors as cab drivers . . . 300 *medical* doctors. Nobody realizes what the Depression meant in large urban centers. These men pleaded for the chance to earn that pittance. It meant that they at least could bring some milk or bread into the house. There were hundreds of stories like that."[7] To qualify for WPA jobs, fifteen hundred lawyers declared themselves paupers in 1934.[8]

Countless thousands of Jews with lesser academic credentials also searched futilely for work. In 1930 and 1934, New York's Jewish employment agencies found jobs for a bare fifth of those who registered.[9] Jews across the country blamed more than the national economic emergency for their trouble finding work. Frances Halpern of Minneapolis, for example, had sought a teaching job back in the prosperous 1920s. Armed with her University of Minnesota degree, she attended numerous interviews. But every time, according to Frances's sister Blanche Halpern Goldberg, the same question would arise: "'And what is your religion?' And when she said, 'Jewish,' . . . that would interfere" with getting hired. Finally Frances wrote to a man she knew who worked as a teacher in the town of Grand Rapids, Minnesota. "How did you get your job?" she asked. "It seems that I can't get a job because I am Jewish." Her friend advised, "'Just don't answer that question. Put down anything but Jewish." "And sure enough," Blanche remembered, "as soon . . . as there was another possibility she put down Unitarian" and landed a job. "What else could she do?"[10]

A young New Yorker who had faced similar rejections but did not "look Jewish" took an even more direct approach by enlisting the help of a friendly Episcopal priest. On the strength of a letter naming her as one of his parishioners, she landed a job at an insurance company with a policy of not hiring Jews. Her jobless father objected to the subterfuge but her mother took a more pragmatic view. "Would going around jobless and having to come to her father or mother for a dollar be better?" she asked the *Forward*.

Blanche Goldberg also found that some changes were in order when she began looking for a teaching job of her own. She showed her University of Minnesota mentor the photos she made up to send out with her applications. "You ought to take them over again so you don't look so Jewish," the professor suggested. "Your hair is too curly."[11]

How many Jews decided to "pass" will never be known, but the number was probably substantial. Others took a different course. Fannie Schwartz hoped to learn to run a particular business machine to improve her chances of landing an office job. "If a girl finished comptometer school she earned $35 a week, big money" during the Depression, Fannie remembered. Fannie went to a business school to apply for the training. She "was received by this lovely-looking Nordic," who politely asked "about experience and grades in school and what I hoped to do. Then she said, 'I have just one last question to ask you. Are you Jewish?' And I said, 'Yes.' After a pause she said to me, 'We don't have any Jewish students.' I said, 'I'm sorry about that. I don't mind being the only one.' She said, 'We don't place Jewish students.' And I said, 'You don't have to place me; just train me. I'll get my own job.' And she paused, and pretty soon she said, 'I'm sorry, but I can't accept you or your money.' And that was the end of the conversation. My money was returned to me, pushed back across the desk and I was asked to leave the office."[12]

Amid the forest of signs proclaiming "Not Hiring Today" and "Jews Need Not Apply," one of the only bright spots for Jews was the growth of civil service work, which in many places depended not on employers' personal preferences but on test scores and other objective criteria that favored those with good academic records. In 1933, for example, New York's Mayor Fiorello LaGuardia reformed the civil service, transforming many jobs from patronage handed out by Tammany politicians into posts awarded through written exams. Much to the chagrin of the Irish community, Jews soon had 74 percent of those posts, up from 55 percent under the old system.[13] The chance to enter federal service in the expanding "alphabet soup" of New Deal agencies also drew thousands of Jewish degree holders to Washington, D.C.

Jewish families generally managed to scrape by. "During the Depression, from 1929 on, things were rough for almost everyone" in the South Portland neighborhood where Frieda Gass Cohen grew up. "We didn't feel any different; we never considered ourselves poor; we just didn't have any money. My parents were very frugal, and again we never ate out, but we didn't lack for anything. Things were difficult as far as money was concerned, but my friends did not have money to spend either . . . so we did not particularly feel the lack of money."[14] Compared even with Jews like the Gass family, many Gentiles suffered worse hardships. Heavy industrial workers, small farmers, and the unskilled were hit hardest of all, and few Jews belonged to those categories. White-collar people needed government relief less often than those who worked with their hands. Still, the beleaguered working class included many thousands of Jewish families. The left-wing stalwarts of Irving Howe's boyhood East Bronx neighborhood considered relief "suspect as both gentile and bourgeois" and many "would have starved—and perhaps some did a little, rather than go on 'relief.'"[15]

Despite such ideological qualms, in the mid-1930s 12 percent of New York City Jewish youths belonged to families taking the government dole; among Italians, the comparable figure reached 21 percent. Jews forced to apply for government assistance felt "embarrassed," Ida Barnett remembered. "In order to put food on the table," in 1934 she and her husband took that dismaying step. "We tried to keep it quiet. . . . you have a certain pride. . . . We did not want the neighbors to know that we were on home relief. Maybe they were too, but it wasn't common knowledge."[16]

Jews avoided this humiliation more often than some other groups because their ethnic economy of countless small businesses provided niches and cracks where the unemployed could at least hang on. Entrepreneurs going bust in one line of business could try to shift to a related one, reupholstering old furniture instead of selling new pieces, for example, or repairing old shoes instead of retailing the latest styles, or cleaning and reblocking hats to make them last another season, or recutting and restyling worn clothing and furs instead of fashioning new ones. If need be, small businesses could take on an extra unpaid or poorly paid employee. Even if the unemployed relative had no actual work to do and received little or no income, he or she at least had somewhere warm to stay and some way of passing the hours. Large Jewish firms that stayed afloat, department stores like Glosser Brothers, for example, often helped significant portions of their communities to do likewise.

The Jewish habit of communal self-help, well honed in the immigrant quarters, provided a lifeline for many. Not only did established philanthropies, benefit associations, loan societies, and *landsmanshaftn* continue their work during the Depression, but relatives also organized to meet the emergency. The Joseph Nudelman family of Portland, for example, established the Nudelman Family Association. All the grown sons and daughters "paid five dollars a month dues," according to one member. "Whenever someone had a problem and needed some money, they could borrow it from the association and pay it back if and when they could. The fund ... lasted for at least twenty years." In addition, the association "would meet every two weeks in a different home in the family. [It] really held the family together."[17]

Merchants and landlords also often helped customers over rough spots. Countless small stores carried struggling clients on credit. When Rebecca Augenstein's husband lost his fur industry job, for example, the family faced the embarrassment of taking home relief. "At the beginning, before my husband started to work [for the WPA] and earn a little money," she remembered, "the grocer said to me, 'You can trust all you want.' And so it was. I bought food to eat. He used to have a *tzetl* [list]. . . . Everything I bought when I didn't have the money to pay, he wrote it down. . . . Then, when we got the [relief] check every month, I went to the grocery and he took off what I owed him."[18] Another grocer told a relief investigator that he had extended credit in the substantial amount of $25 to a family named Berger "because they are the type of family who does their best. He knows they would not apply for assistance unless their need was great."[19] Some grocers even let men run tabs for the carfare they needed to travel about the city looking for work. The storekeepers' generosity fit the ancient mitzvah of *tzedakah,* but it also fulfilled the modern, nonaltruistic purpose of helping the little groceries to stay in business. Credit customers did not pay immediately, but at least they eventually paid, and when they did, they paid higher prices than those charged by the cash-only chain stores like A&P. Thus merchants unable to compete on price could still keep a loyal customer base.

Landlords sometimes allowed leeway on due dates for rent, although not as often as mom-and-pop groceries. With fewer tenants able to pay promptly than there were during the 1920s building boom, owners sometimes concluded that keeping a tenant who would eventually pay his arrears made more sense than letting a unit stand vacant. Sometimes simple humanity inspired leniency. One day Rebecca Augenstein's landlord, making the monthly rounds of his Bronx apartment building, found her distraught. "*Host deveynt, mein kind?* [Have you been crying, my child?]," the rent collector asked. "So I said, 'Yes,' and he said to me, '*For vas host du gevant?*' He said, 'Why do you cry?' and I said, 'My son, every boy in the Boy Scouts has a uniform. He is the only one that has no uniform.' You know what he said to me, '*Gib mir nit di dire gelt.*' 'Don't give me the rent. Go out and buy that child a uniform. This is much more important . . . As soon as you'll have, you'll pay.'"[20]

But tears and credit were not the only strategies that Rebecca and women like her used to stretch meager family budgets. When merchants and landlords failed to show compassion for their creditors' woes, women, especially in left-leaning neighborhoods, once again resorted to meat strikes and rent strikes to force prices down or forestall evictions. "Fists were flying, bricks and fragments of concrete were hurling through the air and nightsticks were describing forceful arcs" as a crowd of four thousand tried to prevent the police from evicting seventeen families from the building at 2802 Olinville Avenue, the *Bronx Home News* reported in January 1932. "As each piece of furniture was taken to the streets, tenants in the other apartments uttered loud boos from their windows. Off in the distance, the boos were echoed by the crowd," which the police had succeeded in pushing back.[21] Within days, a "swarm of women" was standing their ground against police in front of 665 Allerton Avenue, also in the Bronx, according to the *New York Times*.[22] "The strike is organized by the men but it is led by the women," the *Forward* observed. "Such is the way in all the rent strikes that are going on today in greater New York. The women are the fighters, the pickets, the agitators. A remarkable bravery and battle-cheer is displayed by the women in the rent strikes."[23] Ordinarily these "housewives from large families, mothers of small children . . . could not go out of the house for a minute," the paper rhapsodized, "but now they stand half the day in the picket line [and] attend strike meetings."[24] They could do so because neighbors often shared child care, cooking, and housekeeping during a strike. When one striking *balebuste* was jailed on a Friday, friends in her building saw to it that her family's Sabbath dinner did not suffer.

The basic survival strategy of the Jewish wife, as it had always been, was to bring in money to feed her family. Rebecca, for example, found a job clerking part-time in a bakery near her home. Her wages were low, but "I needed that 85 cents an hour very badly at the time."[25] The same went for countless other wives. "Poor Jewish women now look for all kinds of ways to make a living," reported the *Forward* in 1931, bemoaning the ground that so many hardworking families had so suddenly lost. Once again "they peddle; they take in boarders; they raise other people's children." Even more dispiriting, "still others return to the factory. Fifteen years ago they . . . dreamed they would ultimately 'find their destined mates and be free of the factory. Now they have their mates, but after fifteen years' time, they must go back to the factory.'"[26] That step backward, the *Forward* acknowledged, indicated far more than just an unexpected need for cash; it meant that a family had fallen back into the working-class penury that many Jews only recently thought they had escaped.

Rebecca managed to avoid the indignity of factory work by taking a job that fit with her *balebuste* role. She worked only while her children were at school, and although her small earnings probably made a big difference, she didn't see herself as "really" working, in the sense that a factory hand did. Decades later, talking with an interviewer about how the Augensteins got through the Depression, she did not even initially remember the hours she spent at the bakery, recalling them only midway through their talk. Another wife, whose Depression earnings had also figured in her family's survival, remarked that the jobs she found in those days always paid poorly, but she always had one. "If I didn't help out, we couldn't manage at all."[27]

Like their foremothers in the immigrant districts and the Pale, Jewish wives in Brooklyn and the Bronx, in Roxbury and Lawndale, in Johnstown and Portland and Los Angeles worked to put bread on the table. But now, as members of (or at least aspirants to) the American middle class, they "helped out." An immigrant husband could without embarrassment accept that his wife made up a shortfall in the family exchequer, just as women had done in Europe. But an American man who had attained middle-class income and status, or was struggling to hang on to them, often felt shamed by needing a woman's income, though many needed it nonetheless. Even if a middle-class wife stepped in to assume the *balebuste's* burden of seeing that the bills were paid, she had to do it, if at all possible, in a way that did not violate American middle-class expectations.

Whether she held a paying job, was active in the family business, or ran a business of her own, propriety required that she merely "help out." As the jobless rolls rose, so did the numbers of women, children, and young people scrambling for whatever work they could find. Lower-paying and relatively plentiful clerical, sales, and light-industrial jobs were often considered "female." The better-paid "male" heavy-industrial and skilled craft jobs that could support a family were hardest hit by the Depression. To make ends meet, more married women found employment as the Depression decade advanced. Wives constituted 29 percent of the female American workforce in 1930 but 35 percent a decade later.[28] At any given time during the 1930s, a quarter of America's married women held paid employment. The official statistics probably missed others "helping out" in small businesses, their family's or their own. And Jewish women, with their long breadwinning tradition, probably exceeded the general American rate.

One approach to earning within the confines of middle-class domesticity was doing work that was outwardly invisible. A resourceful Washingtonian named Mrs. Goldstein, for example, combined two impeccably feminine activities, shopping at the city's best department stores and calling on prosperous ladies in their homes. Her hostesses belonged to the city's substantial African American middle class, a group that since the Civil War had held government posts, taught at Howard University and the city's segregated public schools, staffed Freedmen's Hospital, and run businesses and professional practices serving a largely black clientele. They had middle-class tastes and the means to afford them. One thing they did not have in a legally segregated southern city, however, was the right to try on clothes in the stylish downtown stores also patronized by whites. Rather than submit to the limitation of patronizing only small Negro stores or buying garments they had not tried on, they would call for a visit from Mrs. Goldstein. Arriving at a home with a suitcase or two of the latest fashions culled from chic downtown racks, she helped her clients try on and select the most flattering looks. She would then return any rejected outfits.

Marriage Partners, Business Partners

A very popular strategy among American-born wives with high school and even college credentials was "helping out" in ventures far more sophisticated those their immigrant mothers had managed. From the 1920s through the 1950s, enterprises involving both spouses provided vehicles for Jewish wives to work under cover of conventional domesticity in an enormous variety of fields. Brooklyn-born Mollie Parnis, for example, watched her mother support four children on the Lower East Side after their father, a butter and egg dealer, died in 1915, when Mollie was ten. Mollie had started working even before that, teaching English to immigrants at twenty-five cents an hour at the age of eight. After finishing high school and starting Hunter, eighteen-year-old Mollie took a sales job with a Seventh Avenue blouse company. Selling wholesale to store buyers, she showed a flair for style that had been evident in high school, when she had remade her only dress, a drab blue serge, into a party frock by altering the neckline and adding an artificial flower and a row of lace. This same attention to crucial fashion detail made her a standout saleswoman. Suggesting small changes in her employer's line, she found ways to offer clients a range of varied and distinctive styles. In lieu of a raise, the company added "Mollie Parnis, 4th floor" to its listing in the lobby directory. Public recognition on the main thoroughfare of the New York fashion business made Mollie feel "like an actress having her name up in lights for the first time."[29]

At twenty-four, not long before the stock market crashed, she took a job as a stylist for a well-known dress company, a move that changed her professional and personal lives. Among the textile salesmen who called on the firm was Leon Livingstone (né Levinson), whom she wed in 1930. She spent the first years of her marriage keeping house and caring for their son, Robert. Despite the deepening Depression, the young couple decided that they could succeed as clothing manufacturers while most established firms were going under. In 1933, with Leon running the business side and Mollie overseeing design, Parnis Livingston Incorporated went into the business of making silk dresses.

Mollie had never formally studied design or learned the mechanics of clothing construction, but her shrewd fashion sense enabled her to direct the designers whom the company hired. Focusing on the over-thirty market, she perfected a refined and elegant look that raised the company to the top rank of Seventh Avenue fashion houses. From the 1940s on, leading photographers shot Parnis Livingston creations for the chic pages of *Vogue, Harper's Bazaar*, and other major magazines. Prestigious clients included first ladies Bess Truman, Mamie Eisenhower, Lady Bird Johnson, and Pat Nixon. The daughter of the Lower East Side took great pride in meeting presidents and their wives. When Mrs. Eisenhower once encountered a fellow guest at a Washington function in an identical Parnis taffeta, Mollie eased the ensuing uproar by remarking that the company made clothes for a democratic nation, not a privileged elite. She and Leon remained business and personal partners until he died in 1962. She closed the company briefly but returned and soon expanded into such new lines as affordable clothing for working women and casual leisure wear.

Beatrice Alexander also spent a career designing distinctive fashions, but for a younger clientele. As a twenty-eight-year-old wife and mother, she began selling the dolls she had for years been making and outfitting at home. This kitchen-table craft grew from the trade she had seen her immigrant father, Maurice, practice in his New York doll hospital, probably the nation's first. In those days the finest toys were handmade and imported from Germany. Beatrice, one of four daughters growing up in the apartment over the workshop, waited on the prosperous parents who paid Maurice to repair their children's expensive and highly breakable porcelain playthings.

Then World War I cut the flow of European dolls, and their mother suggested that Beatrice and her sisters try their hand at making some. Beatrice put together a cloth figure with a three-dimensional painted cloth face and clothed her in a Red Cross uniform. In 1923 she began selling her creations, and by the end of the 1920s the operation had outgrown Beatrice's kitchen. Her husband of more than a decade, Phillip Behrman, joined her in the business, then located in a nearby workshop. In the 1930s and 1940s, the authenticity and finesse of her costumes won the Madame Alexander Doll Company recognition as one of the world's leading creators of high-quality dolls. Eventually, their Harlem factory became the neighborhood's largest employer, with 650 people crafting dolls by hand.

In the 1930s, Madame Alexander began acquiring the rights to make dolls based on famous people, both fictional and real. First came Alice in Wonderland, followed by Louisa May Alcott's Little Women, various figures invented by Dickens, and then, in a major coup, the Dionne quintuplets, the little Quebec girls whose birth and survival created a worldwide sensation in the mid-1930s. Scarlett O'Hara of the best-selling book *Gone with the Wind* also appeared as a Madame Alexander doll, as did real-life stars actress Margaret O'Brien and first lady Jacqueline Kennedy. Even the British royal family was portrayed, first in a trio including Queen Elizabeth (now the Queen Mother) and her daughters, Princesses Elizabeth and Margaret. To celebrate Princess Elizabeth's coronation as queen at her father's death in 1953, Madame Alexander produced a set of thirty-six dolls, including Her Majesty, Winston Churchill, and other dignitaries, all meticulously dressed in exact replicas of the outfits they wore to the lavish Westminster Abbey ceremony, one of the first great state events televised to a mass audience. In addition to making the Behrmans wealthy, Madame Alexander Dolls pioneered technical innovations in doll making. In the 1930s it led the way in making unbreakable composition heads with eyes that appeared to open and close. During the 1940s, it introduced the new plastics and synthetics into its dolls, scoring a hit with vinyl-headed models whose hair their young owners could style. For seventy-five years, doll making was a family affair for the Behrmans, as it had been for the Alexanders. Both Beatrice and Phillip's daughter, Mildred, and their grandson, William Alexander Birnbaum, grew up surrounded by dolls. William was the company's president when it was sold in 1988, two years before Beatrice died at the age of ninety-five.

Sadie Marks, on the other hand, went into her husband's business. The couple met one Passover when a cousin who worked as a touring vaudevillian, Herbert Marx (known in business as Zeppo), brought a colleague, born Benjamin Kubelsky, to a family seder. Earlier in his career the young guest had changed his name to Jack Benny. After appearing on Jack's show—for decades among the nation's most popular, first on radio and then on TV—in the role of Mary Livingstone, Sadie legally adopted her stage name. In another branch of show business, writers Fay and Michael Kanin collaborated for twenty years on film and theater scripts that included the Oscar-winning *Teacher's Pet* and the Broadway hit *Rashomon*. Eventually, the couple "decided we would have to keep the working collaboration or the marriage. We decided on the marriage," Fay explained.[30] Another agile pen, belonging to composer, lyricist, and pianist Sylvia Fine Kaye, produced more than a hundred songs, a number of which helped her husband, comedian and singer Danny Kaye (born David Daniel Kaminsky), rocket to fame on the New York stage and then in films. Both Brooklyn born, the couple met when Danny auditioned for a part and Sylvia happened to be working as the producer's rehearsal accompanist. Married in 1940, they joined forces to advance his performing career; she produced his shows while continuing to write songs. Though their personal relationship was often rocky, they established a film production company. Sylvia's work on *The Moon Is Blue* and *The Five Pennies* earned her Oscar nominations.

Lee Krasner, like Sylvia a respected creative talent, also spent prime professional years promoting her husband's fame rather than her own. Her career took her from Brooklyn, where she grew up watching her mother actively manage the family's fruit and vegetable store, to Manhattan. But the distance between her girlhood in an observant immigrant family and her adulthood at the fulcrum of the New York art scene was greater by far. Lee spent years struggling to get serious artistic training at a time when female artists got little attention. She had matured into an accomplished thirty-year-old painter when, in 1938, she met a relative beginner named Jackson Pollock. Lee's teacher, Hans Hofmann, had pronounced her work "so good you would not know it was done by a woman."[31] But the brilliant, erratic, and alcoholic Pollock soared to the pinnacle of the art world as the creator of abstract expressionist "drip painting" and became a major figure in the all-male group known as the New York School of modern painters. Lee found her reputation as artist submerged by her identity as the notorious Jackson Pollock's wife. In the late 1940s and early 1950s, instead of nourishing the artistic vision that had won her exhibitions at prominent New York galleries, she spent most of her time and energy managing the hard-drinking Pollock's increasingly chaotic life and increasingly complicated business affairs. After he died in a 1956 auto wreck, the art world regarded her as the widow in charge of the Pollock estate, not as the artist in charge of the Krasner talent. Two decades passed before her work began to attract attention and recognition in its own right.

Even the first Jewish woman to serve in the U.S. Congress got there by "helping out." Florence Prag Kahn ran her husband Julius's office for a quarter century. When he died in 1924, she succeeded to the job in her own right and made a name for herself by effectively representing San Francisco in the U.S. House of Representatives from 1924 to 1937. Her immigrant father arrived in the California gold fields in 1849 and helped found the Shearith Israel synagogue two years later. Her mother arrived in San Francisco at the age of five. After graduating from the University of California in 1887, Florence taught high school and religious school until she married in 1899 and followed Julius to Washington for his first term. During his political career, the column she wrote for the *San Francisco Chronicle* generated an income. "The equal of any man in Congress and the superior of most," according to Washington doyenne Alice Roosevelt Longworth, the "shrewd, resourceful, witty" legislator succeeded Julius on the decidedly unfeminine Military Affairs Committee and served as a canny advocate for her home region, introducing the bills that created the Moffett Field, Alameda Naval Air Station, and the Bay Bridge between San Francisco and Oakland. Policies she did not support included movie censorship and prohibition. Like all the eminent and accomplished professional women mentioned here (except Lee Krasner) and countless others like them, Florence Kahn raised a family while "helping out."

American Beauty

By making their work appear secondary to their husband's, countless Jewish wives strove to maintain American standards of respectable femininity. But another of the relevant criteria, physical appearance, presented a challenge to substantial numbers of Jewish women. Good-looking Americans, as seen in films, ads, and magazines, were slender and shapely with crisp, compact facial features; high cheekbones; small, straight noses; long jaws; high, arched foreheads. They also had shiny hair with only the slightest wave, preferably blond, possibly light brown, perhaps touched with reddish highlights. Neither kinky black hair, long curved noses, almond-shaped dark eyes, nor any hint of peasant plumpness marked the all-American girl next door. Generations of Jewish women therefore struggled to force their faces and their forms into a mold constructed along Anglo-Saxon lines.

Fannie Brice (née Fania Borach), a major comedy star from 1900 until her death in 1951, gained immense popularity on stage, in films, and as the long-running radio rascal, *Baby Snooks*. But even she resorted to plastic surgery to attain more classic looks that she thought might land her the serious dramatic roles she craved. In a widely reported operation, she "cut off her nose to spite her race," according to the half-Jewish Dorothy Parker, the reigning queen of the acerbic witticism.[32] Denying her origins was probably not Brice's main motivation, even had it been possible. She began her career doing a broad Yiddish accent and understood that for her audiences, "I *am* the race, and what happened to me on the stage is what happened to them."[33] Like most of those watching, she never attained the all-American looks she craved.

By the 1930s and 1940s, though, old-fashioned ethnic stereotyping—and identifiably Jewish characters—had passed from vogue in entertainment, and even in the Hollywood film industry, which East European Jews had built and still dominated. Nonetheless, a number of Jewish women who, unlike Brice, could convincingly acquire "non-Jewish" looks and identities made successful careers as all-American movie stars. Wearing their ethnically neutral stage names as faultlessly as their elegant costumes, they played "regular" Americans as convincingly off-screen as on. From the raw sexuality of Sophie Tucker (Sophie Abuza), "the last of the red-hot mamas," in the late 1920s, to the languid, ash-blond elegance of Lauren Bacall (Betty Joan Perske) in the late 1940s and 1950s, Jewish women projected an image of WASPish womanhood. Sylvia Sydney (Sophia Moscow), Luise Rainer, Paulette Goddard (Marion Levy), June Havoc (Ellen Hovick) and her sister, the stripper Gypsy Rose Lee, Betty Hutton (Betty Thornberg), the aptly named Joan Blondell, Judy Holliday (Judy Tuvim), Shelley Winters (Shirley Schrift), and Lee Grant (Lyova Rosenthal) were the more successful of these actresses.

In those days, film personalities of all backgrounds, even such authentic Anglo-Saxons as Archie Leach (Cary Grant) and Marion Morrison (John Wayne), customarily adopted new names as they began their careers, but Jewish performers felt a need to disguise their origins. In 1944 director Howard Hawks cast Bacall, an unknown twenty-year-old model who adopted her mother's maiden name, as the love interest of Humphrey Bogart, the forty-five-year-old box-office idol who became her husband, in *To Have and Have Not*. She "didn't tell . . . Hawks I was Jewish, because he was an anti-Semite and scared the hell out of me. He made me so nervous I didn't say anything." Brought up to speak plainly, Bacall "was not proud of myself."[34]

The "leggy blonde huntress"—a reporter's description of Bacall that applied equally well to many other cinema beauties—captivated the American imagination for decades.[35] From Clara Bow to Marilyn Monroe, the movies and the magazines glorified platinum hair and sinuous limbs. By the late 1950s, with Monroe ascendant, Americans pondered whether "blondes [truly do] have more fun." Little girls dreamed of someday resembling the impossibly long-legged, improbably slender, inimitably yellow-tressed figure of the Barbie doll. The plastic paragon's pert nose and Nordic coloring could hardly have reassured many Jewish preteens, though Clairol offered some comfort to their mothers. But, like the topflight professional hidden inside the *balebustish* Molly Goldberg, these apparent icons of unattainable Gentile beauty concealed a Jewish female business brain every bit as insightful and incisive as Gertrude Berg's. Two married Jewish mothers, Shirley Polyakoff and Ruth Mosko Handler, made their own stellar careers selling the very aspects of mythic American femininity that bedeviled so many Jewish women.

Brooklyn-born Shirley—initially named Leo by a father who ardently wanted his second child to be a son—discovered, at the age of twelve, the route that would carry her to the heart of the American dream. Ultimately granted a feminine name by immigrant parents eager for her to be an American and an earner, she sought guidance toward the first goal by studying advertisements. In pursuit of the second, she entered a Campbell's Soup jingle contest. Though she did not win a prize, she received something far more valuable in the long run: a note acknowledging her entry from the advertising agency running the contest. Ads, she realized, were composed by real people who earned their living writing them. At twenty-one she was writing copy for a women's store in Brooklyn. Slogans like "Rhinestones, a girl's next best friend" made her an immediate success.[36] Before long she was top copywriter for Bamberger's and Kresge's, Newark's top department stores. In 1933, employed by a fashionable Fifth Avenue fur salon, twenty-five-year-old Shirley married lawyer George Halperin, who encouraged her to continue her career after their two daughters were born. By 1955, she achieved heights almost unprecedented for a Jew, let alone for a woman. Foote, Cone & Belding, a leading Madison Avenue advertising firm hardly noted for hiring either women or Jews, offered her a major job and a particularly delicate assignment: to change America's attitude toward women who dyed their hair. When Shirley took on the challenge, a mere 7 percent did so. Only Hollywood starlets, Monte Carlo socialites, cover girls, and others with at least slightly risqué reputations would consider having hair that obviously "came out of a bottle." Neither respectable matrons nor girls hoping to make good marriages would do anything so blatantly "fast."

In the service of Clairol, Shirley astutely married Main Street wholesomeness to chemical coloration in photographs of demure young mothers cherishing their angelic offspring. "Does she . . . or doesn't she?" the headline coyly asked, going on to confide, "Only her hairdresser knows for sure." Reading this sly double-entendre in the pages of *Life* and other family magazines, women across the country decided that no one would know for sure about them either, and they called their hairdressers by the millions. Within several years, half of American women were coloring their hair.[37] "Is it true that blondes have more fun?" Shirley's Clairol ads asked next, and millions decided to find out.[38] By 1961, she was a new widow and Foote, Cone's highest-paid staffer. In her mid-sixties, she started her own ad agency and won all of the major awards in the advertising business before retiring ten years later.

But the true fair-haired girl of American popular culture was probably Barbie, the anatomically impossible teenager that replaced the traditional baby doll in toy boxes and dollhouses nationwide. The tenth and last child of Polish immigrants, Ruth Mosko(witz) got her first business experience in a Denver drugstore run by a sister and brother-in-law. At sixteen she met Izzy Handler, an art student whose career prospects did not inspire her family in the Depression year of 1932. Several years later Ruth, then a student at the University of Denver, visited Los Angeles and decided to take a job at Paramount Studios instead of returning to school. Izzy came west and married her in 1938. At Ruth's urging Izzy began to go by Elliot, his middle name. While she worked at the movie studio, he studied at the Art Center College of Design and held a job designing light fixtures, which led him to an interest in the new materials known as plastics.

The young couple took a chance and produced some of the designs Elliot had been doodling, which Ruth proceeded to market. They had their first big success with a model of the DC-3 airliner, which the plane's manufacturer, Douglas Aircraft, bought in large numbers as a corporate Christmas gift. The onset of the war, however, cut their access to plastic, which was considered a vital military material. The Handlers had been using it to make picture frames but quickly shifted to wood, which proved even more popular. Along with their associate Harold "Matt" Matson, who managed production, they celebrated their new product line with a new company name that combined the men's first names: Mattel. No one suggested that the trademark should also honor Ruth's crucial role in sales and product development.

When World War II ended, the Handlers not only had a successful business but two children, Barbara and Kenneth. With wartime shortages over, Mattel went back to making plastic toys, including a popular ukelele based on the instrument played by hit radio personality Arthur Godfrey. In 1955 Ruth and Elliot, who had bought out Matson's interest, took a step that would revolutionize the toy industry when they sponsored Walt Disney's new *Mickey Mouse Club* on TV. Suddenly parents found their children asking for specific toys all year round instead of only at Christmas. In three years Mattel's sales tripled. In 1956, while traveling in Switzerland, Ruth and her fifteen-year-old daughter looked into a shop window and had a billion-dollar epiphany. There stood six sexy plastic female figures, each just under a foot tall, modeling a variety of alluring ski ensembles. Obviously intended for adults, these seductive playthings had the contours of curvaceous grown-up women. But Ruth saw beyond the sexual overtones to an American marketing possibility. For some time she had been toying with the idea of a potentially very profitable variant on the popular costume dolls then available. Rather than an immature form and a single outfit, her doll would have a woman's figure and an ever expanding wardrobe of clothes that could be purchased separately.

Three years later, Barbie hit the market, joined soon by her boyfriend, Ken, and eventually there was a coterie of other chums and kinfolk, each equipped with an inexhaustible, ever changing array of outfits and accessories. Barbie and company proved extraordinarily adaptable to changing times because they could adopt any or all of a huge range of roles and activities. Young owners simply had to choose among a constantly expanding line of ball gowns, career outfits, athletic togs, leisure wear, and other ensembles as well as various residences, workplaces, sporting gear, vehicles, and a host of other consumer products, all cunningly sized to Barbie's world and even more cunningly marketed. Within a decade, Barbie had a million-and-a-half-member fan club and Mattel had a tenth of the country's toy sales.[39]

In her trip from that European display window to toy chests across America, Barbie underwent a sea change, keeping her European prototype's womanly body but losing its aggressive sexuality. She became at once chaste and voluptuous, busty and innocent. She mixed girl-next-door charm with a figure that embodied the American fascination with slenderness, legginess, and breasts. Indeed, "when I conceived Barbie, I believed it was important to a little girl's self-esteem to play with a doll that had breasts," Ruth recalled.[40] Despite her concern with boosting youngsters' self-esteem, some critics argued that Barbie became instead an icon of unattainable beauty. By combining dauntingly perfect looks with the apparent ability to achieve almost any goal a child might aspire to, some observers noted, Barbie increased the pressure that girls felt to attain a specific type of appearance.

The need to conform to another standard of appearance inspired a second business venture of Ruth's, after she suffered breast cancer. Her difficulty in finding a satisfactory prosthesis convinced her to found Nearly Me to manufacture an improved prosthesis and "return that self-confidence to women who have lost theirs" through mastectomy.[41]

The Ideal Occupation

Despite the remarkable success a working woman might attain, however, American Jews overwhelmingly considered marriage and family the truest role for a woman. "Papa thought like most American fathers then, that his daughters should work only until they married," Sarah Rothman remembered from her New York girlhood during the first third of the twentieth century. His opinion "that an education for his girls, with all the sacrifices that went along with it, would be wasted when we married" was, Sarah knew, the mark of an immigrant's progress toward accepting the mores of his chosen homeland.[42] Luckily, her mother had a different idea of respectable female adulthood—and one that she shared with many other Jewish mothers across the city. "Becoming a teacher was drummed into me at an early age," recalled Goldie Cohen, whose mother held the same view as Sarah's. Encouragement to "study, study, so that you can become a teacher" went as far back as Goldie could recall.[43] "The only time that I could remember my mother taking a stand against my father," added their contemporary Myn Silverman, was when she insisted that Myn have a chance to try for teaching credentials.[44]

For many East European immigrant mothers, in fact, the encounter with the commanding Yankee and Irish spinsters who taught their children to speak English and become Americans revealed a world of possibilities. Traditional East European culture held teaching in high esteem, but it never envisioned women in charge of classrooms where boys and girls learned together. In America, though, women whom circumstance had kept from studying realized that their bright and determined daughters could one day stand in the prestigious place held by those admirable female professionals. Native-born daughters could perhaps realize their mothers' thwarted hopes at the same time as they boosted themselves— and, by extension, their entire families—into the category of Americans whose work commanded respect.

American-born girls also saw in those well-spoken schoolmarms an image of a tantalizing future. "I remember how I admired them, for I loved the way they dressed and the way they spoke," said Rachel Berkowitz, who went on to join their ranks. "I wanted to be just like them."[45] Seventy years later, Ethel Cohen, who also realized the dream of a teaching career, warmed at the memory of the "third grade. I can still see Miss Jensen. She was my ideal."[46] To gain the approval of these paragons of success, "we all vied for the lavish praise of our teachers. We literally basked in it," remembered Lily Gordon, who succeeded in joining the profession.[47]

Throughout the nineteenth century, America's school systems insisted that female teachers be spinsters, and some employed only single women for five decades into the twentieth. In other places, New York among them, a teacher could continue her respected, secure career after she married and had children. In 1904 Kate M. Murphy, who at the time had eleven years of experience with the New York City public schools, successfully challenged the policy of dismissing teachers who wed. In 1915, a new mother named Bridget Peixotto won reinstatement after the school system had dismissed her for neglect of duty during a leave of absence to have her baby. Her case established the principle that childbirth did not automatically end a teaching career. This precedent had special importance for young Jewish women because, unlike the Yankee bluestockings and Irish maiden ladies who had long dominated the profession, the vast majority of first-generation Jewish daughters had every intention of marrying.

In cities that kept wives and mothers on the teaching staff, the profession became by far the most desirable one for able, ambitious Jewish girls. Americans considered teaching quintessentially feminine and indisputably middle class, embodying just about every value that big-city Jewish culture cherished during the first two-thirds of the twentieth century. And beyond that, it admirably fit women's personal needs. Unassailably respectable, proudly white-collar, conspicuously academic, well-paid, and secure, a teaching job offered a daily schedule and a yearly calendar that meshed well with family responsibilities. To accommodate its female employees, the New York school system provided maternity leaves and even encouraged teachers to work in schools near home. The city's free public colleges put this enticing occupation within the reach of students who had more brains and gumption than money. Until the early 1930s, a mere three years at a city teachers training school qualified a beginner for an elementary school post. From then on, the requirement for a four-year college degree went into force.

In the eyes of most young Jewish women, teaching's advantages surpassed those of any of the other conventional middle-class female occupations. It had more prestige than business, offered better hours and less arduous physical demands than nursing, took less training than social work, and afforded far more job opportunities than librarianship. Its work hours and vacation schedule were unmatched. Jewish women accounted for more than a quarter of the New York public school system's new hires by 1920, 44 percent a decade later, and 56 percent the decade after that.[48]

Throughout the 1920s, teaching was a growth industry. New York's system, by far the nation's largest, added students at a rapid pace, expanding from a million children in 1925 to a million and a quarter in 1932. As new neighborhoods sprang up in the outer boroughs, so did hundreds of new school buildings and thousands of new jobs. Nor did the end of prosperity mark the end of hiring opportunities. High school enrollment nearly doubled during the Depression. Until then, students had only stayed in school beyond the age of fourteen because they chose to, not because the law required attendance or they had little chance of finding work. But with grown men competing for the jobs that youngsters used to do, in 1936 the city decided—as did communities across the country—to get teenagers off the labor market by raising the legal school-leaving age to sixteen. Additional education seemed to improve a youngster's chances at whatever employment openings did exist. By 1938 the city employed thirty-nine thousand teachers.[49] Its one thousand school buildings ranged from a teacher and fourteen children in Staten Island's one-room P.S. 2 to a faculty of 347 teaching 9,965 students in Brooklyn's New Utrecht High.[50]

During the Depression, landing one of those positions was no easy undertaking. Of all the jobs a Jewish woman could get in those dark years, few held more allure. At the time of the stock market crash, elementary teachers earned between $1,600 and $3,500 for their ten-month year and their secondary colleagues between $2,040 and $4,200. Though city budget shortfalls forced two pay cuts during the 1930s, a teacher's salary could buy a middle-class lifestyle amid the Depression's falling prices, and a married couple lucky enough to bring in two such salaries could live in real comfort—or support a great many relatives. What's more, tenure ensured income security and the law prevented open discrimination against Jews. As the job situation worsened in the 1930s, men as well as women found teaching an increasingly desirable career. Ethnic competition for the jobs also sharpened, as the numbers of Jewish teachers increased at the expense of Irish ones, who had previously dominated the system.

But when Mildred Herman and her parents had joyfully celebrated her teaching degree on that spring day at Carnegie Hall, she was only one of the thousands of other potentially qualified candidates hoping to land one of those coveted posts. The four years of labor and sacrifice that went into earning the degree represented the first leg on the long journey to a classroom job. Completing the trip took energy and determination. An applicant for a New York City job needed to present, in addition to the required college degree, proof of U.S. citizenship, a letter from her college dean attesting to her good moral character, and excellent reports from those who supervised her student teaching. Once she had submitted those documents, she could sign up to take an extremely difficult written exam in pedagogy and, if she aspired for a high school post, one in her subject area as well. Next came a wait of up to six months for the results. If she passed, an oral exam then tested the quality of her speaking voice and an interview evaluated her appearance, poise, and cultivation.

Many found these last two tests the most stringent of all. Many Jews suspected that anti-Semitism may have been the reason why. The examiners searched for "imperfect" speech, especially for such signs of a "foreign" accent as a Yiddish-sounding D where a T belonged, a G missing from the end of a word, or a telltale rising inflection. Students who had labored for years to reach this point saw their dreams evaporate in the course of a single conversation, often for defects they could not discern. Turned down for supposedly inadequate diction, Marion Rosenstein decided to sign up for a speech course at New York University so that she could try again. The speech professor, however, would not admit her to the class because he could find no flaw when he spoke with her. He wrote to the school system's examiners telling them so, but they nonetheless required Marion to pass two more evaluations before granting her their approval. An Irish lilt, many Jews believed, weighed not nearly as heavily against a candidate as a hint of Yiddish.

The applicant who passed these hurdles next presented a demonstration lesson and submitted the lesson plan she had prepared for it. Should she survive to this stage, she finally received her license, which qualified her to go on the list of people awaiting appointment to a specific opening. As the Depression advanced, the lists lengthened to thousands and the number of male candidates increased. Males and females waited on separate lists. The women had generally been aiming at teaching since childhood, but the men rarely considered it their first career choice. The women had usually ranked at the top of their college classes, but the men generally came from the bottom third. The men totaled about a tenth of the applicants but got a quarter of the jobs assigned.

At the beginning of the Depression, an applicant stayed on the waiting list for three years before eligibility expired. Because of Depression-related budget constraints, thousands of New Yorkers never moved off these lists into the jobs they had worked so hard to win. Between 1936 and 1939, for example, the city appointed only eleven hundred new teachers.[51] Political pressure from candidates fearful of having to repeat the whole difficult qualification process eventually convinced the legislature to extend the period of eligibility. Competition for the relatively few jobs available during the 1930s became so severe that unscrupulous officials ran a lucrative scam, fleecing scores of gullible women candidates of thousands of dollars with promises of appointments that never materialized. Not all cities faced budgetary problems as bad as New York's, however, and in Chicago, Boston, Newark, Philadelphia, and some other places the odds of being hired were somewhat better. Still, teaching jobs were not easy to get in those systems, and not all of them permitted women to continue teaching after marriage.

A Jewish woman who landed a teaching appointment in a system that permitted wives and mothers usually considered herself to be embarking

on a lifetime career. Few relinquished their hard-won positions when they
married or had children. One study found that close to 90 percent of New
York teachers who took maternity leave in the 1920s and 1930s returned
to the classroom, most going on to retire after thirty years of service.[52]
Many agreed with Anne Kunstler, who felt she had "invested too much of
my family's resources, and of myself and all my dreams, not to mention
money into my pension plan, for me to abandon teaching."[53]

For the first American generation, becoming a teacher—or, for that
matter, a secretary, a bookkeeper, a social worker, or a nurse—was a family affair. It remained one after the career got under way. Working women
saw a salary not as a license to strike out on their own but a means to help
other family members, either the ones who had sacrificed to help them or
the ones still struggling to get their own start in life. Half of Depression-
era Jewish women teachers supported out-of-work relatives and two-thirds
helped support their parents, one study found.[54] As long as a working
woman lived in her parents' home—and the great majority did until marriage—she contributed to the family budget. "Young people had a conscience in those days," remembered Leah Parnes, who finished high
school just as the Depression began. "We pitched in and did our bit. My
mother never said to me, 'Leah, you have to go out and work.' I automatically helped. There was no question."[55]

Like 90 percent of Jewish New Yorkers under twenty-five, and like the
great majority of young adults across the country, Leah lived at home until
she married.[56] Households across America were crowded and often dis-
cordant during these years when finances forced families to double up
with relatives. The desertions that had plagued so many couples during the
immigrant period fell sharply, and some formerly wayward husbands even
came home. "The wife" and not the husband, the Forward acerbically
noted, "has credit with the butcher and grocer."[57]

Even marrying did not necessarily mean leaving home. Newlyweds
hard pressed to afford a place of their own routinely moved in with one
set of parents. When New Yorker Roland Baxt married in 1937, he had
a college degree and a WPA job. His wife had a high school diploma and
a position as a saleswoman. But they spent the first years of their marriage with her parents because they could not afford an apartment of
their own. "When we got married, my parents helped us make a small
apartment on the third floor of our house," recalled a Philadelphian
named Shoshana, who also married in the 1930s. "We lived there for
eight years. Times were tough."[58]

So tough, in fact, that marrying—even dating—became a luxury that many young people could not afford. "Nowadays," the *Forward* lamented in 1933, "there are thousands and thousands of families where only one family member earns anything and brings a few dollars to the household. The ten or fifteen or thirty dollars a week that one [person] earns must maintain the whole family. If that one is a boy or a girl of marriageable age, he or she cannot get married."[59] Even with multiple earners in the home, a young person's wages often could not be spared. "My father is out of work and I must help out my family with my earnings," one dutiful Jewish daughter explained to a social worker. "I have a young man who I would like to marry, but under such circumstances I can no longer think of getting married."[60] So many Americans gave up on the idea that 1932, the Depression's worst year, saw the lowest marriage rate ever recorded in the United States, only 7.9 weddings per thousand persons in the country, 27 percent below the 10.1 per 1000 persons performed in prosperous 1929.[61]

Despite the hardship and frustration, the Depression did not derail the start of new Jewish families. Girls grew up knowing that they "had to get married; otherwise there was a terrible stigma," Leah remembered.[62] Jews tended to marry a bit later than other groups because they often stayed in school longer, but women in their twenties felt pressure to find a beau. Leah undertook a concerted campaign after she finished high school, joining a club that held parties and dances where she hoped to meet nice young men. She felt the need to spend money on the dues because "we didn't have places where we could go to meet. A young lady couldn't go anywhere unescorted, and when I was growing up I was instilled with respectability. We had to do the right thing. . . . A fella that took a girl out in the thirties would try things, but if a girl came from a respectable home she was expected to reject his advances . . . and of course no girl made advances to men. Morality was well-defined. Women didn't sit by themselves at restaurant tables. They never, never went into bars. And they never went all the way."[63]

Her investment in the social club paid off. One evening a fellow named Morris "walked in with my girlfriend's boyfriend, and I looked up and said to myself, 'That's the man I'm going to marry.'"[64] Soon they were "keeping company" and finally they wed. But for many young couples like Leah and Morris, hard times lengthened the wait for the wedding, and in an era of strict sexual mores, that often imposed considerable hardship. "Boys and girls went together sometimes for four or five years and sexually didn't go beyond a certain point until marriage," Leah noted. "I think that was the way it was for millions of us." The fear of pregnancy, the disgrace of a forced marriage, hung over them all the time. Still, "we all accepted this. I know that boys were wary of girls who were loose in the their morals. I knew of cases where a girl would 'get loose' out of love for a boy—and she was dropped, like that. . . . like a hot potato."[65]

In the end, the overwhelming majority of young Jews made it to the *chuppah*, and they almost always married other Jews. Boys and girls living in densely Jewish city neighborhoods or attending heavily Jewish colleges had relatively little chance to meet, let alone date, eligible Gentiles. Smaller Jewish communities afforded more frequent contact with Gentiles but intermarriage rarely occurred. Young Johnstowners sometimes dated across religious lines, but "would never think of marriage [with a non-Jew]" a town resident remembered. "It was understood that [inter]marriage was out of the question," added another.[66]

Not only the marriage rate but the birthrate in America dropped during the Depression decade, from 21.3 births per 1000 people in 1930 to 18.4 per 1000 people in 1933. Native-born Jews, by far the nation's most effective contraceptors, had a lower rate still, producing only 69 babies for every 100 borne by white women of the general population. Among the unemployed, went a popular joke, were many *mohelim* (ritual circumcisers). By 1938 half of all Jewish family had no more than two children, with professional families the smallest of all. Low fertility, accomplished by scrupulous birth control, played an important role in upward mobility. Families that concentrated their resources on educating fewer children, Jews believed, could give each one a better start, and mothers of fewer children had an easier time arranging to work.

But the drop in family size did not indicate a slackening wifely concern for domestic life. Married women who didn't live in the same house or apartment with parents and siblings often lived nearby, perhaps in separate apartments in the same building, on the same block, or in the same neighborhood. This provided working wives a handy network of sisters, mothers, aunts, and cousins available for child care. Yetta Yuretsky and her husband, for example, invited Yetta's sister and unemployed brother-in-law to share their home. Yetta taught school and rejoiced that she "now had [her] own sister to watch my child. My sister was already homebound with a little one, and insisted on watching mine as well. What could be better than my own sister?"[67] Care by relatives seemed incomparably superior to care by any "stranger." Worst of all was institutional care in a nursery school or day care center. For Ida Rubenstein, who briefly placed her son in a city-run nursery school, "the shame lasted far beyond the four months he attended. I knew these schools were for underprivileged working women and I was embarrassed to be lumped with them." Providing her three-year-old care that so violated the reigning middle-class standard made her feel "less than adequate."[68]

A working mother, even one with a professional job, did not relinquish the tradition of her *balebuste* forebears. Her family role remained central to her life. While Charlotte Printz was off teaching school, she still felt it "vital that no one be given the opportunity to even suggest that perhaps I was slacking [in household duties], that maybe it was too much for me. My windows had to shine like everyone else's."[69]

Women at War

As abruptly as the stock market crashed in 1929, Japanese bombers brought the Depression to an end in 1941. The years of scrimping and patching and skipping meals were over. The years of overtime shifts and oversubscribed bond drives and overseas duty had begun. Anxiety about the next paycheck gave way to anxiety about loved ones away in uniform. Suddenly America was fighting a total war, and suddenly Americans were doing things that only recently they could never have imagined.

Stephanie Markowitz, for example, descended from ancestors who left Europe to escape anti-Semitic rulers. But she found herself in an ordeal that lasted six times as long as the typical steerage crossing and managed to elude a brutal, anti-Jewish tyranny. An American army nurse, she survived a plane crash in Nazi-occupied Albania. Her route to freedom lay across hundreds of miles of snow-covered terrain scourged by harsh winter weather and by German bombing runs. For sixty days—including five without sleep—she trudged up to seven hours daily through drifts and blizzards to become the first Allied woman to make her way safely out of Nazi-held territory.

The first member of the WAVES (Women Accepted for Volunteer Emergency Service, the navy's female branch) and the first member of the American Red Cross to die on active wartime duty were Jewish, as well as the first American servicewoman to be taken prisoner by the Japanese. Seaman Elizabeth Korensky of Philadelphia perished in an explosion at the Norfolk Naval Air Station. American Red Cross volunteer Esther Richards of San Francisco, on overseas assignment to serve American troops, was killed by a German bomb on the beachhead at

Anzio. Army nurse Lieutenant Magdalene Eckman of Pine Grove, California, was taken captive during the horrific fall of Bataan and Corregidor in the Philippines.

Men did the fighting that would "smash the Nazis and the Japs," the patriotic posters proclaimed to the nation's women. But "to support our men and keep them fighting, there are other jobs which must be filled. Vital military jobs which *you* can fill. . . . *You* are needed. Needed now!"[70] Jewish women joined with others across the country to take factory jobs and enlist for military service. But their parents did not always agree. Despite the crucial national need, for example, former soldier Isaac Bloch, who had served with Pershing in World War I, objected when his nineteen-year-old daughter, Miranda, wanted to volunteer for World War II right after Pearl Harbor. "What is a nice Jewish girl going to do in the Marine Corps?" he demanded. Enlisting just after she reached the age of legal majority, twenty-one, in 1943, Miranda soon gave him the answer: become an aircraft radio technician responsible for installing and maintaining equipment in the air, skills she used on frequent training flights for bomber pilots.

Other Jewish daughters wrote home about other far-flung adventures and hardships. WAC (Women's Army Corps) officer Eva Kritzer received the Bronze Star personally from General Eisenhower for her work as a legal adviser at his Supreme Allied Headquarters in Europe. Lillian Bloomberg, a WAC and an air traffic controller, helped oversee flights in Germany and France. Selma Kantor Cronan, who had become a certified civilian pilot before the war, accepted an invitation from celebrated aviator Jacqueline Cochran and joined the brand-new Women's Air Force Service Pilots, the American military's first female flyers. Selma had initially experienced flight when her mother paid two dollars to take her "on an airplane ride in Asbury Park, New Jersey in the 1920s." At that first seaside taste, she "fell in love with flying and knew I was going to be a pilot someday."[71] Lillian Levine, on the other hand, began her WAC service as a Morse code operator but later switched to flight training at a superior's suggestion. As a flight instructor, she taught male pilots to fly bombers while she mourned her brother, killed fighting in Europe under General Patton.

Though she was not a pilot, army flight nurse Yetta Moskowitz received the Air Medal for the one hundred–plus hours she spent over South Pacific combat zones, evacuating wounded soldiers from battlefield aid stations to hospitals. Her close friend and classmate at Air Evacuation

School in Lexington, Kentucky, Lieutenant Beatrice Memler, died doing this dangerous work. Army nurse Anita Gold, among the first to arrive in the Pacific theater of operations, served for three and a half years, mostly at a frontline hospital in New Guinea that suffered twenty-six months of daily shelling or air raids. As the war ended, she helped care for three hundred survivors of the brutal Japanese POW camps aboard a hospital ship bringing them home to San Francisco. Most of the men's comrades had "died of starvation or ate lizards and rats to survive," she recalled, expressing her disgust at seeing the "pampered, well-fed Nazi prisoners" at a camp she visited near San Francisco.[72]

At about the same time, army nurse Gertrude Shapiro arrived in Hiroshima with the first American medical unit sent to care for Japanese survivors of the atomic bomb. She eventually became a victim of the bombing herself, dying in 1972 of a cancer probably caused by her exposure to nuclear radiation. After the war ended in Europe, army nurse Ruth Karsevar of the 136th Evacuation Hospital's communicable disease unit in Bad Kreuznach, Germany, turned from treating troops under combat conditions to caring for inmates just liberated from POW and concentration camps. She quickly understood that her "fellow Jews were massacred" and filled letters home with descriptions of the appalling conditions she had seen. She made a point of telling the German civilian workers at the hospital how "proud she was to be an American Jew."[73] Behind the battle lines, Jewish women did many other military jobs: predicting the weather; decoding enemy messages; running kitchens, offices, and supply rooms; commanding WAC battalions; even developing improved artificial eyes for wounded veterans.

Postwar Plenty

As the nation was celebrating victory and the troops came home, American Jews threw themselves into the postwar boom as enthusiastically as they had into the war effort. With the dislocations and privations over, with wartime factories converting from tanks and bombers to cars and washing machines, with suburban developments mushrooming around all the major cities, Jews of the GI generation were perfectly positioned to join the suburban middle class. Under the GI Bill, education and home mortgages were easier to get than they had ever been. Discrimination in housing and employment still existed but had begun to ease. In 1948, for example, the Mayor's Commission on Human Relations in Minneapolis focused attention on anti-Semitism in hiring, and Jewish women began landing jobs that had previously been denied them as teachers, dental hygienists, and clerks in banks and insurance companies. Still, as late as the early 1950s, over a quarter of firms explicitly barred Jews, according to a Chicago study, with banks, utilities, and insurance companies the worst offenders.[74] Chicago's Bureau on Jewish Employment uncovered blunt comments, for example, "desperate but not desperate enough to hire Jews" and "can't use Matzo-ball queens" on job orders.[75]

By the 1950s, the sacrifices to get all those years of schooling were paying off handsomely. Jews now found themselves in the most middle class of all the nation's ethnic groups. Fully 15 percent of Jewish workers were professionals, and attending college was now commonplace among their children. Like all other middle-class Americans in the postwar years, Jews underwent a wave of intense domesticity. With an abundance of well-paying jobs, a single white-collar breadwinner could support a family in middle-class comfort. With huge numbers of young families ensconced in the single-family tract houses filling the new bedroom suburbs, wives found themselves raising young children far from the grandmothers and aunts who had made jobholding possible during the Depression and war—and also from the downtown offices and stores where many had worked. In the baby boom years of the late 1940s and 1950s, Jewish college women married younger than their mothers had—sometimes even before they finished college—and had children sooner than their mothers too. The national birthrate soared in the 1950s, and Jewish couples—along with everyone else—produced more offspring than during the 1930s or 1940s. But Jewish women continued to have fewer babies than comparable Gentiles. In Providence and Detroit, to take two typical cities, Jewish families had an average of 2.3 children, about 70 percent fewer than their non-Jewish neighbors.[76]

The family patterns established in the 1920s and 1930s persisted through the 1950s and into the 1960s: high rates of marriage, high levels of education, and low numbers of children. As in decades past, Jewish women thought about "helping out," though now they looked for work that suited the educated wives of men on the way up. New Yorker Joyce Bauer, for example, graduated from Cornell in 1947 and took a Columbia master's degree in psychology in 1949, the same year she married a medical student named Milton Brothers. By the time she earned her Ph.D. in 1953, she had had a baby daughter and had decided, in keeping with her times, to stay at home as a full-time mother. But Milton's medical residency paid only $50 a month and money was tight. In 1955, Joyce saw a way of earning more.

To please Milton, she had turned her scholar's mind to learning about his favorite sport, boxing. Now the demure young woman with her smooth blonde pageboy hairdo decided to put that unexpected store of information to an equally unexpected use. She tried out, as an expert on prizefighting, for a TV quiz show called the *$64,000 Question*. In a seven-week run that riveted the nation's attention, she answered question after question about this most masculine of sports, becoming only the second person to take the top prize, in those days a very large sum of money. Two years later she repeated her feat on the *$64,000 Challenge*. The quiz show scandals of the late 1950s temporarily cast doubt on whether a petite, soft-spoken woman could have known enough about the ring to win such a fortune honestly, but investigators vindicated her victories in 1959. In fact, she revealed, the producers had wanted her off the program, but, unlike some notorious cheats, she had refused to throw a match and had continued winning in spite of them.

Like Bess Myerson before her, Joyce Brothers parlayed her odd celebrity into a continuing media career, but minus any overt indication of her Jewishness. She cohosted a sports program and in 1958 began an advice show on which she answered questions in her real area of expertise, psychology. Among the first to discuss sexuality openly in the mass media, she covered impotence, the ramifications of menopause, the causes of frigidity, and other issues until then considered far too intimate and shameful for the public airwaves. But her frank, dignified, scientific treatment attracted listeners. Letters arrived by the thousands, and soon she added a syndicated newspaper column and later a column in *Good Housekeeping* magazine. She also authored a number of successful books.

While Joyce Brothers was helping open the airways and newspapers to topics until then taboo, she carefully stayed within her era's conventions of respectable middle-class femininity. Like Gertrude Berg a generation before her, this canny media professional used the protective coloration of marriage and motherhood. A female scientist could not be wholly feminine, her era believed, but the radio and TV personality who always introduced herself as "Dr. Joyce Brothers" resembled not a mannish denizen of a laboratory or research library but the elegant wife of a successful businessman or professional man. With her smooth, stylish hair, her restrained yet fashionable clothing, her perfect makeup, and her soft, feminine voice, she wrapped disarmingly traditional packaging around an innovative, even daring, message. Though she explored the terrain of intimate personal issues, her appearance assured her fans that she was a wife and mother first, and a psychologist only secondarily. She had no intention, or so it seemed, of being anything other than ladylike. She went far beyond "helping out" her family budget to helping millions of listeners and viewers better understand their lives. Her career began with serious intellectual attainments and it earned her serious amounts of money. But Joyce never went beyond the symbolic boundaries of her period's expectations about women. That task awaited the generation of girls who grew up watching her.

14

"SOMETHING OF THE ARTIST"

Reinventing Tradition — East European Style

In the last days of November 1950, a serious problem struck Temple Beth Israel. Dr. William Ackerman, their beloved rabbi for twenty-four years, had just died, leaving them in urgent need of a new spiritual leader. Meridian, Mississippi, was hardly a place used to radical change. But that winter the temple board made a very radical decision. They unanimously decided not to begin an immediate search for a new rabbi from out of town, but to turn instead to a local person who for a quarter of a century had taught the temple's children and led its services when Dr. Ackerman, the area's only Jewish clergyman, had been sick or traveling. The congregation president, Sidney Kay, wrote to the Reform movement's central office that "practically all" of the 150 members favored this choice.[1]

One of the few who did not was Paula Herskovitz Ackerman, the rabbi's widow. When the board asked her, shortly after William's shivah, to step into his place and "carry on the ministry until [Beth Israel] could get a Rabbi," she declined. They needed someone with proper credentials, she told them, someone whose religious learning was deeper and broader than hers. A long-term Hebrew teacher who had never even been to college simply lacked the necessary standing and expertise.

But they persisted. As far as the congregants were concerned, their president stated in a letter to Rabbi Maurice Eisendrath, head of the Union of American Hebrew Congregations, "she is qualified and we want her."[2] Eisendrath did not at first discourage them. He himself had earlier stated that "women should not be denied the privilege of ordination." He could see "nothing in the practice and principles of Liberal Judaism which precludes the possibility of a woman serving as a rabbi."[3] By January the board had convinced Paula to take the post.

Concern that the little congregation could weather the crisis of William's death appears to have weighed heavily in her decision. It would take some time, she knew, to locate an able rabbinical graduate willing to take an isolated Mississippi pulpit. Nearly three decades in Meridian had taught her that the congregants did not expect profound or deeply scholarly sermons. Nor did they need a highly skilled administrator to run a small synagogue with a school for fewer than twenty children. Rather, they lacked someone to "give them some of the faith I have in my own heart" and show them "the Jewish way of life I've lived every day of my life."[4] She fully recognized "how revolutionary the idea [of her taking the pulpit] is—therefore it seems to be a challenge I pray I can meet. If I can plant a seed for the Jewish woman's larger participation . . . then my life would have some meaning."[5]

Before long, though, Eisendrath thought the better of the situation. Discussions with colleagues persuaded him that the congregation required a leader with the training and official credentials to carry out all rabbinical functions. Other problems could also arise, argued Rabbi Samuel Goldenson, former president of the Reform rabbinical body, for example, the "considerable embarrassment" that would exist in "other communities" if other rabbis' "exceedingly able wives," including some who lacked Paula's "personal and mental qualities," decided that they could emulate her example.[6] Eisendrath wrote to tell the temple of his change of mind.

But in the best tradition of American congregational independence and lay governance, the people of Beth Israel disregarded these warnings. In January 1951, they officially appointed Paula Ackerman their spiritual leader, making her, at fifty-seven, the first female to head an American Jewish congregation belonging to one of the three major doctrinal streams. For the next two and a half years, now dubbed "America's first Lady Rabbi" by the media, she performed all of public duties of her new position.[7] Though she never claimed the title that the press mistakenly bestowed on her, the people of Beth Israel called on her to lead their services, deliver sermons from their pulpit, perform their marriages, bury their dead, welcome converts into their community, offer pastoral guidance to members in trouble, and generally explain the role of the Jewish tradition in everyday American life to both Jews and non-Jews. She retired for the first time in the fall of 1953, when a permanent, ordained rabbi arrived, but she continued teaching and lecturing, now to audiences across the country. Nine years later she took up a similar interim post while Temple Beth-El, her childhood congregation in her native Pensacola, Florida, sought a new rabbi. Later she returned to Meridian for another stint as full-time spiritual leader of Beth Israel.

Not until Paula reached her nineties did her work receive formal recognition from UAHC. By then, of course, the Jewish world in which she had grown up and played her exceptional part no longer existed. Such a role for herself was unthinkable when she had first arrived at Beth Israel in 1924 not as the rabbi but as the *rebbetzin*, not as the congregation's leading intellectual and religious figure but as that person's consort. She did not busy herself with the weighty matters that concerned the men, but with the seemingly trivial affairs of the women and children. She raised a son and served as a model for Meridian women on how to run a Jewish home. She took leadership roles (though never the presidency) in Beth Israel's sisterhood, the National Federation of Temple Sisterhoods, and other community activities open to females. Like so many talented and knowledgeable women of her era, in her efforts she served to enhance her husband's effectiveness, strengthen his stature, and solidify his career. Like countless Jewish wives before her, Paula "helped out."

She was doubtlessly used to such a secondary role. By the time she, William, and their fifteen-month-old Billy arrived in Meridian, social convention had stifled Paula's first attempt at professional and intellectual independence. Born in 1893 into an immigrant home, she had early shown a scholarly bent and an interest in Judaism nourished by the pious example of her mother, Dora. Her father, Joseph, the product of an Orthodox upbringing in Romania, chose in America to affiliate his family with Reform. Even so, he wanted a more complete religious education for his sons than Temple Beth-El's weekly classes provided and arranged for an Orthodox rabbi to give them private lessons. True to the teachings of his chosen denomination, he also allowed his bright and eager daughter to join in. By the time Beth-El confirmed Paula, she knew enough to teach in its religious school.

Joseph's educational tolerance had limits, however. For a girl to take extra religious training was one thing, but for her to pursue a serious—and masculine—professional education was something else. Paula let him know that she yearned to study medicine; he let her know that teaching was the only career he would allow her to pursue. When she graduated as high school valedictorian, New Orleans' prestigious Sophie Newcomb College awarded her a scholarship. But if she could not be a doctor, Paula decided, she would not go. Soon family finances forced her to go to work in any case. Drawing on her outstanding academic background, she taught math and Latin in high school, gave private music lessons, and continued as choir director and teacher at Beth-El. William Ackerman had recently become the congregation's rabbi, and the talented young staff member caught his eye. After a seven-year acquaintance, he and twenty-six-year-old Paula married in 1919. Perhaps mindful of his newly acquired financial obligations, William accepted the higher salary offered by a congregation in Natchez. After several years there, the young family, now numbering three, moved on to Meridian and Beth Israel.

In retrospect it is tempting to see Paula as a precursor of coming change in the more liberal reaches of Judaism. Her unexpected late-life career, however, was an isolated episode unfolding in a pair of small, provincial towns far from the centers of American Jewish life. Neither lasting precedent nor institutional change flowed from her work. Nor, despite press accounts, was Paula even the first American woman to almost become a rabbi. In the 1920s and 1930s, a handful of women had attempted to get rabbinical training, the lack of which supposedly constituted Paula's main deficit as a spiritual leader.

In 1939 Helen Levinthal, a University of Pennsylvania graduate, a former graduate student at Columbia, and the Jewishly well-educated daughter of a prominent Brooklyn Conservative rabbi, successfully completed the entire rabbinical program at the Jewish Institute of Religion, a Reform-leaning New York seminary. The males who passed those courses with her received a master's degree and were ordained as rabbis. The faculty awarded Helen the degree but withheld the ordination. Nearly twenty years before, Martha Neumark, daughter of a Reform rabbinic eminence, had enrolled at Hebrew Union College, the Reform movement's seminary, on the blithe assumption that finishing the same curriculum as the men would earn her the same credentials. Equally blithely, she requested one of a seminary student's normal privileges, an assignment to lead High Holy Day services in an outlying Jewish community that had no permanent rabbi.

This inquiry kicked off a debate on female ordination that roiled through HUC for two years. The faculty did not reject the idea outright. Finally the question reached the college's governing board, composed of both lay and rabbinical members. Rabbi Jacob Lauterbach and layman Oscar Berman denounced the "absurd and ridiculous" notion that, "contrary to all Jewish tradition," women could serve as rabbis. Apart from the logistical difficulties HUC would face in providing them proper restrooms and dormitory accommodations, the two objectors warned, such a change would "outrage the feelings of a large part of the Jewish people." It also would expose Reform, "the majority" of whose regular temple-goers already were female, to the "danger of the Synagogue and Judaism becoming altogether an affair of women."[8]

Why a female-dominated synagogue in the present day was inherently worse than the male-dominated synagogues of old (or, indeed, than a male-dominated rabbinical seminary in the twentieth century), they did not explain; presumably they considered the reasons too obvious to require explanation. One conclusion is inescapable, however. Paula Ackerman was not disqualified from the rabbinate solely by her lack of education. Leading a congregation was simply not a woman's place.

Leaving the Old Ways Behind

But if women were unwelcome in the pulpit during the middle decades of the twentieth century, their influence in other aspects of American Jewish religious life was growing steadily. As the East European immigrants' American children moved into their middle-class adult lives, they, like the American generations before them, devised new versions of the tradition—Conservative Judaism and Modern Orthodoxy—that met their needs, both in the middle-class Jewish city neighborhoods and in the postwar suburbs. As in all previous American transformations of Jewishness, women played a critical and creative role.

By the 1920s, many of the places where middle-class East Europeans worshiped were becoming very noticeably American. The old established families descended from Central Europe—by now a small majority of the nation's Jewry—still maintained their loyalty to Reform. Many East European immigrants meanwhile clung to the outward forms of Orthodoxy, even if they had abandoned many of its practices and rarely if ever set foot in a shul. The least prosperous immigrant synagogue-goers— who constituted the largest percentage of immigrants maintaining formal observance—usually favored congregations with a distinctly old-world flavor that were, as one progressive rabbi sniffed, "American by geographic location only."[9]

But the muttering, mumbling, and wailing of the old-fashioned service, the increasingly alien customs and superstitions transported from the Pale, and the tedious, heder-style study of Hebrew and Scripture held little appeal for the rising generation of American-born Jews. As they came of age, they discarded religious folkways that they saw as un-American.

When, for example, a Marshall Street girl "began to menstruate," a Philadelphian remembers, "her friends . . . knew how superstitious her family was based on their reaction. If the girl was slapped three times, to remove the devil from her, the family was not Americanized yet. Some families spit three times to keep evil away from her. Some families made no fuss whatsoever. They were more modern, forward-thinking people."[10]

Even practices with a more solid religious basis were passing rapidly from the scene. "Before Yom Kippur," another former Marshall Streeter recalls, her devout mother "twirled a live chicken over our heads to *shlug kipporas,* chase away our sins." This ancient ritual, reminiscent of the scapegoat sent out from biblical Jerusalem to carry the inhabitants' sins into the desert, had for centuries been commonplace in the Pale. Even in Philadelphia, "I would go to the live chicken store with my grandmother and carry home that hen, whose feet were tied, sticking up from the shopping bag. Oh, those prayers she'd intone. All the while, she waved that chicken over my head. I was sure it would land right in my long hair. She did that for many years. And then we refused because we hated it. We didn't commit any sins. Maybe we felt we were becoming more Americanized."[11]

Modern, forward-looking, Americanized people preferred a form of worship that suited their advanced habits and views. Still, for East European sons and daughters reared on the sounds and symbolism of hectic, cozy, deeply traditional Yiddish-style shuls, the strict decorum, stripped-down spirituality, and rationalism of Reform simply did not *feel* Jewish. Although these first-generation Americans were often no more devout in their beliefs or personal habits than Central European descendants who prayed bareheaded to the accompaniment of an organ, for many of them, authentic Judaism had a certain plaintive, minor-key, tallis-covered, comfortingly Semitic look and feel.

And so, between the two extremes of Pale-style traditionalism and American-style enlightenment, some congregations began to seek a compromise. Their services still proceeded largely in Hebrew, the cantor still intoned the old-country melodies, men still donned tallis and yarmulke. But women sat with them in family pews. The congregation faced the *bimah* as in a Christian church, instead of surrounding it as in a traditional shul. The rabbi was a man educated in English as well as Hebrew and offered an English sermon. Girls as well as boys got Hebrew and religious training. Major holidays retained two days of celebration, but the actual services grew shorter. Sabbath was ushered in, as in Reform temples, by an after-dinner Friday evening service that the entire family could attend rather than by the all-male prayer meeting at sundown that went on while the women prepared dinner at home. Customs involving live poultry, spit directed against the forces of evil, dips in dank water tanks located in dreary basements, or other things that enlightened Americans found weird or distasteful or embarrassing, simply and unceremoniously vanished.

Many of the congregations feeling their way toward this modernized form of East European tradition were attracted to an organization founded in 1913 by Solomon Schechter, president of New York's Jewish Theological Seminary, an American-style graduate school that trained rabbis who were neither doctrinaire Reform nor unyielding Orthodox. Initially Schechter hoped that the United Synagogue of America would speak for congregations across the spectrum of practice and belief that sought "tradition without Orthodoxy" and wished to continue *halachah* but help it evolve into modern times.[12] In effect, the twenty-two congregations—in Syracuse, Sioux City, Norfolk, and Birmingham, Alabama, as well as in more obvious locales like Chicago, New York, and the Boston suburb of Newton—that initially joined his group became the nucleus of the Conservative movement.

In congregations across America, however, it was still the men who busied themselves with any lofty questions of liturgy, doctrine, and interpretation. The women "helped out" by seeing to many of the details of making things run. In 1918, three years after Solomon Schechter's death at sixty-eight, his widow, Mathilde, had founded an organization to help likeminded female congregants do that more effectively. She viewed her Women's League of the United Synagogue as an extension of Solomon's work and an expression of his belief in women's active role in Jewish religious life.

For Mathilde, then entering her sixties, the league crowned decades spent in Jewish intellectual and cultural life. Born in the small Silesian town of Guttentag in 1857, she had been a teacher before studying at Queen's College in London. There she met and in 1887 married Solomon, a brilliant Romanian-born scholar ten years her senior, and became doyenne of a salon at the center of Jewish London's intellectual life. There, and in their home in Cambridge, where Solomon later taught at the university, they frequently welcomed leading lights of modern Jewish thought and scholarship. While he pursued his scholarly work on the Continent and in the Middle East, she stayed at home raising their three children and rendering his and other Cambridge figures' writings into graceful prose in her adopted English.

In 1902 Solomon accepted the presidency of the Jewish Theological Seminary in New York, which put Mathilde at the center of liberal Jewish thought in America. During "vivid days" there, Henrietta Szold later wrote to the Schechters' son, Frank, Mathilde, Solomon, and their "house were a stimulating creative center in whose genial warmth" many of leading Jewish luminaries "—so many, many of us—basked and were transformed."[13] Mathilde also wrote a pioneering book of hymns called *Kol Rina: The Hebrew Hymnal for School and Home*, which helped introduce the use of congregational singing into non-Reform American synagogues. She also devoted herself to the immigrant poor, founding a girls school on the Lower East Side.

This combination of practical work and love of Judaism molded the conception of "helping out" that Mathilde embodied in the league. "The absolute unselfishness and utter forgiveness of mother-love" might be a woman's highest calling, she believed, but the outer forms of religious ritual were also necessary to hear the "song of our soul's communion with God."[14]

Making Jewishness American

Few American Jews, however, were listening to the holy song that rang in Mathilde's ears. Indeed, to many it seemed that Judaism itself was passing from the metropolitan scene. In the late 1920s, 80 percent of the New York Jewish youngsters surveyed denied knowing the Hebrew alphabet or having had any religious training at all.[15] Only a quarter had been to a synagogue service in the preceding year, a 1935 survey found.[16] This mirrored the estimated 23 percent of New Yorkers who belonged to congregations, although membership rates varied widely among the huge city's neighborhoods. In the least devout districts, only 2 percent of Jews were synagogue members as opposed to 44 percent in the most devout.[17] On the affluent Upper West Side, Christmas trees "for the children" were commonplace, on the theory that they were an American, rather than a Christian, custom.

Practices far less bizarre in American eyes than *kaporos*—Sabbath candles, for example—were also slipping into disuse; by 1931, only 40 percent of big-city Jews still lit the Friday night lights.[18] In many families, Sabbath observance had become a matter of traditional foods at a Friday night dinner for those family members who could get off from work. By 1938, only 30 percent of the families on New York's Staten Island observed the ban on cooking during the Sabbath.[19] The silver kiddush cups, embroidered challah covers, and special Sabbath candelabras that once graced the table each week, as well as the Hanukkah menorahs that once stood on the shelf displaying the family's proudest possessions, now gathered dust at the back of cabinets. Amid their tastefully chosen furniture and reproductions of famous art works, middle-class householders rarely found room for the pictures of Moses, Theodore Herzl, or a particularly revered rabbi that had adorned parents' and grandparents' walls.

Outside of the major cities, in places like Johnstown, Meridian, and Pensacola, where Jewish populations numbered under two thousand, observance and education remained vigorous and synagogue membership a nearly essential sign of Jewish identity. Two-thirds of small-town youngsters attended religious school (upward of 80 percent in particularly observant communities like Johnstown and certain agricultural settlements in New Jersey.) In Johnstown, synagogue membership topped 80 percent and Christmas trees were simply out of the question.[20] Sabbath was almost universally observed, though not always with traditional rigor. Friday night dinner, complete with candles and the kiddush prayer over wine, occurred in the great majority of homes, but sometimes in the absence of the father, who arrived late after closing up the store. But in the great cities, where the overwhelming majority of America's Jews lived, Jewishness and Judaism had by the 1920s become increasingly detached. In both the old immigrant districts and the new, middle-class neighborhoods, with more successful immigrants and especially their American children, Jewishness was now an ethnic identity every bit as much as, or even more than, a religion.

Still, the upwardly mobile families flocking to the new middle-class enclaves included some who regarded actual religious practice as central to their ethnicity, indeed, to their lives. They wanted to worship in places suiting their status and tastes. Along boulevards in Brooklyn and the Bronx, on the West Side of Chicago, in Hartford's North End and Newark's South Ward, in Northeast Philadelphia, in Brookline and Roxbury, near Baltimore's Druid Hill Park, and in similar places throughout the country rose large, dignified, conspicuous structures of granite or marble or brick. Between 1924 and 1927 alone 162 new synagogues went up in the United States, at a cost of over $40 million—an enormous sum at a time when an income of $3,000 to $5,000 placed a family solidly in the middle or even the upper middle class.[21]

These new synagogues far outdid the old immigrant *chevrah* and *shtiebel shuls* in more than architectural grandeur. Those modest venues—often simply rented halls or storefronts—had housed a prayer room and perhaps a room or two where men gathered to study Torah or Talmud or where a hard-pressed *melamed* attempted to pound the rudiments of Hebrew and Scripture into boys unwillingly sitting through after-school heder classes. But the new buildings, some called not merely synagogues but "Jewish centers" or "community centers," included a panoply of facilities, including a large and majestic sanctuary; a smaller chapel where a minyan of stalwarts could recite weekday prayers; a social hall for wedding and bar mitzvah receptions and other festive gatherings; a sizable kitchen where those feasts could be prepared; an auditorium with a stage; a set of up-to-date school rooms; an office or a study for the rabbi and cantor; office space for administrative staff; and often meeting or conference rooms, a library, a gymnasium equipped for basketball and other sports and exercising, a swimming pool, and the requisite locker rooms. This was no mere house of worship, but, in a joke current at the time, "a pool with a school and a *shul*."[22]

Filling these facilities, day and night, ideally were people of all ages and interests. Shooting baskets or dancing the foxtrot or practicing the backstroke or earning Scout merit badges had no Judaic content, but these American activities became ethnically Jewish by the magic of being carried out in a Jewish setting among Jewish people. As its first native generation came of age, East European Jewry evolved from an immigrant community into an American ethnic group, from an alien enclave grafted onto America into a category of middle-class American, a Hebraic version of Americanness. In the new, multipurpose synagogues of the new middle-class neighborhoods, Jewishness was no longer a way in which people were foreign, but rather the context in which they were American. Even in little Johnstown, Congregation Rodeph Shalom became the Jewish Community Center/Rodeph Shalom in 1931, with the introduction of a social hall that housed such innovative gatherings as a community Passover seder, a New Year's Eve party, and a confirmation pageant, as well as private social events on a rental basis.

Orthodoxy Goes Modern Too

Many of these august new edifices housed Conservative congregations. The movement gained rapidly among the middle-class residents of the new

Jewish neighborhoods, quickly outpacing Reform in numbers of families joining, if not yet in numbers of congregations, as well as in members' feeling that they belonged to the Judaism of the future in its most progressive, enlightened and authentically American version. But some upwardly mobile members of the first America generation rejected Conservatism and wanted to remain actively, *halachically*, Orthodox. They saw that the traditional Orthodox service in no way resembled the dignified and formal assemblies that educated Americans admired. A scattering of women sat off to the side while men in an assortment of prayer shawls and head coverings prayed near but not with one another. Many were draped or encased or engulfed in great woolen sheets that often trailed down their backs or flopped over their hair and faces. Their heads bore a yarmulke or a fedora or a workman's soft cloth cap. Worshipers read from a variety of personal prayer books, all containing the same liturgy but each edition paginated differently, making reciting in unison impossible. Men prayed individually, often in an undertone, but sometimes in a singsong or even a wail, each swaying in time-honored fashion to his own personal rhythms. On the *bimah,* which often stood in the middle of the main floor, the cantor meanwhile floridly intoned the prayers, oblivious to the proceedings around him. Congregants who had finished their own recitations, or had not yet started, or had simply lost interest, strolled about or dozed or hobnobbed with friends. Children, unsupervised by their preoccupied fathers and grandfathers, scampered around.

When time came to read the Torah, a scene unfolded that modern Americans found particularly unseemly. The privilege of ascending to the *bimah* to recite the prayers before and after each of the several segments read—an honor known as an aliyah, or "going up"—went at impromptu and often lively auction to the highest bidders. So did such honors as lifting, adorning, and returning the scrolls to their places in the *aron ha-kodesh* after the reading was done. Although handling money was strictly forbidden on Sabbath and festivals, calling out pledges of money was not—if they concerned worship and not business and if payment, when promptly rendered, went into the synagogue coffers. Publicly peddling honors, *shnuddering* in Yiddish, provided a significant portion of some synagogues' revenues, and thus for some were a way of performing the mitzvah of supporting Judaism. To right-thinking moderns, however, it appeared offensively old-fashioned and crass, an embarrassing vestige of Pale primitiveness.

Remaining Orthodox in Flatbush or Olney obviously required a Judaism that blended *halachic* correctness with the decorum and decor of the American middle class. By the 1920s, that Judaism was coming into being, invented by groups such as Young Israel, a movement of first-generation Americans determined to be both authentically traditional and acceptably American. Adherents of what came to be called Modern Orthodoxy held firm to *halachic* law, including scrupulous observance of the Sabbath and festivals, regular synagogue worship, and *kashrut*. As educated, white-collar Americans, many found it far easier to keep to their principles than had many pious immigrants. Uneducated laborers often had to spend their Saturdays toiling in sweatshops, but a schoolteacher or civil servant could conveniently spend the day in piety and rest.

However Jewish the Modern Orthodox may have been in their homes or shuls, though, they were unmistakably American to the outside world. Any teaching or practice that would publicly mark them as different from their fellow citizens—whether their immigrant ancestors' beards or wigs, or *halachic* injunctions about modesty that might be interpreted as forbidding mixed swimming and dancing, sleeveless dresses, or stylishly short skirts, or requirements to do such things as cover male heads at all times or erect a sukkah outside one's house—was quietly disregarded. In dress the Modern Orthodox were indistinguishable from those around them.

In architecture and deportment they also resembled other Americans. A goodly number of the palatial synagogues erected in the new neighborhoods were Modern Orthodox. Within the ample, well-appointed sanctuaries, services proceeded in an emerging American style. *Shnuddering* was banished in favor of membership dues. Young Israel of Newark, at four hundred families the largest Orthodox congregation in New Jersey, typified synagogues with a clear notion of what constituted proper devotional deportment. In a booklet entitled *Synagogue Etiquette and Procedure*, it informed worshipers of the behavior expected in its splendid new building in Weequahic. One should not "take back seats. Come forward. You will find more inspiration in the service.

"Do not mumble . . . Read unitedly and distinctly. Do not be afraid to sing out in the congregational singing. . . .

"On Sabbath and Holidays, the display of pocketbooks, the jingling or open display of money, chewing gum, reading of secular literature, and driving to the synagogue, are indeed violations of good taste. . . .

"Proper dress ties, no sweaters, should be worn to the synagogue."[23]

In most Modern Orthodox congregations, uniformity of attire was as much a mark of modernity as uniform prayer books and responsive reading. "If you attended a formal party," Rabbi Joseph Lookstein pointed out, "you would be asked to wear formal clothes. If you were a soldier in the army, you would have to dress in accordance with the regulation of uniform."[24] Instead of coming to shul in what one happened to have on, as many davening immigrants had to do, the propriety-conscious Modern Orthodox congregant, whether adult or child, was urged to don a dignified outfit suitable to a formal daytime occasion. In addition to a tie, the male dress code required a dress shirt and suit or sport coat. A black silk yarmulke complemented the look in most congregations, although some accepted or preferred black felt hats instead. In place of the copious, cape-like old-fashioned woolen tallis, the enlightened worshiper preferred a smaller silk model that hung around his neck or over his shoulders rather like a gentleman's dress scarf. Those who did not own their own ritual gear could use yarmulkes and tallesim provided in convenient bins or racks near the sanctuary entrance.

Ladies were encouraged to appear on Sabbath in dressy daywear, either a smartly tailored suit or a stylish dress, accented, of course, by the hat, gloves, and high-heeled shoes that completed every finished look in those days. Those who owned impressive pieces of jewelry took this occasion to wear them. For important holidays, ladies chose even dressier ensembles, and for the Kol Nidre service on the eve of Yom Kippur, "cocktail dress was de rigeur," along with accompanying jewels and furs, a fashion-conscious worshiper recalled.[25] Little girls wore dressy party frocks, shiny Mary Janes, gloves, and hats. Any female without a head covering of her own used a lace circlet provided at the door.

But even more important than the fact that women were encouraged to come to service in fashionable dress was the fact that they were encouraged to come to services at all. Previously they had appeared only occasionally, perhaps on one of the major festivals when the Yizkor prayer for departed loved ones was recited. Rather than try to follow the distant davening from the cramped women's section, they would more often recite prayers at home in private, reading perhaps from one of several female-oriented Yiddish inspirational books that were in wide circulation.

In the fine new Modern Orthodox synagogues, the women's section was no longer a curtained-off nook or a narrow, closed-in gallery but an ample balcony or a spacious, conveniently located main-floor area separated from the men by a handsome *mechitza* screen reaching no more than waist high. Seating was comfortable, sight lines unobstructed and acoustics clear. "Women have much to be thankful for in this new type of synagogue," one female worshiper noted. "To be sure, they still are not counted toward a quorum but they are not hidden behind a curtain. They have plenty of elbow room," as well as a much better vantage point to observe the happenings on the *bimah*. Unlike old-fashioned congregations that enforced the traditional ban on men hearing women's voices while at prayer lest impure thoughts distract them from their devotions, Modern Orthodox leaders encouraged women to join in the congregational recitations and songs. Thanks to this new, more welcoming regime, "the synagogue finds in woman not only a most generous supporter, but also a far more frequent worshipper than it finds in man," the ever enthusiastic Rabbi Lookstein observed.[26]

Sisterhoods Are Powerful

No group worked harder to fashion this new-style Jewishness than women. By the 1940s, no up-to-date synagogue of any denomination lacked a congregational sisterhood. As early as the mid-1920s, the National Federation of Temple Sisterhoods, representing Reform, had 317 chapters and 50,000 members.[27] The Women's League for Conservative Judaism, the renamed distaff arm of that growing movement, grew from 230 sisterhoods with 23,000 members organized into six branches in 1925, to 100,000 members in a total of twelve branches in 1939, and to 800 sisterhoods in twenty-eight branches enrolling 200,000 women by the late 1960s.[28] The Union of Orthodox Jewish Congregations had its own Women's Branch to help local groups with organizing and program planning. Orthodox Jewry could "not but be impressed by the invasion of all institutions and movements in Jewish life by the ever increasing numbers of women," noted Rabbi Lookstein in 1935.[29]

Housekeeping concerns occupied much of the sisterhood's time, since refreshments—often provided and served by members—were central to many synagogue occasions. During the Depression, keeping a congregation's house in order took on a broader meaning. Memberships dropped drastically as unemployment rose and disposable income fell. Even at Manhattan's Emanu-El, the very toniest of Reform temples, the pool of dues payers shrank by 44 percent.[30] But the huge mortgages so blithely assumed during the 1920s building boom had to be paid. Although fewer families contributed to synagogue coffers, more individuals came to the synagogue centers to pass the endless, empty, jobless hours playing chess or swimming laps or even studying Hebrew or Scripture. Keeping the congregation housed and the building heated, lighted, and repaired fell more and more to the fund-raising efforts of the sisterhoods. Playing an increasingly crucial financial role, women gained new confidence and influence. In a skit presented by the ladies of Manhattan's Park Avenue Synagogue in 1939, for example, the all-male board of directors pondered an innovative way to assure the financial future: turn the synagogue over to the sisterhood. "Splendid," cried a fictitious board member. "They're the only ones who have any money. They're the only ones who know how to raise money. They're the only ones who use the synagogue anyway. . . . Well, then, why should we worry—let's vote to give the shuel [sic] to the sisterhood."[31]

Women, however, held far more than purse strings. It was they, Rabbi Lookstein believed, who could "weld [a] congregation into a happy family unit" that would bind together adults and children of all ages.[32] Modern Orthodox synagogues, many of them synagogue centers, sought to play a central role in the family life of their members by making the concerns of middle-class families central to the synagogue. Instead of a prayer house for adult men, the Modern Orthodox shul intended to be a clubhouse for all ages and both sexes, with many congregations grafting such nontraditional but ideologically appropriate occasions as Mother's Day, Father's Day, and Thanksgiving onto the congregational calendar.

But as central as women were to the new-style congregations, Americans concerned with Jewish life and continuity agreed, their role in the community was more crucial still: they created the homes in which the next generations grew up; they transmitted the tradition into the future while the men were busy working. "The Jewish ideal of womanhood is not the entrancing beauty of the queen of a knightly tournament nor the ascetic life of a virgin saint but wifehood and motherhood," proclaimed a male speaker at a convention of the National Federation of Temple Sisterhoods.[33] The wife and mother presided over "the grandest of all institutions," rhapsodized a writer on the Jewish home.[34] Just as it had among the Central Europeans, the responsibility for Jewish education had passed from the father to the mother, from male heder and Talmud Torah teachers to female synagogue school teachers, from males to females generally. "The Jewish woman who presides over her home is entrusted with a great and noble responsibility," exhorted the prominent writer Trude Weiss-Rosmarin. "The Jewish fate, past and present, and the Jewish future are in her hands."[35]

But as the founders of Council and Hadassah had noted decades before, the exalted priestess of the Jewish home could not carry out her holy office of inculcating religion in the young if she herself knew little or nothing about it. Even in families that remained observant through the 1920s and 1930s, few of the mothers had received much religious training. "What have most American-born observant Jewish women been taught?" lamented an Orthodox critic in the 1920s. "The reading of a few prayers? A few Biblical stories? Some superstitions of the East European ghetto?"[36] This might have sufficed in the shtetl, where religion was part of a seamless Jewish whole, or on the Lower East Side, where the old Yiddish culture still endured. In those places, "the primary concern of Jewish education has been the Jewish boy," admitted Rabbi Lookstein. "His Jewish sister had to be content with a few private lessons and with rudimentary instructions in the religious duties of Jewish wifehood and motherhood. The inevitable result was generation upon generation upon generation of righteous women, but not of learned women."[37]

In Midwood or Olney or Clinton Hill, among women with high school diplomas or even college degrees, this would no longer do. Judaism no longer simply passed automatically from grandparent and parent to child by osmosis. Observance no longer formed part of the fabric of community life. Women no longer carried out home rituals because that was simply what women did. Many, in fact, had not even seen their mothers perform them. "Why should a Jewish girl maintain a kosher home after she marries when she has never been taught the meaning of the dietary laws?" mused Rebecca Goldstein, a Barnard graduate married to an Orthodox rabbi, in 1935. "Why kindle the Sabbath lights . . . Why maintain Family Purity?"[38] Only education could ensure that she would. Educators had to "get off the educational double standard and offer to women the educational advantages hitherto seen to be only man's prerogative," Lookstein urged.[39] The Jewish mothers of the future had to be consciously taught, and families interested in religion increasingly sent their daughters to the same religious schools their sons attended.

As part of this educational campaign, English-language children's books on Jewish themes began to appear, consciously patterned after their American counterparts. K'tonton (from the Hebrew *k'ton,* "small"), the "Jewish Tom Thumb" whose exploits enlivened children's bedtime for at least three generations, made his debut in 1935; sixty-six years later, he remained in print. First published by Mathilde Schechter's Women's League in 1935, the stories by Conservative *rebbetzin* Sadie Rose Weilerstein recount how the tiny boy, adopted by an observant couple, learns Judaism's fundamental values and the meaning of its holidays through a series of scrapes and adventures in a contemporary city.

K'tonton's lasting success inspired Weilerstein to write several additional books. Another rabbi's wife, Elma Ehrlich Levinger, combined the insights into children gained as a schoolteacher in rural Iowa and Illinois, the literary skills acquired studying English at Radcliffe and the University of Chicago, and the Jewish lore learned working at New York's Bureau of Jewish Education to bring out a series, *In Many Lands*, that highlighted the traditions of Jewish communities around the world. Her other books of history and biography for children, as well as *Jewish Child*, a magazine she edited, aimed to build Jewish identity in children growing up in the 1920s, 1930s, and 1940s. Her *Great Jewish Woman* and *Fighting Angel*, a life of Henrietta Szold, explicitly encourage girls to serve the Jewish community.

But if the mothers of the future could gain the preparation they needed from Hebrew school and bedtime stories, the mothers of the present represented a different challenge. They needed not whimsical tales or long-term intellectual stimulation but immediate, on-the-job training in the practicalities of being Jewish. In addition to those long-standing champions of adult education, Council and Hadassah, various other organizations took up the task. In 1926 a well-to-do New York social worker and former teacher, Julia Horn Hamburger, for example, founded Ivriah as a women's section of the Jewish Education Society. The name meant "Hebrew woman" and the society believed that "the way to make the home Jewish is to make the mother Jewish."[40] To help form and encourage this household paragon, it offered instruction in Hebrew and Jewish culture and religion, as well as attractive and affordable ritual objects, including Hanukkah menorahs bearing the organization's name, to beautify home observances.

But for most synagogue women, the major source of information on Jewish homemaking was the sisterhood. "Education is the lifeline of sisterhood," proclaimed the education department of the Women's League, organized as a national resource for local Conservative activities. Written by yet another rabbi's wife, a Hunter classics graduate and former high school teacher aptly named Deborah Marcus Melamed ("teacher" in Hebrew), and published by the Women's League in 1927, *The Three Pillars: Thought, Worship, and Practice* became a basic textbook for Jewish living so popular that it went through nine printings. Deborah had done graduate work in Semitic languages at Philadelphia's Dropsie College, where her husband, Raphael, received his Ph.D. for a study of an Aramaic-language commentary on the Song of Songs. Nonetheless, *Pillars*, her best-known book, took a less scholarly approach. It explained all that a woman needed to know to carry out and understand the important home rituals, as well as why she should want to do them.

In educated middle-class homes, ritual often had a stylistic as well as a spiritual dimension, not only fulfilling religious requirements but also reflecting elevated taste. The esthetic possibilities of the Sabbath table, the Passover seder plate, and other design opportunities got prominent and prestigious display at the 1940 World's Fair. First presented in the Temple of Religion pavilion, a pageant entitled The Jewish Home Beautiful was repeated countless times over the next three decades in synagogue social halls and auditoriums and at interfaith programs across the nation.

An array of formal dining tables graced the stage, each set for a particular holiday with fine linen, china, crystal, and silver, as well as elegant floral arrangements and candles in ornamental holders. Several refined matrons in fashionable suits or afternoon dresses and hats stood at the ready. A spotlight illuminated first one table, then another. As the beam rested on each display, the pageant's narrator explained the holiday's historic background, described its modern customs, and suggested appropriate menus. The onstage ladies meanwhile demonstrated each observance as a female singer intoned suitable songs. The pageant's originators, Betty Greenberg and Althea Osber Silverman, issued instructions for conducting the pageant in a 1941 book of the same name, published by the Women's League and complete with suitable recipes.

Making Kashrut *Modern*

The role of sisterhood women was even more crucial in the effort to modernize Orthodoxy. In 1930 the Women's Branch issued *Symbols and Ceremonies of the Jewish Home,* a detailed instruction manual that allowed even the rankest beginner to understand and, even more importantly, to fulfill the detailed requirements of Sabbath and holiday observances, running a kosher kitchen, and maintaining marital purity. What her grandmother had known simply from growing up in an observant household, a Modern Orthodox housewife could now find printed between covers.

Kashrut became a cornerstone of the campaign to make Orthodoxy modern. Though once an unquestioned commonplace of Jewish life, the dietary laws were becoming dead letters for many Americans. *Oysesn* (Yiddish for "eating out") grew in popularity along with incomes in the century's first decades, and many families began the slide from *kashrut* by deciding to observe the ancient rules at home but not away. "Kosher-style" restaurants—a new category of cuisine that offered the traditional *haimish* flavors without the encumbrance of strict observance—attracted many diners who wanted to be modern without disdaining tradition. Even in homes where the spirit of the law was still honored, the execution had often become lax.

Johnstowners, for example, considered separate dishes for meat and milk a given. "Everyone had them," a longtime resident recalled, but "there was no constant vigilance [about] which plate may have been used for what," and few housewives made the effort to get out the boiling water to rekosher a dish or pot or utensil that might have become contaminated by touching the wrong class of food.[41] In St. Paul, Minnesota, Anne Garon Greenberg started marriage "with four sets of dishes, not five. One for Passover, glass dishes for Passover" which, being nonporous according to religious law, could be more easily rekoshered for use with either milk or meat. She had "a good set for fleishig [meat] and an everyday set" as well as "a good set for milchig [milk] and an everyday one. And gradually they merged. I don't know what happened, but they all merged. . . . And the same with the silver."[42]

Apart from keeping dishes separate, *kashrut* also requires buying only kosher meat. The move away from that habit was not always clean or ideologically consistent either. Florence Shuman Sher, for example, remembers how her father "gradually wore down my Mother's wish to have nothing but kosher meat in our house." The Shumans lived in a small Iowa town, and in the days before refrigerated railway cars, meat shipped from Dubuque often arrived in a condition "fit for neither man nor beast! Gradually then, my Mother's inbred beliefs were put aside but my Mother never set a foot inside a 'traye' (unkosher) meat market. She always insisted that my father do this shopping (perhaps as a sly punishment). But even though the meat came to her unkosher, she still used to salt and soak [it] in the orthodox way she had been trained to do, and thus she lived up to her religious beliefs as best she could."[43]

As the first American generation came of age, many made a conscious decision to ignore the old ways. Cecyle Eirinberg Marsh's mother, for example, had struggled to keep kosher in rural South Dakota, feeding her family mostly cheese, eggs, and canned salmon because the kosher meat sent by rail from Sioux City, Iowa, often arrived inedible. When Cecyle married, her mother offered her some surprising advice. "'Daughter, I couldn't change, but I don't want you to keep kosher.' She knew I was going to live in a small town. She told me not to."[44]

Many brides of the 1920s, 1930s, and 1940s decided for themselves not to bother with what they considered antiquated requirements. Others found that the food restrictions imposed by World War II made *kashrut* overly onerous. Even though Cecilia Rose Waldman began married life determined to emulate her mother's and mother-in-law's kosher kitchens, wartime shortages convinced her husband to suggest, "'Let's forget the whole thing about *kashrut*,' so I mixed my dishes and I didn't keep kosher." But then Cecilia's mother came to live with the Waldmans. "I said, 'How are we going to manage? My husband doesn't want it, my children don't know from it. My dishes are mixed.' I'll never forget her answer for a woman of her generation. She said, "'Cec, I eat in restaurants. I really don't care about your pots and pans or your silverware, but I would choke to death if I had to eat nonkosher meat.' So I said, 'There is no problem. Whenever we sit down as a family I'll buy kosher meat, and you cook it.' So that was how we lived for over twenty years."[45]

For many families, Passover, with its special restrictions on leavened foods in addition to the ordinary restrictions on milk and meat, was the last bastion of *kashrut*. "We did not keep Kosher," Marion Newman remembered of her parents' home in the 1930s. "Except for one week, the week of Passover. Every dish in our home was out. . . . Any rabbi in America could eat in our home for one week a year. . . . The rest of the year there was one set of dishes in the house and in the early years we didn't serve butter with meat but in due course we got over that and butter was served with meat, milk and so on."[46] And in Dorothy Moscow Hurwitz's home, "The only time I kept strictly kosher was the week of Passover, because Grandma Kruger would come." In addition to buying kosher meat, "we used all grandma's pots. We had an old bake box that had come from the Old Country, and in there were the *pesadicka* [Passover dishes and the silver and the pots and pans]. . . . There weren't three dishes alike."[47]

But if the great majority of Jewish households were eating more and more like other Americans, Modern Orthodoxy made *kashrut* a matter of principle. Conservatism also encouraged adherence to the dietary laws, but only a minority of its members complied. Achieving or increasing kosher kitchens in modern America, *kashrut*'s proponents realized, would mean making it attractive to modern, middle-class American women, a project that became an important focus of educational efforts. Many modern high school and college graduates resisted the appeals to custom or tradition or Scriptural commandment that had convinced their grandmothers, so reasons for keeping kosher were rephrased into the language of the aspiring middle class. The kosher family was more refined, civilized, and healthier than its nonkosher counterpart, publicity campaigns claimed. "On the whole, nothing has refined the Jewish character as much as the dietary laws," confided Deborah Melamed in *The Three Pillars*. What was more, "abstinence from foods permitted to others develop[s] and strengthen[s] self mastery and control."[48] In addition, some authors argued, kosher food promoted stronger resistance to disease.

But, most importantly, *kashrut* called on the creative and esthetic side of the woman practicing it. As Jews' social status rose, so did their desire for greater elegance in their meals as well as their surroundings. "In a Jewish home, a perfectly prepared meal, daintily served is not enough," Betty Greenberg and Althea Osber Silverman warned their readers. "It may satisfy the physical desires and the aesthetic sense but to be *perfect* it must be kosher."[49] The "art" of kosher cooking, a crucial element in creating the "Jewish Home Beautiful," took ingenuity, taste, and skill, their influential volume explained. "Living as a Jewess is more than a matter of faith, knowledge and observance," they assured their readers. "To live as a Jewess, a woman must have something of the artist in her."[50]

Like any other artist, the creator in the kosher kitchen needed excellent tools and expert techniques, and in the 1920s and 1930s, the Modern Orthodox movement set out to provide them. This effort coincided with a transformation in how American food got to the table. Before the mid-1920s, the average American woman had made at home, alone or with the help of servants, almost everything she fed her family. She baked from scratch, she canned and preserved, she bought chickens with their feathers on and fish still in their fins. She hulled and shucked and peeled and pared fruits and vegetables. She rolled pie dough and noodles. She mashed potatoes with a fork and chopped liver with a knife. She ground meat by forcing it through a metal mill. She rendered cooking fat from the meat and poultry she boiled or roasted. She soaked beans. She filled pickle barrels with vegetables and brine. She might even churn her own butter and wash the dishes in soap she herself had mixed and poured into molds. To her, cooking kosher meant buying or growing fresh produce, meats, fish, and dairy products and then killing and preparing them according to the restrictions of *kashrut*. Flour, condensed milk, rice, and a few other staples represented the totality of the packaged food in the typical pantry.

Forty years later, between 70 percent and 90 percent of the food that that woman's daughter or granddaughter served was commercially processed before she bought it, and a great proportion of it would bear some nationally known brand name. Canned, frozen, and packaged goods crowded store and home shelves and refrigerators. In the 1920s and 1930s, just as the overwhelming majority of Jewish women were learning to cook like Americans, Americans of all religions were learning to cook with prepared or partially prepared foods. The observant housewife thus faced the daunting task of deciding which of the countless products now available in the ultramodern new chain markets she could buy. Were canned soups kosher? Packaged bread? Chocolate syrup? Boxed crackers? Prepared noodles? Cake mixes? Peanut butter? Pancake batter? Bottled ketchup? Could she wash her dishes in Ivory soap? Could she wrap her children's sandwiches in waxed paper?

The rows of shelves filled with products were too long, the listed ingredients too numerous, and the rules of *kashrut* too complex for each housewife to puzzle the matter out for herself. She had to depend on the judgment of qualified rabbis who examined the food's production and determined whether it adhered to *halachah*. Such supervision had been the rule since time immemorial in the slaughter and butchering of meat and the baking of matzah for sale. But it was something quite unfamiliar to American food companies.

But observant *balebustes* understood something of market power. If the manufacturers understood the potential of a whole new, and very loyal, market, Orthodox women believed, these shrewd businessmen would certainly respond with items that met kosher standards. In fact, through their movement's magazines and congregational newsletters and networks, "We have within our power to give these kosher products nation-wide sanction and publicity," Women's Branch members read in one such publication.[51] Under Women's Branch auspices, Orthodox sisterhoods took the initiative in contacting many food companies, visiting their facilities, and financing the technical studies needed to investigate and sometimes alter production techniques when necessary. They were also instrumental in acquainting non-Jewish executives with a discreet little symbol developed by the Union of Orthodox Jewish Congregations, the letter *U* within the letter *O*. Printed in small type in some inconspicuous corner of a label or package, it went unnoticed by non-Jewish shoppers but was plainly visible to Jews. Many major manufacturers responded enthusiastically to these overtures.

Though the percentage of kosher households was dropping, they still represented a formidable purchasing block, spending $200 million on kosher food, excluding poultry, in New York City alone in 1934.[52] By then a wide variety of popular American brands was consumed regularly in kosher homes, and each new addition to the approved list was trumpeted in Orthodox publications. Twenty-six of Heinz's 57 varieties were listed, readers of *Orthodox Union*, a movement publication, were informed, as were Wrigley's gum, Dugan's baked goods, Pepsi-Cola, and dozens of breakfast cereals, soups, macaronis, shortenings, and other products. Some inherently *treif* products were offered in new, kosher forms. Pork and beans, for example, reemerged as "vegetarian" baked beans.

When Loft's, then a major producer of ice cream and candy, decided in 1935 to go kosher, the Orthodox press praised this "historic event for the Jews of America," and the company's Gentile head was feted at a testimonial banquet at the prestigious Hotel Biltmore.[53] Manufacturers made sure that kosher housewives knew of their wares. "Orthodox Women Hail New White Shortening," a 1936 ad for Spry brand proclaimed. "No Wonder! For now you can use a beautiful White shortening and still keep the Dietary Laws."[54] Thanks to the OU seal on the can of hydrogenated vegetable oil, kosher food could be as American as apple pie but without forbidden lard or limiting butter in the crust.

Of course, merely having access to a range of kosher products did not guarantee an up-to-date, all-American diet. The home cook needed to know which products to buy as well as how to use them. A variety of cookbooks, many written and published by sisterhoods, presented hundreds of recipes that suited American tastes and met *halachic* rules. These volumes generally highlighted not the familiar kosher foods of the Ashkenazic tradition but new, American treats. Readers learned that in addition to kasha, cholent, brisket, and other boringly familiar dishes, such American delicacies as fried chicken, devil's food cake, corn fritters, chile con carne, spaghetti and meatballs, chocolate chip cookies, and deviled eggs could grace the Orthodox table.

But if updated *kashrut* became a mark of sophistication in Orthodox circles, the other ceremonial foundation of the traditional home, the rules of family purity, did not. But try as they might, such rabbi-written marriage manuals as *The Duty of the Jewish Woman* or *A Handbook for the Jewish Woman* failed to convince middle-class wives that concern about *niddah* had any place in their modern, enlightened lives. These books delicately suggested that the alternating periods when contact was and was not allowed added piquancy, romance, and even excitement to a couple's sex life. Restraint had an important spiritual value, they argued. But women seem not to have agreed. There was nothing sophisticated, refined, or artistic about the monthly resort to the *mikvah*, especially a dingy, unappetizing basement water tank of the type that had customarily served three hundred people before each water change and that the New York Board of Health had termed a "menace" as far back as 1912. Yet the new, modern, tiled, hygienic, and luxuriously equipped "ritualariums" constructed in the 1930s did not attract women either.

By 1942, the Committee on Traditional Observances of the Rabbinic Council of America declared the practice of monthly purification "on the verge of extinction," although no hard data exist on the custom's actual incidence.[55] All the world could see who kept a kosher home, but who used the *mikvah* and when was known only to the women themselves, their husbands, and the *mikvah* attendants. Rarely discussed openly in an age that enforced severe discretion on sexual subjects, and seen by many women as an archaic throwback, "the use of the *mikvah* at the prescribed periods is more honored in the breach than in the observance," noted Mrs. Moses Hyamson, an Orthodox rabbi's wife, in 1927.[56] Which factor weighed more heavily in the decline of *niddah*—the immersion itself or the nearly two weeks of sexual abstinence that preceded it—is not known.

Education for the Future

Notwithstanding efforts to inform observant wives, the long-term future of observant Jewish motherhood clearly lay in the deep education of girls, not the stopgap training of grown women. New York offered the first opportunities for girls to attend all-day Jewish schools. In 1927 the Center Academy, an adjunct of the Brooklyn Jewish Center, a largely upper-middle-class Modern Orthodox synagogue center, began accepting girls into an all-day program it called "a progressive school for the American Jewish child."[57] The following year, the coeducational Yeshiva of Flatbush enrolled its first students, as did the all-female Shulamith School the year after that. Eight years later, in Manhattan, the Ramaz School opened for both boys and girls. Each school provided a program that combined traditional Jewish studies, including Hebrew language, with the same secular curriculum that children followed in public school. They attempted to produce knowledgeable, observant Jews at home in modern American culture.

Stern College for Women, established in 1954 at the hitherto all-male Yeshiva University, sought the same objective. Providing a modern baccalaureate program with a strong emphasis on Jewish studies, it gave girls from observant homes the opportunity to earn a degree in a Modern

Orthodox atmosphere and, incidentally, to meet a wide range of potential husbands who shared their religious orientation. Like other Modern Orthodox schools, it strove to make Orthodox Jews and Orthodox Jewry comfortable and successful in middle-class America.

The Bais Ya'akov School, founded in the Williamsburg section of Brooklyn in 1937, had quite a different goal: to inculcate into its girl students the traditional Orthodoxy of the Chassidic communities of Eastern Europe while giving them the secular training they needed to survive economically. Begun in Cracow, Poland, in 1917 by a scholarly, thirty-five-year-old dressmaker named Sarah Schenirer, the first Bais Ya'acov (House of Jacob) school gave young girls the thorough religious education that tradition had denied Sarah in her girlhood. Though Orthodox families in Poland took care to educate their sons in Judaism in those days, they had no Jewish schools for their daughters. Instead, they sent them to local secular or even Christian schools and then expected them to function as observant Jewish wives and mothers. Without spiritual knowledge, Sarah feared, modern girls were left to wander alone in "a world which is wide open, unfenced, and pitiless."[58] She yearned to give them the religious grounding that boys received in school and in the synagogue. Several prominent rabbis, including the Belzer Rebbe, the Gerer Rebbe, and the Hafetz Hayyim, approved of her plan to start an appropriate Jewish girls' school and even devised a justification for breaking with tradition in order to strengthen it. Though the *Shulkhan Arukh*, an authoritative law code, barred women from the study of Torah, the rabbis reasoned that women born to Judaism had the right to receive the same instruction in law and ritual that female converts had to master.

In its first year, Sarah's little school grew from twenty-five to eighty pupils. The influential Orthodox movement Agudat Israel adopted her philosophy and techniques, and within seven years twenty-five Bais Ya'acov Schools had been started. Sarah died suddenly in Vienna in 1935 at the age of fifty-two, but the Bais Ya'acov network continued to flourish. Two years after her death, when refugees from increasing persecution in Europe started the first American branch, a Brooklyn elementary school, Sarah's vision had grown to encompass thirty-five thousand students in 284 schools. Additional hundreds of schools were founded by the time Hitler invaded Poland in 1939 and began the destruction of East European Jewry. Transplanted to Brooklyn, Bais Ya'acov served as an early beachhead of the ultra-Orthodox refugee immigration that started slowly before World War II broke out and intensified after it ended.

But the small band of decidedly old-world Orthodox painfully recon-
structing a shattered world out of the remnants of catastrophe were not a
focus of American Jewish attention in the 1930s, 1940s, and 1950s.
Instead, Americans of all three denominational streams put their hope in
modern Jewish education modeled on secular educational programs.
Women became increasingly prominent in religious education during
those years, both in the few existing day schools and in the widespread
after-school programs.

By the 1930s, women constituted a third of New York's afternoon
Hebrew teachers, and the American schoolmarm was rapidly replacing the
heder-style *melamed* in the nation's Jewish classrooms. Teacher training
institutes run by the Jewish Theological Seminary, the Women's Branch,
community-based programs in Cleveland, Pittsburgh, Detroit, Denver, St.
Louis, Newark, and more than two score other places prepared young
women for this work. One of the most prestigious programs was developed in New York by Dr. Samson Benderly of the Bureau of Jewish
Education. Born in the holy city of Sfat and educated at the American
University of Beirut before coming to Baltimore to study at Johns Hopkins
University, Benderly abandoned a medical career to pioneer modern
Jewish education in America. Among the cadre of his enthusiastic disciples
who called themselves "Benderly Boys" were quite a few girls.

Continuing Community Service

As prominent as sisterhoods became in the lives of synagogue women,
women without synagogue ties also worked to aid the Jewish community.
Council, Hadassah, and several newer organizations channeled their charitable impulses into activities that women controlled. Hadassah's projects
in Palestine became increasingly ambitious as the organization's numbers
grew in America. By the late-1920s, Henrietta Szold's energies were concentrated abroad and Hadassah's American operations were in the hands
of a younger generation of dedicated female Zionists who sponsored crucial social welfare and public health programs for the yishuv. In the mid-
1930s, alarmed by the growing persecution of Jews in Europe, Hadassah
began to support Youth Aliyah, an effort begun in Germany to bring
refugee youth to Palestine to live in kibbutzim and youth villages. It also
joined with the Rothschild family to build the Rothschild-Hadassah
Hospital on Jerusalem's Mount Scopus. Together with Hebrew University,
the hospital's neighbor on the mount, Hadassah sponsored the graduate

medical school. During World War II, it also established a girls vocational school. After the war, it strongly supported the establishment of a Jewish state. On April 13, 1948, when Arab attackers killed seventy-five doctors, nurses, and technicians trying to reach Scopus by convoy, Hadassah decided that the hospital had to be evacuated. Construction of a second Hadassah Medical Center in the safer Jerusalem neighborhood of Ein Kerem began in 1952.

For its American members Hadassah remained an engrossing, even consuming, interest that often passed from mother to daughter. In 1919, for example, North Carolinian Jennie Nachmanson founded the first southern chapter. Fourteen years later she and her eldest daughter, twenty-eight-year-old Sara Nachmanson Evans, visited Palestine together. Sara went on to became chapter president in Durham, where her husband, E.J. ("Mutt"), served as mayor for twelve years starting in 1951 and the couple ran Evans United Department Stores, which had grown out of a Nachmanson family business. While Sara raised two sons, she worked to build Hadassah throughout the South, greatly aided by her seven younger sisters, each of whom also chaired a local Hadassah chapter. In 1942 Sara began a forty-five-year tenure on the national board and rose to be national vice president in 1954. In 1968 a *Jerusalem Post* photo taken in the Hadassah hospital chapel, world-renowned for its Chagall windows, recorded the visit of all eight Nachmanson sisters to celebrate Sara and Mutt's fortieth wedding anniversary.

Throughout the first half of the century, Council retained both its dynamism and its focus on service to American communities. Through the Depression and World War II, it worked to aid women affected by the national crises. The Portland chapter, for example, in cooperation with the local B'nai B'rith Women, opened the Opportunity Bake Shop, which made noodles, caramels, bagels, strudel, pickles, and other foods and provided jobs for up to eighteen women working two to three days a week. During World War II, when the problem was too many rather than too few work hours, Washington, D.C., Council provided day care for children of women war workers.

Founded in 1909, B'nai B'rith Women had twelve thousand members in 103 chapters by 1935 and forty thousand members in 248 chapters during World War II.[59] Mizrachi Women (now called AMIT) began in 1925 as an organization of Orthodox Zionists. With "Tikva teas" and "Palestine evenings," it had fifty chapters by the mid-1930s and fifty thousand members in 1950 raising money for girls' education and refugee relief. Pioneer Women, also begun in 1925, catered to secular, socialist Zionists. Women's American ORT (Organization of Rehabilitation through Training), the New World division of a group founded in 1880 in Russia, raised money to provide vocational education to needy Eastern European Jews. The Women's Division of the American Jewish Congress, founded in 1933 by Louise Waterman Wise, wife of a prominent Reform rabbi, devoted its major efforts in its early years to aiding refugees from European persecution.

The gathering crisis in Europe became an increasingly important focus for American women's service groups as the 1930s advanced. The "grievous conditions" of German Jews in 1933 already required Americans to make "personal sacrifices in order to be able to forward monies to the Joint Distribution Committee for Germany," Dora Spiegal, president of the Women's League exhorted Conservative sisterhood members.[60] Some families brought European Jews to safety by sponsoring their entry into the United States. Sara and Mutt Evans, for example, personally took financial responsibility for fifty-five people.

Council, with over forty years experience serving immigrants, became especially active in attempting to rescue mortally threatened Jews. As Sadie American had worked at the national and international levels on Council's behalf to protect vulnerable women from white slavers, now Cecilia Razovsky became Council's woman on the spot in the struggle to snatch men, women, and children from Hitler's clutches. Like Sadie, a native-born midwesterner, Cecilia grew up in an immigrant home in St. Louis. She sewed on buttons, waited tables, and did various other jobs to help the family finances while she went to high school. After graduation she worked as a clerk at the *St. Louis Star* and also did community work as a teacher and club leader and took courses at Washington University and the Corliss School of Law. Several years as a legal secretary and several more teaching public school night courses preceded a move to Washington, D.C., in 1917. There, at twenty-eight, she began enforcing child labor laws for the U.S. Children's Bureau.

The following year, a Supreme Court decision overturning federal child labor legislation ended that job. Taking a position with Council, she began her life's work of aiding endangered refugees and immigrants. In the 1920s, she worked to reform the Cable Act of 1922, which made citizenship harder for many immigrant women to obtain. After the Immigration Act of 1924 was enacted, she sought alternative destinations for Jewish refugees unable to enter the United States, helping establish a program in

Cuba. Neither her 1927 marriage to Dr. Morris Davidson nor the birth of their son, David, slowed her professional work.

As the European situation drastically darkened, Council's efforts intensified and Cecilia coordinated various agency efforts to integrate the refugees who managed to arrive into American life. She was one of many working desperately but ultimately futilely to convince the United States to loosen the rules preventing many refugees from obtaining visas. In the spring of 1939, when the Cuban government reneged on a prior agreement to admit the 930 Jewish passengers fleeing Hitler aboard the steamship *St. Louis*, Cecilia traveled to Havana vainly seeking a change of policy. As she and the world watched in horror, the ship was refused in port after port, including American ones, and finally bore its doomed cargo back to Europe, where many perished.

Later that year the port of Vera Cruz, Mexico, turned away the SS *Quanza,* also laden with refugee Jews. Determined to prevent another *St. Louis* disaster, Cecilia joined forces with Evelyn Hersey of the American Committee for Christian Refugees. They met the ship when it attempted to land its passengers at Norfolk, Virginia, but was rejected by U.S. officials. From the deck, a local newspaper reported, women shrieked to the people on shore, "begging piteously that they and their children be given a chance to live again in the sunshine of a free land."[61] Not everyone aboard the *Quanza* got that wish, but the State Department reluctantly admitted the children, the adults who met the requirements of refugee status, and those who had South or Central American visas. Commitments from Cecilia and Evelyn that their organizations would financially guarantee those admitted ultimately gained their rescue.

Cecilia next worked with the Dominican Republic, whose dictator, Rafael Trujillo, had agreed to accept 100,000 Jewish refugees as settlers on twenty-six thousand acres in the coastal area of Sosua. Cecilia took part in the complicated negotiations and again provided crucial financial guarantees. Then Italy entered the war on the Axis side, cutting off the escape route of the initial thirty thousand. About five hundred ultimately got to Sosua, where support that Cecilia arranged again proved vital. Council also played a part in the only other sizable American wartime refugee rescue effort, the temporary 1944 admission of a thousand refugees interned in an unused army camp at Oswego, New York. By that time, though, Cecilia had moved on to another organization.

When the United States went to war, Jewish women's organizations threw themselves into the struggle for victory. Eleanor Roosevelt addressed the 1941 Women's League convention on women in defense. "Over 100,000 of our members are working in every single branch of the war effort," league president Dora Spiegel announced in 1943, "giving of their blood, selling bonds, turning assembly halls into emergency hospitals, enlisting in motor corps, serving in canteens, taking first aid courses, and teaching first aid."[62] All around the world for those four years, the young American Jews who served in the military found themselves living, generally for the first time, among Gentiles of every kind. No longer comfortable members of the dominant group in their neighborhoods, they suddenly found themselves a tiny, scattered handful among the millions of their countrymen also called to service. The military had long considered Jews a legitimate category of Americans, but a religious rather than a cultural group. Every branch provided the means to practice Judaism. Jewish chaplains, themselves military officers, ran services on the major holidays that Jewish personnel could freely attend. Being Jewish in uniform, unlike being Jewish in Brookline or Weequahic or Flatbush, was to go to shul. Many a homesick young man or woman who had not been to synagogue for years, or perhaps ever before, now attended services to assert their Jewishness in a sea of Gentiles or simply to feel yet once again the familiar comfort of Yiddishkeit, the warmth of being among a crowd of their own kind.

For four Rosh Hashanahs, Yom Kippurs, Hanukkahs, and Passovers, young Jews of various religious backgrounds (and of none at all) gathered not in neighborhood synagogues among their families and old friends, but under canvas tarps, in massive mess halls, or in the open air with *landsleyt* gathered almost randomly from across the United States. Belle Goldman, a supply clerk from Milwaukee, atoned for the sins of 1944 as part of an ad hoc military congregation at Buna Buna on New Guinea. Lieutenant Mildred Scheier of the Thirty-Fifth Army Field Hospital was the officer who led a thousand enlisted men in a Passover seder in Bari, Italy. Army Nurse Corps Lieutenant Revelyn Prebluda joined American nurses and sailors for a seder in Wales. Since most of the chaplains leading Jewish troops in prayer were Conservative, many servicemen and women came to know, often for the first time, the Conservative style of worship.

Being Jewish in the Suburbs

That knowledge would soon prove useful. Once the war ended, the newly demobilized veterans had hardly arrived stateside before the race to the suburbs was on. In those muddy subdivisions, the sons and daughters of the old Jewish neighborhoods found a world as different from the one in which they grew up as military service had been. "When you live in a suburban community like we do, you have to identify yourself with the Jewish organizations," one new Essex County, New Jersey, suburbanite explained. "How else can you show you are a Jew?" Back in Newark, you had showed it simply by where you lived. But here, beyond the city limits, "the only way you can achieve anything is through united action. As Jews, we have to stand together just like the non-Jews do. This is life in the suburbs."[63]

The most visible and obvious organization to join was a synagogue. Belonging to a "church" was acceptable—almost mandatory—as a way of showing that one was a reputable, responsible, member of the middle class, but belonging to a non-American ethnic group most decidedly was not. By the late 1940s, Americans had begun to accept Judaism, if somewhat gingerly, as one of three "American" religions, along with Protestantism and Catholicism. As the photo magazines and newsreels revealed to a horrified world the true extent of the Nazi atrocities, the casual anti-Semitism formerly permissible in "polite society" lost its respectability. The 1947 Oscar winner, *Gentlemen's Agreement*, signaled this important change. In this daring film, the strikingly un-Semitic but extremely popular Gregory Peck played a courageous non-Jewish reporter who posed as a Jew to get the painful lowdown on anti-Semitism in America. In the postwar world, Jews who appeared outwardly American and conformed to middle-class norms could live unhindered in many very pleasant, religiously mixed neighborhoods. They still did not find themselves welcome in prestigious Gentile clubs and resorts or in the most exclusive residential areas. But those who passed middle-class muster no longer needed to fear the crude stereotyping and blatant restrictions of the past.

As soon as suburban Jews moved into their new homes, registered their children in the local school and Little League, and seeded their lawns, they embarked on a frenzy of synagogue building unmatched since the 1920s. As Jews had throughout American history, families on the suburban frontier tended to cluster in certain suburbs—Scarsdale in New York's Westchester County and Great Neck on Long Island, to name two of the most prestigious, as well as South Orange, New Jersey; Shaker Heights, Ohio; Cheltenham, Pennsylvania; and others. Between 1947 and 1959, ninety-nine new congregations began in the New York suburbs alone, but

some of the glass and stone pavilions rising among the housing developments belonged to older congregations following their members out of the
city. Between 1945 and 1952, Jews spent between $40 million and $50 million building synagogues, and twice that much in the following decade.

Unlike the Classical and Moorish palaces that their parents had erected
along city avenues, the new generation of congregational boards adorned
suburban roads with bold, boxy examples of postwar modern design.
These structures looked not back to any imagined Mediterranean or
Oriental past, but forward into the American future, away from the
anguished history of their people and toward the promise of an unencum-
bered life in a new land of freedom. Sleek lines, blond brick, bright colors,
light wood, picture windows, abstract sculptures and paintings set the tone
for a Judaism not of outmoded tradition but of enlightened, up-to-date
thought. Often set on expansive lawns, these bastions of progress boasted
parking lots, school rooms, meeting rooms, social halls, and kitchens that
together took up much more space than the sanctuary. The Hebrew
school, nursery school, scout troops, sisterhood, men's club, teen groups,
and other activities kept the building busy throughout of the week.

Most of the new suburban synagogues, whether recently founded or
established for generations, were Conservative. By the 1950s,
Conservatism was the largest stream of Judaism. Until the 1940s, the great
majority of American synagogue members had favored Orthodoxy, but by
late in that decade, Conservatism had outpaced both it and Reform. Some
Modern Orthodox congregations even moved over to Conservatism. For
the native-born East European sons and daughters who built, paid for, and
sent their children to the suburban congregations, Orthodox was "too
Jewish" and Reform not Jewish enough. Lacking Orthodoxy's insistence
on preserving tradition and Reform's rejection of the modern validity of
halachah, Conservatism attempted to adapt to modern circumstances
while maintaining *halachic* justification without proclaiming an overarching ideology. In 1950, for example, the Conservative rabbinate voted to
permit congregants to drive to Sabbath services, on the theory that suburban distances were too great for many people to walk, attending synagogue
was an overriding value, and driving a modern automobile, though it did
involve combustion, did not constitute the same kind of physical "work"
as a horse- or donkey-drawn carriage.

So well did the suburban congregations meet their congregants' needs
that by 1960, fully 60 percent of American Jews were synagogue members,
nearly triple the rate of thirty years before. Yet even as synagogue rolls rose

dramatically, observance continued to fall. Despite the denomination's teachings, most Conservative households neither kept kosher nor observed Sabbath. Religious observance was not even a major reason that most people joined. A 1959 survey of three Newark suburbs, for example, found that 22 percent of synagogue members cited religion as their main reason, but 27 percent named the desire to have a bar mitzvah for their sons, a ceremony that congregations did not perform for nonmembers.[64] In Los Angeles, the lure of religion was even weaker, with a mere 2 percent citing it as their main motivation for membership.[65]

The synagogue was now not so much a house of prayer as the new Jewish neighborhood, where middle-class men and women could find for themselves and convey to their children the sense of peoplehood and belonging that they had simply absorbed from the air when they were young. It became a way of identifying as a Jew and establishing a respectable Jewish presence in their new, non-Jewish hometowns. To accomplish these tasks, the suburban synagogues chose to emphasize, from the vast array of Jewish culture and religion, a symbolic shorthand, a set of observances and customs that preserved a sense of Jewishness and harmonized with suburban modernity: Hanukkah, Passover, the High Holy Days, Hebrew school, and the bar mitzvah.

In part to prepare for that rite, the Hebrew school became the suburban synagogue's central activity. Enrollments rose drastically as the leading edge of the baby boom children neared the crucial age, more than doubling between 1947 and 1957 in the suburbs of Newark, for example. Significantly, girls now attended religious school as often as boys, and for as long—in some cases, all the way through high school. Torah reading and the accompanying celebration on turning thirteen remained an almost exclusively male prerogative through the 1960s. But except for missing bar mitzvah training, girls in Reform and Conservative schools followed exactly the same curriculum as boys. By the 1950s, Americans were raising the first generation of Eastern European-descended Jewish girls who had the chance to become adults as Jewishly knowledgeable as their brothers and husbands. Back in the old ethnic enclaves Hebrew school had been an educational adjunct chosen by observant families, but in the suburbs it became many children's central—and often only—experience of Jewish community. With carpools and school buses replacing street life and television replacing the old neighborhood's corner candy stores, suburban youngsters did not simply inhale Jewish identity. Fostering and maintaining it now took conscious effort.

Some families worked hard at the task, attending late Friday evening services, lighting candles and singing kiddush, sending their youngsters to Jewish summer camps, and adorning their homes with the new, clean-lined copper ritual objects coming out of Israel. The brand-new and astonishingly vibrant Jewish state now provided a dynamic, romantic, inspiring focus for Jewish identity. The hideous, unfathomable, irreparable losses of World War II, the utter and savage destruction of the thousand-year-old Eastern European Yiddish world and of the millions of their kinfolk who inhabited it, was more than surviving world Jewry could emotionally absorb in the immediate postwar decades. And the Yiddish culture of the center cities had also become, over the years, irredeemably outdated and lower-class.

Better by far, many believed, to attach the next generation's loyalties to the valiant pioneers planting trees in the desert, to the bracing vigor of their songs and dances, to the sleek yet touchingly authentic handicrafts they exported. Usually made of hammered copper patinated in greenish blue, the new style of menorahs, candlesticks, kiddush cups, seder plates, mezuzahs, wall plaques, and serving platters cunningly combined the contours of fashionable Danish modern with references to the ancient Jewish past—not the poverty of the now ruined Pale but the glories of biblical days. In place of battered brass or silver heirlooms carried in steerage trunks and bundles, Jewish wives now often lit Friday or *yom tov* candles in holders adorned with urn-bearing maidens or the bunch of grapes Israel had adopted as a national symbol. Many families now gathered at Hanukkah not around a brass menorah from the Lower East Side emblazoned with the rampant lions of Judea but around a bluish copper one adorned with a Greek-style oil jar. No longer did families light the orange, New York–made Hanukkah candles that had been customary for generations. Now multicolored Israeli twists stood in their place. In addition to national pride, a central factor in the spread of the new decor was the sisterhood shop. In the past it was a mere fund-raising project located in a little nook somewhere in the synagogue that provided various utilitarian ritual objects—Sabbath and Hanukkah candles, inconspicuous tin mezuzahs meant to be painted over. Now it had become a source of tasteful, exotic, conspicuous decorative objects for the sophisticated Jewish home.

Though Israeli arts and crafts proudly ornamented the walls, shelves, and doorposts of countless split-levels and ranch houses, Yiddish culture, and the dense weave of organizations and ideologies that it once represented, did not make the move. Yiddish passed increasingly out of use from the 1940s on. Although Jews remained politically more liberal than other suburbanites, socialism, radicalism, and labor activism found no home among the well-kept lawns and mortgage-covered ramblers. By 1951, when Sydney Taylor's children's book *All-of-a-Kind Family* appeared, the immigrant world of the Lower East Side had acquired a nostalgic glow it never possessed while penniless newcomers crowded its streets, lofts, and sweatshops. The five sisters in Taylor's stories shared a tenement bedroom, a pair of loving parents, and a number of innocent adventures. In reality, Taylor had been the middle sister in just such a family. A graduate of NYU, a professional actress and dancer in modern dance pioneer Martha Graham's company, she married in 1925 at twenty-one and gave birth to her only child, Joanne, ten years later. She began to entertain Jo at bedtime with reminiscences of her lively family, and eventually wrote them down for her own satisfaction.

Then, "satisfied, [she] promptly put the manuscript away and the years rolled over it."[66] Jo was well past bedtime stories when Sydney's husband, Robert, found the manuscript and sent it, without its author's knowledge, to the Charles A. Follet Award writing competition. The collection of stories won the prize and was soon published to great acclaim, as well as a prize from the Jewish Book Council. To satisfy the many young readers, not all of them Jewish, enchanted by her gentle tales of challah baking and family seders and Purim costumes and Hanukkah lights and the family's eventual move uptown to more prosperous Harlem, Sydney wrote four additional *All-of-A-Kind Family* books, which also achieved great commercial success and have remained in print for decades. Sydney succumbed to cancer just before the final volume in the series appeared in 1978. The following year the Association of Jewish Libraries named its children's literature award for her.

Nostalgic images were all that remained of the Yiddish world in midcentury suburbia. The organizations and institutions that succeeded in the suburbs were those that projected their members into the American middle class. Sisterhoods formed the backbone of everyday life at many of the new synagogues functioning in bedroom communities largely devoid of adult males during the weekdays. "It is women who really run the congregation anyway—and they certainly run our homes," Reform Rabbi Maurice Eisendrath commented. "Jewish life is matriarchal."[67] For the educated women who populated those towns full-time, fashioning the institutions they needed for their young families became the focus of their

Jewish lives. New York native Marjorie Weiss, for example, arrived in the Bannockburn neighborhood of Bethesda, Maryland, with her husband, Abraham, after World War II. With an undergraduate degree from the University of Michigan and a graduate degree in mathematics earned at American University in nearby Washington, she began a career as a bio-mathematician at the National Cancer Institute, minutes from her home, in 1957, when she was nearly forty. By the time she retired twenty-one years later, she had worked in the first generation of computer modeling in biology.

Before Marjorie became a technical expert at a world-class research institution, she had already put in an entirely different career in Bethesda. An early resident of Bannockburn, whose ranch houses sheltered young couples with university degrees, she and other mothers founded a neighborhood nursery school. Marjorie taught there for six years while her two children were small. At the recently formed Conservative Congregation Beth El she helped start a second, Jewish-oriented nursery school and served as sisterhood president.

Many women less comfortable with synagogue life found similar vehicles for Jewish identity in organizations like Council, Hadassah, and B'nai B'rith Women. Because these groups engaged seriously in political, cultural, and civic concerns, their members could view themselves as intelligent, educated, active citizens, not mere extensions of their husbands and children. Nine such women got together in 1950 to start a Council section in Montgomery County, Maryland, the northwestern frontier of greater Washington, D.C. Along with Bethesda, it included a growing Jewish presence in Silver Spring and part of Chevy Chase. Within two years, the section had 102 members, 153 the year after that, and 200 in 1955. It continued growing, though more slowly, for many more years.

Some of the women who joined had had "little religion in [their] background" and had "always been embarrassed and awkward around people who know more religious stuff than I do," one remembered.[68] Council allowed her and others like her to simultaneously meet Jewish women, associate themselves with the Jewish people, and become part of an active, literate group of suburbanites involved in important local issues. The typical Council member, a college graduate, wife, and mother who had worked, often as a teacher, before becoming a full-time homemaker, and who intended to do so again, did not see herself as a mere housewife. "We required gratification beyond the nursery. . . . We were professional women. . . . We wanted to serve our communities, local, state, national and international," one explained.[69] Though many of their functions took the guise of luncheons, teas, or fashion shows, Council women were not deceived about the serious intent of these activities. Under the conventions of ladylike respectability, they meant to make a difference in the communities and the world. For many, in fact, during the years that they were at home, organizational work became a career. "My whole life used to be the organizations," a Council woman recalled.[70]

Nor was Council the only group actively recruiting lively, intelligent Jewish members. "Those were the days when if you sat next to a woman, your first question was, 'Are you a member of Hadassah?' If the answer was 'no,' you signed her up on the spot," active member Rose Dorfman remembered.[71] "When I joined the great 'exodus' to ... suburbia, Hadassah found me—to my eternal gratitude," said Irene Ruza, a Hunter graduate who eventually rose to the presidency of the Hollis Hills chapter in suburban Queens and membership on the national board.[72] Even those who did not achieve national prominence gained a new awareness of self through organizational work. "In a way, I received my first introduction to the idea of women's lib many years before it was a household word," said Hadassah member Sara Rosen. "I never imagined, nor had I ever seen, so many independent, accomplished women working together for a cause that did not in any way benefit them personally."[73]

It would be these women's daughters, however, who would bring this idea to full fruition, in both their Jewish and their American lives. The women who built suburban Jewry had done so within the conventions they learned when they were young. Before the seeds of a new Jewish womanhood had time to sprout, however, the ground in which they had been planted, which had supported the first American generation's homes and married lives, would shift. The world that generation had made would tremble. By the late 1950s, the faintest, earliest rumblings of a coming earthquake had begun.

Among the first to notice was a Jewish son of the midwestern heartland. Not many years after his mid-1950s bar mitzvah in little Hibbing, Minnesota, where his family ran a store, Robert Allen Zimmerman followed the example of countless American Jews before him. He dropped his parents' old-country surname and adopted one that had originated in the British Isles and seemed closer to the life he wanted to live. His choice was the moniker of a colorful Welsh poet. And, along with most small-town Jews of his generation, he headed for a big city where the future he foresaw for himself seemed more likely to happen.

He chose to begin his career as a musician and songwriter in New York, but he eschewed Tin Pan Alley, the traditional Jewish route to songwriting success. He began performing his compositions in the smoky basements and grubby bars of Greenwich Village, where a new Bohemian generation born just before and during World War II was rediscovering the traditional acoustic music of rural America. Before long, people began to notice as he intoned his original pieces in a flat, nasal, northern plains voice that he tried to make sound like folk singer Woody Guthrie's. His songs announced his, and, by extension, his generation's, rejection of their parents' conformist, consumerist, middle-class values.

Like all rising generations, this one had little notion of what it had cost their elders, the men and women who had survived the great Depression and won World War II, to achieve the lives of apparently stifling conformity and seemingly empty material comfort that their children now disdained. A song penned by Bob Dylan in 1963 warned parents that the younger generation now flamboyantly choosing its own way of living was decidedly "beyond your command" in a world that was rapidly changing.[74]

PART FIVE

"Beyond Your Command"

Remaking Womanhood, 1964–Onward

15

"NO ONE WILL STOP YOU"

Feminism's Second Wave

In 1963, a thirty-year-old lawyer who held honors degrees from Cornell and Columbia and had served on the *Harvard Law Review* accepted a faculty job at the Rutgers law school. Midway through her second academic year, she learned that she was pregnant. Though she had clerked with distinction for a federal judge, had tied for first place in her law school class, had written a book on legal procedure, and had won the glowing recommendations of distinguished professors, she feared that she would lose her post if her superiors found out about her pregnancy. Since this was the only teaching position she could find, dismissal would end her budding academic career. Thanks to "a wardrobe one size larger than mine" on loan from her husband's mother, she "got through the spring semester without detection," she recalls.[1] The baby, her second, arrived at the end of summer vacation. That fall saw her back in the classroom.

Hard experience made her fear firing. "Not a single law firm in the entire city of New York [had] bid" to hire this top graduate of the city's top school.[2] Her first pregnancy had cost her a job. Eleven years earlier, right after being elected to Phi Beta Kappa and receiving her bachelor's degree, she married a fellow Cornellian and followed him to his military service in Lawton, Oklahoma, where she went to work for Social Security. She soon conceived, however, and did not keep it secret. Her superior decreed that no expectant mother could make the trip to a required training session. She took the only other available job, which ranked lower and paid less.

But this daughter of first-generation Jewish Brooklyn wanted to live up to the hopes and sacrifices that her parents, whose firstborn died at age six, had invested in their only surviving child. Neither Nathan Bader, a Russian immigrant who landed in New York at thirteen, nor Celia Amster, a native American whose parents arrived from their shtetl near Cracow four months before her birth, could afford to go to college. They were determined that their daughter, Ruth—high school baton twirler, newspaper editor, and star student—would have that chance. Jobs as a furrier and clothing salesmen earned Nathan only a modest living, but Celia shopped and scrimped with her daughter's college fund always in mind. She also constantly encouraged the girl to read and do her best. Celia, however, did not live to see Ruth go to Cornell on a combination of scholarships and part-time jobs. Sick with cervical cancer during Ruth's high school years, she died the day before she was to give the graduation speech.

And so, when Ruth, her husband, Martin Ginsburg, and their baby, Jane, returned to the East Coast after their Oklahoma sojourn, Ruth entered Harvard Law School, where Martin had already finished his first year. By way of welcome, Dean Erwin Griswold invited the nine female class members to dinner and demanded that each tell why she deserved to deprive a man of a place in the school. Martin, though, already knew the answer; Ruth, he told friends, would make *Law Review.* A standout in her class of five hundred, she did just as he predicted.

When Martin graduated in 1958, twenty-five-year-old Ruth had a year to go, but again she followed him, this time to New York, where he went to work at a well-known firm. Ruth spent her third year at Columbia, caring for Jane and working for the law review. Harvard declined to award her a degree, despite her two stellar years there, but Columbia agreed to bestow one. Another rejection came from Supreme Court Justice Felix Frankfurter, who refused to hire women law clerks, no matter how brilliant their record or enthusiastic their Harvard professors' recommendations.

But if her life had taught Ruth the reality of women's place in midcentury America, her years at Rutgers revealed the possibility that the law could change it. In those days, "well, sex discrimination was regarded as a woman's job," she later recalled.[3] In 1971 she wrote a brief that convinced the U.S. Supreme Court unanimously to overturn a law giving men preference in administering wills. The next year the Court accepted her argument that the air force could not discharge an officer for pregnancy. In the next three years Ruth won five of the six sex discrimination cases she argued before the Court. In 1972 she became Columbia's first tenured female law professor and in 1980, a judge on the federal Court of Appeals for the District of Columbia. In 1996, when the Supreme Court ruled that the Virginia Military Institute must admit women students, Ruth Bader

Ginsburg, the Court's first Jewish female associate justice and its second female of any background, wrote the decision.

Celia's daughter wore her mother's earrings and brooch as she made her Supreme Court arguments. Celia's courage and determination, as well as the limited opportunities available to that generation, were in her heart and mind her mind as she accepted President Clinton's nomination to the High Court in June 1993. Ruth recognized that she and her own generation were traveling into social, spiritual, and religious territory unimaginable to their mothers. Thousands upon thousands of educated, independent-minded women would no longer content themselves with "helping out" in the affairs of men or with defining themselves in relation to males. They were dismantling both the notion of a special female sphere and the restrictions it imposed on their public and private lives. They crossed the boundaries that had long reserved the most powerful, prestigious, respected, and lucrative positions for men.

In the three decades between Ruth's first term at Rutgers and her appointment to the Supreme Court, women in unprecedented numbers became doctors, lawyers and Indian chiefs, carpenters and astronauts, scientists and racehorse jockeys, military pilots and police patrol officers, university presidents and professional basketball stars. Female judges, professors, surgeons, district attorneys, accountants, stockbrokers, architects, and members of countless other formerly male professions would become commonplace. In 1984, Democratic presidential nominee Walter Mondale picked New York congresswoman Geraldine Ferraro as his running mate, the first female candidate on a national ticket.

Now the entire range of human endeavor seemed to lie open to women, including Jewish ones. Thus Twentieth Century-Fox film studio chose Sherry Lansing, daughter of a refugee from Nazism, as its president. The University of Pennsylvania chose Judith Seitz Rodin to be the first permanent female president in the Ivy League. (A fellow Jew, Claire Fagin, preceded her as interim president.) The space shuttle *Challenger* exploded shortly after takeoff on January 28, 1986, killing, among other crew members, Judith Resnick, who had an engineering Ph.D. from the University of Maryland, a bat mitzvah in Akron, and the distinction of being the nation's first Jewish astronaut. Two women, both Jewish, simultaneously represented the nation's most populous state in the U.S. Senate. Women served as U.S. attorney general and secretary of state. As the twenty-first century dawned, a new generation of girls could assume that only their ambition, ability, and dedication limited the heights they could attain. As this epochal transformation of American society unfolded, and continues to unfold, Jewish women played, and continue to play, pivotal parts. They also wrought equally drastic changes in their ethnic and religious community, adding new depth and vigor to American Jewish life.

To many who lived through this social revolution, its onset seemed abrupt. But that apparent suddenness masks a deep continuity in the American Jewish story. Rather than a break with the past, the feminist transformation elaborated on themes that have sounded from the beginning. The same drive for achievement, education, and a life of meaning, the same pragmatic self-confidence and practical idealism, the same belief in their right and ability to affect the world that animated generations of their foremothers now carried the American Jewish generations of the late twentieth century toward definitions and expressions of their womanhood and their Jewishness at once deeply traditional and strikingly original.

The overall outline of this dynamic era is clear, but the scholarship that will clarify its details has hardly begun. The forces underlying so vast a metamorphosis, building since before World War II but first unleashed in the 1960s, continue to reverberate through society to this day. The generations that lived through these dislocations—ourselves, our mothers, and our daughters—are still largely alive, active, and struggling to understand the import of what they have seen and done. Not until historians examine this turbulent age will we obtain real perspective on its mechanics and its meaning. For now, we can only begin to understand or explain the tsunami that bore Americans from the middle of the twentieth century to the dawn of the twenty-first, from Ruth's long-ago humiliations to the place where she, and American Jewry, stand today.

A Second Feminism

During the 1960s, about the time Ruth Ginsburg began drafting briefs on sex discrimination, many other bright, educated young women also found themselves increasingly drawn into a renascent feminism that grew stronger and more turbulent as the decade advanced. While Ruth explored the possibilities available in the law, women—many of them Jewish—were coming together in small groups to examine their personal experience through the lens of a new sensibility. These new feminists coalesced into a formal movement with the founding of such institutions as the National Organization of Women in 1966 and *Ms.* magazine in 1972.

The radical monthly, named for a controversial new title used by daring young women, instantly became the movement's national voice. Insisting that adult women had identities apart from their relationships to men, they rejected the titles Mrs. and Miss. The startling appellation that they used instead gave women the ability—enjoyed by men since time immemorial—to present themselves as individuals without regard to their marital status. Those using it boldly refused to label themselves as anything other than themselves.

But for all their revolutionary rhetoric and radical designs, movement members had major differences from Jewish women activists of yore. They were neither penniless immigrants carrying the banner of rebellion through an icy winter nor hard-pressed housewives battling Depression-era evictions. Rather, they were women like Ruth, educated products of the urban or suburban middle and upper-middle classes. Unlike sweatshop girls who had maintained pickets during the long, desperate uprising or rent strikers who had pummeled policemen in 1930s, they were not struggling for survival or minimally decent treatment. Rather, they were prosperous, articulate, native-born college graduates demanding the two things that their materially comfortable lives had thus far not provided: treatment that fully recognized their abilities rather than their gender and equality of respect and opportunity with men of their own background.

The public face of *Ms.,* and to a great extent of the movement at large, was Gloria Steinem, her signature aviator glasses and silky long hair the nationally recognized symbols of resurgent feminism. Her grandmother, Pauline Perlmutter Steinem, had also been a prominent (if much less glamorous) feminist, an early leader of both the suffrage movement in Ohio and Toledo's section of Council, an activist who telegraphed her congratulations to Hannah Greenebaum Solomon as the congress opened. Raised in Germany, Pauline, a nineteen-year-old wife and mother, accompanied her husband, Joseph, to America in 1884. More than a decade older than his bride and already established in this country as a brewer, he had returned to the Old County to make a suitable match. In her new home Pauline became active in Reform Judaism but switched her loyalties to the mystical teachings of Theosophy, an Eastern-inspired sect that also influenced Gloria's girlhood. Leo, the youngest of Pauline and Joseph's four sons, married Ruth, a Presbyterian of Scottish descent who had Gloria baptized a Congregationalist but nonetheless taught her pride in her Jewish ancestry and revulsion at the Nazi atrocities. During the Hitler era the widowed

Pauline spent more of her small income than her family thought prudent on ransoming relatives out of Germany and into Palestine.

Gloria grew up with no real connection to Judaism, but half of those who founded *Ms.* were at least secular Jews. So were nine of the twelve founders of the Boston Women's Health Book Collective, which wrote the immensely influential feminist health handbook, *Our Bodies, Ourselves.* It was a Jewish woman, and one also alienated from Jewish life, who first ignited modern feminism by identifying "the problem that has no name," the unhappiness of bored, anxious housewives unfulfilled by lives of middle-class domesticity.

Millions of them now lived in single-family tract dream houses eagerly bought in the years after World War II. The Freudian orthodoxy then in vogue taught that a depressed or lonely woman, disillusioned or ungratified by the PTA, the carpool, and a gleaming kitchen floor, caused her own misery through unreasonable neurosis. According to the reigning ideology, soon to be universally known as the "feminine mystique," making a suburban home for a husband and kids provided satisfaction bounteous enough for any normal woman. But then a restless wife and mother in Rockland County, New York, coined that phrase as the title of a 1963 book, and women across the country realized with a flash of unforgettable recognition that the fault for their unhappiness was not entirely their own.

In writing that volume, Betty Friedan created both an instant best-seller and a publishing perennial. *The Feminine Mystique*, still in print, has sold over 3 million copies. It transformed the frustrations and anxieties of middle-class wives from the personal foibles of inadequate individuals into the talk of the nation. It transformed Betty Friedan from one of their anonymous numbers into a national figure. Three years after the book appeared, she founded the National Organization of Women, a flagship of feminism reborn. The new association boldly rejected "the traditional assumption that a woman has to choose between marriage and motherhood on the one hand and serious participation in industry or the professions on the other."[4] It demanded both equality in the workplace and all the facilities needed to make it possible: day care, maternity leave, legal abortion, and an Equal Rights Amendment to the Constitution to outlaw discrimination based on gender.

But if the problem that clouded Betty Friedan's suburban adulthood was initially nameless, the one that helped blight Bettye Naomi Goldstein's small-town girlhood had the old, familiar name of anti-Semitism. Born in Peoria, Illinois, in 1921, Bettye, as her name was originally spelled, grew up in material comfort and social unease. Her father, Harry, forty years old at his eldest child's birth, had come to America as a boy from the hinterland of Kiev. His family settled in St. Louis, but Harry was a peddler in Peoria by the age of thirteen. The fashionable jewelry business that he built there placed him among the town's most prosperous merchants. He married well, winning the hand of the beautiful Miriam Horowitz, eighteen years his junior and the daughter of a successful doctor who was also town health commissioner. Though Miriam had social aspirations and nourished them as society editor of the local newspaper, she abandoned journalism when she married. She appears to have spent the rest of her life mourning that loss.

From then on, neither Miriam nor the marriage was happy. Her husband, as well as Bettye, a second daughter, and their son became butts of her frustration. "Nothing we did was good enough" for her, the Goldsteins' eldest child remembered.[5] But the mother's thwarted ambitions soon focused on Bettye's outstanding academic ability. "She could not wait for me to get into junior high to put it into my mind to try for the school newspaper," then write for the high school literary magazine, and go off to college and become editor of the campus paper.[6]

Nothing Miriam tried in Peoria ever really fulfilled her. She dabbled in charity work for the synagogue, Hadassah, and the Community Chest. She grieved for her truncated career but never resumed it despite constant resolutions to resume writing. The Depression further sharpened conflict in the family, as Harry struggled to keep the jewelry store afloat and Miriam resisted any restrictions on her spending. She blamed him for the failure of her social ambitions. Though ranking among Peoria's better-off citizens, the Goldsteins never won social acceptance from prestigious Gentiles or membership in the country club to which their children's classmates belonged. Harry moved in the town's top business circles during the day but the invitations and good fellowship stopped at nightfall. Miriam, however, never faulted the local elite's anti-Jewish attitudes or sought a more satisfying social life within the Jewish community. Instead she berated her self-made immigrant husband for lacking the country clubbers' education, unaccented English, and social graces.

Harry understood, and explained to Bettye, that simple prejudice, not deficiencies in his speech or schooling, caused the snubs. He praised the "passion for justice" that grew out of her experience with discrimination.[7] He took an active part in the Peoria Jewish community and saw that Bettye was confirmed in the local Reform temple. In high school, as the only

Jewish girl in her class, she was the only one overlooked when bids to join sororities went out. Formerly popular but now isolated and miserable, she compiled an outstanding school record. Although she "suffered the actuality of anti-Semitism, [she] didn't experience [her]self as Jewish with either the solid strengths or the expectations of rejection of the Jewish girls from New York or Chicago or Cincinnati. I was never part of a Jewish crowd, a Jewish community, a group of Jewish friends."[8] With little grounding in Jewish tradition, she had no one to show her the sacred work of Jewish womanhood or how it gave meaning to the mundane female tasks of home and community.

At seventeen, she fled Peoria for prestigious Smith College in Massachusetts, where she fulfilled her mother's ambitions—and her own—by editing the newspaper, founding the literary magazine, and earning her psychology degree summa cum laude. In the fall she moved west to continue her psychology studies at another top school, the University of California in exciting, cosmopolitan Berkeley. Dropping the *e* from her first name and taking up a research fellowship, she began working toward a graduate degree. But her academic career lasted only a year. Still an excellent student, she worried that her brains would keep her from attracting a husband. After two semesters she left Berkeley for New York and a career in journalism. She lived in Greenwich Village and worked as reporter for a news service with decidedly left-wing views. A long-standing concern for social justice soon attracted her to the labor movement, and by 1946 she was a staff writer at *UE News*, a publication of the United Electrical, Radio and Machine Workers of America, whose communist leadership placed the union at the far left of the American labor movement.

The following year she married a Jewish ex-GI, Carl Friedan, who had an interest in the theater but found a career in advertising. Betty stayed at *UE News* until 1952. Pregnant with the second of their three children, she was fired from her full-time job, no reason given. "It's your fault for getting pregnant again," the head of Betty's Newspaper Guild unit told her.[9] "There was no word for sex discrimination, no law against it," she remembers. "But I bitterly felt the injustice of it, being fired because I was pregnant."[10]

In a way she was relieved to take up the housewifery that books and magazine articles assured her were woman's only true calling.[11] "'Career woman' in the fifties became a pejorative," she remembered, "denoting a ball-busting harpy from whom man and child should flee for very life."[12] Like countless contemporaries, the Friedans moved to the suburbs, where babies replaced the politics that had formerly engrossed her. Like Miriam, she found herself unhappily married to a man of lesser education than her own. Nonetheless, for ten years she focused her main energies on home-making. Choosing to live in Rockland County, which had only scant Jewish life, Betty and Carl identified themselves as Jews just strongly enough to provide their two sons "aesthetic bar mitzvahs" but their daughter neither a bat mitzvah nor a confirmation.[13]

Betty later described herself as leading the boring life of a housewife, but in fact, however, she remained active as a professional writer, albeit part-time, producing articles even as she fixed TV dinners and drove car-pools. With McCarthyism raging, however, she published her freelance pieces in mass-market women's magazines, not the politically engaged labor union organs of old. But commercial journalism did not satisfy the former scholar and labor activist. Her frustration was probably fortified when she learned, through a 1957 survey answered by several hundred of her Smith classmates, that others from her class of '42 also felt that they had made a poor bargain when they traded their intellectual aspirations for station wagons and split-levels. Many reported the very feelings of depres-sion, anxiety, and boredom that assailed Betty. And most blamed their unhappiness on their own inadequacies, not the on hollowness of the cur-rent domestic ideal. Pondering this widespread failure to find the prom-ised felicity in domesticity, Betty began to look elsewhere for the cause.

Perhaps she used methods of social analysis learned during her radical New York days, at Berkeley and at Smith to discern that societal and cul-tural forces, not personal failings, were driving women out of paid employ-ment and into full-time homemaking. Or perhaps, as she would later recount, a sudden epiphany revealed the role that the reigning ideal of all-consuming domesticity played in influencing all those millions of appar-ently individual choices. However it happened, her study of the survey results convinced her that the pervasive suburban ideology of male bread-winning and full-time female housekeeping—the idea that she shrewdly and euphoniously dubbed "the feminine mystique"—lay at the root of her and her classmates' malaise. Soon she was writing about what the survey results had taught her. In September 1960, *Good Housekeeping,* one of the nation's most popular and highest-paying women's service magazines, published her article "Women Are People Too!" An extraordinary flood of letters from readers revealed that "the problem that has no name" afflicted not only fellow alumnae of elite Seven Sister colleges but women from a wide range of backgrounds all over the country.

Though Betty claims to have experienced her life as housewifery, writing for an outlet as prominent and lucrative as *Good Housekeeping* testifies to professional journalistic skills and contacts of a high order. She soon put them to use expanding the article into her epoch-making book. Written in a sure-handed, smoothly commercial style, it demolished both the "mystique" and the advertisers, magazines, TV shows, writers, educators, Freudian psychologists, and others who fostered and spread it. Women suffered not because of their personal failings, she explained, but because American society forced them into subservience and kept them from becoming the autonomous adults their education supposedly prepared them to be. The pervasive ideology of domesticity—her "feminine mystique"—brainwashed women to seek happiness not by developing their talents in the world of work but in subordinating their ambitions in the service of husband and children.

For Betty, wifely existence in America was essentially Miriam's Peoria writ large. Alienated, like Gloria Steinem, from Judaism's ancient vision of homemaking as a sacred and surpassingly important calling, Betty argued that housewifery produced frustration, depression, futility, and despair. Separated by both distance and social status from the need or even the possibility of playing a crucial role in the family economy, women's work had become servile, isolated, and trivial. Unaware of the countless Jewish forebears who had combined homemaking and earning into lives of service to family and community, Betty saw household responsibilities as inimical to women living lives of meaning and respect. For her, womanly fulfillment, satisfaction, and self-esteem lay in neither home nor community, but in the wider world of publicly recognized professional achievement. Only equality with men, not significant accomplishment in specifically womanly pursuits, could provide true scope for individual ability. Rather than something nurturant or sanctified or creative or vital to larger purposes, "there is," Betty wrote, "something dangerous about being a housewife."[14]

Once the volume containing those words appeared, neither America's nor Betty's life would ever be the same again. Suddenly she was not an anonymous suburbanite at the supermarket or the Little League, but a national figure, symbol and leading exponent of an explosively controversial ideology. Women by the thousands rapturously devoured the book, instantly recognizing in it a misery they had not realized that they suffered. Thousands of others, including many of her neighbors, angrily rejected an analysis that profoundly threatened the lives and identities they had built around their suburban homes. And across the country, couples who had gone to the altar or the *chuppah* to make the middle-class bargain—he would go out to work and she would stay at home—suddenly, and often painfully, found themselves renegotiating the very basis of the their daily lives together.

Arrangements that women had deemed perfectly acceptable, even desirable, in the postwar era of suburban nest building all at once appeared outmoded, even oppressive, in light of Betty's insight. Until then, middle-class American women who worked for pay had generally paid homage to the domestic ideology by phrasing their careers as subservient to "true" womanliness. On the airwaves, in print, and in kitchens and bedrooms everywhere, Americans were suddenly arguing about the role gender should play in society. "Suddenly my wife got bitten by the feminist career bug," one professional-class Jewish ex-husband recalls. "First she started making all kinds of demands on me to take care of the children and the house. Then she wanted to leave the marriage altogether."[15]

Many couples managed to reach new understandings, but many others did not. Opponents of change argued that liberating women from their postwar preoccupation with housewifery—a notion widely trivialized as "women's lib"—posed a major threat to the traditional American home. Soon the equality of women was not only a topic for marital bickering or theoretical debate, but a plan for political and social action. In addition to spearheading NOW, Betty helped found the National Women's Political Caucus to elect women to political offices at every level. She worked with Bella Abzug, who in 1970 won a congressional seat after an overtly feminist campaign.

A Long Revival

Betty Friedan is widely credited with firing the opening shot in the second campaign of American feminism. The first campaign, after decades of struggle, secured women the vote in 1920 but subsided under the onslaught of Depression and world war. The second campaign began with a broader goal than formal political equality. Feminists now sought full equality with men in political, social, legal, and economic opportunity and power. Driving the mighty movement that, over the next several decades, utterly remade American society and life was something far deeper and more powerful than any reaction to any single book. Beneath the surface of postwar convention and conformity, potent social forces had been working largely unnoticed.

By the 1960s, American colleges enrolled as many women as men.[16] White-collar jobs suitable for female workers multiplied rapidly in the prosperous economy. To be sure, thousands of female war workers had traded their hardhats and workboots for frilly aprons and dust cloths when the GIs came home to reclaim their old jobs. Nonetheless, between 1940 and 1960 the long-term trend in female employment rose steadily, the percentage of all women working jumping from 25 percent to 35 percent. The proportion of wives working soared even more sharply, doubling from 15 percent to 30 percent.[17] Jewish women, with their higher than average education and smaller than average families, were especially well suited to find jobs. Although American birthrates remained at historic highs, the postwar baby boom had only a few more years to run. By the time Betty's book was in wide circulation, so were the first oral contraceptives. So stunning was the impact of easy, esthetically pleasing, and essentially foolproof birth control that Americans immediately and universally called the revolutionary tablets in the little plastic cases The Pill.

The mood of the country and its attitude toward established custom were also changing quickly. In the early 1950s, black Americans began to demand an end to the legalized segregation that for generations had barred them throughout the South from schools, colleges, hotels, restaurants, waiting rooms, parks, restrooms, drinking fountains, and every other kind of public facility used by whites. In Montgomery, Alabama, ordinary working people had discovered the power of concerted action by merely refusing to ride the segregated city buses. The simple determination by thousands of citizens to walk until they could ride in dignity forced an end to the practice of confining black riders to the back of the bus. In 1954, a legal team headed by attorney Thurgood Marshall, who later became the first African American U.S. Supreme Court justice, used the landmark case of *Brown v. Board of Education of Topeka* to destroy the legal basis of racial segregation. Jurisdictions across the South had to choose between accepting black students (often in token numbers) in formerly all-white public schools and shutting their school systems down altogether. Some for a time picked the latter course, and President Eisenhower used federal troops to safeguard the handful of black students who first enrolled at Little Rock's Central High School. President Kennedy did the same at the University of Alabama.

Beyond legal and governmental maneuvering, private citizens of both races bucked stiff and often violent resistance from southern whites and organized for change. Black high school and college students devoted to the philosophy of nonviolence took the lead. Across the South, in polite, neatly dressed groups, they "sat in" at dimestore lunch counters formerly restricted to whites, quietly waiting, sometimes for hours, and often in the face of heckling, harassment, and physical assault, for service that never came. Integrated bands of male and female "freedom riders" traveled together on interstate buses, trying to sit together in still segregated waiting rooms, eat together at still segregated lunch counters, and together use still segregated restrooms. Across the South, peaceful demonstrators marched, sang, and knelt in prayer before stores, schools, and other institutions that would not admit, hire, or otherwise treat blacks equally with whites. As desegregation marches filled TV screens, as arrested civil rights demonstrators filled southern jails, as appalled evening news viewers watched policeman attack unresisting demonstrators with dogs and firehoses, as whites across the nation began taking sides in the controversy, civil rights zoomed to the top of national consciousness.

As victims of similar, though admittedly far less severe, discrimination, Jews had a long-standing concern about equality. At least since the early decades of the twentieth century, some had joined forces with blacks to end legalized racism. Jews helped found the National Association for the Advancement of Colored People and other civil rights organizations, gave crucial financial backing to the desegregation effort, and worked on the NAACP legal team that prevailed in *Brown*. As northern white youngsters swelled the student wing of the civil rights movement in the early 1960s, young Jews, who constituted 3 percent of the nation's college-aged population and 10 percent of its collegians, accounted for well over a third of the white student activists.[18] The hundreds of Jewish youths who went south during the 1960s in the cause of civil rights included many women. Dorothy Miller, a staffer with the Student Nonviolent Coordinating Committee for several years during her twenties, ultimately married a SNCC colleague, Robert Zellner. Harriet Tanzman, twenty-five, spent six months as a Selma, Alabama, field worker for Martin Luther King's Southern Christian Leadership Conference. Twenty-three-year-old Carol Ruth Silver joined an otherwise all-male Freedom Ride in 1961 and spent over a month in the racially segregated Jackson, Mississippi, jail. More than half of her thirteen freedom-riding white female cell mates were fellow Jews. A year later, the "Albany nine" activists, including Joni Rabinowitz, faced charges in

Georgia. Harvard law student and future congresswoman Elizabeth Holtzman, then twenty-two, worked on their defense.

In 1964, the student movement's most ambitious project to date led to perhaps the most savage and notorious outrage of the civil rights struggle: the murder of three young members of the Freedom Summer campaign. As hundreds of white volunteers fanned out across Mississippi to register voters and teach literacy, James Cheney, Andrew Goodman, and Michael Schwerner, all in their early twenties, disappeared while driving one night near Meridian. James was the son of a poor local black family, but Andrew and Michael came from prosperous, liberal, upper-middle Jewish class homes in Manhattan and the New York suburb of Pelham, respectively. Their bodies were eventually discovered buried in an earthen dam. Rita Levant Schwerner, Michael's 22-year-old widow and partner in his civil rights work, and a Jewish daughter of suburban Mount Vernon, New York, became, thin and haggard in her cotton summer dress, a national icon of horror and grief. And in addition to students such as Rachel Brown Cowan, who would later adopt her husband Paul's Judaism and become the first female convert to enter the American rabbinate, civil rights workers in Mississippi that year included adult professionals such as June Finer, M.D., who ran a clinic, and Florence Howe, a college professor who headed a "freedom school."

The movement grew and its demonstrations swelled in the wake of that bloody student season. Later in 1964 it achieved a major goal, passage of the national Civil Rights Act, which outlawed racial and religious discrimination in public accommodations, housing, and employment. Along with dismantling racial segregation aimed at blacks, it opened may new opportunities for Jews. Corporations, law firms, and other employers that had routinely excluded them now faced legal consequences if those policies continued. Neighborhoods and apartment building previously off-limits to Jewish residents opened to those with the means to pay the same prices as gentile purchasers or renters. Well into the 1960s, the ascendancy of white male Anglo-Saxon Protestants over the nation's elite institutions remained virtually complete. The Ivy League universities, for example, presented a solid phalanx of presidents who could trace their ancestry to the British Isles. Men of similar background occupied the executive suites of the nation's major industrial companies.

Over time, the civil rights law allowed Jews to land jobs and then promotions in a wide range of organizations previously closed to them. The immense and long-standing investment that Jewish families had made in education now greased the new generation's way into the national upper-middle and even upper classes. By the 1970s, Jewish adults had, on average, fourteen years of schooling, half a year more than the average Episcopalian, who belonged to the nation's most prestigious and prosperous denomination.[19] Four out of five Jewish youngsters went to college, but fewer than half of non-Jews. Jews were likelier than other students to attend elite schools, composing 17 percent of students at private universities in 1971.[20] They were likelier to get good grades, producing twice as many Phi Beta Kappas as their share of the student population.[21]

The faculties as well as the student bodies of leading universities, once largely Protestant preserves, now welcomed Jewish talent. People who once would have happily become Depression-era public school teachers now sought careers as professors. By the mid-1970s, Jews accounted for one in five of those teaching at elite universities and one in four of those in the Ivy League. The younger faculty cohorts and the schools of law and medicine were even more strongly Jewish. Progress in the world of big business was less conspicuous, but Jews, who had long shunned large corporations in favor of their own enterprises, now began to succeed there as well.

The rise of two men named Shapiro signaled the new world of opportunity. In 1973, Irving Shapiro, a son of Minneapolis whose immigrant father made his living pressing pants, became the chief executive officer and chairman of the Du Pont Corporation, the nation's largest chemical producer and its oldest major industrial firm. Harold Shapiro, a Montreal-born economist, and no relation to Irving, became Princeton's president in 1986. Though once the most socially restrictive of the Ivy League schools, with a Jewish enrollment of 2 percent in the 1930s, the Princeton that Shapiro would lead had a student body one-fifth Jewish.[22] So commonplace were Jews in high places by then that the *New York Times* did not bother to mention his religion in either of its two articles noting his selection. Even in the world of entertainment, overt Jewishness, long taboo, was becoming acceptable, even sexy. In 1964, twenty-two-year-old Brooklyn-born Barbra Streisand won the Academy Award for her portrayal of Fannie Brice in the hit film *Funny Girl*. Unlike Brice, though, Streisand refused to alter either her name or her unmistakably Jewish looks. Over four decades as a bankable movie star, Grammy-winning singer, and film director, she would model for millions of women a vividly dark-haired, almond-eyed, prominent-nosed version of glamour.

A Revolution for Women

The Civil Rights Act's epoch-making bans on racial and religious discrimination attracted the major attention, but a provision called Title VII also outlawed job discrimination based on gender. In 1966 President Lyndon Johnson issued an executive order requiring firms seeking government business to do more than merely refrain from discriminating against nonwhite job applicants and employees. To get federal contracts, companies now had to take "affirmative action" to make their workforce resemble the racial makeup of their local labor pool. The next year, the requirement was expanded to include women. Employers now not only accepted applications from women and blacks they might formerly have automatically rejected but began seeking them out. Qualified members of both groups were actively encouraged to take jobs and enter fields previously limited to white men. Despite significant resistance, various well-paid, and often unionized, skilled trades also began opening to formerly rejected people who began earning incomes that could support a middle-class lifestyle.

No group in America was better situated to profit from these new opportunities than Jewish women. With their college degrees and middle-class polish, they had the skills and credentials that many employers sought. With their belief in women's right and ability to act in the world—inherited from foremothers who had pioneered Council and Hadassah, marched on picket lines, worked beside men in factories, organized religious schools and synagogues, made careers as teachers, run stores and boarding houses, and crossed the plains and the ocean—they had the confidence that careerists need. Larger and larger numbers of young Jewish women began aiming higher, at such heavily male professions as law, medicine, journalism, accounting, and college teaching. A 1970 lawsuit challenging federal contracts with colleges and universities not practicing effective affirmative action intensified the search for female academics, at least at the lower faculty ranks. Two years later, Title IX of the 1972 Education Act banned educational programs receiving federal funds from discriminating on sexual grounds. Educational, athletic, and other programs available to men now became available to women too. The year after that, the Supreme Court handed down the precedent-shattering decision in the case of *Roe v. Wade*, overturning the generations-old ban on legal abortion and affirming each woman's right to the privacy to decide when and whether she would reproduce.

The civil rights movement overturned more than antiquated laws. Its highly successful tactics—marches, sit-ins, and nonviolent civil disobedience—quickly spread as other youthful causes began to catch fire. By the late 1960s, turmoil swept the campuses, fueled by intense resistance to the Vietnam war and by student demands for reforms in curriculum and college life. Once again, Jews filled both the ranks and the leadership of the protests. With rebellions and liberation struggles flaring everywhere, female activists, at first gradually and one by one, began reflecting on their experience in the liberal and radical movements. Men, they began to notice, exercised the leadership, devised the strategies, held the press conferences, made the speeches, planned the demonstrations. Women ran the mimeograph machines, typed the manifestos, made the coffee and, in keeping with the new ethic of sexual freedom, often shared their male comrades' beds. Some of the young people struggling for equality, women activists increasingly realized, were, in George Orwell's familiar phrase, decidedly more equal than others. A movement devoted to equality of the races had ignored equality of the sexes. The struggle to free men from unwanted war service subjected women to unwanted subservience. When female activists pointed out these apparent inconsistencies, their male comrades often answered them with derision and scorn.

The Personal Is Political

Radical young women now became doubly radicalized. They began applying to their own situation the leftist analytical tools they had learned in class and in antiwar teach-ins. American society, they concluded, made females an oppressed group needing liberation as badly as any racial minority. Education and intelligence equal or even superior to men's, as Ruth Ginsburg had discovered a decade earlier, did not entitle women to equal influence, power, or opportunity in the larger society.

Having just watched organized righteous anger overturn decades-old segregation laws and hamper an ongoing war effort, young women determined that the rules governing their own position in society must also change. They were determined to use their energies in a struggle for what they called women's liberation. First in New York, Boston, and other major intellectual centers, and then on campuses and in cities and towns across America, young, white middle-class women began to meet to discuss their situation. These gatherings had the goal of making women aware—in the parlance of the day, of raising their consciousness—about the injustice toward females—the sexism—pervasive in American society. Recognizing this structural injustice—making the personal political, as the saying went—was, according to fashionable revolutionary doctrine, the first step toward destroying it. Along with disillusioned veterans of the student movement and Friedan's disgruntled housewives, other tributaries of the American left also flowed into the new feminism. These included middle-aged campaigners for peace and nuclear disarmament such as Bella Abzug, who in the 1950s had joined with friends from her Hunter College days during World War II to organize Women Strike for Peace.

As in the civil rights and antiwar movements that preceded it, a striking number of new feminists were Jews. Along with Betty Friedan, prominent Jewish feminists included Abzug; psychologist Phyllis Chesler, author of a seminal feminist critique of Freudian psychology called *Women and Madness;* and writers Robin Morgan, Vivian Gornick, Shulamith Firestone, and Andrea Dworkin, among many others. Feminist opinion ranged from demanding equality within the context of family life to totally rejecting traditional marriage, motherhood, and sexual relations as means of oppressing and exploiting females. Though some of the leading Jewish activists and theorists came from actively Jewish backgrounds, those who took the more radical positions were generally secularists, unfamiliar with and even hostile to religious tradition and ignorant of the notion of motherhood and homemaking as special, sacred callings. Many defined legitimate female accomplishment solely in terms of professional achievement. Most, however, retained a residual Jewish sense of social justice, often in messianic form and frequently transmitted to them by leftist or communist parents.

Bella Abzug was a notable exception. Three decades before, as thirteen-year-old Bella Savitzky, she had insisted on saying Kaddish for her beloved father Emanuel, an immigrant butcher. The men objected on the grounds that this was a male duty and prerogative. But she ignored them, praying in the women's section of her family's Orthodox shul each morning before school for the entire year that tradition commands a son to mourn. Emanuel, however, had only daughters. Her defiance taught Bella a lifelong lesson about doing what she thought was right. "People may not like it," she said years later, "but no one will stop you."[23] Independent thinking she had learned at home. Emanuel, proprietor of the Live and Let Live Meat Market in Manhattan's Chelsea neighborhood, used his shop sign to protest the carnage of World War I; her mother, Esther, backed Bella's rebellions and supported the family as a department store clerk after her husband died.

Bella had already also learned Hebrew and the prayers from attending services with her grandfather and from years of Hebrew school. Her religious studies continued through supplementary Hebrew high school and classes at the Jewish Theological Seminary while she attended Hunter. Gifted with musical ability and a fine singing voice, young Bella gained recognition as the star davener of the women's section. By eleven she was a stalwart of Hashomer Hatzair (Hebrew for the Young Guard), a left-wing Zionist youth group. With fellow adolescent socialists, she hiked, danced, hung out, planned their future lives as kibbutzniks in Palestine, and collected money for the homeland, often orating to passersby at subway stops.

An outstanding student and leader, she served as president of her class at Walton High School and on the Hunter student council. After her first choice, Harvard Law School, rejected her—as it did all women until 1952—she attended Columbia Law School on scholarship. Elected to the law review, she nonetheless married Martin Abzug, an aspiring writer and ex-GI whose family owned a profitable garment business. The easygoing Martin had no objection to his dynamic bride continuing her studies. He agreed that she could work after they wed and became parents, and he even typed her law school papers because she never learned how—a tactic used by some educated young women to avoid being shunted into secretarial work. Forty years later, the National Women's Political Caucus, created by Bella, inaugurated the annual Martin Abzug Memorial Award for husbands who helped their wives realize their ambitions.

As good as his word, Martin stood by Bella as she began her career in labor law. He worked in his family's company and later as a stockbroker. He also wrote two published novels. Bella quickly found, however, that a pretty, redheaded young woman did not get the respect due the legal representative of auto, restaurant, and mill workers' union locals. But no one asked her to get the coffee, she discovered, when she wore a hat. Large-brimmed headgear that distinguished her from clerks and secretaries would be her trademark throughout her subsequent legal, political, and congressional careers.

Bella gave birth to their first daughter in 1949 and to their second in 1952. She continued practicing law, now as a solo practitioner defending intellectuals and performers snared in the anti-Communist cases of the 1950s. She famously defended Willie McGee, a black Mississippian ultimately executed for allegedly raping a white woman who was actually his willing lover in an extended affair. McGee's repeated trials and appeals attracted worldwide attention and brought Bella before the U.S. Supreme Court, where she won a stay on the grounds that "Negroes were systematically excluded from jury service."[24] The pregnant Bella traveled to Jackson, Mississippi, on her client's behalf, once spending a night in the local bus station when no hotel in town would rent to her. Neither her passionate advocacy nor the protests erupting at home and abroad saved McGee's life. Miscarriage claimed Bella's pregnancy.

Despite busy work lives, Bella and Martin enjoyed an active family life with their children in suburban Mount Vernon, the same bedroom town where Rita Levant was growing up. But in 1965, the Abzugs defied upper-middle-class convention and abandoned suburban serenity for bustling, dynamic Greenwich Village. Bella plunged into local Democratic reform politics and five years later her neighborhood, along with Chelsea, Little Italy, the Lower East Side and the West Side, sent her, now fifty, to Washington for the first of three congressional terms. She won on the slogan "This woman's place is in the House."[25]

Casting her maiden congressional vote for the Equal Rights Amendment, which passed both the House and Senate but ultimately failed to win the required number of state ratifications, Bella quickly emerged as a leading national spokeswoman for the political branch of resurgent feminism. She organized a congressional caucus on issues relating to women, worked successfully to outlaw sex discrimination in credit and mortgages, and supported many bills on feminist causes such as child care, abortion rights, and Social Security eligibility for homemakers. The legal basis for female equality expanded during her years in Congress, partially through legislation and partially because of a battery of court decisions won by lawyers like Ruth Bader Ginsburg.

An Unexpected Turning

In 1975 Bella's feminist activities took her and many other Americans to Mexico City for the first of a series of international conferences marking the United Nations International Women's Decade. Thousands of female delegates from countries around the world convened to discuss their common struggle for equality in their homelands and in the world at large. But instead of the solidarity they had expected to feel with their sisters from every continent, Bella and other American Jews felt a shocking sense of isolation and rejection, this time not from the men of their religious community but from the women of their beloved feminist movement. In the aftermath of two recent Arab-Israeli wars, many Third World delegations wanted to include in the conference's official declaration an Arab-instigated claim that "Zionism is racism." Bella, the congressional adviser to the U.S. delegation, denounced as "totally unacceptable" the proposal "that Zionism must be eliminated along with colonialism and apartheid."[26] At her behest, the Americans, Jews and Gentiles alike, voted solidly, though futilely, against the declaration's passage. For the first time, Jewish feminists began to suspect that their much vaunted sisterhood, though powerful, might not be free of ancient religious bigotry. For the first time in years, even decades, some began to wonder whether they were not only women but also Jews.

Five years later, the second U.N. Women's Conference in Copenhagen "was even worse," recalled *Ms.* editor and writer Letty Pogrebin. Ironically, in the capital of a nation that during World War II rescued virtually its entire Jewish population from the Nazis, "Jewish women of every nationality" found themselves "isolated, excoriated, and tyrannized" by blatant, casual, pervasive anti-Semitism.[27] One evening, at a briefing by the American delegates on the day's events, "an American black woman rose to accuse our delegation of deferring to the Jews," remembers Barbara Leslie, who was representing the International Council of Jewish Women. "She said she couldn't understand what was wrong with saying that Zionism is racism. Women of all races applauded her statement."

Bella Abzug, however, rose to her feet. "'I'll tell you what Zionism is,' she said. 'It is a liberation movement for a people who have been persecuted all their lives and throughout human history.'"[28] Few other Americans rose to Bella's defense, and some feared that "Gloria Steinem, Betty Friedan, and Bella Abzug all being Jewish gives the American women's movement a bad name," Letty Pogrebin recalls. Some people even said in her hearing that "the only way to rid the world of Zionism is to kill all the Jews."[29] Novelist E. M. (Esther Masserman) Broner had a similar experience. A U.N. staffer told her that "Denmark is wonderful, but the Germans take it over in the summer, and I hate them. They only did one thing right—they killed the Jews." Appalled, Broner made "choking sounds" and the woman asked in dismay, "Oh, did I hurt your feelings . . . are you German?"[30]

Feminists who felt bound to the Jewish people, even if by long-forgotten ties, could no longer ignore the deep strain of anti-Semitism among many in their movement. By 1982, Letty Pogrebin had written in *Ms.* about the taint of bigotry among women's liberation activists. Nor did feminist antipathy to Jews and Jewish life end with the political. Some Christian religious theorists blamed Judaism for dethroning the beneficent goddess figure that had allegedly ruled Middle Eastern religions before the Hebrew Bible replaced her with a vengeful, masculine, Mosaic God.

For the first time in years—and in some cases, for the first time in their lives—some of the nation's leading feminists began to explore not only how to be a woman seeking equality and meaning but a Jewish woman on that search. Women of nominally Jewish background often did not feel the pull of this ancient tie. For others, though, the tug back to observance, to the tradition of their mothers and fathers, proved irresistible. Many feminists committed to Jewishness found that being a woman equal to men was not enough. They also needed to find ways to be Jewish among their fellow Jews. To find them, they would have to remake American Judaism.

16

"RESPONSIBLE FOR
THEIR OWN JUDAISM"

Demanding Religious Equality

One evening in 1955, fifteen-year-old Letty Cottin of Queens, New York, was abandoned by—and abandoned—the faith of her ancestors. The break with the tradition her family revered happened soon after her mother died. Letty's father, Jacob, an observant Jew active in his Conservative congregation, followed the full rites of shivah for his wife. The customary quorum of friends and relatives gathered at their home for the Kaddish, which can be offered only as part of public prayer. By reciting these ancient words, immediate family members would both honor Cyral Halpern Cottin's memory and fulfill their personal obligations to mourn her formally.

Raised in Cyral and Jacob's traditional household and educated in part at the Yeshiva of Central Queens and the Jamaica Jewish Center Hebrew High School, Letty hoped to join in this deeply symbolic ritual. She had celebrated her bat mitzvah only two years before and had attended synagogue often. But still, the men asked Cyral's daughter to leave the room as they began the prayer expressing grief for her loss. They intended no personal hurt or insult. As a female, even a Jewishly well-educated one who had reached the age of majority, Letty simply did not count in the minyan. In a flash of anger at that offhand rejection, the grieving girl abruptly turned her back on the "male-run religion personified by my Daddy," she remembered years later. A few words severed her emotional link to a community that had in its turn "excise[d] women from the healing of Jewish mourning rituals and prevent[ed] closure."[1]

Long afterward, Letty would recognize her feelings that evening for what they were: an early stirring of the impulses that would lead her to feminism. But in that pivotal moment she had no idea that a new age had begun. She only knew that, despite being the intellectual and educational equal of Jewish boys her age, she was not their equal in respect. And she knew with equal certainty that this inequality was unjust and intolerable. Any minyan would have welcomed as a chief mourner a son of her age who had only a fraction of her extensive Jewish education or even none at all. The men would have put comforting arms around his young shoulders, patted his kippah-covered head, spoken kindly as they helped him pronounce the soothing, singsong words.

But her sex alone banished her from formal, liturgical recognition of her bereavement. "For the next fifteen years," she has recounted, she "did nothing" formally Jewish, even as she went about marrying and establishing her own family, "except for celebrating the holidays in my house to honor [both] my mother's memory" and the elaborate home celebrations that Cyral had arranged.[2] "Rebellion was one thing; giving up the Jewish holidays was something else. I wasn't going to let my alienation from my father's religious institutions cut me off from the rituals . . . associated with my mother and the home-based Judaism in which my heritage seemed . . . most real."[3]

A lawyer's daughter, she went on to Brandeis University, where she paid little attention to the active religious life on campus. After graduating with honors in 1959, she returned to New York to work in publishing. Four years later she married a young lawyer named Bertrand Pogrebin. Her editing and writing continued after she and Bertrand became parents of twin daughters and a son. As a founding editor of *Ms.* magazine, she helped articulate the discontent of her educated American generation. Not until the epiphany of Mexico City did she make a connection between her American feminist present and her Jewish past.

Feminists of Letty's time belonged to the first generation of female East European descendants to receive essentially the same Jewish training as males and to an American generation that grew up in postwar material comfort. They felt confident and comfortable in their American identities but stymied in their Jewish roles. As awareness of feminist anti-Semitism grew, as well as the tug of recollection, simply denouncing the Judaism of their childhood as outdated patriarchy would no longer do for many women like Letty. As she herself had long realized, renouncing the rituals redolent of past generations, the customs rich with memory of the beloved dead, deadened rather than liberated the spirit. Only by finding new, modern, spiritually and intellectually satisfying ways to be Jewish, only by blazing routes back to the sources of their peoplehood, could these women continue to grow as feminists and as human beings.

And so, just as American Jews in every generation had devised ways of being Jewish that matched the American lives they lived, women of the second feminist generation began to do the same. Striding toward equality in their educational and professional lives, they rejected as intolerable the old restrictions imposed by Jewish ritual and custom. Just as Rebecca Gratz and her contemporaries almost completely took over one of traditional Judaism's central male roles, just as the club women of Council, Hadassah, and the sisterhoods taught not only their children but themselves; just as the first American-born East European generation brought women visibly into Conservative and Orthodox worship, this new generation began to demand what they considered their rightful place in the American Jewish world. And that place, many of them insisted, was on the *bimah*, in the board room, in the seminary—everywhere men exerted power and leadership.

A Jewish Feminism, a Feminist Judaism

This meant rethinking—refeeling—many aspects of Jewish life in female terms. Letty and a number of friends, including, for example, Bella Abzug, the Orthodox-raised Phyllis Chesler, and others, felt a need to read the story of the Exodus from Egypt differently and more deeply than they had at their families' Passover table—in a sense "raising their consciousness" about the possible meanings of freedom. Many had experienced the festival as weeks of cleaning and cooking done by women followed by two nights of ceremony conducted by men. But in 1976 a group of feminist "seder sisters" gathered for their first women's seder to discuss and witness the Jewish people's freedom through female eyes, through the exploits not only of Moses and Aaron but the ingenuity and courage of other figures central to the liberation: Miriam, her mother, Yochevet, and the midwives Shifra and Puah.

Attending this first Jewish religious ceremony of her life, Gloria Steinem realized that "there was room in the women's movement for the spiritual."[4] One of the earliest of the many groups that now regularly hold women's seders, the New York circle has continued the custom for a quarter century, reserving the third night of the festival for this observance. E. M. Broner's *Women's Haggadah*, published in *Ms.* in 1976, provided a ritual framework for continuing explorations. That same year *Lilith: The*

Independent Jewish Women's Magazine began appearing, dedicated to fostering "discussion of Jewish women's issues and put[ting] them on the agenda of the Jewish community, with a view to giving women—who are more than 50 percent of the world's Jews—greater choice in Jewish life."[5] Named for Adam's mythic consort before the creation of Eve, it takes an irreverent, female-centered but knowledgeably Jewish perspective on modern life. By the 1990s, about twenty-five thousand well-educated, prosperous, mostly married middle-class women—who read almost one book a week—saw each quarterly issue.[6]

As the founders of the national feminist movement were feeling their way back to Jewish tradition and seeking ways to fit Judaism into feminism, women who had never left the tradition were working on the problem from the other end: how to make room for the women's movement within Judaism. Jewishly committed readers of *Ms.* and *The Feminist Mystique* began to question ever more sharply why the equality and respect they sought at home and on the job should not be theirs in the synagogue as well. Reform Judaism, of course, had long considered male and female worshipers equals in regard to seating, education, confirmation, appearing on the *bimah,* and the like. By the 1960s many congregations permitted bat mitzvah, though it had not yet become widespread. But for all this apparent evenhandedness, positions of leadership, both religious and administrative, eluded Reform's women.

As Paula Ackerman's sojourn in the pulpit had shown, not even the nation's most liberal denomination would admit women to the ultimate equality—rabbinic status. Still, attitudes were gradually shifting. Several women had served as congregational presidents during the 1950s. In the year following Paula's appointment, Beatrice Sanders replaced her recently deceased husband, Gilbert, as the lay prayer leader at Temple Aaron in little Trinidad, Colorado, a former mining town that could no longer support a rabbi. The year after that, Temple Israel in Akron, Ohio, asked Libbie Levin Braverman, who had headed the religious school at another local Reform congregation, to fill in for a rabbi who had just been fired.

In 1955 Temple Avodah, a Reform congregation in suburban Oceanside, New York, marked another first by hiring Betty Robbins. The *New York Times* reported on its front page that Robbins was, in the opinion of "a spokesman for the School of Sacred Music of the Hebrew Union College-Jewish Institute of Religion . . . the first woman cantor in 5000 years of Jewish history."[7] Like the appointments of Paula and Beatrice, however, this arrangement arose from an exceptional set of circumstances, not from a formal change in policy. Born in Greece and raised in the town of Sopot, Poland, Betty (née Berta Abramson), as a child, so loved the recordings of the famous cantor Yossele Rosenblatt that she asked to join her synagogue boys' choir. Initially refused, she sang at services so loudly and fervently that the rabbi relented. She also talked her way into the all-male heder on the condition that she sit apart from the other students and behind a curtain. Trading her braids for a short bob, she sang solos with the choir from the age of eight until she was fourteen.

That same year, 1938, her father moved the family from Poland to Australia. Four years later, at a synagogue dance in Sydney, Betty met Corporal Sheldon Robbins, a GI medic on leave from the U.S. Army Air Force in New Guinea. They married in 1943, and she reached the United States a year later on a transport for war brides. By the early 1950s, Betty, Sheldon, and their three (soon to be four) children had moved to suburban Oceanside and joined Temple Avodah. Betty's extensive liturgical knowledge made her a standout in the congregation. When, just before the High Holidays, the temple unexpectedly needed a new cantor, she seemed an obvious choice. The board checked with their rabbi and other experts who concluded, as reported in the *Times*, that "there was no religious law, merely a tradition, against women becoming cantors."[8]

For Conservative Jews, however, the law did present a real obstacle to ritual equality. Women sat with men in the sanctuaries of most congregations, but they did not count in the minyan or generally appear on the *bimah*. But Saturday after Saturday, year after year, in synagogue basements and social halls across the country, Conservative girls and boys in the movement's coed Hebrew schools led weekly "Junior Congregation" Sabbath services for their fellow students. Summer after summer, in camp rec halls or under the open sky, both girls and boys gave sermons during daily or Sabbath prayers. Why, wondered the female products of these religious education programs, could they not do in the main sanctuary as grown women what they had always done in the social hall or at the lakeside as girls?

Such disabilities, of course, had been part of Jewish life from time immemorial. But many of the mothers and grandmothers who had climbed the stairs to the women's section and deferred while the men davened and divided up the Torah honors had cultivated their own special, and often highly spiritual, ways of being Jewish. Shul represented only one, and in many ways far from the most important, arena of Jewish expression. The home and the world of womanly community action provided bountiful opportunities for sanctity and sacred purposefulness. Making Sabbath and the holidays, raising the next generation, keeping the laws of *kashrut*, and fulfilling the specifically female mitzvot of lighting candles, preparing challah, and guarding marital purity had connected the believing woman to the law. A rich devotional literature in Yiddish and other Jewish vernaculars had connected her to her God, especially the loving, nurturing qualities associated with the Shechinah, the deity's feminine side or, in some interpretations, His consort. The pious traditional woman may never have recited the full Hebrew liturgy in shul, but no day passed without her reciting *tekhinnes*, special devotions that sanctified the events and emotions of her life.

By the 1960s, as surely as the notion of a separate and valid female sphere was vanishing from the larger society, it was disappearing from Judaism too. For most educated, middle-class suburban Americans, religion no longer pervaded daily life but happened mainly in the synagogue. Lighting candles at home no longer held a candle to participating fully in public prayer. Nor did serving in Council, sisterhood, or Hadassah quench the thirst for participation among women aspiring to formerly male-only careers. With the sacred female realm now a vague memory and the institutional synagogue now the sole vessel of Jewish life and identity, with traditional careers in unpaid Jewish communal service increasingly discredited as professional opportunities opened, the old restrictions rankled ever more severely. Separate spheres, the new generation had learned in *Brown v. Board of Education*, were inherently unequal. To have a role and realm different from men's was to have a status inferior to theirs. For the knowledgeable, committed young women who cared enough about Judaism to remain Conservative, full religious personhood now required full ritual equality with men.

In 1972, as the U.S. Congress was outlawing gender discrimination in higher education and *Ms.* editors were putting the finishing touches on their first issue, a group of young women arrived at the Concord Hotel in Lake Kiamesha, New York, for the annual convention of the Rabbinical Assembly, the professional association of Conservative rabbis. Like Hannah Greenebaum Solomon's committee in Chicago eighty years before, they were not deemed worthy of inclusion in the official schedule of the men's meeting. So, like Hannah and her friends, they proceeded to organize a meeting of their own, attended largely by women, primarily wives accompanying the rabbis to this leading "borscht belt" resort. And like the organizers of the congress in Chicago, they issued a manifesto calling for drastic change in Jewish life and women's role within it.

These insurgents called themselves, with a touch of irony, Ezrat Nashim, which literally means "help of women." In ancient times, it referred to the temple court where the women congregated and, in later centuries, to the women's section of the synagogue. Knowledgeable, earnest, impassioned young alumnae of Conservative Hebrew schools and summer camps, they told their approving audience that the days when "Judaism views women as separate but equal" must soon end.[9] "Jewish tradition regarding women, once far ahead of other cultures, has now fallen disgracefully behind," they proclaimed. "Life-patterns open to women, appropriate and even progressive for the rabbinic and medieval periods, are entirely unacceptable to us today."[10] Jewish marriage law must be equalized, they insisted. Not only the man but also the woman deserved the right to initiate divorce. Husbands who deserted without granting a religious divorce should no longer be allowed to leave women *agunot*, "chained" wives unable to remarry. It was "time that . . . women be allowed full participation in religious observances," and also "encouraged to perform Rabbinical and Cantorial functions in synagogues."[11] Rabbinical authority, in the eyes of many religious feminists, was the key to genuine equality. Only when females—properly trained, of course—led worship and rendered decisions on religious questions could women and girls enjoy the relationship to their tradition that men attained by the simple fact of birth.

Conservative Judaism had already been responding tentatively to these complaints. As far back as 1955, the Committee on Jewish Law and Standards had approved calling women to the Torah, but even in the early 1970s, fewer than one congregation in ten actually took advantage of this decision to grant them aliyot. The year after the Ezrat Nashim manifesto, the committee accepted women as full minyan members. The year after that, it declared them ritually equal to lay male worshipers, with the right to serve as synagogue lay prayer leaders, though not as rabbis. Now, if she could read the siddur well enough, a girl past bat mitzvah age could not only recite the Kaddish but lead the minyan in prayer. All congregational leadership positions as board members, officers, and the like, were opened to women as well as men. But for Conservative Judaism in the early 1970s, overturning millennia of tradition and law by ordaining women as rabbis was simply too large a step.

On to Ordination

Reform, however, was moving much more quickly toward that goal. Given its general approach toward both gender and *halachah,* of course, it had a shorter distance to go. The first serious push to prepare women for the rabbinate had begun two generations earlier, in the first bright dawn of feminist triumph. In 1918, as American women pressed for the vote, four-teen-year-old Martha Neumark enrolled in the preparatory program of Hebrew Union College, the Reform movement's rabbinical seminary in Cincinnati. The German-born daughter of HUC philosophy professor David Neumark was both scholastically able and "deeply and sincerely religious," according to her own description.[12] So fine were Martha's Hebrew skills that during her sixteenth summer, at a Michigan summer resort where her father served as seasonal rabbi, he let his daughter lead the prayers. The astounded congregants mostly responded favorably, and the "witchery and charm" of the "ancient service" touched the sensitive, spiritual Martha very deeply.[13] She would, she decided, become a rabbi.

After three years at HUC, she asked for an assignment to lead High Holiday services as the male students routinely did, never doubting that her professors would grant her a practice pulpit and, when the time came, the chance for a real one as a fully ordained rabbi. Though a committee of rabbis studying the issue concluded, with four in favor and two opposed, that "since Reform Judaism teaches the equality of women with men in the synagogue, [they] could see no logical reason why women should not be entitled to receive a rabbinical degree." Nonetheless, unspecified "practical considerations" stood in the way of putting their conclusion into practice at the moment, they continued. And the dissent-ing committee members dissented very strongly from the "absurd and ridiculous" proposal "contrary to all Jewish tradition."[14] Unlike Reform's previous moves to alter tradition, which had been "absolutely necessary for the preservation of Judaism," this one represented the mere whim of "two or three girls" with unsuitable ambitions.[15] Furthermore, admitting female students would necessitate costly remodeling and replumbing of its dormitory to create appropriate accommodations as well as hiring chaperones. Since Martha would doubtlessly marry and become pregnant and thus unable to "appear in public and perform public functions" at various times, training her added up to a "very bad investment" for the college. More studies and more debates ensued. Eventually the faculty acknowledged that, given Reform's many deviations from accepted

Talmudic precedent, no basis in fact existed to "logically and consistently refuse the ordination of women."[16]

But Martha still did not get her assignment. Despite detailed arguments against female rabbis by leading Talmudists, the Central Congress of American Rabbis, in effect the HUC alumni society, decreed that "women cannot be justly denied the privilege of ordination," and Martha believed that when she finished her program she would in fact be ordained.[17] She proceeded to HUC's upper division while also, as was customary, pursuing undergraduate studies at the University of Cincinnati. But neither she nor the CCAR had bargained on the decision of the HUC board, which held ultimate authority over college enrollment and graduation. At a meeting in February 1923, its two rabbinical members voted for female ordination, but its six lay members voted against. There would be no change in the college policy of limiting ordination to males.

Martha persevered at HUC a while longer, the only woman among the hundred members of her class. But in 1925 she gave up her struggle, a year and a half shy of finishing the nine years required for the rabbinical degree. Though the board's vote closed off HUC as women's road to the rabbinate, another possible avenue for female ambition opened at just about the same time. In 1922 Rabbi Stephen Wise, the dynamic founder of New York's Free Synagogue and one of the most charismatic figures in Reform, established the Jewish Institute of Religion, a liberal seminary that, unlike HUC, took a pro-Zionist stance. The following year, three women enrolled in its inaugural class. Irma Levy Lindheim, a thirty-three-year-old mother of five when she began her studies, descended from a wealthy old southern family with Central European Jewish ancestry but little Jewish knowledge. For the next three and a half years she devoted herself to study. She applied for a change of status from special student to rabbinical candidate, and eventually the faculty agreed, in Wise's words, "to admit women on the same terms as men."[18]

Illness and family difficulties, however, ended her academic ambitions. Neither of Irma's female classmates finished the program either, although Dora Askowith, a Hunter history professor with a Ph.D., persevered part-time for fifteen years. She withdrew in 1937, probably because she never adequately mastered Hebrew. She did not, however, aspire to ordination. Helen Hadassah Levinthal, daughter of a prominent Conservative rabbi, a scion of a rabbinic lineage stretching back twelve generations and a graduate of the University of Pennsylvania, did complete the entire rabbinical curriculum. Her father, Israel, actively lobbied Wise to ordain her. Wise once jokingly remarked that if Israel's father, Rabbi Bernard Levinthal, founder of the Union of Orthodox Rabbis, concurred in Helen's ordination, then JIR would certainly proceed. As things stood, though, "the time was not ripe" for such as step.[19] When the class of 1939 finished the curriculum, ten students received the master of Hebrew literature degree and ordination as rabbis. With Israel and Bernard looking on, an eleventh student, who had completed exactly the same program, received the M.H.L. along with a second diploma bestowing on her the newly invented but essentially meaningless Hebrew title of *musmakah,* a feminine form meaning "authorized." Though derived from the same word as *smicha* (ordination), it did not denote elevation to the rabbinate.

For the next decade or so, the question of female ordination attracted only sporadic attention, mainly when Paula Ackerman ascended her temporary pulpit. It broke back into the headlines in 1957, as Jane Evans, executive director of the National Federation of Temple Sisterhoods, raised it in an address in Toronto before a combined meeting of NFTS and the Union of American Hebrew Congregations, the association of Reform temples. Little happened until 1961, however, when NFTS met in Washington and Jane proposed that "sisterhood women take a definitive stand on the question of opening the rabbinate to women."[20] She believed that NFTS, two years shy of its fiftieth anniversary, should pass a resolution demanding change. The membership resolved to spend the next two years studying the question in their own sisterhoods and to vote definitively at the next convention, when the organization reached its half-century mark. As that climactic meeting began, a procession of speakers revealed the hidden history of the women who tried for ordination at both HUC and JIR, which in 1950 had merged into a single institution with campuses in Cincinnati and New York. Then a thousand women sent as representatives from communities across the country resolved that the entire Reform movement, its rabbis, its congregations, its seminary, and its sisterhoods, must send delegates to a meeting to take final action on the issue.

But before any such epochal convocation could take place, a handful of young women forced the issue. In the mid-1950s, the HUC Cincinnati campus had begun allowing candidates for ordination to cut a year off the lengthy program by simultaneously matriculating, directly out of high school, as University of Cincinnati undergraduates and HUC rabbinic students. Three of the twenty-four students in the combined program's first class were women, and others enrolled in subsequent years. None, however, stayed long enough to approach ordination. In the year that Reform sisterhoods united to demand change and Betty Friedan published her book, Anne Blitzstein arrived in Cincinnati, determined to be a rabbi. She spent that year as the sole female student in the HUC/U of C program. The following year others joined her, one of them preceded by an article in her hometown paper, the *Cleveland Plain Dealer.* "Girl Sets Her Goal to be First Woman Rabbi," the headline declared.[21]

Sally Jane Priesand had cherished that ambition for at least three years, a long time in the life of an eighteen-year-old. Daughter of an engineer and his wife, she spent her early years in a Conservative synagogue where women played little role in worship. In junior high school Sally first encountered Reform. Her parents moved from Cleveland's east side to a new neighborhood in the west and joined Beth Israel—The West Temple. Much about the new congregation surprised Sally: bare male heads in the sanctuary; small, lively classes in the Sunday school; and girls saying Torah blessings on the *bimah.* Suddenly she connected with Judaism in a brand-new way, plunging into youth group activities, delivering a sermon at a youth service, and winning a sisterhood scholarship to a movement summer camp where her plans for the pulpit quickly became obvious to her fellow campers. She continued to prepare for her revolutionary future with confirmation, Hebrew high school graduation, and teaching in the Sunday school.

Born in the first year of the baby boom and entering HUC and U of C as the first baby boomers flooded campuses, Sally felt her generation's characteristic optimism and assurance. Cheered on by her parents and friends, she had little doubt that hard and earnest work would attain her goal. But HUC made no promises, encouraging her to consider teaching, the field that "most women prefer to enter."[22] Sally ultimately became a historic figure and the forerunner of a powerful movement within Judaism, but as she undertook her studies she did not view herself as an ideologue. Indeed, she took pains to prove herself no radical "women's libber." Though she thought feminism "a very important movement," she was not one of its active supporters, she explained, and "didn't go into the rabbinate to break down barriers."[23] She was simply a sincerely devout girl who saw herself affirming her "belief in God, in the worth of each individual, and in Judaism as a way of life." Entering HUC was "a tangible action declaring my commitment to the preservation and renewal of our tradition."[24]

Sally made friends among both the handful of other girls at HUC and those at U of C interested in Jewish studies. She accepted many invitations to give speeches on the issue of women in the rabbinate, depending on classmates to tape the classes she missed. Being the best possible student was always on her mind. "Undoubtedly, many believed I was studying . . . to become a *rebbezin* rather than a rabbi," she recalled. One professor tried to speed that process along by encouraging a student she was dating to pop the question—and, the professor believed, remove the college's awkward problem. But Sally held "very high standards" about her work, which remained her top priority. "If they were going to get rid of me," she said, "it wouldn't be because of my grades."[25]

In 1968 Sally's class completed the undergraduate portion of their program. The men proceeded automatically into the second year of graduate rabbinical studies. Although she had followed the same program, Sally had to make a formal application and submit to a mandatory psychological examination, as if she were an applicant unknown to the school. Classmates urged her to protest these indignities. She preferred to quietly await her acceptance, which arrived in due course.

Now officially a rabbinical student, she next approached the obstacle that had derailed Martha Neumark more than forty years before. Twenty members of the second-year class drew lots for five congregations seeking High Holiday prayer leaders. Sally drew number one. When Congregation Beth Jacob of Murphrysboro, Illinois, was informed to expect Ms. Priesand, its president insisted that a mere student would not do. This rejection ignored Sally's gender but provided "merely a first taste of the problems that [she] will be facing and that we all recognize in advance," warned Kenneth Roseman, coordinator of the holiday assignments.[26] Implicit in his concern, however, was the assumption that Sally would one day face other such rebuffs; that she would, in other words, become a rabbi.

Ultimately Sally successfully served three temples during her student years: B'nai Israel of Hattiesburg, Mississippi, whose board voted to accept her by a margin of one vote; Sinai Temple of Champaign–Urbana, Illinois, and a congregation in Jackson, Michigan. Much had changed since HUC refused to assign Martha Neumark a High Holidays pulpit or Helen Levinthal's JIR classmates unanimously petitioned the faculty to present her diploma at a separate commencement ceremony lest her presence "detract from the dignity and force of our ordination."[27] Now the president of UAHC, a classmate of Martha's in both high school and college, advised his colleagues to "face the realities of life." Indeed, continued Maurice Eisendrath, who had initially encouraged Paula Ackerman,

"Women are here to stay." With Sally less that two years from the date of her class's ordination, he bemoaned the male tendency to "cop out . . . with snide jokes about Women's Lib and the like."[28] Perhaps he had in mind such wits as the CCAR convention speaker who "dreamed I preached a sermon in my Maidenform Bra."[29]

Nor was Eisendrath the only rabbi rethinking old prejudices. As publicity mounted in the year before Sally's graduation, a seminary classmate of Helen Levinthal's wrote to the president of HUC-JIR about the injustice done her all those years ago. Even now, more than a generation later, Rabbi Earl Stone hoped that "something could be done" to accord her the honor she deserved as the first woman to finish a rabbinical program.[30] Though a hunt through the seminary archives turned up no transcript of her work, her achievement, and the fact that it had fully equaled the men's, had been common knowledge at JIR. Rabbi Alfred Gottschalk, a former JIR student and now president of HUC-JIR, had told as much to her father. But without an official record of Helen's grades, Gottschalk decided, the seminary could not ordain her now. Not until 1988 did her alma mater present Helen Levinthal Lyons, by then near death, with a certificate recognizing her singular accomplishment.

So, Sally Priesand, though not the first American woman to finish a rabbinical course, became, on June 3, 1972, the first to be ordained a rabbi by a mainstream Jewish denomination. Two years later the Reconstructionist Rabbinical College in suburban Philadelphia ordained its first woman graduate, Sandy Eisenberg Sasso. Growing out of the teachings of Rabbi Mordechai Kaplan, the charismatic Jewish Theological Seminary professor who had arranged the first bat mitzvah ceremony for his daughter Judith in 1920, Reconstruction had gradually grown from a philosophy into a separate, fourth denomination. From its founding in 1968, RRC accepted men and woman on an equal basis. Only men applied for the new seminary's inaugural class, but Philadelphia-born Sandy Eisenberg entered in the second in the fall of 1969, the year after Sally began her studies.

A year younger than Sally Priesand, Sandy had been a devout, active, and knowledgeable participant in youth activities at her family's Reform congregation, Keneseth Israel. She had led services and had won the top prize—a trip to Israel—in an essay contest. Next came a bachelor's degree in religion from Temple University. At the end of her first RRC year she married fellow student Dennis Sasso in the world's first wedding at which two future rabbis stood under the *chuppah* as bride and groom. In her penultimate seminary year *Response* magazine published an original ceremony that Sandy composed to be used to celebrate the birth of a daughter, a occasion traditionally marked by a single prayer in the synagogue, not the elaborate ritual and party afforded a son. The male rite of *brit milah* commemorated God's promise that Abraham would father a great people. His wife, the matriarch Sarah, also heard that promise, Sandy pointed out, and she had played just as crucial a role in the birth of the Jewish people.

Sally and Sandy's progress riveted the American Jewish world. As the Conservative members of Ezrat Nashim prepared for their declaration at Lake Kiamesha in March of the spring when Sally would graduate, they were intensely aware that Reform's historic step was weeks away. Their own denomination would struggle for another eleven years before Amy Eilberg received the first Conservative *smicha* ever granted a woman. Though the debate within Conservatism lasted a shorter time, it was more intense and bitter than in Reform because *halachic* arguments and liturgical tradition carried far more weight. For years Jewish Theological Seminary faculty members probed the sacred literature, finding arguments for and against the possibility of female rabbis. In 1978, a fourteen-member commission appointed to study the issue sharply split, eleven finding "no direct *halachic* objection" and three arguing that the step would split the movement.[31] By the time the report came to a vote of the seminary faculty in 1979, opposition had hardened, led primarily by the seminary's most distinguished Talmudic scholars. Threatened by a boycott of sixteen renowned professors who argued that "Jewish law forbids the participation of women as rabbis,"[32] the faculty put off balloting.

That same year the Sassos accepted joint appointments to Beth El Zedeck, an Indianapolis congregation that belonged to both the Reconstructionist and Conservative movements, making Sandy technically a rabbi of a Conservative synagogue. This does not appear to have influenced the JTS debate, nor did a 1983 attempt at an end run by the Rabbinical Assembly, the association of JTS alumni that constituted the Conservative rabbinate. In 1980 it declared itself, by a 156–115 vote, in favor of female ordination. A proposal to admit Rabbi Beverly Weintraub Magidson, a 1979 HUC-JIR graduate, failed by four votes to receive the required three-quarters of the membership. Even without the official RA seal of approval, but with the help of several RA members, Beverly soon landed a job at a Conservative congregation, becoming for all practical purposes a Conservative rabbi.

Such overwhelming support by the nation's active Conservative rabbis ultimately forced the seminary's hand. During the month before the RA vote almost admitting Beverly, Rabbi Saul Lieberman, the towering Talmudist who had most forcefully enunciated the *halachic* objections, had died. This immensely respected scholar had never objected to women pursuing advanced Jewish studies, even at JTS, and his female students recalled him as helpful and encouraging. His conclusion arose solely from what he found in the texts. His absence, rather than any flaws in his reasoning, permitted the JTS faculty to take the climactic vote. It happened in an atmosphere "filled . . . bitterness and acrimony," according to Ohio teacher Judy Kanfer, a JTS Talmud student during the long struggle.[33] Many of Lieberman's colleagues in the Talmud department refused to participate. Finally, on October 24, by a margin of 34–8, the professors of the Jewish Theological Seminary of America agreed to admit women to its rabbinical program on an equal basis with men. In the fall of the following year, twenty-five women enrolled.

Some of these new rabbinical candidates had been studying at the seminary through the years of wrangling. The most advanced, Amy Eilberg, had completed an M.A. and the course work for a Ph.D. in Talmudic studies. Shortly after she entered the JTS rabbinical program in the first female class, it was clear that she had done nearly all the work needed for ordination. In May 1985, she received her rabbinic degree and the first Conservative *smicha* granted to a woman. The RA soon welcomed her, as well as Beverly Magidson, Jan Kaufman, and other Reform female rabbis.

Despite her Reform *smicha,* Jan had not set out to serve Judaism's most liberal stream. The product of an observant Baltimore home and the city's Beth Tefilloh Jewish day school, she had decided in seventh grade to become a rabbi and had followed the only available path to get there. After receiving her undergraduate degree jointly from Goucher College and Baltimore Hebrew College, she went on to HUC's New York campus. But she never gave up her dream of becoming a rabbi in *halachically* more rigorous Conservatism. She was only one of a number of highly observant women who entered HUC because they were unwelcome at JTS. Many believe that they helped spark a significant movement within Reform to return to more traditional observance. The cantorate also afforded a platform for female influence on Reform ritual. In 1975, the HUC-JIR School of Sacred Music graduated Barbara Ostfield-Horowitz as the first female cantor. JTS certified Marla Rosenfeld Barugel and Erica Lipitz as cantors two years later. By the mid-1990s, women constituted the majority of those graduating each year from the Reform, Reconstructionist, and Conservative seminaries.

But, as was already obvious in many other occupations, the most prestigious, best paying, and most visible rabbinical posts largely eluded them.
Sally Priesand began her career at New York's Stephen Wise Free
Synagogue, first as an assistant and then an associate rabbi. Her fame did
not easily land her a pulpit of her own, however. Applications to twelve
different congregations yielded only three interviews. Finally, in 1979, she
became the part-time rabbi of Congregation Beth El in Elizabeth, New
Jersey, meanwhile also serving Lennox Hill Hospital in Manhattan as
Jewish chaplain. Two years later, she moved on to Tinton Falls, New Jersey,
as the spiritual leader of the 250 families of Monmouth Reform Temple.
Congregations have shown more willingness to name women as their senior or sole cantors, perhaps because a *hazzanit* leads a synagogue's prayers
but not its overall program.

At the start of her career, Sally had expected to measure her success
by the speed of her rise up the career ladder, ministering to ever larger
congregations until she reached a conspicuous, influential post in a large,
famous temple. The first female rabbi, she felt, owed a duty to her sex to
reach the top of her profession. But the frustrations and burdens of
being simultaneously a historic figure and an oddity, along with her daily
life among her congregants, taught her something very different. The
true mark of her success, she came to believe, lay in her increasing ability to empower people spiritually and to help them "become responsible
for their own Judaism."[34] Many other women in the pulpit also emphasize the rabbi's role as a spiritual guide or example rather than as religious authority and arbiter, believing that concern for individuals rather
than structures, for relationships rather than rules, marks a typically
female style of leadership. Rabbi Sandy Eisenberg Sasso cites the pioneering 1982 feminist analysis of moral reasoning, *In a Different Voice:
Psychological Theory and Women's Development*, by Harvard psychologist Carol (Friedman) Gilligan as evidence that "women's center of focus
is on people rather than principles."[35] Female leaders often "seek to con-
nect with others, to be together at the center," Sasso says, rather than follow a more traditionally masculine "hierarchical model" with a goal of
standing alone at the top.[36] Although women have not reached the rabbinate's pinnacle of prestige, their arrival as rabbis signaled new opportunities and options for many Jewishly involved women. The
countercultural ferment of the 1970s produced another model of thor-
oughgoing Jewish egalitarianism: intentionally small, earnestly participa-
tory groups called *havurot*. Within these fellowships students and other

young people sought an intense, authentic, often homemade, experience of Jewish community unmediated by bureaucracy, stale custom, or hierarchy. The Ezrat Nashim prayer and study group, for example, grew from one such collective, the New York Havurah.

Finding a New Female Spirituality

A year after Ezrat Nashim electrified the Rabbinical Assembly convention with their manifesto—and mere weeks after the Supreme Court handed down the *Roe v. Wade* decision legalizing abortion—five hundred women from all parts of the country, all branches of Judaism, and all levels of knowledge gathered in New York for perhaps the first meeting expressly intended to catalyze a new era in American Jewish life since Hannah Greenebaum Solomon put together her congress in Chicago exactly eighty years before. The national Jewish feminist women's conference showcased Bella Abzug and other speakers as well as workshops on family, social roles, education, religion, politics, and other aspects of Jewish life. As in Hannah Solomon's Chicago, women previously isolated in their feelings of powerlessness found in each other, in their great numbers, and in their deep feeling of peoplehood the power to transform their situation and their lives. Blu Greenberg, a thirty-six-year Orthodox *rebbetzin* and mother of five, had read *The Feminine Mystique* a decade earlier, tasting in it "the fruit of the tree of knowledge" from which "there was no going back."[37] Like previous eaters of forbidden fruit, she gained little joy from what she learned through her new insight. She could see, disturbingly, the deep gender inequality in the Judaism she devotedly practiced, but she could not bring herself to embrace what she considered the offensive radicalism of "women's lib."

At the conference, among hundreds of fellow feminists who were also fellow committed Jews, she discovered that "you could still be a mild-mannered yeshiva girl and a card-carrying feminist and not feel out of whack all the time."[38] You could both question practice and remain loyal to Jewish faith; you could rethink your position but not reject your beliefs. You could, in fact, be exalted and exhilarated. These powerful feelings flooded over her at an all-female service when, for the first time in her life, she performed an act she had beheld in synagogue thousands of times. As the ritual for reading the Torah drew to its close, she, and not a man, lifted the sacred scroll before the people as they sang, in Hebrew, "This is the Torah that Moses placed before the Children of Israel, according to the

Lord, by Moses's hand." Never before had she even held a Torah. The depth of that moment moved her to deeper thinking and study of issues that troubled her for years and ultimately led to her 1981 book, *On Women and Judaism: A View from Tradition*, a bold and probing synthesis of feminism and Orthodoxy.

As the women who gathered in Chicago in 1893 had done, those who came to New York had a vision of change and solidarity that permeated communities across the continent. Conservative and Reform congregations everywhere revised their policies on aliyot, selection of officers and board members, and distribution of labor and power. The bat mitzvah, complete with girls reading from the Torah just as boys had always done, became a universal part of growing up Reform, Reconstructionist, and Conservative. Women began to don the tallis and kippah for prayer, and before long independent fabric artists, commercial manufacturers, and individual needle women were producing these ancient ritual garments from modern designs suited to a feminine sensibility. Congregations, and then whole denominations, began experimenting with the liturgy itself, trying to modify the overwhelmingly masculine language that had since time immemorial been the Jewish path to the divine. Translators now strained to construct sentences without the gendered pronouns. Worshipers now praised the "sovereign" rather than "king" of the universe, appealed to their heavenly "parent" rather than their "father" and intoned the names of the matriarchs Sarah, Rebecca, Rachel, and Leah along with those of their patriarch husbands Abraham, Isaac, and Jacob.

But as Reform, Reconstructionist, and Conservative women strove to be men's religious equals, they increasingly noticed that they were not their spiritual equivalents. Judaism's formal liturgy, traditionally intended to be recited in public by males, and Jewish law, written and administered by men, have for millennia ignored certain profound experiences specific to female lives. *Halachah,* for example, considered the personal cataclysm of a baby's birth only insofar as it renders the mother for a time sexually unavailable to her husband. But for many an observant women like Miriam Klein Shapiro of the Union for Traditionalist Judaism, a group that favors *halachic* stringency within Conservatism, the births of children are the "most religious experiences" of her life. "Five times from an act of love I have felt life growing inside me," says Miriam, a mother of five. From this "I know what a miracle is. Crossing the Red Sea is nothing compared to that."[39]

To sanctify their deepest moments, to bless events and feelings that the prayer book ignores, women began to compose prayers and ceremonies drawn from female lives—in effect to reinvent the rich female spirituality that had vanished, along with much of the old-world Jewish culture, during the passage to the New World. Where once pious shtetl housewives had recited psalms in Yiddish as they went about their daily tasks, where once mothers birthing in tenements and sod huts had prayed that "the life of [their] child [would] not be [their] death" and their pain would be reborn as delight in a healthy newborn, now descendants of theirs who had law degrees and master's degrees, comfortable homes and professional jobs, composed new texts to mark the same timeless hopes and fears. In Philadelphia's old Marshall Street, as in homes across the Pale and Central Europe, mothers and grandmothers not yet "Americanized" had known what holy things to do to protect a girl at her first period and to prepare a bride for the sexual side of marriage. But on the way to becoming modern, along with the lost grammar of the Yiddish in which these women had dreamed and prayed, along with habits of the women's culture in which they had lived, their granddaughters and great-granddaughters had discarded or forgotten their rituals and prayers.

As feminism gained ground in American Judaism, so did a new excitement in restoring this specifically female sphere of spirituality and reviving or creating rituals that mark and express the holiness that happens only to women. Creators of such liturgies often explored such qualities of the Shechinah as mercy, compassion, creativity, and loving kindness. Groups of women began developing ceremonies to revive the observance of Rosh Hodesh, the new moon. At least since biblical times, strong symbolism has connected the monthly cycles of waxing and waning in both the heavens and in each female body. By the mid-1970s the first feminist seder celebrations had also begun. As word of these services spread, so did interest in the females who made crucial contributions to liberation of the People Israel. The *kos Miriam* (Cup of the Prophetess Miriam) joined that of the Prophet Elijah on many seder tables.

From the hearts and pens of observant feminists also have come many other new ceremonies: rituals to mark menarche and menopause and to help heal the emotional pain of miscarriage, rape, and abortion. Many of these use the *mikvah* for both spiritual and physical cleansing. Female rabbis and rabbinical students, having overturned one of Judaism's most ancient traditions, are also now leading the way back to one that had been widely discarded, the monthly visit to the *mikvah*. In assuming the previously male mantle of the rabbinate, female rabbis and seminarians often voluntarily take on the male obligation to perform such time-bound male mitzvot as thrice-daily prayer. Being "very serious about their spiritual and religious lives," says Anne Lapidus Lerner, a dean at JTS, these women also "feel deeply that they should [also] maintain those obligations which Jewish women have maintained—sometimes with great difficulty— throughout Jewish history."[40]

Orthodox Feminism

Some women, of course, never stopped fulfilling the old obligations. Despite the spread of Conservatism and Reform through most of suburbanizing Jewry, Orthodoxy rebounded vigorously after World War II, with the arrival of ultra-Orthodox, often Chasidic, survivors of the European calamity. Many Americans saw them as mere remnants of the shattered past, but these new arrivals soon reconstituted a European world of small but dedicated communities devoted to *halachic* observance far stricter and more conspicuous than anything American-style Modern Orthodoxy had practiced. Large families and tightly knit congregations made for rapidly rising populations and high morale. Distinctive attire—beards and head coverings for men, wigs or head scarves for married women—marked them off from both Gentiles and less observant Jews. Active outreach to the Jewishly less engaged swelled their numbers. Newly Orthodox men and women (known as *ba'alei t'shuva* and *ba'alot t'shuva*, respectively, literally masters and mistresses of return) abandoned the liberal Judaism or assimilationist secularism of their youth to "return," often via an interlude of yeshiva study and a marriage arranged by a Chasidic rebbe, to a new world of strict practice.

The feminist message penetrated even to women living amid the gender roles of resurgent tradition. The commitment that Orthodoxy, both modern and traditional, had made to educating girls was genuine and vigorous. By the 1970s, two generations of young women had grown up with rigorous religious training. Though few had studied Talmud nearly as thoroughly as their brothers, still, "the average twelfth-grade yeshiva girl often has a more extensive and deeper knowledge of traditional Jewish texts than the traditional Reform rabbi," according to Orthodox activist Rivka Haut.[41]

Blu Greenberg had been just such a girl. Daughter of an Orthodox New York home of the 1940s and 1950s, she received "a fine Jewish education, the best a girl could have."[42] Indeed, for her Jewish studies took precedence over secular subjects. She spent a college year in Israel studying with

Nechama Liebowitz, widely considered the twentieth century's greatest teacher of Bible. Blu reveled in her time with this charismatic woman scholar and hoped to extend it when it neared its end. Her parents and friends disapproved, however. A "nice Orthodox Jewish girl," she returned home convinced that a similar request by a "a nice Orthodox boy" would have received a different answer. For Blu, as for growing numbers of knowledgeable Orthodox women, the turbulent 1960s and 1970s brought growing unease. Though deeply devoted to the tenets and discipline of *halachic* Judaism, many had begun suspecting that the law, if properly interpreted, provided far more scope to female intellect and spirituality than traditional practice allowed.

Some rabbis, including Yeshiva University professor Saul Berman, agree. Judaism strongly distinguishes the roles of males and females, he notes, and its "necessary" prescriptions "can and have created many undesirable side effects and consequences. We must differentiate between what are the necessary aspects of role differentiation and what are the undesirable consequences—and eliminate them. . . . to expand spiritual opportunities for women within the framework of Jewish law."[43] The traditional prohibition on men and women praying together in the synagogue does not, for example, mean that groups of women cannot pray together in public, Berman and others argue. By the late 1960s, Orthodox feminists had begun meeting in small, all-female *tefila* (prayer) groups.

In the late 1960s, Rabbi Shlomo Riskin, then the influential spiritual leader of Manhattan's Lincoln Square Synagogue, gave his blessing to a women's celebration of the Simchat Torah festival separate from the men's. Literally "Rejoicing in the Torah," the holiday fully deserves its name. Adult synagogue-goers, accompanied by children waving special flags, joyously parade their Torah scrolls, often breaking into dance as they carry their richly bedecked burdens up and down the sanctuary aisles and even out into the streets. Orthodox women, however, have traditionally watched the festivities from the gallery or behind the *mechitza*. For the first time ever, Rabbi Riskin allowed Torahs to be brought to the women's section for dancing and then reading in a separate female gathering. Other synagogues began to do likewise, and before long separate women's Simchat Torah services, complete with aliyot for everyone in attendance, were marking the festival. Over the next decade, *tefila* groups in several cities began meeting monthly, often on Rosh Hodesh, at first in private homes and often without rabbinical approval. Though many of their colleagues objected, Rabbi Avi Weiss of the Hebrew Institute of Riverdale

(New York) and Rabbi Haskel Lookstein of Manhattan's Kehillat
Jeshorun, opened their synagogue doors to the innovative prayer circles.
Tefila groups continued to proliferate in cities across the country, num-
bering several dozen by the late 1990s and performing such rituals as read-
ing the Megillah of Esther at Purim and lighting the candles at Hanukkah.
They carefully refrain from reciting particular prayers, including the
Kaddish and Barchu, that by law require the presence of a minyan which,
in the Orthodox view, can include only men.

Much less controversial are efforts encouraging study so that girls and
women can strengthen Jewish life and ensure its survival across the generations. Talmud, long considered inappropriate for women, now appears
on the curriculum of Stern College and the educational programs of many
Orthodox congregations. Even Rabbi Menachem Schneerson, the late
Lubavitcher Rebbe, recommended Talmudic learning for the mothers and
future mothers of his community. Women, he noted, have the intellectual
ability, and married couples can particularly benefit from studying
together. To provide opportunities for advanced study of sacred texts,
Orthodox Rabbi David Silber founded the Drisha Institute in New York
in 1979. Hundreds of women attend each year, from high school students
to graduate-level scholars, and take everything from individual lectures to
full-day programs that last for years. A three-year program taught at the
level of a rabbinic seminary leads to certification to teach Talmud at the
high school level, a credential never before available to women. Giving
women the skills and knowledge for teaching and independent research is
not, Rabbi Silber insists, "a feminist issue. It is a community issue. The
more thoughtful and knowledgeable men and women we have active in the
Jewish community, making good ethical decisions and setting good goals,
the better community we have."[44] Traditionally, however, male students not
only listen to lectures and hear interpretations but immerse themselves in
the original texts, meeting each passage in the company of a long-term
study partner. Pairs of students, bent over the original Hebrew words of
the law, discussing, debating, and deliberating the import of every phrase,
have filled yeshiva study halls for centuries. Shalhevet: A Torah Institute
for Women, a new school in Hillcrest, New York, offers female students
the same opportunity to wrestle with text that males have long enjoyed.

All this new female knowledge, some Orthodox argue, should be used,
as men's always has been, to help decide the proper course of action
according to religious law. Orthodox religious authorities universally dis-
miss the possibility of women in the rabbinate. In 1993, the Rabbi Isaac

Elchanan Theological Seminary of Yeshiva University, Modern Orthodoxy's main rabbinical training school, rejected its first-ever female applicant, Haviva Krasner-Davidson. But Rabbi Weiss sees "aspects of the rabbinate—the teaching of Torah and counseling—in which women can participate in on the same level as men."[45] Certain aspects of Jewish life, such as sexual purity and *kashrut,* hold special meaning for women. A woman with proper training, some people have asserted, could decide issues in these areas perhaps even better than a man; she might even usefully occupy a formal position as a *poseket* (decider) for the women of her community. By the late 1990s, a handful of women were serving with Orthodox congregations as "rabbinical assistants," teaching, counseling, making pastoral visits, and sometimes preaching. So rapidly has religious education advanced among Orthodox women that Blu Greenberg feels "optimistic" that she will live to see women rabbis leading Orthodox congregations. In the "not-too-distant future," she believes, Orthodoxy will accept "the model of women in leadership positions in the other denominations. When that happens, history will take us where it will take us. That holds much promise for the likes of me."[46]

But history has not yet arrived to sweep Orthodox women into the rabbinate. The ancient distinction between the sexes, and the venerable customs that enforce it, still structure Orthodox life. Many Orthodox women see that clear demarcation as a precious spiritual and personal bulwark. The sacred work of wife and mother, the indispensable labor of womanhood, retain in many of today's Orthodox communities the same high esteem and deep richness that glorified them in the shtetl. Indeed, it is precisely the distinctive and essential feminine sphere that attracts many young *ba'alot teshuva* into the ultra-Orthodox fold. The special sanctity of woman's work, still clearly recognized and highly valued, gives their new, observant lives a depth of meaning that their old, secular lives utterly lacked. The rules of family purity, for example, by subjecting sexual desire to spiritual discipline, afford them a dignity and control they did not find in the secular world of constant, and often casual, sexual access.

Doing Women's Work

Orthodox women may still live religious lives that their great-great-grandmothers would easily recognize, but in other respects they closely mirror their less observant modern sisters, pursuing higher education and white-collar careers. Just over half of Orthodox married couples had two working spouses in 1990, the year of the most recent available statistics, a bare 3 percent below Conservative and Reform couples.

As the twenty-first century begins, Jewish women have come closer than any other group in America to realizing the feminist dream that captivated Betty Friedan four decades ago. They long ago surpassed the general male population in education. Almost three times as many of them hold professional or academic jobs as white American women generally, nearly a third more have managerial or technical ones, and only a quarter as many do service work.[47] Even more impressively, they almost equal Jewish men in education; college is essentially universal for both sexes. Virtually no position seems beyond the reach of their ambition. Young Jewish women no longer simply get married and "help out." They no longer get married young and teach school. Many plan prestigious careers in lucrative professions, the arts or business, exactly as their brothers have done for three generations. As diligently and meticulously as their great-grandmothers stitched shirtwaists in stifling sweatshop lofts, the daughters of the baby boomers now tailor their credentials and their careers.

But also like those indefatigable factory girls, the new generation of young Jewish women wants more from life than working for pay. They too want roses along with their sourdough baguette bread. Today's Jewish professional women may marry and give birth later than those with lesser credentials—and a decade or more later than those long-ago Jewish girls who wed small-town shopkeepers and big-city garment workers—but the current Jewish generation still overwhelmingly wants a husband and children. Of all American religious and ethnic groups, Jewish women least hope to avoid parenthood. Education increases rather than decreases the number of children Jewish women hope to bear, unlike more educated Christian women, who want fewer offspring.[48] Among Jews, the long-sacred tasks of motherhood and homemaking—in the sense of creating and raising a family, though not necessarily of cleaning and maintaining the house they inhabit—remain integral to many people's conception of fulfilling womanhood—even among those who have shed *Shabbat, kashrut, niddah,* and nearly everything else that marks the traditional faith. The more strongly a modern woman feels her Jewishness, the more intensely she wants to make a Jewish home.

In an irony worthy of a Yiddish humorist, though, the age of feminist liberation has greatly complicated the Jewish woman's path toward that once straightforward goal. Until the late 1960s, marriage to a Jewish man of good prospects, followed by the rearing of a small family, was not only the sign of a Jewish girl's success in life but almost her unavoidable fate. For the first two postwar decades, the search for a suitable—meaning Jewish—spouse simply shifted from the neighborhood to the college campus, from the family circle to the sorority or fraternity house. But now, with virtual educational equality and vastly improved career opportunities, schooling can stretch far into the twenties, and many young people seek to establish a career while their hard-earned credentials are fresh. For three generations now, Jewish men have been devoting the bulk of their first three decades to education and professional apprenticeship; for two of those generations, young wives often worked to support their husbands through medical or law school, residency or clerkship, and the first lean years out on one's own.

But now young women often seek the same kind of lengthy, specialized training and the same kind of competitive careers. The work of getting started, combined with the sexual revolution based on virtually foolproof contraception and easily available abortion, have pushed upper-middle-class marriage into the late twenties or even the thirties. For increasing numbers of the ambitious and educated, in fact, marriage may not come at all. And of those who do find spouses, many eventually divorce. For the first time in Jewish history, a community that since time immemorial has seen wedlock as the normal state for everyone past adolescence now contains significant numbers of adults who remain single during the most marriageable and fertile years of their lives. But so strong is the lure of motherhood, that, also for the first time, a small but growing number of mature and prosperous women who lack male partners are intentionally bearing or adopting children on their own. Jewish women, often highly committed to religion and community, form the majority of at least New York's chapter of Single Mothers by Choice.[49]

As Jews marry later and later, they are not finding their spouses where their parents and grandparents and great-grandparents did—at dances in Jewish fraternity houses, or in their solidly Jewish neighborhoods, or at cousins' club meetings, or the next sewing machine, or through helpful relatives or professional matchmakers or family friends. The spouses that they find in their law offices and consulting firms and university departments, through their professional conferences or condominium board meetings or personal ads, are less often fellow Jews. More than half of marriages now involve a partner from outside the Jewish community, making a Jewish home problematic for many couples and future Jewish generations increasingly problematic for the community at large. A quarter or more of non-Jewish wives convert to Judaism, according to some estimates, but many fewer non-Jewish husbands—perhaps as few as 10 percent. For the first time since before the *Illinois* tied up at Philadelphia, being Jewish is for increasing numbers of Americans a matter of personal choice rather than a simple fact of family history.

Jewish women, nonetheless, still overwhelmingly choose to be Jewish and to be the mothers of Jewish children. Because a Jewish woman's children are Jewish regardless of the father's religion, and because male conversion, at least to Conservatism and Orthodoxy, can involve awkward and painful questions of circumcision, the small number of men formally joining the Jewish people may not reflect a family's desire to abandon tradition, but only to avoid needless difficulties. Interfaith families without conversion, however, tend to produce children with more attenuated Jewish identities than those with two parents who are Jewish either by birth or by choice. Jews who choose the faith, of course, generally rank among the community's more active and committed members.

Also like their factory-worker foremothers, many of today's Jewish women leave paid employment, but when they become mothers, not wives. Jewish women are more likely than other Americans to withdraw from the workforce while their children are small, though many return, at least part-time, as school age approaches.[50] Well-educated themselves and married to educated men, they probably enjoy more freedom to stop working than many other women. They more often have husbands who can support the family alone, at least for a few years. They often have established careers to which they can fairly easily return. And the hiatus is often brief because Jewish families mostly number one, two, or three children; only the very Orthodox generally have four or more. Today's Jewish mothers have made large investments of time, money, and emotion in their professional training. Family planning, which generations of American Jewish wives have used expertly, thus plays a large part in their career success.

As in centuries past, combining work and family goes without saying in today's Jewish homes. Only a third of Jewish women, but almost half of the general female population, believe that a mother at home full-time necessarily does a better job.[51] A study of Jewish women who "have it all"— three or more children and active careers—found that 85 percent thought themselves "successful" mothers, 80 percent thought themselves "successful" workers, and 75 percent felt "satisfied" or "very satisfied" with their lives overall.[52] In their assumption that a woman plays an active role in her family's economic well-being, today's American Jewish generations continue the pattern set by three and a half centuries of their predecessors on this continent. With the pragmatic self-assurance of Rycke Nounes, who sued to salvage what she could of her savings, fifteen generations of American Jewish women have set their minds and hands to the goal of economic survival. But with the spiritual devotion of Rebecca Samuel, who abandoned a thriving business to find a Jewish life, today's self-consciously Jewish women put their financial success to the larger purpose of building Jewish homes and communities.

But, like every one of those generations, the women who will inhabit the twenty-first century will face unique challenges. There has never been a permanent solution to the problem of making a Jewish life in America. Each generation has had to invent a version of Jewishness that fit its needs. Unprecedented social freedom and openness now make Jewishness, whether ethnic or religious, not a mandatory inheritance but a chosen affiliation. Career opportunities unimaginable mere decades ago, combined with nearly infallible reproductive control, now make motherhood and marriage conscious lifestyle choices, not inevitable destinies. Whether present and future generations of Jewish women and men—the prosperous, educated, fully American offspring of two or more American generations—will themselves choose to be Jewish, to have children, and to raise them as Jews, will determine the fate of the largest, richest, and arguably the most creative and dynamic Jewry in the history of the world. That large numbers still do so testifies to the vitality of the tradition that millions of hopeful newcomers carried to America in sailing ships and emigrant liners and nurtured in colonial towns, sod shanties, and mining camps, in city slums and army posts, in suburban developments and college dorms, and everywhere a people restlessly pursuing happiness has carried it.

As a new millennium began—or an old one ended—Jewish Americans pondered a staggering possibility: that the vice president's house, the official residence of the person second in line to the most powerful position in the world, might soon have, of all unthinkable improbabilities, a kosher kitchen. Joseph and Hadassah Lieberman, as things turned out, will not be celebrating their Passover seders or lighting their Hanukkah candles in the mansion on the National Observatory grounds. They will not be walking under Secret Service guard through the streets of Georgetown to their shul each Shabbat. But only a few hundred votes kept this Modern Orthodox couple—the son of a deliveryman and the daughter of Holocaust survivors—from becoming the first Jewish Second Family of the land. That both Joseph Lieberman and the man who defeated his ticket graduated from Yale testifies to the almost limitless opportunity that America has offered its Jews. That the election's great controversy involved dangling chads and not the Liebermans' religion testifies to the extraordinary acceptance it has afforded them.

Peter Stuyvesant, it turns out, had it right after all. Admitting the tiny storm-tossed band forever changed his colony and the city and nation that grew from it. As his supporters foresaw with dismay, a great many more of that lot did follow, first in scores and then hundreds and ultimately in fleeing millions. And as Stuyvesant may well have intuited, it was the arrival and labor of women that made their presence permanent and transforming. It was by bearing and raising and sustaining families; by building communities through *tzedakah* and teaching; by caring for their own and other people's children; by tackling the bottomless troubles of the poor and powerless; by educating themselves for citizenship and devotion; by moving ever forward toward the common American and Jewish dream of a better, more just, and more meaningful future; by demanding their dignity and taking their destinies in their own hands, that three and a half centuries of American Jewish women have taken the opportunities that a new land offered and turned them to the purposes of an ancient tradition. Doing the sacred work of Jewish womanhood, fifteen generations of Jewish grandmothers, mothers, and daughters have built companies, hospitals, synagogues, schools, bodies of legal precedent, social service agencies, industries, works of art, and, ever and always, families and communities.

But in ways that no one could have predicted, as generation after generation of newcomers came down the gangway into the land that was their future, America changed the Jewish people and Judaism far more profoundly than they changed it. It made them free people, full citizens, partners in the building of the nation, no longer outcasts depending on the sufferance of Gentile overlords but equal human beings endowed with inalienable rights. It made their tradition one of many accepted faiths in a land where all manner of beliefs could flourish, no longer a hated heresy barely tolerated by the powers of a hostile state. It gave persecuted people the freedom to become who they wanted to be. It gave committed people the power to make their religion into what they needed it to become. Through centuries of dedication, hardship, and sacrifice, they remade it in the image of their new land. Judaism has become not the unitary tradition of old but a diverse congeries of communities, each pursuing its own image of the good, each choosing ancestral elements that serve its purposes, and all carrying values and loyalties from an ancient past forward into an unknown future.

Like the women of every past American Jewish generation, those of the coming century will invent in their own image authentically American ways of being Jewish, distinctively Jewish ways of being American. Just as Rachel Levy blended her ancestry with that of Isaac Seixas into a single American strain, they will continue grafting New World dynamism onto undying tradition. Like three centuries of their foremothers, they will provide much of the creativity that fuels American Jewish life. Like Hetty Hays in her boardinghouse and Rebecca Gratz in her Sunday school, like Lillian Wald in her settlement and Mathilde Schechter in her salon, like Hannah Solomon on the platform and Sally Priesand on the *bimah*, and like countless others across the centuries and across the continent, who conceived, created, and sustained the institutions and observances that are American Jewish life, they will make an ever changing Jewish present out of the eternal Jewish past. As it has since 1654, the work that women do and the works that they create will compose the essence of what it means to be Jewish in America.

NOTES

Chapter 1

1. Egon Wolff and Freida Wolff, "The Problem of the First Jewish Settlers in New Amsterdam, 1654," *Studia Rosenthaliana* 15 (1981): 170.

2. Jacob Rader Marcus, *The Jew in the American World: A Source Book* (Detroit: Wayne State University Press, 1996), 29–30.

3. Marcus, *Jew in the American World,* 30–31.

4. Marcus, *Jew in the American World,* 32.

5. Eli Faber, *A Time for Planting: The First Migration, 1654–1820,* vol. 1 of *The Jewish People in America* (Baltimore: Johns Hopkins University Press, 1992), 31.

6. Marcus, *Jew in the American World,* 27.

7. Arnold Wiznitzer, "The Exodus from Brazil and Arrival in New Amsterdam of the Jewish Pilgrim Fathers," *in The Jewish Experience in Latin America: Selected Studies from the Publications of the American Jewish Historical Society,* vol. 2, ed. Martin A. Cohen (Waltham, Mass.: American Jewish Historical Society, 1971).

8. Marcus, *Jew in the American World,* 29–30.

9. Genesis 26:18; Jewish Publication Society translation (1917).

10. Faber, *Time for Planting,* 11–12; Wiznitzer, "Exodus from Brazil," passim.

11. Marcus, *Jew in the American World,* 32.

12. Wolff and Wolff, "Problem of the First Jewish Settlers," 170.

13. Marcus, *Jew in the American World,* 33.

14. Marcus, *Jew in the American World,* 32.

15. Carl Bridenbaugh, *Cities in the Wilderness: The First Century of Urban Life in America, 1625–1742* (New York: Oxford University Press, 1966), 6.

16. Bridenbaugh, *Cities in the Wilderness,* pl. 2.

Chapter 2

1. Abraham Karp, ed., *The Jews in America: A Treasury of Art and Literature* (Southport, Conn.: Hugh Lauter Levin Associates, 1994), 48–50.

2. Jacob Rader Marcus, *The Jew in the American World: A Source Book* (Detroit: Wayne State University Press, 1996), 142–143.

3. Eli Faber, *A Time for Planting: The First Migration, 1654–1820,* vol. 1 of *The Jewish People in America* (Baltimore: Johns Hopkins University Press, 1992), 74.

4. Marcus, *The Jew,* 43.

5. Doris Groshen Daniels, "Colonial Jewry: Religion, Domestic and Social Relations," *American Jewish Historical Quarterly* 66 (1976–1977): 393–394.

6. Faber, *Time for Planting,* 65.

7. Faber, *Time for Planting,* 66.

8. Faber, *Time for Planting,* 65.

9. Faber, *Time for Planting,* 65.

10. Jacob R. Marcus, *The Jewish American Woman: A Documentary History* (New York: KTAV, 1981), 37–39.

11. Hyman B. Grinstein, *The Rise of the Jewish Community of New York* (Philadelphia: Jewish Publication Society of America, 1947), 373.

12. Morris A. Gutstein, *The Story of the Jews of Newport* (New York: Block, 1936), 138.

13. Marcus, *Jewish American Woman,* 52–53.

14. Marcus, *Jewish American Woman,* 53.

15. Faber, *Time for Planting,* 88.

16. Grinstein, *Rise,* 26.

17. Daniels, "Colonial Jewry," 385.

18. Karp, *Jews in America,* 22.

19. Faber, *Time for Planting,* 34.

20. Gutstein, *Jews of Newport,* 138.

21. Marcus, *Jewish American Woman,* 35.

22. Marcus, *Jewish American Woman,* 36.

23. Faber, *Time for Planting,* 69.

24. Faber, *Time for Planting,* 88.

25. Marion Bodek, "Making Do: Jewish Women and Philanthropy," in *Jewish Life in Philadelphia,* ed. Murray Friedman (Philadelphia: Institute for the Study of Human Issues, 1983), 145.

26. Bodek, "Making Do," 145.

Chapter 3

1. Abraham Karp, ed., *The Jews in America: A Treasury of Art and Literature* (Southport, Conn: Hugh Lauter Levin Associates, 1994), 73.

2. Eli Faber, *A Time for Planting: The First Migration, 1654–1820,* vol. 1 of *The Jewish People in America* (Baltimore: Johns Hopkins University Press, 1992), 15.

3. Faber, *Time for Planting,* 14.

4. Faber, *Time for Planting,* 14.

5. Robert P. Sweirenga, *The Forerunners: Dutch Jews in the North American Diaspora* (Detroit: Wayne State University Press, 1994), 48.

6. Jacob R. Marcus, *The Jewish American Woman: A Documentary History* (New York: KTAV, 1981), 30.

7. John Bartlett, *Familiar Quotations,* ed. Emily Morison Beck (Boston: Little, Brown, 1980), 392.

8. Marcus, *Jewish American Woman,* 29.

9. Barnett A. Elzas, *The Jews of South Carolina* (Philadelphia: J. B. Lippincott, 1905), 44.

10. Irene D. Neu, "The Jewish Businesswoman in America," *American Jewish Historical Quarterly* 66 (1976–1977): 138.

11. Morris A. Gutstein, *The Story of the Jews of Newport* (New York: Block, 1936), 41.

12. Sweirenga, *Forerunners,* 48.

13. Faber, *Time for Planting,* 48.

14. Faber, *Time for Planting,* 48.

15. Faber, *Time for Planting,* 155 n. 48.

16. Faber, *Time for Planting,* 42.

17. Francine Klagsbrun, *Voices of Wisdom* (New York: Pantheon, 1980), 161.

18. Faber, *Time for Planting,* 46.

19. Doris Groshen Daniels, "Colonial Jewry: Religion, Domestic and Social Relations," *American Jewish Historical Quarterly* 66 (1976–1977): 400.

20. Carl Bridenbaugh, *Cities in the Wilderness: The First Century of Urban Life in America, 1625–1742* (New York: Oxford University Press, 1966), 124, 303.

21. Karp, *Jews in America,* 55.

22. Faber, *Time for Planting,* 89.

23. Karp, *Jews in America,* 55.

24. Daniels, "Colonial Jewry," 392.

25. Faber, *Time for Planting,* 159 n. 3.

26. Daniels, "Colonial Jewry," 391.

27. Daniels, "Colonial Jewry," 390.

28. Grinstein, *Rise,* 246.

29. Daniels, "Colonial Jewry," 390.

30. Karp, *Jews in America,* 56.

31. Jacob Rader Marcus, ed., *The Jew in the American World: A Source Book* (Detroit: Wayne State University Press, 1996), 121.

32. Sheldon Hanft, " Mordecai's Female Academy," *American Jewish Historical Quarterly* 19 (1989): 80.

33. All Mordecai materials are drawn from Hanft, "Mordecai's Female Academy."

Chapter 4

1. Steven Lowenstein, *The Jews of Oregon, 1850–1950* (Portland: Jewish Historical Society of Oregon, 1987), 25–26.

2. Lowenstein, *Jews of Oregon,* 65.

3. Quoted in Lowenstein, *Jews of Oregon,* 26.

4. Quoted in Lowenstein, *Jews of Oregon,* 12.

5. Quoted in Hasia R. Diner, *A Time for Gathering: The Second Migration, 1820–1880,* vol. 2 of *The Jewish People in America* (Baltimore: Johns Hopkins University Press, 1992), 16.

6. Quoted in Lowenstein, *Jews of Oregon,* 12.

7. Quoted in Diner, *Time for Gathering,* 37.

8. Quoted in Diner, *Time for Gathering,* 39.

9. Quoted in Diner, *Time for Gathering,* 42.

10. Diner, *Time for Gathering,* 47.

11. Quoted in Diner, *Time for Gathering,* 43.

12. Quoted in Diner, *Time for Gathering,* 53.

13. Diane Ashton, *Rebecca Gratz: Women and Judaism in Antebellum America* (Detroit: Wayne State University Press, 1997), 33.

14. Quoted in Lowenstein, *Jews of Oregon,* 12.

Chapter 5

1. Amelia Ullmann, quoted in Jacob Rader Marcus, *Memoirs of American Jews, 1775–1865* (Philadelphia: Jewish Publication Society of America, 1955), 2:354.

2. Ullmann in Marcus, *Memoirs,* 2:353.

3. Ullmann in Marcus, *Memoirs,* 2:354.

4. Ullmann in Marcus, *Memoirs,* 2:353.

5. Quoted in Jacob Marcus, *The Jewish American Woman: A Documentary History* (New York: KTAV, 1981), 191.

6. Ullmann in Marcus, *Memoirs,* 2:355.

7. Ullmann in Marcus, *Memoirs,* 2:355.

8. Quoted in Marcus, *Documentary,* 193.

9. Quoted in Robert P. Sweirenga, *The Forerunners: Dutch Jews in the North American Diaspora* (Detroit: Wayne State University Press, 1994), 231.

10. Quoted in Hasia R. Diner, *A Time for Gathering: The Second Migration, 1820–1880,* vol. 2 of *The Jewish People in America* (Baltimore: Johns Hopkins University Press, 1992), 58.

11. Ira Rosenwaike, "The Jews of Baltimore: 1810–1820," *American Jewish Historical Quarterly* 67 (1977–1978): 105.

12. David G. Dalin and Jonathan Rosenbaum, *Making a Life, Building a Community: A History of the Jews of Hartford* (New York: Holmes & Meier, 1997), 35.

13. Dalin and Rosenbaum, *Making a Life,* 11.

14. Quoted in Harriet Rochlin and Fred Rochlin, *Pioneer Jews: A New Life in the Far West* (Boston: Houghton Mifflin, 1984), 93.

15. Quoted in Linda Mack Schloff, *"And Prairie Dogs Weren't Kosher"* (St. Paul: Minnesota Historical Society Press, 1996), 58.

16. Quoted in Marcus, *Documentary,* 192.

17. Quoted in Marcus, *Documentary,* 195.

18. Quoted in Deborah Goodman, "Jewish Settlement History in the United States and in Champaign-Urbana" (unpublished paper, Champaign County Historical Archives, Urbana Free Library, Urbana, Illinois, 1970), 9–10, passim.

19. Quoted in Marcus, *Documentary,* 192.

20. Quoted in Marcus, *Documentary,* 194.

21. Quoted in Rochlin and Rochlin, *Pioneer Jews,* 95.

22. Quoted in Schloff, *Prairie Dogs,* 71.

23. Quoted in Marcus, *Memoirs,* 2:364.

24. Quoted in Marcus, *Documentary,* 238.

25. Quoted in Marcus, *Documentary,* 239.

26. Rochlin and Rochlin, *Pioneer Jews,* 90.

27. Diner, *Time for Gathering.*

28. Rochlin and Rochlin, *Pioneer Jews,* 92.

29. Quoted in Rochlin and Rochlin, *Pioneer Jews*, 99.

30. Rosenwaike, "Jews of Baltimore," 116.

31. Sweirenga, *Forerunners*, 136.

32. Quoted in Charlotte Baum et al., *The Jewish Woman in America* (New York: New American Library, 1975).

33. Quoted in Diner, *Time for Gathering*, 83–84.

34. Quoted in Paula E. Hyman and Deborah Dash Moore, eds., *Jewish Women in America: An Historical Encyclopedia* (New York: Routledge, 1997), 243.

35. Quoted in Hyman and Moore, *Jewish Women*, 807.

36. Quoted in Hyman and Moore, *Jewish Women*, 666.

37. Quoted in Hyman and Moore, *Jewish Women*, 1165.

38. Smith, in Jonathan A. Sarna and Ellen Smith, eds., *The Jews of Boston* (Boston: Combined Jewish Philanthropies of Boston/Northeastern University Press, 1995), 57.

39. Marc McCutcheon, *The Writer's Guide to Everyday Life in the 1800s* (Cincinnati: Writer's Digest Books, 1993), 161.

Chapter 6

1. Quoted in Hasia R. Diner, *Jews in America* (New York: Oxford University Press, 1996), 31.

2. Diner, *Jews in America*, 32.

3. Quoted in Irving Cutler, *The Jews of Chicago: From Shtetl to Suburb* (Urbana: University of Illinois Press, 1996), 13.

4. Quoted in Robert P. Sweirenga, *The Forerunners: Dutch Jews in the North American Diaspora* (Detroit: Wayne State University Press, 1994), 231.

5. Quoted in Cutler, *Jews of Chicago*, 12–13.

6. Sweirenga, *Forerunners*, 278.

7. Quoted in Cutler, *Jews of Chicago*, 13.

8. Quoted in Sherri Goldstein Gleicher, "The Spiegelbergs of New Mexico: A Family Story of the Southwestern Frontier," *Southwest Jewish History*, 1992; a publication of the Leona G. and David A. Bloom Archives, University of Arizona.

9. Quoted in Jacob R. Marcus, *The Jewish American Woman: A Documentary History* (New York: KTAV, 1981), 256.

10. Quoted in Marcus, *Documentary*, 259.

11. Quoted in Gleicher, "Spiegelbergs of New Mexico," 3.

12. Quoted in Linda Mack Schloff, *"And Prairie Dogs Weren't Kosher"* (St. Paul: Minnesota Historical Society Press, 1996), 80.

13. Quoted in Hasia R. Diner, *A Time for Gathering: The Second Migration, 1820–1880*, vol. 2 of *The Jewish People in America* (Baltimore: Johns Hopkins University Press, 1992), 128.

14. Quoted in William R. Helmreich, *The Enduring Community: The Jews of Newark and Metrowest* (New Brunswick, N.J.: Transaction, 1999), 18.

15. Quoted in Charlotte Baum, Paula Hyman, and Sonya Michel, *The Jewish Woman in America* (New York: New American Library, 1975), 29.

16. Quoted in Schloff, *Prairie Dogs*, 182.

17. Quoted in Diner, *Time for Gathering*, 99.

18. Quoted in Diner, *Time for Gathering*, 99.

19. Quoted in Herbert T. Ezekiel and Gaston Lichtenstein, *The History of the Jews of Richmond: 1769–1917* (Richmond: Herbert T. Ezekiel, Printer, 1917), 253.

20. Quoted in Hyman and Moore, *Jewish Women*, 230–231.

21. Quoted in Hyman and Moore, *Jewish Women*, 230.

22. Quoted in Hyman and Moore, *Jewish Women*, 232.

23. Diane Ashton, *Rebecca Gratz: Women and Judaism in Antebellum America* (Detroit: Wayne State University Press, 1997), 94.

24. Quoted in Ashton, *Rebecca Gratz*, 96.

25. Jacob R. Marcus, *The Jew in the American World: A Source Book* (Detroit: Wayne State University Press, 1996), 153–154.

26. Marcus, *The Jew*, 156.

27. Marcus, *The Jew*, 156.

28. Quoted in Marcus, *Documentary,* 225–227.

29. Quoted in Marcus, *Documentary,* 173.

30. Marcus, *The Jew*, 154.

31. Quoted in Diner, *Time for Gathering*, 130.

32. Quoted in Diner, *Time for Gathering*, 130.

33. Quoted in Diner, *Time for Gathering*, 130–131.

34. Quoted in Diner, *Time for Gathering*, 116–117.

35. Quoted in Marcus, *Documentary*, 187.

36. Quoted in Diner, *Time for Gathering*, 120.

37. Quoted in Marcus, *Documentary*, 188.

38. Quoted in Marcus, *Documentary*, 188.

39. Quoted in Paula E. Hyman, *Gender and Assimilation in Modern Jewish History: The Roles and Representation of Women* (Seattle: University of Washington Press, 1995), 28.

40. Quoted in Hyman and Moore, *Jewish Women*, 667.

41. Quoted in Marcus, *Documentary*, 188.

42. Quoted in Baum et al., *Jewish Woman.*

43. Quoted in Hyman and Moore, *Jewish Women*, 281.

44. Quoted in Marcus, *Documentary*, 230.

45. Quoted in Marcus, *Documentary*, 231.

46. Quoted in Marcus, *Documentary*, 271.

47. Quoted in Marcus, *Documentary*, 269.

Chapter 7

1. Quoted in Gerald Sorin, *A Time for Building: The Third Migration, 1880–1920,* vol. 3 of *The Jewish People in America* (Baltimore: Johns Hopkins University Press, 1992), 40.

2. Quoted in Sydney Stahl Weinberg, *The World of Our Mothers: The Lives of Jewish Immigrant Women* (Chapel Hill: University of North Carolina Press, 1988), 71.

3. Quoted in Linda Mack Schloff, *"And Prairie Dogs Weren't Kosher"* (St. Paul: Minnesota Historical Society Press, 1996), 30–31.

4. Quoted in Schloff, *Prairie Dogs,* 28.

5. Quoted in Schloff, *Prairie Dogs,* 21.

6. Quoted in Schloff, *Prairie Dogs,* 22.

7. Quoted in Charlotte Baum, Paula Hyman, and Sonya Michel, *The Jewish Woman in America* (New York: New American Library, 1975), 68.

8. Quoted in Schloff, *Prairie Dogs,* 22–23.

9. Weinberg, *World of Our Mothers*, 30.

10. Quoted in Sorin, *Time for Building,* 26.

11. Weinberg, *World of Our Mothers,* 55.

12. Quoted in Sorin, *Time for Building,* 32.

13. Quoted in Sorin, *Time for Building,* 32.

14. Irving Cutler, *The Jews of Chicago: From Shtetl to Suburb* (Urbana: University of Illinois Press, 1996), 50.

15. Andrew R. Heinze, *Adapting to Abundance: Jewish Immigrants, Mass Consumption, and the Search for American Identity* (New York: Columbia University Press, 1990), 185.

16. Weinberg, *World of Our Mothers,* 32.

17. Quoted in Cutler, *Jews of Chicago,* 54.

18. Quoted in Weinberg, *World of Our Mothers,* 8.

19. Weinberg, *World of Our Mothers,* 32.

20. Cutler, *Jews of Chicago,* 50.

21. Quoted in Susan A. Glenn, *Daughters of the Shtetl: Life and Labor in the Immigrant Generation* (Ithaca: Cornell University Press, 1990), 77.

22. Weinberg, *World of Our Mothers,* 54.

23. Quoted in Sorin, *Time for Building,* 34.

24. Quoted in Sorin, *Time for Building,* 33.

25. Quoted in Irving Howe, *World of Our Fathers* (New York: Harcourt Brace Jovanovich, 1976), 40.

26. Quoted in Howe, *World of Our Fathers,* 40–41.

27. Quoted in Howe, *World of Our Fathers,* 41.

28. Quoted in Heinze, *Adapting to Abundance,* 41.

29. Quoted in Sorin, *Time for Building,* 41.

30. Quoted in Sorin, *Time for Building,* 41.

31. Quoted in Weinberg, *World of Our Mothers,* 60.

32. Glenn, *Daughters of the Shtetl,* 47.

33. Heinze, *Adapting to Abundance,* 41.

34. Hasia R. Diner, *Jews in America* (New York: Oxford University Press, 1996), 52.

35. Quoted in Schloff, *Prairie Dogs.*

36. Quoted in Schloff, *Prairie Dogs,* 34.

37. Quoted in Sorin, *Time for Building,* 43.

38. Sorin, *Time for Building,* 44.

39. Sorin, *Time for Building,* 46.

40. Sorin, *Time for Building,* 47.

Chapter 8

1. Quoted in Charlotte Baum, Paula Hyman, and Sonya Michel, *The Jewish Woman in America* (New York: New American Library, 1975), 96.

2. Quoted in Baum et al., *Jewish Woman,* 96.

3. Quoted in Baum et al., *Jewish Woman,* 97.

4. Quoted in Baum et al., *Jewish Woman,* 97.

5. Quoted in Baum et al., *Jewish Woman,* 97.

6. Quoted in Baum et al., *Jewish Woman,* 97.

7. Quoted in Baum et al., *Jewish Woman,* 97.

8. Quoted in Baum et al., *Jewish Woman,* 97.

9. Susan A. Glenn, *Daughters of the Shtetl: Life and Labor in the Immigrant Generation* (Ithaca: Cornell University Press, 1990), 64.

10. Quoted in Baum et al., *Jewish Woman,* 105.

11. Quoted in Baum et al., *Jewish Woman,* 104–105.

12. Quoted in Baum et al., *Jewish Woman,* 105–106.

13. Quoted in Baum et al., *Jewish Woman,* 105.

14. Gerald Sorin, *A Time for Building: The Third Migration, 1880–1920,* vol. 3 of *The Jewish People in America* (Baltimore: Johns Hopkins University Press, 1992), 70–71.

15. Abraham Karp, ed., *The Jews in America: A Treasury of Art and Literature* (Southport, Conn.: Hugh Lauter Levin Associates, 1994), 15.

16. Quoted in Sorin, *Time for Building,* 72.

17. Sorin, *Time for Building,* 70–71.

18. Quoted in Sorin, *Time for Building,* 71.

19. Quoted in Sorin, *Time for Building,* 71.

20. Quoted in Sorin, *Time for Building,* 71.

21. Quoted in Karp, *Jews in America,* 218.

22. Harriet Rochlin and Fred Rochlin, *Pioneer Jews: A New Life in the Far West* (Boston: Houghton Mifflin, 1984), 216; William R. Helmreich, *The Enduring Community: The Jews of Newark and Metrowest* (New Brunswick, N.J.: Transaction, 1999), 20.

23. Sorin, *Time for Building,* 137.

24. Glenn, *Daughters of the Shtetl,* 92.

25. Glenn, *Daughters of the Shtetl,* 92.

26. Glenn, *Daughters of the Shtetl,* 92.

27. Glenn, *Daughters of the Shtetl,* 93.

28. Sorin, *Time for Building,* 74.

29. Glenn, *Daughters of the Shtetl,* 92.

30. Baum et al., *Jewish Woman,* 109.

31. Glenn, *Daughters of the Shtetl,* 65.

32. Glenn, *Daughters of the Shtetl,* 65–66.

33. Baum et al., *Jewish Woman,* 147.

34. Quoted in Karp, *Jews in America,* 221.

35. Quoted in Karp, *Jews in America,* 221–222.

36. Quoted in Sydney Stahl Weinberg, *The World of Our Mothers: The Lives of Jewish Immigrant Women* (Chapel Hill: University of North Carolina Press, 1988), 91.

37. Quoted in Glenn, *Daughters of the Shtetl,* 64.

38. Quoted in Paula E. Hyman and Deborah Dash Moore, eds., *Jewish Women in America: An Historical Encyclopedia* (New York: Routledge, 1997), 55.

39. Quoted in Joyce Antler, *The Journey Home: Jewish Women and the American Century* (New York: Free Press, 1997), 23.

40. Quoted in Antler, *Journey Home,* 21.

41. Glenn, *Daughters of the Shtetl,* 80.

42. Quoted in Glenn, *Daughters of the Shtetl,* 83.

43. Quoted in Marcus, *Documentary,* 573.

44. Weinberg, *World of Our Mothers,* 190.

45. Quoted in Weinberg, *World of Our Mothers,* 191.

46. Quoted in Weinberg, *World of Our Mothers,* 191.

47. Quoted in Sorin, *Time for Building,* 52.

48. Andrew R. Heinze, *Adapting to Abundance: Jewish Immigration, Mass Consumption, and the Search for American Identity* (New York: Columbia University press, 1996), 43.

49. Quoted in Sorin, *Time for Building,* 179.

50. Quoted in Glenn, *Daughters of the Shtetl,* 155.

51. Quoted in Glenn, *Daughters of the Shtetl,* 159.

52. Heinze, *Adapting to Abundance,* 118.

53. Quoted in Weinberg, *World of Our Mothers,* 182.

54. Paula E. Hyman, *Gender and Assimilation in Modern Jewish History: The Roles and Representation of Women* (Seattle: University of Washington Press, 1995), 105.

55. Quoted in Weinberg, *World of Our Mothers,* 182.

56.Hyman and Moore, *Jewish Women,* 1268.

57. Quoted in Glenn, *Daughters of the Shtetl,* 180.

58. Quoted in Glenn, *Daughters of the Shtetl,* 167.

59. Quoted in Hyman and Moore, *Jewish Women,* 632.

60. Baum et al., *Jewish Woman,* 140.

61. Quoted Hyman and Moore, *Jewish Women,* 1433.

62. Glenn, *Daughters of the Shtetl,* 168.

63. Quoted Hyman and Moore, *Jewish Women,* 1433.

64. Quoted in Baum et al., *Jewish Woman,* 142.

65. Quoted in Baum et al., *Jewish Woman,* 143.

66. Quoted in Glenn, *Daughters of the Shtetl,* 205.

67. Irving Howe, *World of Our Fathers* (New York: Harcourt Brace Jovanovich, 1976), 299.

68. Quoted in Howe, *World of Our Fathers,* 299.

69. Hyman and Moore, *Jewish Women,* 1434.

70. Quoted in Glenn, *Daughters of the Shtetl,* 207.

71. Glenn, *Daughters of the Shtetl,* 172.

72. Quoted in Howe, *World of Our Fathers,* 300.

73. Quoted in Hyman and Moore, *Jewish Women,* 675.

74. Quoted in Baum et al., *Jewish Woman,* 144.

75. Quoted in Howe, *World of Our Fathers,* 300.

76. Quoted in Sorin, *Time for Building,* 130.

77. Quoted in Jacob R. Marcus, *The Jewish American Woman: A Documentary History* (New York: KTAV, 1981), 592.

78. Quoted in Marcus, *Documentary,* 592, 594.

79. Quoted in Marcus, *Documentary,* 591.

80. Quoted in Baum et al., *Jewish Woman,* 151.

81. Quoted in Baum et al., *Jewish Woman,* 151.

82. Quoted in Baum et al., *Jewish Woman,* 151.

83. Quoted in Baum et al., *Jewish Woman,* 152–153.

84. Quoted in Hasia R. Diner, *Jews in America* (New York: Oxford University Press, 1996), 66.

85. Quoted in Glenn, *Daughters of the Shtetl,* 205.

86. Quoted in Glenn, *Daughters of the Shtetl,* 205.

87. All quotes in paragraph from Sydney Stahl Weinberg, *The World of Our Mothers: The Lives of Jewish Immigrant Women* (Chapel Hill: University of North Carolina Press), 199.

88. Quoted in Jacob Rader Marcus, *The Jew in the American World: A Source Book* (Detroit: Wayne State University Press, 1996), 694–697, passim.

89. Quoted in Howe, *World of Our Fathers,* 98.

90. Quoted in Howe, *World of Our Fathers,* 97.

91. Quoted in Baum et al., *Jewish Woman,* 175.

92. Quoted in Howe, *World of Our Fathers,* 97.

93. Quoted in Baum et al., *Jewish Woman,* 175.

94. Quoted in Weinberg, *World of Our Mothers,* 92.

95. Quoted in Baum et al., *Jewish Woman,* 175.

96. Quoted in Sorin, *Time for Building,* 85.

Chapter 9

1. Quoted in Sydney Stahl Weinberg, *The World of Our Mothers: The Lives of Jewish Immigrant Women* (Chapel Hill: University of North Carolina Press, 1988), 211.

2. Quoted in Jacob R. Marcus, *The Jewish American Woman: A Documentary History* (New York: KTAV, 1981), 506.

3. Quoted in Weinberg, *World of Our Mothers,* 211.

4. Quoted in Marcus, *Jewish American Woman,* 503.

5. Quoted in Marcus, *Jewish American Woman,* 504.

6. Quoted in Weinberg, *World of Our Mothers,* 208.

7. Quoted in Paula E. Hyman, *Gender and Assimilation in Modern Jewish History: The Roles and Representation of Women* (Seattle: University of Washington Press, 1995), 101.

8. Quoted in Weinberg, *World of Our Mothers,* 207.

9. Quoted in Weinberg, *World of Our Mothers,* 208.

10. Quoted in Weinberg, *World of Our Mothers,* 208.

11. Quoted in Weinberg, *World of Our Mothers,* 205.

12. Quoted in Joyce Antler, *The Journey Home: Jewish Women and the American Century* (New York: Free Press, 1997), 80.

13. Quoted in Hyman and Moore, *Jewish Women,* 1342.

14. Quoted in Hyman and Moore, *Jewish Women,* 1343.

15. Quoted in Antler, *Journey Home,* 81.

16. Quoted in Weinberg, *World of Our Mothers,* 110.

17. Quoted in Weinberg, *World of Our Mothers,* 110.

18. Weinberg, *World of Our Mothers,* 110.

19. Quoted in Charlotte Baum, Paula Hyman, and Sonya Michel, *The Jewish Woman in America* (New York: New American Library, 1975), 117.

20. Quoted in Marcus, *Jewish American Woman,* 487.

21. Quoted in Marcus, *Jewish American Woman,* 488–489.

22. Quoted in Weinberg, *World of Our Mothers,* 211.

23. Andrew R. Heinze, *Adapting to Abundance: Jewish Immigrants, Mass Consumption, and the Search for American Identity* (New York: Columbia University Press, 1990), 23.

24. Heinze, *Adapting to Abundance,* 24.

25. Heinze, *Adapting to Abundance,* 22.

26. Quoted in Heinze, *Adapting to Abundance,* 23.

27. Quoted in Heinze, *Adapting to Abundance,* 44.

28. Quoted in Heinze, *Adapting to Abundance,* 44.

29. Quoted in Marcus, *Jewish American Woman,* 497.

30. Heinze, *Adapting to Abundance,* 46.

31. Quoted in Heinze, *Adapting to Abundance*, 136.

32. Quoted in Heinze, *Adapting to Abundance*, 140.

33. Quoted in Heinze, *Adapting to Abundance*, 127.

34. Gerald A. Sorin, *A Time for Building: The Third Migration, 1880–1920*, vol. 3 of *The Jewish People in America* (Baltimore: Johns Hopkins University Press, 1992), 158.

35. Quoted in Sorin, *Time for Building*, 158.

36. Quoted in Hyman and Moore, *Jewish Women*, 820.

37. Quoted in Heinze, *Adapting to Abundance*, 95.

38. Quoted in Hyman and Moore, *Jewish Women*, 462.

39. Quoted in Marcus, *Jewish American Woman*, 500–501.

40. Quoted in Heinze, *Adapting to Abundance*, 112.

41. Quoted in Heinze, *Adapting to Abundance*, 110.

42. Quoted in Marcus, *Jewish American Woman*, 500.

43. Quoted in Sorin, *Time for Building*, 94.

44. Quoted in Sorin, *Time for Building*, 94.

45. Quoted in Marcus, *Jewish American Woman*, 658.

46. Quoted in Marcus, *Jewish American Woman*, 660.

47. Quoted in Marcus, *Jewish American Woman*, 661.

48. Quoted in Marcus, *Jewish American Woman*, 661.

49. Quoted in Marcus, *Jewish American Woman*, 661.

50. Quoted in Marcus, *Jewish American Woman*, 662.

51. Quoted in Marcus, *Jewish American Woman*, 681.

52. Heinze, *Adapting to Abundance*, 196.

53. Quoted in Baum, *Jewish Woman in America*, 100.

54. Quoted in Baum, *Jewish Woman in America*, 114.

55. Linda Mack Schloff, *"And Prairie Dogs Weren't Kosher"* (St. Paul: Minnesota Historical Society Press, 1996), 125.

56. Quoted in Hyman and Moore, *Jewish Women*, 348.

57. Quoted in Hyman and Moore, *Jewish Women*, 886.

58. Quoted in Weinberg, *World of Our Mothers*, 220.

59. Quoted in Marcus, *Jewish American Woman*, 680.

60. Quoted in Marcus, *Jewish American Woman*, 678.

61. Quoted in Weinberg, *World of Our Mothers*, 222.

62. Weinberg, *World of Our Mothers*, 220.

63. Quoted in Marcus, *Jewish American Woman*, 541–542.

64. Quoted in Marcus, *Jewish American Woman*, 547, 546.

65. Quoted in Marcus, *Jewish American Woman*, 545.

66. Quoted in Marcus, *Jewish American Woman*, 547.

67. Quoted in Marcus, *Jewish American Woman*, 545.

68. Quoted in Marcus, *Jewish American Woman*, 548.

69. Quoted in Baum, *Jewish Woman in America*, 123.

70. Weinberg, *World of Our Mothers*, 174.

71. Quoted in Baum, *Jewish Woman in America*, 126.

72. Weinberg, *World of Our Mothers*, 170.

73. Quotation and statistics, Hyman and Moore, *Jewish Women*, 661.

74. Weinberg, *World of Our Mothers*, 196.

75. Marcus, *Jewish American Woman*, 745–749, passim.

76. Quoted in Marcus, *Jewish American Woman*, 747.

Chapter 10

1. Gerald Sorin, *A Time for Building: The Third Migration, 1880–1920*, vol. 3 of *The Jewish People in America* (Baltimore: Johns Hopkins University Press, 1992), 137.

2. Quoted in Paula E. Hyman and
Deborah Dash Moore, eds., *Jewish Women
in America: An Historical Encyclopedia* (New
York: Routledge, 1997), 684–685.

3. Quoted in Irving Cutler, *The Jews of
Chicago: From Shtetl to Suburb* (Urbana:
University of Illinois Press, 1996), 95.

4. Hyman and Moore, *Jewish Women,*
926.

5. Quoted in Sorin, *Time for Building,*
181.

6. Sorin, *Time for Building,* 18.

7. Susan A. Glenn, *Daughters of the
Shtetl: Life and Labor in the Immigrant
Generation* (Ithaca: Cornell University Press,
1990), 140.

8. Quoted in Paula E. Hyman, *Gender
and Assimilation in Modern Jewish History:
The Roles and Representation of Women*
(Seattle: University of Washington Press,
1995), 117.

9. Quoted in Heinze, *Adapting to
Abundance,* 58.

10. Quoted in Cutler, *Jews of Chicago,* 95.

11. Quoted in Cutler, *Jews of Chicago,* 95.

12. Quoted in Marion Bodek, "Making
Do: Jewish Women and Philanthropy," in
Jewish Life in Philadelphia, ed. Murray
Friedman (Philadelphia: Institute for the
Study of Human Issues, 1983), 156.

13. Quoted in Hyman and Moore, *Jewish
Women,* 235–236.

14. Quoted in Hyman and Moore, *Jewish
Women,* 1264.

15. Quoted in Hyman and Moore, *Jewish
Women,* 1231.

16. Hyman and Moore, *Jewish Women,*
1231.

17. Hyman and Moore, *Jewish Women,*
878.

18. Quoted in Bodek, "Making Do," 155.

19. Quoted in Jacob R. Marcus, *The
Jewish American Woman: A Documentary
History* (New York: KTAV, 1981), 542.

20. Quoted in Joyce Antler, *The Journey
Home: Jewish Women and the American
Century* (New York: Free Press, 1997), 49.

21. Quoted in Marcus, *Jewish American
Woman,* 401–402.

22. Quoted in Irving Howe, *World of Our
Fathers* (New York: Harcourt Brace
Jovanovich, 1976), 91.

23. Quoted in Marcus, *Jewish American
Woman,* 402.

24. Quoted in Howe, *World of Our
Fathers,* 91.

25. Quoted in Howe, *World of Our
Fathers,* 91.

26. Quoted in Howe, *World of Our
Fathers,* 93.

27. Howe, *World of Our Fathers,* 93.

28. Quoted in Hyman and Moore, *Jewish
Women,* 1447.

29. Quoted in Howe, *World of Our
Fathers,* 94.

30. Quoted in Hyman and Moore, *Jewish
Women,* 1448.

31. Hyman and Moore, *Jewish Women,*
717.

32. Quoted in Beth S. Wenger, "Jewish
Women and Voluntarism: Beyond the Myth
of Enablers," *American Jewish Historical
Quarterly* 79 (1989): 24.

33. Quoted in Wenger, "Jewish Women
and Voluntarism," 25.

34. Quoted in Wenger, "Jewish Women
and Voluntarism," 25.

35. Wenger, "Jewish Women and
Voluntarism," 24.

36. Quoted in Wenger, "Jewish Women
and Voluntarism," 35.

37. Quoted in Wenger, "Jewish Women
and Voluntarism," 32.

38. Quoted in Wenger, "Jewish Women
and Voluntarism," 32.

39. Quoted in Wenger, "Jewish Women
and Voluntarism," 33.

40. Quoted in Wenger, "Jewish Women
and Voluntarism," 34.

41. Quoted in Marcus, *Jewish American
Woman,* 599–600.

Chapter 11

1. Quoted in Charlotte Baum, Paula
Hyman, and Sonya Michel, *The Jewish
Woman in America* (New York: New
American Library, 1975), 169.

2. Quoted in Baum, *Jewish Woman,* 169.

3. Quoted in Faith Rogow, *Gone to Another Meeting: The National Council of Jewish Women, 1893–1993* (Tuscaloosa: University of Alabama Press, 1993), 10.

4. Quoted in Rogow, *Gone to Another Meeting,* 11.

5. Quoted in Rogow, *Gone to Another Meeting,* 10.

6. Quoted in Rogow, *Gone to Another Meeting,* 17.

7. Quoted in Rogow, *Gone to Another Meeting,* 14.

8. Quoted in Rogow, *Gone to Another Meeting,* 14.

9. Quoted in Rogow, *Gone to Another Meeting,* 14.

10. Quoted in Rogow, *Gone to Another Meeting,* 14.

11. Quoted in Rogow, *Gone to Another Meeting,* 20.

12. Quoted in Rogow, *Gone to Another Meeting,* 20, 19.

13. Quoted in Rogow, *Gone to Another Meeting,* 22.

14. Quoted in Rogow, *Gone to Another Meeting,* 22.

15. Quoted in Rogow, *Gone to Another Meeting,* 23.

16. Quoted in Rogow, *Gone to Another Meeting,* 24.

17. Quoted in Rogow, *Gone to Another Meeting,* 24.

18. Quoted in Rogow, *Gone to Another Meeting,* 24.

19. Quoted in Beth S. Wenger, "Jewish Women and Voluntarism: Beyond the Myth of Enablers," *American Jewish Historical Quarterly* 79 (1989): 36.

20. Quoted in Marion Bodek, "Making Do: Jewish Women and Philanthropy," in *Jewish Life in Philadelphia,* ed. Murray Friedman (Philadelphia: Institute for the Study of Human Issues, 1983), 159.

21. Quoted in David G. Dalin and Jonathan Rosenbaum, *Making a Life, Building a Community: A History of the Jews of Hartford* (New York: Holmes & Meier, 1997), 74.

22. Quoted in Abraham Karp, ed., *The Jews in America: A Treasury of Art and Literature* (Southport, Conn.: Hugh Lauter Levin Associates, 1994), 134.

23. Quoted in Karp, *Jews in America,* 134.

24. Susan A. Glenn, *Daughters of the Shtetl: Life and Labor in the Immigrant Generation* (Ithaca: Cornell University Press, 1990), 52.

25. Quoted in Baum, *Jewish Woman in America,* 166.

26. Glenn, *Daughters of the Shtetl,* 48.

27. Quoted in Baum, *Jewish Woman in America,* 169.

28. Quoted in Baum, *Jewish Woman in America,* 173.

29. Quoted in Dalin and Rosenbaum, *Making a Life,* 74.

30. Quoted in Baum, *Jewish Woman in America,* 171.

31. Quoted in Baum, *Jewish Woman in America,* 50.

32. Quoted in Hyman and Moore, *Jewish Women,* 1193.

33. Quoted in Hyman and Moore, *Jewish Women,* 1194.

34. Quoted in Rogow, *Gone to Another Meeting,* 103.

35. Quoted in Rogow, *Gone to Another Meeting,* 104.

36. Quoted in Rogow, *Gone to Another Meeting,* 107.

37. Quoted in Joyce Antler, *The Journey Home: Jewish Women and the American Century* (New York: Free Press, 1997), 103.

38. Quoted in Hyman and Moore, *Jewish Women,* 571.

39. Quoted in Hyman and Moore, *Jewish Women,* 572.

40. Quoted in Antler, *Journey Home,* 106.

41. Quoted in Antler, *Journey Home,* 107.

42. Quoted in Hyman and Moore, *Jewish Women,* 878.

43. Quoted in Baum, *Jewish Woman in America,* 51.

44. Quoted in Baum, *Jewish Woman in America,* 52.

45. Quoted in Wenger, "Jewish Women and Voluntarism," 36.

Chapter 12

1. Quoted in *Women in the Military: A Jewish Perspective* (Washington, D.C.: National Museum of American Jewish Military History, n.d.), 26.

2. Quoted in *Women in the Military,* 26.

3. William R. Helmreich, *The Enduring Community: The Jews of Newark and Metrowest* (New Brunswick, N.J.: Transaction, 1999), 217.

4. Quoted in Elaine Krasnow Ellison and Elaine Mark Jaffe, *Voices from Marshall Street: Jewish Life in a Philadelphia Neighborhood, 1920-1960* (Philadelphia: Camino, 1994), 114.

5. Quoted in Ellison and Jaffe, *Voices from Marshall Street,* 47.

6. Quoted in Ellison and Jaffe, *Voices from Marshall Street,* 47.

7. Henry L. Feingold, *A Time for Searching: Entering the Mainstream, 1920–1945,* vol. 4 of *The Jewish People in America* (Baltimore: Johns Hopkins University Press, 1992), 127.

8. Feingold, *Time for Searching,* 125.

9. Feingold, *Time for Searching,* 145.

10. Feingold, *Time for Searching,* 127.

11. Beth S. Wenger, *New York Jews and the Great Depression: Uncertain Promise* (New Haven: Yale University Press, 1996).

12. Feingold, *Time for Searching,* 126.

13. Ewa Morowska, *Insecure Prosperity: Small-Town Jews in Industrial America, 1890–1940* (Princeton: Princeton University Press, 1996), 61.

14. Wenger, *New York Jews,* 16.

15. Wenger, *New York Jews,* 63.

16. Quoted in Ellison and Jaffe, *Voices from Marshall Street,* 129.

17. Quoted in Ellison and Jaffe, *Voices from Marshall Street,* 130.

18. Quoted in Ellison and Jaffe, *Voices from Marshall Street,* 33.

19. Hasia Diner, *Jews in America* (New York: Oxford University Press, 1996), 83.

20. Ruth Jacknow Markowitz, *My Daughter, the Teacher: Jewish Teachers in New York City Schools* (New Brunswick, N.J.: Rutgers University Press, 1993), 20.

21. Diner, *Jews in America,* 82.

22. Quoted in Feingold, *Time for Searching,* 17.

23. Wenger, *New York Jews,* 23.

24. Wenger, *New York Jews,* 6.

25. Quoted in Morowska, *Insecure Prosperity,* 180.

26. Morowska, *Insecure Prosperity,* 182.

27. Quoted in Morowska, *Insecure Prosperity,* 181.

28. Morowska, *Insecure Prosperity,* 85.

29. Quoted in Markowitz, *My Daughter,* 32.

30. Morowska, *Insecure Prosperity,* 182.

31. Quoted in Markowitz, *My Daughter,* 27.

32. Quoted in Markowitz, *My Daughter,* 38.

33. Quoted in Markowitz, *My Daughter,* 31.

34. Markowitz, *My Daughter,* 44.

35. Quoted in Markowitz, *My Daughter,* 43.

36. Quoted in Edward S. Shapiro, *A Time for Healing: American Jewry since World War II,* vol. 3 of *The Jewish People in America* (Baltimore: Johns Hopkins University Press), 8.

37. Quoted in Elinor Slater and Robert Slater, *Great Jewish Women* (Middle Village, N.Y.: Jonathan David, 1998), 183.

38. Quoted in Slater and Slater, *Great Jewish Women,* 184.

39. Quoted in Slater and Slater, *Great Jewish Women,* 184.

40. Deborah Dash Moore, *At Home in America: Second Generation New York Jews* (New York: Columbia University Press 1981), 42.

41. Quoted in Moore, *At Home in America,* 24.

42. Quoted in Moore, *At Home in America,* 29.

43. Quoted in Moore, *At Home in America,* 29.

44. Quoted in Moore, *At Home in America,* 23.

45. Moore, *At Home in America,* 24.

46. Moore, *At Home in America,* 19.

47. Jonathan A. Sarna and Ellen Smith, eds., *The Jews of Boston* (Boston: Combined Jewish Philanthropies of Boston/Northeastern University Press, 1995), 142.

48. Quoted in Steven Lowenstein, *The Jews of Oregon, 1850–1950* (Portland: Jewish Historical Society of Oregon, 1987), 190.

49. Quoted in Wenger, *New York Jews,* 81.

50. Wenger, *New York Jews,* 85.

51. Irving Cutler, *The Jews of Chicago: From Shtetl to Suburb* (Urbana: University of Illinois Press, 1996), 127.

52. Moore, *At Home in America,* 31.

53. Quoted in Helmreich, *Enduring Community,* 61.

54. Cutler, *Jews of Chicago,* 244.

55. Quoted in Ellison and Jaffe, *Voices from Marshall Street,* 132.

56. Quoted in Ellison and Jaffe, *Voices from Marshall Street,* 132.

57. Quoted in Ellison and Jaffe, *Voices from Marshall Street,* 64.

58. Quoted in Moore, *At Home in America,* 62.

59. Cutler, *Jews of Chicago,* 23.

60. Quoted in Moore, *At Home in America,* 63.

61. Quoted in Diner, *Jews in America,* 84.

62. *Women in the Military,* 53.

63. Diner, *Jews in America,* 101.

64. Quoted in *Women in the Military,* 7.

65. Shapiro, *Time for Healing,* 121.

66. Diner, *Jews in America,* 104.

67. Quoted in Sarna and Smith, *Jews of Boston,* 155.

68. Quoted in Sarna and Smith, *Jews of Boston,* 156.

69. Sarna and Smith, *Jews of Boston,* 155.

70. Diner, *Jews in America,* 104.

71. Diner, *Jews in America,* 116.

72. Lowenstein, *Jews of Oregon,* 190.

73. Diner, *Jews in America,* 105.

74. Shapiro, *Time for Healing,* 134.

Chapter 13

1. Quoted in Joyce Antler, *The Journey Home: Jewish Women and the American Century* (New York: Free Press, 1997), 237.

2. Quoted in Antler, *Journey Home,* 236.

3. Quoted in Beth S. Wenger, *New York Jews and the Great Depression: Uncertain Promise* (New Haven: Yale University Press, 1996), 10.

4. Quoted in Wenger, *New York Jews,* 14.

5. Henry L. Feingold, *A Time for Searching: Entering the Mainstream, 1920–1945,* vol. 4 of *The Jewish People in America* (Baltimore: Johns Hopkins University Press, 1992), 147.

6. Wenger, *New York Jews,* 17.

7. Quoted in Jacob R. Marcus, *The Jewish American Woman: A Documentary History* (New York: KTAV, 1981), 774.

8. Feingold, *Time for Searching,* 148.

9. Wenger, *New York Jews,* 25.

10. Quoted in Linda Mack Schloff, *"And Prairie Dogs Weren't Kosher"* (St. Paul: Minnesota Historical Society Press, 1996), 149–150.

11. Quoted in Schloff, *Prairie Dogs,* 132.

12. Quoted in Schloff, *Prairie Dogs,* 147.

13. Feingold, *Time for Searching,* 201.

14. Quoted in Steven Lowenstein, *The Jews of Oregon, 1850–1950* (Portland: Jewish Historical Society of Oregon, 1987), 188.

15. Quoted in Wenger, *New York Jews,* 45.

16. Quoted in Wenger, *New York Jews,* 45.

17. Quoted in Lowenstein, *Jews of Oregon,* 189.

18. Quoted in Wenger, *New York Jews,* 98.

19. Quoted in Wenger, *New York Jews,* 98.

20. Quoted in Wenger, *New York Jews,* 101.

21. Quoted in Wenger, *New York Jews,* 112.

22. Quoted in Wenger, *New York Jews,* 114.

23. Quoted in Wenger, *New York Jews,* 114.

24. Quoted in Wenger, *New York Jews,* 115.

25. Quoted in Wenger, *New York Jews,* 37.

26. Quoted in Wenger, *New York Jews,* 37.

27. Quoted in Wenger, *New York Jews,* 36.

28. Quoted in Wenger, *New York Jews,* 38.

29. Quoted in Hyman and Moore, *Jewish Women,* 1032.

30. Quoted in Hyman and Moore, *Jewish Women,* 718.

31. Quoted in Hyman and Moore, *Jewish Women,* 753.

32. Quoted in Antler, *Journey Home,* 149.

33. Quoted in Antler, *Journey Home,* 149.

34. Quoted in Antler, *Journey Home,* 437.

35. Quoted in Elinor Slater and Robert Slater, *Great Jewish Women* (Middle Village, N.Y.: Jonathan David, 1998), 38.

36. Quoted in Hyman and Moore, *Jewish Women,* 1093.

37. Hyman and Moore, *Jewish Women,* 1092.

38. Quoted in Hyman and Moore, *Jewish Women,* 1093.

39. Hyman and Moore, *Jewish Women,* 29.

40. Quoted in Hyman and Moore, *Jewish Women,* 593.

41. Quoted in Hyman and Moore, *Jewish Women,* 59.

42. Quoted in Ruth Jacknow Markowitz, *My Daughter, the Teacher: Jewish Teachers in the New York City Schools* (New Brunswick, N.J.: Rutgers University Press, 1993), 13.

43. Quoted in Markowitz, *My Daughter,* 12.

44. Quoted in Markowitz, *My Daughter,* 13.

45. Quoted in Markowitz, *My Daughter,* 10.

46. Quoted in Markowitz, *My Daughter,* 10.

47. Quoted in Markowitz, *My Daughter,* 10.

48. Markowitz, *My Daughter,* 2.

49. Markowitz, *My Daughter,* 17.

50. Markowitz, *My Daughter,* 16.

51. Markowitz, *My Daughter,* 89.

52. Markowitz, *My Daughter,* 135.

53. Quoted in Markowitz, *My Daughter,* 135.

54. Markowitz, *My Daughter,* 139.

55. Quoted in Marcus, *Jewish American Woman,* 769.

56. Wenger, *New York Jews,* 42.

57. Quoted in Wenger, *New York Jews,* 52.

58. Quoted in Elaine Krasnow Ellison and Elaine Mark Jaffe, *Voices from Marshall Street: Jewish Life in a Philadelphia Neighborhood, 1920-1960* (Philadelphia: Camino, 1994), 61.

59. Quoted in Wenger, *New York Jews,* 74.

60. Quoted in Wenger, *New York Jews,* 74.

61. Wenger, *New York Jews,* 73; Markowitz, *My Daughter,* 134.

62. Quoted in Marcus, *Jewish American Woman,* 769.

63. Quoted in Marcus, *Jewish American Woman,* 770.

64. Quoted in Marcus, *Jewish American Woman,* 770.

65. Quoted in Markowitz, *My Daughter,* 771.

66. Quoted in Ewa Morowska, *Insecure Prosperity: Small-Town Jews in Industrial America, 1890–1940* (Princeton: Princeton University Press, 1996), 210.

67. Quoted in Markowitz, *My Daughter,* 146.

68. Quoted in Markowitz, *My Daughter,* 147.

69. Quoted in Markowitz, *My Daughter,* 147.

70. Quoted in *Women in the Military,* 7.

71. Quoted in *Women in the Military,* 35.

72. Quoted in *Women in the Military,* 31.

73. Quoted in *Women in the Military,* 22.

74. Irving Cutler, *The Jews of Chicago: From Shtetl to Suburb* (Urbana: University of Illinois Press, 1996), 132.

75. Quoted in Cutler, *Jews of Chicago,* 132.

76. Hyman and Moore, *Jewish Women,* 394.

Chapter 14

1. Quoted in Paula E. Hyman and Deborah Dash Moore, eds., *Jewish Women in America: An Historical Encyclopedia* (New York: Routledge, 1997), 11.
2. Quoted in Hyman and Moore, *Jewish Women,* 11.
3. Quoted in Pamela S. Nadell, *Women Who Would Be Rabbis: A History of Women's Ordination, 1889–1985* (Boston: Beacon Press, 1996), 123.
4. Quoted in Nadell, *Women Who Would Be Rabbis,* 123.
5. Quoted in Nadell, *Women Who Would Be Rabbis,* 122.
6. Quoted in Nadell, *Women Who Would Be Rabbis,* 124.
7. Quoted in Hyman and Moore, *Jewish Women,* 11.
8. Quoted in Nadell, *Women Who Would Be Rabbis,* 64.
9. Quoted in Jenna Weissman Joselit, *New York's Jewish Jews: The Orthodox Community in the Interwar Years* (Bloomington: Indiana University Press, 1990), 27.
10. Quoted in Elaine Krasnow Ellison and Elaine Mark Jaffe, *Voices from Marshall Street: Jewish Life in a Philadelphia Neighborhood, 1920–1960* (Philadelphia: Camino, 1994), 110.
11. Quoted in Ellison and Jaffe, *Voices from Marshall Street,* 53.
12. Quoted in Gerald Sorin, *A Time for Building: The Third Migration, 1880–1920,* vol. 3 of *The Jewish People in America* (Baltimore: Johns Hopkins University Press, 1992), 186.
13. Quoted in Hyman and Moore, *Jewish Women,* 1201.
14. Quoted in Hyman and Moore, *Jewish Women,* 1203.
15. Henry L. Feingold, A *Time for Searching: Entering the Mainstream: 1920-1945,* vol. 4 of *The Jewish People in America*

(Baltimore: Johns Hopkins University Press, 1992), 55.
16. Beth S. Wenger, *New York Jews and the Great Depression: Uncertain Promise* (New Haven: Yale University Press, 1996), 184.
17. Ewa Morowska, *Insecure Prosperity: Small-Town Jews in Industrial America, 1890–1940* (Princeton: Princeton University Press, 1996), 136.
18. Hyman and Moore, *Jewish Women,* 395.
19. Morowska, *Insecure Prosperity,* 155.
20. Morowska, *Insecure Prosperity,* 137.
21. Wenger, *New York Jews,* 85.
22. Quoted in Deborah Dash Moore, *At Home in America: Second Generation New York Jews* (New York: Columbia University Press, 1981), 135.
23. Quoted in William R. Helmreich, *The Enduring Community: The Jews of Newark and Metrowest* (New Brunswick, N.J.: Transaction, 1999), 247.
24. Quoted in Joselit, *New York's Jewish Jews,* 38.
25. Quoted in Joselit, *New York's Jewish Jews,* 102.
26. Quoted in Joselit, *New York's Jewish Jews,* 101.
27. Feingold, *Time for Searching,* 158.
28. Hyman and Moore, *Jewish Women,* 1493.
29. Quoted in Joselit, *New York's Jewish Jews,* 99.
30. Wenger, *New York Jews,* 167.
31. Quoted in Wenger, *New York Jews,* 177.
32. Quoted in Joselit, *New York's Jewish Jews,* 104.
33. Quoted in Joselit, *New York's Jewish Jews,* 97.
34. Quoted in Joselit, *New York's Jewish Jews,* 97.
35. Quoted in Hyman and Moore, *Jewish Women,* 395.
36. Quoted in Joselit, *New York's Jewish Jews,* 108–109.
37. Quoted in Joselit, *New York's Jewish Jews,* 109.

38. Quoted in Joselit, *New York's Jewish Jews,* 100.

39. Quoted in Joselit, *New York's Jewish Jews,* 109.

40. Quoted in Hyman and Moore, *Jewish Women,* 396.

41. Quoted in Morowska, *Insecure Prosperity,* 161.

42. Quoted in Linda Mack Schloff, *"And Prairie Dogs Weren't Kosher"* (St. Paul: Minnesota Historical Society Press, 1996), 99–100.

43. Quoted in Schloff, *Prairie Dogs,* 98–99.

44. Quoted in Schloff, *Prairie Dogs,* 99

45. Quoted in Schloff, *Prairie Dogs,* 101.

46. Quoted in Schloff *Prairie Dogs.*

47. Quoted in Schloff, *Prairie Dogs,* 108

48. Quoted in Joselit, *New York's Jewish Jews,* 110.

49. Quoted in Joselit, *New York's Jewish Jews,* 112.

50. Quoted in Joselit, *New York's Jewish Jews,* 110.

51. Quoted in Joselit, *New York's Jewish Jews,* 113.

52. Feingold, *Time for Searching,* 129.

53. Quoted in Joselit, *New York's Jewish Jews,* 113.

54. Quoted in Joselit, *New York's Jewish Jews,* 111.

55. Quoted in Joselit, *New York's Jewish Jews,* 115.

56. Quoted in Joselit, *New York's Jewish Jews,* 116.

57. Quoted in Hyman and Moore, *Jewish Women,* 364.

58. Quoted in Elinor Slater and Robert Slater, *Great Jewish Women* (Middle Village, N.Y.: Jonathan David, 1998), 244.

59. Hyman and Moore, *Jewish Women,* 164.

60. Quoted in Hyman and Moore, *Jewish Women,* 1300.

61. Quoted in Joyce Antler, *The Journey Home: Jewish Women and the American Century* (New York: Free Press, 1997), 220.

62. Quoted in Hyman and Moore, *Jewish Women,* 1300.

63. Quoted in Helmreich, *Enduring Community,* 57.

64. Helmreich, *Enduring Community,* 41.

65. Edward S. Shapiro, *A Time for Healing: American Jewry Since World War II,* vol. 3, *The Jewish People in America* (Baltimore: Johns Hopkins University Press, 1992), 14.

66. Quoted in Hyman and Moore, *Jewish Women,* 1381.

67. Quoted in Nadell, *Women Who Would Be Rabbis,* 264 n. 159.

68. Quoted in Laurie Sokol, "My Whole Life Used to Be Organizations: A Case Study of Jewish Women in Montgomery County, Maryland, 1950–59" (unpublished manuscript, 1996), 4.

69. Quoted in Sokol, "My Whole Life," 35.

70. Quoted in Sokol, "My Whole Life," 4.

71. Quoted in Hyman and Moore, *Jewish Women,* 579.

72. Quoted in Hyman and Moore, *Jewish Women,* 578.

73. Quoted in Hyman and Moore, *Jewish Women,* 589.

74. From "The Times They Are A-Changin," *Great Songs of the Sixties,* 276.

Chapter 15

1. Quoted in Elinor Slater and Robert Slater, *Great Jewish Women* (Middle Village, N.Y.: Jonathan David, 1998), 97.

2. Quoted in Slater and Slater, *Great Jewish Women,* 97.

3. Quoted in Paula E. Hyman and Deborah Dash Moore, eds., *Jewish Women in America: An Historical Encyclopedia* (New York: Routledge, 1997), 518.

4. Quoted in Hyman and Moore, *Jewish Women,* 483.

5. Betty Friedan, *Life So Far* (New York: Simon & Schuster, 2000), 18.

6. Friedan, *Life So Far,* 17.

7. Quoted in Joyce Antler, *The Journey Home: Jewish Women and the American Century* (New York: Free Press, 1997), 264.

8. Friedan, *Life So Far,* 35.

9. Friedan, *Life So Far,* 79.

10. Friedan, *Life So Far,* 79.

11. Friedan, *Life So Far,* 79.

12. Quoted in Antler, *Journey Home,* 265.

13. Quoted in Antler, *Journey Home,* 267.

14. Quoted in Antler, *Journey Home,* 266.

15. Quoted in Sylvia Barack Fishman, *A Breath of Life: Feminism in the American Jewish Community* (New York: Free Press, 1993), 32.

16. Hyman and Moore, *Jewish Women,* 265.

17. Pamela S. Nadell, *Women Who Would Be Rabbis: A History of Women's Ordination, 1889–1985* (Boston: Beacon Press, 1985), 119.

18. Hyman and Moore, *Jewish Women,* 265.

19. Edward S. Shapiro, *A Time for Healing: American Jewry Since World War II,* vol. 3 of *The Jewish People in America* (Baltimore: Johns Hopkins University Press, 1992), 100.

20. Shapiro, *Time for Healing,* 100.

21. Shapiro, *Time for Healing,* 100.

22. Shapiro, *Time for Healing,* 95, 97.

23. Quoted in Hyman and Moore, *Jewish Women,* 6.

24. Quoted in Hyman and Moore, *Jewish Women,* 8.

25. Quoted in Hyman and Moore, *Jewish Women,* 9.

26. Quoted in Antler, *Journey Home,* 274.

27. Quoted in Antler, *Journey Home,* 275.

28. Quoted in Antler, *Journey Home,* 275.

29. Quoted in Antler, *Journey Home,* 276.

30. Quoted in Fishman, *Breath of Life,* 10.

Chapter 16

1. Quoted in Sylvia Barack Fishman, *A Breath of Life: Feminism in the American Jewish Community* (New York: Free Press, 1993), 140.

2. Quoted in Fishman, *Breath of Life,* 141.

3. Quoted in Paula E. Hyman and Deborah Dash Moore, *Jewish Women in America: An Historical Encyclopedia* (New York: Routledge, 1997), 1087.

4. Quoted in Joyce Antler, *The Journey Home: Jewish Women and the American Century* (New York: Free Press, 1997), 307.

5. Quoted in Hyman and Moore, *Jewish Women,* 854.

6. Hyman and Moore, *Jewish Women,* 854.

7. Quoted in Hyman and Moore, *Jewish Women,* 1159.

8. Quoted in Hyman and Moore, *Jewish Women,* 1159.

9. Quoted in Pamela S. Nadell, *Women Who Would Be Rabbis: A History of Women's Ordination, 1889–1985* (Boston: Beacon, 1985), 170.

10. Quoted in Nadell, *Women Who Would Be Rabbis,* 170–171.

11. Quoted in Nadell, *Women Who Would Be Rabbis,* 170–171.

12. Quoted in Nadell, *Women Who Would Be Rabbis,* 63.

13. Quoted in Nadell, *Women Who Would Be Rabbis,* 63.

14. Quoted in Nadell, *Women Who Would Be Rabbis,* 64.

15. Quoted in Nadell, *Women Who Would Be Rabbis,* 64.

16. Quoted in Nadell, *Women Who Would Be Rabbis,* 66.

17. Quoted in Nadell, *Women Who Would Be Rabbis,* 71.

18. Quoted in Nadell, *Women Who Would Be Rabbis,* 73.

19. Quoted in Nadell, *Women Who Would Be Rabbis,* 82.

20. Quoted in Nadell, *Women Who Would Be Rabbis,* 135.

21. Quoted in Nadell, *Women Who Would Be Rabbis,* 136.

22. Quoted in Nadell, *Women Who Would Be Rabbis,* 149.

23. Quoted in Nadell, *Women Who Would Be Rabbis,* 155.

24. Quoted in Elinor Slater and Robert Slater, *Great Jewish Women* (Middle Village, N.Y.: Jonathan David, 1998), 216.

25. Quoted in Slater and Slater, *Great Jewish Women,* 216.

26. Quoted in Nadell, *Women Who Would Be Rabbis,* 156.

27. Quoted in Nadell, *Women Who Would Be Rabbis,* 85.

28. Quoted in Nadell, *Women Who Would Be Rabbis,* 159.

29. Quoted in Nadell, *Women Who Would Be Rabbis,* 264 n. 159.

30. Quoted in Nadell, *Women Who Would Be Rabbis,* 111.

31. Quoted in Nadell, *Women Who Would Be Rabbis,* 194.

32. Quoted in Nadell, *Women Who Would Be Rabbis,* 194.

33. Quoted in Fishman, *Breath of Life,* 213.

34. Quoted in Antler, *Journey Home,* 297.

35. Quoted in Antler, *Journey Home,* 297.

36. Quoted in Antler, *Journey Home,* 297.

37. Quoted in Antler, *Journey Home,* 292.

38. Quoted in Antler, *Journey Home,* 292.

39. Quoted in Fishman, *Breath of Life,* 128.

40. Quoted in Fishman, *Breath of Life,* 137.

41. Quoted in Fishman, *Breath of Life,* 192.

42. Quoted in Hyman and Moore, *Jewish Women,* 552.

43. Quoted in Fishman, *Breath of Life,* 162.

44. Quoted in Hyman and Moore, *Jewish Women,* 340.

45. Quoted in Fishman, *Breath of Life,* 215.

46. Quoted in Fishman, *Breath of Life,* 216.

47. Moshe Hartman and Harriet Hartman, *Gender Equality and American Jews* (Albany: State University of New York Press, 1996), 118.

48. Fishman, *Breath of Life,* 49.

49. Fishman, *Breath of Life,* 57.

50. Hartman and Hartman, *Gender Equality,* 95.

51. Fishman, *Breath of Life,* 88.

52. Fishman, *Breath of Life,* 89.

BIBLIOGRAPHY

Antler, Joyce. *The Journey Home: Jewish Women and the American Century.* New York: Free Press, 1997.

Ashton, Diane. *Rebecca Gratz: Women and Judaism in Antebellum America.* Detroit: Wayne State University Press, 1997.

Bartlett, John. *Familiar Quotations.* Edited by Emily Morison Beck. Boston: Little, Brown, 1980.

Baum, Charlotte, Paula Hyman, and Sonya Michel. *The Jewish Woman in America.* New York: New American Library, 1975.

Bodek, Marion. "Making Do: Jewish Women and Philanthropy." In *Jewish Life in Philadelphia,* edited by Murray Friedman, 143–162. Philadelphia: Institute for the Study of Human Issues, 1983.

Bridenbaugh, Carl. *Cities in the Wilderness: The First Century of Urban Life in America, 1625–1742.* New York: Oxford University Press, 1966.

Cutler, Irving. *The Jews of Chicago: From Shtetl to Suburb.* Urbana: University of Illinois Press, 1996.

Dalin, David G., and Jonathan Rosenbaum. *Making a Life, Building a Community: A History of the Jews of Hartford.* New York: Holmes & Meier, 1997.

Daniels, Doris Groshen. "Colonial Jewry: Religion, Domestic and Social Relations." *American Jewish Historical Quarterly* 66 (1976–1977): 375–401.

Diner, Hasia R. "German Immigrant Period." In *Jewish Women in America: An Historical Encyclopedia,* edited by Paula E. Hyman and Deborah Dash Moore, 1:502–507. New York: Routledge, 1997.

_____. *Jews in America.* New York: Oxford University Press, 1996.

_____. *A Time for Gathering: The Second Migration, 1820–1880.* Vol. 2 of *The Jewish People in America.* Baltimore: Johns Hopkins University Press, 1992.

Ellison, Elaine Krasnow, and Elaine Mark Jaffe. *Voices from Marshall Street: Jewish Life in a Philadelphia Neighborhood, 1920–1960.* Philadelphia: Camino, 1994.

Elzas, Barnett A. *The Jews of South Carolina.* Philadelphia: J.B. Lippincott, 1905.

Ezekiel, Herbert T., and Gaston Lichtenstein. *The History of the Jews of Richmond: 1769–1917.* Richmond: Herbert T. Ezekiel, Printer, 1917.

Faber, Eli. *A Time for Planting: The First Migration, 1654–1820.* Vol. 1 of *The Jewish People in America.* Baltimore: Johns Hopkins University Press, 1992.

Feingold, Henry L. *A Time for Searching: Entering the Mainstream: 1920–1945.* Vol. 4 of *The Jewish People in America.* Baltimore: Johns Hopkins University Press, 1992.

Fishman, Sylvia Barack. *A Breath of Life: Feminism in the American Jewish Community.* New York. Free Press, 1993.

Friedan, Betty. *Life So Far.* New York: Simon & Schuster, 2000.

Gleicher, Sherri Goldstein. "Flora Spielberg: Grand Old Lady of the Southwest Frontier." *Southwest Jewish History* 1 (1992): 5–6. *Southwest Jewish History* is a publication of the Leona G. and David A. Bloom Southwest Jewish Archives at the University of Arizona.

——. "The Spielbergs of New Mexico: A Family Story of the Southwestern Frontier." *Southwest Jewish History* 1 (1992): 1–7.

Glenn, Susan A. *Daughters of the Shtetl: Life and Labor in the Immigrant Generation.* Ithaca: Cornell University Press, 1990.

Goodman, Deborah. "Jewish Settlement History in the United States and in Champaign-Urbana." Unpublished manuscript, Champaign County Historical Archives, Urbana Free Library, Urbana, Ill., 1970.

Grinstein, Hyman B. *The Rise of the Jewish Community of New York, 1654–1860.* Philadelphia: Jewish Publication Society of America, 1947.

Gutstein, Morris A. *The Story of the Jews of Newport.* New York: Block, 1936.

Hanft, Sheldon. "Mordecai's Female Academy." *American Jewish Historical Quarterly* 19 (1989): 72–93.

Hartman, Moshe, and Harriet Hartman. *Gender Equality and American Jews.* Albany: State University of New York Press, 1996.

Heinze, Andrew. *Adapting to Abundance: Jewish Immigrants, Mass Consumption, and the Search for American Identity.* New York: Columbia University Press, 1990.

Helmreich, William R. *The Enduring Community: The Jews of Newark and Metrowest.* New Brunswick, N.J.: Transaction, 1999.

Howe, Irving. *World of Our Fathers.* New York: Harcourt Brace Jovanovich, 1976.

Hyman, Paula E. *Gender and Assimilation in Modern Jewish History: The Roles and Representation of Women.* Seattle: University of Washington Press, 1995.

Hyman, Paula E., and Deborah Dash Moore, eds. *Jewish Women in America: An Historical Encyclopedia.* New York: Routledge, 1997.

Johnson, Paul. *A History of the Jews.* New York: Harper Perennial, 1987.

Joselit, Jenna Weissman. *New York's Jewish Jews: The Orthodox Community in the Interwar Years.* Bloomington: Indiana University Press, 1990.

Kaplan, Marion A. *The Making of the Jewish Middle Class: Women, Family, and Identity in Imperial Germany.* New York: Oxford University Press, 1991.

Karp, Abraham, ed. *The Jews in America: A Treasury of Art and Literature.* Southport, Conn.: Hugh Lauter Levin Associates, 1994.

Klagsbrun, Francine. *Voices of Wisdom.* New York: Pantheon, 1980.

Levitan, Tina. *First Facts in American Jewish History.* Northvale, N.J.: Jason Aronson, 1996.

Lowenstein, Steven. *The Jews of Oregon, 1850–1950.* Portland: Jewish Historical Society of Oregon, 1987.

Marcus, Jacob R. *The Jewish American Woman: A Documentary History.* New York: KTAV, 1981.

_____. *The Jewish American Woman: 1654–1980.* New York: KTAV, 1981.

Marcus, Jacob Rader. *The Jew in the American World: A Source Book.* Detroit: Wayne State University Press, 1996.

_____. *Memoirs of American Jews, 1775–1865.* Vol. 2. Philadelphia: Jewish Publication Society of America, 1955.

Markowitz, Ruth Jacknow. *My Daughter, the Teacher: Jewish Teachers in the New York City Schools.* New Brunswick, N.J.: Rutgers University Press, 1993.

McCutheon, Marc. *The Writer's Guide to Everyday Life in the 1800s.* Cincinnati: Writers Digest Books, 1993.

Moore, Deborah Dash. *At Home in America: Second Generation New York Jews.* New York: Columbia University Press, 1981.

Morowska, Ewa. *Insecure Prosperity: Small-Town Jews in Industrial America, 1890–1940.* Princeton: Princeton University Press, 1996.

Nadell, Pamela S. *Women Who Would Be Rabbis: A History of Women's Ordination, 1889–1985.* Boston: Beacon, 1985.

Neu, Irene D. "The Jewish Businesswoman in America." *American Jewish Historical Quarterly* 66 (1976–1977): 137–153.

Okun, Michael, ed. *The New York Times Great Songs . . . of the Sixties.* Chicago: Quadrangle Books, 1970.

Rochlin, Harriet, and Fred Rochlin. *Pioneer Jews: A New Life in the Far West.* Boston: Houghton Mifflin, 1984.

Rogow, Faith. *Gone to Another Meeting: The National Council of Jewish Women, 1893–1993.* Tuscaloosa: University of Alabama Press, 1993.

Rosenwaike, Ira. "The Jews of Baltimore: 1810–1820." *American Jewish Historical Quarterly* 67 (1977–1978): 101–124.

Sarna, Jonathan A., and Ellen Smith, eds. *The Jews of Boston.* Boston: Combined Jewish Philanthropies of Boston/Northeastern University Press, 1995.

Schloff, Linda Mack. *"And Prairie Dogs Weren't Kosher."* St. Paul: Minnesota Historical Society Press, 1996.

Seltzer, Robert M. *Jewish People, Jewish Thought.* New York: Macmillan, 1980.

Shapiro, Edward S. *A Time for Healing: American Jewry Since World War II.* Vol. 3 of *The Jewish People in America.* Baltimore: Johns Hopkins University Press, 1992.

Shepard, Richard E., and Vicki Gold Levi. *Live & Be Well: A Celebration of Yiddish Culture in America.* New Brunswick, N.J.: Rutgers University Press, 2000.

Slater, Elinor, and Robert Slater. *Great Jewish Women.* Middle Village, N.Y.: Jonathan David, 1998.

Sokol, Laurie. "My Whole Life Used to Be the Organizations: A Case Study of Jewish Women in Montgomery County, Maryland, 1950–59." Unpublished manuscript, 1996.

Sorin, Gerald. *A Time for Building: The Third Migration, 1880–1920.* Vol. 3 of *The Jewish People in America.* Baltimore: Johns Hopkins University Press, 1992.

Sweirenga, Robert P. *The Forerunners: Dutch Jews in the North American Diaspora.* Detroit: Wayne State University Press, 1994.

Weinberg, Sydney Stahl. *The World of Our Mothers: The Lives of Jewish Immigrant Women.* Chapel Hill: University of North Carolina Press, 1988.

Wenger, Beth S. *New York Jews and the Great Depression: Uncertain Promise.* New Haven: Yale University Press, 1996.

Wiznitzer, Arnold. "The Exodus from Brazil and Arrival in New Amsterdam of the Jewish Pilgrim Fathers." In *The Jewish Experience in Latin America: Selected Studies from the Publications of the American Jewish Historical Society,* edited by Martin A. Cohen, 313–330. Waltham, Mass.: American Jewish Historical Society, 1971.

Wolf, Edwin. "The German-Jewish Influence in Philadelphia's Jewish Charities." In *Jewish Life in Philadelphia,* edited by Murray Friedman, 125–142. Philadelphia: Institute for the Study of Human Issues, 1983.

Wolff, Egon, and Freida Wolff. "The Problem of the First Jewish Settlers in New Amsterdam, 1654." *Studia Rosenthaliana* 15 (1981).

Women in the Military: A Jewish Perspective. Washington, D.C.: National Museum of American Jewish Military History, n.d.

INDEX

Printed in the United States
113767LV00001B/1/A

9 780465 017126